INTRODUCTION TO SOCIAL WELFARE
AND SOCIAL WORK:
Structure, function, and process ໒

The Dorsey Series in Social Welfare

Introduction to social welfare and social work

STRUCTURE, FUNCTION, AND PROCESS

Beulah Roberts Compton, Ph.D.

University of Minnesota, Minneapolis

1980
THE DORSEY PRESS   Homewood, Illinois   60430
Irwin-Dorsey Limited   Georgetown, Ontario   L7G 4B3

Cover photos (from center outwards):
U.S.D.A. Photograph by Fred S. White
U.S.D.A. Photograph
U.S. Department of Housing and Urban Development
U.S. Department of Housing and Urban Development

© THE DORSEY PRESS, 1980

ISBN 0-256-02093-0

Library of Congress Catalog Card No. 79–56079

Printed in the United States of America

1 2 3 4 5 6 7 8 9 0 K 7 6 5 4 3 2 1 0

Dedicated to three teachers who have, over the years, been model and inspiration:

- ❧ Professor Emeritus Samuel C. Ratcliffe, Illinois Wesleyan University
- ❧ Professor Emeritus Mary Houk, Indiana University School of Social Work
- ❧ Professor Grace Browning, who was Director of the Indiana University School of Social Work at the time of her death.

✌️§ Preface

This book is intended as an introductory text for students interested in acquiring a beginning knowledge of social welfare and of social work. It attempts to pull together and to organize the literature of social work and social welfare in such a way that the student who covers the material should finish the book with a basic understanding of the development, structure, and function of social welfare as an institution, and of social work as a profession. The book should provide the student with a base from which to pursue further knowledge in these areas. It is hoped that it raises enough questions for readers, and leaves enough unfinished, to interest them in pursuing the cited sources and other works in greater depth over time.

The questions that guided and focused the selection of the material included in the text, and the way in which that material was organized and presented were: (1) Will this contribute to an understanding of the profession of social work—and of the institution in which it is lodged—that will be helpful and usable for beginning social workers, as they pursue their development? (2) Will this help the student to understand something about the nature of change in a democratic society composed of a large and heterogeneous population spread over a large and diverse landmass? (3) Will this give the student an opportunity to develop some beginning notions both of social policy and of social policy analysis, through the history of such policy development and change? (4) Will this help the student to understand something about the decisions that must be made as program develops out of policy? and, (5) Will this help the student to achieve a beginning knowledge of present programs?

The text is organized in four parts. The purpose of Parts I and II is to offer students an opportunity to develop a framework for the analysis of the development of social welfare and of the functioning of the social work profession. Part III gives students an account of how the institution and the profession developed. This part is presented as a case example of social change, giving students an account of the actual development of policy, programs, and the profession that can be examined as an exercise in the use of a framework for the analysis of change. Part IV summarizes the issues we face today.

I am indebted to so many people who have helped me in my development, challenged my thinking, and supported me in the writing of this book that I cannot possibly mention them all. Certainly, one is always indebted to the patience of one's family and friends who understand when writing must come before pleasure. And there is no way to adequately thank all the teachers who have served as stimulators and models as one struggles toward learning.

I wish to thank both my colleagues and those doctoral students who raised questions and offered comments, insights, and ideas during the process of writing. Two MSW students, Pam Luienberg and Gene Hysjulien, and Peter Hettinga, a doctoral student, and his wife, Patricia Hettinga, were invaluable assets in helping in any way they could with library research and with the myriad of details that such work involves.

I owe special thanks to Robert Constable of the University of Illinois, Chicago Circle Campus, who reviewed and commented on the manuscript as it was in progress and on the final draft of the manuscript. His willingness to take time to read the work and to share his thinking about it strengthened the manuscript. Those who generously gave me permission to quote from or paraphrase their writings deserve acknowledgment and gratitude. Without their willingness to share, this book would indeed be quite different. In spite of such generous help from others, the author must accept the sole responsibility for the content of this text.

March 1980   **Beulah Roberts Compton**

Contents

Part I

Introduction to social welfare as a social institution and to its function in society

International Year of the Child 1979

U.S. Committee for UNICEF 331 East 38th Street New York, New York 10016

The care and nuture of children is
a worldwide social welfare concern.

Courtesy UNICEF

Chapter 1 🦢

🦢 Introduction

This book is about social welfare, social services, and social work as they have developed in the United States over the past centuries. It is written for the person who has not been introduced to the institution of social welfare, to social services as a system found within that institution, and to social work as the dominant profession involved in delivering those social services to consumers. This book is intended to provide a base upon which further understanding of social welfare can be developed, and it has been written to provide breadth rather than depth of comprehension. It is recognized that social welfare problems and programs are worldwide. However, the difficulty of forming an initial comprehension of our social welfare system and of social work as a profession necessitates limiting this book to a consideration of social welfare and social work systems in the United States of America to the exclusion of other systems.

The goals of the book are to offer the student the kinds of information that will support the development of (1) a beginning ability to think analytically about the organizational patterns and the professional roles within the American social welfare system, (2) some comprehension of the relationship of such patterns and roles to the larger social structure, (3) some concrete knowledge of central social welfare, programs and their functioning, and (4) some ability to fit all of this within a theoretical framework. However, it is recognized that no one introductory book, and no one course, can serve as a sole basis for the development of competence in the areas set forth above. There are many ways in which to approach the study of social welfare and many frameworks of analysis that may be used. Hopefully, this book will serve as one contribution to a beginning knowledge of the phenomenon.

It is hoped that the student will not end the search for an understanding either of individual welfare needs or of how societies operate to meet such needs with what is written here. The reader should continue to search within a wider circle and at greater depth for increasing knowledge and for other methods of analysis. The study of social welfare is a fascinating and complex investigation of a phenomenon that affects us all. The modern industrial state in which each of us holds membership operates in such a way that no one of us can determine his or her destiny independent of all others; thus in the course of our lives all of us depend in various ways on the social welfare programs and policies of our society.

Students beginning the study of the social welfare system encounter a most confusing tapestry—a cloth that over years of service has become torn and full of holes. Woven at an earlier time for different needs, it fails to cover and protect us as it should in today's complex industrial society. Yet the tapestry is never totally discarded for a new one or unraveled and rewoven to make it more adequate. Rather, it is patched, often with very different materials, giving it a strange and wild design, and it is added onto so that it becomes longer and wider, with designs that depart significantly from those of the original work. Puzzling and complex, constantly changing in both internal patterns and outer shape, the social welfare system is often a frustrating subject for students who find that it changes and develops even as they seek to understand it.

Although the policy underlying social welfare programs often seems to be unchanging, the development of such programs in this country has never paused long enough for a student to feel that comprehension has really been achieved "as of this point in time." And so it is with this text—even as it is written, changes are being made in the material with which it deals. Another frayed spot is being patched here, and a significant new strip is being added there. To have real expertise in this subject, one must study it continuously and unremittingly. Many students, seeing themselves as primarily interested in serving individuals in trouble, think the struggle to understand social welfare development is not worth the work it demands. Yet the comprehension of this subject is essential for those who would practice effectively in the social services because, to a large extent, the social welfare system

shapes the form of professional practice and determines which client systems are served and which client needs are met. Also, individual practitioners affect organizational policies since they are actively involved in making decisions as to how general policies shall be interpreted and operationalized. In the final analysis, these practitioners determine what policies, laws, and directives shall mean to the individuals who seek to use the social welfare systems.

This book is concerned with both the present and the future in a very special way. It is not futuristic in terms of predicting the shape of the welfare system in the 21st century, but rather in the sense that many of the students who study it may very soon be directly involved as professionals in the delivery of social services. *Without exception,* each reader will be among those who determine the policies of tomorrow by virtue of his/her professional, economic, and/or political activity—or *lack of activity.* In the latter case, the readers of this work will participate by electing to leave to others the complex choices to be made. For such readers, this work will have failed. Its ultimate mission is to help readers come to grips with some of the complexities of social choice in the hope that it will not only equip them to appraise and further develop their own stance on social welfare policy but that it will also be a factor in their commitment to concerned and informed action as members of society. In that sense, reader and author are inextricably bound together within the same society and affected by the same social welfare system—each making choices that affect the other, each making choices that affect everyone in our nation.

Students who are looking for specific answers to questions as to the "rightness" or "wrongness" of a particular social welfare policy and/or program may find this book frustrating, as it provides no such answers. Rather, it seeks to help the reader develop a way of thinking about and analyzing social welfare systems that, hopefully, will be applicable to responsible, participatory choices in the future. This book attempts to introduce students to the challenges, the discomforts, and the range of knowledge and understanding that are associated with the study of the social welfare institution. It also attempts to introduce students to the process of social change through the use of our own social welfare history as a case example, and it introduces a framework of analysis to help readers come to grips with the complexity of such choices. In a recent book on social policy Gilbert and Specht, social work professors who have become recognized experts in the area of social policy, state so well the position of this text that we quote them here:

> Good and righteous answers to the fundamental questions in social welfare policy are not come by easily. Addressed seriously, they require a willingness to abide complexity, and ability to tolerate contradictions, and a capacity to appraise empirical evidence and social values critically, which is to say that professionals who are engaged in the business of making social welfare policy choices will require patience, thought, and intelligent curiosity to fulfill their commitment well. (1976, p. xi)

Though this book is concerned with the future, a major portion of its contents is devoted to the past via: (1) a tracing of the processes of social policy development, (2) a description of various programs that were the product of such processes, and (3) a discussion of the effectiveness of those programs in meeting their stated goals. Thus we shall study the "past as process" in an effort to help the student understand how the development of the social welfare system of today and the social welfare choices for tomorrow are affected by: (1) the social context (the available knowledge, values, and social philosophies and the existing economic and political pressures); (2) the behaviors, motivations, and goals of the various actors; (3) the various programs already in existence; and (4) the policy choices of the past. No student of social welfare can fail to note the recurring parallels: in the current and past attitudes toward persons in distress; in our search for causes in the same areas that we sought them before; and in the development of means similar to those that were previously taken to relieve the distress. Those who would work ef-

fectively within the social programs of today, and those who would reform them for the betterment of humanity, have no choice but to deal with the past.

We are concerned here with two different but interrelated pasts. One is the struggle of individuals and groups to move a nation, bit by bit and choice by choice, toward their vision of an adequate program of social welfare, trying to reconcile social needs with their convictions and with the resources and the social philosophies of their times. The other past is the history of social work as it has developed in America over the last 100 years through the struggles of individual practitioners to competently serve clients within a social welfare system—into which the profession has often had relatively minor input.

The development of the profession of social work and the growth of the institution of social welfare can hardly be discussed separately. Actually the profession can be seen as growing out of the institution, and they can both be viewed as organized efforts to cope with the problems of life in an industrial society. The profession developed from the institution's need for agents to carry out the welfare programs that were developing. However, today the profession is much more than the agent of the welfare system. It is charged both with the delivery of services to individuals, families, and groups and with attending to the institutional structure within which such services are offered—"creating, maintaining, and reforming the institutional context within which it operates" (Gilbert and Specht, 1976, p. 4).

This text is not presented as a scholarly treatise on welfare policy. Rather, it should be considered as an attempt to help beginning students of the social welfare field by presenting some concrete and accurate information about social welfare programs and how they developed and by raising questions for future study.

The book is divided into four major parts. The first part develops the notion of social welfare as an institution. It provides the reader with a description of certain social welfare services and with certain ways to think about those services. It attempts to answer the question "What is social welfare?" It gives students a way of thinking about the description of social welfare programs and their development that will follow. The second part is brief but significant. It attempts to answer the questions "What do we mean by social services?" and "What is social work?" It develops some concepts about the profession of social work, and it lays the foundation for understanding social work as a profession within the institution of social welfare.

The third part is organized around the historical development of social welfare and social work. The purpose of this part is to give students an example of social change through examining how and why our present social welfare system developed. Although not presented under these topical headings, the chapters in this part seek to give the student an understanding of: (1) how the social welfare institutions and the profession of social work develop, operate, relate to each other, and change over time; (2) how the concerns, commitments, knowledge, and technology of individuals affect the development and operationalization of the systems within the social welfare institution and the shape of social work as a profession; (3) the effects of the social welfare organizations upon the individuals working within them; (4) the effects of the professional organizations and educational patterns upon the practitioners; and (5) how the development and operationalization of the agencies, services, and organizations within the American welfare system relate to the values, the social phi-losophy, the resources available, and the political and economic system which exist at the time of their establishment.

The chapters that make up the concluding part constitute a summary that seeks to examine some issues and to draw some conclusions about the changing structure and function of social welfare as an institution and about the future of the social work profession. These chapters explore the question of what sort of social welfare programs and professional competences are required in today's world.

It is not an easy task to determine what should be included in a study of the development of such a complex institution as social welfare. Any structure that one attempts to develop results in a certain amount of overlapping and in much untidiness. There are, of course, many ways to organize a textbook on social welfare and many ways to develop an analytic approach to any institution. Given the increasing complexity of this phenomenon called social welfare, one must recognize that it is impossible for any one volume to "tell it all." Any author, particularly an author of an introductory text, must select on the basis of some conceptual framework. The approach developed here will be useful only as it (1) helps to explain certain relationships and processes in the emergence of today's social welfare system and social work profession, (2) gives students some concrete knowledge about certain programs, and (3) helps the student to raise relevant questions.

Courtesy ACTION

Two participants in a Senior Companion Program show a social welfare program in operation.
Every day 69 year-old Frank Dixon visits 89 year-old Oscar Mallet and takes him to lunch. Lunch,
in this Iowa program, is provided by the Hawkeye Valley Area Agency on Aging.

Chapter 2 ૐ

๐ Social welfare—
some concrete examples ૐ

ๆ **Introduction**

As indicated in Chapter 1, each of us inevitably, during the course of our lives, conducts transactions, voluntarily or involuntarily, with a whole range of organizations that provide critical resources which assist us in improving, maintaining, or restoring our well-being. These resources are provided by a society for the purpose of meeting social needs recognized as necessary to the well-being of its members. Taken as a whole, they comprise the social welfare institution of that society. We will consider the definition, description, and structure of the social welfare institution in greater detail in the next chapters.

In this chapter we have two other important purposes. The first is to help readers of this text to recognize some of the organizations and systems that make up the American social welfare institution today. We will do this by presenting some very concrete examples of the operation of such systems in the lives of two families. We present these examples so that they may be available to illustrate the definitions and concepts of social welfare when these abstract notions are introduced in the next chapters. The second purpose of this material is to illustrate through examples the impact of certain social welfare programs upon people's lives—to demonstrate the impact of social welfare programs upon all of us. This book is not about someone else. It is about us—each and every one of us—and about the way that social welfare programs will affect our quest for actualization in a complex, largely urban, industrialized society. One caution—the examples presented here are highly simplified to facilitate a beginning understanding of certain programs. They do not by any means illustrate the totality of social welfare or even of the programs mentioned. They are only used for purposes of illustration and to present certain questions that will be dealt with later.

The Poor family

What is the mental picture that most people have when we say the words *social welfare?* Perhaps most people would think immediately of poor people and of relief. Such notions confuse the institution of *social welfare* with *public welfare,* one of the programs (or systems) found within it. Both social welfare and public welfare are concerned with more than the poor. Upon hearing the words *public welfare,* many people might think immediately of a drab-looking woman (let us call her Mrs. Poor) holding a baby in her arms and with two poorly dressed and perhaps grimy, children beside her. Some people might color the woman and her children black, or brown, or red. Most people would see this family as being on welfare because of the irresponsibility of the man who fathered the children and the woman who bore them. Many people would see this woman as receiving a generous relief check, food stamps, and medical care, all paid for from their taxes. They may believe that the woman prefers being on welfare to working for her own support and that she neglects her children. Some persons would suspect that Mrs. Poor, while posing as a deserted mother, is really living with the father of her children, who is working, and that they conceal this from the welfare authorities.

While there may be people who utilize the resources of social welfare organizations for illegal and fraudulent gains, the Poor family picture is more likely to conform to the following description than to the mental image that many people have. It is true that Mrs. Poor is a woman struggling to exist and to raise her children by herself. She is more likely to be white than she is to be black, brown, or red, and to have two children rather than three. Because of her husband's desertion during her second pregnancy, she found it necessary to turn to public welfare for money to support herself and her first child and for medical care during her pregnancy. The program under which Mrs. Poor received assistance is known as Aid to Families with Dependent Children. It is set up to help families in which there is need for financial support because of the handicap, death, or continued absence from the home of one parent and in which the remaining parent is needed in the home to provide child care for minor children. In some states, the continued unemployment of the father in a two-parent family qualifies the family for AFDC. As a rule, funds for the program come from federal, state, and local general tax revenues.

Mrs. Poor hates having to turn to welfare for support, and she looks forward to the day when she can find a job that pays enough to allow her to pay for adequate child care and to support herself and her two children. She hates the process of having to prove that she has nothing in order to receive help. If she is representative of the average AFDC family, she will find some way to support herself within three years of receiving her first grant. Mrs. Poor has no work experience (having married just before high school graduation) and no easily marketable skills that would bring her a paycheck large enough to support her two children. She has been enrolled in a public welfare program that was set up to teach persons new work skills, but so far that has not resulted in a job. Her husband has disappeared. Her father has no resources. Her in-laws live in a different state, and they seem to have little interest in Mrs. Poor. Because of the many difficulties she faces as a lone parent, because the younger child has shown some behavior difficulties, and because of her depression and a sense of worthlessness that seems to stem from her husband's leaving her and her need to apply to welfare, Mrs. Poor also looks to public welfare for psychological support and help. To aid her in dealing with this need, she has a social service worker, a social worker to help her with psychosocial problems, as well as her eligibility technician, who determines her level of need and her continued eligibility, and an employment counselor. Mrs. Poor's lack of skill and lack of resources may mean that her family will become one of the 30 percent of the AFDC families that are dependent on welfare for long periods (Rein and Rainwater, 1978, pp. 511–34).

Mr. Olds

Mrs. Poor's father, Mr. Olds, is retired. He lives across town from his daughter. He had owned and operated a small grocery store all his life. A self-employed man with a very minimal income, he had contributed only a minimum to social security. Unfortunately, just after Mrs. Olds's death, he fell ill of a long and very disabling illness. The cost of the longtime care forced Mr. Olds to sell his store and to exhaust his resources. So he, like his daughter, is in need of some kind of support in order to live. Also, he can no longer pay for his medical care. Since he is over 65 years of age, he will be supported in part by funds from OASDI (commonly called social security) and in part by funds from general tax revenue for which he, like his daughter, will have to prove need. However, the process of applying for help will be very different for Mr. Olds than for his daughter. First, the basic cost of his support will be paid entirely from federal funds. To receive these, Mr. Olds does not go to the local welfare office but rather to the social security office. Here he will receive a minimal amount from social security (OASDI) and a supplemental income (SSI) grant of up to $167 a month. The grant covers Mr. Olds's needs according to the standards of his state (this will be discussed later).

Part of Mr. Olds's medical care (medicare) is included in social security, so he must now go to the county welfare office and once again prove need in order to receive help in paying for the remainder of his medical care (medicaid). Since Mr. Olds has no income but minimal social security, the county welfare agency will pay all of his other medical costs. The agency also suggests that he is eligible for food stamps to aid in purchasing food. Both Mr. Olds and his daughter see themselves as being "on welfare," and they feel a certain stigma from the fact that they must "take help." Mr. Olds will talk with a sympathetic listener about what he sees as the injustice of working hard all one's life, of trying to take care of one's own, and of now finding oneself at the mercy of others. It seems a bitter injustice to him that he tried so hard and gained so little to support himself in his old age. But the reality of life for his daughter is even harder, for she must stretch an amount no larger than her father's monthly grant to cover the needs of three people. She looks at her children and thinks

of all she would want for them that she cannot supply and wonders how their lives will be damaged in the future because of the deprivation of today. We will come back to the Poor and Olds families in following chapters and use their situation to illustrate our discussion. However, for now, let us examine very briefly the situation of another family.

The Comfortable family and Mrs. Affluent

Mr. Comfortable is a junior executive working for a large multinational corporation. He has just been transferred to head a new plant in Centerville. As a result of the transfer, Mr. and Mrs. Comfortable had to find a new house for their family, which consists of two boys—10 and 12 years of age—and Mrs. Comfortable's mother, Mrs. Affluent. The Comfortables agreed in advance that they wanted to find a house in a neighborhood with good schools, with a park and a library easily available, and, hopefully, close to their church and to some recreational and developmental resources for the family, such as a YWCA or YMCA or a community center. When they found a house they liked in such an area, it was necessary for them to take a large mortgage to cover the cost of purchase.

Before buying the house, Mrs. Comfortable visited the school to see what programs and resources it had. Mr. and Mrs. Comfortable also explored the level of health and the available medical services in the community. They felt that this was particularly important because of their two children and Mrs. Affluent. Mrs. Affluent has had one minor stroke, and she is frail and sometimes confused. She is a widow. Part of her support is derived from social security. Her medical needs are also partly covered through medicare, a part of the social security program. Actually, Mrs. Affluent has never worked outside the home, but she receives social security because her husband was a chemical engineer who was covered at the maximum level of benefits. In addition, he had a company pension and some investments. Mrs. Affluent receives the maximum widow's level of benefits. She also receives a widow's benefit under the company pension, and, of course, she received her husband's investments under his will.

Mr. and Mrs. Comfortable think of themselves as very adequate and planful people. They pride themselves on utilizing many resources of the community to support their effort to be good parents. They might be very disturbed by the notion that they may very well be utilizing more welfare resources than the family in our first example. However, the reality is that their family does receive more support from the social welfare resources of the community than does the Poor-Olds family. The resources that they receive may have a different source of funding, and they do not apply to the public welfare office or have to prove need in order to receive them. Nevertheless, their family is a heavy user of social welfare resources.

In addition to the public welfare and social security programs we have discussed, we should look at the educational system of society as a part of the social welfare institution. Families utilize the schools of their community for their children's education and to support their efforts as parents to socialize their children to appropriate roles and responsibilities as members of society. Public schools are a tax-supported resource serving the purposes of normal human development because society has arrived at the conclusion that both society and the individual need this type of help if either is to survive. An industrial society, dependent on a changing technology, must have citizens who possess certain attitudes, skills, and knowledge if the economic system is to exist and grow. At the same time, in today's world only a very few families possess the capacity to educate their children adequately for competent functioning in either today's world or tomorrow's. Thus, industrial societies develop and financially support a social welfare resource to carry out this necessary function of education.

✌§ The use of social welfare resources

If we analyze the use that these two families make of the educational system, we will discover that in the course of their lives the Comfortable family members will use this welfare resource far more than the members of the Poor family. In the first place, the Comfortable family lives in a school district that offers a much richer (and thus more expensive for the community) educational experience than that offered Mrs. Poor's children. Also, the Comfortable children will probably continue in school much longer than the Poor children. College and graduate education is very expensive for the community. We will discuss this issue in greater detail later, but for now we would like to point out that no person pays the full cost of her/his education. In private colleges and universities, the *highest rate of contributions* by individuals through their fees and tuition costs is approximately 80 percent. The rest of the costs are paid by contributions of members of society. For society, education for the professions is among the most expensive types of education. Although many medical students think that they pay a great deal for their education, the members of society may well pay as much as 95 percent of the costs of educating a student in a public medical school.

The Comfortable family also makes full use of other "developmental" resources that are supplied by social welfare organizations. The two boys regularly participate in groups sponsored by the community center. This type of activity is supported by the community to aid families in giving their children developmental experiences. Mrs. Affluent relied heavily on community center activities developed by social workers for older persons to help her find new friends in the community, and she now spends a great deal of time at the community center participating in activities with these friends. In fact, as an elderly semi-invalid living in her daughter's family in a strange community, she finds that the center makes her life bearable.

Mrs. Comfortable has also found the move very difficult. She had a very active social life and was a valued and active member in the community that she had to leave behind. Faced with her own unhappiness and anger at the loss of her friends and with the problem of her mother's loneliness and the boys' disturbance over the move, Mrs. Comfortable has found herself increasingly unable to cope with the demands of family life. Her attempt to obtain support from her husband was rebuffed. Deeply involved in the demanding new responsibilities he had taken on at work and confronted with an unhappy family at home, he was spending more and more time at the office. Mrs. Comfortable, thinking that the stimulation of outside interests might help, and as a way of getting into the community, enrolled in some extension courses that were offered by the local university and were housed in the community center, thus utilizing two social welfare organizations. She also volunteered her time to work with patients at Children's Hospital, thus giving her time to support a social welfare resource in the community. When these activities did not seem to help her with her depression and with her anger at her husband for what she regarded as his desertion, Mrs. Comfortable consulted a social worker at Centerville Family and Children's Service, and she has been going to the agency each week for help in coping with her feelings and with the crisis of moving.

Mrs. Poor, alone with two children and probably needing support and help to a far greater extent than does the Comfortable family, which has three adults to interact with the children and to do family tasks, uses much, much less of the types of social welfare resources that we have discussed above. There may be several reasons for this: (1) Mrs. Poor probably knows much less than does the Comfortable family about the existence of such resources and how to gain access to them; (2) the area Mrs. Poor lives in will be less affluent than that of the Comfortable family, so less community-supported resources will be available; (3) Mrs. Poor, alone with her two children, has neither the time nor the money that is often necessary for the effective use of such resources. The one resource that Mrs. Poor does use, in addition to the social work help, medicaid, and income maintenance supplied by the county welfare agency, is Big Brothers. This social agency, supported by the United Fund, recruits and trains volunteers to work with boys from families without fathers. In this case, a man from the community occasionally picks up her boys and takes them out for an afternoon of recreation and companionship. Mrs. Poor's county social services worker suggested this resource to her, and she has found it extremely helpful to her and meaningful to her sons.

Mr. Olds is as isolated as his daughter. The one service he does use is the support provided by the medical social worker. He often talks with her about his loneliness and anger when he visits the hospital. The social worker has tried to find other social supports for Mr. Olds, but he has not used any of her suggestions. He feels that he doesn't have money for activities. And he has never been active in social groups.

In telling the story of our families, we have discussed the use of medicaid and medicare—programs to supply medical care to individuals either at no cost or at much below cost. A nation's medical system should also be considered part of the institution of social welfare. Certain parts of this institution—such as your visit as a private patient to a doctor in private practice—may be largely paid for from your individual funds. However, the health-care system is supported and organized by society as a social resource needed by all of us. For the Poor and Olds families, the pattern of medical care is relatively simple. Their health care and their illnesses are usually handled by the staff at Centerville Public Hospital. After eligibility for care has been determined and care has been approved by the county welfare agency, Mrs. Poor and her family and Mr. Olds are free to go to this hospital for all care. The costs are paid for through some combination of local, state, and federal funds. Mrs. Poor often hesitates to go for medical care. It is so difficult to get her children organized for the long bus trip; bus fare costs so much out of a tight budget; and she has to wait so long to be seen. Besides, she often feels that the medical personnel who serve her are critical of her and her family as inadequate and unworthy. She also has some reservations about the competence of the interns and residents on whom she usually must rely for help.

The Comfortable family also pays a relatively minute part of the costs of its medical care, but it uses different resources, and the sources of the funds from which the payments are made are different. Mr. Comfortable and his family are "covered" by a health-care plan paid for by his company. Mr. Comfortable pays nothing for this coverage, which reimburses him for any medical and dental care needed by his wife and children. The Comfortables go to any doctor and hospital of their choice, and a private insurance carrier, paid by the company for which Mr. Comfortable works, will reimburse the family for the costs of all medicine, appliances such as glasses, health and dental care, and hospital bills. In this case, the Comfortables are required to pay the first $50 of doctor bills and the first $50 of dental bills each year. Not only does Mr. Comfortable not pay for this coverage, but he pays no tax on the value of such care to his family.

Mrs. Affluent does not pay for most of her medical costs either. Her costs are, in part, covered by medicare, for which she became eligible as a recipient of social security. However, in financial terms she is the least well covered of the individuals in our stories. Certain deductibles and limitations on medicare limit the amount of financial support it gives. In many situations in which social security is the sole form of income, these uncovered costs could be paid for out of medicaid funds. However, as we said before, medicaid has a means test, which requires the individual to be in serious financial need before he or she can get help. Mrs. Affluent has a significant personal income in addition to social security, and this would bar her from the use of medicaid to supplement her medicare benefits.

Publicly supported programs to assure adequate housing for people will also be considered a part of the social welfare institution (see Chapters 3–5). Mrs. Poor does not live in a housing project, but her AFDC grant pays for her $175 monthly rent in an extremely crowded and inadequate apartment. Mr. and Mrs. Comfortable consider that they pay for their own housing. However, property taxes and the interest on the large loan for their housing is tax deductible, which means that they save $2,400 a year on their taxes because of this housing expense. Thus, their housing is subsidized

at the rate of $200 per month, or $25 more than Mrs. Poor's rental allowance.

This completes our example of the impact of various social welfare programs upon two specific family groups. Although the example may have failed to detail all the social welfare supports used by these families, it touched on the most common ones. It is not expected that most readers will have a working knowledge of the specifics of the programs mentioned in the example. We present the stories here for the purpose of introducing a concrete example to illustrate the breadth of social welfare services and to give us some basic material that can be used later to illustrate and integrate certain concepts. It is hoped that the readers will be finding answers throughout this book to the questions raised by the stories of these families.

◁§ Direct and indirect benefits

One principle that we hope the above stories illustrate is that in our daily lives all of us are directly or indirectly dependent on and subsidized by our government, and that many of us benefit directly and indirectly from the support of nongovernmental social welfare as well. We all benefit, both directly and indirectly, from the social welfare programs of our society. However, the social welfare institution as we know and experience it in the United States is a complex, multidimensional phenomenon loosely held together by public policy, legal sanctions, and administrative regulations. The public welfare programs of our society are diverse, conflicting, and sometimes contradictory, and the various privately supported welfare programs are even more disparate. Furthermore, average members of our society view the various parts of the social welfare institution differently, depending on who benefits from the programs, how the benefits are determined, and how the financing is secured.

For example, Mrs. Poor and Mr. Olds benefit directly in that they receive the principal part of their life supports from public welfare programs that are established to help people who have no other defined sources of financial support. Since the programs are *means tested,* Mrs. Poor and Mr.

Olds must prove that they are without enough resources to purchase minimal food, clothing, and shelter for themselves. The benefits they receive are seen as given by society, not earned. The programs are financed by general tax revenues, and the benefits are given at the discretion of authorities who find Mrs. Poor and Mr. Olds needy. These are examples of *residual* programs. Because of the nature of the programs they use, Mrs. Poor and Mr. Olds are seen by many people as "dependent." Thus, in terms of one of the value systems found in our society (value systems and their impact will be discussed further in Chap. 5), Mrs. Poor and Mr. Olds are considered of less worth and deserving of less respect than other people. People want to be sure that Mrs. Poor and Mr. Olds are not given something that they do not need and feel that Mrs. Poor and Mr. Olds are less honest than the rest of us.

Mrs. Affluent benefits directly from the welfare programs of government when she accepts her social security check. However, most people would not consider her to be on welfare. Although her benefits are paid for by a very regressive tax on the presently employed (this point will be developed in detail in later chapters), the benefits she receives are based on her husband's earning record; therefore, they are considered earned, not given. The benefits she receives are centralized, are governed by clear rules of entitlement, and are administered by employees who have a minimum of discretion about the benefits. The social security program was developed for a particular population that is specifically defined. It is an example of an *institutional welfare program.* (We will discuss the concepts *residual* and *institutional* in the next chapter.)

Mr. and Mrs. Comfortable receive a number of *institutional, indirect welfare benefits.* Their medical care is indirectly financed by society in that Mr. Comfortable's employer pays its costs and is then able to include that amount in the costs of doing business. This allows the employer to deduct such costs from the taxes paid to the government. Somehow the budget for government operation has to be met; therefore, the less the employer pays,

---

A fable

A young man lived with his parents in a public housing development.

He attended public school, rode the free school bus, and participated in the free lunch program.

He entered the Army and upon discharge kept his national service life Insurance. He then enrolled in the state university under the GI Bill, working part time for the state to supplement his GI check.

Upon graduation he married a public health nurse and bought a farm with an FHA loan, then obtained an RFC loan to go into business. A baby was born in the county hospital. He bought a ranch with the aid of a GI loan and obtained emergency feed from the government.

Later he put part of his land in the Soil Bank, and the payments helped pay off his debts. His parents lived very comfortably on the ranch with their social security and old-age-assistance checks.

The county agent showed him how to terrace it, then the government paid part of the cost of a pond and stocked it with fish. The government guaranteed him a sale for his farm products.

He signed a petition seeking federal assistance in developing an industrial project to help the economy of his area. He was a leader in obtaining a new federal building, and went to Washington with a group to ask Congress to build a great dam costing millions so that the area could get cheap electricity.

Then, one day, he wrote his congressman a letter of protest:

"I wish to protest excessive government spending and high taxes. I believe in rugged individualism. I think people should stand on their own two feet without expecting handouts. I am opposed to all socialistic trends."

Source: *Around the Clock,* Minneapolis Civil Service Commission, March 1970.

the greater the amount of the budget costs that must be met by other sources of revenue or the higher the tax rate that must be set. Mr. and Mrs. Comfortable see the benefits as supplied by the employer, and the benefits are seldom considered welfare. More and more employers are contracting with social workers and members of other helping professions to offer therapy to troubled employees. This, too, is a welfare benefit to the employees.

However, such benefits are not only of help to the employee. They are also an indirect support to the employer, and thus to the economic institution of society, in that they help support a stable, well-functioning work force that is absolutely necessary for the success of the business, which, in turn, may be a source of financial support for many stockholders, of whom Mrs. Affluent is one. The tax regulations that permit the deduction of interest on loans from our income taxes mean that a certain amount of our borrowing, particularly for the housing of middle- and upper-income groups, are supported by the general tax base. Our expensive public educational programs from kindergarten through advanced university education are indirect welfare benefits that contribute immensely to the opportunities and future security of those who utilize them.

As an example of the difficulties we have in comprehending the full extent and meaning of our public welfare programs, we are reproducing a fable which appeared in a bulletin published by the Civil Service Commission of Minneapolis. The boxed example leads us directly into the questions of cost. The costs of welfare activities have been rising rapidly over the last three decades. Certainly, in this dimension alone, social welfare touches all our lives. We pay for it.

✑§ Social welfare costs

According to the *Social Security Bulletin,* the total for all of the social welfare expenditures in the nation reached $389 billion in the fiscal year 1975. This means that in the fiscal year 1975 27 percent of the *total market value of all the goods and services produced by the nation* (often referred to as GNP—gross national product) was uti-

lized to pay for social welfare activities. In that fiscal year, public social welfare spending accounted for 73 percent of all social welfare outlays.

The *Bulletin* defines public social welfare expenditures as the cash benefits, services, and administrative costs of all the programs operating under public law that are of direct benefit to individuals and families. The programs included are those for income maintenance provided by social insurance programs, public assistance, and the public provision of health, education, housing, and other welfare services. Private social welfare expenditures are defined as direct consumer expenditures for medical care and education; expenditures of private employee-benefit plans, including group health and life insurance for government employees; and other welfare services (*Social Security Bulletin,* 1976, pp. 6–8). Table 2–1 shows social welfare expenditures under public programs for selected fiscal years from 1929 through 1975.

We would suggest that the reader look closely at the listing of the programs in Table 2–1—remembering that this listing represents only *public expenditures* for social welfare and that the programs listed are only those provided for under public law. Is it possible to locate in the table some of the programs that were a source of help to the Poor family? What about Mr. Olds? Mrs. Affluent? Does the listing include programs that were of help to your family? What programs aid all the families of the nation?

We do not have similar tables that detail all the expenditures and services of private social welfare. However, as shown by Table 2–2, expenditures in this sector are increasing too. It has been estimated that in 1975 as many as 6 million voluntary U.S. groups could be classified as social welfare organizations. The core group of the traditional philanthropic organizations numbers more than 37,000 (Commission, 1975, p. 36). For those readers who are interested in social work as a profession, it has been estimated that by 1980 we will need 400,000 social workers, of whom 200,000 will need a master of social work degree (MSW). This estimate is up 100,000 from that for 1974 (Siegel, 1975).

Table 2-1
Social welfare expenditures under public programs, selected fiscal years, 1929–1975[1] *(in millions)*

Program	1929	1950	1955	1960	1965	1970	1972	1973	1974	1975[2]
					Total expenditures					
Total	$3,921.2	$23,508.4	$32,639.9	$52,293.3	$77,175.3	$145,761.1	$191,413.6	$214,389.9	$239,302.6	$286,547.0
Social insurance	342.4	4,946.6	9,834.9	19,306.7	28,122.8	54,691.2	74,810.2	86,152.7	98,952.1	123,444.1
Old-age, survivors, disability, and health insurance [5]		784.1	4,436.3	11,032.3	16,997.5	36,835.4	48,229.1	57,766.6	66,286.6	78,456.3
Health insurance (Medicare)[4]					7,149.2	8,819.2	9,478.8	11,347.5	14,781.4
Railroad retirement [3]		306.4	556.0	934.7	1,128.1	1,609.9	2,141.2	2,477.5	2,692.6	3,085.1
Public employee retirement [5]	113.1	817.9	1,388.5	2,569.9	4,528.5	8,658.7	11,921.3	14,010.8	16,692.1	20,000.0
Unemployment insurance and employment service [6]		2,190.1	2,080.6	2,829.6	3,002.6	3,819.5	7,651.0	6,065.9	6,660.7	14,396.5
Railroad unemployment insurance		119.6	158.7	215.2	76.7	38.5	86.0	45.2	25.6	41.5
Railroad temporary disability insurance		31.1	54.2	68.5	46.5	61.1	42.1	34.9	31.5	33.0
State temporary disability insurance [7]		72.1	217.5	347.9	483.5	717.7	783.7	848.2	915.4	904.2
Hospital and medical benefits [8]		2.2	20.0	40.2	50.9	62.6	68.3	69.8	70.7	73.3
Workmen's compensation [9]	229.3	625.1	943.0	1,308.5	1,859.4	2,950.4	3,955.7	4,903.6	5,647.6	6,437.5
Hospital and medical benefits [8]	75.0	193.0	315.0	420.0	580.0	985.0	1,185.0	1,335.0	1,560.0	1,830.0
Public aid	60.0	2,496.2	3,003.0	4,101.1	6,283.4	16,487.7	26,077.0	28,696.5	31,997.0	40,536.3
Public assistance [10]	59.9	2,490.2	2,941.1	4,041.7	5,874.9	14,433.5	21,895.0	24,002.6	23,827.4	26,610.6
Vendor medical payments [11]		51.3	211.9	492.7	1,367.1	5,212.8	7,751.6	9,208.6	10,371.9	12,968.0
Social services [11]						712.6	2,160.5	2,306.2	2,155.0	2,522.5
Supplemental security income [13]								45.7	2,799.9	6,036.4
Food stamps					35.6	576.9	1,865.6	2,218.1	2,818.4	4,677.4
Other [13]	.1	6.0	61.9	59.4	373.0	1,477.3	2,316.4	2,430.2	2,551.3	3,211.9
Health and medical programs [14]	351.1	2,063.5	3,103.1	4,463.8	6,246.4	9,752.8	12,681.6	13,187.5	14,359.7	16,635.7
Hospital and medical care	146.3	1,222.3	2,042.4	2,853.3	3,452.3	5,176.4	6,634.2	7,180.5	7,802.0	8,502.7
Civilian programs	117.1	886.1	1,297.6	1,973.2	2,515.5	3,416.8	4,293.2	4,712.5	5,061.0	5,491.7
Defense Department [15]	29.2	336.2	744.8	880.1	936.8	1,759.6	2,341.0	2,468.0	2,741.0	3,011.0
Maternal and child health programs [16]	6.2	29.8	92.9	141.3	227.3	431.4	495.3	455.3	493.4	540.0
Medical research [8]			.2	.6	4.3					
Medical research		69.2	132.8	448.9	1,165.2	1,561.4	1,772.0	2,001.0	2,092.0	2,424.0
School health (education agencies)[17]	9.4	30.6	65.9	101.0	142.2	246.6	281.3	300.0		
Other public health activities	88.8	350.8	383.7	401.2	671.0	1,405.0	2,075.3	2,151.7	2,625.3	3,457.0
Medical-facilities construction	100.4	360.8	385.4	518.1	588.3	932.1	1,423.5	1,099.0	1,347.0	1,712.0
Defense Department		1.1	33.0	40.0	31.1	52.5	100.0	76.0	86.0	157.0
Other	100.4	359.8	352.4	478.1	557.2	879.6	1,323.5	1,023.0	1,261.0	1,555.0
Veterans' programs	657.9	6,865.7	4,833.5	5,479.2	6,031.0	9,078.0	11,522.4	13,026.4	14,112.4	16,660.8
Pensions and compensation [18]	434.7	2,092.1	2,689.7	3,402.7	4,141.4	5,393.8	6,209.3	6,605.8	6,777.4	7,578.3
Health and medical programs	50.9	748.0	761.3	954.0	1,228.7	1,784.0	2,431.4	2,766.1	2,983.6	3,468.9
Hospital and medical care	46.7	582.8	721.5	879.4	1,114.8	1,651.4	2,255.6	2,587.3	2,786.6	3,242.3
Hospital construction	4.2	161.5	34.1	59.6	77.0	70.9	109.8	104.8	118.9	135.7
Medical and prosthetic research		3.7	5.6	15.1	36.9	61.8	66.0	74.0	78.0	91.0
Education		2,691.6	706.1	409.6	40.9	1,018.5	1,924.6	2,647.9	3,206.8	4,420.6
Life insurance [19]	136.4	475.7	490.2	494.1	434.3	502.3	523.7	532.2	538.5	556.1
Welfare and other	35.8	858.3	186.5	218.8	185.8	379.4	433.3	474.4	606.1	637.0
Education [20]	2,433.7	6,674.1	11,157.2	17,626.2	28,107.9	50,905.0	59,626.2	65,379.1	70,149.5	78,438.5
Elementary and secondary	2,216.2	5,596.2	9,734.3	15,109.0	22,357.7	38,632.3	44,524.0	48,376.9	52,083.5	57,905.4
Construction [8] [21]	377.0	1,019.4	2,231.9	2,661.8	3,267.0	4,659.1	4,458.9	5,008.4	5,259.3	5,487.0
Higher	182.1	914.7	1,214.4	2,190.7	4,826.4	9,970.3	11,850.8	13,259.2	13,893.6	15,972.5
Construction [8]	.2	310.3	196.6	357.9	1,081.4	1,629.1	1,736.7	1,793.4	1,758.7	1,942.0
Vocational and adult [21]	34.9	160.8	204.9	298.0	853.9	2,145.9	3,034.8	3,496.4	3,900.3	4,295.6
Housing		14.6	89.3	176.8	318.1	701.2	1,332.4	2,179.6	2,553.8	2,954.0
Public housing		14.5	74.7	143.5	234.5	459.9	731.1	1,101.9	1,232.9	1,456.0
Other		.1	14.6	33.2	83.6	241.3	601.3	1,077.7	1,320.9	1,498.1
Other social welfare	76.2	447.7	619.0	1,139.4	2,065.7	4,145.2	5,363.9	5,768.2	7,178.1	7,877.5
Vocational rehabilitation	1.6	30.0	42.4	96.3	210.5	703.8	875.5	911.7	926.8	950.0
Medical services [22]	.1	7.4	9.1	17.7	34.2	133.8	179.2	175.0	185.2	190.0
Medical research [22]			.3	6.6	22.4	29.6	17.0	15.0		
Institutional care [23]	74.7	145.5	195.3	420.5	789.5	201.7	251.1	263.5	284.8	301.8
Child nutrition [24]		160.2	239.6	398.7	617.4	896.0	1,502.3	1,707.0	2,023.0	2,517.7
Child welfare [26]		104.9	135.1	211.5	354.3	585.3	532.0	526.0	510.0	480.0
Special OEO and Action programs [26]					51.7	782.8	782.7	894.9	766.7	602.3
Social welfare, not elsewhere classified [27]		7.1	6.5	12.4	42.3	1,005.6	1,420.2	1,465.1	2,666.8	3,025.7

[1] Expenditures from federal, state, and local revenues (general and special) and trust funds and other expenditures under public law; includes capital outlay and administrative expenditures unless otherwise noted. Includes some payments abroad. Fiscal years ended June 30 for federal government, most states, and some localities.

[2] Preliminary estimates.

[3] Excludes financial interchange between OASDHI and railroad retirement.

[4] Included in total directly above; includes administration.

[5] Excludes refunds of employee contributions; includes noncontributory payments to retired military personnel and survivors. Administrative expenses for federal noncontributory retirement not available.

[6] Includes unemployment compensation under state programs, programs for federal employees and ex-servicemen, trade adjustment and cash training allowances, and payments under extended, emergency, disaster, and special unemployment-insurance programs.

Table 2-1 *(continued)*

Program	1929	1950	1955	1960	1965	1970	1972	1973	1974	1975 [3]
					From Federal funds					
Total	$798.4	$10,541.1	$14,622.9	$24,956.7	$37,711.7	$77,334.4	$106,312.5	$122,611.2	$137,654.5	$165,943.5
Social insurance	55.9	2,103.0	6,385.0	14,307.2	21,806.6	45,245.6	61,249.4	72,249.4	82,828.5	99,209.5
Old age, survivors, disability, and health insurance [3]		784.1	4,436.3	11,032.3	16,997.5	36,835.4	48,229.1	57,766.6	66,286.6	78,456.3
Health insurance (Medicare) [4]						7,149.2	8,819.2	9,478.8	11,347.5	14,781.4
Railroad retirement [3]		306.4	556.0	934.7	1,128.1	1,609.9	2,141.2	2,477.5	2,692.6	3,085.1
Public employee retirement [5]	51.9	507.9	808.5	1,519.9	2,780.5	5,516.7	7,648.4	8,878.1	10,785.1	12,725.0
Unemployment insurance and employment service [6]		328.6	320.8	473.5	699.8	1,036.1	2,486.9	1,869.1	1,720.9	3,513.5
Railroad unemployment insurance		119.6	158.7	215.2	76.7	38.5	86.0	45.2	25.6	41.5
Railroad temporary disability insurance		31.1	54.2	68.5	46.5	61.1	42.1	34.9	31.5	33.0
Workmen's compensation [9]	4.0	25.1	50.5	63.1	77.6	147.9	615.7	1,178.1	1,286.2	1,355.1
Hospital and medical benefits [8]	.6	5.2	6.9	9.0	11.3	20.7	26.9	32.3	36.1	50.6
Public aid		1,103.2	1,504.2	2,116.9	3,593.9	9,648.5	16,290.1	18,066.2	20,834.0	26,634.4
Public assistance [10]		1,097.2	1,442.3	2,057.5	3,185.4	7,594.3	12,108.1	13,372.3	13,307.2	14,103.2
Vendor medical payments [11]			23.3	199.8	555.0	2,607.1	4,166.2	4,997.4	5,833.2	6,966.4
Social services [11]						522.0	1,598.2	1,718.6	1,562.9	1,891.9
Supplemental security income [12]								45.7	2,157.1	4,641.9
Food stamps					35.6	576.9	1,865.6	2,218.1	2,818.4	4,677.4
Other [13]		6.0	61.9	59.4	373.0	1,477.3	2,316.4	2,430.2	2,551.3	3,211.9
Health and medical programs [14]	46.7	603.5	1,150.3	1,737.3	2,780.6	4,775.2	6,321.8	6,697.7	7,129.7	8,403.6
Hospital and medical care	37.7	382.6	811.5	983.5	1,074.7	2,045.4	2,960.3	3,272.7	3,562.0	4,100.6
Civilian programs	8.5	46.4	66.7	103.4	137.9	285.8	619.3	804.7	821.0	1,089.6
Defense Department [15]	29.2	336.2	744.8	880.1	936.8	1,759.6	2,341.0	2,468.0	2,741.0	3,011.0
Maternal and child health programs [16]	1.2	20.1	23.7	35.3	73.4	196.0	259.0	221.0	234.7	277.0
Medical research [8]				.2	.6	4.3				
Medical research		69.2	132.8	425.9	1,110.2	1,485.4	1,693.0	1,913.0	2,000.0	2,327.0
Other public health activities	6.9	63.8	65.0	57.3	222.9	590.3	968.0	911.0	959.0	1,201.0
Medical-facilities construction	.9	67.8	117.4	235.1	299.3	458.1	441.5	380.0	374.0	498.0
Defense Department		1.1	33.0	40.0	31.1	52.5	100.0	76.0	86.0	157.0
Other	.9	66.8	84.4	195.1	268.2	405.6	341.5	304.0	288.0	341.0
Veterans' programs	657.9	6,386.2	4,771.9	5,367.3	6,010.6	8,951.5	11,405.2	12,903.3	13,873.8	16,505.2
Pensions and compensation [18]	434.7	2,092.1	2,689.7	3,402.7	4,141.4	5,393.8	6,209.3	6,605.8	6,777.4	7,578.3
Health and medical programs	50.9	748.0	761.1	954.0	1,228.7	1,784.0	2,431.4	2,766.1	2,983.6	3,468.9
Hospital and medical care	46.7	582.8	721.5	879.4	1,114.8	1,651.4	2,255.6	2,587.3	2,786.6	3,242.3
Hospital construction	4.2	161.5	34.1	59.6	77.0	70.9	109.8	104.8	118.9	135.7
Medical and prosthetic research		3.7	5.6	15.1	36.9	61.8	66.0	74.0	78.0	91.0
Education		2,691.6	706.1	409.6	40.9	1,018.5	1,924.6	2,647.9	3,206.8	4,420.6
Life insurance [19]	136.4	475.7	490.2	494.1	434.3	502.3	523.7	532.2	538.5	556.1
Welfare and other	35.8	378.8	124.9	106.9	165.4	252.9	316.2	351.3	367.6	481.4
Education [20]	36.5	156.7	485.1	867.9	2,469.8	5,873.1	6,707.6	7,399.1	7,076.0	8,670.1
Elementary and secondary	9.6	47.1	309.2	441.9	776.8	2,956.8	3,417.8	3,548.3	3,675.0	4,337.1
Construction [8][21]	(20)	5.2	139.9	70.6	77.0	35.9	20.3	20.0	22.4	21.0
Higher	12.1	48.5	101.8	293.1	1,217.0	2,155.7	2,233.2	2,659.2	2,193.6	2,972.5
Construction [8]	.2	5.7	5.1	1.2	324.0	466.3	351.0	393.6	213.7	225.0
Vocational and adult [21]	14.3	58.7	70.5	104.5	406.2	604.1	840.1	945.0	935.3	1,095.6
Housing		14.6	74.7	143.5	238.2	581.6	1,183.2	1,749.7	2,008.9	2,354.0
Public housing		14.5	74.7	143.5	234.5	459.9	731.1	1,101.9	1,232.9	1,456.0
Other		.1			3.6	121.7	452.1	647.8	776.0	898.1
Other social welfare	1.4	174.0	251.7	416.7	812.0	2,258.9	3,155.1	3,545.9	3,903.5	4,166.6
Vocational rehabilitation	.7	21.0	27.1	64.3	143.3	567.4	719.6	753.2	796.8	798.0
Medical services [22]	.1	5.1	5.7	11.2	21.2	107.0	143.4	140.0	154.0	157.0
Medical research [22]				.3	6.6	22.4	29.6	17.0	15.0	
Institutional care [23]	.7	20.5	40.3	20.5	34.5	22.5	25.8	27.4	24.8	18.0
Child nutrition [24]		121.2	170.7	306.1	503.7	710.9	1,232.1	1,409.4	1,611.0	2,037.7
Child welfare [25]		4.2	7.1	13.4	36.5	44.7	44.7	45.9	47.4	49.8
Special OEO and Action programs [26]					51.7	752.8	782.7	894.9	766.7	602.3
Social welfare, not elsewhere classified [27]		7.1	6.5	12.4	42.3	160.6	350.2	415.1	656.8	660.7

[7] Cash and medical benefits in five areas. Includes private plans where applicable and state costs of administering state plans and supervising private plans. Administrative expenses of all private plans and all data for Hawaii not available.

[8] Included in total directly above; excludes administrative expenses, not available separately but included for entire program in preceding line.

[9] Cash and medical benefits paid under federal and state laws by private insurance carriers, state funds, and self-insurers. Includes Alaska and Hawaii beginning 1959–60. Administrative cost of private carriers and self-insurers not available. Starting 1970, federal expenditures include "black lung" benefit programs administered by the Social Security Administration and the Department of Labor.

[10] Represents categorical programs under the Social Security Act and (from state and local funds) general assistance. Starting 1969, includes work incentive activities.

[11] Included in total for public assistance above; vendor medical payments include administrative expenses of medical assistance (medicaid) program.

[12] Benefits began January 1974; fiscal year 1973 data represent administrative expenses only.

[13] Work relief, other emergency aid, surplus food for the needy,

Program	1929	1950	1955	1960	1965	1970	1972	1973	1974	1975 [2]
	From State and local funds [29]									
Total	$3,122.8	$12,967.3	$18,017.1	$27,336.6	$39,463.5	$68,426.7	$85,101.1	$91,778.7	$101,648.1	$120,603.5
Social insurance	286.5	2,843.6	3,449.9	4,999.4	6,316.2	9,445.6	13,560.8	13,903.3	16,123.5	24,234.6
Public employee retirement [3]	61.2	310.0	580.0	1,050.0	1,748.0	3,142.0	4,272.9	5,132.7	5,907.0	7,275.0
Unemployment insurance and employment service [6]		1,861.5	1,759.9	2,356.1	2,302.8	2,783.4	5,164.1	4,196.8	4,939.7	10,883.0
State temporary disability insurance [7]		72.1	217.5	347.9	483.5	717.7	783.7	848.2	915.4	994.2
Hospital and medical benefits [8]		2.2	20.0	40.2	50.9	62.6	68.3	69.8	70.7	73.3
Workmen's compensation [9]	255.3	600.0	892.5	1,245.4	1,781.8	2,802.5	3,340.0	3,725.5	4,361.4	5,082.4
Hospital and medical benefits [8]	74.4	187.8	308.1	411.0	568.7	964.3	1,158.1	1,302.7	1,523.9	1,779.4
Public aid	60.0	1,393.0	1,498.8	1,984.2	2,689.5	6,839.2	9,786.9	10,630.3	11,163.0	13,901.9
Public assistance [10]	59.9	1,393.0	1,498.8	1,984.2	2,689.5	6,839.2	9,786.9	10,630.3	10,820.2	12,507.4
Vendor medical payments [11]			51.3	188.6	292.9	812.1	2,605.6	3,585.4	4,211.3	4,538.7	6,001.7
Social services [11]						190.6	562.3	587.7	592.2	630.6
Supplemental security income [13]									642.8	1,394.5
Other	.1									
Health and medical programs [14]	304.4	1,460.0	1,952.8	2,726.8	3,465.8	4,977.6	6,359.8	6,489.8	7,230.0	8,232.1
Hospital and medical care	108.6	839.7	1,230.9	1,869.8	2,377.6	3,131.0	3,673.9	3,907.8	4,240.0	4,402.1
Maternal and child health programs [16]	5.0	9.7	69.2	106.1	153.9	235.3	236.3	234.3	258.7	263.0
Medical research				23.0	55.0	76.0	79.0	88.0	92.0	97.0
School health (educational agencies) [17]	9.4	30.6	65.9	101.0	142.2	246.6	281.3	300.0		
Other public health activities	81.9	287.0	318.8	343.9	448.1	814.7	1,107.3	1,240.7	1,666.3	2,256.0
Medical-facilities construction	99.5	293.0	268.0	283.0	289.0	474.0	982.0	719.0	973.0	1,214.0
Veterans' programs		479.5	61.6	111.9	20.4	126.5	117.1	123.1	238.6	155.6
Education	2,397.2	6,517.5	10,672.1	16,758.3	25,638.1	45,031.9	52,918.6	57,980.0	63,073.5	69,768.4
Elementary and secondary	2,206.6	5,549.1	9,425.1	14,667.1	21,580.9	35,675.5	41,106.3	44,828.6	48,408.5	53,568.4
Construction [8][21]	377.0	1,014.2	2,091.9	2,591.2	3,190.0	4,623.2	4,438.1	4,988.4	5,236.9	5,466.0
Higher	170.0	866.3	1,112.6	1,897.7	3,609.4	7,814.6	9,617.6	10,600.0	11,700.0	13,000.0
Construction [8]	(28)	304.6	193.4	355.7	757.4	1,162.8	1,385.7	1,399.8	1,545.0	1,717.0
Vocational and adult [21]	20.6	102.1	134.4	193.5	447.7	1,541.8	2,194.7	2,551.4	2,965.0	3,200.0
Housing			14.6	33.2	80.0	119.6	149.2	429.9	544.9	600.0
Other social welfare	74.8	273.7	367.3	722.8	1,253.6	1,886.3	2,208.8	2,222.3	3,274.6	3,710.9
Vocational rehabilitation	.8	9.0	15.3	32.1	67.1	136.3	155.8	168.5	130.0	152.0
Medical services [8]	.1	2.3	3.5	6.6	13.0	26.8	35.8	35.0	31.2	33.0
Institutional care [34]	74.0	125.0	155.0	400.0	775.0	179.3	225.3	236.1	260.0	283.8
Child nutrition [24]		39.0	69.0	92.6	113.7	185.1	270.3	297.6	412.0	480.0
Child welfare [25]		100.7	128.0	196.1	317.8	540.7	487.3	480.1	462.6	430.2
Social welfare, not elsewhere classified [27]						845.0	1,070.0	1,050.0	2,010.0	2,365.0

repatriate and refugee assistance, and work-experience training programs under the Economic Opportunity Act and the Comprehensive Employment and Training Act. See footnote 26.

[14] Excludes state and local expenditures for domiciliary care in institutions other than mental or tuberculosis and services in connection with OASDHI, state temporary disability insurance, workmen's compensation, public assistance, vocational rehabilitation, and veterans' and antipoverty programs (included in total expenditures for these programs).

[15] Includes medical care for military dependent families.

[16] Includes services for crippled children.

[17] Starting 1974, data not separable from expenditures under "education."

[18] Includes burial awards. Starting 1965, includes special allowances for survivors of veterans who did not qualify under OASDHI. Starting 1974, subsistence payments to disabled veterans undergoing training shifted from veterans' pensions and compensation to veterans' education subgroup.

[19] Excludes the Servicemen's Group Life Insurance program.

[20] Federal expenditures for administrative costs (Office of Education) and research included in total only.

[21] Construction for vocational and adult education included with elementary-secondary school construction.

[22] Medical services and research included in total; excludes administrative expenses.

[23] Federal expenditures represent primarily surplus food for institutions.

[24] Surplus food for schools and programs under National School Lunch and Child Nutrition acts, State and local funds represent direct appropriations.

[25] Represents primarily child-welfare services under the Social Security Act. Starting 1969, excludes administrative expenses.

[26] Includes domestic programs consolidated in fiscal year 1972 under Action (former VISTA, Foster Grandparents, and other domestic volunteer programs) and special OEO programs such as community action and migrant workers. Other OEO programs listed in appropriate subsection under public aid and education.

[27] Federal expenditures include administrative and related expenses of the secretary of health, education, and welfare and of the Social and Rehabilitation Service; Indian welfare and guidance; aging and juvenile delinquency activities; and certain manpower and human development activities. State and local expenditures include amounts for antipoverty and manpower programs, day care, child placement and adoption services, foster care, legal assistance, care of transients, and other unspecified welfare services; before 1970, these amounts included with institutional care.

[28] Not available.

[29] Except as otherwise noted (see footnotes 7 and 9).

Source: Treasury reports, federal budgets, Census of Governments, and reports of federal and state administrative agencies. For detailed description of programs and for single-year historical data, see Social Welfare Expenditures under Public Programs in the United States, 1929–1966 (Research Report no. 25).

Source: Social Security Bulletin, 1976, 39 (1), pp. 6–8.

☙ Cost benefits

In social welfare programs one is concerned not just with the costs of the programs but with the benefits realized in relation to some established priority. As social welfare costs have grown larger over the years, increasing concern with accountability has developed. Does the program as implemented achieve the objectives that were set when it was funded? How does it meet those objectives?

The attempt to measure the benefits realized through social welfare programs and the costs they incur is difficult and complicated. It is difficult to obtain agreements on the way benefits should be defined. Education benefits individuals in that it offers them opportunities for better jobs and higher income. Hopefully, it enables individuals to enjoy their leisure more. It also benefits the community in that individuals who earn higher wages pay greater taxes to support the general welfare, and in addition the community gains from the ability of those individuals to appreciate the world around them. Moreover, education operates to assure the economic system a supply of the appropriately trained workers who are necessary for its operation. Among all of these benefits, which are to be defined as important goals?

Once we have defined our goals, how are we to measure the benefits? In the case of education, we can measure the amount of money a person earns and make some estimate of how this would differ from the amount that would have been earned without the education. But what are the intangible benefits of education? These may be even more important than the tangible benefits, but how are we to measure them? An additional problem is found in the length of time that elapses between the expenditure of money to support a program and the reaping of the benefits from the program. The measurement of benefits requires information, and in most situations the administrators of programs do not know what they have accomplished. Can doctors prove that medical care does in fact make people healthier? Do educators have any notion of what their efforts really contribute to the lives of their students?

The benefits from social welfare programs cannot be measured on a common scale applicable to all the programs. Mrs. Poor receives direct money payments that meet her family's basic needs. How are these benefits to be weighed against the medical care that Mr. Olds and Mrs. Affluent receive? And how will the benefits of the educational programs that the Comfortable and Poor children attend compare with the benefits of the medical programs? And how does one compare the benefits of the money spent on higher education that is utilized largely by the affluent with the benefits of the money that goes to support the poor?

There are other complications. If we could measure benefits on a common scale, it would not necessarily follow that programs should be established and funded in the same order as the ratio of benefits to costs. There are broad social and political objectives that we may choose to implement, regardless of the costs of attempting to do so. Our value judgments about the benefits of social welfare programs may have little to do with the costs.

☙ Summary

In this chapter we have furnished the reader with some very simplified examples of the impact of social welfare programs upon two families and two older individuals. We are going to summarize these examples below. We will introduce some new words in this summary. These words will be italicized so that they can be identified easily. The words will reappear with definitions in the next three or four chapters. We use them now so that they can be connected with the concrete examples which will appear later.

We have looked at Mrs. Poor and Mr. Olds, whose need for income to maintain life (income maintenance) is met by basically *residual* public welfare programs in which eligibility for the necessary funds is established by what is known as a *means test.* This makes proof that one is without significant resources of one's own a condition for getting help. The Poors' and Mr. Olds's need for medical care is met primarily through a similar

◦§ Table 2–2
Public and private expenditures for social welfare programs, selected years, 1950–1975*

Fiscal year	Total† (public- private)	Public			Private
		Total	Federal	State-local	
Amount (in billions)					
1950	$ 35.7	$ 23.5	$ 10.5	$ 13.0	$ 12.2
1955	50.6	32.6	14.6	18.0	18.0
1960	80.1	52.3	25.0	27.3	27.8
1965	119.9	77.2	37.7	39.5	42.8
1970	213.8	145.8	77.3	68.4	68.0
1975‡	394.3	286.5	165.9	120.6§	107.8
As percent of GNP					
1950	13.5	8.9	4.0	4.9	4.6
1955	13.3	8.6	3.8	4.7	4.7
1960	16.1	10.5	5.0	5.5	5.6
1965	18.2	11.7	5.7	6.0	6.5
1970	22.3	15.2	8.1	7.1	7.1
1975‡	27.4	19.9	11.5	8.4	7.5
Percentage distribution					
1950	100.0	65.8	29.4	36.4	34.2
1955	100.0	64.4	28.9	35.6	35.6
1960	100.0	65.3	31.2	34.1	34.7
1965	100.0	64.4	31.4	32.9	35.7
1970	100.0	68.2	36.2	32.0	31.8
1975§	100.0	72.7	42.1	30.6	27.3

Source: Advisory Commission on Intergovernmental Relations (ACIR) staff compilation based on U.S. Department of Health, Education, and Welfare, *Social Security Bulletin,* January 1976; Alfred M. Skolnick and Sophie R. Dales, *Social Welfare Expenditures, 1950–75;* and U.S. Department of Commerce, Bureau of Economic Analysis, *Benchmark Revision of National Income and Product Accounts: Advance Tables, March 1976.* From ACIR, *Significant Features of Fiscal Federalism, 1976* (Washington, D.C.: U.S. Government Printing Office, 1976), pp. 19–41. From R. Morris, *Social Policy of the American Welfare State: An Introduction to Policy Analysis* (New York: Harper & Row, 1979), p. 24.

* Includes income maintenance, health, education, and welfare and other services.
† Includes the following amounts of duplication resulting from the use of cash payments received under public and private social welfare programs to purchase medical care and educational services: 1950, $0.4 billion; 1955, $0.6 billion; 1960, $1.4 billion; 1965, $2.0 billion; 1970, $2.8 billion; 1975, $5.6 billion.
‡ Preliminary.
§ Federal general revenue sharing is included as state-local expenditure. In fiscal year 1974 an estimated $3.1 billion in general revenue-sharing receipts was spent for social welfare purposes. Estimates for 1975 are not available.

residual, means-tested process. One important distinguishing factor of the programs that employ this process is that they serve persons who are without certain specified ties to work.

We have also looked at Mrs. Affluent, who receives income and medical care primarily from a welfare program that is commonly known as social security. Mrs. Affluent receives this support as a result of her age and of her late husband's employment in a *covered work situation.* She did not have to prove need—in fact, she has the largest personal income of any of the individuals in our

examples. Mr. Comfortable also has help with the medical needs of his family, received because of his ties to his work. His eligibility for this care has nothing to do with his need for such support. These people receive help because they fall into certain categories of individuals who have defined ties to the work force.

In addition to these social welfare programs, we have seen how both the Poor and the Comfortable families use the educational resources of the community: how the Comfortables use certain programs in a *privately supported* community center and how the Poors use a *private agency*—Big Brothers. Both Mrs. Poor and Mrs. Comfortable also use social work counseling. Mrs. Poor receives this help through a *public agency,* and Mrs. Comfortable goes to a *private agency* for it.

We ended the chapter with a brief look at the costs of social welfare programs as of the fiscal year 1975. This was done as a way of developing, through concrete examples, a comprehension of the complexity and extent of public programs of social welfare.

✌§ A look ahead

In the next chapter we will discuss the many attempts that have been made to define social welfare. The examples that we have given in this chapter should have served to raise questions in your minds about how this complex, wriggling monster can be described and classified. We hope that the next chapter will begin the process of clarifying some of the confusion raised by the examples and discussion of this chapter.

✌§ Study questions

1. Think about the stories of the families. How do you respond to Mrs. Poor? Do you think she should be working? What would be necessary if she should be required to work?
2. Mr. Comfortable could afford to contribute to Mrs. Affluent's support. Do you think *social security* is a better solution than her dependence on her son-in-law? What are your reasons for and against this solution?
3. Can you select from the programs in Table 2–1 those that benefit you and members of your family? Have you ever thought of yourself as benefiting from welfare?
4. Do the costs of welfare disturb you? If so, what programs from Table 2–1 would you eliminate? What population group of groups would this affect? Why do you think the programs could be eliminated?
5. What programs in Table 2–1 show an increase in supporting funds? What kinds of programs are these?
6. Before you begin to read the next chapter, try to write your definition of social welfare from what you

have learned from this chapter and from your own previous experiences.
7. Make a list of the questions that you have after reading this chapter. Keep the questions, and try to write the answers to them as you encounter those answers in the text. Do the same with the new words that you have found in the chapter.

✌§ Selected readings

Morales, A., and Sheafor, B. *Social Work: A Profession of Many Faces.* Boston: Allyn & Bacon, 1977. Pp. 161–66.

A welfare mother tells the story of her battle with the system. Her account should raise many questions about how the client negotiates the public welfare system.

Wilcox, C. *Toward Social Welfare.* Homewood, Ill.: Richard D. Irwin, 1969.

Although this book was published ten years ago and does not include the most recent programs of social welfare, it is an excellent book that we will refer to many times in our text. As a beginning, we would recommend that the student read chaps. 1–4 to gain an understanding of the social problems of the United States.

Wilensky, H. L., and Lebeaux, C. N. *Industrial Society and Social Welfare.* New York: Free Press, 1965.

A number of references to this book will appear throughout this text. We would recommend using only the paperback edition. This has a new introductory statement by Wilensky, "The Problems and Prospects of the Welfare State," which we are recommending for reading along with this chapter. The statement may raise several questions about social welfare that are not dealt with in this chapter. Readers should list those questions and hold them for later. One mark of a good student is the ability to tolerate ambiguity. Thus, students do not need to have their questions answered immediately. They should hold them and pursue them over time. This is a good experience in scholarship, and besides it makes learning more interesting if you pursue your own questions over a period of time.

Federico, R. *The Social Welfare Institution.* 2d ed. Lexington, Mass.: D. C. Heath, 1967.

We are recommending that students read the material on pages 16–30, including the accompanying exhibits 1–4. This should further the material in our text.

Zastrow, C. *Introduction to Social Welfare Institutions.* Homewood, Ill.: Dorsey Press, 1978.

The example given on pages 5–6 in this text should further illustrate the material in our chapter.

An example of social welfare activities directed at the development and change of social systems.

The Spanish Speaking Unity Council (SSUC) of Oakland, California, was founded in 1969 by Arabella Martinez and others from Oakland's large Mexican-American community. The SSUC, one of three Chicano community development corporations funded by the Ford Foundation, is successfully working to develop Chicano leadership, to win recognition of that leadership by the community at large, and, as a consequence, to make social, economic, and political institutions more responsive to the needs of the Chicano community.

Ms. Martinez, shown above, is a social worker, and former Assistant Secretary of Family and Children's Services, H.E.W.

Chapter 3 ?∾

∾? Social welfare—
Definition and purpose ?∾

∾? **Introduction**

In this chapter we shall discuss the concept of social welfare and examine some definitions found in social work literature that has been written over the last 15 years. Further, we shall develop and discuss a concept of social welfare and its functions that will be useful in understanding the material in this text. In doing so, we shall also discuss several notions about the purpose of social welfare in our society.

Even though social welfare activities are a very important part of our lives, and of the lives of people in every industrialized nation in the world, we find it hard to reach agreement on a definition of the activities that fit within the concept. Perhaps this is difficult because the term *social welfare* expresses a changing view of a changing institution. Social welfare is a relatively new institution that began with the breakup of feudalism as a substitute for what the community as a whole, the church, or the extended family once did. But we have never really accepted social welfare programs and services as necessary to individual functioning in a modern world. We in the United States have continued over the years to see the emergence of social welfare (so necessary in an industrial society that every industrial nation has developed such an institution and most industrial nations have committed a far greater proportion of their resources to it than has the United States) as an illicit encroachment on the functions of the older and more traditional societal institutions. Thus we often feel that there is something seriously wrong either with a society that must maintain this institution or with the individuals who utilize it, or both. We are in the curious situation of having a new and still-emerging institution to which we have given a most broad and diffuse responsibility in critical areas of individual and societal life without having really legitimated it by developing a commonly accepted definition that speaks to its purpose, function, and parameters.

✎§ Concepts of social welfare

In a book written in 1965, Wilensky and Lebeaux (1965, pp. 138–47) identified two differing concepts of social welfare as dominant in the United States. It is our belief that these two notions of social welfare are still prominent in our society. The first is the conviction that social welfare activities should be called upon only when the ordinary, expected, and normal structures of society break down. This view assumes that the individual's needs are "naturally" met through the channels of the family or the market economy—the preferred sources that should be utilized to meet individual needs. However, when these channels do not function properly or when the individual through some personal handicap is unable to use them, the social welfare structure is brought into play as a temporary substitute. This way of conceptualizing social welfare views it as a *residual* institution, "attending primarily to emergency functions" and "expected to withdraw when the regular social structure is again working properly." (Wilensky and Lebeaux, 1965, p. 139).

One might add that this notion implies that it is the moral duty of the people using social welfare agencies to do everything in their power to make themselves able once again to utilize the "normal" channels of meeting needs. The very fact that social welfare agencies are seen as coming into play following a breakdown of the usual ways of meeting need means that the persons utilizing such agencies are considered abnormal or deviant. They are seen, therefore, as weaker, or less adequate, than their fellows, and the acceptance of help under these conditions carries the stigma of dole or charity. The programs used by the Poors and Mr. Olds were of this nature. One is not eligible for the benefits of these programs until one has no other resources.

The second view of social welfare has been labeled the *institutional* conception. This notion sees social welfare as an accepted, legitimate function of the modern, industrial society, designed to serve individuals and groups as they seek to attain satisfy-

ing standards of life and health for themselves. It aims at the fullest possible development of the capacities and well-being of the individual as a way of serving both the individual and the social group. According to this view, seeking to use the social welfare institution implies no stigma, no weakness, no moral failure. The institutional conception considers a modern industrial society to be one in which all persons are so closely interdependent and interactive that the inability of individuals to provide fully for themselves or to meet all their own needs through the family or the marketplace is a normal state of membership in that society. Each and every member of such a society will, as a normal part of human life, find it helpful or necessary to utilize the social provisions or social services of social welfare. As a result of such use each individual will be a more effective member of the society that establishes and supports the social welfare institution. The helping agencies, in this view, are seen as having a regular or *institutional* status in society.

While these two views seem very divergent, in practice we find agencies and programs in today's social welfare structure representing both of them. Mrs. Poor receives public assistance (means-tested money payments to meet maintenance needs) from a public welfare agency. Underlying this program is the *residual* concept that her support should come through her family or a job, and she may receive benefits only if she can prove that she has needs that cannot be met through these channels. Mrs. Affluent, in contrast, receives OASDI regardless of her need. It comes to her because she belongs to a particular, defined group of people for whom this program was established. This more nearly meets the concept of an *institutional* program. Although Mrs. Affluent proved "normality" through marrying a man with a proper attachment to the work force, there is also an assumption that it is normal for elderly people to need some basic economic support, that Mrs. Affluent's service to society as a wife and mother gives her a natural and normal claim on the resources of society.

Wilensky and Lebeaux have served us well in naming and defining the two differing conceptions of social welfare. These two widely divergent notions have been and still are the cause of much of the struggle between the various groups concerned with the development and functioning of social welfare. We will be dealing with the impact of these two notions on the development of social welfare programs in the remainder of the text. The residual concept was born during the transition of our society from mercantilism to industrialism. One may question it as a base upon which to build the social welfare system for a modern society, but one must also ask why it has been around so long if it is an ineffective way to view social welfare.

It is important to understand that notions about the purpose of social welfare, as about all of its other aspects, do not develop or continue to exist in a vacuum. It is our position in this text that social welfare can best be understood as an *institution* made up of *interacting systems*. These systems and the institution, or larger system, are affected by a range of factors in the society in which the institution develops: the various views of the nature of human beings found in society; values and value systems; social philosophies; economic and political supports and pressures; economic and political resources; the behaviors, motivations, and goals of certain individuals in society; the available knowledge and technology; and (last, but certainly among the most powerful) past solutions and notions as to the effectiveness of those solutions. All of these things in complex interaction bear on the kind of social welfare system that any nation develops; and perhaps they bear most heavily on the development of such a system in a democratic society. Just when one thinks one understand this complex, wriggling, squirming, growing monster, something occurs to challenge all over again all of one's hard-earned knowledge.

In order to examine the concept of social welfare, many authors have struggled to define it. As no one of these efforts has resulted in a commonly accepted definition, we shall examine several definitions here. These were selected to introduce readers to the range of the notions found in the literature.

✌§ Definitions

Social workers often turn to the *Encyclopedia of Social Work* as a source of authoritative statements about social work matters. The 1971 edition defined social welfare as follows:

> "Social welfare" generally denotes the full range of organized activities of voluntary and governmental agencies that seek to prevent, alleviate, or contribute to the solution of recognized social problems, or to improve the well-being of individuals, groups, or communities. Such activities use a wide variety of professional personnel such as physicians, nurses, lawyers, educators, engineers, ministers, social workers, and paraprofessional counterparts of each. (p. 1146)

The 1977 edition of the *Encyclopedia* put it somewhat differently:

> Social welfare is an organized effort to insure a basic standard of decency in relation to the physical and mental well-being of the citizenry. . . . [It] includes considerably more than assuring the necessities to support life . . . is characterized by a large complex of interlocking preventive and protective laws and organizations designed to provide, at the least, universal access to the mainstream of society . . . [involves] the ever-present, active assistance to individuals and groups to facilitate their attaining and maintaining a respectable lifestyle. (p. 1503)

Both of these definitions see social welfare as an *organized effort* to improve the well-being of individuals, groups, or communities. The 1977 statement adds a new element to the job of social welfare—that of *active assistance* to persons who are having difficulty in obtaining access to ways of developing a "respectable" life-style. However, one cannot help but wonder what may be meant by "respectable." Does this mean that the recipient is expected to conform to the judgments of others, or is the word a substitute for "satisfying," meaning something sought by the individual? The 1971 statement seems clearer in its view that the purpose of welfare is to enhance the welfare of the whole population by developing programs that improve the well-being of all individuals, groups, or communities. It sees welfare as seeking to prevent, alleviate, or contribute to the resolution of social problems rather than to support failing individuals. When individuals need help to maintain themselves, this is seen as a social problem rather than individual failure. This definition tends to see social welfare as *institutional*.

Philip Klein, writing in 1968, formulated a much narrower definition of social welfare as "the administration of certain services to individuals and families who find it *difficult or impossible to maintain themselves* and their dependents in *material solvency* and in *health by their own efforts*" [Italics added for emphasis.] (Klein, 1968, p. 7).

This definition expresses a very different concept of social welfare. Klein sees the purpose of social welfare as the supplying of financial assistance or material goods and health care to families or persons that have failed individually in coping with the essential tasks of life. According to this view, social welfare measures come into play only when individuals can no longer fend for themselves and have no resources within themselves or their families to support them and solve their problems. This is an example of the *residual* view of social welfare.

In his text on social welfare, Walter A. Friedlander has developed a much-quoted definition that goes thus:

> Social welfare is a system of laws, programs, benefits, and services which strengthen or assure provisions for meeting social needs recognized as basic for the welfare of the population and for the functioning of the social order. The system is undergoing rapid transformation in response to the transition of our society from scarcity to relative abundance and to the revolution of rising expectations. (1961, p. 4)

Friedlander first presented this definition in 1955, and he repeated it in the 1961 edition of his book. A government agency, the Social Security Administration, offered the following definition in 1950:

The concept of social welfare in the United States of America is not constant, but rather it alters with changing conditions. Most recently, social welfare has been defined as encompassing the development and administration of (1) Social Insurance, (2) Social Assistance, and (3) other social services designed to strengthen family life and to provide care and protection for special groups such as children, the aged, and mentally, socially, or physically handicapped persons. (Social Security Administration, *Social Security Bulletin*, 1950, p. 1).

In 1965 Elizabeth Wickenden defined social welfare as "including those laws, programs, benefits and services which assure or strengthen provisions for meeting social needs recognized as basic to the well-being of the population and the better functioning of the social order" (p. vii). In *Social Welfare: Charity to Justice,* John M. Romanyshyn, a student of social welfare development and a teacher of social work courses in the subject, defines social welfare as

> including all those forms of social intervention that have a primary and direct concern with promoting both the well-being of the individual and of the society as a whole. Social welfare includes those provisions and processes directly concerned with the treatment and prevention of social problems, the development of human resources, and the improvement in the quality of life. It involves social services to individuals and families as well as efforts to strengthen or modify social institutions. Looking at it from a sociological point of view, social welfare functions to maintain the social system and to adapt it to changing social reality. From an ideological point of view, it is society's answer to that ancient and ever-recurring question, "Am I my brother's keeper?" (1971, p. 3).

Elsewhere Romanyshyn says that social welfare is "a field of activities and policies directing efforts to deal with social problems" (1974, p. 70).

All of the above definitions recognize that social welfare is not a static concept and imply that this fact makes definition difficult. However, these definitions do have some things in common. First, they see social welfare as being composed of laws, programs, benefits, and/or services which would indicate some formal organization and a social sponsorship. Second, they emphasize the purpose of welfare as being to further the well-being of the population as well as the better functioning of the social order. In other words, social welfare has as its purpose the support of the stability of society as well as the development of the individual. We believe that the authors of the definitions did not see these two aspects of welfare as two different things. The individual cannot exist with any peace or sense of control in a society that does not have a certain minimum of stability and order. And the organized human groups that make up society cannot function without individuals who have a certain sense of purpose and who possess skills needed by the society. Thus, there is an interaction between the individual and society that is necessary to both.

There are, however, other definitions that take up one aspect or the other of this interrelationship. In a provocative paper on the systemic nature of welfare, Martin Wolins says: "Social welfare is a device for maintaining or strengthening the existing social strucuture of an industrial society" (1976, p. 1). Here the purpose of welfare is seen as totally related to the strengthening of a particular model of society.

A text in social welfare defines the concept as an institution of society which has as its purpose "improving social functioning and minimizing suffering through a system of socially approved financial and social services at all levels in the social structure." Federico, the author of this text, goes on to say that the "focus of the social welfare system may be on solving existing problems (curative), preventing the future occurrence of problems (preventive), or rehabilitating those with problems to prevent future problems (rehabilitative)" (1976, pp. 17–18). This definition puts primary emphasis on individuals and their development.

Crampton and Keiser define social welfare as "a system that embodies a multifaceted approach to social and economic problems, reflecting social values and using the expertise of interrelated disciplines for the collective good" (1970, p. 5). In a very brief and simple statement defining social welfare, Smith and Zeitz write that "the social services

institutionalize, as public policy, the philanthropic impulse" (1970, p. 3). This definition appears to be the very opposite of Wolins's in that it puts the emphasis on welfare as help from the better off to those in need.

In writing the U.S. Committee Report for the 1974 International Conference on Social Welfare, John Turner describes social welfare as including

> (1) the wide range of services designed to attain ways of life acceptable to individuals and the community, sometimes thought of collectively as the "social aspects of development" and including services designed to strengthen the individual confronted with economic, physical, mental or social disabilities, together with (2) those aimed at including the remedy of conditions leading to dependency.
>
> The scope of social welfare in the U.S. is not as broad as social work professionals concerned with the question would like it to be. While the preferred definition suggests improvements in social conditions for all, [and] support and enhancement of the social well-being of the total population, in actual practice the scope of social welfare has a narrower and more residual orientation. . . . The principal targets of social welfare are then, in spite of our preferences for a broader view, special groups in the population whose social situation is problematic [that is] . . . the poor, the handicapped, the dependent, the deprived, the deviant, the disadvantaged, the alienated. (p. 19)

Of all the definitions, John Turner's discussion of the scope of social welfare most closely parallels the conceptions of Wilensky and Lebeaux. First, Turner includes in the purpose of social welfare the "enhancement of the social well-being of the total population." This deals with welfare from an *institutional* perspective. But it is only half of the definition. The second notion discussed by Turner, "in actual practice the scope of social welfare has a narrower and more residual orientation," takes account of the fact that the *residual* view of social welfare is still found in our society. However, Turner's statement does not seem to consider the possibility that social welfare can serve the structure of society itself.

✑§ Further consideration of residual and institutional concepts

At the dawn of the industrial era, confronted with the problem that the older institutions (family, religious, political, economic) were not meeting certain human needs, society gradually and painfully began to develop social welfare as a new social institution. However, in the struggle over the shape and purpose of the new institution, societal leaders have constantly asked, "Why social welfare?" Why were human needs not being met by the older institutions? The simplest explanation was that something was wrong with either the individual or the institutions—something that, given the right answers, could be fixed so that things would once again be right without any major, ongoing work. Thus the earliest notion was that the new institution should serve as a temporary substitute for the failures of the major older institutions or failures of the individual (most often the latter). It was thought that once the failures had been identified and remedied, social welfare activities would no longer be needed. We have previously labeled this view as residual in that it sees the social welfare institution as a correction of failure, rather undesirable, and certainly not of equal standing with the major societal institutions.

As we have noted earlier, certain leaders have become concerned with this notion, feeling that it was an inaccurate view of this emerging institution. These persons held that social welfare should be seen as the normal and accepted means by which individuals, families, and communities fulfilled needs and attained a satisfying life in the new society that was evolving in the industrial and post-industrial age. However, it has been difficult for persons espousing this concept to spell out exactly how this notion should differ from the earlier notion in the actual functioning of the institutional approach. How were the resources and services of the social welfare institution to be allocated, given the fact that the resources to support human life are not infinite? As long as we distribute certain services and resources because individuals have presumably failed to gain or husband their own

resources, it will be hard to make Wilensky and Lebeaux's, institutional concept of social welfare a viable one. The later chapters of the text will examine this central problem in some detail.

However, to state this problem in a very simple way, it would appear that the fundamental issue in the definition of social welfare is the extent to which the institution is seen as (1) a temporary one reflecting the deficiencies of some individuals or reflecting some small problem in institutional functioning that can be put right in a defined period of time by a defined action, as opposed to (2) the notion that social welfare is a regular institution necessary to life in a modern industrial society. Such institutional programs and resources are necessary because of the inherent limitations of both institutional adaptations to change and the individual's efforts to achieve self-development and fulfillment in a complex and changing world.

Which view of social welfare one adopts depends in large measure upon how one, or one's group, defines the problems of unmet need in our society. *How we define a problem sets the parameters of our consideration of its causes and of the ways in which it can be approached.* We would point out that both views of social welfare rest to some extent on the idea that something is ineffective in meeting individual needs. This leads to the position that something is wrong somewhere and that someone is at fault—something and someone that can be corrected without affecting the rest of us—something that will return our way of operating to its previous balance and pace of change.

But perhaps it is time that we accepted the notion that human life in both its individual and its organized components is a developmental process. As this development proceeds, we find that certain changes and adjustments have to be made by individuals, their organized groups, and society. These changes are made necessary by growth and not by failure. An example of such change from the perspective of the individual is adolescence. When a person grows from childhood to adolescence, a process the individual cannot change or alter, the family's response to him must change. This change comes from productive growth and from the problems that growth and difference bring to the family, not from failures in either the adolescent or the family. In fact, if the family treats such development as the individual's problem, then the family, the adolescent, and, to some extent, society will inevitably be hurt.

✅§ An interstitial institution

Accepting this view of human beings and their society—this notion of development, growth, and change that inevitably require some changes in previously stable ways of meeting needs—we propose that social welfare be viewed as a very special type of social institution. Social welfare needs to be viewed as an *interstitial institution*—an institution concerned with the development of both society and the individual.

As an institution

There are two concepts here that need discussion: (1) the concept of social welfare as an institution and (2) the concept of interstitial. The reader may have been aware that from the beginning of the text we have written of social welfare as an *institution* (not to be confused with Wilensky and LeBeaux's special use of the term). Although the reader may not have been aware of it, we have been using the term *social institution* in a very special way. We see social welfare, as we will use it in this text, as a social institution in that it encompasses an aspect of social life in which distinctive value orientations and interests (this does not mean that some value orientations are not in conflict) center upon a very large and important social concern. These concerns generate and are accompanied by distinctive modes of social interaction and relationships that are of strategic structural significance. We are speaking of an institution in the sense that W. G. Sumner defines it: "An institution consists of a concept (idea, notion, doctrine, interest) and a structure. . . . The structure is a framework or apparatus, or perhaps only a number of

functionaries, . . . [which] holds the concept and furnishes instrumentalities for bringing it into the world of facts and action" (Gould and Kolb, 1964, p. 338).

Federico (1976, p. 19) also defines social welfare as an institution. He believes that this is helpful because all definitions of social welfare attribute social functioning to it and because it is internally structured. Social functioning and internal structure are key concepts in the definition of a social institution. He says: "These characteristics . . . allow us to talk about it as a social institution, meaning that it embodies a set of norms clustered around a societal function and operationalized by a social structure of positions and roles."

We are in agreement with this way of regarding the concept of social welfare. In Chapter 5 we will discuss a way of conceptualizing the structure of the institution's positions and roles. For now, we would like to discuss the distinguishing characteristics of the agencies, organizations, and activities that fall within our notion of social welfare.

The distinguishing charactertistics of the institution

Ideological base. We need to recognize that social welfare as an institution involves value orientations and interests that are a reflection of the broader cultural and societal conditions within which the institution operates. This ideological base is not unitary, but however conflicting its ideological base may be, social welfare cannot exist without such a base.

Formal organization. As we shall conceive of social welfare activities, they are formally organized and assume a "degree of social distance between helped and helper" (Wilensky and Lebeaux, 1965, p. 141). This means that intermittent handouts or individual acts of charity do not fall within our definition of social welfare. Neither do services or aid given to a person with whom we have a bond of friendship, or kinship, or group association. We recognize that it is often difficult to draw a sharp dividing line that separates certain mutual aid welfare activities or the the welfare activities of small church groups or neighborhood agencies from help given within the parameters of personal bonds. However, in this text we are discussing the regular, full-time, and recognized social welfare activities of the community.

Socially sanctioned purposes and methods; accountability. The formal organizations found within the social welfare institution are sponsored by the community through some sanctioning process and are accountable to the community for the services they render. In the case of a public agency, this is accomplished through some sort of legislative action establishing the agency. In a case of a voluntary agency, accountability is achieved through the establishment of a governing board of some sort and sometimes through permissive legislation or other public licensing or approval.

Absence of profit motive. "The services and goods produced by the market economy and purchased by individuals with money derived from competitive participation in the economy are not social welfare" (Wilensky and Lebeaux, 1965, p. 142). Thus, although we will discuss the health system as a part of social welfare, when the medical practitioner, as an individual, charges what she/he thinks the individual can pay for the service, her/his income is clearly nonwelfare in nature. This is as true for private social work practitioners as for any other individual professionals. The professional in private practice may scale fees so as to put services within the user's ability to pay. However, this is done under the mandate of professional ethics rather than as a part of the social welfare concept.

A greater problem is presented by the recreational facilities, pension plans, or health care that a profit-making enterprise may offer its employees. It is possible to take the position that such services are not central to the mission of the organization and that they do not alter the nature of the central profit-making activity. Such benefits offered by companies are usually set up separately from the financial operations of the companies, usually have or are paid from a separate trust fund, and usually come under some degree of government operation.

Also, the social welfare purposes of such activities are recognized by the taxing policies of the government. However, it is possible to take the position that such programs are only a substitute for wages and are thus established specifically for the purposes of furthering the profit-making enterprise. However, it is clear that the programs affect the development of other social welfare programs. Most pension plans, for instance, give some recognition to the role of OASDI, and there is legislation that provides tax benefits for employees who, having no employer-provided pension plan, decide to establish individual plans. Thus we feel some need to take account of industrial welfare programs in our discussion of social welfare services.

Concern with human needs. Social welfare activities are primarily concerned with the consumption needs of individuals and families. This should in no way be taken to mean that social welfare activities are not concerned with changes in the larger social structure. However, the social changes with which social welfare is concerned are those that contribute to the welfare of individuals and families rather than those that are a part of the functioning of the nation-state, and such as national defense, the preservation of law and order, and the administration of criminal justice. Social welfare is concerned with social change and with the development of programs in which there are direct benefits to individuals and families as well as general benefits. The difficulty in distinguishing social welfare services from other socially sponsored services brings us to the discussion of social welfare as an *interstitial institution.*

As an interstitial institution

Interstitial is defined as that "situated between the cellular elements of a structure or a part" *(American College Dictionary,* 1973, p. 638). We consider it helpful to regard social welfare as interstitial institution. Welfare services are found attached to, or performing in place of, the family, the economy of the marketplace, and the church. Welfare activities often serve the political institution of society while they serve the individual. Since human needs and human capacities are almost countless, social welfare activities are infinitely varied and social welfare as an institution is extremely diffuse. Social welfare operates in the spaces between individuals, families, and other institutions of society when their differences or lacks appear to handicap individual development and problem solving.

This notion presupposes a relationship between the individual and society in which each reaches out for the other through a mutual need for self-fulfillment. The individual and society need each other for life and growth—neither can survive without the other. The institution of social welfare is charged with functioning at the place where the individual's push toward health, growth, and belonging meets the social institutions of society that have been developed primarily to meet the needs of society.

The charge of the social welfare institution then becomes one of integrating societal and individual needs, and societal and individual struggles toward growth and change, into a productive and dynamic whole. Thus social welfare as an institution is quite properly charged with a supporting role in relation to (1) all social institutions and (2) all individuals as both social institutions and individuals struggle with life and change. It is only as both are tended to that social welfare meets its charge as an institution in today's complex society.[1] As such an institution, social welfare should be routinely available to individuals and groups, as a resource of equal merit and standing with other institutions, whenever the functioning of other institutions and the needs of the individual do not mesh effectively. Of all the social welfare organizations, the educational system has perhaps come closest to achieving this type of recognition. It is generally accepted that in our highly diversified society the family and the church lack the technology needed to import all the knowledge and skills that are required for

the effective socialization and integration of the individual into society, although they once carried the full burden of these functions. However, the respective roles of the school and the family may still be a problem when the school and the family conflict over the proper content and methods of socialization.

In today's world, social welfare organizations lack the resources, the means, or the personnel that would enable them to completely substitute for any, or all, of the other social institutions. This is called to our attention by the recent literature which holds that children have difficulty in achieving appropriately in school when the family fails to perform certain basic socialization functions. Thus, one of the most complete and best-accepted of social welfare systems finds that it cannot fully perform the functions or totally substitute for the functioning of the institutions it stands beside. Perhaps one of the reasons that social welfare organizations are regarded as failures by certain groups is that they have verbally accepted the responsibility for totally substituting for the functioning of selected societal institutions in the lives of individuals without actually being able to carry out that charge. It would seem important, given the above conceptual formulation, for social welfare to become increasingly aware of the importance of its interaction, as an interstitial institution, with the parallel first-line institutions whose functioning it supplements.

✑ Functions of social welfare

This leads to some consideration of the functions of social welfare. It is our position that the social welfare institution must be concerned with three types of activities.

1. *Maintenance activities* that act to protect the individual by supplying necessary limits, supports, and resources to enable adequate coping with life and also act to ensure the coherence, continuity, and stability of the other social institutions of society as they struggle to cope with change and provide for individuals and groups within their areas of concern.

---

[1] This notion rests on William Schwartz's views on the function of social work as originally developed in "The Social Worker in the Group," National Conference on Social Welfare, *Social Welfare Forum, 1961* (New York: Columbia University Press, 1961), pp. 146–71.

2. *Developmental activities* that, within the prevailing social values and political structure, work to aid the orderly growth both of the individual and of the established political, economic, familial, and religious institutions within the framework of national plans and aspirations in order to furnish a foundation for the optimal development of individuals and families.

3. *Change activities* that aim directly at changing individual, family, and group functioning when the individual wants to change and when change is necessary for the protection of self and others and also aim directly at changing significant elements in the social structure even if this means challenging existing values and organizational investments in the status quo. Such change activities seek, through pressure within the bounds of existing law, to change the workings of other social institutions when these workings are identified as hurtful to the individuals or groups within society.

That social welfare is charged with helping individuals in these ways is generally recognized, but we do not always see the importance of social welfare's charge in relation to that of other social institutions. Writing in *Social Service Review* about the functions of social welfare in regard to social systems, Herman Stein (1976, pp. 1–11) sees these functions as system maintenance, system development, and system change. He defines the functions as follows:

> System maintenance sustains social stability and cohesion through meeting needs of people in accordance with prevailing social values and institutions. Developmental functions aid in the orderly growth and change of established institutions, . . . System change challenges significant values and elements in the social structure including distribution of wealth and power. (p. 1).

✑§ A proposed definition

Given the concept of social welfare developed above, perhaps the following definition will be helpful. Social welfare is a social institution charged with the necessary function of helping both individuals and the other social institutions to move to-

gether more productively for the sake of individual and family welfare. This is accomplished by offering the other social institutions and individuals certain services that are designed for the support and maintenance of present or previous functioning, the development of the capacity to function more productively, and the solution of significant problems within either individuals or social institutions.

We would propose the following way of establishing the functional limits of the social welfare institution. The functions of social welfare are (1) those having a direct impact on the welfare of individuals by providing them with social services, social provisions, and income and (2) those aimed at enhancing the quality of human life and ameliorating its hardships by interaction with other institutions toward improved ways of meeting individual, family, and small-group needs. Programs included in the social welfare institution under this definition are those "socially sponsored programs and activities that reflect social policy decisions," carried out through public or voluntary means that meet socially recognized needs not provided through other channels (Romanyshyn, 1971, p. 51).

The following statement sets forth the important components of the social welfare institution as it has been described in this chapter.

✑§ (1) Social welfare is an *institution*

✑§ (2) comprising *policies and laws* that are

✑§ (3) operationalized by *organized activities* of *voluntary (private)* and/or *governmental (public)* agencies

✑§ (4) by which a defined minimum of *social services, money,* and *other consumption rights* (medical care, education, and public housing, for example)

✑§ (5) are *distributed* to *individuals, families, and groups* by criteria *other than those of the marketplace or those prevailing in the family system*

✑§ (6) for the *purposes of* preventing, alleviating, or contributing to the solution of recognized social problems so as to improve the well-being of individuals, groups, and communities directly.

✤ Summary

In this chapter we have examined and discussed various definitions of the institution of social welfare. We have also examined the principal components of social welfare and have been introduced to the notion of social welfare as a residual institution and how that differs from the notion of social welfare as an institutional system. It is suggested once again that the reader return to the case examples in Chapter 2 and see whether it is possible to identify which of the resources mentioned are examples of residual functions and which are examples of institutional functions. These two notions as to the purpose of the social welfare institution will appear again and again in the following chapters.

We have taken the position that social welfare is a social institution and that it is best understood as an interstitial institution. We have also formulated a definition of social welfare from this perspective.

✤ A look ahead

The next two chapters will further develop the central issues introduced in this chapter. In the next chapter we will briefly discuss the social institutions of society and the need for an interstitial institution. In Chapter 5 we will discuss in a more concrete manner the structure, roles, and services that form the internal operations of the institution of social welfare.

✤ Study questions

1. Go back to Chapter 2. Make a list of the programs used by the families described there. Identify the services as residual or institutional, utilizing Wilensky and Lebeaux's formulations. Now identify them as maintenance activities, developmental activities, or change activities according to your understanding of those functions of social welfare as developed in this chapter.
2. In this chapter we have discussed social welfare as a social institution. Can you name the other major social institutions of society?
3. Do you think that benefits to employees, such as the pension plans found in industry, should be considered a part of social welfare? What are your arguments for this stand?
4. How do you think most people see social welfare in our society—as a special, residual function or as a social institution? What do you think?

✤ Selected Reading

Wilensky, H. L., and Lebeaux, C. N. *Industrial Society and Social Welfare.* Paperback ed. New York: Free Press, 1965.

We strongly recommend the use of chap. 6, "Conceptions of Social Welfare" and chap. 7, "Welfare Auspices and Expenditures," as a good source for expanding and supporting the material in this chapter.

Jeffers, C. *Living Poor.* Ann Arbor, Mich.: Ann Arbor Publishers, 1971.

This report describes some of the harsh meanings of living poor today. It sheds some light on the interplay between being poor and the problems of public housing, one system in the social welfare institution. It should help to raise further questions for students.

Turner, J. B., et al. *Encyclopedia of Social Work, 1977.* New York: Columbia University Press, 1977. See vol. 2, pp. 1463–97.

The material in these pages discusses the definition of social policy and the relationship between social policy and economic planning. Also, beginning on page 1611 and continuing to the end of the book are a series of tables relating to social welfare issues. It might be a very interesting assignment for students to analyze and to discuss certain of these tables of their findings on the material that they have read in our text.

Illustrated here is a social welfare program fulfilling an integrative activity that was formerly a family responsibility.

Louise Plenty Holes, 79, is a Foster GrandParent (FGP)—one of 46 volunteers with the two all-Indian FGP programs in the nation. The volunteers work with children in hospitals, schools, and Head Start centers.

Chapter 4 ❧

❧ Social welfare—An interstitial institution ❧

❧ Introduction

In this chapter we are going to discuss the scope and function of the social welfare institution as an interstitial institution. We will develop a functional statement formulating the particular assignment drawn by the social welfare institution in the society which creates and sustains it. In the next chapter we will convert this functional statement into some of the typical patterns of activity by which this function is implemented.

❧ The purpose of social institutions

When individuals come together to form an on-going human group they find that certain things must be accomplished in order to exist individually within the group and as a group. First, there must be individuals—members for the group. If the group is to continue over time there must be provision for reproduction and for the nurture of children. There must be a way of producing and distributing food and other supports for human life. People have to learn to give and take in social and nurturing relationships with each other as well as in the tasks of organized group life. There must be a division of labor and allocation of authority. The group must achieve some level of solidarity and morale. This means that certain behavior patterns and values must be developed, taught, and monitored. Over time the activities of the group become organized in some way into structured networks of relationships to carry out these functions. The structures that are generally accepted as ways of carrying out the large and essential functions of society (those necessary for the preservation of group life) conceptualized as social institutions.

This implies that the purpose of social institutions is the preservation of group life and social order. This notion of social order (patterns of regular structure, process, and change occurring in and arising from human interaction) and social control (the monitoring and influencing behavior of individuals to achieve conformity with group norms or with the social order) is often seen by students and others as a negative thing, as an oppressive force that would deny the humanity and creativity of the individual in the interest of the group. However, one must recognize that individuals only become creative, free human beings as the group is able to provide them with certain essentials that support life. Among these essentials is social order.

Human beings are social animals, and social relationships with others are necessary to an individual's very existence. The human infant, unlike the offspring of other species, cannot exist or grow to possess the qualities that most of us evaluate most highly in ourselves (the ability to perceive, to interpret symbols, to reason, to love and be loved by others) without intimate relationships with nurturing persons who are themselves supported by some kind of group relationships. Thus, the group and the social structures growing out of group life are necessary if we are to grow and develop as human beings.

Complex societies usually develop more than one way of meeting essential needs. Thus, there may be several institutions that have as their charge the meeting of similar needs, although one institution will often be primary and preferred. These different institutions are usually structured and patterned so that they respond in somewhat different ways to similar needs, and society often attaches different meanings to the use of different institutions to meet similar needs. In fact, one institution is usually seen as the primary or preferred one for use, and certain definitions of status, as well as rewards or sanctions, may be attached to the use of different institutions. For example, one can satisfy hunger by purchasing food with money earned from a job; one can also satisfy hunger by securing food through the efforts of a member of the family group. In addition, a neighbor might be asked to supply food to the hungry individual, or one might purchase food with funds secured from a social welfare agency. Each of these ways would meet the need of the body for food, but each would involve different activities and would have a differ-

ent meaning to the individual and the social group. Given the complex beings we are, it is also entirely possible that one dinner would nourish better than another because of the meaning attached to the source of supply by the individual who consumes the dinner.

The more complex a society becomes, the more complex become the structure of its social institutions and the roles within them. In fact, one might well define an advanced society as one in which there are many complex, overlapping structures and relationships. Societies become more complex both in the structure and function of their social institutions and in the relationships between and among social institutions. In addition to the increasingly complex interrelationships among institutions, there are increasingly complex relationships between and among the operating parts (agencies and organizations) of each institution as the institution's functions become increasingly differentiated and as the institution is assigned new and developing units.

The more complex the social system and its institutions, the more difficult it is for individuals to have direct input into those societal arrangements that will affect their lives and the more power, knowledge, and status individuals will need if they are to be heard. Yet even as individuals find it difficult to make themselves heard in the critical decisions and operations of the social institutions, they find those institutions more and more essential to satisfactorily coping with life needs. This shift reflects, on the one hand, the growing knowledge and technology available to the production-consumption-distribution organizations of society, which offer us increasingly complex consumption experiences produced by increasingly complex production and distribution methods. On the other hand, it reflects the development of complex knowledge about human life and a growing technology of socialization and social control methods that, at least in the present, is seen as needing skills and resources not easily available to the institutions of family, church, and neighborhood that were formerly central to the discharge of the functions of socialization, integration, support, and social control.

✒§ Institutional functions

We have said that in order to exist both individually and as a group, human beings usually live in groups and find it necessary to develop certain organized ways of accomplishing certain functions that are necessary to ongoing individual and group life. Now that we have established something of the purpose of social institutions, we will discuss the functions of the group (society) around which the major social institutions develop.

Production-distribution-consumption

In order to exist at the most basic level, human beings must have food and protection from the elements in the form of clothing and shelter. However, as the group develops, food, clothing, and shelter begin to serve certain aesthetic and social needs as well as the simple support of human life at its most basic level, and methods of producing goods become more sophisticated and specialized. If different persons produce different things to meet different needs, ways of exchanging these various things must develop. Thus, we have society concerned with and developing organized ways of distribution. Certain standards and rituals of consumption also develop, so we have organized and approved ways of consumption. You do not take another's bread. The bread you earn is more approved than bread given to you by welfare. The primary institution that fulfills the distribution function in the United States is the marketplace, where work is exchanged for money and money is used to purchase the necessary and desired goods and services. However, the institution of social welfare also shares a part of this function in our society. It operates through a set of organizational arrangements by methods, or on the basis of principles, which result in the production and distribution of economic output to consumers "which differ from those of the free economic market or prevailing under the family system" (Burns, 1974, p. 89).

Socialization

If society is to have any stability and if the life of any organized group is to go on, individuals who enter the group must be inducted into the knowledge systems, social values, roles, and behavior patterns of its members. Before the industrial revolution, the family and the church were the primary institutions that fulfilled these socialization functions. With the coming of the industrial revolution, however, there also came a demand for individuals with new and special skills. The family and the church were no longer able to fulfill the socialization functions in a way that met the needs of society. These institutions have become less and less able to meet the demand for the training that has become necessary as our increasing technology and our rising level of consumption have brought changes in work and in marketable skills with ever-increasing rapidity. As knowledge systems, values, and social roles change rapidly, the family and the church become less effective agents of socialization. Thus the socialization functions have become increasingly a responsibility of the institution of social welfare. In today's society, three systems of organizations within the social welfare institution have been assigned these functions: education, corrections, and the social services.

Social integration

Social integration has to do with the processes by which individuals come to value their membership in their particular group and to feel a responsibility for abiding by its rules. These processes are aimed at developing a level of solidarity and morale that is necessary to the ongoing life of any social group. In this way people come to believe that they belong to something larger than themselves and come to feel a moral commitment to the group. They want to see the group continue to exist at the highest possible level for the group's good. The institutions that society depends upon to fulfill the social integration functions are the family, the church, and social welfare. The social welfare systems usually involved are education and social services.

Mutual support

Mutual support is also necessary between members of any social group if individuals within the group are to grow, develop, and function comfortably and effectively as human beings. No one of us is able to meet all of his/her needs alone; we depend on others for affection, for approval, for help when we are ill, for a listening ear when we are confused and worried, and for food and shelter when we are unable to provide them for ourselves. In turn, we offer the same to others. The very use of the term *mutual* implies an exchange of supporting provisions and services among the members of a society. Mutual support is usually thought of as involving a give-and-take between individuals in intimate social groups. However, it is also necessary to the ongoing functioning of society and thus may be thought of as a societal process. The institutions primarily charged with providing for the processes of mutual support are the family, the church, and certain other indigenous groups. Once again, however, the social welfare institution is also charged with fulfilling the mutual support function. It does this in two ways: through the provision of concrete resources and through the provision of social services.

Social control and social order

Social control refers to the arrangements by which a society attempts to assure that its members behave in conformity with its generally accepted norms of social behavior. The political institution, through its lawmaking and law-enforcing function, performs this task. However, institutions usually thought of as functioning primarily as agents of socialization and social integration have, through history, also served a secondary function as agents of social control (the family and church are examples). The more effectively the institutions charged with the functions of socialization, integration, and

mutual support carry out those functions, the less society needs to rely on agents of social control. In today's society the social welfare institutions, through the operation of correctional agencies and certain social services, are an explicit part of the social control process. Implicitly, socialization, social integration, and mutual support processes all have some implications of social control, as has been noted above. Thus, some organizations within the social institution that would claim other functions as their primary charge must also recognize their importance in the functions of social order and social control.

Social change

If human groups are going to survive in any but the must undifferentiated states, they must develop means to provide for orderly, lawful change in the ways in which the institutions of society function and interrelate. These changes are not always forward-looking and they do not always achieve the "most good for the most people." They are often attempts to get the maximum stability at the minimum cost, given the problem confronted. Old ways of doing things are patterned in the internal relationships of the social institutions and at the individual levels that usually have been profitable for certain members of society. All new solutions to social problems contain new rewards for certain groups and new deprivations for other groups.

The political institution of society is usually seen as the central agent of orderly social change. However, in industrial societies, where there is a constant and rapid development of technology, the economic institution of society may, quite outside the political institution, be responsible for far-reaching social change. In modern industrial states the social welfare institution has gradually assumed responsibility for the social-change efforts directed at optimizing the experiences and relationships of the individuals in those states.

Now that we have outlined the six major needs of a human society, we will discuss the social institutions that have developed as organized and patterned ways of meeting those needs.

ᦁ Social institutions

We will begin this discussion with a look at the institution that has developed from the patterning of roles and relationships around the production, distribution, and consumption of the necessary resources for the physical maintenance of life.

The economic institution

The functions of the economic institution are the production, distribution, and consumption of goods and services. Given the inadequacy of easily available life-sustaining resources for the human population in the natural environment and the necessity for human labor to wrest the required life-sustaining resources from nature and to process them in usable form, every human society has had to devise some system for: (1) organizing and assuring the performance of the labor needed to develop the resources and (2) distributing the produced goods to members of the society (Gil, 1976, pp. 11–30). In other words, a society must organize a system to assure the production of enough goods and services for its own survival and must arrange for the distribution of the fruits of its production so that more production can take place.

Organized pattern of work. If people do not live by bread alone—and increasingly we have evidence that bread alone does not adequately sustain the life of individuals (Lynch, 1977)—they certainly cannot live without bread. Thus, in all human groups there develops an organized pattern of work and the distribution of the results of work, a pattern structured to take account of different skills and roles. Probably the first human group was the family (probably an extended family that later developed into a tribe), and in that group the pattern of work roles and distribution was very simple. Not only was the pattern simple, but it was closely intertwined with the tasks of mutual support and socialization of the family.

However the bread was divided, in the intimate, early human groups in which everyone lived close to extinction it was self-evident that neither the group nor its individual members would survive unless a certain number of people were willing, or were forced under penalty of sanction, to undertake certain types of labor. It was also recognized that there had to be some ordered pattern for the distribution of the results of this toil. Not only were those who brought home the bacon entitled to eat, but also those who cooked it and those undefined others who contributed to integration, mutual support, and socialization as well as those unable to labor.

The distribution of goods. In a human group one no sooner produces bread than one has the problem of how to distribute it among the members of the group. Should the children have the best because they are the future of the group? Should the direct producers have the best because they labored to bring the bread into existence? Should the support personnel (the mothers who worked to care for the children and process the food, the priests who served as links between the group members and the spiritual meaning of life, or the persons who cured the ills of human flesh) have the best because without integration and social order the group could not survive? What about those persons who seemed to contribute nothing to the group welfare? Were they entitled to eat? Could the group afford to feed them?

These may seem to be simple questions, but simple or not, these basic questions of the adequacy of resources and of the basis for their distribution have been asked throughout human history and continue to plague us in our questions about and our concern with equality, security, and access to opportunity. Although considered a concern of the economic institution in the modern industrial world, they are, and have been throughout history, also related to the functions of integration, mutual support, and the social control of the family, the church, and the political system. At no time in human history has complete equality in labor been required from the members of a society or have the results of labor been distributed equally. The level of living of the individuals within a social group, their relationship to one another and to their group as a whole, will depend to a significant extent on the specific tasks that they perform within the total array of tasks to be done, the value that the group attaches to those tasks, and the rights to goods and services granted to individuals by the group in return for the performance of tasks or work roles.

Although rights earned through the performance of productive task roles within society may be distributed directly in kind (for example, in the form of land or particular services), in a modern, industrial society the consumptive rights and rewards earned by the performance of certain tasks are usually expressed in terms of money payment. The worker who earns a certain amount of money as a laborer may then purchase in the marketplace the resources needed or wanted to support a certain level of living. Within the limits of income (consumptive rights), each worker and those dependent on the worker may spend as they wish to. Given this method of determining the rights of individuals to goods and services, we tend to accept the decisions of the individual who is both an income producer and a consumer of goods and services as a satisfactory principle on which to determine what shall be produced. In other words, the power of the consumer to spend will determine what goods and services society will produce and how such goods and services will be distributed.

Two points need to be made about this system of rights distribution. Since the economic institution relies on people's ability to purchase consumptive rights through the use of money, it does not differentiate between needs and wants. Moreover, the market does not respond to demand alone. It responds only to demand as that demand is made effective through the power to spend. This way of distributing consumptive rights means that some persons can not only avail themselves of high-quality necessary goods and services but can purchase unnecessary luxuries while other persons cannot secure even the basic necessities of life. It may also mean that no consumer has the range of choice he/she desires or that society's resources may be directed to the production of goods and services that are actually harmful to the individuals who purchase them (Burns, 1974, p. 91).

Consumption rights. Under this system, the totality of the individual rights to the goods and services available for distribution to the members of a society will depend on the money income of individuals and on the money value of the resources, goods, and services generated by the labor of the members of that society. As a means of determining the totality of the goods and services available in modern societies, economists have designed a measure of the market price of all the goods and services produced in any given period. This measure is called the gross national product. The gross national product is not a measure the social value of any product, nor does it make allowance for hidden costs or damage to people or the environment. It is a measure of value within the marketplace.

In speaking of the free use of consumption rights, we need to recognize that in no organized group are the rights and freedoms of the individual absolute. Thus, in addition to granting rewards or entitlements, the social group through the political institution may decide to impose specific or general limitations on the rights a person may enjoy. Even in a free money society, certain things are held to be so vital to the society's interests that the consumer's freedom of choice not held to be absolute and the individual is forced through taxation to spend part of his or her income as society decides. Taxation for public services within social welfare are an example of this.

Society may decide that its welfare requires the development of an educated group of citizens, and it may be unwilling to entrust such a vital task to individual parents. Everyone who receives an income or possesses certain kinds of wealth (such as real property) may be required by law to pay taxes, some of which may be used to support public education that is required of all children in jurisdictions having compulsory school attendance laws. Thus, in financing the functions of the institution of social welfare, reliance on the judgment of the individual consumer is generally abandoned. Decisions as to what shall be spent toward what ends become the decisions of political processes in public services and of other organized groups in the case of private expenditures. These groups use some principles or criteria to arrive at social priorities.

Equality of opportunity. One more notion regarding the place of people in our economic society needs to be developed before we consider the operation of the marketplace and social welfare.

Because of the connection between work roles and the level of income earned, society has been concerned not only with the inequality of the distribution of wealth but with equality of opportunity. The extent to which all work roles (statuses) are open to all members of society and the nature of the criteria that determine which persons will fill those roles are important questions for any society. In a democratic society, what is society's role in assuring equality of opportunity? The criteria by which these decisions are made bear heavily on the opportunities of all persons for life-enhancing and life-sustaining activities. Thus, the distribution of opportunities within our society has become a concern of social welfare policies. The availability of certain work roles and the rewards that accrue from those roles give certain members of society the economic and political power not only to control their own life satisfactions but also to control the level of living and the opportunities of others.

We will now discuss the notion mentioned above that the institution of social welfare distributes certain resources and opportunities outside the pattern by which resources and opportunities are purchased through money earned.

Social welfare and the economic institution

Eveline M. Burns, a professor of economics who is widely known and respected for her work on social welfare policy, says in a recent article:

> . . . the most significant fact about social welfare as an institution is that it is a set of organizational arrangements which results in the production and distribution to consumers of economic output by methods, or on principles, which differ from those of the free economic market or prevailing under the family system. (1974, p. 89)

One of the central functions of social welfare is to distribute goods and services by criteria other than those of the marketplace in order to produce results that the operation of the marketplace cannot produce. Services or payments to those who benefit from such transfers are not offered in exchange for services rendered (or paid for) by the recipients but rather to add to the quality of life enjoyed by the individuals or families so benefited. Thus, social welfare stands between the producer and the consumer to allocate resources outside market exchange, collecting money from one group and distributing it to another group in cash, goods, and services. This process is often discussed in social welfare literature as *income transfer.* Income moves from one group to another, not in payment by the buyer of services to the seller of services, but as a transfer that is effected through the offices of social welfare programs. Not all of these transfers are money payments—the payments may also be in services, in the creation and distribution of opportunities, in credits, and in power incrementals—although all involve resource-exchange distribution and consumption outside the market place. Not all of these benefits go to the pretransfer poor. Mrs. Affluent received OASDI although she was not nor had ever been poor. Not all such transfers are in the public domain. Mr. and Mrs. Comfortable received medical care under such a transfer. Table 4–1 lists broad federal, state, and local expenditures for fiscal year 1972 that went to pretransfer poor.

Because social welfare policies involve benefit allocations outside the market economy, many persons see these policies as involving a unilateral exchange from society to the individual. However, this is an inaccurate notion. The transfer of goods and services through the welfare system involves a reciprocal exchange—but one that is different from that found in the market. Rather than a direct, voluntary, face-to-face, well-defined interaction between buyer and seller, exchange in the social welfare system is indirect in that the social welfare

◄§ Table 4-1

Antipoverty budget, including federal and state-local expenditures, fiscal year 1972

	Total expenditures ($ millions)	Benefits to pretransfer ($ millions)	Percentage spent on pretransfer poor
Total	184,871	78,653	42.5
Cash transfers	80,110	42,719	53
Social security and railroad benefits	40,426	23,367	58
Public employee retirement	11,692	4,443	38
Unemployment insurance	6,751	1,424	21
Workers' compensation	3,794	1,248	33
Public assistance	10,828	9,511	87
Veterans' benefits	6,215	2,641	43
Temporary disability	404	85	21
Payments to farmers	3,234	162	5
Nutrition	3,688	2,582	70
Food stamps	1,866	1,586	85
Other	1,822	996	55
Housing	1,834	1,016	55
Public housing	744	551	74
Rent supplement	75	56	75
Model cities	500	210	42
Other	514	200	39
Health	24,574	13,826	56
Medicare	7,023	3,371	48
Medicaid	7,548	5,690	75
Veterans' medical care	2,377	523	22
State—local hospitals and public health	5,039	2,671	53
Other	2,587	1,571	61
Welfare and OEO services	5,290	3,822	72
Public assistance social services	2,161	1,750	81
Community action	458	440	96
OEO health and nutrition	180	173	96
OEO legal services	60	58	96
Other	2,431	1,401	58
Employment and manpower	3,904	2,796	72
Employment services	450	228	51
OEO manpower programs	1,337	1,319	99
Other manpower and vocational rehabilitation	1,559	1,093	70
Public employment program	559	156	28
Education	62,238	11,730	19
Student support	1,688	347	21
Local schools	42,148	7,376	18
Elementary and Secondary Education Act	1,836	879	48
Other federal elementary and secondary education	1,632	695	43
State-local higher education	9,700	970	10
Federal aid to higher education	518	96	19
Veterans' education	1,889	623	33
Vocational-adult education	2,828	744	26

Note: Entries may not sum to totals because of rounding. Also, in some instances the percentage appearing in column 3 diverges considerably from the ratio of column 2 to column 1. The percentage is correct; the divergence results from rounding of the dollar entries.

Source: Plotnick and Skidmore, 1975, p. 56.

agency or organization stands between the recipient and the giver. The social welfare exchange is often involuntary in that there is usually little leeway for the recipients to choose between vendors or because the recipient must either accept the services offered or face a further sanction (as in correctional services). Moreover, social welfare benefits are often given in the expectation that the recipients will change their behavior or themselves (Gilbert and Specht, 1974, pp. 28–29).

Another problem governing exchange under these conditions is that the conditions of reciprocity are unclear and open-ended. Although the recipients do not pay money, or at least the full costs of the goods and services they receive, they often do incur heavy obligations, such as getting a job (any job), being a good mother, behaving in a special way, being grateful. Thus, there is a reciprocal exchange, but the method of payment is so indirect and different that it is not seen as one. It is further pointed out by Wolins that in this type of indirect exchange the welfare organization functions to keep "the demanding recipient and the grudging donor from expressing direct, face-to-face confrontation" (1976, pp. 1–2).

Burns writes that even though social welfare determines the distribution of goods and services on principles that differ from those prevailing in the free economic market, social welfare expenditures have a bearing on the economic growth and "full employment of the nation's resources." Social welfare affects and is affected by the economic policies of the nation in various ways. Social welfare expenditures for such things as unemployment insurance, veterans' benefits, and social security payments, are a way of getting purchasing power into consumers' hands and may run counter to the nation's efforts to control inflation. On the other hand, certain welfare spending can be seen as a way of utilizing otherwise idle personnel and thus can serve as a built-in stabilizer for the economy. If government spending needs to be reduced, social welfare finds itself in conflict with all other public spending for necessary financial support (Burns, 1974, pp. 100–101).

Among the questions that Burns raises regarding the interaction between the economic system and the social welfare system are:

1. "If in the economic market power to consume is conditioned on participation in production, what happens to incentive (and, therefore, the volume of production) if goods and services are received without this participation?" (Burns, 1974, p. 97).
2. If work were not required in order to receive a minimum income, how many persons would choose leisure in preference to work?
3. Would the number of persons choosing welfare over work be reduced if unpleasant conditions were attached to receiving welfare or if the level of welfare payments were significantly below what the lowest paid worker could earn in a free market?
4. What is the effect of heavy taxes on the initiative of workers and entrepreneurs?
5. "On what principles are decisions made on who is to benefit from . . . social welfare programs and on who is to get less than they would under the free market system?" (Burns, 1974, p. 100).
6. How do we make priority decisions within the welfare institution itself as to allocation of resources if a country should decide to allocate a certain percentage of its gross national product to social welfare?
7. What in social welfare can be substituted for the profit-and-loss system in the economic institution to ensure that what is provided for people is in fact what people want?

Throughout the historical section of the text we will be seeing how the economic institution and the social welfare institution have struggled with these questions of production and consumption in ways that will bear on the future answers to these questions. We need to recognize that the superior productivity of American workers is not based on their greater talents or skills or industry but on the superior tools they work with and on the technical staff work that organizes production. And automation may continue to reduce individual workers' contributions. Given the present economic system, workers must be paid more and more as their distinctive contributions become less and less. Other-wise we would not have a market large enough to absorb the goods produced (Rose, 1958, pp. 605–6).

The political institution

The parameters of the social welfare institution are shaped primarily by its interrelationships with the economic institution and the political institution. The central issue for the economic institution is the allocation of scarce goods and services. For the political institution, the central issue is the exercise of power. The charge to the political institution is that it act both to maintain the stability of society and to develop orderly processes of change through the use of its power to control behavior. Its principal function is to ensure the continued existence of society by prescribing the ways in which social stability will be assured and the processes of change will operate. The term *political power* as used here refers to the ability of some persons or groups to impose their preferences on all other persons or groups within the society (Heffernan, 1979, pp. 27–30). Political power emerges from the ability to impose change on people or to prevent change in desired ways of acting and interacting. Since political power involves the ability to compel persons to act in particular ways, regardless of their agreement with the actions taken, it is intimately involved with the concept of liberty. How can we allow for individual autonomy and yet fulfill the legitimate interests and obligations of society?

To understand the development of social welfare in the United States, it is important to remember that the framers of our Constitution were deeply concerned with the protection of the people's individual rights against their own democratically elected political leaders. Rights were defined negatively as "freedom from" rather than "freedom to." The Founding Fathers were more concerned with the need to limit the government's power to do harm than to bestow on it the power to do good. It was not that they saw government as evil but that they saw it as dangerous. This concern with

the danger of power for the welfare of the governed led them to enumerate in a Bill of Rights the powers that government officials should never be allowed to exercise, to limit the powers of the federal government to those specifically given in the Constitution, to vest all other powers in the states, and to divide the various powers of the federal government among its three branches.

In fact, the American political institution might be said to be partial to the "rule of three." There are three branches of government—executive, legislative, and judicial; three levels of government—national, state, and local; and three aspects of law enforcement—the police, the courts, and the correctional system. The functions, interrelationships, and conflict among these various parts of the political system have had a tremendous impact on the development of the social welfare institution. As we proceed to analyze the historical development of social welfare programs in the Part III the text, many of these conflicts will become clear. Given their complexity and diversity, it is difficult to summarize them in this brief discussion. However, a few basic concepts may be developed here.

Ideals of freedom and equality are deeply embedded in American life. A central value of many Americans has been the belief that society is composed of individuals, each of whom is the best judge of his/her own interests, and that any interference with the freedom of the individual's behavior in his/her own interests is a blow, not only at the individual's good, but at the social good of the nation. This belief in freedom and in equality and opportunity for all has posed many unanswered questions to the political institution of society. The belief that society should provide certain resources and rights to its members, because each one of them holds equal membership in society, conflicts with the notion that institutions of control, such as government, are dangerous, if not essentially evil. The actual abundance of wealth and opportunity in our society, the fact that so many persons do live lives marked by greater ease than the lives of their parents, has served to support the notion that everybody can do this. The belief that American institutions in an expanding society offer all people an equal opportunity if only they have the initiative and the will to grasp it has been deeply cherished by many of us.

In spite of the institutionalization of the value of equality, there is, nevertheless, an uneasy feeling on the part of American citizens that equality may be a myth. Americans find that they have high status primarily in the role of buyers or voters but not as individuals. The political system of the United States reflects a constant struggle to preserve freedom for or impose freedom on one set of interest groups even though this may be at the expense of another set. The continuing effort to find some balance between the ideals of freedom and equality among the numerous competitive and conflicting interests is a fundamental key to understanding the political institution and the conflicts between the social welfare institution and other societal institutions. As each party or coalition of interest groups has achieved power—or countervailing power—it has attempted to set up, by law, certain rules, regulations, and agencies to protect its interests. Labor, management, consumers, producers, minority groups, and business competitors all seek to have governmental agencies established in their own behalf in order to protect themselves against the exertion of power by others. The legislative branch of the government finds itself at war with the executive branch. And the executive branch is a wilderness of agencies, oftentimes in conflict with one another.

One irony of the early concern with freedom on the part of our founders is that the leading protagonists of liberty were themselves slaveholders. Perhaps it was safe for these aristocrats to preach equality and freedom because they could see to it that slaves had no chance to demand it. Perhaps it is as Lincoln said:

> With some the word liberty may mean for each man to do as he pleases with himself and the product of his labor; while with others the same word may mean for some men to do as they please with other men and the product of other men's labor. (Nicolay and Hay, 1894, p. 513)

In an article on liberty and social policy, Jack Otis discussed freedom from as follows:

Traditional liberalism defines liberty as negative, universal, and abstract. Liberty is negative since it means the absence of governmental restraint; it is universal since law, or its absence, should apply equally for all individuals and groups in society; it is abstract in that it is concerned with the *formal* ability to do something rather than the *practical* or *substantive* ability to do something. Thus, the absence of a law forbidding any members of society from obtaining a university education means that all have the freedom to pursue this goal. The three criteria are met in that no individual is legally prevented from acquiring a higher education (negative); it applies to all (universal); and the means by which this goal might be attained by all members of society are not taken into account (abstract). (1976, p. 37)

Strict adherents of this view of liberty tend to regard any governmental activities in the area of social welfare as destroying liberty, although they are willing to allow for government intervention in certain functions having to do with public safety, the protection of public property, and the enforcement of contracts. Otis points out that throughout history governments have operated to deprive the governed of liberty and have been despotic and tyrannical. However, according to Otis, to say that "government, necessarily, merely out of its participation in the affairs of men, destroys liberty is a contention that does not necessarily follow" (1976, p. 38). Otis argues that in revolting against and rejecting certain forms of authority, the traditional liberal has revolted against the principle of authority itself and consequently has "tended to deprive individuals of the direction and support necessary for both individual freedom and social stability" (1976, p. 39). In arguing, as many of our early political leaders did, that people have *natural rights which are independent of society,* these leaders viewed liberty as a natural possession or gift and not as an achievement that people had to struggle for. This sanctioned the right of individuals to act as they pleased as private citizens and to be responsible only to themselves in seeking to fulfill their needs and desires. Otis contends that this has worked to create a "principle of disorder—the public be damned—whose effects are readily apparent today in the business of crime and the crimes of business" (1976, p. 39).

Otis goes on to say:

> The modern liberal assets that this negative theory of liberty no longer fits the social realities of our day, except in the limited sense that the actions of government may be antilibertarian, and that its persistence in our thinking is due to cultural lag and to the power of vested interests for whom this theory serves as a bulwark for present privileges. To meet these social realities, modern liberalism provides a theory of liberty which, by way of contrast, is positive, particular, and concrete. It is sometimes called the "power to do" or the "power of effective choice" conception of freedom.
>
> *   *   *   *   *
>
> This theory of liberty, then, is positive in that it refers to the power to do something, not merely to the absence of restraint; it is particular in that it refers to particular individuals and groups in a particular time and place; and it is concrete in that it is concerned with the practical ability to do that which the individual or group wishes to do. Thus, the opportunity to obtain a university education is a function not only of the absence of a law forbidding the individual from attaining this goal, but of his physical, emotional, and intellectual capacities, and of the social, legal, and economic arrangements which exist at that time. Furthermore, liberty and control are not inherently antithetical: they are two sides of the same coin. The artist is free to produce works of art only in so far as he has developed adequate control of his material and techniques; the social worker is free to help people through a relevant methodology to the extent to which his involvement is professionally disciplined; women, Chicanos, and blacks have attained greater freedom as a result of affirmative action policies and requirements of the federal government, and so on. The issue involved is rarely ever answered by the single question of liberty versus control, since liberty is attained through personal and social controls. Rather there are questions which need to be asked in connection with who shall have liberties and who restraints, what these liberties and restraints shall

consist of, and for what purposes they are to be granted or taken away by society. (1976, pp. 40–41):

John Dewey, in writing of liberty and social controls, makes three important points:

> Well, in the first place, liberty is not just an idea, an abstract principle. It is power, effective power to do specific things. There is no such thing as liberty in general. . . . If one wants to know what the condition of liberty is at a given time, one has to examine what persons *can* do and what they *cannot* do. The moment one examines the question from the standpoint of effective action, it becomes evident that the demand for liberty is a demand for power, either for possession of powers of action not already possessed or for retention and expansion of powers already possessed. The present ado in behalf of liberty by . . . beneficiaries of the existing economic system is immediately explicable if one views it as a demand for the preservation of the powers they already possess. . . .
>
> In the second place, the possession of effective power is always a matter of the *distribution* of powers that exists at the time. . . . There is no such thing as the liberty of effective power of an individual, group, or class, except in relation to the liberties, the effective powers, of other individuals, groups, and classes. . . . You cannot discuss or measure the liberty of one individual or group of individuals without thereby raising the question of the effect upon the liberty of others. . . .
>
> In the third place, this relativity of liberty to the existing distribution of powers of action . . . means necessarily that wherever there is liberty at one place there is restraint at some other place. *The system of liberties that exists at any time is always the system of restraints or controls that exists at that time.* No one can do anything except in relation to what others can do and cannot do.
>
> These three points are general. But they cannot be dismissed as mere abstractions. For when they are applied in idea or in action they mean that liberty is always a social question, not an individual one. (1935, p. 41)

Nowhere are the political ideals of the nature of the concept of freedom more clearly illustrated than in the decisions of the Supreme Court. In discussing this matter, Jessie Bernard writes:

> The first ten amendments of the American Constitution protect citizens against the invasion of their rights by the federal government; the fourteenth amendment protects them against invasion by the several state governments. And increasingly the tendency is to protect individuals against the invasion of their rights by other individuals and groups, as well as by governments. As former President Truman once said, "The extension of civil rights today means not protection of the people against the government but the protection of people by the government." The new governmental protection is increasingly against the violation of rights by other individuals and groups. The effect is to deprive some segments of the population of certain kinds of rights or freedoms and to bestow new kinds of rights or freedoms on other segments. (1958, p. 617)

These political positions are critical of the way in which the social welfare institution develops. If one believes in the traditional position, then one also believes that social welfare interventions should be residual and remedial in nature. If one believes that rights are social, then one believes that the institution of social welfare should be empowered to increase the power to do of individuals and groups and to work toward the development and modifications of institutional structures that fail to support the power to choose of all individuals in our society. This latter notion of liberty means that freedom may be limited by the unequal opportunities in the social and political environment, by the unequal access to those opportunities, and by the problems, conflicts, and lacks in the individual that prevent or distort such access and use. The function of social welfare then becomes one of supplying the knowledge and tools by which individuals and groups may be enabled to change their environment, to change the rules of access to opportunities in that environment, or to change themselves so that they may more effectively use the available opportunities and access.

Thus, many activities of the public sector of social welfare are attempts to assure people greater freedom of choice by providing all kinds of enlarged opportunities and by providing greater security and equality, primarily through various income maintenance programs and through devices to provide credit and power to certain groups.

Because of their distrust of the powers of government, the framers of the Constitution not only specifically limited what the federal government could and could not do, but they conceived of dividing its powers among three branches. Thus, each branch of the sovereign state could act as a check on the powers of the other. This division of power has operated over the years to offer certain protections for the liberties of people, but it also can and does work to limit individual rights. As we shall see, the division of powers between state and federal governments and among the three branches of government has had a tremendous effect on the development of social welfare in the United States.

Although the operation of public social welfare programs is lodged in the executive branch of the government, these programs are authorized and funded by the legislative branch and are supported or weakened by the court decisions of our society. Also, the conflict between the rights, authorities, and functions of the levels of government—federal, state, and local—are reflected in all public welfare programs. We shall see how these develop and are worked out in Part III of the text.

In any society, there are always established patterns to deal with the people who do not conform to the mores of the society. In the United States, this function is thought of as being lodged primarily in the criminal justice and correctional system. In this system we often find that the social service aspects of social welfare are an active part of the correctional process. Here, too, there are built-in conflicts, especially a conflict between the notion of punishment and the notion of rehabilitation in our correctional institutions. That conflict will be discussed later in the text. Social welfare is involved with deviance in some other ways. Many social service programs involve socialization activities, and these may well be viewed as a part of our concern with the control of individual actions. In addition, the health system within the social welfare institution is engaged in the treatment of mental illness. Many of these treatment activities have been thought by social welfare leaders to represent another attempt to control deviance.

Thus social welfare activities come into play in relation to the political institution to: (1) offer people equality of opportunities and choices, (2) offer people a degree of security not provided by other institutions of society, and (3) make the knowledge and skills of the various staffs of social welfare organizations available for the prevention and correction of deviance. Many of the conflicts and forces that shape these activities may be found in the values and patterns of the political institution.

The church as a social institution

Perhaps the most striking characteristics of the religious institutions of the United States are their separation from the state. The complete separation of the religious and the political institution as known in the United States is almost unique among nations. However, organized religious groups do act on the political institution as pressure or veto groups. This conflict is reflected in a recent Supreme Court decision relating to the use of tax funds by parochial schools. Although the abortion issue is much more than a religious one, we also see certain aspects of this conflict in the reaction of religious groups to the Supreme Court decisions relating to abortion.

Social welfare and the church have interacted from the beginnings of modern social welfare, and one function of the church before that time, charity to the needy and nuture to the helpless, is now seen as belonging in part to social welfare. Down through human history, the religious institution in society has sought to answer our questions about the meaning and purpose of life. The central religious beliefs shared by all members of a certain human group have fulfilled that group's need for integration, mutual support, social order, and socialization. Many of the voluntary activities of social welfare came into being and are at present implemented with the support of the church. Many

public social welfare activities became necessary as the church could no longer meet the needs of individuals.

Americans are a diverse lot, and perhaps this becomes most ovbious on weekends when we attend different churches on different days and at different times. Given the heterogeneity of our population and the right of people to worship as they please, the church has found it impossible to further the integration and socialization of our population. In fact, it often seems that our divisions as a people as to the central mission of human life and the meaning of human experience are intensified because the many organized churches within the religious institution do not agree on what our belief system should be. The powers of the organized churches in our society are considerable, but it is in no way as great as those of the earlier church or of the church in other societies. Some of the earlier powers of the church have been assigned in our society to the political institution and some to the family, but some of those powers and much of the earlier church functions that supported integration, socialization, and mutual support have become a part of the responsibility of social welfare.

The family as a social institution

Throughout history, the family as a social institution has been charged with broad responsibilities in the areas of production, distribution, and consumption; has been the major source of both the socialization of its younger members and the maintenance of that socialization among its older members; has been the primary source of our sense of membership in a meaningful society; and has been the principal source of the most meaningful forms of our mutual giving and receiving of nurture and care. The family has been and will continue to be the institution in society that is most vulnerable to, and influenced by, changes in other social institutions. The rapid changes in our society affect the family and all of its members in a most direct manner.

The impact of these changes is felt as stresses by the family unit as a whole and by members of the family as individuals. In turn, each individual member's feelings of stress has an impact on the family as a unit. The meaning of these stresses to the family will vary with the age and sex of family members, with the social position of the family, and with the education and the psychological makeup of its members. Although values change more slowly than other aspects of social life, new stresses and changes do bring changes in values. Values and value conflict, in turn, relate very directly to family patterns of intimate human interaction and to family patterns of socialization, integration, and mutual nurturing and support. They bear very directly on our notions of freedom, power, equality, responsibility, and all other elements of family interaction. Given these facts, it is understandable that much of the early social welfare activities was focused on the family as it was stressed by rapid social change. And it is to be expected that many of the social service activities of today are developed to help the family with its functioning or around the need for, or the problems that arise from a lack of, effective education, socialization, integration, nurturing, and mutual support of individuals who are suffering because of the family's inability to effectively offer these to its members.

Functions of the family

First, let us examine some functions of the family. Through the ages, the family institution has been viewed as an economic unit in that much of the labor of production took place within the family, the family determined the distribution of resources among members, and the family was responsible for maintaining the economic stability of its members. The family was also the unit charged with the education and socialization of children into productive adult roles. In addition, the family served its individual members as a source of emotional support.

These functions are critically important to the welfare of society. However, in the course of our development as an industrial society and in the history of our development through immigration and migration, certain forces impinged upon the

U.S. family in a way that resulted in critical changes in its functions.

Socialization functions. The industrial revolution resulted in the movement of certain types of labor from the home into the factory. The types of labor that moved out of the home were those designated by society as paid work. As the labor performed outside the home has become increasingly technical, the family has proved incompetent to educate its members in work skills. Thus, the formal education and socialization of children moved from the family as a social institution to the educational system that was part of the emergent social welfare institution. Society no longer entrusted parents with the task of making judgments about the needs of their children in this area.

A second force that pushed certain aspects of socialization, including education, out of the home was the pattern of settlement and migration in the United States. Through the ages of human development, it had been taken for granted that parents, who had lived longer than their children and had had more experience with life, had valuable knowledge and moral authority that should serve their children well. However, in the United States this assumption was challenged. Immigrant parents, representing other cultures, found their experience of little value to their children. They felt helpless to function as effective agents of socialization to a culture that they often did not understand. Many immigrant parents urged their children to live differently than they had and supported teachers as appropriate models for socialization. (This was often recognized in the standards that the community set for teachers' behavior.) To some extent the same processes occurred among rural parents who migrated to the cities. In addition, in the United States each generation of children has attended school longer than the preceding generation. The rate of vocational and technological change as well as the differences in the types and amounts of knowledge has been so great that even parents who were born in the United States may feel inadequate as socialization agents for their children.

Thus, the authority of parents as socializers and educators for their children has been weakened and these functions have become the responsibility of social welfare through the use of both the social services system and the educational system. This change has generated a good deal of conflict in the home and between the family and certain social welfare organizations. And it may be that children, caught in and aware of the conflict and of their parents' lack of authority and security, suffer from that conflict and insecurity.

Economic functions. It is interesting to note that while certain economic functions of the family were being transferred to the institution of social welfare, in other areas of social welfare (particularly income maintenance) society continued to insist that families be effective economic units. In spite of the vulnerability of the family to economic changes and in spite of all the noneconomic functions that families are responsible for, there is a tendency to evaluate the family as effective to the degree that it is able to maintain the economic stability of its members. The fact is that the conflict between older patterns of family functioning and the changing forces that bear on the family have created problems in the relationship between the social welfare system and the needs of the family. There is no social policy that overtly supports family integrity as a goal in itself.

An important trend in family life that is both social and economic is the large and rapidly increasing number of wives and mothers who work outside the home. An equally important trend is the increase in single-parent families—mostly headed by women—in which the only parent must work to support the family. The economic and legal systems have not yet been able to adjust to these changes in the customary patterns of family life. Many women face severe problems as a result of the discrepancy between the real world and the general notion of the family's operation as an institution and the family's relationship to the economic and political institutions. This conflict between the institutionalized systems of family life and law and economics is, and has been over the years, a concern of the social welfare system. Many activities in family and child welfare and in income maintenance have specifically developed as ways of offer-

ing economic support to women and children who have been seen as particularly vulnerable to a lack of economic support.

Political functions. The family is involved in problems of economic and social equality as well as problems of interpersonal support. The institution of the family has legal, economic, and social aspects. The legal aspects focus on the need of society for a continuing membership and involve regulations as to marriage, divorce, and child care. So far as the legal aspects of the family are concerned, there are 53 separate jurisdictions—the 50 states, the District of Columbia, Puerto Rico, and the Virgin Islands—all enforcing their many separate legal provisions for marriage, family relations, and divorce. Most of the legal aspects of family relationships require a great deal of pressure if one wants to bring about innovations. None of our social institutions feels the impact of custom and tradition in greater force than does the family.

In the United States it has never been the custom for parents to select mates for their children or for mates to be selected for utilitarian or family reasons. The ideal has been the free choice of a partner on the basis of love. However, during the earlier part of the 20th century, one of the more striking legislative trends concerning the family was a trend toward increasing legal restrictions and qualifications for marriage. Beginning in about 1938, states began to pass laws requiring physical examinations, blood tests, and waiting periods before marriage. There was also a trend away from the recognition of common-law marriage, a trend which may now be changing. Courts are increasingly recognizing that two people who live together may have certain obligations to each other even when there is no legal marriage.

Another trend has been in the direction of equalizing the duties and responsibilities of marriage partners. However, such equalization is contrary to the traditional roles and relationships found both within the family and between the family and other institutions, and it is far from complete, either factually or legally. Thus, although a husband is required to support his wife even if she has independent means, a wife is not usually required to support her husband unless he is unable to support himself. Because of this general expectation, we have had social security regulations under which wives and widows had certain accepted rights to benefits earned by their husbands, but until recently husbands had no right to benefits from their wives' contributions unless they could prove that they were dependent on them for their support. This regulation has been set aside by the courts, but it took years to get them to do so. There are many other equally problematic regulations in the social security program—putting the family with the working wife who contributes to the program equally with the working husband, at a very real financial disadvantage in relation to the family in which the wife does not work. At the same time, wives who stay home have complained bitterly that they have no rights in this program except as dependents of their husbands. To illustrate a similar situation in another sphere, we might note that until recently it has been all but impossible for a wife, even one with substantial income of her own, to establish her own right to credit apart from her husband.

Important changes in society that affect the family

Of the many changes which are occurring in society, five will be identified and examined here because of their impact on the family and on the interaction between the family and the social welfare institution.

1. The long economic dependence of young persons on their families.
2. The capacity of more and more persons to live to an advanced age in a society that has not developed an honorable role for the old.
3. The new militancy among women, marked by their demands that their rights be equal to those of men.
4. A marked shift in sexual mores.
5. An emphasis on individual rights.

The dependence of the young

In a technological society, particularly one that suffers wide swings in economic activity, young people remain a part of the family and are economically dependent on their parents for a long period of time. Because the positions in society that command good wages and access to other rewards demand long periods of education, youths find the opportunities for satisfying adult roles increasingly delayed into adulthood and increasingly tied to the family's economic status. So, in addition to the development of education, social welfare encompasses many programs aimed at the provision and equalization of vocational and educational opportunities for people over an increasing part of the life span. In addition to inadequate access to vocational, educational, and developmental opportunities, the financial dependence of children and youth through years marked by energy, enthusiasm, and productivity plays a part in family disputes and in conflicts between parents and children. This problem within the family results in calls for the development of social welfare programs to deal with conflicts between parents and children, the rebelliousness of children, and failures of socialization that are manifested in violent behavior among the young and in antiauthoritarian youth cultures.

In families today, children represent something different to parents than they did a century ago. They are no longer an economic asset or insurance against want and loneliness in old age. Also, there is a growing sophistication regarding the population limits of the planet Earth. These things, given the greater knowledge of contraception, have caused more and more families to limit the number of children they produce.

The increase of the life span

At the same time that the number of children per family has been decreasing, advancement in our knowledge of human physical needs plus medical technology has resulted in a tremendous increase in the number of people who live longer. This expanded life span has not meant just the adding of years of inactivity to the end of life. Although an ever larger number of people live into the years of phsical helplessness, we are also the first generation in the history of the world to have significant numbers of people in late maturity who are still actively interested in productivity, still active in the lives of their families and their communities, and still in control of a significant portion of the world's resources. We are facing a new demographic reality with tremendous impact on the family as a social institution and on the interrelationships among the individuals within the family.

The tendency to have fewer children, closer together and earlier in life, results in an acceleration of the generational wheels. There tends to be a small group of brothers and sisters, born close together, who form a group of peers rather than a set of children spanning a decade or more of family life. Increasingly, parents and their children are middle-aged together—the child in early middle age and the parent in late middle age. We see children today who are functionally older than their parents. Of women today who have sons at 20, one in four will outlive at least one son who will die at 65 years of age. There are an increasing number of parents and children in nursing homes together.

Even though it may not fit our mental notions about life, grandparenthood today is a phenomenon of middle age. The grandparents we see on television and the images we carry in our head are really those of today's great-grandparents. The grandmother of today is more likely to be a "chick in blue jeans" running off to class before she stops by to see her mother in a nursing home than she is to be an elderly woman peacefully sitting by the fire. Increasingly, people of 45 and 50 years of age will have living grandparents. This means that the family will involve the interaction of three generations of adults over a 40-year span. It means that different generations of adults will be spending long years together in what we all believe should be a loving and caring relationship. In the families of our industrial society, women have been the care givers, charged with tending the development and maintenance of the family's social interrelationships. What will these facts mean to individual women and their families when women are seeking greater freedom from family demands in the interests of individual achievement?

In addition to the greater number of active middle-aged people, there is a rapidly increasing number of the very old who cannot carry an active share of responsibility in society. At the same time that the numbers of the very old are increasing, and perhaps because of the rapid increase in this population group, there is a growing antipathy against the aging process and sometimes against the aged themselves.

Over the centuries of human history, the aged have usually had a place of honor in society because there was usually only a small number of the old and because aging was associated with the accumulation of wisdom. However, today, given rapid technological changes, it is almost impossible for the aged to possess wisdom about the new conditions of life. Thus, the aged become largely separated from the rest of society, and long life comes to mean loneliness and loss of power and esteem. The middle-aged members of the family are caught in a special conflict, as they are expected to offer both dependent young adult children and dependent older members a certain degree of material and/or emotional comfort. This creates a world in which the young and the middle-aged must constantly compete with each other for financial advantage in order to try to protect themselves against the economic problems of growing older. As the family's ability to meet these conflicting needs breaks down, the responsibility for supporting the older person is being borne increasingly by the social welfare institution. This responsibility is considerably greater than the simple economic support of earlier years. It now involves a wide array of social services designed to offer emotional support and nurture to the old as well as efforts to construct a respected place for the aged individual in our society.

Women's liberation

The development of a money economy and the movement of the work that produced earned income out of the home meant that the work of men and women became separate and differently valued. At the same time that this gave men a greater responsibility for the economic welfare of their families, it also gave them greater freedom and power than women. It meant that women who had always worked beside their husbands as part of an economic team charged with carrying out family responsibilities now took the primary responsibility for much of the nurturing, socializing, and integrating functions of the family while men assumed the economic burdens. Women who wanted or needed to share in the economic support of the family had to leave the home in order to do so and were seen as intruders in the economic system. They were also seen as neglecting their family responsibilities, although women who left the home to work were seldom relieved of the other functions necessary to the welfare of the family.

The women's movement can be seen as an effort to provide women with access to freedom and power or equality with men. In terms of impact on the interrelationships of family members, there is probably no more significant movement than this one. Unlike other struggles for liberation, this struggle tends to be an unremitting 24-hour-a-day battle from which neither men nor women can withdraw. It is often surprising to discover how deeply even the most liberated of husbands may resent the demands of his liberated wife or to discover the inner conflict of women who are seeking new roles and responsibilities when nothing in their life experience has trained them to desire them or to see them as acceptable for themselves (Halleck, 1976, p. 488).

We need to recognize the role of a developing and changing technology in the development of this movement. Contraception gave women the possibility of control over her own body. The washing machine and the dishwasher freed her from time-consuming household tasks. The automobile gave her both greater mobility and a new role— chauffeur for the family. The development of the school freed her from the tasks of education.

However, the women's liberation movement has resulted in the development of new social services to aid women in their search for their rights as members of society and to help family groups deal with the conflict and struggle that the new demands bring to the family.

Individualism and sexual freedom

In many ways the family is a small political institution. Just as there are differences in the ways we regard the concept of liberty on the national scene, so there are differences in the meanings we attach to notions of individuality, autonomy, spontaneity, and equality as they apply to the integrating and nurturing ties of the family. At present, it appears that members of the family are increasingly concerned with the rights of individuals within the family to the freedom to be themselves, to pursue their own course, without concern for the meaning of their actions to the others with whom they have been involved in close and nurturing relationships.

Society needs to be concerned that the new demands for freedom on the part of one member of the family unit do not result in the exploitation of other, less powerful members of the unit. For example, men, especially those who have considerable social and economic power, are considered desirable sexual objects through their middle years. The freedom to divorce a longtime mate leaves the man free to pursue a younger woman. But "sexual freedom to women over forty may be only the freedom to be lonely" (Halleck, 1976, pp. 483–93). A very basic question in this area relates to the place of children as valueless, powerless, and needy individuals in their parents' struggle for freedom and autonomy. Parents are still held legally responsible to care for their children. But social workers are very aware that such legal responsibility without caring on the part of parents and without the social support of society is really meaningless.

People need ongoing, dependable, caring relationships in order to maintain mental health. Certain research tends to support the view that the more losses in intimate relationships one endures, the more vulnerable to depression one becomes. When the freedom to have multiple relationships is exercised, there will be an increase in the number of painful separations and in the amount of stress that one will face over a lifetime. How much of the violence in the family system stems from the parents' lack of security with each other is an important question.

The family has been seen as the small, informal social unit in society that has been not only a nurturing unit but also a source of care for its members when they confront trouble and distress. Society cannot survive without population replacements, and men and women cannot really survive as individuals if they must face the world alone. As the family fails to provide nurture and care to the individual, or as individualism takes precedence over the concern for meaningful others in one's life, a more formal unit, the social agency, may assume these functions to an increasing extent. Only the future can tell us what this will mean to the shape of the institution of the family, to the development of children deprived of long-term nurturing relationships within a family, to the mental health of individuals as they are increasingly deprived of the support that commitment to long-term relationships gives, and to the shape of social welfare as it is called upon to deal with these changes.

✦§ Summary

In this chapter we have discussed the tasks that must be done by a group of people if they are to remain a group and to meet the necessary needs generated by their relationship. We have looked at how these various tasks became organized into functions and structured relationships that could be called social institutions. We have also examined the problems of these institutions as they operate in a rapidly changing technological, capitalist, democratic society. As the structured and patterned ways of functioning fail to meet the new developmental needs of society and the stress of individual change, the functions of the social welfare institution become larger and more diverse.

Social welfare acts in relation to all the other social institutions of society. It develops economic transfers of various kinds in order to meet economic needs and to distribute consumptive rights among the population in order both to meet survival needs and to effect changes toward a greater equality of people and a greater access to opportunities. We have examined the two ideas of liberty found in our society and have seen how many of the developments in social welfare have been based on the concept that in modern societies liberty is operationalized through the maximization of choice and how the tasks of providing access to opportunities for choice have become a part of social welfare. With the changes that have come to the church and the family, social welfare has been increasingly charged with the activities that contribute to the integration, social supports, and socialization of members of the group.

✦§ A look ahead

The institution of social welfare functions through the development and maintenance of socially sponsored programs and agencies to meet the needs of individuals and society. If one is to understand the institution, one must understand these programs and agencies. In the next chapter we shall begin to develop material that will contribute to the student's understanding of the structure and operations of social welfare systems and organizations.

✦§ Study questions

1. In this chapter we have often referred to the social changes brought about by changes in technology. Can you name some inventions and discuss how they have affected our ways of life?

2. In this chapter we discussed the fact that the production of goods rests on the demand for them as expressed through purchasing power. Can you give some examples of harmful goods that are produced because of such demand? How is the demand created and expressed?

3. What examples can you think of that illustrate the use of the power to tax for social purposes?

4. Table 4–1 in this chapter gives the total amount of income transfers and the amount that goes to the pretransfer poor. Calculate the amount of the transfers that go to the nonpoor based on the information in the table.

5. We have discussed some of the changes that have occurred in the family. How do you evaluate these changes? What functions of the family do you believe that social welfare cannot take over?

✑ Selected readings

Wilensky, H. L., and Lebeaux, C. N. *Industrial Society and Social Welfare*. New York: Free Press, 1965.

It would be helpful if students were able to read all of part 1 (pages 27–138). Some of the issues raised by this chapter will be discussed later in our text as we develop the historical material, but this reading serves nicely to further our discussion of institutions and their function in society and to raise more questions for students.

Macarow, D. *The Design of Social Welfare*. New York: Holt, Rinehart & Winston, 1978.

This text deals with social welfare as an institution in a way similar to ours. We would suggest part 1—on meeting human needs—as helpful reading.

Weinberger, P. E., ed. *Perspectives on Social Welfare*. New York: Macmillan, 1969.

There is an edited book. We would suggest that all the articles in section 1, "The Scope of Social Welfare," would be helpful in expanding the material in this chapter. In addition, the Schottland article, "Changing Roles of Government and Family," pages 132–46, would be interesting reading for the student.

Gilbert, N., and Specht, H., eds. *The Emergence of Social Welfare and Social Work*. Itasca, Ill.: F. E. Peacock. 1976.

Chapter 6, which includes a reprint of Wilensky and LeBeaux and three other articles, sets forth various ways of regarding social welfare. These articles should raise some interesting concepts for student discussion. The Wolins article contains some material that we have used in this and earlier chapters.

U.S.D.A. Photograph by Jack Schneider

These photographs illustrate two types of social welfare systems, and their sources of funding. In the picture on the left, federal tax money funds building improvements. Above, Red Cross workers feed flood victims in an example of a personal social service supported by voluntary giving.

U.S. Department of Housing and Urban Development

Helping Develop the Nation's Capital

The O Street Market

Federal Funds being used for Land Purchase and Substantial Rehabilitation

U.S. Department of Housing and Urban Development

Chapter 5 ﾞ

ﾞ Social welfare services, programs, and organizations ﾞ

The purpose of this chapter is to help the reader gain a way of understanding the specific services that fall within the parameters of social welfare and how they are delivered to eligible individuals. This is not an easy task, and it will require some patience on the part of the reader. We will begin our discussion by reminding readers that the word *institution* is commonly used at two levels of abstraction. We have used it and will continue to use it to mean the overall network of structured relationships that have been accepted by society and designated to carry out certain essential social functions. In addition, the term is often used to refer to a particular organization, such as the First Avenue High School. We shall avoid this use and shall use the term only to refer to the sum of the organizational units found within social welfare.

When we speak of a single unit, involving a formal structure and having a defined purpose that involves the delivery of certain specified services, social provisions, or resources to defined populations, we shall use the term *organization*. Thus, the First Avenue High School is an *organization*. In many instances, such *organizations* found within the *institution of social welfare* are called agencies. Thus, we shall use the term *agency* as synonymous with *organization*. *Organizations* carry out their function through *programs*. *Programs* may be considered the *structure, plans, and processes* developed to assure the delivery of *certain specified services, social provisions, or resources* to eligible consumers of such services, provisions, or resources.

Another term that needs to be understood is the abstraction *system*. We shall use this term to apply to a *collection of organizations* that have things in common, such as sources of funding or types of programs (for example, the public welfare system is the collection of all the public welfare agencies and the programs they administer). We shall also use the term *system* to mean a *collection of common programs,* and in this case we shall usually talk about *social service systems,* such as the *income maintenance system.* We shall use the term *delivery systems* to refer to an agency or groups of agencies that actually deliver services to clients. In addition, we shall use the term *social welfare systems* or *social service systems* to refer to all programs of a particular kind without regard to the organizational lines of the individual agencies in which the programs are located, although as a rule, organizations deliver one type of service as their primary function.

There is one other term that readers need to become familiar with: the term *policy* or *social policy.* Just as there are many definitions of social welfare, so there are many definitions of policy. For our purposes in this text we will use a definition found in Robert Morris's *Social Policy of the American Welfare State:*

> . . . social policy can be seen as a guide to action in future unanticipated situations. Policy identifies the general principles which an individual party or a government uses to make choices and decisions in unfamiliar circumstances which may arise in the future. Policy is, therefore, a guiding principle. It is a guide to action to be taken by individuals or groups capable of influencing the course of events. (1979, pp. 15–16)

Thus, policy is a guide to action in the future, whereas programs are specific rules, regulations, and processes for dealing with the known, concrete duties of service delivery. All levels and types of social welfare systems, organizations, and programs have policies—or general principles—to guide further action.

⋨ Classification of programs

It helps in comprehending the diverse and complex social welfare institution if one can organize the units that make up the whole of the institution in some way. There are different ways of organizing our thinking about social welfare. Social welfare programs may be classified according to: (1) the clientele, (2) the nature of the service, (3) the pur-

pose of offering the resource, (4) the source of support and sanction, and (5) in the case of public agencies, the arrangement among the levels of government. Discussions of welfare programs and services often involve a mixture of these various classifications.

By clientele

If we were to attempt to classify programs and services by clientele, our list would look something like this:

⋨ Programs by clientele

The aged.
Dependent children.
Neglected and abused children.
Delinquents.
Offenders.
The unemployed.
The emotionally disturbed.
The physically handicapped.
The mentally retarded.
The mentally ill.
The veterans.
The railroad workers.
The disabled.
The community special-interest groups.

The above categories are far from mutually exclusive. A black man may be a member of a social action group largely limited to black people that has as its purpose the advancement of social justice and equality for blacks. He is, however, also a veteran, and he has recently lost his job. The fact that he is operating as an active citizen in one group and is classified as a veteran of military service by another does not exempt him from problems that may result in his being served by other agencies and classified in other groups. A railroad worker might also be a veteran and might have a child with a special handicap. An aged person, served under certain programs for the aged, may apply for this service because of a disability rather than age. Clientele is, obviously, a variable basis for classification.

By source of funding

If we attempt to classify organizations and programs by source of funding, we will have two major divisions. As a rule, organizations are primarily supported either by tax funds or by voluntary contributions from private individuals and groups that support certain programs. However, similar programs are often found in different organizations and supported by different funding arrangements. For example, one finds programs of adoption, day care, homemaker services, and family counseling supported by both public and voluntary or private funds and lodged in separate organizations. Or one may find a mingling of funds in that the public agency charged with mounting a program of adoption may enter into a contract with a private agency under which the private agency is reimbursed for serving public agency clients who seek service under the adoption program.

Given the fact that there are only two large divisions of organizations and that if a classification by source of funding were used, similar programs would need to be put in both groups, this would not seem to be a productive classification. Understanding the source of funding is very important to our analysis of the functioning of social welfare organizations and the development of programs, but such large classifications do not help us in looking at programs and services. If we were to use a classification by source of funding, it would look something like the list below. This list is very incomplete.

By level of administration

If one is concerned only with the public agencies and organizations, one could classify them by the level of government responsible for their administration. Some public programs are administered directly by the federal government, some by cooperative arrangements between the federal government and state governments, and some by state,

---

✑ Programs by source of funding

Public	Private or voluntary
Old-age, survivors, and disability insurance (social security)	Adoption
Medicare	Child welfare services
Medicaid	Foster homes
Unemployment insurance	Family services
Maternal and child health programs	Day care
Services to veterans	Homemaker
Parole	Community action groups Scouts–YMCA–YWCA
Vocational rehabilitation	Community councils
Supplemental Security Income	Big Brothers
Aid to Dependent Children	Community centers
General Assistance	
Stipends for educating social welfare personnel	
Homemaker	
Day care	
Housing and redevelopment	
Urban renewal	
Social service	
Adoption	
Foster care	

state and local, or entirely local programs. Below are some examples of this type of classification.

Federally administered programs

Old-age, survivors, and disability insurance
Medicare
Supplemental Security Income
Railroad workers' insurance
Most services to veterans
Federal probation and parole
Administration of federal prisons

Federal-state programs

Aid to Dependent Children
Unemployment compensation
Vocational rehabilitation
Mental health services (public)
Crippled children's services
Child welfare services
Maternal and child health services

State, state-local, and local programs

Workers' compensation
Disability insurance
General Assistance
Local probation
Parole
State and local prisons and reformatories
Institutions for juvenile delinquents

By nature of service

Within recent years a frequently utilized system for classifying social welfare programs is that of categorization by the nature of the service. Like other methods of classification, this method has its problems, but we believe that it will be the most productive of understanding. The method was first suggested by Kahn (1973) and was further developed by Kammerman and Kahn (1976). They listed six categories:

1. Income maintenance.
2. Health care.
3. Housing.
4. Education.
5. Manpower.
6. Personal social services.

In his discussion of social policy, Robert Morris (1979, p. 117) implies two additional categories: corrections and rehabilitation. We would add a ninth: social-change activities. Thus we have nine classes of social welfare programs. Each of these broad categories will be considered a social welfare system.

Social welfare systems, which are essentially collections of programs, do not always coincide with the boundary lines of delivery systems or agencies. An agency may offer programs that fall into two or more categories. Social services and social-change activities, are often found as auxiliary services, or coservices, within organizations that are organized primarily to deliver other types of resources or social provisions. For example, the local public welfare agency will have at least two major divisions: (1) programs relating to the income maintenance system and (2) programs of general social services. The combining of income maintenance programs with social service is common to all welfare agencies. This is accounted for by the fact that these two programs developed together historically. It was not until 1965 that social services and income maintenance were separated as distinct programs within public welfare. In order to further illustrate this concept, we are reproducing an organization chart of the Ramsey County Welfare Department (Figure 5–1). You will note that it is divided into two portions—one of them is a part of an income maintenance delivery system, and the other is a part of the social service delivery system.

☙ Human services

For purposes of this discussion, we would like to divide the list of nine delivery systems into three parts. In the first part, which we have labeled human services, we would list income maintenance, health care, housing, education, manpower, and vocational rehabilitation. These broad services have become so elaborate and comprehensive as to be considered freestanding systems. They are publicly underwritten areas of modern life which require governmental sanction and support. They are primarily concerned with supplying persons

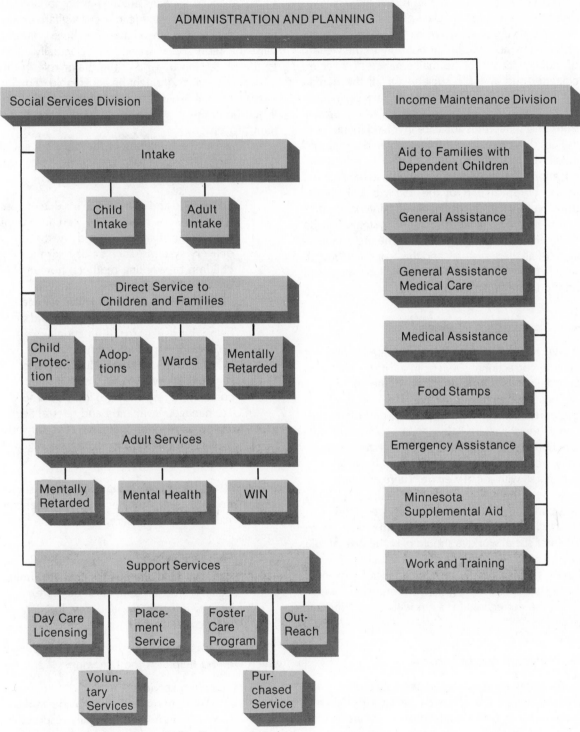

~§ Figure 5–1
Organization chart of Ramsey County Welfare Department

ADMINISTRATION AND PLANNING

Social Services Division

Intake

Child Intake

Adult Intake

Direct Service to Children and Families

Child Protection

Adoptions

Wards

Mentally Retarded

Adult Services

Mentally Retarded

Mental Health

WIN

Support Services

Day Care Licensing

Placement Service

Foster Care Program

Out-Reach

Voluntary Services

Purchased Service

Income Maintenance Division

Aid to Families with Dependent Children

General Assistance

General Assistance Medical Care

Medical Assistance

Food Stamps

Emergency Assistance

Minnesota Supplemental Aid

Work and Training

Source: Supplied by Ramsey County Welfare Department, St. Paul, Minn.

with social provision or social resources. They address themselves to the ideal goals of social security, social justice, and social opportunity. These goals make them important not only to the welfare of individuals but to the maintenance of a secure citizenry and a stable society. Of all the human services, only the means-tested part of income maintenance is considered welfare. Many professions and semiprofessions are involved in and central to these services: for example, doctors and nurses in health services, teachers in education, vocational counselors in vocational rehabilitation. In the historical part of the text we will discuss the development of the income maintenance programs in some detail. The other systems will be dealt with in a more general way. The present operation of all these systems and the programs through which they are operationalized will be discussed briefly in the final part of the text.

✑§ Correctional services

We recognize that some authorities would not include correctional services in a list of social welfare delivery systems. We have done so because we believe that the correctional system is a relatively freestanding system that is part of the institution of social welfare. We view it as a government-sanctioned and -supported welfare system. Historically, correctional services have been closely connected with social welfare. There are some who regard the primary tasks of correctional services as a part of the personal social services. However, there is considerable dispute in the field as to whether social workers should play the central role in corrections. In addition, the correctional services have as their goal the control of social deviance, a task that, at least in degree, confronts social workers in the correctional system with some different issues.

✑§ Personal social services

The term *personal social services* comes from England, where these services are a fifth delivery system that is considered equal in stature to the other four: income, health, housing, and education.

Personal social services are also an important and growing part of the American social welfare institution. However, here they have often been confused with the term *social work,* which actually refers to the profession that plays the major role in this system of services. It might be acceptable to define personal social services as a set of basic and established programs in which social work is the dominant profession.

In England the functions of the personal social services are defined as follows (Morris, 1979, pp. 117–19):

1. To provide and manage the residue of concrete services required by certain groups but not ordinarily provided by the other delivery systems, such as day care for the children of working mothers, homemaker services, and adoptions.
2. To provide psychotherapeutic services to individuals and families that need and want help with psychosocial functioning.
3. To provide an advocacy function that will alter or moderate the rigidities of the other social delivery systems so that they become more responsive to individual needs.
4. To manage information and referral activities so as to coordinate activities for individuals or reduce the overlap of agency functions.

Kahn (1973, p. 16), a leading authority on social service programs and activities in both American and international social welfare, classifies the functions as:

1. Socialization and development services.
2. Therapy, help in rehabilitation (including social protection and substitute care).
3. Access, information, and development of new services.

A way of classifying the personal social services which we find helpful is the following:

1. Protection services
   a. Adoption services to provide families for children without legally responsible parents.

b. Foster home care for children who need temporary living arrangements apart from parents.

c. Services in neglect and abuse situations to the end of protecting and assuring adequate parenting for the children at risk.

d. Services to other victims of family violence.

e. Protection services for the vulnerable aged.

f. Services to provide alternative living situations for persons who need them.

2. Social care services

a. Access and information services.

b. Coordination of the differing services for individuals.

c. Advocacy services for individuals.

d. Supportive counseling or other services which enhance individuals' capacity for satisfying self-care.

e. Provision of such social utilities as day care and homemaker services.

3. Development and socialization services

a. Services that contribute to normal development.

b. Services that contribute to the socialization of individuals.

4. Rehabilitation or psychotherapeutic services

a. Services aimed at bringing about a change in the psychosocial functioning of individuals and families.

b. Services aimed at resolving problems in areas of psychosocial functioning.

These services may be found as freestanding services in agencies devoted to one or more of them as their central purpose or as adjunctive services in the programs classified above as human services, such as income maintenance, health care, and education. Here the services are charged with assistance to individuals who need certain kinds of help and change if they are to use the services of the host programs effectively. Examples of such assistance are found in medical social services and school social work. In this type of program, social services are manned by social workers and operate as departments of social work or social service within a host agency or organization, such as a hospital. Social services are not always easily identifiable functions. Even within a single community, given social service programs may have different activities and different target populations. Similar services will have different sources of funding or will operate under different auspices within the same geographic area. A partial list of personal social services would include:

Family services.

Child welfare services, including foster care and adoption.

Probation and parole work.

Group therapy.

School social work with troubled children.

Medical social work.

Mental health programs for children and adults.

Protective services for vulnerable persons, particularly children and the aged.

Day care.

Homemaker services.

Family planning.

Centers for senior citizens.

Child development programs.

Parent groups.

Day-care activities.

Day care.

Residential treatment.

✑ Social development and change activities

Social development and change activities involve programs that are directed at system change rather than individual change. In certain ways these programs may be seen as complementary to social services. While social services are aimed at *changing people* so that they may cope more effectively with life events, including the impact of unresponsive systems upon them as individuals, social development and change activities are aimed at changes in the policies of larger social systems. These two types of activities are often interrelated. In the process of participating in social action groups in their own interest, many persons may find that their self-esteem is altered so that they are better able to handle their personal problems. Or effective help with personal problems may help individuals to gain the kinds of knowledge or skills that will encourage involvement in social action.

Efforts at social reform involve many different professionals and a wide range of expert knowledge. Most social workers would claim the central role in such action. Like social service programs, social development and change programs are often found in conjunction with other programs. Thus, in a hospital an evaluation and policy program may coexist with health and medical programs. The evaluation and policy program may operate to change the health and medical programs, which are the principal programs of the hospital. Usually social development and change activities require the coordination of the expert knowledge and skills of professionals with the commitment and work of citizens. Some examples of such activities are: Model Cities programs, urban renewal programs, certain legal aid and advocacy programs, and the Community Action Program of the Economic Opportunity Act.

ᴥ§ Organizational structure of programs

In every community the programs discussed above are organized and structured in ways that bring them to the consumers. The people who use the services provided by these programs do not apply to programs—they go to public welfare, the social service administration, social agencies, clinics, hospitals, probation offices, and so on. Thus we have the delivery systems of social welfare services. These systems, or organizations, are usually bureaucratic structures, but the specifics of the structures and the ways in which they operate will differ from one type of organization to another and from one specific organization to another. For example, the Divine Redeemer Hospital will differ from Public Hospital, and Public Hospital may differ from Public Medical Center—which may include many clinics not found in a public health agency simply called Public Hospital. However,

all health agencies will have structures and processes in common which make them significantly different in organization from the agencies that deliver personal social services or income maintenance programs.

The Family and Children's Service, the Catholic Social Services, and the Jewish Family Service will all look very much alike in that they all deliver only personal social services under private or voluntary auspices. The Jewish Community Center and the Teen Canteen are also agencies that are structured primarily to deliver personal social services, though some health services may be attached to the Teen Canteen. These are privately funded community centers. They offer mainly group experiences, so their structure will be somewhat different from that of the agencies offering individual and family personal social services, and their internal processes may be very different. And these privately funded agencies will operate very differently from the public welfare agencies that also deliver personal social services, and will often feel very different to the applicant.

In the following sections we will discuss very briefly the typical organization of personal social service delivery systems and certain income maintenance agencies.

ᴥ§ Personal social service organizations

The programs and activities of the personal social services are administered by organizations that are often called agencies. Three major factors affect the organization of agencies: their source of support; the source of their sanction, or right to operate; and the areas of their concern which are operationalized through the programs and activities they offer.

Funding. As a rule, agency funds come from 1) public or tax funds (public welfare agencies or public schools) or from 2) privately given, voluntary contributions (the Family Service Association), although agencies supported primarily by private contributions may utilize tax funds through various contracts and grants. Agencies using primarily tax funds are called public agencies, and agencies using primarily voluntary contributions are known as private or voluntary agencies. One of the important public contributions to the support of private agencies is the provision in the tax law that allows contributors to deduct the amount contributed to private agencies when they compute their tax liability.

Any agency's policy and structure, procedures, and flexibility will be determined by the source and adequacy of its funding. As a general rule, the available funds are never adequate to the demands upon the agency, so that difficult choices among needs and purposes must be made. Ideally, the use of funds would be determined by policy. However, in both public and private agencies, persons who control funding sources can often impose their notions of the services needed upon the agency.

Policy. The public tax-supported agency usually operates within legislation and is usually dependent on some legislative body (for example, county commissioners or the state legislature) for its broad policy and for the appropriation of public funds for its support. In some cases the board or commission of a public agency and/or its chief executive may be appointed by an elected executive officer (for example, the governor). The programs of such agencies are usually administered by individuals who are required to prove their competence by passing a civil service or merit system test. These administrators will determine procedures and more detailed program issues within the broad legislation or the policy that established and maintains the agency.

Private agencies usually operate under the general policy directives of a board of directors. Such a board has three primary functions: 1) it establishes the right of the agency to carry on its program, and it sanctions the agency's activities; 2) it is responsible for the agency's overall policy; and 3) it oversees fund-raising activities. Until very recently almost all of these boards were composed of an elite group of members who had little understanding of the realities of the lives of the persons for whom they developed policy. The boards of private agencies almost always operate by consensus. Their members are volunteers who give a great

deal of free time to agency matters. Sometimes these members are independently wealthy people, private professionals, or representatives of community corporations which see this service as a contribution to the community. Only those who have a commitment to certain goals of the agency and/or are supported by their fellow members tend to remain active. In most situations the board hires the executive of the agency. The executive usually controls staff access to the board and the flow of information to the board about the agency's work.

Some personal social service organizations are really departments of larger organizations with a differing function, such as the medical social work department of a large hospital or the school social work department of a school system. In such cases the department that administers personal social services is part of a host organization. In such situations the financial support and overall policymaking processes will be determined by the host agency, which generally operates under a structure similar to the one described here.

Function and program. Agencies have both a function and a program. For the professional person working in an agency, this distinction may have some meaning in that the program of the agency may change while the function remains constant. Thus, an agency whose function is the care and treatment of children may have initially cared largely for orphaned dependent children in an institutional facility that it administered. But today it may care mostly for disturbed and delinquent children in a series of group foster homes. Perhaps it sold the building in which the children of an earlier day were lodged to an agency that now offers nursing-home care for the aged population.

Organizational structure. Each agency has an organizational structure (usually bureaucratic) by which it delegates responsibilities and tasks and stabilizes and systematizes its operations. The executives of each agency are the primary administrative officers. They have the direct responsibility for the day-to-day functioning of the agency. They are usually responsible for agency funding, which may take most of their time. They are further responsible for relationships with the boards of directors or public policymaking bodies. They are usually responsible for working with other agencies toward the social welfare goals of the community and for overseeing the public relations functions of the agency.

Below the executive on the organization table of a large agency, one may find a bewildering array of division directors, unit supervisors, consultants, and line supervisors. In most agencies, these persons are social workers who are responsible for the service rendered to the people who come to the agency to take advantage of the program it offers (Compton and Galaway, 1979, pp. 487–88).

As was discussed, the programs that agencies offer may be focused on a special population, usually a population that is considered vulnerable in some special way to special problems in living, such as children or the aged, or they may be focused on a special problem in living, such as family counseling to prevent or alleviate family conflict or the counseling of children who are having difficulty in school. The private social agencies offer primarily social services. In addition to social services, certain means-tested income maintenance programs are found primarily in public agencies. Organizations that offer other kinds of maintenance services, such as hospitals, clinics, schools, and employment offices, are known by titles other than "agency."

✑ Public welfare agencies

An agency found in every U.S. county is the public welfare agency. In fact, this agency and the public welfare programs it administers are so well known that when one speaks of "the welfare" one is inevitably speaking about this agency and its function. (We will follow the same pattern in this book.) The agency is so well known that it is often difficult to separate the term *social welfare,* which we understand to mean a total societal institution with a broad function, from the term *public welfare,* which refers to either the public welfare agency or its function. We will discuss the Public Welfare Agency and some other major agencies usually found in communities very briefly here. We

will trace the development of agencies and their programs in Part III, ending with a much more detailed account of the present-day agency structure.

Public welfare agencies are invariably among the largest social agencies in the community, and they usually administer some of the more diverse programs (see Figure 5–1). They either operate as county agencies under the supervision of the state agency or they are administered directly by the state. They are supported by a combination of local, state, and federal funds. The diverse programs of the public welfare agencies include both personal social services and income maintenance programs, and the regulations under which these agencies work are complex and ever changing. Most county welfare agencies offer services of income maintenance, such as Aid for Dependent Children (AFDC) and General Assistance (GA). They also offer food stamps, and they pay for the medical care of those who are unable to pay for their own care, for example, Mr. Olds.

In addition to these maintenance-type services, which will be discussed briefly in the next section, the public welfare agencies offer a host of personal social service programs. Perhaps the best known of these are the following: counseling offered to families and children, discharged mental patients, and the parents of the retarded; and the services known as protective services under which social workers try to assure that vulnerable populations such as children and the aged are neither neglected nor abused.

✑ Privately supported agencies

Larger urban communities will have a range of privately supported agencies that offer programs of personal social services aimed both at the specific troubles of people and at the development and self-actualization of people. In rural communities, particularly in the South, private agencies may be scarce or nonexistent. One of the larger and more prominent agencies in the urban community is usually called Family and Children's Services. Supported by fees, contributions, and the United Fund, it is a very old agency that originally offered both income maintenance and personal social services. Large communities may, in fact, have several such agencies offering almost identical programs for different populations. These agencies may bear such titles as Catholic Social Services, Lutheran Social Services, or Jewish Family Service. The agencies usually offer social services aimed at helping troubled families and individuals with problems of family life, individual adjustment, crisis situations, and child care. They often offer developmental services, such as family planning and family-life education. Other private agencies, usually thought of as community centers or as recreational agencies, will offer services aimed at the personal and social development of children and families plus many of the other services listed above when these services can be effectively delivered through small groups of consumers.

◄§ Income maintenance and distribution of wealth

Considering the fact that it is through income that we all buy our existence, our social and physical environment, and to some extent our social status, it is not surprising that the social arrangements and the social welfare policies affecting income distribution should be the most important and sensitive area of social welfare.

When we speak of "welfare," most people think of either money or goods given individuals who are in need. In this text we use the term *income maintenance* to cover goods, services, or money that is transferred to individuals from public funds in order to meet actual or assumed socially approved needs of individuals. However, two other governmental programs that are seldom considered by the general public affect the maintenance of wealth and income in widespread population groups in our society. These are the programs involving grants and subsidies and tax and tariff policies. Not only do most people not consider these programs as "welfare," but most people are generally uninformed about the ways in which the programs operate and about their public cost.

It is interesting to look at the underlying assump-

tions that support the different ways in which the public views income maintenance for the poor and subsidies and tax policies. The general public accepts the last two programs as desirable, appropriate, and necessary because of the general belief that they "are in the national interest" and that they "trickle down" to all segments of the population (Turner and Starnes, 1976, p. 115). But it seldom views the programs of income maintenance to the AFDC mother as being in the national interest, though it is hard to understand why the highest national interest is not served by the care and nurture of children.

Tax codes are extremely complex, and they operate in conjunction with allowable deductions and credits in ways that are difficult to understand. Under the present tax code, the cost to *all* taxpayers of special credits or deductions for the few does not appear in the federal budget—thus we seldom view tax codes as instruments of income maintenance for the affected groups. The federal income tax, which is steeply progressive on *taxable* income, is especially complex in the way it operates to offer income maintenance opportunities to various levels of taxpayers. For the wealthier taxpayers the ability to exclude income from *taxable income* results in a lower rate of taxation that offers significant opportunities to preserve income. For example, let us take the fact that we can all deduct our medical expenses above 3 percent of our income. Suppose that a congressman, concerned about the aged, introduces a bill that would allow older persons to deduct all medical expenses. This seems to be a very sound proposal because, as we all know, the elderly on fixed incomes are suffering severe economic problems. However, the proposal would cost all of us over $200 million. Persons with incomes above $40,000 per year would receive $90 million of that amount, and persons with incomes of less than $4,000 per year would receive only $8 million. Or consider the married couple with a taxable income of $200,000. Because of the provision that people may deduct the interest paid on loans for the purchase of housing, the actual cost to the couple of the mortgage on their home will be $30 for each $100 of interest.

However, a couple with an annual income of $10,000 will actually pay $81 for each $100 of interest (Turner and Starner, 1976, pp. 115–16).

There are five general types of laws that operate to reduce basic taxes: (1) exclusions from gross income; (2) deductions from gross income; (3) tax credits; (4) special tax rates; and (5) tax shelters. Most of us, like the Affluent family, are wage earners. We are now allowed *to exclude* from our income the benefits we receive from our employers, such as sick pay, contributions to medical insurance, social security, and retirement. Most of us are happy that we do not have to pay taxes on the value of these benefits. However, what we do not realize is that the more income we have, the greater the value of these exclusions becomes, because they result in our being in a lower bracket and our being taxed at a lower percentage. For individual consumers, certain costs in earning a living, or in just living, such as the interest on housing loans that we discussed above, are *deductible,* with the same results. *Tax credits* allow individuals or corporations to receive a percentage of credit on taxes for certain kinds of expenditures and income. Under the tax laws certain types of income are *taxed at lower rates* than other types. This holds true for capital gains—that is, the profit from selling some tangible asset, such as real estate or stocks. Under the tax laws relating to capital gains, one half the profit is automatically excluded from taxation. Various tax laws allow individuals to defer paying taxes on income to a later time. For example university professors, among others, are allowed to put a certain amount of their income into a *tax-sheltered fund,* which allows them to exclude that amount of income from taxation until their retirement, when they will presumably be in a lower income bracket, and thus the income that was deferred will be taxed at a lower rate (Turner and Starnes, 1976, pp. 92–99). Only taxpayers with a high income and money beyond the daily costs of living have money to invest. Average taxpayers often do not have money to invest, and if they do invest, it is a relatively modest amount that does not allow them to take full advantage of this type of support for income and wealth.

The federal government also provides loans and grants to individuals and corporations in the form of subsidies, in the belief that such expenditures will serve the national interest by stimulating the economy, providing or preserving jobs, and supporting farmers so that agriculture can continue to provide us with our abundant food. It would be foolish to take the position that subsidies to industry and agriculture are not needed. The basic questions are: Does our present pattern of subsidies serve the national interest, and does it unnecessarily increase the present pattern of inequality in America (Turner and Starnes, 1976, pp. 116–17)?

But what is most important for students of social welfare to understand is that governmental activities and expenditures in social welfare are not all devoted to the poor. In fact, the largest amounts not only go to the nonpoor, but to the *wealthy.* In this text we will not discuss these types of social welfare supports to the economic system and to individuals in any detail. However, we should recognize that the present welfare system, though it may offer succor to the poor and support many nonpoor through the social security system, also operates to maintain income and wealth for the more privileged segments of society and to perpetuate inequality. An example of the operation of subsidies is provided by a newspaper report on subsidies for agriculture in which Senator James Eastland of Mississippi was listed as receiving more than $150,000 in federal subsidy payments in 1967 for allowing his land to lie idle. He did not work to earn this. The payments came because he possessed wealth—land. Further the subsidy meant that many black agricultural workers ordinarily employed in tending and harvesting the crops who did not work that year. A single mother with children who was unable to secure work to support herself and her children in Mississippi that year could receive no more than $500 from public welfare for that purpose.

> Unequal distribution of wealth is of critical significance because wealth conditions the exercise of power and, through power, determines much of the inequality of social life. Among the consequences of wealth inequality is income inequality. Income refers to a flow of money or in-kind goods. Wealth refers to a store of the same. Income also

refers to payment or compensation for something as a part of an exchange. Wealth, however, refers essentially to control over something—not merely some thing, but something of central instrumental value. (Turner and Starnes, 1976, p. 45)

Turner and Starnes go on to point out that economic inequality (inequality of wealth and income) reflects differences in political power among a population and that such differences often determine access to prestige, health, education, and other resources. In every society, those who possess the most political power also have the greatest capacity and opportunity to disseminate the social theories and value positions that they espouse.

America is a democratic state in which people are relatively free to express themselves as they wish. However, the impact of their opinions on the course of the nation is significantly unequal. America has a capitalist economic system which

has operated to allow most people to live better than their parents, and many live in an affluence beyond their wildest early dreams. However, from its earliest days the United States has been "neither a land of equality nor a land of equal opportunity" (Turner and Starnes, 1976, p. 14). In order to lift oneself by one's own bootstraps, one had to have boots. During the early days of our country, there were examples of great wealth in the midst of the abject poverty of the great mass of people. In 1810 in Brooklyn, the richest 1 percent of the population owned 22 percent of the wealth and the poorest 54 percent owned 3 percent of the wealth. It is extremely difficult to secure reliable information on the distribution of wealth in this country. However, the two accompanying tables show the distribution of wealth in selected American cities in 1860 and 100 years later. The last table presents the latest data available.

The distribution of wealth in America for selected cities

Level of wealth	Percentage of population	Percentage of wealth held in 1860 in:		
		Baltimore	New Orleans	St. Louis
Highest fifth	20	94.7%	92.9%	92.7%
Second fifth	20	4.4	5.7	6.0
Middle fifth	20	0.9	1.3	1.1
Fourth fifth	20	0.0	0.0	0.2
Poorest fifth	20	0.0	0.0	0.0

Source: Robert E. Gallman, "Trends in the Size Distribution of Wealth in the Nineteenth Century: Some Speculation," in *Six Papers on the Size Distribution of Wealth and Income*, ed. Lee Soltow (New York: National Bureau of Economic Research and Columbia University Press, 1969), pp. 1–25.

Distribution of wealth, 1962: Percentage of total wealth held by fifths of units

By size of wealth		By income		By age of head	
Fifths of units	Percentage of total wealth	Fifths of units	Percentage of total wealth	Fifths of units	Percentage of total wealth
Total	100.0%	Total	100.0%	Total	100.0%
Lowest fifth	0.2	Lowest fifth	7.2	Youngest fifth	6.0
Second fifth	2.1	Second fifth	8.6	Second fifth	14.3
Middle fifth	6.2	Middle fifth	11.4	Middle fifth	20.7
Fourth fifth	15.5	Fourth fifth	15.6	Fourth fifth	29.2
Highest fifth	76.0	Highest fifth	57.2	Oldest fifth	29.8

Source: Board of Governors of the Federal Reserve System, "Survey of Financial Characteristics of Consumers, 1962," as reported in the Department of Commerce's *Social Indicators, 1973* (Washington, D.C.: U.S. Government Printing Office, 1973).

✒ Purposes of income maintenance

There are many authors who would hold that the functions of the direct individual-income maintenance programs are very different from those usually recognized. Although such authors would agree that the primary goals include relieving at a minimum cost the suffering of the destitute poor and maintaining the functioning of special population groups that may fall into poverty, they feel strongly that three other goals should be recognized.

1. Maintaining the existing political and economic order by: *(a)* expanding public relief somewhat in times of protest, *(b)* utilizing public assistance to maintain a work force for seasonal, unskilled industries, and *(c)* removing from the work force certain groups—the elderly, the mothers of young children—so as to make opportunities available to others.
2. Reforming the work attitudes and morals of the very poor and encouraging or ensuring maximum work effort from key groups among the poor.
3. Offering people subsistence while they attempt to rehabilitate themselves so that they may join the work force.

There are authors who see these three goals as the *primary goals* of our income maintenance system. However, we believe that although there is much concern about the impact of relief on the morals of the poor and about the importance of rehabilitating people or getting people off welfare, the principal concerns of the people who are involved in the local income maintenance and personal social services delivery systems are to protect the weak, to provide supportive resources to individuals and families at times of crisis or stress, and to enhance the well-being of the needy poor.

Public assistance

As we stated earlier, most of the means-tested income maintenance programs are delivered by county welfare agencies. The programs are called public assistance (relief, the dole), and they may be administered by the county, or they may be delivered at the county level but administered at the state level. Given the value placed on the importance of having individuals take care of themselves economically through the operation of private effort in the marketplace, the continued belief in the saving virtues of work, and the optimistic view that there are opportunities in an ever-expanding society for people who will but grasp them (these notions will be discussed in detail in our next chapter), it is perhaps to be expected that the applicants for public assistance have had to endure a lengthier list of restrictions to obtaining aid than any other group of recipients of social welfare services.

Public welfare programs are usually under constant attack from certain groups in the community which feel that all welfare recipients are cheaters and that the money such persons receive allows them to live in idle luxury, and on the other side, these programs are also criticized by other groups for expecting persons to live in conditions of deprivation and destitution. It is beyond dispute that such programs offer, at best, minimal levels of aid and that they often offer totally inadequate assistance. The truth is—as we shall see later in this text—that many reforms are needed in public welfare. Under the AFDC program, however, hundreds of thousands of children have been enabled to live in their own homes with their own parents instead of being placed in foster homes or institutions, and thus they have had a minimally adequate opportunity for a normal childhood experience.

One of the famous, or infamous, and much-discussed local attempts to respond to the notion that the welfare rolls were full of "bums," "cheats," and "chiselers" was an effort made in Newburgh, New York, in 1961 by the Newburgh city manager. In order to eliminate "chiselers," he required all public assistance recipients to pick up their checks at the city police department. No "chiselers" were found. Thirteen additional eligibility requirements were set up, including the requirements that applicants new to the city show that they had moved to the city because of a concrete offer of employment, that all able-bodied "loafers" work, that persons who voluntarily left jobs not be entitled to receive relief, that mothers who received AFDC show that they maintained a "suitable home for their children." The city manager became a national hero; many prominent officials at all levels of government supported his efforts; and mail supporting the new eligibility requirements poured into Newburgh from all parts of the country. The New York State Welfare Board ordered Newburgh not to implement these requirements; the Supreme Court issued an injunction on the ground that the rules deprived people of certain rights; and eventually all but one of the requirements was found illegal. A careful combing of the welfare rolls for able-bodied men who could support themselves disclosed *one possible case*. Nonetheless, the impact of this punitive attack on public assistance recipients continued long after it was legally stopped. Many people continue to believe that hundreds of applicants had been found to be "cheaters" or "chiselers" (May, 1964, p. 31).

A further example of the attitudes of people toward those who are supported by public assistance is provided by the article reproduced in the accompanying box. In this article we find many different views of the problem.

It is inevitable that there will be mistakes in any program, public assistance or otherwise, in which individual eligibility status is based on criteria of such a personally sensitive nature as family relationships, income, personal expenditures, and household conditions. (We would submit as one example, the conflicts with the Internal Revenue Service that result from the efforts of individuals to reduce their income taxes.) There are obviously cases of individuals who are dishonest in the information they share with the public welfare agency and who defraud public welfare programs by concealing substantial income or assets. However, most abuses of the programs come from either (1) minor errors in which income changes were reported later than they should have been or (2) administrative errors in which the staff failed to assess needs and income properly. Incidentally, such administrative errors cut both ways. It may be that through staff

errors as many persons are deprived of funds they are eligible for as are given too much (Morris, 1979, pp. 65–66).

However, there are other reasons for public criticism of public assistance programs. One stems from the fact that people see long lists of job openings in the newspapers without realizing the skills or capacities that these jobs require. Another comes from the complexity and overlapping of programs. There are claims made by individuals that are entirely legal but result in certain families receiving more aid than do other families. For example, a worker may receive unemployment benefits even though all the other members of the family are working, and the income of such a family will be considerably higher than that of a family in which the only wage earner is an elderly man who has been denied social security because his income from wages is above the allowable maximum. It is also possible that adult children who go to college and set up independent households will be eligible for income support if they cannot find work, even though their parents may be able to aid them. Such situations offend the public's notion that aid should go only to people in dire distress and should only be temporary.

Social insurances

Every county in the United States is served by another large agency—the Social Security Administration office. This agency operates under federal auspices and administers money from the federal government. It is purely an income maintenance program, determining individuals' eligibility for cash payments under two programs—social security (OASDI) and supplemental security income (SSI)—and eligibility for medicare (HI and SMI), a program under which certain persons are eligible for prepaid medical care. These are extremely complicated programs whose major outlines will be discussed later.

The social security program is often thought of as being only for the older, retired person and that person's dependents. But it is a great deal more than that. It covers persons who have worked in

~§ Stricter welfare screening favored

By George Gallup
Director, American Institute of Public Opinion, Princeton, New Jersey

In an initial assessment of the public's attitudes regarding welfare reform, which is being debated in Washington, these important observations emerge:

1. The response people give most often (52 percent) when asked what changes they would like to see in the welfare system, is to improve the investigative and screening process.

A 31-year-old student said, "I think welfare is justified, but I'd like to see some abuses eliminated. There are too many on the rolls who are not really in need. They are taking advantage of the system and should go to work."

A 48-year-old unemployed Pennsylvania resident said, "The welfare system is way out of hand. It needs more investigation. People are on welfare who could be working. People on welfare make out better than we do."

2. The response given next most often in the survey (28 percent) is that those who are able to work should work.

A 44-year-old business executive from Belleville, Ill., wants to "crack down": "Confine it to poor and needy; people able to work should be made to work!"

A 22-year-old civil servant from Georgia said, "Instead of giving it away, let them work for it. For example, remodel apartments so they can take pride in receiving the money."

3. The change sought third most often (26 percent) is that more aid should be given to the deserving. Often overlooked in discussions of welfare is that 90 percent of welfare recipients are old or disabled or are women with small children.

A 22-year-old nurse from Pennsylvania commented, "A lot of social programs such as food stamps and welfare should be put together. It should be streamlined to make it easier for people who need it to get it. Make welfare less accessible to those misusing it."

A 30-year-old Atlanta man, currently unemployed, complained, "I would like to get it. There should be a less degrading method of applying for welfare. The system degrades those who apply by abusing them and their privacy."

4. Instituting work programs is a change mentioned by 12 percent. Gallup surveys in recent decades have found solid majorities of people of all ages in favor of a revival of Depression-era Civilian Conservation Corps (CCC) camps or their urban counterpart.

President Carter has said that the existing federal welfare systems should be replaced by a program that would guarantee jobs for those who can work, a "decent income" for those who cannot, and income tax credits for the working poor.

The Carter administration's plan to revise the welfare system, including tightening the eligibility requirements, is to be submitted to Congress in August.

This question was asked in the survey reported: *"Congress will soon begin to consider many reforms in the way welfare is handled in the United States. What changes, if any, would you like to see made?*

Better investigative/screening methods	52%
Better screening/eliminate cheaters	23
Those who don't need it shouldn't get	16
Tougher requirements	9
No aid for unwed mothers	2
Other	2
Those who can work should be taken off welfare	28
Not enough aid for the deserving	26
General	17
Elderly/children	6
Some people don't get welfare who need it	3
Work programs (such as modern version of CCC)	12
Changes needed (general)	5
Reduced costs (general)	2
Eliminate welfare altogether	2
Fine as is; no changes needed	2
Miscellaneous	25
Don't know, no answer	10

The total adds to more than 100 percent because of multiple responses.

The results reported are based on interviews with 1,548 adults, 18 or older, in more than 300 scientifically selected localities across the nation May 20–23, 1977.

covered employment for a certain number of quarters and then become permanently and totally disabled. The dependents of such workers are also eligible for benefits. The program also covers the spouse (under certain conditions) and the children under 18, or 18 to 21 if in school, of workers in covered employment who die before becoming eligible for retirement benefits. The eligibility pattern for medicare follows closely that for social security.

In addition to these two programs, the social security office administers the supplemental security income program, under which the aged, the blind, and the disabled can receive money for necessary living expenses by proving that they qualify and that they have no other significant or reliable source of income. These programs are all complex, with many details that must be considered in establishing eligibility. However, those who meet the qualifications are entitled to the income provided under law.

The public views the programs administered by the Social Security Administration under OASDI differently from public assistance. These programs are viewed by the public as *social insurance,* and thus they have the trappings of earned rights rather than something given. Most people believe that social security is a program under which workers contribute while working and receive their earned benefits later. It is true that most workers pay into this program while working, but on the average, the persons who are now receiving social security benefits in no way earned the return they are getting. Rather, their benefits are paid for by people who are currently employed and are currently paying social security taxes. These taxes fall proportionately heavier on lower-wage earners than they do on higher-wage earners, but the benefits go routinely to persons who have certain attachments to the work force, regardless of need. Thus, the social security program is regarded by some as benefiting mainly the nonpoor at the expense of the poor. We will discuss the present operation of this program in Part IV of the text and the development of the program in Part III. Our purpose, for now, is to give the reader a general notion of the Social Security Administration as a delivery system within the income maintenance system.

✍§ Other organizations

In addition to having access to the agencies discussed above, persons in every community will have access to hospitals, schools, and manpower agencies, though in rural communities these agencies may be at some distance from one's home. Larger communities will have housing authorities as well as several organizations that aim at community development and social change.

In addition to these agencies, most areas will have available certain agencies of control and rehabilitation, such as mental hospitals, prisons, and programs of probation and parole. As the reader can see from this brief discussion, most communities, or at least most areas, have a number of social welfare organizations that offer interrelated programs. These programs may be overlapping and poorly coordinated, and in every area there will be persons in need of service who do not fit within the developed programs. These are some of the problems with which this book is concerned.

✍§ Summary

In this chapter we have considered the various programs found within social welfare and their classification. In addition, we have very briefly discussed the different agencies that will administer such programs in a community or a geographic area.

We would hope that this chapter has also begun to give the reader some notion of the frustration that may await an individual who would like to use the programs offered by social welfare. It is a problem of some magnitude to correctly identify the agency that offers the facilities or services one wants. One must then understand enough of the agency's program to state one's problem in such a way that it fits the program. All agencies have some ways of determining eligibility for their services, and an applicant to the agency must fit this standard in order to receive service. For example, one must define oneself as sick in order to gain admission to a hospital, where one is then defined as a patient. Beneficiaries of programs are expected to assume roles (client or patient or member) that may fit poorly with their concept of themselves and their goals. These problems will also be a part of our concern as we trace the development of social welfare.

A look ahead

In the next chapter we shall develop and discuss a framework for the analysis of social welfare programs and agencies. If we are to understand social welfare as an institution, we must comprehend something of the issues and concerns that have shaped it. In order to do this we need to have some way of approaching this complex phenomenon.

Study questions

1. Return to our families whose use of social welfare programs was discussed in Chapter 2. Try to identify the types of programs and the organizations used by these families according to the classifications set forth in this chapter. Which agencies are public, and which are private? Which programs of income maintenance are considered assistances, and which are insurances?

2. Can you identify the various social welfare systems illustrated in the families? What programs used by the families would be considered personal social services? Were any social action programs discussed in these examples?

3. Identify the privately supported personal social service agencies in your community. Have a member of your class secure the organization chart of such an agency. What programs do you find in this chart (or charts, if you do this for more than one agency)?

4. Are there probation services in your community? How are they structured, and what are the qualifications of the service delivery staff?

5. Go through the material in this chapter and the glossary at the end of the book. Can you define what is meant by public assistance as opposed to social insurance? What is meant by the terms *means-tested service delivery systems* and *social welfare systems*?

Selected readings

Brieland, D., et al. *Contemporary Social Work*. New York: McGraw-Hill, 1975.

Part 1 of this book offers material that should help students further understand the organizations found in social welfare and the ways in which they are organized. Part 2, which is organized around major problem areas and thus differs from our approach, is helpful in illustrating the activities of social workers as part of the social service system in the various fields of practice.

Glasser, I. "Prisoners of benevolence: Power versus Liberty in the Welfare State." In *Doing Good: The Limits of Benevolence,* by W. Gaylin, I. Glasser, S. Marcus, and D. Rothman. New York: Pantheon Books, 1975. Pp. 99–168.

An excellent discussion of the meaning of the Bill of Rights in the Constitution. Raises many questions about the meaning of liberty.

Halleck, S. L. "Family Therapy and Social Change." *Social Casework,* 57 (1976):483–93.

This article deals with changes in our society that impact the family. It is a very interesting article for discussion.

Frankel, C. "The Impact of Changing Values on the Family." *Social Casework,* 57 (1976):355–65.

A good companion to the Halleck article above.

Kahn, A. J. *Social Policy and Social Services*. New York: Random House, 1973.

Chaps. 1 and 2 in this book are an explication of some of the beginning material on the development of the concept of personal social services as a separate system within the institution of social welfare. This is an important foundation reading.

Morris, R. *Social Policy of the American State*. New York: Harper & Row, 1979.

We are recommending chaps. 1 and 2 in this book. The material in these chapters bridges Chapters 5 and 6 in our text. It might be better for students to read this material after they finish Chapter 6. The material deals with the scope of social policy and establishes a foundation for analyzing social policy, which is what our next chapter is about.

Otis, J. "Liberty, Social Work and Public Policy Development." In *Social Welfare Forum: Proceedings of the National Conference on Social Welfare, 1976.* New York: Columbia University Press, 1976. Pp. 36–46.

An excellent article on the meaning of liberty as "freedom to." It is strongly recommended that this be assigned reading.

Wilensky, H. L., and Lebeaux, C. N. *Industrial Society and Social Welfare*. New York: Free Press, 1965.

To accompany our material, we are recommending that the student read chap. 10, which deals with agency structure and social welfare policy.

An example of social change is found in the passage of the Civil Rights Act of 1964. The photo was taken at signing ceremonies for that Act.

Chapter 6 ❧

❧ Framework for analysis

❧ **Introduction**

In the first five chapters of this book, we have considered several definitions of social welfare found in the literature, discussed the social institutions of our society, and presented some brief descriptive material about the structure of the social welfare institution. The purpose of these chapters was to help readers develop an understanding of the operation of the institution and to establish a certain common knowledge and vocabulary. We recognize that readers have only a beginning comprehension of social welfare.

Any basic comprehension of this complex phenomenon will rest on some understanding of: (1) the societal forces and conditions that interact with one another and with the institution to set certain parameters of change and push toward further development, (2) the processes through which the programs and policies that make up the institution have developed, (3) the processes through which the various programs within the institution continue to change, (4) the structure of the agencies that carry out the policies and programs, and (5) how effectively the various policies and programs meet the objectives set for them.

In this chapter we will develop and discuss a framework that will serve as a guide to examining the societal forces that bear upon the development and change of the social welfare institution. In addition, this framework should also serve as a guide to examining the processes through which social welfare policies and programs have developed over time and to understanding the present structure of social welfare organization. Although we will consider the notion of accountability here, the general effectiveness of policies and programs in meeting objectives will be discussed throughout the text as we examine their historical development.

Earlier we discussed the functions of social welfare as being to maintain present functioning, to provide resources for development toward more productive functioning, and to provide stimulus toward the change of nonproductive functioning. These functions of maintenance, development, and change are critical to the satisfying existence of both individuals and society. Social welfare has a responsibility for the maintenance of stability in certain areas of human life and for movement toward change in these same areas. Both stability and change are necessary in human life and social organizations.

People cannot live and grow, plan or produce, unless they are a part of a social system that offers them a certain level of predictability. There must be a pattern of life on which people can depend—a certain stability and certain limits to change. In addition, however, a society and its institutions must also be involved in growth and change if the society is to remain viable. The significant questions about change, whether that of an individual or of a social institution, are:

1. What forces or conditions push any system, individual, or society toward change?
2. What forces or conditions limit and restrict change?
3. Does the change result in better life experiences for the individual or for the society?
4. What is the rate of change?

⤳ Limiting conditions

There are three significant conditions that limit societal change: (1) the natural resources and properties of the surrounding world, (2) the biological and genetic properties of individuals, and (3) chance events. Human beings constantly struggle to understand more about themselves and the world. One reason for doing this is so that they can with an increasing reliability predict the results of courses of action and thus control themselves and their living conditions. However, even though we have through the centuries achieved increasing comprehension of ourselves and our world, there seem to be certain biological and natural forces that are unchangeable and unalterable and others that are alterable only at great expense.

People cannot live without oxygen or water, and they need a supply of food that will support life. These facts limit where people can live and how much of the resources of a society will have to be devoted to securing the necessary supplies of food and water. Thus, an arid land cannot naturally support a large population. If the population exceeds this optimal amount, there are two directions that a society may take: (1) a large amount of the people's resources may be directed toward finding and distributing water from some available source; or (2) members of society or groups may be allowed to compete for the available water, allowing those who cannot gain an adequate supply to die. If the society decides to pursue the first alternative, it will not be effective unless some additional source of water can actually be found, and if an acceptable source is found, the resources that the society devotes to distributing this necessary commodity may mean that the society will have to limit other uses of resources. Human beings are capable of living in many diverse environments and of surviving in many very difficult societal structures. However, some absolute limits set by nature—our own biological nature and that of the world around us—restrict the extent of societal change.

As we wrote earlier, people struggle to understand themselves and their world in order to control certain natural forces and to be able to predict and plan for certain events that are beyond their control. Thus, the Weather Bureau attempts to predict the weather. Weather is a natural force that we do not yet know how to control, but we can protect ourselves from the worst natural disasters if we know in advance that they may occur and how to deal with them if they do. However, in all human societies, chance events occur—some of these chance events may be great disasters, and some may be great opportunities. These chance events may involve natural forces, unforeseen discoveries, unforeseen consequences of plans gone awry, or international developments. Such unexpected events may very well create a crisis and result in the disruption of previously patterned relationships. They demand new and different ways of coping, and thus they may operate to push societies toward change. But they may also set the limits within which change can take place if they result in the destruction of resources, if they are too great and too sudden a break in old patterns, or if they overwhelm people. If we are to comprehend the development of social welfare in the United States, we will need to understand the interaction of such limiting conditions with the other forces discussed below.

Two other limiting conditions that are of a different quality than those previously mentioned, and that are very frequently overlooked when we try to understand the past from our perspective in the present, are the limits of the knowledge that is available for use and of the technology that develops from such knowledge. For instance, 200 years ago the best doctors recommended bloodletting for many illnesses. Today we know that under certain conditions no action could better assure death and that such treatment was helpful to no one. Yet we cannot accuse these men (and all the doctors of that time were men) of being evil or of desiring either the death of their patients or the oppression of women. They were creatures of their time, and they acted on the basis of the biological knowledge and the social patterns that were then accepted as correct. At that time many children died of diphtheria. Children with diphtheria could not be saved until we understood how diphtheria was transmitted among people and had developed a technique of immunization. There is so much knowledge available to us today, and it is increasing so rapidly, that it is difficult for us, as creatures of our time, to really understand the level of knowledge that existed only two centuries ago. But we may be able to comprehend how a lack of knowledge and technology can affect us if we think of some recent unexpected consequences of the use of powerful drugs without adequate knowledge of their effects on fetuses or of the current struggle for appropriate sources of energy, including nuclear power. Perhaps in the not-too-distant future our children will wonder why we were so ignorant in dealing with malignancies.

Human knowledge is always finite, always subject to further investigation and change. We also need to remember in discussing the limits of knowledge that what knowledge we do have may be distorted or deflected in behalf of values or vested interests. Often such deflection is not conscious, but lies in the way we define our questions, select our raw data, and put facts together to arrive at our empirical generalizations, as well as in the things we don't see or distort in organizing our generalizations into theories (Loewenberg, 1974, pp. 62–63).

In addition to acquiring knowledge, we need to develop a knowledge-based technology which makes the use of knowledge effective. (Even after we understood the cause of diphtheria, we could not prevent it until we had developed a way of immunization.) Our ability to develop an effective technology rests on our ability to predict that certain manipulations will be effective in achieving certain outcomes. We have not yet reached the stage at which we can predict outcomes in human social interaction with any degree of confidence. One of the problems we should always be aware of in our espousals of social change is the possibility of unintended effects of such change. A second difficulty in designing social change is that, inevitably, any social change brings its own problems. We must try to predict the possible problems that the change will bring and to anticipate the meaning of these new problems for society. In espousing change, we need to bear in mind that the unanticipated consequences of the change we espouse may be more problematic than the original difficulty. Examples of unanticipated consequences are the twin problems of rapid population growth and assuring the aged a place in society. These problems followed the reduction of infant deaths and early adult deaths that was brought about by the growth of knowledge and technology in dealing with maternal and child health and with certain types of illnesses.

✑ Conservative forces

As we have pointed out several times, neither individuals nor their society can exist without some stability, some consistency of action and reaction patterns, that allows some assurance that we can accurately predict the behavior of others. There are forces within individuals and within society that act to assure stability and to slow the pace of change. The first and perhaps the most potent of these is past (or historical) solutions.

Historical solutions, customs, and traditions

All human behavior, whether group or individual, tends to follow repetitive patterns. The difference between groups and individuals is that we consider individuals to have serious personality problems if they are unable to give up past patterns of behavior and relationships that are unsuccessful in dealing with new problems or demands. It is not this simple at the level of society. In group patterns of interaction, certain people benefit and are satisfied. The demand for a change in the interactive patterns of society inevitably shifts the patterns of rewards and benefits. Thus, the individuals who perceive that they will be hurt, or even those who just do not believe a better way is possible, will resist change.

Social change rests on the experiences of the past. Old solutions, even those proven time and time again to be ineffective, do not just fade away. They reappear again and again in slightly new garments. In studying social welfare development, we must understand the development of both the needs of the past and the solutions that were developed to meet those needs. It has been said that those who do not remember the past are doomed to repeat it, and certainly students of social welfare movements will often be confronted by inadequate past solutions in the guise of new answers. They need to understand the influence of ineffective proposals and programs of the past as an expected force of resistance so that they do not become bitter. In addition, persons who would take some leadership in policy formulation and program development need to know the past solutions thoroughly so that *they* do not repeat those that have proven ineffective. We are increasingly surprised and troubled by professional people who announce

as "new" a program which anyone with even a rudimentary knowledge of the past would know is not new and is probably doomed to failure. There are so few opportunities for social change, and it takes so much time and effort to dismantle a plan once it is in place, that it is criminal for professionals to "reinvent the wheel" out of ignorance of past efforts.

Much of our sense of identity, our sense that there is a meaning to life and that it will continue to nourish us, is found in myths, customs, and traditions. These offer us a sense of continuity, of being something greater than ourselves. Many of the transitions in our lives are marked by ceremonies that are a part of our culture and our tradition. Too rapid change can destroy a society, partly because it destroys the sense of integration that comes from customs and traditions. However, the great importance of customs and traditions in helping us to feel part of a whole and in offering us a sense of mutual support operates to slow the forces toward change that impinge on our lives.

The patterns of functioning of social institutions

The functioning of social institutions is patterned both in terms of the network of relationships between and among individuals and the institutions and in terms of the relationship of one institution to another. A most significant set of forces that serve to restrict social change is found in the structural and operational processes within social institutions and in the patterns of interactions and relationships among the social institutions of a society. Although there is a push within all human beings toward growth and change, the need for security that was discussed earlier may also result in our being more comfortable with old structure and habit patterns. The same is true of institutions. Institutions have a built-in need to continue their existence. New patterns of action and new notions of structure often appear to pose a threat to the continued existence of institutions. Thus, there is a push to continue doing things in the way one has done them previously even if that way no longer serves people's welfare. People often are afraid of the new because it involves the unknown.

Beliefs, values, and ideologies

Although we have included beliefs, values, and ideologies among the conservative forces, they are different from the forces discussed above in that they can operate either as forces toward change or as conservative forces. For example, the view that a society has of itself can work to prevent change when the society feels that it offers the best possible life to its members. But tremendous forces toward change will accumulate if the view society has of itself is that things aren't well with it, that its members are not reaping the satisfactions that they should.

As to the role of beliefs, we would remind readers that it was in the service of their beliefs that the people who began the colonization of America left their roots in a settled country and made their way into the totally unknown, equipped with little but their own hands and brains. Although there may be readers who feel that humanity would be better off if there had been no such trip to America, we cannot doubt that it represented a tremendous change, both for the individuals involved and for the world. Certainly, while social philosophies are often conservative and argue against change, some of the greatest changes in human life that the world has known have been generated by a commitment to a new social philosophy, to new ideas of the meaning of human life and of how people should relate to one another.

Some of the great changes in social welfare, imperfect as we may consider those changes of the past, came about because of determined individuals who insisted that society face the fact that the operations of the social institutions of the time were contrary to the values that society espoused. Although values and long-held social ideologies may operate to slow change, they can also be used to demand that society live up to its accepted beliefs. This may be a more effective way of bringing about change than to struggle to alter the underlying beliefs. A challenge to live up to our beliefs may bring

change more quickly than an attack on the legitimacy of those beliefs. Although we may be very unhappy about the operation of our society today in relation to social justice and equality, it is important to recognize that despite our miserable failure to live up to our values and our ideologies about the relationships of people to one another and to society, it is our values and our belief that life should be good for the majority of the people in our society that have pushed us toward the tremendous improvements we have achieved. We also need to recognize that the underlying motives of men and women are mixed and often contradictory. We should not blind ourselves to the struggle we all make to maximize our self-interest, but should also realize that without our concern with others and our desire to contribute to the welfare of the vulnerable and the helpless, our lives today would be much less meaningful than they are.

Because actual social conditions are at variance with expressed values does not mean that values are empty words of hypocritical cant. One of many problems in performing in ways consistent with our words and our beliefs is that neither our words nor our beliefs are always consistent. For example, freedom may conflict with security, family values with equality. As we consider the development of social welfare in the United States, we will have examples of such conflict.

Our values and beliefs represent identity and security for all of us, and these are difficult emotional states to sacrifice to change. It may not be easy to see values as a part of the process of the development of social welfare programs. However, they do have a significant impact both on the way in which questions are defined and on the answers sought. What is meant by values? One dictionary defines value as follows: "something intrinsically valuable or desirable" (*Webster,* 1970, p. 1414). Muriel W. Pumphrey, who has made a special study of social work values (which will be discussed in Chapter 7), has written that values

> imply a usual preference for certain means, ends, and conditions of life often being accompanied by strong feeling. While behavior may not always be consistent with values held, possession of val-

ues results in strain toward consistent choice of certain types of behavior when alternatives are offered. The meaning attached to values is of such impelling emotional quality that individuals who hold them often make personal sacrifices and work hard to maintain them, while groups will mobilize around the values they hold to exert approval and disapproval in the form of rewards and penalties (sanctions) (1959, p. 23).

Along with its definition of the concept of values, this statement contains two notions that are important to anyone who would attempt to introduce change into any group's way of life. First, one must know how and to what degree the proposed change is congruent with the value system of the "changee." One must expect that the more incongruent the change is with the value system of the changee, the more resistance one will encounter from the changee. One should further expect that if the change rests upon a value system that is extremely divergent from that of the group, the person who introduces it and works for it will be the focus of penalties and sanctions. This in no way implies that persons who have a commitment to certain changes should not fight for those changes with all their strength and skill. But it does mean that the "movers and shakers" should not see themselves as being treated unfairly when they encounter resistance and when penalties are invoked against them because of their activities.

Values and knowledge

The second notion contained in Pumphrey's statement is that values have an emotional quality. Values are neither rational nor based on knowledge. They are articles of faith—things preferred rather than things known. The measure of a person's commitment to values is the price, effort, or sacrifice that the person will make for those values and the force and extent of the sanctions that the person will impose on anyone who threatens them. People often expect knowledge to be more effective in changing a value-ridden situation than it is because they do not understand that knowledge as a cool, objective tool often fails

against belief and faith. It should be recognized that when we invoke objectivity and rationality in our efforts to change a situation, we are attempting to utilize knowledge. There are times when knowledge can work to produce change. New knowledge can produce change when a society values knowledge and believes that it should be given a central place in life. Our country is a good example of such a society. Our faith in technology and science makes us unusually willing to accept knowledge as a sufficient base for constructing social interaction. New knowledge can also be effective in changing social institutions and society itself at a time of crisis. When people are dying all around us, we may be willing to accept an injection from a doctor although we have no confidence in either the doctor or the injection. In those circumstances, doing anything may seem better than doing nothing. However, if our values forbid injections, we may refuse it even then. For persons who would work in the area of social welfare and human change (whether individual or organizational), it is imperative to understand the difference between knowledge and value as a force for or against any proposal.

Knowledge may be conceived of as the notion that we have of the world and ourselves *as they are, not as we would wish them to be or would prefer them to be.* Knowledge refers to what seems to be derived from "the most rigorous interpretation one is capable of giving to the most objective sense data one is able to obtain" (Gordon, 1965, p. 33). What we know we should be willing to submit to reevaluation and testing by others without a sense of personal violation and with a minimal sense of personal threat. It is true we do not always feel this way about the concepts we put forth as knowledge. But to the extent that we feel personally violated and threatened by an examination of a notion we hold—to that extent we are imbuing the notion with value. Here are two examples of the difference between knowledge and value:

Value: The individual is of primary concern to society.

Knowledge: There is interdependence among individuals.

Value: A democratic form of government is the best form of government for humanity.

Knowledge: A democratic form of government leaves the ultimate power in the hands of the people (Gordon, 1965, p. 33).

We should be able to differentiate between beliefs and values. Beliefs are what we accept as true, and values are the preferences we base on our beliefs. Thus, values imply courses of action based on beliefs. In this chapter we will be discussing both beliefs and values.

There are different levels of values. Values that relate very clearly to beliefs are considered basic. However, there are also operational values that guide daily actions. Such values relate more to norms of social behavior than to beliefs in the purpose of human life.

Self and values

In Chapter 7 we will examine from a somewhat different perspective the value system of a profession, but in this chapter we are discussing social welfare. It is important for students of social welfare and social work to examine their own value stance and to be especially aware of a central value that most students and the author hold in common. That value is a certain commitment to rational thought and action and to knowledge as a base for change. Most university students and university graduates have a strong feeling about the importance of knowledge in human life. This should be recognized as a value stance that is not shared by all persons.

A very difficult question, one that haunted our Founding Fathers (our government was established as a republic rather than a democracy) and that still plagues us, relates to the authority of knowledge and expertise in a democratic society. As we struggle to develop knowledge and understanding, we often assume that our struggle and pain entitles us to be authorities on certain matters and certain methods of action—to be listened to and to be heeded. We assume that because we "know" we

are right, that we are the "good guys." To work effectively in and with social welfare programs, to study them with understanding rather than bitterness, we must comprehend the role of values and knowledge in human life and the ways in which they interact in all our lives and all our decisions. We must recognize that knowledge is truth, not right.

Value system and culture

American culture has a number of value systems, which is natural given the heterogeneity of our population. A value system needs to be viewed as a social phenomenon in the sense that any individual is likely to select the value system that is predominant in his or her primary social group. This is a circular phenomenon. Once a person's value system is in place, which occurs very early in life, that person tends to support it and to keep it in place by associating with those who hold similar beliefs.

However, people do change their basic belief and value systems. This usually occurs in one of four ways: (1) individuals move into new and valued social groups where they desire acceptance and are confronted with somewhat different value systems; (2) individuals come into close association with a person whom they trust or want to please, or whose opinion they regard highly but whose value system is different from their own; (3) individuals are exposed to crises so strange and so different that their value systems no longer serve as reliable guides; or (4) individuals hold a value system which views "the new" as better than "the old."

Although any "in" group may disparge an "out" group's value system in private conversation, it is well to respect the power of values and to understand that other individuals are as committed to their values as we are to ours. We must remember that in a democratic society we can hardly attempt to make changes because we are "right." The change we seek may be brought about through conflict, through persuasion, through demonstration, through holding up to conscious analysis the conflicts in value systems, through trust and caring, through crisis, and in other ways, but it seldom comes about from an announcement that we know the "right" way.

Alan Keith-Lucas, a professor of social work who has been deeply concerned about the role of values in professional life, has written a book about the meaning of giving and taking help. In this book he discusses the complexity of societal values. He takes the position that our social welfare structure is built upon the values in our society, that the heterogeneity of our value systems is the primary problem in constructing a coherent social welfare system. Keith-Lucas argues that three basic belief systems (logical sets of assumptions) underly the value systems in our society. He recognizes that there may be variations on these three systems that some people may hold to be distinct systems in themselves (Keith-Lucas, pp. 138–43).

American value systems

Keith-Lucas calls the first of the three belief systems, which may be the most powerful belief system in our society, the capitalist-puritan system, or CP. He points out that this system is often thought of as common sense, or sometimes even as American, and that it is a part of the heritage of most of us. He summarizes the basic assumptions of the system as follows:

1. Human beings are responsible for their own success or failure.
2. Human nature is basically evil, but it can be overcome by an act of will.
3. The primary purpose of people is to achieve material prosperity, which is done through hard work.
4. The primary purpose of society is to maintain law and order, which make material prosperity possible.
5. Unsuccessful or deviant persons are not deserving of help, though efforts should be made, up to a point, to rehabilitate them or to spur them to greater efforts on their own behalf.
6. The primary incentives to change are to be found in economic or physical rewards and punishments (Keith-Lucas, 1972, pp. 138–43).

The second belief system identified by Keith-Lucas is almost diametrically opposed to the first. He calls it the "humanist-positivist-utopian" system, or HPU. He writes that this is the belief system of most social scientists and many liberals and that it is sometimes held to some degree by people who profess CP views. Although there is some conflict between the HPU system as he sees it and religion, Keith-Lucas states that many religious people adhere to the HPU view. These are the basic HPU assumptions:

1. The primary purpose of society is to fulfill man's material and emotional needs.
2. If man's needs were fulfilled, then he would attain a state that is variously described, according to the vocabulary used by the specific HPU system, as goodness, maturity, adjustment, or productivity, through which most of his and society's problems would be solved.
3. What hampers man from attaining this state is external circumstances that are generally not under his individual control. This difficulty has, in various HPU systems, been ascribed to his lack of education, his economic status, his childhood relationships, or his social environment.
4. These external circumstances can be manipulated by those who possess significant technical and scientific knowledge, using, in general, what is known as "the scientific method."
5. Consequently, man and society are ultimately perfectible (Keith-Lucas, 1972, pp. 138–43).

Keith—Lucas points out that it is often difficult to recognize the HPU view as a unitary theory, as leading advocates of this position have relied on various specifics as the key to utopia. He gives as examples Dewey, who saw education as the key; Marx, who felt that utopia rested on the overthrow of the economic system; and Freud, who in the earlier stages of his life saw the removal of repressions as the answer.

The basic assumptions of the third system, which is labeled the Judeo-Christian value system, might be summarized as follows:

1. Man is a created being, one of whose major problems is that he acts as if he were not such a being and tries to be autonomous.
2. Man is fallible, yet capable of acts of great courage and unselfishness.
3. The differences among men, in terms of being good or bad, are insignificant as compared with the standard demanded by their Creator, and consequently man cannot judge his fellows in such terms.
4. Man's greatest good lies in his relationships with his fellows and with his Creator.
5. Man is capable of choice, in the "active and willing" sense, but he may need help in making his choices.
6. Love is always the ultimate victor over force.

Probably most people are influenced to some extent by all three of these sets of assumptions. They are not presented here from the point of view that one set is bad and another good but in the interest of exploring which set is more likely to preserve the kinds of values that we see as important in and compatible with what we observe are needed changes in the social welfare system.

Keith-Lucas goes on to develop a set of assumptions that he feels has become, since the 1930s, a model of the assumptions about human beings that underlie much of the activity of individuals who are concerned about helping others and about the social welfare system. He argues that these are basically Judeo-Christian values but that they have become acceptable to the humanists and utopians as well:

1. A sense of man's common vulnerability. One of Freud's greatest contributions was to help people whom he no longer regarded as "sick" or "well" but as experiencing greater or lesser difficulty with problems that trouble us all.
2. A habit of looking at problems from the point of view of the helped person rather than from the outside; that is, of treating him or her as a subject rather than as an object.
3. An emphasis on relationship as the principal means of help.

4. At least in the earlier stages a degree of awe in the face of new knowledge of a somewhat mysterious nature (1972, pp. 138–43).

Given the roots of American culture in a Judeo-Christian heritage, when we strip away certain conflicting notions we find that most Americans believe in the essential dignity of the individual, in the fundamental equality of all persons, and in the rights of all members of society to freedom, justice, and a fair opportunity.

We have written very briefly of the heterogeneity of the values of the American people. However, despite that heterogeneity the central character of the social welfare institution in the United States has been and continues to be shaped by certain norms, or operational values, about how needs should be met in our society. Most citizens and most elected officials appear to share the following ideas as to the proper social policy base: they believe that solutions to problems should be found through the "interactions of many decisions made privately, if at all possible"; they share "a vague confidence that individual decision making is preferred above all other forms of action." (Morris, 1979, p. xi.)

Despite preference for allowing the marketplace (private decision making mediated through economic exchange) as much freedom as possible, there is a recognition that individual choices are negated by the need of the corporations that produce our goods and services to show a profit and thus satisfy their stockholders and managers. The incongruity between individual and collective wants leads to a concern with the fact that the market does not serve all individuals equally. Thus we have a second, generally accepted norm that there should be some recognized and legitimated way in which society can act on the behalf of vulnerable individuals or groups. However, there is disagreement over how active government should be in providing such protection and what groups should benefit. The generally accepted definition of vulnerable individuals is narrow, encompassing only those whom we tend to see as being in serious trouble that does not result from their own actions or decisions.

The social welfare institution is also shaped by three other important norms that are generally accepted in our society. One of those norms is a continued belief in the saving virtues of work. For any society to exist, the members of that society must be productive. However, people may work because they see work as necessary to society and thus an obligation that they owe to their fellows, or people may work because they believe that work is moral and that it should, regardless of what it contributes to others, bring about conditions of life that are satisfying to them as individuals. In other words, if we work hard, life owes us something— we have behaved morally, and we are entitled to tangible signs of approval. This leads directly to the belief that people who are poor are poor because they are lazy and do not try hard enough. If we can fulfill our needs just by trying hard enough, then certainly private actions to help those in need are to be preferred to the intervention of society. Only those who are unable to make the necessary efforts in their own behalf should have their needs met in other ways. This is a particularly optimistic view of human life which we also find expressed in a belief in progress through technology. This view leads us to choose short-term policies over long-term commitments to action. Since technology will abolish our current difficulties or point the way to a solution of our problems, it is not necessary to seriously consider our present dilemma. A better way will come along.

One of the most basic norms of our society is a preference for a division of responsibility among the various layers of government. This norm rests on a belief that we explored earlier about the dangers of government. An extension of the norm is found in our desire to keep as many decision-making and operational activities as possible at the local level, where there can be direct input and surveillance by individuals. At the same time, we have a decided preference toward shifting the responsibility for paying for public programs as far from individual consciences as possible. Thus we have

payroll deductions for our federal income taxes (Morris, 1979, pp. 19–23).

It is critically important that students understand the material presented in this discussion and that they work at truly comprehending the meaning of their own basic beliefs and value systems for the positions they take. It is essential to avoid a simplistic notion of what is said here. Individuals as well as heterogeneous societies often build on conflicting and contradictory values. In particular, those of us who would work in the social welfare field are confronted with the gap that exists between our values and reality and with our attachment to conflicting values. Given our plural and conflicting values, we cannot simultaneously maximize all of them. This forces us to make moral choices that are often painful and difficult.

Value systems are a critical variable that will be referred to again and again as the reader is asked to examine the development and the present operation of the social welfare system and the social work profession. Indeed, it is probably correct to say that we define welfare according to our moral ideals as we make judgments about the proper purposes of life (Pusic, 1968, p. 85; Frankel, 1968, p. 164).

The problem is not that we act on beliefs and values, but that these are implicit rather than explicit. Because they are not dealt with directly, they become even more powerful than they would be otherwise. The better we understand the principles that guide public actions, the better we can use them and the more effectively we can change them. Certainly, recognizing the role of implicit values and their conflicts and the limits of our knowledge of consequences should move us away from the notion that social policy develops as the result of a comprehensive and logical design which is introduced by conscious decision after careful calculation of all the consequences. One can find some patterns and continuities in social designs and social behavior, but these come in part from our need to repeat the known and from other emotional needs rather than from conscious design. Even so, much remains unexplained. We only partly understand the dynamics of the behavior of individuals and their social organizations. And we are certainly limited in our knowledge of the interaction between individuals and society (Morris, 1979, p. xiv). We must remember that most members of our society share only a few values and that these values are only changed slowly as the result of the operation of a number of other social factors.

৯§ Mediating forces of change

The forces which push toward change and the forces that resist change are in constant interaction in any society. Standing between these forces and in constant interaction with them are certain mediating forces. One of these is the size of the area occupied by a nation. In a large country, we will find that the land and climate make a difference in the way social institutions operate. In such a country, there will be more diversity and thus more conflicting pressures to be dealt with, than in a smaller country. In the same way, the heterogeneity or homogeneity of a population is an important factor in generating different interests. The shape of social institutions in the United States reflects the influence of both these factors.

Also of critical importance as mediating forces are the stage of a society's cultural, economic, and technological development and its institutional differentiation or complexity. When a society is diverse, when geography presents different population groups with different conditions of nature, when the social institutions are complex, it is more difficult to make national social policy changes because so many and such diverse interests are in interaction that it becomes difficult to influence enough of those interests at the same time and in the same direction. However, more conflicts and discontent are found in a diverse and complex society, and this may be a force toward change because a leader can seize on such conflict and discontent and use it as a push to do things differently.

An important factor to consider in evaluating the meaning of diversity is the positions and interests of societal leaders. Are there leaders who are able to exercise power within more than one social institution? Such leaders may play a critical role in effecting change or in resisting change. They can use the elements of diversity or difference for their own ends. However, the more complex the social institutions and the more complex the society, the more difficult it is for one person or one small group to make an impact. Of recent concern is the notion that, given the small number of our corporate leaders and their common interests, we may have less conflict at the center of our nation than would be most productive. This concern becomes particularly marked when we find that clusters of the leaders among our social institutions are united by common goals. President Eisenhower warned of this when he spoke of the common interests among the industrial and military leaders and of the tendency of this group to act as a unit. Such unified action is a very powerful force and negates the emergence of conflict that can be used to effect change.

The course of the social change that takes place within a nation may not always be within that nation's control. International events may be mediating forces that make unexpected impacts on a society. The resources used in a war are unavailable for social programs.

৯§ Forces toward change

Actually, we have been discussing the forces that move us toward social change all through this chapter. As we have pointed out, many of the forces that can be conservative may also be important for change. There are, however, some factors that generally result in change. For example, the invention of an industrial technology resulted in tremendous changes in the economic institution of society. Those changes are still taking place. In fact, their pace seems to be accelerating as technology offers us new and previously unimagined ways of communicating. The changes in our economic institution have also enabled us to generate the resources to pay for some of their costs.

As we discussed earlier, chance events that present society with a crisis almost inevitably alter the operation of social institutions. New knowledge may result in the recognition of new needs or in different ways of defining problems. The understanding of how certain diseases were transmitted resulted in a struggle to make milk safer for children to drink. With the pasteurization of milk came a significant decrease in infant deaths. However, we could not reduce the deaths that resulted from unpasteurized milk until we had the knowledge that enabled us to define the problem of infant deaths in a way different from the way we had defined it previously.

Throughout history, one of the most effective forces toward change has been the emergence of charismatic leaders who, as individuals, define problems differently and have the courage, the strength, and the power to force a consideration of new ways of regarding problems. Such persons do not always accomplish all they hope to, and they may become the center of criticism and repression, but they often create a crisis for society that must eventually be dealt with by the rest of us.

It is important to remember that a change in the functioning of one social institution almost inevitably brings a change in another, and that no lasting or basic change comes about without change in one or more social institutions. Social welfare, as an interstitial institution, finds its function deeply affected by such changes. In fact, it was in the changes of more traditional institutions that social welfare found its function and developed as a modern institution. And given our concept of the institution, social welfare will always be fluid and in change.

Perhaps one of the most important forces for change, as we discussed earlier, is the notion that society has of itself. A society which views itself as being in trouble will make strenuous efforts to change, whereas the notion of significant change will hardly be politically acceptable in a society which feels that its institutions are functioning effectively.

Another factor affecting the acceptability of change is the cost of such change as it relates to the level of a society's economic output. If the times are good and people feel confident that there are enough resources to go around, they will be willing to finance many changes that would be rejected in times of hardship or shrinking resources. In other words, how we react to a proposed change depends on how we perceive it as affecting our standard of living. Other considerations relate to how the proposed change will affect social and political stability and to our knowledge of how to go about implementing the change. If we are going to be effective in making change, we must have the knowledge and the tools needed to take the necessary action.

✑ Process of change

We have been discussing the various forces in a society that bear on change. The action and interaction of these forces will be illustrated in our discussion of the historical development of the social welfare institution. At this point, we will move on to consider two other important aspects of social welfare development. The first of these is the process through which decisions are made and actions taken to implement change, and the second is the decisions that must be made about structure.

In discussing these notions of process and structure, we would make one caution. Although it would be very desirable for all change in social welfare to come about through a conscious consideration of the factors we shall discuss, change seldom takes place that way. It is important to remember that although the process of change and the decisions about structure may occur as we depict them, the persons involved in the process may have no conscious knowledge of the process and decisions about structure may be made in many ways that depart considerably from careful consideration of the factors introduced in this discussion.

The process of social change begins with the identification of a problem or issue in society. A problem comes to the fore and is then defined in some way. This phase is critically important to the kinds of programs developed. The objectives of any program, the data collected about it, and the focus and shape of any policy or program that is developed, will be determined by how the problem, in turn, is critically affected by the values and knowledge of a society as well as the stance of the other institutions of that society.

As an example, let us consider the issue of poverty in an industrial society. First, how do we define poverty? Are we poor if we earn less than a specified amount, say, $3,000 a year? Or are we poor if our income is less than the income of most of the other members of our society? Or should we assume that money income relates to poverty at all? Do the poor live poorly? Let us assume that we know what poverty is and that we think it should be eliminated. Is poverty to be defined as a problem of the malfunctioning of the economic institution of our society, or is it to be seen as an individual social problem? What causes poverty? Furthermore, do we see poverty as a lack of money or as a lack of employment? If we see poverty as a social problem that results from a lack of money, we will attempt to design an acceptable program to give persons living in poverty more money; and we may have a guaranteed income program. If we see poverty as a lack of employment, the government may try to stimulate the businesses of the country so that they expand and provide greater opportunities of employment. Or the government may decide to become an employer itself and to provide opportunities for people to work on public projects. However, if we define poverty as a problem within the individual person, we will have programs of social services and training that are aimed either at increasing the individual's skill in doing a job or at changing something within the individual's psychological functioning. The issue is poverty. How do we define the problem?

Once a problem has been defined, we will find ourselves involved in setting objectives. If poverty has been defined as a lack of money, our desired outcome will be to see that all people have a certain amount of money at their disposal. If poverty has been defined as a lack of employment, we will set the objective of a job for everyone.

Once we have defined the problem and set the objectives, we will begin a process of data collec-tion, an assessment of the relevant realities and resources. We will call upon the knowledge we have available to help us pull all of these things together and determine a course of action. However, we would point out that the data we collect, the realities and resources that we consider relevant, the sources of knowledge we tap will all be determined by the way in which we define the problem and the objectives we set. Once the problem has been defined and the objectives set, we have narrowed our field of observation in a way that makes it difficult for us to be open to conflicting data or assessments of reality or to different theories. This narrowing of our field of observation is necessary in that we can accomplish nothing if we wait until we collect all possible data before we define a problem. However, we need to be very aware of what happens in the process of defining the problem and setting the objectives. Our values and our beliefs about the nature and purpose of human life will have a critical impact on how we view the problem and the desired outcome.

Once we have assessed the problem as defined and filtered our assessment through society's value screen, we will then go about the business of determining what changes are necessary and what (or who) are to be the targets of change. If we decide that the best thing is to stimulate business, the target of change will be the business community. If we decide that the problem is individual, we will see the individual as the target of change.

Once we have selected our target of change, we will use our knowledge and our assessment to determine the shape and costs of the program and the strategy to bring the change about. The last step in the process is the plan for evaluating whether the policies and program really resulted in effective action.

✑ The organized structure of activities

We wrote earlier that social welfare consists of those "socially sponsored programs and activities that reflect social policy decisions, carried out through public or voluntary means, that meet socially recognized needs" (Gilbert and Specht,

1974, p. 29). We also talked about programs and agencies. This says that social welfare is structured in some way and that structure is determined and supported by social policy decisions. These decisions are essentially choices among principles or guidelines to determine "what benefits are to be offered to whom, how these benefits are to be delivered, and how they are to be financed" (Gilbert and Specht, 1974, p. 29). Four major types of decisions determine the design of the programs that make up the structure of social welfare. These decisions concern: (1) the basis of social allocations, (2) the types of social provisions to be made, (3) the strategies for the delivery of services, and (4) the methods of financing the services.[1] The dimensions of these choices cut across the entire field of social welfare and provide the framework for one way of analyzing social welfare programs and services within the larger framework of social welfare as a social institution. One can also ascertain the why of social welfare programs by searching out the values, theories, and assumptions that are implicit in these choices. These values, theories, and assumptions will be discussed briefly here and will be explicated further in our examination of the development of social welfare programs in Part III of this book.

The basis of social allocations

Social welfare programs always designate who is to benefit from, or be served by, the programs. Such designation results in the differential distribution of program benefits among the population. The literature of social welfare dealing with problems of benefit allocation usually discusses the principles of universalism and selectivity as a way of conceptualizing the answers to the question of who gets welfare benefits. Benefits made available to an entire population as a social right, such as social security and public education, are usually thought

of as meeting the criterion of *universalism* (which is somewhat similar to Wilensky and Lebeaux's concept of institutionalization). Benefits made available to persons on the basis of some judgment as to individual need, such as public assistance or food stamps, are usually thought of as meeting the criterion of *selectivity* (which is somewhat like Wilensky and Lebeaux's concept of residual).

There have been many arguments around these two principles of allocation, and these principles offer a useful starting point from which to examine the notion of allocation. But the principles become very fuzzy when one attempts to apply them beyond the realm of public assistance. Therefore, other authors have proposed other ways of examining the allocation of benefits. It has been suggested that a broader range of alternatives might be: attributed need, compensation, diagnostic differentiation, and means-listed need.

Attributed need. This method of allocating benefits assumes that certain categories or groups of people have certain common needs that are not met by the present functioning of societal institutions. It is assumed that it is important for society to meet these needs, either for the present maintenance of individuals or in the interests of society's development. Thus society's welfare is furthered through the contributions *to* individuals. Given this principle, need is established by certain normative criteria, such as membership in an identified demographic group. An example of benefit allocation based on attributed need is the establishment of the public school system on the assumption that all children need a certain basic education. Recently states and cities have taken the position that adults also need ongoing education. However, the older concept was that the need of all persons for education ended with high school. True, higher education has been supported by society for many years, but the base of need has been different. Higher education has been available to a population group that (1) could pay part of its cost and (2) had demonstrated certain capacities to achieve. Day care that is available to all working mothers would be a further example, as would a program of public medical care, the income tax deduction

---

[1] The discussion of the conceptual development of these decisions and their impact on programs is based upon Gilbert and Specht's *Dimensions of Social Welfare Policy* and upon the seminal study by Eveline Burns, *Social Security and Public Policy*.

allowed for families with children below a certain age, or services to crippled children. This type of allocation rests on the principle of categorical allocations based on normative criteria of need. Social security rests in part on this notion.

Compensation. To be eligible for this method of allocation one must belong to certain categories of people who: *(a)* have made social and economic contributions to society in the past or *(b)* have suffered unmerited disservices at the hands of society. The allocation for the disservice, or unmerited handicap, that the individual suffers may be one of two types: *(a)* as a partial compensation for identified disservice caused by society, such as unemployment, some categories of industrial injuries, and services in the armed forces; or *(b)* as partial compensation for unidentifiable disservices caused by society, as is the case for many benefits related to public health and other services that have been created to aid minorities. Here the assumption is that society has not served such minorities equally over time. Compensation rests on the principle of categorical allocations based on some notion of equity restoration.

Diagnostic differentiation. Benefits based on this method of allocation are available to persons as *individuals* rather than through membership in identified groups. Benefits of this kind are based on professional judgments, founded on professional or technical diagnostic criteria, that special goods and services are needed in certain identifiable individual instances. Examples are found in the various programs offering social work help to disturbed or disturbing individuals, educational programs for retarded children and adults, and so on. Some of these programs involve society's insistence that individuals accept services or suffer a sanction of some sort. In such cases, it has been decided that certain problems of individuals threaten the welfare of other individuals. Examples are found in protective services to children and in correctional programs.

Means-tested need. This method of allocating benefits is based on the ability of individuals to demonstrate that their access to necessary goods and services is limited by their economic circum-

stances. The best examples are programs of relief, public assistance, and supplemental security income. This type of allocation rests on the principle of basing individual allocations on economic criteria of need (Titmus, 1968, pp. 129–32; Gilbert and Specht, 1974, pp. 54–76).

During the remainder of this text, we will consider the ways in which these principles operate in the various welfare programs we discuss. We will discover that, although the principles look nice and orderly on these pages, the differences between them are not always self-evident. Thus, although public medical care is listed under "attributed need," on the assumption that all sick persons need care, one cannot achieve membership in the group that receives such care except through a diagnostic process. This makes a program of public medical care somewhat different from a program of children's allowances, under which any family having children of certain ages will receive payment. Here membership in a group is determined by demographic characteristics. Thus, the principles of benefit allocation may be mixed in various ways.

The nature of social provisions

In addition to answering the question of who, social welfare programs must answer the question of what. Who gets what? From the very beginning of welfare programs in early mercantile society, there have been two forms of social provision. These are generally labeled *benefits in kind* and *benefits in cash.* The names are descriptive of what is involved. Should unemployed persons be given groceries and rent vouchers, or should they be given money with which to purchase these things on the open market?

Well-reasoned arguments have been made for both types of programs, as we shall see when we examine the welfare programs of the past. Those who support benefits in kind usually note that a cash subsidy may be misused. They also point out that a standard item, such as a particular kind of food or a place to live (as in public housing), may be produced and distributed with greater efficiency and at less cost by the government than by the free economy. Thus, it is more economical to give benefits in kind. Persons who oppose benefits in kind are usually concerned with the individual, of the right of all persons in a democratic society to make their own choices. If this right is taken from persons who suffer need, they are being deprived of certain civil rights and are no longer full participants in society. Further, it can be theoretically demonstrated that people given a certain amount of money to spend as they wish will invariably achieve more satisfaction from the goods they buy than they would if they were given those goods in kind.

Essentially, these arguments become very heated on both sides because of the issue of social control. Through benefits in kind, society is able to exercise a greater control over the final utilization of the tax dollar. Some of us respond negatively to any suggestion of social control, as was mentioned earlier. However, we should remember that social controls are necessary to operate a complex and interdependent society. "The question is not whether we will have controls but whether they will be deliberately designed to realize our ideals of human dignity and justice or to serve pernicious ends" (Gilbert and Specht, 1974, p. 84).

Becoming too involved in these arguments may blind us to the fact that social provisions come in a variety of ways and involve a variety of forms. In terms of form and transferability, social provisions may be classified broadly into six categories: opportunities, services, goods, credits, cash, and power.

Opportunities. Opportunities are "sets of sanctions in which incentives and sanctions are employed to achieve desired ends" (Gilbert and Specht, 1974, p. 88). Opportunities may be conceived of as an "extra chance." Examples are the extra effort that some schools make to recruit minority students and the special advantage that may be given to women and minority groups in obtaining public employment. Scholarships offered to outstanding students constitute an extra chance. Opportunities must be used within the context in

which they are offered and thus have no direct transfer value to the individual. One cannot trade a scholarship to attend a school of social work for a job in a public welfare agency, for example.

Services. Services involve the performance of functions in behalf of certain persons. Examples are teaching, counseling, and social work treatment. The market value of these benefits, like that of opportunities, is nontransferable.

Goods. Goods are just what one would expect them to be—concrete commodities such as food and clothing. They are also nontransferable through the regular channels of the marketplace. However, they may be exchanged through certain marginal channels, such as pawnshops and informal barter.

Credits. Credits may be tax credits or vouchers for goods and services. These have a structured exchange value, and they may be transferred for choices among certain types of resources. Food stamps that may be exchanged for the recipient's choice of food within certain limits, and tax credits may be used to make purchases of one's choice. Credits cannot be used outside their defined purpose. One cannot use food stamps to pay taxes.

Power. Power involves the redistribution of influence over the control of goods and services. Although power cannot be spent as cash or credits, it offers a high degree of latitude to command social and economic choices.

Cash. Cash involves the redistribution of money. This type of social provision offers the greatest latitude for consumer choice in that it has universal exchange value. Money offers its possessors a command over resources equal to that of all other persons offering similar payment for goods and services, regardless of the source from which it was received.

Once we have determined who is supposed to get what, we are confronted with the question of how. Social provisions and social services are dependent for their implementation on a complex system of interrelated programs and structures. Once the benefits have been decided upon, some sort of organizational structure must be created to connect the benefits with the recipient. The form of such structures, the ease of access to them, and the pattern of staffing will all have critical impact on the value of any benefits to the recipients.

The structure of the delivery system

The delivery system, as defined in Chapter 5, refers to the organizational arrangements among the distributors and between the distributors and the consumers of social welfare benefits. The distributors of the benefits may be individual professionals, professional groups, and public or private agencies, acting separately or in concert to provide services in private offices, settlement houses, welfare departments, and so forth. Stated in simpler terms, this means that the structure of the organizations to which persons must go in order to secure the benefits of social welfare is considered a delivery system. Persons who have had some real-life experiences in applying for welfare benefits often tell of difficult and frustrating attempts to secure social provisions or social benefits.

The first problem these persons face in obtaining such provisions or benefits is access to resources. It may be extremely difficult to appear at the agency at the specified office hours; rules and regulations about who may apply are sometimes couched in language that is difficult to understand; and, once the applicants enter the system, they may find themselves shuffled from one department to another, or one agency to another, in what appears to be great confusion. This situation does not necessarily arise out of the ignorance or ill will of the planners, or out of the unwillingness of those who operate the programs to be of service. The choices that must be made in operationalizing any system of benefits are varied and difficult to untangle.

In the modern world, most formal organizations are structured in a particular way that has become known as bureaucracy. Bureaucracy is usually seen as the most efficient way to organize any large group of people in order to get any complex job done. We will consider bureaucracy as a form of organization in the next chapter. Here, we would like to concentrate on some other issues. Should we establish services as decentralized units, or

should we employ consumers of services to give the service? Do we place the major decision-making authority in the hands of experts or professionals, or do we allot it to the community? Do we attempt to coordinate our efforts, or do we never work together? Should we locate all agencies centrally, or should we disperse agencies throughout the community, and if so, what agencies, if any, should we place under one roof?

Broadly speaking, it is possible to identify three kinds of questions that relate to the basic decisions regarding service delivery organizations: (1) Where is it best to locate the authority for decision making, and what controls shall be instituted? (2) Who will carry out the tasks involved in offering service, and what will the qualifications of the staff be? (3) What numbers and types of units will be developed to make up the delivery system? One may easily take the position that delivery systems should be easily accessible to the consumers; that they should be integrated, so that the consumers are not shuffled about; that they should be continuous, so that consumers may move easily through the network; and that they should certainly be accountable. However, doing this is not easy. As you open new channels of communication and referral, as you work to reduce fragmentation and provide for integration, as you eliminate duplication of services, you may well increase both the inaccessibility of agencies and the problems of accountability. These problems and the bases for choices will be illustrated as we study the development of the social welfare system in Part III.

The source of funds

The problem of how welfare services are to be financed has plagued planners since the beginning of social welfare. Basically, the choices to be made here are what sources of funds to use (recipient fees, earmarked taxes, general revenues, or voluntary contributions) and how to have those funds flow from the sources to the persons who will distribute it to the recipients in the form of goods, services, cash, or credit. The problems related to these choices will be explored further as we examine the development of social welfare services.

✑§ Accountability

Since welfare programs are socially sponsored activities that reflect social policy decisions, they must answer publicly for their performance toward their designated ends. All social institutions are accountable to society for their functioning, and society is concerned when such institutions do not function adequately. For example, note the many articles about the malfunctioning of the family, and note that parents who fail to function adequately with regard to the care of their children face the sanction of losing the children. Accountability is an increasing problem of social welfare organizations. As social welfare's share of the nation's resources grows, people become more and more interested in the adequacy of its performance. When social welfare programs that reflect social policy decisions are established, there is some notion as to what the outcome of such programs should be. Increasingly, it is expected and demanded that social welfare programs will develop formal accountability measures and a method of accountability.

In the free marketplace, profit is a visible, quantitative measure of whether an organization has met its goal. Also, both the buyer and the seller know how much is being exchanged, when payments will begin, how much interest is being charged, and when each of the participants in the transaction will have discharged his or her obligations to the other. These criteria are unambiguous and usually quantitative, or quantifiable, and they permit a direct evaluation of the exchange.

This type of evaluation is difficult in social welfare transactions for a number of reasons. The consumer may not pay directly for the service rendered or may pay in relation to ability to pay rather than in relation to the value of the service. The criteria by which we measure the outcome of the service are difficult at best. How do we decide whether education has been a good service? Do we measure the ability of the child to learn or the ability of the teacher to teach? Do we measure the resources

for learning controlled by the child or those controlled by the teacher? Is motivation a factor? Or is education the product of all of these? In that case, how do we decide what has failed if education is unsuccessful? Because of the complexity of such measurements, we sometimes define effectiveness in terms of something that is easy to measure, such as the attendance of the child or the absence of the teacher. The move toward accountability in social welfare is important. We should be accountable. But how and for what? There is a growing danger that we may decide that accountability means doing something we can measure.

✑§ A further consideration

For now, we need to propose one further framework for examining social welfare programs. As we discuss the development of the various welfare programs, we should attempt to answer two further sets of questions. One set may be phrased as follows: (1) How was the problem recognized and defined? (2) What were the goals toward which the effort was focused? (3) What were the means of accomplishing the goals? (4) What types of organizations were developed? A second set might well examine organizations from the point of view of the following questions: (1) What kind of recipient? (2) What kind of trouble? (3) What kind of help? (4) What kind of giver?

This has been a long discussion of what is involved in the characteristics of the formal organization of social welfare systems. We will now discuss four other characteristics of the social welfare institution. These can be developed in a much shorter discussion than some of the earlier characteristics.

Directly concerned with individuals

Although it works through an organized structure, social welfare is directly concerned with altering something about the individual or the group or the social institutions in which individuals find themselves in order to benefit the individuals in some way. The overall purpose of social welfare organizations is to provide critical programs, resources, or new social structures not available else-where that enable individuals to live better lives, not only as members of society but as individuals. Thus, the product of social welfare is proper service to each individual.

The centrality of agency-client relationships

Although the centrality of agency-client relation-ships in social welfare would appear to be a self-evident fact, it needs to be stated here because it has profound implications for the character of so-cial welfare. More than anything else, the patterns of staff-consumer relationships mark the social cli-mate, the distinctiveness, and the effectiveness of the services of the social welfare organization. The greater the reliance on such relationships by the organization, the more difficult is the direct control and evaluation of the services it renders. Yet more than any other characteristic of the organization, this factor is low in visibility. Because it is difficult to supervise and direct the use of relationships, social welfare organizations rely on professional staff. There is an assumption that professionals have had, among other things, long training and social-ization to a value system and to self-evaluation and self-direction. These matters will be discussed in more detail in the next two chapters.

Interactive systems network

As has been mentioned in other places, the or-ganizations within the institution of social welfare constitute an interactive systems network. It is not only the function of any individual social welfare organization that needs to be understood, but the quality and patterns of the interaction among social welfare organizations. This variable is also very im-portant in determining the level of the service given by such organizations.

Emergent character

The growing, emergent character of social wel-fare has been alluded to earlier. As we trace the development of the social welfare organizations in Part III, readers will become increasingly aware of this quality.

๛ Summary

We have now reached the end of this chapter.

The chapter examined the forces that affect so-cial change, the process of change, and the charac-teristics of the social welfare delivery systems.

The process of social change, the development of social policies, and the social welfare structure were seen as resting on certain choices determined by value, knowledge, power, and conflict. The ma-terial covered by the chapter is summarized in Fig-ure 6–1.

๛ Study questions

1. What do you think is the nature of human beings? Are we basically comfort seekers, or do we welcome crisis? How would your answer to this question affect the social welfare programs that you might like to see developed?

2. What do you think is the primary purpose of human existence? How does this idea affect your relation-ships with others?

3. Can you think of some recent advances that have affected how we live? Were the examples you thought of advances in knowledge or advances in technology? What is the difference between these two concepts?

4. Go through some recent issues of your local newspa-pers. Count the number of articles dealing with wel-fare. Now select three major articles and write an analysis of the beliefs about people and the values that are illustrated by the articles.

5. Give some examples from your experience of unfore-seen consequences of new ways for doing things.

6. Think of a person who, as an individual, made an impact on our way of life. What factors enabled this person to have such an impact?

7. Make an outline of the material that deals with *social provisions* in this chapter. Select a social welfare pro-gram found in an agency in your community. Apply the outline to the program you selected. Do you find this a helpful way to analyze and understand social welfare programs?

Conditions that limit range of possibilities	Conservative forces	Mediating forces	Forces toward change	Process	Structure
Natural resources and properties of environments	Customs and traditions	Stage of cultural, economic, and technological development	Beliefs, values, and ideologies	Identification and definition of issues or problems	Basis of social allocations
Biological and genetic properties of individuals	Patterns of functioning of social institutions	Geographic size of nation	View society has of itself	Definition of objectives	Attributed need
Chance events	Historical solutions	Institutional differentiation or complexity of society	Significant changes in functioning of one or more social institutions	Collection of data	Compensation for identified and unidentified disservices
Limits of knowledge	Beliefs, values, and ideologies	Positions of societal leaders	Chance events	Assessment of relevant realities, objectives, preferences, available theoretical knowledge, and resources	Diagnostic differentiation
Limits of technical ability to manipulate and control environmental and individual factors	Social philosophies	Interaction between intra- and extrasocietal forces	New and developing knowledge	Identification of necessary changes and their targets	Means test
			New and developing technology: technical ability to manipulate and control environmental and individual factors	Consideration of intended and possible unintended effects and costs of proposed changes	Nature of social provision
			Recognition of new needs	Consideration of strategy and adoption of program and plan	Opportunities
			Emergence of charismatic leaders	Plan of evaluation	Services
			Conflicts of interest groups		Goods
					Credit
					Power
					Money
					Structure of delivery system
					Where located in social structure
					Who has authority for decisions
					Staffing requirements
					Basic units
					Access provisions, definition of user, guarantee of right
					Source of funds
					Fees
					Voluntary contributions
					Taxes
					Local–state
					National
					Specific
					General
					Provisions for accountability

Source: The above framework rests in part on David C. Gil, *Unraveling Social Policy* (Cambridge, Mass.: Schenkman, 1976). Gil's framework was developed to guide the construction of social policy. This framework is developed for the purposes of guiding the analysis of critical variables in social welfare policies and programs already in existence and of helping beginning students to acquire an understanding of how a social institution develops.

✑ Selected readings

Feagin, J. R. *Subordinating the Poor.* Englewood Cliffs, N. J.: Prentice-Hall, 1975.

The chapter on the historical background of social welfare is a bit premature. We shall treat history in much greater detail in Part III of our text. However, it may be that this book will provide a good overview, provided that it is treated as a survey of what is to come. Chaps. 3 and 4 should supply the student with an excellent statement on welfare as a means of keeping the poor under control.

Gil, D. C. *Unraveling Social Policy.* Rev. ed. Cambridge, Mass.: Schenkman, 1976.

The material being recommended is that found in part 1, chaps. 1–3 (pages 1–56). This material is written for students with a good background in social welfare. It is presented here because it has been used as the basis for some of our thinking.

Gilbert, N., and Specht, H. *Dimensions of Social Policy.* Englewood Cliffs, N.J.: Prentice-Hall, 1974.

Chaps. 1–7 (pages 2–176) present some of the material used in developing Chapter 6 in our text. The material is written for somewhat more knowledgeable students than those for whom we are writing, but aspects of this material may prove helpful. The book deals with some of the notions we have discussed earlier as well as the subjects taken up in this chapter.

Gilbert, N., and Specht, H. *The Emergence of Social Welfare and Social Work.* Itasca, Ill.: F. E. Peacock, 1976.

The three articles in section 3 of this book cover certain aspects of the material developed in the latter part of our chapter.

Keith-Lucas, A. *The Giving and Taking of Help.* Chapel Hill: University of North Carolina Press, 1972.

Although this book is thought of primarily as a text on methods of helping, Keith-Lucas develops one of the best statements of our society's value system to be found in the literature. Chaps. 8–10 (pages 109–85) should be very interesting to the student.

৽ Part II

৽ Introduction to social work: A profession within the personal social services ৽

A VISTA volunteer at work. Sharon Gromala, from Chicago, Illinois, has a degree in social work, and is a member of the National Association of Social Workers.

Chapter 7

Social workers as deliverers of social services

Introduction

In the first six chapters of this text, we have discussed something of the definition and the structures of social welfare as an institution in our society. However, the structures of social welfare need people to carry out the mission of the institution. In Chapter 5 we identified nine social service systems within the social welfare institution and we stated that these social service systems were structured so as to be composed of various delivery systems (organizations). These delivery systems are linked to the users of their services through people who work within them to give the required services. A social welfare system is usually served by identifiable groups of people who have become central to the service of that particular system. For example, teachers are central to educational delivery systems, doctors and nurses to medical delivery systems, rehabilitation counselors to rehabilitation systems. Over the years such special groups have developed into professions.

The personal social services

In the development of both social services and social work, the rather diverse services offered by social workers came to be identified as social work and the professionals were usually not differentiated from the services they offered. In public welfare, public assistance and social services both were offered to clients through one person who, it was held, should be a social worker. In reality, only a minuscule number of persons working in the social welfare program had received social work education. But for half a century financial assistance was seen as a part of social work and the general public saw social workers principally as relief givers and/or child placers. In the 1960s the notion that people who needed financial aid also needed other assistance— that people who needed financial help also had character disorders—was challenged and pub-

lic assistance became a part of the income maintenance system. Social workers were no longer to
be involved in the actual delivery of such services
to clients, though they remained heavily involved
in policy and administrative decisions.

If social workers no longer gave money, what
did they do? Since the early 1900s, social work
professionals have struggled with this problem. Social work and social services both were defined
as what social workers did. It was like saying that
the health service system consisted of what doctors
do. It was obvious that the social services needed
to be differentiated from the social work profession.
This need was felt more strongly in 1967, when
the Department of Health, Education, and Welfare,
accepting the notion that poor people did not automatically suffer from personality deficits, separated
public assistance from the public social services.
The eligibility technicians who staffed public assistance were to be clerical people, and social workers
were to staff the social services.

Troubled by the possibility that it had created
a whole new public service (although, in reality,
it had only separated programs already in existence), HEW established a Task Force on the Organization of the Social Services. Charles I. Schottland
was in charge of staff work, and Alvin Schorr, the
deputy assistant secretary of HEW, was the chairperson. The committee was charged with developing information and a point of view about the planning and organization of social services. However,
the task force was unable to define social services
in a way that allowed the charge to be implemented
effectively. In reading the committee report, one
can almost sense the frustration of the members
who finally decided to describe the services they
could not define satisfactorily. They believed that
these services should be classified as follows: ac-
cessibility (information, referral, complaint, and
perhaps some legal services), treatment (casework
services to families, corrections, rehabilitation,
health care, and socialization), developmental services (such as day care and group activities), and
equalization (services that should be developed to
compensate for handicaps and discrimination). An
appraisal of the activities of the task force was writ-

ten by Winifred Bell in the July 1970 issue of *Social
Work,* the publication of the national professional
organization of social workers.

Bell's rather general statement was followed by
letters from other social workers that were published in the October 1970 and January 1971 issues. In the July 1970 issue, Alvin Schorr, the editor,
commented on the Bell article and offered the following as possible definitions:

> Professional definition
> Social services are services rendered or
> controlled by social workers.
> The imperialistic definition
> Social services are services we should like
> to have rendered or controlled by social
> workers.
> Paternalistic definition
> Social services are services rendered to
> the poor or disadvantaged in order to
> compensate for their disadvantage or to
> rehabilitate them.
> Definition by exclusion
> Social services are services that are left
> over when income maintenance and serv-
> ices are separated.
> The European definition
> Social services are the major forms of
> provision for the welfare of citizens under-
> taken by the state or community. (Bell,
> "Comments," 1970, pp. 102–3)

These definitions appeared in the October 1970
issue of *Social Work* as an answer to Schorr:

> Generally, in Western culture, social services are
> those activities calculated to prevent, ameliorate,
> or solve the problems of a socioeconomic-psycho-
> logical order for individuals, groups, and commu-
> nities in our society (Kidneigh, "Letters," 1970,
> p. 119)
> Social services are acts authorized by public law
> or private charter, performed by designated per-
> sons capable of working effectively with individu-
> als and/or groups toward solutions of social and/
> or personal problems so that every willing con-
> sumer, no matter who or what he is, may fare
> well himself and contribute to the welfare of soci-
> ety. These acts coordinate and complement ac-

ceptance, utility, and availability of services provided by health, education, income maintenance, and so forth; create new awareness for enhancement, enrichment, and enablement in other consumer-chosen community-accepted areas; and correlate individual and societal ways, means, and ends. (Owen, "Letters," 1970, p. 119)

Social services are the services rendered or supervised by social workers in response to a need expressed by an individual or a family and related to their social adjustment. The provision of social services is inherent in the community responsibility for the enhancement of social functioning and the reduction of dependency. (Mostwin, "Letters," 1970, 119)

Schorr found the Mostwin definition unacceptable in that it classified services according to who did them. Thus, counseling would be considered social work if social workers did it but not if others did it. Schorr felt that the other two definitions were too broad and would include such services as trash collection. He invited more definitions, and in the January 1971 issue of *Social Work* the following attempts were published without comment.

Social services are those activities that help an individual to solve his problems related to his relationship with another significant person or persons. (Wilcox, "Letters," 1971, p. 128)

Social services refers to activities performed with the goal of assisting individuals and groups in their efforts to readjust to society in order to live "normal" lives. (Sowers, "Letters," 1970, 128)

Social services reflect recognition and responses by social workers, along with other professionals in the helping professions, toward meeting specified human needs under the auspices of both private and publicly funded agencies and programs, with a focus of enabling the consumer of these services to become more functional, effective, and/or adaptive—whatever might be appropriate in his individual situation. (Davis, Jr., "Letters," 1970, p. 128)

As we discussed in Chapter 5, Kahn and Morris have given thought to the question of defining a separate delivery system that could be called not just social services but personal (Kahn uses the term *general*) social services. For example, hospitals are a part of the health system. However, hospitals accredited by the American Hospital Association must have social service departments within which social workers, as separate professionals, offer personal social services related to health problems.

As social welfare systems other than public assistance systems developed, those systems, too, began to see the need to use social workers in the delivery of their services. Very early in our history, hospitals began to hire social workers to help patients to better understand and utilize medical services and, perhaps even more important, to serve as consultants to doctors and other medical personnel about how to meet the needs of people and to humanize medical services. After World War I, social workers became important as members of the psychiatric team and schools began to use social workers as a link between teachers and pupils. From the very beginning of the correctional system, social workers were an important part of that system. In fact, the early meetings of social workers as professionals were called the Conference of Charities and Corrections, establishing the early roots of the profession in income maintenance and corrections as well as in the personal social services. At that time, income maintenance and social services were considered one system called charities. It may be that there are people who still see corrections as a part of personal social services. We have conceptualized these as separate social welfare systems because they differ in focus and purpose from the rest of the personal social services and also because they employ large numbers of professionals other than social workers in decision-making positions. In the personal social service delivery systems, the major, central profession, and the profession that makes the practice decisions central to services, is social work.

Social work carries the broadest assignment of any profession across all the programs of social welfare. In some instances—for example, the freestanding personal social services—they carry the central role. In others, as we have seen, they play a supporting role to other professions in individualizing and humanizing the delivery structures as well as serving the consumers. Because of the historic development of social work as an agent of the social welfare institution and because of its interaction with that institution over time, the understanding of that interaction and of the development of the social work profession seems necessary to understanding social welfare and its development. It is assumed that most of the students reading this material are interested in social work as a career choice. For all of these reasons we will concentrate in this book on the development of income maintenance, social change, and personal social services, and on the development of social work as a profession.

This text does not discuss in any detail the how of the methods that social workers use. Instead, it seeks to examine the interaction of social welfare and social work as a major profession providing the critical knowledge, skills, and leadership that are needed to carry out the purposes and functions of the social services. Social welfare and social work are both emergent, and both have developed together out of some common societal and individual problems. Social work came out of social welfare's need for agents to carry out its programs. To understand either social welfare or social work, one needs to understand something of the development of both.

✑§ Social work: some examples

To get some notion of the functions of social work, let us return to our examples of the families in Chapter 2. The Poor family has had contact with three social workers. When Mrs. Poor applied for AFDC, she confided to her eligibility technician, who was responsible for establishing her right to receive assistance, how troubled she was at her husband's desertion and her concern at having to raise her sons alone. The eligibility technician suggested that she might like to talk to a social worker about her problems. Mrs. Poor has been meeting regularly with the social worker in the public welfare department of social services. Within the climate of concern, understanding, and support that

the worker offers, Mrs. Poor is able to talk with freedom and relief about her worries. The worker helps her understand something of herself and supplies helpful information about child development, parental functioning, budgeting, and other aspects of living. The worker recognizes with Mrs. Poor that it is natural and to be expected for her to feel overwhelmed by her responsibilities and the demands of her life.

In the course of working with Mrs. Poor, the social worker suggested that one way in which she might supply her sons with some different social experiences would be to ask an agency called Big Brothers for help. Big Brothers is a private agency that is supported principally by the United Fund for the purpose of recruiting and training men from the community to act as "big brothers" to boys who are without the championship and the role model of a father. (There is also a group called Big Sisters, which does the same for girls without mothers.) The director of Big Brothers is a social worker. He talked with Mrs. Poor, whose sons were eligible for service because of the absence of their father, and he selected a volunteer who was interested in being helpful to the two brothers in their need for growth experiences that their mother could not supply. The boys have enjoyed their new friend, and Mrs. Poor has found it helpful, too, to have an interested person who can give her sons experiences that she would find difficult to manage alone, such as weekend canoe trips. The "big brother" picks up the boys at their home, so Mrs. Poor does not have transportation problems and she has found that this provides some time to herself that she, as a lone parent of two youngsters, really needs. Mrs. Poor's sons receive free lunches at school because of their income level. When a new principal initiated a special lunch line for those receiving such aid, Mrs. Poor talked to the school social worker, who was able to consult with the principal about the meaning this practice had to the students (both those who received aid and those who didn't) and their parents. The principal changed the practice, although he saw it as the most efficient way to administer the free lunch program.

Mr. Olds has also found social workers helpful. During his wife's illness and following her death, he came to know the medical social worker, Miss Willoby, at the hospital. She helped him with the anger, the pain, and the sorrow of his wife's loss, and she visited him regularly when he was later admitted to the hospital. As Mr. Olds's illness dragged on and his savings were exhausted, the medical social worker offered to help him apply to and qualify for support from SSI and medicaid. Now when Mr. Olds comes to the hospital for a checkup, he often asks to see Miss Willoby and he feels better for a few minutes' exchange with another human being who cares about him and seems to understand his feeling of helplessness and hopelessness.

The Comfortable Family and Mrs. Affluent also have contact with social workers. The community center used extensively by the family is a social agency whose primary function is to offer members of the community opportunities for self-actualization and development. It is supported partly by the United Fund and partly by the primary religious group in the community. The senior citizens programs that Mrs. Affluent attends are carried on with the help of a social worker who possesses special skills in working with groups and has special interest in the older adult. One group that Mrs. Affluent has joined is interested in organizing senior citizens for political action to support programs and laws that give the older person certain special considerations, such as increased social security and free rides on the public transportation system in Center City. This group often consults with a social worker in the mayor's office as to political-change strategies.

The extension course that Mrs. Comfortable attends was planned by a social worker in cooperation with the university. It is a course on parenting skills that is taught by Dr. Jan Weller, a social worker who is a faculty member from the university's school of social work. In her volunteer work at the hospital, Mrs. Comfortable meets another social worker who supervises the volunteer activity. Still other social workers participate along with medical and hospital personnel in training and ad-

vising volunteers in their work with patients. When Mrs. Comfortable went to Family Service for help with her struggles to cope in a satisfying way with her family's move, she was using the services of a social agency supported by client fees, memberships, and the United Fund. Here Mrs. Comfortable became the client of a social worker who possessed special competence in working with family problems.

✎§ What is social work?

The problem of developing a definition that deals with all of these diverse activities that are considered social work has plagued the profession for 100 years. Wilensky and Lebeaux have defined social work as "an occupation or profession, a group of people with more or less specified training and skills, who occupy key positions, along with other groups, in the provision of welfare services" (1965, p. 17 n). Certainly, it is possible to define social work as the profession that delivers the personal social services devised by social welfare programs and guided by social policy to the consumer of such services. However, neither of these definitions really tells us much about who social workers are or about what they do that differentiates them from people who are not social workers. Social workers do so many things in so many different places. Wherever one looks one finds them: in high-level positions in the department of Health, Education, and Welfare helping to plan for services of all kinds, from aging to infant, maternal, and child health; in the mayor's office; as the commissioner of corrections and/or social welfare and perhaps as the commissioner of equal opportunity; in the state as directors of local agencies offering help to a terminally ill patient around issues of life and death, working with a family that has troubles in living together as a family, being a probation officer for an angry youngster, working in a mental health clinic, and helping to plan camp experiences for girls and boys. Where are the limits of what social workers do? How do we know what social work is? It is interesting to look at definitions that have been developed over time. We have listed some of them here for your consideration. The first definitions refer to social casework, rather than social work, because at the time they were formulated the other methods of social work had not yet developed.

Definitions of social work

. . . the art of doing different things for and with different people by cooperating with them to achieve at one and the same time their own and society's betterment. (Richmond, 1915, p. 43)

. . . the art of bringing about better adjustments in the social relationships of individual men, or women, or children. (Richmond, 1917, p. 389)

. . . the art of bringing an individual who is in a condition of social disorder into the best possible relation with all parts of his environment. (Jarrett, 1919, p. 507)

. . . those processes which develop personality through adjustments consciously effected, individual by individual, between men and their social environment. (Richmond, 1922, p. 98)

. . . the art of changing human attitudes. (Lee, 1923, p. 119).

. . . a method of helping people out of trouble. (de Schweinitz, 1924, p. ix)

. . . individual therapy through a treatment relationship. (Robinson, 1930, p. 187)

. . . a particular way of assisting people to meet their personal and social needs. (Lowry, 1937, p. 264)

. . . helping the client to use whatever capacity he has to deal actively and responsibly with some specific problem which he is encountering in reality. (Marcus, 1938, p. 103)

. . . those processes involved in giving service, financial assistance or personal counsel to individuals by representatives of social agencies according to policies established and with consideration of individual need. (de Schweinitz, 1939, p. 39)

. . . a process through which we use the understanding of the individual in society in the rendering of certain social services supported by the community and applied for by members of it. (Gartland, 1940, p. 126)

. . . a therapeutic discipline for encouraging ego-development. (Wilsnack, 1946, p. 303)

. . . one method by which certain special services are made available in areas of unmet need. (Towle, 1947, p. 447)

. . . an art in which knowledge of the science of human relationships and skill in relationship are used to mobilize capacities in the individual and resources in the community appropriate for better adjustment between the client and all or any part of his environment. (Bowers, 1949, p. 317)

Social casework is a process used by certain human welfare agencies to help individuals to cope more effectively with their problems in social functioning. (Perlman, 1957, p. 4).

Social work seeks to enhance the social functioning of individuals, singly and in groups, by activities focused upon their social relationships which constitute the interaction between man and his environment. These activities can be grouped into three functions: restoration of impaired capacity, provision of individual and social resources, and prevention of dysfunction. (Boehm, 1958, p. 18)

Casework has always been a psychosocial treatment method. It recognizes both internal psychological and external social causes of dysfunctioning and endeavors to enable the individual to meet his needs more fully and to function more adequately in his social relationships. (Hollis, 1964, p. 1)

By provision of certain services and material resources and by psychologically therapeutic supports and counsel, casework modifies either the problem experienced in the individual case or the person's modes of coping with it or both. The aim of casework is to restore or reinforce or refashion the social functioning of individuals and their families who are having trouble with person-to-person or person-to-circumstance encounters. (Perlman, 1965, p. 607).

Social work is: a helping activity directed to problems which affect economic and social well-being, a non-profit activity, and a liaison activity concerned with maximizing resources for well-being and facilitating their use. (United Nations Commission, 1959, p. 13)

William Gordon concluded that

the central target of technical social work practice is matching something in person and situation—that is, intervening by whatever methods and means necessary to help people be in situations where their capabilities are insufficiently matched with the demands of the situation to "make a go of it." (1969, p. 6)

Of all the above definitions, the one most quoted is probably Boehm's. Another definition of interest is a working definition published by the Commission on Practice of the National Association of Social Workers (1958, pp. 5–6) which defined social work practice as a "constellation of value, purpose, sanction, knowledge, and method." The working definition identified three purposes of social work practice:

1. To assist individuals and groups to identify and resolve or minimize problems arising out of disequilibrium between themselves and the environment.
2. To identify potential areas of disequilibrium between individuals or groups and the environment in order to prevent the occurrence of disequilibrium.
3. In addition to these curative and preventive aims, to seek out, identify, and strengthen the maximum potential in individuals, groups, and communities. (p. 6)

In 1970 the National Association of Social Workers (the professional social work organization) adopted a formal definition of social work. This definition may be stated as follows:

Social work is the professional activity of helping individuals, groups, or communities to enhance

or restore their capacity for social functioning and to create societal conditions favorable to their goals.

Social work practice consists of the professional application of social work values, principles, and techniques to one or more of the following ends: helping people obtain tangible services; providing counseling and psychotherapy for individuals, families, and groups; helping communities or groups provide or improve social and health services and participating in relevant legislative processes.

The practice of social work requires knowledge of human development and behavior; of social, economic, and cultural institutions; and of the interaction of all these factors (1973, pp. 4–5).

More recently the West Virginia Undergraduate Social Work Curriculum Development Project conceptualized social work as

concerned and involved with the interactions between people and the institutions of society that affect the ability of people to accomplish life tasks, realize aspirations and values, and alleviate distress. These interactions between people and social institutions occur within the context of the larger societal good. Therefore, three major purposes of social work may be identified:

1. To enhance the problem-solving, coping, and developmental capacities of people.
2. To promote the effective and human operation of the systems that provide people with resources and services.
3. To link people with systems that provide them with resources, services, and opportunities. (Baer and Federico, 1978, p. 68)

Earlier we quoted Schwartz's viewpoint that a social worker's job assignment is to "mediate the process through which individuals and society reach out for each other through a mutual need for self-fulfillment" (1961, pp. 154–55). We particularly like Schwartz's statement because of its focus on the needs of both the individual and society. However, it is really a statement of purpose rather than a complete definition. We would like to propose the following definition: Social work is a process that operates to assist individuals (as individuals or as groups and as members of groups) in increasing their control over their own lives through making satisfying choices, coping satisfactorily with the results of life choices and life events, and working to provide the societal changes that will make available to individuals and groups the social resources and support necessary for the selection of meaningful alternatives and for the making of meaningful choices.

We once asked a class of students the following question: What do you see as the major purpose of social work? Listed below are the statements of the 16 students in the class:

1. To help individuals make decisions that will help them lead happier and more productive lives.
2. To help people who are willing to help themselves but do need extra assistance. To understand the existence of many human differences in culture, family background, and education.
3. To provide the client with another human contact that is exclusively his.
4. To improve the clients' ability to live in their environment and to improve the environment.
5. To mediate between an individual and the client system and society in order to effect the best possible development of the potentialities of both.
6. To help individuals or groups to help themselves to understand their problems and to work out those problems.
7. To identify the concerns of individuals, groups, and families and take positive steps to resolve them in the best interest of the client.
8. To set up change processes with socially dysfunctioning individuals, groups, and communities.
9. To assist people in changing their environment or their circumstances so that they can function to their highest potential and satisfaction.
10. To help people change what they want to change about themselves or their situations.
11. To assist the client in reaching his or her goals and potential.
12. To facilitate the giving of help to specified populations that generally meet certain criteria.
13. To help facilitate change or to help overcome crises in an individual's life with mutually acceptable goals.
14. To facilitate relationships among individuals, families, and individuals within communities and other large systems which recognize and meet human needs to the fullest possible extent.
15. To help clients state their feelings by regarding how they view a particular situation.
16. To mediate between needs of individuals and needs of society. To help people to be aware of choices in their lives and to find their own awareness.

It is interesting to study these definitions. In many ways they reflect the changing emphases and the growth of the social work profession. First, we will examine the verbs used in the definitions: *to help, to improve, to change, to endeavor to change, to restore, to bring about, to assist, to mediate, to facilitate, to enable.* One of the most used verbs is *to help.* We suspect that it is one of the most used words in the social work literature and in daily discussions by social workers. It may be the word that attracts people to the profession in the first place. "It carries idealistic overtones: to be of service to humanity. It carries altruistic overtones: to transcend one's own needs in the cause of others. It carries self-gratifying overtones: to become stronger by aiding others and/or to exercise power" (Tropp, 1974, p. 23).

Help has many meanings in our language. It can mean to succor or to save, to relieve someone in need, sickness, pain, or distress. It can also mean to cooperate effectively with a person or to assist. Let us look next at the object of the verb in the definitions. The earlier definitions, by and large, focus on helping the individual change something within that individual's own skin. It would appear that in the earlier definitions the work *help* essentially meant to relieve someone in need, sickness, or distress. This appears to be a logical interpretation of the early uses of the word, since the roots of the profession are deeply embedded in caring about those who are considered less able than ourselves and in attempting to better their lives. There are many ways to regard these efforts of the early (but not yet professionalized) social workers.

If we look at later definitions, we will see less use of *help* as the verb. This seems to stem from conflicts about the motives of helpers. Social work has come to reject the notion of help as the giving of aid or succor to persons who are unable to help themselves, and thus less capable of self-help than we are. We have come to reject much of the idealistic and altruistic overtones of the term *help* and have begun to ask in suspicious tones what lies behind the stated good impulses of people who hold themselves out as wanting to help others. We have become very aware that "some paradox in our nature leads us, once we have made our fellow men the objects of our enlightened interest, to go on to make them the objects of our pity, then of our wisdom, ultimately of our coercion" (Rothman, 1978, pp. 67–96). We have become increasingly aware that the benevolence of our motives combined with the recognition of the distress and despair of others does not automatically guarantee that our efforts will really benefit others. We have become more aware of the power problems that hide behind the word *help* in all the "helping professions." It has come to the point at which expressing a concern for the well-being of others, or suggesting a better way of coping with a problem, leaves us open to the charge of having dark and evil hidden motives.

We would remind the readers that "the power drive is given freest rein when it can appear under the cloak of objective and moral rectitude. People are the most cruel when they can use cruelty to enforce the 'good' " (Guggenbuhl-Craig, 1976, p. 10). We need to recognize that probably no one acts out of only one motive. Even the noblest things we do are based on motives that we might label both pure and impure. People who sacrifice to aid others are almost always hoping to be respected and honored for their generosity or, at the least, to convince themselves that they are good. These needs of givers do not make their help any less

valuable to receivers. There will always be need for compassion in human society, and the compassionate impulse should be respected, not rejected. The most meaningful elements that link us to one another are our notions of our responsibility and obligation to care. Caring is necessary for the development of humanity in human beings. If we are not cared for by others, we cannot care for ourselves. "We do not choose to live in social relations; we are obliged to. . . . the unity of man is no romantic myth. It is a biological fact that we ignore with peril" (Gaylin, 1978, pp. 34–35). Therefore, we need to recognize that in social work one of our motives for helping stems from our identification as human beings with the pain of others and from our impulse to relieve that pain because it hurts us as fellow human beings. This ability to identify with others is at the center of all we value in being human. We will discuss these notions further when we speak of the value systems of social work.

Perhaps because of our concern with the motives of helpers and because we began to understand more about human problems, beginning with Boehm in 1958 we begin to find a different use of the verb and the object in most attempts to define social work. Boehm speaks of *enhancing* the social functioning and says that this includes the "providing of social resources." Perhaps Richmond foresaw this change when in 1922 she spoke of helping to develop the individual through adjustments in the social environment, but it is in the definitions of 1958 and the following years that we find a greater use of verbs—for example, *enabling, enhancing,* and *facilitating*—that try to convey the notion that social work involves worker and client in some sort of interaction toward some change.

✺§ The focus of practice

In the definitions of social work that were formulated after 1958, there is a rejection of the notion of the worker as the subject and the client as the object and a movement toward the notion of two people working together. In addition, the "working together" begins to be seen as a process, meaning a series of actions, functions, or changes, rather than as static "doing." Moreover, we find in the definitions a growing emphasis on the interaction of individuals and their environments. The focus of social work intervention is increasingly seen as in some way mediating between people and their social environments in order to correct some disequilibrium. The notion of being concerned with people's social functioning or with the disequilibrium between persons and their environments moves social workers away from the idea of the illness or inadequacy of the person and away from the idea that the central mission of social work is to correct individual psychological pathology.

The later definitions change the focus of the problems with which social workers deal. Gitterman and Germain say:

> Social workers focus on problems in living which fall into three areas: (1) problems and needs associated with tasks involved in life transitions; (2) problems and needs associated with tasks in using and influencing elements of the environment; and (3) problems and needs associated with interpersonal obstacles which impede the work of a family or a group as it deals with transitional and/or environmental tasks. (1976, pp. 602–3)

Compton and Galaway write:

> . . . the focus of social work activity is directed toward the interaction of people and their environments in accordance with Schwartz's view of the social worker as a mediator (1961, pp. 154–55). This process of mediation requires the ability to direct change strategies toward person and environment and the interaction between them. The debate as to whether social workers should be stretcher-bearers or social engineers fails to account for a dual focus on both person and situation. (1979, p. 8)

> . . . social workers seek to strike a balance between people's coping ability and environmental demands. Social workers may at times (1) direct change strategies toward individuals, (2) direct change strategies toward the environment, and (3) direct change strategies toward the interaction of individual and environment. But in all cases, these strategies are directed toward changing the nature of the person-situation interaction.

> But does changing the nature of the interaction mean changing the individual or changing the environment? This is an old issue in social work which was enunciated at an early date by Porter Lee (1929) in his distinction between social work as cause and social work as function. Our contention is that social workers do both and that the debate as to whether the profession should focus primarily on individual change or on environmental change results from a largely incorrect formulation of the focus of social work intervention. The parties to this debate tend to perceive social workers as either focusing on the individual or on the environment and miss the central focus on the interaction of the two. (1979, p. 7)

৵ Knowledge and competence

What should social workers know in order to carry out the tasks just listed? Social workers need to master knowledge of how individuals and their social groups develop and function. They need to have some notion of what causes people trouble in the business of living and what to look for when trouble does not respond to ordinary efforts to bring about change. They need to understand organizational behavior and administrative processes. They need to know something about the political process at all levels of government and how one intervenes in that process to bring change. They need to know something about research methods in general and about methods of evaluation in particular. They need to know how to organize data and to plan for intervention. They need to be able to select situationally appropriate actions from a repertoire of skills. They need to be competent in the use of intervention skills. This is a large and demanding body of knowledge. Social workers seldom master it all, but they must continue to learn as long as they are active professsionally. The amount of knowledge is so great and some of it is so uncertain that social workers are constantly faced with the need to act on incomplete knowledge.

The West Virginia Undergraduate Social Work Curriculum Development Project identified ten competences which can be seen as necessary for social work practice within an ecological framework:

1. Identify and assess situations where the relationship between people and social institutions needs to be initiated, enhanced, restored, protected, or terminated.
2. Develop and implement a plan for improving the well-being of people based on problem assessment and the exploration of obtainable goals and available options.
3. Enhance the problem-solving, coping, and developmental capacities of people.
4. Link people with systems that provide them with resources, services, and opportunities.
5. Intervene effectively on behalf of populations most vulnerable and discriminated against.
6. Promote the effective and human operation of the systems that provide people with services, resources, and opportunities.
7. Actively participate with others in creating new, modified, or improved service, resource, and opportunity systems that are more equitable, just, and responsive to consumers of services, and work with others to eliminate those systems that are unjust.
8. Evaluate the extent to which the objectives of the intervention plan were achieved.
9. Continually evaluate one's own professional growth and development through assessment of practive behaviors and skills.
10. Contribute to the improvement of service delivery by adding to the knowledge base of the profession as appropriate and by supporting and upholding the standards and ethics of the profession. (Baer and Federico, 1978, pp. 86–89)

ᴥ§ The organization of social work practice

Because of the manner in which social work developed as a profession as well as because of the diversity of the demands in social work practice, social work practice has been organized in two ways. One way has been to divide it by fields of practice, which means that social workers became specialists in working within certain delivery systems. For many years these specialists took their

names from fields of practice and were known as child welfare workers, probation officers, public welfare workers, visiting teachers, medical social workers, psychiatric social workers, or family workers. As a result of the division by fields of practice, supported by separate professional associations, many social workers felt a primary identification with the delivery system in which they worked rather than with the social work profession. The division also resulted in status differentials among workers of relatively similar competence. Thus, there was a movement away from this type of specialty toward a common identification. The various special professional organizations were joined with the overall association. For many years, there has been an emphasis upon the commonness of social work practice. Recently, however, there has been a new interest in specialties. This was recognized in a statement by the National Association of Social Workers that attempted to develop a framework, principles, and criteria for the development of specializations. It said that the profession should:

a. Follow reasonably and logically from a commonly accepted and understood social work perspective.
b. Be anchored principally in institutions which assure continuity with social work's historic commitments.
c. Focus on a broader level than that of a particular service delivery institutional structure where the specialist practices.
d. Not inhibit the creative evolution of new specializations.
e. Allow for use of all social work methods.
f. Be able to spell out the knowledge and skills required.
g. Be viewed as preparing *beginning specialists* with plans made for continuing education offering post M.S.W.
h. Incorporate minority content. (NASW, 1979, pp. 20–31)

Social workers have also divided themselves according to the methods they use and have thought of themselves as caseworkers, group workers, or community organizers. Each of these groups has been assumed to use methods characterized by distinctive skills and change strategies. It is interest-ing to consider that the primary variable in this division is related not to what the social worker does or to the purpose of the action but to the number of persons involved in the interaction. This way of thinking about social work practice has come under severe attack over the last decade of social work development. Others ways of thinking about methods of practice have been proposed. As an alternative to the casework–group work–community organization model. Herbert Bisno (1969, pp. 9–12) conceptualized nine social work methods which might be utilized with any size of client system: adversary, conciliatory, develop-mental, facilitative-instructional, knowledge devel-opment and testing, restorative, regulatory, role im-plementing, and rule making.

Systems in social work practice

Another way to conceptualize social work prac-tice is to organize the groups and people with whom social workers work into practice systems. When we think about social work practice we often think of clients or groups of clients. However, social workers do some of their most important, time-consuming, and demanding work with people other than those traditionally viewed as clients. Practi-tioners who are involved with the protection of children will find themselves working with persons other than the children and their parents. They will be involved with court services, medical services, neighbors, police, attorneys, perhaps the school system, and foster parents and/or institutional staff. The social worker whom Mr. Olds met at the hospi-tal was involved on his behalf, with the medical, nursing, and business office staff as well as the administrators of social security, the eligibility tech-nician at public welfare, and the staff of Meals on Wheels. Pincus and Minahan (1973, pp. 54–74) were the first to suggest this way of approaching social work practice. They suggested that the peo-ple with whom the social worker interacted in the practice of social work could be classified into four systems: the client system, the target system, the action system, and the change agent system.

Compton and Galaway (1979, p. 84) suggested that two more systems were important to what social workers did and how they did it. Borrowing from Pincus and Minahan, Compton and Galaway discussed the systems in social work as follows:

The change agent system. Social work-ers may be viewed as change agents, who are specifically employed for the purpose of planning and working with the six systems toward the planned change. The agency or organization that employs them or of which they are a part can be thought of as the change agent system. Obviously, the change agent system heavily influences the worker's behavior through various policies and re-sources that represent sanctions, constraints, and resources. . . .

The client system. People may be con-sidered to be a part of a client system when (1) they have either asked for or sanctioned the worker's services; (2) they are expected to benefit from those services; and (3) they have entered into an explicit or implicit con-tract with the worker. . . . This definition leads to a brief consideration of the nature of the first coming together of client and worker. There are clients who come to the agency voluntarily seeking the help of the worker, but there are large numbers of situa-tions in which the worker approaches the client because the agency function calls for it to assume this type of responsibility in be-half of the community (which should be con-sidered the client at this point), for example, corrections, child welfare, protection for the aged and incompetent, and so on. Also a neighborhood center staff (a change agent system) may identify what they see as a neighborhood need and ask a staff member to attempt to form an organization to deal with it. In all these instances the community or the change agent system itself may more appropriately be considered the client than the people the worker approaches "to help." The people identified as targets of the work-er's efforts are more appropriately regarded as *potential clients* until some sort of agree-ment is reached in which potential clients sanction the worker's intervention in their lives and transaction. . . .

The target system.   The people that the change agents "need to change or influence in order to accomplish their goals" are the target system (Pincus and Minahan, 1973, p. 58). The target system and the client system often overlap when it is the client, or the client's part in an intersystem transaction, that needs to be changed. However, much of social work practice involves the social worker working with the client system toward some desired change in some other system (a target system).

The action system.   The action system is used to describe those with whom the social worker interacts in a cooperative way to accomplish the purposes of the change effort. There are an endless number of different action systems in which the worker may be engaged. . . . However, action systems may be a neighborhood group, a family group, or others that the worker works with toward bringing about a change helpful to the client.

The professional system.   This system is made up of the professional association of social workers, the educational system by which workers are prepared, and the values and sanctions of a professional practice. The values and the culture of the professional system strongly influence both the required and the permitted actions of the worker as change agent. In working to change their own agency or in acting as an advocate of social change, practitioners often utilize the professional system.

The problem identification system. This system is the system that acts to bring a potential client to the attention of the worker. At the initiation of its contact with the worker, or the change agent system, it might be considered (as Pincus and Minahan discuss) the client system. However, it usually does not consider itself a client, and

if, in the course of things, it should appear that it should be the focus of the helping effort, the worker will need to treat it more as a potential client until it makes a role transition. (1979, pp. 84–85)

The terms and notions discussed above may seem strange and artificial to readers. We believe that they are a very helpful way to think about social work actions, and they are being used more and more widely in social work practice. It might be helpful to the reader once again to go back to our earlier examples. Let us consider Mr. Olds's situation.

Mr. Olds would be our client system and also our target system in that the social worker is trying to help him function with greater satisfaction. The other professionals in the hospital, together with the worker, make up the change agent system, and the other agencies that the worker contacts on behalf of Mr. Olds are the action system. The worker is also a part of the professional system of social work. If Mr. Olds lived in a public housing project and certain housing authority regulations about the use of its facilities created difficulties for him, he and the worker might decide that an effort should be made to change the regulations. In that case Mr. Olds would still be the client system, but the housing authority would become the target system, as the goal of the worker and the client system would be to change it. Mr. Olds and the worker might organize the residents of the project to bring pressure for change. These residents would then be an action system.

The process of social work practice

The dynamics of all that goes on between the client system and the worker is encompassed by the phrase *social work process,* meaning the whole series of actions, changes, or functions that go on between the client and the worker in the course of their being together. For this process to be helpful, it must proceed in an orderly manner and be accompanied by attitudes of respect, caring, and belief in the competence of the client to participate as a partner with the worker in the problem-solving work.

Problem or issue definition

Before client and worker can begin to do something about the obstacles that seem to be preventing the client system from accomplishing desired goals, they have to decide what the problem or issue is. In other words, they must define the problem. Sometimes this is the most difficult and time-consuming part of the social work process. But unless the worker and the client can agree on the problem, they cannot work together. Without some agreement, they will go their own ways and work at their own things. This often happens in social work when workers assume that they know best and have notions about "the real problem" that they do not share with clients. We do not mean that the worker and the client will see the problem that brought them together in the same terms, but in order to work together they need to reach an agreement on the problem to be worked on—the issue or problem that is going to occupy the focus of their attention and their joint action. The way in which the worker and the client system define the problem will determine all that happens from that time on. The way we define a problem affects the way we observe the data of the problem, and the data we collect will affect the plans we make and what we do to solve the problem.

Goal setting and assessment

The second critical part of the social work process is the *determination of the goals*. What do clients see as the problem that has to be solved? What have they done about the problem? How did that turn out for them? In other words, once the problem has been defined, a decision has to be made about the desired outcome. What are the goals of being together?

Once the problem and the goals have been determined, we are free to go about collecting information that appears to bear on them. At this point, after having explored the problem and the goals,

the client and the worker will need to decide whether they want to go on together. We call this the *preliminary contract*—a decision to proceed with the collection of data about the problem, the client system, and the situation. After the collection of data, if the worker and the client are to go on together, it is necessary for the two systems (the client and the change agent) to conceptualize why the problem persists in spite of the fact that the client system wants to solve it. We have usually called this the *diagnosis,* though we would prefer to use the term *assessment*. It means putting together the data about the problem, the goal, the resources available to the client and the worker, the blocks and lacks that will handicap the necessary action, and the costs of the action as well as making some decision about what this means to the client system. Following the assessment, the worker and the client will need to think about what has to be done to affect the problem in the direction that the client seeks. A plan for achieving this has to be formulated. At this point, the client and the worker must consider whether they want to go into action together. If they do, they will agree to work together toward the agreed-upon goals in the agreed-upon way. This agreement is called the *contract*.

Contracting

The notion of *contracting* is a recent one in social work practice, and it is sometimes handled by inexperienced workers with excessive rigidity. In social work, contracting simply means stating as clearly as possible orally or in writing the results of a mutual decision to work together in a certain way or of a *decision by the worker or the client that working together is impossible and what the worker's next actions will be*. The contracting notion needs to be used flexibly, as do all procedures in social work. However, because of the issues in the notion of helping that we discussed earlier, we would prefer to have the rule be that a contract is a prerequisite for working together and then to have exceptions treated as exceptions and not as regular procedures.

The first condition of contracting is the full participation of both parties. If the client is reluctant to enter into a contract and the worker insists on one, the work together will fail. If the client is reluctant to join the worker in a specified plan, this needs to be considered seriously. What is the worker missing in pulling things together? A contract does not need to be achieved overnight. It may take weeks or months for the client and the worker to arrive at an agreement.

If they cannot do so, there is no reason for them to continue to work together unless the worker has become involved in the situation because either the client or someone else needs protection from severe injury. In that case the worker will have to inform the client of the action that the worker will take unilaterally and the authority by which the worker will take it. In an emergency or a crisis, the need for action may be immediate. Thus, there will be no time for a long decision-making process. Nevertheless, the client should be involved as much as possible in what is being done. In some situations involving young children, severely retarded persons, or other vulnerable populations, the worker may act unilaterally because of a need to provide protection. In other situations of this kind, the worker may want to include other family members or closely related persons in the decision making.

If the client seeks goals that are beyond the resources of the change agent system and any action system that the change agent can put together, the worker needs to inform the client of this. Sometimes it is possible to agree on subgoals as a way of testing what can be done. At other times the worker must simply inform the client that the worker cannot be involved in the goals that the client seeks or in the actions that the client considers necessary to achieve them. Obviously the worker cannot be involved in actions that the worker sees as seriously harmful to others, and the agency may place limits on what its staff can do. There are other implications of contracting, but we would end with the principle that the worker who engages in contracting uses professional skills to facilitate the client system's participation in the decision-making process. Such a worker is concerned primarily with how involved the client is in the process and with how responsibilities are divided in carrying out the plan and secondarily with the specifics of any individual plan.

Action toward change

The last step in the social work process with the client system are the planning of what actions should be taken and by whom and the evaluation of the work that has been done together. We often hear about treatment plans or treatment in social work. These words are generally used in work with individuals, and they refer to the actions taken to solve the problems. Our decisions on treatment should follow from the earlier steps in the social work process and should not be something we do routinely because we believe in a particular way of approaching people.

Evaluation

Evaluation is the last and an extremely important part of the social work process. It is largely through evaluation that we learn what is effective in solving problems and what is not. We should not consider the social work process complete until there has been an evaluation. In some instances, the evaluation is an interchange between the client and the worker. In other instances, it is a more formal activity, and it may be conducted by someone other than the worker. In all instances, some form of evaluation is necessary.

✑ Practice roles of social workers

A recent way of conceptualizing social work problem-solving (or treatment) actions is to consider the various roles that social workers may perform as part of their professional practice.

Role is a global concept that is not always used consistently. For our purposes we will define role to refer to the behavior that the worker directs toward the accomplishment of the goals that have been set through the interaction of the client and the worker (the contract). The literature of social work lists a large number of possible roles. We will discuss seven roles that we believe an MSW social worker (one who holds a master's degree from an accredited school of social work) should be able to perform in working toward desired goals. These roles are: broker, mediator, advocate, activist, teacher, enabler, and therapist. The first three roles require that the worker operate between the client and another social system. In each of these roles the worker is progressively more active in confronting the other system. The worker may engage in the fourth, activist role on behalf of all people rather than any individual client system. The last three roles involve interaction between the client system and the worker and move in a direction opposite to that of the first four—from the role of teacher, in which the worker is the most active, to the role of therapist, in which the worker serves primarily as a guide while the client struggles to work through certain feelings, thoughts, and/or behaviors. Except for the roles of therapist and activist, these roles may be utilized with any size of client system, and we will use the terms *client system* and *client* interchangeably to mean individuals, groups, or communities.

The therapist and activist roles

The role of therapist is limited to individuals, families, or small groups that are seeking change in themselves as individuals and/or change in their intimate interactions with meaningful people. The role of activist involves nonviolent direct action to change political or social arrangements and thus is limited to the worker's actions with certain kinds of community groups or with groups to which the social worker may belong. In therapy, the client, with the help of the social worker, is seeking some change in self—in feeling, thinking, or behaving, or all three. Such change often involves painful struggle for the client and reaches into the depth of feelings and thoughts about oneself. In the activist role, the goal is to have certain parts of the community or certain social institutions suffer enough pain to make them willing to examine the

problems that a particular way of operating is creating for others. Here the change agent system and the client system are demanding institutional or organizational change. The activist role differs from the therapist role in more than the size of the system. In the therapist role, the client system and the target system are the same. In the activist role, they are different, and the target system has not agreed to the change that the worker seeks. The activist role involves taking a strong position in advocating a generally unpopular or deviant point of view as to the necessity for some social or political change and using such techniques as boycott, demonstrations, leafleting, picketing, and vigils.

The broker role

In *Industrial Society and Social Welfare,* Wilensky and Lebeaux (1965, p. 286) postulated a need for "guides, so to speak, through a new kind of civilized jungle" and saw social work as "an example par excellence of the liaison function, a large part of its total activity being devoted to putting people in touch with community resources they need but can hardly name, let alone locate." In 1976 Carole Meyer wrote:

> . . . bureaucratic structures break down in the area of individualizing when they become too large and too specialized in the function they are established to perform, and . . . as organizational services have come to replace family and other intimate supports, there is a need for . . . that intimate function of individualizing, relating, advocating, and helping people to connect appropriately with the service being offered. (1976, p. 197)

And in another place she wrote: "Most people in the urban complex can use help in negotiation with their lives, and most particularly do those people need help who are under the strain of crisis events in their lives" (1976, pp. 196–97).

These quotations speak to the broker role, in which the activities of the worker are directed toward making effective, usable connections between the client and the community in order to accomplish the agreed-upon objectives of the worker and the client. Referral is a basic part of the social broker role, and assisting a client to find and use a needed resource is frequently the most important service that a social worker can provide (Compton and Galaway, 1979, p. 339).

The mediator role

"Mediation involves efforts to resolve disputes that may exist between the client system and other persons or organizations." When resolving disputes is an important step in helping the client system reach certain goals, the social worker will perform the role of mediator (Compton and Galaway, 1979, p. 341). This role involves assisting the client system and other people or groups involved in a dispute to find a basis for resolving the conflict.

> The social worker in the role of the mediator will use techniques to try to bring about a convergence of the perceived values of both parties to the conflict to help each party to recognize the legitimacy of the other's interests, assist the parties in identifying their common interests in a successful outcome, avoid a situation in which winning and losing are paramount issues, attempt to localize the conflict to specific issues, times, and places, break the conflict down to separate issues, and help parties identify that they have more at stake in continuing a relationship than the issues of specific conflict. (Compton and Galaway, 1979, p. 342)

The social worker as broker will use persuasion and conciliation procedures. But these techniques are not used to get the client system to change. They are used when the goal of the contract is to resolve difficulties that exist between the client system and another system—another agency, an organization, the police, or neighbors.

The advocate role

As an advocate,

> the social worker becomes the speaker for the client in presenting and arguing the client's cause when this *is necessary to accomplish the objectives of the contract*. . . . Advocacy differs from mediation . . . [in that] in mediation the effort is to secure resolution to a dispute through give and

take on both sides. In advocacy the effort is to win for the client; advocacy efforts are frequently directed toward securing benefits to which the client is legally entitled. [italics added] (Compton and Galaway, 1979, pp. 342–43)

Advocacy, like other roles, can be used with client systems of various sizes.

Advocacy is becoming an increasingly popular role for social workers. However, since a similar role is played by the legal profession, we need to consider the similarities and differences between the legal and the social work concept of advocacy. The social work concept is similar to that of the legal profession in that lawyers do not become advocates for their clients until the clients have retained them and have authorized their actions. The same should be true of social workers. Advocacy means standing beside our clients and fighting for their rights. It does not mean that we assume this role without the direct involvement of the client. If advocacy actions go wrong, the result can be more costly to the client than accepting the original situation. Workers must make sure, as lawyers are careful to do, that the client understands the cost of failure.

Advocacy in social work differs from that found in law in that the social worker is often involved in protecting people from actions of their clients. Thus, the worker does not become an advocate for the client in situations in which doing so could result in hurt to others. The attorney stands for the client; the social worker stands between the client and other social systems and must be concerned with the totality of the situation. For example, a social worker would not enter into a contract with an abusing mother to contest a hospital's decision to keep her child overnight unless it were very clear to the worker that the mother would not abuse the child again or that the hospital was not keeping the child in order to make a necessary diagnosis of the injuries it had received.

The teacher role

In the teacher role the social worker provides the client with information that the client needs in order to cope with the problem situation, assists the client in rehearsing or practicing new behaviors or skills, or models alternative behavior patterns (Compton and Galaway, 1979, p. 340).

> Teaching is an important aspect of social work practice. Frequently workers will provide clients with information necessary for decision making; in some situations information may be all that a client needs to accomplish the defined goals. Giving information must be clearly distinguished, however, from giving advice. "Giving information" implies supplying clients with data, input, or knowledge which clients are free to use or not to use on their own behalf; "giving advice" implies that the worker knows what is best for the client. Workers rarely give advice, but providing information is an important service they render to clients. (Compton and Galaway, 1979, p. 341)

There are three important limits to the giving of information:

1. Workers must recognize that the information they offer is only a small part of the available social experience.
2. The information should be related to the problem that brings the client and worker together.
3. Opinions should be clearly labeled as opinions and not represented as facts. (Compton and Galaway, 1979, p. 341)

Workers should always be aware that in their approach to clients and to problem solving, they provide a model of behavior that may be usable by clients. In the sense of providing modeling behavior and new information, teaching is an important interventional role.

The enabler role

The last role that we will discuss is the enabler role. "Workers take the enabler role when their intervention activities are directed toward assisting clients to find the coping strengths and resources within themselves to produce changes necessary for accomplishing objectives of the service contract" (Compton and Galaway, 1979, p. 340). The distinguishing feature of the enabler role is that the client system does the work of effecting the changes necessary to accomplish objectives by using its own coping skills. The worker provides the client system with the support it needs in order to take the required actions, or the worker helps the client system to identify and mobilize strengths that the client system did not know it had available. Thus, the worker facilitates or enables the client's accomplishment of a defined change.

The enabler role can be used to help the client change self or an individual pattern of relating to others or the environment. It can also be used to help the client system change a target system. Here the worker helps the client to identify sources of internal conflict as well as external influences that are blocking the client system from achieving desired changes and then helps the client to discover ways of dealing with these difficulties that are and have been within the client's behavior repertoire but had been unrecognized as usable in the given situation.

~§ The social work relationship

We have discussed the knowledge and competences that social workers need, and we have discussed the process of social work intervention and the roles of social work practice. We now want to speak briefly of the relationship, the feeling climate, that grows between the worker and the client and that makes the social work process possible. Relationship may be considered as the attitudes and emotions that grow between the worker and the client system. We want to discuss very briefly something of its meaning for social workers in their interaction with the client system. Relationship develops out of the purposive interaction between the client and the worker; it has motion and direction and emergent characteristics. The worker should bring to the relationship with the client: (1) concern for the other, (2) commitment and obligation, (3) acceptance and expectation, (4) empathy, (5) authority and power, and (6) genuineness and congruence.

Concern for others—commitment and obligation

Concern for others is an unconditional caring—wanting the client system to be all it wants to be and to do all it wants to do *for its own sake*. The italicized characteristic of unconditional caring is the most critical and the most difficult to achieve. The more we care for others, the more likely we are to want for them what we want for ourselves, not what they want for themselves. Commitment and obligation simply means that when workers enter into interaction with clients, they must willingly and freely accept the commitments and the obligations that such interaction entails.

Acceptance and expectation

In many discussions of acceptance, one finds it equated with a nonjudgmental attitude. It is much more than that. *Accept* is an active verb, meaning to receive as adequate or satisfactory, to regard as true, to believe in, to receive what others offer. To accept others means to receive what they offer of themselves, with respect for their capacity and worth. It is not just a refusal to judge—it is an active seeking to understand. It does not mean that we always agree with other persons or that we forgo our own values to support someone else's values. It does not mean that clients are excused from participating in the world in which they must live. Rather, true acceptance carries with it an assumption that people act as they must in the complexity of their particular human situation and that they are what their nature and their environment, coupled with their vision, permit them to be. It rests on a communicated desire to understand. The social workers who are most effective in working with clients are those who feel that their clients can and will change in their own way, given appropriate support and help. This notion is a real test of our belief in the self-determination and dignity of the client. We believe in the ability of clients to choose directions effectively and to do what is possible to move in the directions chosen.

Empathy

Empathy is the capacity to enter into the feelings of another without losing oneself in the process. It requires that the worker be able to feel an emotion deeply and yet remain separate enough to use knowledge in order to seek solutions to problems or to work out issues. Empathy is one of the central capacities that social workers require in order to work productively with other systems.

Authority and power; congruence and honesty

Not only are the concepts of authority, power, congruence, and honesty difficult to understand, but they interact, so that not understanding and accepting the elements of authority and power in a relationship will lead the client to perceive the relationship as dishonest. Compton and Galaway discuss authority and power as follows:

> The primary characteristic of the concepts of power and authority in the helping relationship is that they are neither good nor bad in themselves. Some aspects of these elements are always present, and the attempt of social workers to abdicate their role and pretend that they carry no authority only leaves clients troubled by suspicions and doubts about why workers are unwilling to admit what they, the clients, are so aware of. This incongruence between what the client feels and what the worker says makes an authentic relationship impossible. The crucial significance of power and authority lies in how they are utilized for help.

In his discussion of authority in social work relationships, Goldstein (1973, pp. 84–86) points out that when persons require what another has to offer "that cannot be obtained elsewhere—whether one is seeking the adoption of a child, financial assistance, help with a personal problem, or professional services to assist in a social action enterprise—the relationship cannot be equalized." As the social worker's needs have no relevance to the task, "the seeker cannot reciprocate or supply the provider with any reward that can restore the balance. The fact that the seeker has limited alternatives to meet personal needs is further heightened by the fact that workers are seen as having competence and knowledge." When social workers say, "We will meet once a week on a Monday, if that is convenient to you," or when they decide to include another family member in treatment, they are setting the conditions of the relationship. Or they may refer clients elsewhere. These are all examples of power and authority.

People who are genuine and congruent in a helping relationship are people who know themselves and are unafraid of what they see in themselves or of what they are. They can enter into a helping relationship without anything of themselves to prove or protect, so they are unafraid of the emotions of others. They do not have to be right or to be the superior in the relationship.

> In order to be congruent and genuine, we must seek three things: (1) an honest knowledge of ourselves, of who and what we really are; (2) a clear knowledge of agency procedures and policies and of the professional role, both in their meaning to the worker and in their meaning to the clients; and (3) an internalization of the first two and our concern for the other, acceptance of clients, commitment to their welfare and to the authority aspects of the worker's role and position, so that these qualities are so much a part of us that we no longer need to be consciously aware of them and can turn our full attention to clients and their situation. (Compton and Galaway, 1979, p. 180)

❧ Summary

We have completed our discussion of social work practice. We have considered the personal social services as the social system within which social workers function. We have discussed the various definitions of social work and how the definitions have changed through the years as the social work profession has developed. These changed definitions have resulted from changed notions of social work practice. After all, we do different things and hold different attitudes if we think of ourselves as aiding people who are less adequate than we are than we do if we see our actions as

generally guided by the purpose of expanding the choices that people are able to make and to implement in their own lives.

We dealt briefly with the competence needed for effective social work practice. We also considered conceptualizing social work practice as work with different types of systems. And, finally, we discussed the process of interaction between the client and the worker, the roles that social workers should be able to perform, and the qualities of the client-worker relationship.

❧ A look ahead

As we have said earlier, social work practice grew within the various delivery systems of the social welfare institution in order to supply the actors who were needed to deliver the services within the various social welfare systems. Thus, social work practice can be conceptualized as an organizational response to needs identified as social welfare. "Social services are the tools of the social worker, and the structure of those services determines precisely what [social workers will do in their] practice. How problems are [organizationally] defined and what services are allocated, when, and to whom are the policy-practice questions that undergird all social work activity" (Meyer, 1976, p. 93).

This is the concern of our next chapter. We shall examine the social work profession and the organizational structure of the personal social services and how they impact each other.

❧ Study questions

1. Go back to Chapter 2. Reread the discussion of the family situations described there, and then refer to the further development of those situations in this chapter. Take each family situation, and label the roles that the social workers played in that situation. Are you able to construct the systems of social work practice that were involved? We recognize that the information provided in these examples is minimal, but see what you can accomplish.

2. Have you thought of social work as an activity to increase the choices of clients? If you were a proba-

tion officer and both you and your client were operating within the limits of the court orders, what would be involved in increasing your client's choices?

3. What do you think is meant by the statement "We can degrade people by caring for them, and we can degrade people by not caring for them"?

4. In addition to suggesting the notion that the clients should be involved in the decision making regarding their contracts with social workers, the concept of contracting also suggests that there are times when the worker and the client may decide not to work together even though the client's problem remains unsolved. How do you feel about this notion? What does your feeling reveal about your view of social work?

5. Can you distinguish between empathy and pity?

6. What ideas about social work practice that were new to you did you find in this chapter?

7. If you were having difficulty in coping with some problem in your life, would you seek social work help? Discuss the reasons for your position.

⊷§ Selected readings

Brieland, D., et al. *Contemporary Social Work.* New York: McGraw Hill, 1975.

Part 3 of this book offers a good statement of social work methods.

Gaylin, W., et al. *Doing Good: The Limits of Benevolence.* New York: Pantheon Books, 1978.

The first two chapters of this book introduce the notions of the problems in "caring" for others.

Guggenbuhl-Craig, A. *Power in the Helping Professions.* Zurich, Switzerland: Spring Publications, 1976.

Although we think that the author of this book discusses something he obviously does not understand very thoroughly, the book could stimulate some interesting discussions.

Keith-Lucas, A. *The Giving and Taking of Help.* Chapel Hill: University of North Carolina Press, 1972.

We have suggested one chapter of this book in an earlier reading list. We would suggest this brief book in its totality as an excellent accompaniment to our present chapter.

Lewis, H. Morality and the politics of Practice. *Social Casework,* 53 (7) (July 1972):404–17.

We strongly recommend this article as a supplemental reading for this chapter. Lewis presents principles that he believes can effectively overcome possible conflict between the client and worker as to the purpose of their relationship.

Morales, A., and Bradford, C. S. *Social work: A Profession of Many Faces.* Boston: Allyn & Bacon, 1977.

This book bridges both this chapter and the next. It is a well-rounded examination of social work, the social work profession, and social work practice. We recommend it highly as a work that extends and explains parts of our two chapters on social work.

Piccard, B. J. *An Introduction to Social Work: A Primer.* 2d ed. Homewood, Ill.: Dorsey Press, 1979.

This book is a concise summary of the basic issues in social work practice and policy. Its organization and division by methods of practice differ from the approach in our text, but there are parts that might be useful in extending what we are saying.

Perlman, H. H. *So You Want To Be a Social Worker.* New York: Harper, 1962.

This book is an older introduction to social work written at a very simple level. It is easy reading, and it should stimulate class discussion about some of the differences between its presentation of social work and that of our text.

A social worker with an innovative program. Ann Laib, a social worker in Bismark, North Dakota, has organized a Regional Lending Library of Toys to be borrowed by foster parents, day care centers, special education classes, and others.

Chapter 8 ❧

❧ The profession and the delivery system: The shape of social work practice ❧

In the last chapter we considered the definition of social work and briefly outlined the elements of social work practice as it comes to life in the interaction between the client and the social work practitioner. In this chapter we will discuss the shape of social work practice as it is impacted by the organization of the social work profession and of the various delivery systems within the personal social service system. Although an increasing number of social workers are practicing privately, the overwhelming majority of social work practitioners work within organized delivery systems. Thus, social work practice must have a continuing interaction with the social welfare institution and with the organization, policies, and programs of the personal social services. In addition, social work practice is professional practice, and as such it is shaped by and shapes the organized social work profession and is dependent on the training offered by the schools of social work attached to colleges and universities. The answers to questions concerning how social problems of human living are defined, what services and resources are allocated to their alleviation, and when and to whom the services are resources will be available set the parameters of most social work activity.

❧ The structure of social services

The resources provided through the delivery systems are the tools of social workers, and the structure of those resources (how they answer the questions about structure raised in Chapter 5) will determine the parameters of what social workers do.

As we have said earlier, social work began with the need for people to administer the functions of social welfare. Thus, from the beginning of social work, the individual social worker's function has been defined and his or her salary has been paid by an agency which receives its sanction from, and is accountable to, the community, whose members differ from, though they may include, the members of the client system. This point is of fundamental importance, since the parameters of the service that any particular social worker can offer are determined by the limits of the agency's social charge. The lack of economic and social power of the people who have traditionally utilized the social services has meant that those who define the priorities and limits of the social services may have interests that differ from, and conflict with, interests of the client group. Often the persons who wield power and influence over social service policymaking have little or no personal understanding of the problems and needs of the persons who come to social workers. Also, given the notion of such policymakers that those who have achieved power and influence know better than those who need help, and given their notion that social services are "gifts" to the beneficiaries, they have shown little concern for the rights of clients. Although public agencies have gradually developed appeals procedures through which clients can challenge agency and worker decisions, these procedures are often not used or prove ineffective in practice. Private agencies have, as a rule, developed no formal appeals procedures.

Social workers use two fundamental types of tools in their work. The first are the tools of internalized knowledge and skills (professional expertise). The knowledge and skills of social workers cannot be used up, and in fact they may be developed and sharpened by practice. But they are costly in that they are what social workers (or any other professionals) sell in order to support themselves. In addition to knowledge and skills, social workers frequently dispense external resources, such as money and services. Now money, whether it is used to pay for the knowledge and skills of the social worker or for concrete resources or is given directly to the client, is usually scarce. And although both the client and the social worker may contribute through taxation or voluntary contributions to the funds that support social work efforts, those funds are not the property of the social worker

or the client, but belong to some identified community. The community, through boards or other devices described in Chapter 6, is responsible for the allocation of these resources and is accountable for their proper use.

Every practicing social worker has been confronted with the harsh reality of the conflict between individual professional judgment as to the ideal interventional actions needed by the client and what is possible, given the resources and the limits of the agency within which both the client and the worker find themselves. At that point, frustrated and angered, social workers confront the fact that they serve a dual function as agents of both the community and the client. Social workers employed by agencies are usually only minimally free to exercise their preferences in terms of clientele, work load, or the problems to be dealt with. Priority decisions as to agency program limit the opportunities of both clients and workers for problem solution (Compton and Galaway, 1979, pp. 479–80).

Another aspect of social work practice should also be recognized. Clients who go to a lawyer for service, or patients who go to a doctor for treatment, may look elsewhere for help if they think that the service they receive is inadequate. Thus, they express their evaluation of the professional's competence by depriving the professional of income. If professionals want to support themselves and their dependents, they must practice in a way that satisfies the users of their services. However, since most client systems do not pay the full cost for social work services, their withdrawal seldom directly penalizes the practitioner. Social workers (and their agencies) are thus well protected from their clients' evaluations. However, they are open to the evaluation of their supporting community. But the supporting community neither pays nor evaluates workers directly. Rather, it gives its money to an organization, usually called an agency, which hires the professional practitioners. Usually it is the agency in interaction with its supporting community through certain representative groups which both sets the parameters of practice within which workers must operate and evaluates their performance within the parameters (Compton and Galaway, 1979, p. 480).

❧ Personal social service delivery systems as bureaucratic organizations

In the modern world most formal organizations are structured in a particular way. This type of administrative organization, known as bureaucracy, has triumphed in modern society because it is thought to operate with an efficiency superior to that of any other form of secondary-group social structure thus far devised. The classical criteria for a bureaucracy were originally set forth by Max Weber as follows:

1. [The employees] are personally free and subject to authority only with respect to their impersonal official [work] obligations.
2. [The employees] are organized in a clearly defined hierarchy of offices.
3. Each office has a clearly defined sphere of competence.
4. The office is filled by a free contractual relationship. (Thus, in principle, each person makes a free selection, or choice, as to whether [the person] will accept the office and its terms.)
5. Candidates [for offices in the bureaucracy] are selected on the basis of technical qualifications. In the most rational case, this is tested by examination or guaranteed by diplomas certifying technical training, or both. They are appointed, not elected.
6. [The employees] are remunerated by fixed salaries in money, for the most part with a right to pensions. . . . The salary scale is primarily graded according to rank in the hierarchy.
7. The [position] is treated as the sole, or at least the primary, occupation of the incumbent.
8. It constitutes a career. There is a system of "promotion" according to seniority or to achievement, or both. Promotion is dependent on the judgment of superiors.
9. The official works entirely separated from ownership of the means of administration and without appropriation of his position.
10. [The worker] is subject to strict and systematic

discipline and control in the conduct of [the] office. (1947, pp. 333–34)

Weber (p. 334) says that the Roman Catholic church, the modern army, and large-scale capitalist enterprise, along with certain "charitable organization, or any number of other types of private enterprises, servicing ideal or material ends are bureaucratic organizations."

Many social workers have been concerned with the problems of the relationship between a bureaucratically organized agency and the social worker as a professional practitioner. However, it is important to recognize that professionals and bureaucrats are not two different sets of people. Some professionals are not bureaucrats, and some bureaucrats are certainly not professionals, but increasingly in our society, there are professionals who operate within bureaucratic structures. At present, there is no known form of organizational structure that offers an organizational model superior to a bureaucratic structure for the delivery of the complex functions required of social services. It is thus not very helpful to simply see bureaucracy as bad and to condemn it. Rather, persons interested in social work need to understand the conflicts between bureaucracy and the social work profession and how to deal with them. Actually, both bureaucracies and professions are expressions of the general trends toward the division of labor and specialization in industrialized society.

Efficiency versus effectiveness

One of the conflicts between the bureaucracy and the practitioner centers on the bureaucratic value of efficiency—making the best possible use of resources in striving toward the attainment of goals. The bureaucratic concern with efficiency is usually expressed in terms of administrative rules budget making, and the circumscription of actions, which appear as the routinization of activity. But professionals tend to place their highest values on the notion of giving the service needed by clients even if doing so demands actions and resources that go beyond the confines of agency policies and procedures. A pervasive type of conflict may thus arise between the practitioner's unlimited commitment to acting in whatever ways may be necessary to achieve client goals and the relatively limited program goals of the agency. In addition to limiting the resources and services that are made available, agency policies will also confine service to problems that are within agency limits. This limitation of service conflicts with professional values.

Professionals are apt to evaluate themselves on the basis of how effectively they provided service rather than on the basis of how efficient they were, though these two values are not unrelated. Workers who are not efficient in utilizing resources for the client's fullest and most immediate benefit are not effective. Another focus of professionals is the development of increasing competence, of becoming more and more effective in what they do.

The routinization of work

The profession values skill and individual judgment rather than procedure and service rather than the performance of routines. The agency imposes a variety of requirements that are necessary to the operation of a complex bureaucracy—paperwork, records, files, verifications of actions taken, and so forth. These requirements are often seen by workers as getting in the way of their work with clients. Certainly, there may be procedures that become only numbing routines in any organization. Yet workers need to understand that paperwork is often necessary in order to assure the client an equal access to services, and that records may enable service to the client to proceed in the absence of the worker in addition to furnishing data for service evaluation.

The structure of authority

Another issue between the professional and the bureaucracy is the structure of authority. All organizations, in order to avoid anarchy and to assure action toward stated goals, have an explicit structure of authority and responsibility. In a bureaucracy, the right to command resides in the position

that one occupies in the administrative hierarchy and in the formalization of relationships. Each person is expected to be proficient in the assigned task and not to intrude into the work assignments of other people. For the professional, however, authority resides in competence, not in position. In addition, in social work the tasks are complicated, require judgment, cannot be concretely determined in advance, and are often unpredictable. These characteristics mean that the social work practitioner, at the lower ranks of the bureaucratic hierarchy, needs to retain greater authority. The authority of knowledge of the client resides at the lowest professional level. Also, the larger the agency, the more divided are the tasks, the greater is the number of professionals hired, and the more difficult it is not to intrude into other people's field of operations. Thus, the need for working cooperatively with others in ways that cannot be concretely defined adds to the resistance of social workers to bureaucratically organized structures.

Size and staffing patterns

The size and patterns of staffing affects the operation of bureaucratic organizations. The larger the organization, the more bureaucratic it may be. In smaller agencies, the informal organization found in every agency is likely to result in a bypassing of rules and procedures in ways that are common knowledge and have the tacit approval of everyone. Even in large agencies, there will be a certain amount of such "slippage," which arises in response to some of the problems of bureaucracies and may well be essential to the survival of the organization. The proportion of the agency's personnel who see themselves as professionals has a strong impact on the bureaucracy. The more central professionals are to achieving the agency's goals, the more influence they can exert on the goals and on the structures of service. As we have pointed out, to be professional is to act in certain ways that run counter to bureaucratic principles. The evaluation of service on the basis of results rather than procedures often enables competent professionals to operate with a relative degree of freedom. The agency accepts this freedom as the price it must pay for their work.

Auspices

Another very important factor affecting bureaucracy is the auspices of the agency. The life of the practitioner is often very different in the public agency than in the private agency. The public agency's policies and programs are framed in law, and the worker often operates under the surveillance of many community groups whose right to such judgment the worker resists strongly. It is perhaps to be expected that the public agency, with its larger size, greater number of nonprofessional employees, rigid operation under law, and insecurity because of constantly being judged by many different interests, usually has fewer MSW social workers among its employees than does the private agency. Yet the public agencies serve the most vulnerable populations, and social workers in public agencies confront the cruelest and most complex problems of modern life. However, not all professional social workers share the concern of the author over the withdrawal of social workers from the social service function of public welfare.

✒️ Agency specialization

Personal social services are delivered by an array of agencies. These agencies, or their supporting publics, have determined the limits of their functions in various ways. As we shall see in Part III of the text, many agencies were established because a particular person or a particular group of people became interested in groups of individuals who were suffering from particular problems. These agencies were developed principally to offer certain services to certain clients. Many social agencies are organized under particular sponsorships. For example, the Lutheran church may believe that Lutherans suffering particular problems can be better served within the parameters of their religion than in nondenominational settings, so it establishes an agency to help Lutherans who are suffering from marriage problems, parent-child problems, or other

problems. The Jews in the community do not see how the Jewish client can receive the best and most understanding service from the nondenominational or the Lutheran agency, so they establish a Jewish agency offering similar services to their own group. Agencies, especially those which are parts of other social systems, can also be developed around purposes such as health and corrections. In addition, agencies are often developed within specified geographic jurisdictions. In fact, most agencies and programs set certain limits to their geographic jurisdictions and boundaries of service. Finally, in large agencies, departments that offer different types of services may operate almost as separate agencies. Although the development of these various types of agencies has in many ways been a result of historical accidents, it has been furthered in modern society by the view that specialization offers greater efficiency of administration. The professional notion of the importance of skill development has also supported specialization in agency services. As we pointed out earlier, one way of organizing social work is by field of practice, which essentially means by program specialization.

Gaps in service

Although specialization may have advantages in making competent services available to clients, it may also pose significant problems that have a constant impact on the activities of the practitioner. Perhaps the first and most serious problem of specialization is the gaps in service that result. We once had the experience of working as a social worker in a police department. While there, we were involved in the case of two small brothers who had run away from home because of beatings by their parents. The parents were contrite, concerned, and interested in getting some help in dealing with the stress that seemed to be at the root of their outbursts. They were referred to the mental health clinic and went there for help. However, as their work with the practitioner proceeded, it appeared that they could probably profit by being relieved of the care of their children for a short period of time. The mental health clinic sent them back to the police for referral to a child-placing agency, as it did not refer clients for child placement. The public agency would not place the children without a court order, which the parents resisted. The local private child-placing agency accepted referrals only from established social agencies. It did not consider the police a social agency, so it would not accept a police referral. Another private agency was sympathetic, but it placed only children under six. A third agency placed only Catholic children. It took several weeks before we could arrange a conference with all of the agencies involved. And it took more time to persuade one of the agencies to accept the children for placement and to agree to work with the mental health clinic.

Many families may be denied services because their income is above that established as the top level for certain public services and because no private agency in the community offers the needed services. In many instances, the programs of a community are structured and specialized in ways that are irrelevant to the problems that its residents encounter in their lives. For agency workers, the roles of broker, mediator, and advocate in social work often involve spending much time in negotiating the wilderness of eligibility requirements of other agencies in behalf of clients who cannot find a service to fit their problem. Although specialization may further skills and the quality of service, it may result in the failure of clients to receive any service at all, or in great demands on the time and effort of workers (Wilensky and Lebeaux, 1965, p. 250).

Dividing the client

When troubled people already burdened by more than enough stress find it necessary to consult with several workers from several agencies, the struggle of these people to get and use help may make their problems worse. The time, effort, and planning that are involved in gaining access to several services, and the emotional toll of telling their problems to different persons drain clients of their ability to cope and certainly do not support the clients' strengths.

Moreover, there may be times when the efforts of different workers are directed to different and conflicting purposes. The worker who is seeing a depressed and lonely mother may urge her to go to work as a way of becoming more active and of raising her living standards. At the same time, however, the school social worker who is seeing her son at school because of his disruptive behavior may be urging her to give him more attention and may be pointing out that her going to work could deprive him of needed attention.

One would hope, of course, that the school social worker would recognize that the mother is depressed and would be concerned with her welfare as well as that of her son, and the school social worker might well want to confer with the mother's worker. But it doesn't always happen that way. We remember a client who was trying to puzzle out why she needed to go to see a worker at Catholic Social Services as well as the eligibility technician at the county welfare agency. She finally concluded that she really did need two workers: one to give her money and tell her how to spend it and the other to console her for the difficulty she had with the first worker. We recognize that the eligibility technician is not considered a social worker, but the client did not know or understand this technical point (Wilensky and Lebeaux, 1965, pp. 252–53).

Segregation and stigmatization

We are always concerned about the questions that specialization poses for justice and equality. On the same day we may encounter two clients who are deeply troubled because they see and hear things that are not real. One of these clients is a member of an affluent and caring family. The family makes immediate arrangements for her admission into a private institution for the disturbed and is able to pay the costs of care from medical insurance. The other client is a mother who is alone with small children and has no economic support other than welfare. She is committed to the public mental hospital, and her children are placed by a public agency. These two patients, suffering from similar problems, are segregated on the basis of their economic resources. And one of them will probably suffer from the stigma of having been committed to a public mental institution.

We have seen how the patterns of segregation by residence and the division of public education by geographic area have resulted in segregation in the schools. In the other social welfare institutions as well, segregation may be introduced by the geographic division of services. We are becoming more and more aware of how services specialized by age can isolate the elderly from the community or can result in services that are poorly financed because there are prejudices against certain age groups (Wilensky and Lebeaux, 1965, pp. 253–54).

The duplication of services

Almost from the time that income maintenance services first began to be administered outside the church, there has been concern about the duplication of social services. Fears of the duplication of services that might enable the client to receive help from more than one agency were the underlying motivation for the early concern with the organization and coordination of social services. Wasteful duplication undoubtedly exists in the programs that have been developed within communities. When the protection worker from child welfare services, the court worker, and the worker who deals with mentally retarded clients are all concerned about the same boy in a family, and all take the same kind of information from a family, and all are working with problems arising from the boy's mental retardation, there may indeed be wasteful effort and damage to the client.

However, sometimes what appears to be duplication of services may not be. Closing the neighborhood offices of the welfare agency because it is better to do all the work downtown, where central records can avoid duplication, may deprive some persons of service. Deciding that a small Chicano agency duplicates the services offered by a larger Anglo agency may deprive the Chicano population of services. Here, having two agencies is not duplication, although services of the agencies may appear to be much the same.

The need to know

We need to know much more than we do about the impact of different patterns of services on the consumers of the services before we can appropriately plan the structure of the personal social service programs. The present structure of these programs are, by and large, marked by a confusion of their goals and by a lack of data on which to plan. The present programs and their structures developed historically as a response to many forces. They are not always logical, and they present the social worker with both support and frustration.

The profession

What do we mean when we speak of social work as a profession? How do we distinguish professional occupations from nonprofessional ones? The literature dealing with occupations generally includes the following elements as important distinguishing marks of a profession:

1. A high degree of generalized and systematic knowledge.
2. Community sanction.
3. A primary orientation to community interest rather than individual self-interest.
4. A high degree of self-control of behavior through codes of ethics that are internalized through formal education, work socialization, and voluntary associations operated by the members of the profession.
5. A culture.
6. A system of monetary and honorary rewards that are primarily an acknowledgment of work achievement and thus ends in themselves, not means to the promotion of individual self-interest.

Although a profession involves practice—the doing of something with a high degree of skill—the chief difference between a professional and a nonprofessional occupation does not lie in the degree of skill required. The crucial distinction is that the skills of the professional are based on a fund of knowledge that has been organized into an internally consistent body of theory. This theory directs the differential application of skill based on the judgment of the professional. It is the quality of such judgment—the possession of knowledge and the capacity to organize that knowledge and to apply it differentially to individual situations—that marks off the professions from other occupations. Thus, not only is professional knowledge generalized and systematic, but it must be available for use in unique human situations. This is what we mean by judgment. Judgment is to be distinguished from intellectual capacity. It may be defined as "the ability to make the most effective choice among alternatives" (Compton and Galaway, 1979, p. 2). Certainly, professional judgment requires a high degree of generalized and systematic knowledge. However, it also requires the capacity to organize that knowledge for use and to apply it in unique human situations.

The search for knowledge

Because the amount of knowledge required by professionals is so great and because some of that knowledge is so uncertain, all professionals are constantly faced with the uncomfortable fact that they are called upon to interfere in people's lives in crucial ways on the basis of incomplete knowledge. This pushes professionals to constantly search for new knowledge. Thus, in the emergence of every profession we find researcher-theoreticians whose role is to seek knowledge and construct theory through the use of scientific inquiry. Social work has not given a less central place to such members of the profession than have other professions. Perhaps one reason is that the majority of social work practitioners are largely concerned with practical and emotional motives rather than intellectual drives. Two other important reasons may be (1) that social work has not as yet perfected a research methodology appropriate to the questions that social workers deal with and (2) that social work has not as yet agreed upon its goals and boundaries.

The power of professionals

The generalized and systematic knowledge possessed by professionals and their control over needed services give them a powerful control over persons and things. We have touched on this earlier. Social workers may exercise great control over services needed by their clients. Such control is often furthered because workers control the only service available. It is important to society that professional expertise be exercised for the welfare of the client and in the interests of the community and that it not be used to satisfy the needs of professionals or to enable professionals to advance at the expense of those they should serve. Thus, as protection to the client, the community usually has some organized way of sanctioning professionals. Such sanctioning is supported by the underlying professional value of community service rather than self-aggrandizement.

The sanctions of professional practice

In all professions the community sanctions the individual practitioner's right to operate through some combination of the following elements: (1) the completion of a certain prescribed course of education; (2) proving a certain level of competence through an examination process; (3) regulations of the practitioner through state licensing, registration, or certification; and (4) employment by an organization authorized by the state to offer certain services. Thus, we have the licensing of teachers and doctors and the registration of nurses. In some states, social workers are required to be licensed in order to offer certain services. However, not all states regulate the individual practitioner. Licensing has posed difficult problems for social work because the exclusive expertise of the profession has never been defined satisfactorily. The National Association of Social Workers has registered the title Certified Social Worker with the federal government. In order to use this title, social workers must possess an MSW (a master's degree in social work), must have worked two years in practice experience under supervision of an ACSW social worker, and must pass an examination. People who meet these requirements may call themselves Certified Social Workers and may use the letters ACSW (Academy of Certified Social Workers) after their names.

Professional associations

All professions are organized into some kind of professional association. These professional organizations serve three purposes: (1) to increase the adequacy of the individual practitioner's performance; (2) to police their ranks so as to ensure competent performance by the individual members; and (3) to protect the members' exclusive right to practice their profession. The professional social work association is the National Association of Social Workers (NASW), a national organization which operates through chapters in each state. NASW accepts for initial membership those persons who have a BA degree in social welfare or social work, though it is attempting to develop and accredit levels of practice.

The local chapters of NASW offer their members and the rest of the social work community opportunities to participate in ongoing learning experiences. The local chapters also often participate actively in state and local political efforts to effect legislation and policies relating to clients or to the well-being of the profession. At the national level, NASW is involved in similar activities. Various leaders and professional experts confer with committees of Congress and with the executive branch, including persons in authority at HEW. The national organization publishes a monthly periodical containing articles devoted to the advancement of social work practice and a newsletter that focuses on various professional matters. It also publishes monographs and pamphlets that are helpful to the individual practitioner.

The local chapters and the national organization have a procedure for sanctioning professional workers or agencies that violate professional standards. Recently a member of a local chapter was expelled from NASW and lost his ACSW because of findings that he had sexually exploited a client. The local chapter saw that this loss of professional membership was widely publicized, so that people would know that the man was no longer considered a capable practitioner. Through its national newsletter, NASW publicizes the agencies that have been sanctioned and urges professional workers not to seek employment with them. Many of the agency sanctions result from agency violations of the rights of social workers.

NASW also contributes financial aid to defend workers who have been fired for activity that was contrary to agency directives but in keeping with the ethical standards of the profession. For example, NASW helped support a court case involving an AFDC worker who refused to make night visits for the purpose of discovering whether mothers had men in their homes. It gave funds to help support another worker who took action against an agency when he was fired for refusing to alter the population of a research study.

In addition to such activities, NASW has a political arm that is financially separate because of tax law. It raises money to support candidates for public office who favor policies that are in agreement with the programs of NASW.

✍§ Professional workers in social welfare

The question of the relevant qualifications for employment in the social welfare field has been a perennial one. Initially social work services were provided by volunteers whose only qualification for practicing social work may have been the availability of time. At no time have all or even most of the jobs in social work been filled by workers with an MSW degree. In fact, in the public services most workers have had only a bachelor's degree, and many have had less. For years, professional social workers looked forward to the day when everyone filling a social work position would possess an MSW. This criterion had two important implications for social work as a profession.

The first is that the day when all social workers

would have an MSW never came. Long before that day arrived, significant developments changed the personnel picture in social welfare. Significant changes in policy and service delivery affected the work force requirements, and NASW therefore decided to admit the BA worker to membership in the profession. This development was followed by the setting up of professional undergraduate courses in social work and the implementation of a program of accreditation by the Council on Social Work Education, the organization that accredits professional social work programs in higher education. These matters will be discussed more fully later in the text.

The second important implication is that social work as an emergent profession never had complete control of who could call themselves social workers and who could do the social work job. In general, the social agencies effectively decided who could be social workers in that the persons they hired to fill social work positions were entitled to call themselves social workers. Thus, there have been wide variations in the education, knowledge, and skill of the people who called themselves social workers and were known to the public and clients as social workers. In general, the private agencies that have usually served the middle class have generally insisted on MSW degrees for employment and the public services have employed workers with a BA degree or less. NASW has developed a statement on the levels of social work practice and the professional qualifications for each level.

◆§ Levels of social work practice

Today, the National Association of Social Workers has identified six levels of social work practice. Two levels—*the social service aide* and *the social service technician*—require less than a college degree in social work. A third level, that of *social worker,* requires a bachelor's degree in social work.

A *Graduate Social Worker* needs a master's degree from an accredited professional school in social work. This usually requires two academic years beyond the BA though it may require less time for persons who have a BSW degree. A Certified

Social Worker must possess an MSW, must have had two years of carefully supervised practice beyond the degree, and must pass an ACSW examination. A *Social Work Fellow* must possess a PhD or a DSW in social work, must have had two years of specialized experience or must have passed the ACSW examination, and must then have two years or two further years of specialized practice. As we trace the development of the profession, we will see how these levels of practice developed and we will learn something about the people who work at these levels.

◆§ Social work, professional autonomy, and bureaucracy

It has long been held that the knowledge required to judge professional performance is available only to those who have themselves been trained in applying such knowledge. That is, the professional knowledge and skill of the professional person are so different from general knowledge and skill that no one outside the profession can judge the professional. This matter is usually discussed under the rubric of professional autonomy.

Thus, every profession has some means for the self-regulation of practice. These "shoulds" of professional practice are generally stated in a formal code of ethics. The social work code of ethics is reproduced later in this chapter. However, certain professionals may engage in unethical or incompetent behavior, and as the community becomes more and more dependent on professional knowledge, the community is increasingly demanding that the people served by the professional should have the right to judge the professional by the outcome of his or her service *as they perceive it.* The community is asking how it is possible for the operation to be a success if the patient dies. This stance may well emanate from unrealistic community perceptions of the capacity of professionals, but it may also evidence a realistic concern with the notion that clients do not have the capacity to know when they have been well served—that only professionals have the ability to judge the outcomes of their actions.

Another element in the concept of autonomy is that professionals are self-directing in their work. As used here, autonomy refers to the control that professionals exercise, through the professional organization, over the content and terms of their work. Clearly, however, autonomy is not a simple criterion of who are to be considered professionals—at least we have never been willing to designate wives and mothers who run their own households as professionals. This introduces the notion that anytime we speak of professional autonomy we are really talking about some kind of organized autonomy—not the autonomy of the individual practitioner. Professionals, even those who practice privately, are not free agents who can do as they please. If their sanction to practice is lodged in their membership in a profession, they are responsible for acting within the profession's practice repertoire.

Thus, the more that a profession as a profession is able to exercise autonomy, the more it represents, and the more its members are controlled by, a hierarchy of professionalized expertise (Friedson, 1979, pp. 71–92). It is possible that mechanistic and authoritarian attributes flow from professional control as well as from bureaucratic control. The health services are often seen as rigid and mechanistic, yet this comes as much from their professional control as from their bureaucratic structure. The notion of professional autonomy often does not refer to the individual practitioner but rather to the fact that a profession as an organized force has gained organized autonomy and is not bound by rules arising outside the profession (Rosengren and Lifton, 1970, pp. 71–92). For the individual practitioner, the dominance of client services by the principle of expertise which is embodied in a professionally ordered division of labor may be fully as problematic as the dominance of the bureaucratic principle. Actually this may present greater difficulties for the client in that a bureaucratic organization usually provides for appeal from bureaucratic decisions, but there is seldom an appeal from professional judgment's, as such judgments are assumed to be an exercise in scientific truth and expertise.

The bureaucratic model of organization and the shortage of professional social workers during most of the profession's history have had important implications for the autonomy of social work as a profession. When the persons recruited to fill professional positions are recruited to the practice of the profession quite independently of the profession's control, it is difficult, if not impossible, for the profession to achieve the control of the right to practice that is necessary to move toward greater professional autonomy.

The culture of a profession

Each profession has its own culture. The interactions of social and professional roles required by professional activities and professional groups generate particular ways of thinking and acting and a language unique to the profession. The value system of the profession in interaction with the value system of the bureaucracy is an important part of the culture of social work. A critical aspect of all professional education and in-service training is the attempt to socialize the workers to the agency and the profession. By this we generally mean the internalization of the values and the culture of the profession so that the professional person is constrained to work in certain ways and to take certain positions.

One of the problems in achieving greater autonomy for the social work profession lies in the fact that when agencies hire younger workers *who have less than the recognized professional training,* these workers lack a well-integrated identification with their profession that will allow them to withstand bureaucratic expectations. Instead, they tend to be socialized to the culture of the agency rather than the culture of the profession. They may see themselves as public welfare employees rather than as social workers. They cannot find employment as social workers elsewhere. They are tied to their positions in the agency rather than to their identification as professionals.

Sound internalization of professional values is critically important as protection to the client system, since in the helping process workers must use themselves and their judgment. There is seldom any way in which another can interfere in the social work process to protect the client in advance of the worker's action. Therefore, the only assurance we have that professionals can be entrusted with their professional tasks is that they can be depended on to act on the basis of deeply internalized feelings and judgments that stem from professional values and knowledge. This value system and the feelings and actions that stem from it become a part of the culture of the profession. The ambiguous position of social work within society in terms of its multiple functions and purposes also contributes greatly to shaping the culture of social work.

These concepts will be illustrated and examined as we trace the development of social work from its roots in the volunteerism of the early days of social welfare, through the period of time when it was more an occupation than a profession, to its present-day development.

✑ Social work values and ethics

All professions have value systems. We have already discussed the meaning and importance of people's values for institutions in society. Value preferences are equally important for professions. The values of a profession are the beliefs that it holds about people, the preferred goals for people, and the preferred instrumentalities for dealing with people. From the values they espouse, professions develop an ethical code—a statement of what ought to be done in professional practice because of the responsibilities that are assumed when one enters the life of another as a professional. Professional ethics are not intended to prescribe the personal qualities or moral standards of individuals; they are a statement of the obligations owed to others. What is expected of social workers in terms of a value stance and ethical behavior is expected of them, not because social workers are human beings, but because they are human beings who do social work.

A profession's values are not usually unique to the profession. They are found in the culture of the society. However, all societies have many di-

verse and conflicting values. Professions select from these values those that seem to support their professional practice. Professions achieve their uniqueness in the way they organize and operationalize values and in their codes of ethics. Thus, "it is not good conduct in universal terms that makes for ethical conduct in social work practice: it is behavior that is consonant with the requisites of the practice situation" (Levy, 1976, p. 45).

> . . . ethics deals with standards or expectations of behavior and action (or inaction) in relation to others and arises out of some definition of individual or collective responsibility to others or for others. This responsibility is based on the nature of this relationship to others.

A problem that confronts the social work practitioner is the conflict of the professional value system with the values of society and the values of the employing bureaucratic organization and the social welfare system as these are operationalized through programs. In addition, there are often conflicts among social work values themselves. The values of a profession are not always internally consistent. There may be problems in operationalizing values as we move from the abstract statement to concrete application to the individual situation. Agreement to the abstract principle of client self-determination is easy to secure. But we may have difficulty in applying this principle to work with a 15-year-old who "rips off" cars. The principle becomes even more problematic when the mother who has severely beaten a child insists that she has a right to take him home from the hospital.

In essence, the two critical moral issues that are the foundation for all values in social work relate to the belief in every person's right to freedom and well-being, which is stated as respect for the dignity and uniqueness of human beings and support of their right to self-determination in conjunction with the equal right of others. Actually, these two values interact in that if you do not accord people the right to make their own choices, you have deprived them of dignity and well-being.

However, acting on this principle is, as we said, more difficult than one might think. If it is essential for us to safeguard the rights of people to freedom and well-being, what do we do when, in practice, we encounter situations in which the acts of one individual harm another? The right of people to freedom of action carries the rather clear assumption that responsible individual decision making takes the well-being of others into consideration—that the responsible exercise of freedom is consonant with the well-being of the social group and with its needs for both stability and change. As social workers stand between society and the individual, they are constantly working with decisions made and actions taken that infringe on the rights of others. When the group deprives the individual of rights and needs, social workers generally recognize that we need to involve ourselves in an attempt to change the response of the group. Barring some clear-cut indication of danger to self or others, however, in their day-to-day contacts with individuals social workers will be concerned with maximizing opportunities for responsible individual self-determination. To believe in and support the right of individuals to make any choices they please, without responsibility to others for the results, is to support the notion that the race is always to the strong and uncaring—the irresponsible.

> Inherent in the concept of client self-determination is the idea of alternatives. Self-determination implies decisions, or the making of choices between one course of action as contrasted with other courses of action. It is fraudulent to think of self-determination without alternatives. If there is only one course of action, how can there be self-determination? The client has no choice and thus no opportunity for self-determining. Much of social work activity with clients consists of a quest for alternatives in order to expand the client's opportunities for self-determination. The quest for alternatives may take various forms—helping the client develop new alternatives and resources within the environment or helping the client find and develop new ways to respond to environmental demands. Thus, interventive activity may focus on removing blockages within the environment which are limiting clients' opportunities or helping clients remove blockages within themselves which limit their abilities to see alternative courses of action. People

> whose range of responses to their environment is limited by their own stereotyped and patterned behavior are as much lacking in opportunity for self-determination as the ghetto client confronted with a lack of environmental opportunities. (Compton and Galaway, 1979, p. 131)

> In most dealings with professionals in our culture the decision-making authority of the client is largely overshadowed by the expertise of the professional and, to a large extent, limited to the decision of whether or not to accept the professional's advice. But not so with the social work profession. The expertise of the social worker lies less in the substantive areas of knowing what is best for the client and more in the process area of assisting clients in developing alternatives for themselves, making a decision among the alternatives, and implementing the decision. (Compton and Galaway, 1979, p. 133)

Social workers are not in the business of forcing people to change behavior: that is a matter for the courts and the legal system. In the interest of protecting persons who cannot protect themselves, social workers sometimes ask the courts to intervene.

A summary of the recently revised social work code of ethics follows on page 138.

In his book on social work ethics, Charles Levy makes an important statement related to the code of ethics. He says:

> . . . a modicum of competence for social work practice of any kind must be assumed before ethical issues can be contended with. Without the basic ability to do the job that the social worker is engaged to do, the social worker can hardly exercise choice concerning the manner in which he [or she] will do it, whether to fulfill professional responsibility, or to avoid infringing on the rights of . . . clientele, or to effect some other moral consequence in the process. (1967, p. 17)

Social workers are expected to serve clients at the highest levels of competence of which they can become capable. Thus, social workers are ethically responsible not only for what they do but for what they might be reasonably expected to consider doing but for the fact that they do not know or do

Code of ethics,* National Association of Social Workers

Preamble

This code is intended to serve as a guide to the everyday conduct of members of the social work profession and as a basis for the adjudication of issues in ethics when the conduct of social workers is alleged to deviate from the standards expressed or implied in this code. It represents standards of ethical behavior for social workers in professional relationships with those served, with colleagues, with employers, with other individuals and professions, and with the community and society as a whole. It also embodies standards of ethical behavior governing individual conduct to the extent that such conduct is associated with an individual's status and identity as a social worker.

This code is based on the fundamental values of the social work profession that include the worth, dignity, and uniqueness of all persons as well as their rights and opportunities. It is also based on the nature of social work, which fosters conditions that promote these values.

In subscribing to and abiding by this code, the social worker is expected to view ethical responsibility in as inclusive a context as each situation demands and within which ethical judgement is required. The social worker is expected to take into consideration all the principles in this code that have a bearing upon any situation in which ethical judgement is to be exercised and professional intervention or conduct is planned. The course of action that the social worker chooses is expected to be consistent with the spirit as well as the letter of this code.

In itself, this code does not represent a set of rules that will prescribe all the behaviors of social workers in all the complexities of professional life. Rather, it offers general principles to guide conduct, and the judicious appraisal of conduct, in situations that have ethical implications. It provides the basis for making judgements about ethical actions before and after they occur. Frequently, the particular situation determines the ethical principles that apply and the manner of their application. In such cases, not only the particular ethical principles are taken into immediate consideration, but also the entire code and its spirit. Specific applications of ethical principles must be judged within the context in which they are being considered. Ethical behavior in a given situation must satisfy not only the judgement of the individual social worker, but also the judgement of an unbiased jury of professional peers.

This code should not be used as an instrument to deprive any social worker of the opportunity or freedom to practice with complete professional integrity; nor should any disciplinary action be taken on the basis of this code without maximum provision for safeguarding the rights of the social worker affected.

The ethical behavior of social workers results not from edict, but from a personal commitment of the individual. This code is offered to affirm the will and zeal of all social workers to be ethical and to act ethically in all that they do as social workers.

The following codified ethical principles should guide social workers in the various roles and relationships and at the various levels of responsibility in which they function professionally. These principles also serve as a basis for the adjudication by the National Association of Social Workers of issues in ethics.

In subscribing to this code, social workers are required to cooperate in its implementation and abide by any disciplinary rulings based on it. They should also take adequate measures to discourage, prevent, expose, and correct the unethical conduct of colleagues. Finally, social workers should be equally ready to defend and assist colleagues unjustly charged with unethical conduct.

Summary of Major Principles

I. THE SOCIAL WORKER'S CONDUCT AND COMPORTMENT AS A SOCIAL WORKER

    A. *Propriety.* The social worker should maintain high standards of personal conduct in the capacity or identity as social worker.
    B. *Competence and Professional Development.* The social worker should strive to become and remain proficient in professional practice and the performance of professional functions.
    C. *Service.* The social worker should regard as primary the service obligation of the social work profession.
    D. *Integrity.* The social worker should act in accordance with the highest standards of professional integrity.
    E. *Scholarship and Research.* The social worker engaged in study and research should be guided by the conventions of scholarly inquiry.

II. THE SOCIAL WORKER'S ETHICAL RESPONSIBILITY TO CLIENTS

    F. *Primacy of Clients' Interests.* The social worker's primary responsibility is to clients.
    G. *Rights and Prerogatives of Clients.* The social worker should make every effort to foster maximum self-determination on the part of clients.
    H. *Confidentiality and Privacy.* The social worker should respect the privacy of clients and hold in confidence all information obtained in the course of professional service.
    I. *Fees.* When setting fees, the social worker should ensure that they are fair, reasonable, considerate, and commensurate with the service performed and with due regard for the clients' ability to pay.

III. THE SOCIAL WORKER'S ETHICAL RESPONSIBILITY TO COLLEAGUES

    J. *Respect, Fairness, and Courtesy.* The social worker should treat colleagues with respect, courtesy, fairness, and good faith.
    K. *Dealing with Colleagues' Clients.* The social worker has the responsibility to relate to the clients of colleagues with full professional consideration.

IV. THE SOCIAL WORKER'S ETHICAL RESPONSIBILITY TO EMPLOYERS AND EMPLOYING ORGANIZATIONS

    L. *Commitments to Employing Organizations.* The social worker should adhere to commitments made to the employing organizations.

V. THE SOCIAL WORKER'S ETHICAL RESPONSIBILITY TO THE SOCIAL WORK PROFESSION

    M. *Maintaining the Integrity of the Profession.* The social worker should uphold and advance the values, ethics, knowledge, and mission of the profession.
    N. *Community Service.* The social worker should assist the profession in making social services available to the general public.
    O. *Development of Knowledge.* The social worker should take responsibility for identifying, developing, and fully utilizing knowledge for professional practice.

VI. THE SOCIAL WORKER'S ETHICAL RESPONSIBILITY TO SOCIETY

    P. *Promoting the General Welfare.* The social worker should promote the general welfare of society.

---

* Preamble and Summary of the NASW Code of Ethics, Revised Edition, approved by 1979 Delegate Assembly; from *NASW NEWS,* Vol. 25, No. 1 (January 1980), pp. 25–26. By permission of the National Association of Social Workers, Inc.

not take the initiative to discover what that is (Levy, 1976, p. 119).

It is important to remember that the ethics of social work demand accountability "for the foreseeable results of the social worker's actions." The social worker has the ethical responsibility "to provide the full measure of . . . expected competence." The social worker who is permitted to practice social work "has the ethical responsibility to be competent as well as to perform competently because [the clients have] been led to expect this" (Levy, 1976, p. 23). Individuals who come to social workers for help with the problems of living come on the assumption that social workers have been prescreened in terms of integrity, ethics, and competence, and thus are willing to give them access to the most meaningful parts of themselves which make them vulnerable to damage. Trust given in the absence of trustworthiness simply enables wrongdoers to increase the damage they do. Actually, the power of the professional person in the life of the client that we spoke of earlier is a function of trust. The power of the worker to develop alternatives for the client is a tremendous instrument for good, but it can also be used as an instrument against vulnerable people (Levy, 1976, pp. 66–67). This danger is especially great when it is more important for the worker that the situation be changed than it is for the client. There is a danger that social workers will evaluate themselves on the basis of their ability to change the client. Such a tendency spells disaster for the client. Unless clients are left free to fail, we have not really left them free.

Much more could be written about social work values and ethics. However, we will deal with only one other important ethical consideration—that of confidentiality. Levy (1976, p. 142) puts it well when he says that the obligation of social workers is to use the confidences of clients for them and not against them. He states that social workers should permit themselves to receive confidences from clients only when they "may be able to do something constructive with them—something consonant with . . . professional function and . . . professional responsibility to the client."

The responsibility for change

Professional workers in a bureaucracy need to recognize that a bureaucratic structure offers some advantages in the service of clients. It gives a form, a consistency, and a stability to work with clients. Workers could not do their jobs as well without these advantages. However, there are often problems in working in a bureaucracy. It is the responsibility of workers to decide how much they owe clients and how much they owe the agency. Where does their primary obligation lie at times of conflict? And workers need to feel some responsibility for changes in procedures that their best judgment tells them are unproductive either for the agency or the client. There are ways of operating within a bureaucracy that are more productive for the client and the worker than are other ways. Pruger (1973, pp. 26–32) has written about them, and Compton and Galaway have summarized his views as follows:

1. "One important property of a good bureaucrat is staying power." This means a recognition that things happen slowly in complex organizations but that whatever changes workers have in mind cannot be implemented if they do not stay in and with the organization.
2. "The good bureaucrat must somehow maintain a vitality of action and independence of thought." Organizational life tends to suppress vitality of action and independence of thought. Workers must resist such pressure.
3. "There is always room for insights and tactics that help the individuals preserve and enlarge the discretionary aspect of their activity and, by extension, their sense of personal responsibility."

And these are tactics the good bureaucrat will employ:

1. "Understand legitimate authority and organizational enforcement." The inescapable degree of generality found in the regulatory policies and codes of the organization allows for considerable autonomy of the individuals if they just recognize it and use it. The organization's

power to control is less than many realize, but if the limits of legitimate authority are recognized, the individuals may expand their discretionary limits.

2. "Conserve energy." Change agents should not thrash around and feel discouraged and unappreciated because they do not receive in a large organization the kind of support they receive from their friends. Also . . . master the paper flow of the organization. This will not only help the client but will also remove from the worker's shoulders the weight of resentment and emotional turmoil one feels as one looks at the uncompleted statistical forms on the desk. Workers should describe what can be changed and work on it rather than spend valuable hours bemoaning what cannot be dealt with.

3. "Acquire a competence needed by the organization."

4. "Don't yield unnecessarily to the requirements of administrative convenience. Keep in mind the difference between that which serves the organizational mission and that which serves the organization." Rules, standards, and directives as to the way things should be done are meant to be means that serve ends. In organizations means tend to become ends so that a worker may be more concerned about turning in the mileage report than the results of the visit to a client. Ends and means should be kept clear.

5. Workers should remember that "the good bureaucrat is not necessarily the most beloved one." (1979, p. 493)

✑§ Summary

"For good or ill, the practice of social work is linked with social agencies, just as . . . surgery is linked with hospitals and teachers with schools; they are, by definition, structurally and functionally connected" (Meyer, 1976, p. 100). The policies and the structures of the personal social services are themselves part of the cases and the problems being served. The individual delivery systems (agencies or divisions or departments) within the personal social services are organized as bureaucracies, as are most formal organizations in modern society. In addition, social work is organized as a

profession, and the stance of the organized profession has tremendous impact on the work of the individual practitioner. Thus, practice is shaped by bureaucratic and professional imperatives.

In this chapter we have introduced the reader to the organized profession of social work as a principal profession engaged in carrying out the activities of the personal social services within a bureaucratic structure. Because of the close interaction of social work and social welfare, it seems important to an understanding of either that we trace the development of the institution and the profession together. The purpose of the last two chapters was to develop enough understanding of social work as an organized profession to give the reader a base for understanding that development. It is important to remember that, although a profession is knowledge based, it should be viewed as the socially organized practice of knowledge by qualified persons who have an ideology and a commitment to the well-being of others.

✑§ A look ahead

We have now finished our brief overview of social welfare and social work, in which we tried to lay some base for understanding the phenomena that we shall examine throughout the remainder of the book. In the next chapter we shall begin to trace the development of social welfare and social work through a history of the development of personal social service programs.

✑§ Study questions

1. Go back to the case examples in Chapter 2. How many different agencies can you identify as being involved with the clients in those examples? What purposes were served by this division? Why do you think the services were divided in this way?

2. Write to NASW and secure material about social work practice that the organization has for people who are interested in careers in social work. What material can NASW offer you about the advantages of joining the professional association? Why does a professional organization distribute such material?

3. Find out whether social workers in your state are licensed. If they aren't licensed, what are their sanctions to practice?
4. List the advantages to clients of the fact that social services tend to be bureaucratically organized. List the disadvantages.

✺ Selected readings

Federico, R. *The Social Welfare Institution.* 2d ed. Lexington, Mass.: D. C. Heath, 1976. Pp. 87–108.

An excellent discussion of planning, structuring, and evaluating social welfare services. It makes a good expansion of this chapter.

Levy, C. Social Work Values and Planned Change. *Social Casework,* 54(10) (1972): 488–93.

An interesting article on values and their relationship to change.

Levy, C. *Social Work Ethics.* New York: Human Sciences Press, 1976.

This book is the best and most complete presentation of social work ethics. For readers interested in pursuing such questions beyond the material in this chapter, we would strongly recommend it.

Lewis, H. Morality and the Politics of Practice. *Social Casework,* 53(7) (1972): 404–17.

This article develops some principles that the author sees as critical to effective social work practice. It is an excellent one for class discussion, although it is not easy reading.

Meyer, C. H. *Social Work Practice: The Changing Landscape.* 2d ed. New York: Free Press, 1976.

We are listing this book here, although it may involve more than can easily be discussed in class and it is beyond the knowledge of many readers of our text. It might be well to use the book as a summary of issues of social work practice at the end of the quarter or semester. However, if there is time, part 2 should contribute a good deal to the student's considerations of the material in our last two chapters.

Morgan, B. Four Pennies to My Name: What It's Like on Welfare. *Public Welfare,* 37(2) (1979): 13–22.

This is strongly recommended as reading to accompany this chapter. It should help students to gain an understanding of the impact of bureaucratic structure on the client.

Pruger, R. The Good Bureaucrat. *Social Work,* 18(4) (1973): 26–32.

An excellent discussion of the principles of professional practice within a bureaucracy.

Wilensky, H. L., and Lebeaux, C. N. *Industrial Society and Social Welfare.* New York: Free Press, 1965.

Part 3 of Wilensky and Lebeaux makes a very fundamental presentation of the issues of bureaucracy and the profession and their impact on practice. We would strongly recommend that this reading accompany this chapter. Some of the differences between our presentation and that of Wilensky and Lebeaux should stimulate class discussion.

The development of social work and the social welfare institution

The "Tichborne Dole" is distributed at Tichborne Manor in Hampshire, England.
Many such privately-endowed philanthropies survive in England to this day—
but as historically interesting ceremonies, rather than pious charitable efforts.

Chapter 9 ᤟

᤟ Foundations of American social welfare ᤟

᤟ Introduction

With this chapter we begin tracing the historical development of social work and social welfare in the United States because we believe that one does not truly understand a social institution without knowing something of its roots. It is in England, during the century before the British began to colonize America and during the two centuries after their first American settlements were established, that we find the roots of our modern social welfare policies. In this chapter we are going to examine the forces of that time in England and to briefly discuss the shape of the early social welfare institution that developed in Britain. In Part I of the text we discussed the forces of change that move to reshape the social institutions of society. We also defined social welfare as an interstitial institution that functions between the other institutions of society and serves both the social institutions and the individual. We see this so clearly at the beginning. The roots of the institution of social welfare lie in the changing social conditions and ideologies of the 16th century, when the established social institutions no longer provided sufficient or satisfactory answers to the need of growing numbers of individuals for economic security. In this chapter we will discuss these roots of our modern social welfare program, their shape, and the forces that led to their development.

In about the 13th century, significant changes occurred in the shape and functions of the social institutions of England and continental Europe. At that time the growth of knowledge and technology allowed European nations to produce the great sailing ships necessary for exploration and trade. The mercantile period of history began. This led in turn to the growth of knowledge and technology—supported by the demands of a growing international commerce in manufactured goods—that resulted in the industrial revolution. This growth of knowledge, technology, and international trade was to result in significant changes in the economic system of medieval society. But the economic system did not change in isolation. The political institution was also changing. Between the kings and their nobles and the people, a group with growing political power was beginning to develop—the industrialists and entrepreneurs. The strength of the national government was growing.

At the same time we find stirrings in the organized church of the day. Such persons as Luther and Calvin found support for their teachings of new spiritual doctrines. Thus the monolithic Catholic church of medieval times, whose rulings had had the force of law in society, began to lose control as the uncontested religious force. The Reformation came as a second powerful religious force that, in changing the religious institution of society, joined with the industrial revolution to change society itself. Faced with a rapidly changing economic, political, and religious order, the family began to change too, as it was no longer the center of the paid work of its members. Given the interaction of these various forces, coupled with certain unforeseen happenings, the societal institutions of the day were no longer able to meet the needs of the people. They began to fail in their patterns of functioning. Some new patterns, new organized ways of meeting certain human problems, had to be developed if an organized society was to continue.

✌§ Status and contract in human relationships[1]

Up to the 12th century there were two primary forces in England—the church and a feudal economic and political society. Under the economic and political system of the time, strongly supported by biblical teachings, church law, and family structure, there existed a certain concept of the community and the common good. Rulers were expected to be concerned with the general welfare. The poor were largely serfs, bound to the soil but having the right of subsistence from their labor on it. In medieval thought, both social and religious law

held that a person's responsibility was first to family, next to neighbors, and finally to strangers. A great deal of emphasis was placed on hospitality for the stranger. While religious motivation was unquestionably paramount in the relief of destitution, strong social pressure to contribute to others was exerted on those who possessed more than enough for their own needs. One of the foundations of medieval society was the notion that each person was born to a particular station in life and that a person's station, acquired by the accident of birth, gave each person certain rights as well as responsibilities. The right to economic support was one of these.

However, given certain economic developments of the mercantile period, landowners began to find it more advantageous to rent out their land and live off the income than to assume the obligations of lifetime responsibility to serfs in return for sharing in the productivity of the serfs' labors. The development of a money economy came as people began to pay for goods and services in money rather than through an exchange of contributions. At no stage in medieval England were the lower classes considered full members of society with political rights comparable to those of other classes; however, the medieval upper classes believed that the purpose of their political and economic position was to enable them to serve as stewards for their people, both their own extended families and their serfs. Because of this belief and because of the economic base of medieval life, little stress was placed on the shortcomings of laborers. People were born to a particular place in society, and they were not evaluated on the efficiency or effectiveness of their labor.

With the coming of a money economy, society in England started to evolve a completely new concept of relationships, a concept based on the relationships of individuals. There came a change from a status to a contract society. Status refers to relationships that are essentially determined by informal, ascribed membership in the group, family, community, society, or any particular institution or association, with place, role, status, security, and opportunity being determined by the accident of birth. Contract refers to "a formal system of rela-

---

[1] The conceptual development of the following notion rests on Samuel Mencher, *Poor Law to Poverty Program* (Pittsburgh: University of Pittsburgh Press, 1967), pp. xv–xix.

tionships specifically and purposefully entered into, with rights and responsibilities determined by their willful acceptance" (Mencher, 1967, p. xvii).

As feudal society was displaced by a mercantile society and later by an industrial society, the development of an open economy became vitally important. Maintaining the right of the lower classes to depend on previous guarantees of support from the manor or the religious communities would have seriously hindered, if not prevented, the changes that were occurring in the economic system. The new industrial and trade leaders wished to free themselves of the traditional patterns of class interdependence. The church found itself torn by the coming of the Reformation, whose religious values also supported individual effort, and in any case the church alone, just as one of the institutions in society, could not have taken on the responsibility for alleviating all of the destitution that existed.

So we find the development of the concept of contractual relationships among people. Each party to a contract knowingly assumes the obligations of the contract, and the obligations of each party toward the other party are limited by the parameters of the contract. The notion of contractual rights in human relationships has continued to grow. Today this concept tends to involve all of our interrelationships with others. When it first developed, however, this view of an individual's relationship to the economic system was supported by and operated to the benefit of the political and economic leaders. The contractual concept, together with the values of individualism, work as a service to God, and the notion of economic independence, prepared the way for the development of modern society and made necessary the establishment of the new societal institution of social welfare.

⌐§ The concept of economic independence

Our modern culture in the United States attaches a great deal of value to the importance of independence and is severely critical of dependence. As Gaylin points out in *Doing Good* (1978, pp. 4–5), dependence is "an ambiguous word with multiple meanings." It is used to refer to "an actual

state of being, whether physical or psychological; to an attitude and a self-evaluation; to a method of coping and adapting; to a description of relationship among people; to a mode of living, whether economic, sociological, or psychological; and more."

In our modern American society, we have mixed the concept of an economic mode of living with the notion of a psychological state and a method of coping and adaptation. Thus, in much literature and in popular writing, dependence relates strictly to the individual's attachment to some source of money income generated in the marketplace. A woman who remains in the home caring for children, husband, and home is considered independent so long as her husband has a source of income from work, pensions, or investments. But let her be without financial support from the efforts of her husband, and she is considered dependent unless she quickly finds her own paid job, although her methods of coping with parental demands may continue at a high level without the support she previously obtained from her husband.

The development of the modern money economy has its roots in the breakdown of the feudal system and the beginning of mercantilism. And with the coming of the money economy, we see the beginning of the relationship between the concept of independence and money, secured not through any evaluation of one's overall contribution to society, but through specified kinds of activities that can be exchanged for money in the marketplace. Somehow the emotional, social, and psychological independence of the individual gets lost in this popular use of the concept. We fail to recognize that in our affluent society based on earned income, individuals are far from independent in their economic life. Actually, one concern that bears most heavily on people in today's society is their helplessness as independent economic individuals if for one reason or another earned income ceases.

Dependence and a money economy

When we turn to the resident of any large metropolitan area of the United States, we find ease of material life coupled with extreme economic dependence on others. The overwhelming majority of Americans have never grown food, caught game, raised meat, ground grain into flour, or even made flour into bread. Faced with the challenge of feeding or clothing themselves or building their own homes, they would be hopelessly untrained and unprepared. Many Americans, dependent on insulin, pacemakers, or other medical technology for life itself, could not exist without the trained assistance of others. Yet there are many people in the world who can sustain life by themselves in a hostile environment, for example, the Eskimo in Alaska. As members of a small self-sufficient community, they have existed through time. Paradoxically, perhaps the richer the nation, the more unable is its average inhabitant to survive alone and unaided.

There is, of course, a reason for this paradox. We survive in a rich nation because the tasks we cannot do for ourselves are done for us by an army of others on whom we call for help. This call for help is generally expressed through the use of money. We live in a money economy in which, given a certain level of the functioning of the economic institution and given, on our part, a certain degree of intelligence, health, status and social acceptance, family support and social place, and luck, we will develop skills and knowledges that can be exchanged for the skills, knowledges, and resources provided by others. No one of us can justifiably claim that by our individual effort or wisdom we, individually and personally, determined the level of economic functioning, our intelligence, our family, our status and social acceptance, or many of our accidents or illnesses.

In a money economy, if we cannot grow food, we buy it; if we cannot provide for our needs ourselves, we can hire the services of persons who can. The enormous division of labor enhances our capacity a thousandfold, for it enables us to benefit from other people's skills as well as our own.

Along with this inevitable gain, however, comes a certain risk:

> 214,000 persons provide all our coal.
> 177,000 persons operate our railroads.
> 83,000 persons fly our airplanes.

Thus, with the abundance of material existence we experience a hidden vulnerability. Our abundance is assured only insofar as our natural resources are effectively husbanded and as the organized cooperation of huge armies of people is to be counted on. Indeed, our continuing existence as a rich nation hinges on the tacit precondition that the mechanism of social organization will continue to function effectively. We are rich, *not as individuals,* but as members of a rich society, and our easy assumption of material sufficiency is actually only as reliable as the bonds that forge us into a social whole. Many bonds support the necessary human integration, and some of these bonds are found in the economic system as well as in the primary systems of family and church. One such bond that unites family, church, and economic system is the value and meaning of work in any society. We will examine this changing value in the next paragraphs.

Work

In early human groups, work typically consisted of a set of activities prescribed by heredity as a part of a particular status position in the community. Asking people in such preindustrial societies why they worked would have been similar to asking them why they stayed alive.

This is not true of individuals today. To ask them what they seek from work is to ask a reasonable question; work means more to them than mere survival or the maintaining of tradition. Indeed, one of the most distinctive characteristics of contemporary urban people is the conscious expectation of deriving meaning from work. Thus, although work has become increasingly segregated from other realms of social life, more people than ever before consciously expect to derive meaning from it (Morse and Wiese, 1962, pp. 29–34). In earlier eras, family, community, and religious activities were expected to give meaning to work; today we expect work to give meaning to other areas of life. The difficulty—perhaps impossibly—of achieving this in an industrial society may underlie the personal and social alienation that exists today. There are many people who work only for economic gain and eagerly look forward to early retirement, only to realize too late the integration that work provided for their lives.

Work changes its meaning with changes in the social order. Industrial society depends on disciplined work and effort and on standardized and interchangeable skills. With the Reformation and the rise of trade and industry there came an emphasis on the value and productivity of labor that represented a radical departure from the attitudes of earlier societies. The mounting attention to efficient work began to be of concern as it became reflected in all the institutions of society. This new attitude toward work was perhaps the most significant psychological change to have occurred since the advent of the Middle Ages and the rise of the feudal states (Mencher, 1967, pp. 6–10).

What is work?

But what is work? The first definition in the *American Heritage Dictionary* (1973, p. 1474) describes it as "physical or mental effort or activity directed toward the production or accomplishment of something; toil, labor." This definition does not attach work to earned income. However, the dictionary's third definition directly relates work to income, stating that work is "the means by which one earns one's livelihood; a trade, craft, business, or profession." This is the generally accepted meaning of work in many of the discussions of social welfare policy. Like the current notion of independence, this definition does violence to the contributions of women in our society. Women who direct their activities toward maintaining a home and socializing their children and women who do much community work outside the home find themselves classified as nonworkers because their work is not directly related to earned income but is focused on freeing their husbands and other men to earn income. In computing the gross national product of the nation, the work of women in the home is not taken into consideration, and it is sometimes questioned whether women seeking work outside the home should be considered in

unemployment statistics, since it is assumed that they could always stay home. But let us look at the development of the meaning of work in the Judeo-Christian societies, recognizing that other societies attach a different meaning to it.

Work in history

The early Hebrews thought of work as a hard necessity. They accepted work as a penalty, an expiation, through which human beings might atone for the sins of their ancestors and reconquer their own lost spiritual dignity. However, both intellectual and manual work took on worth and meaning for them; to work was to cooperate with God in the great task of the world's salvation.

Early Christianity followed the Jewish tradition in regarding work as a punishment laid on humanity by God because of the original sin. But the early Christian teachings added a new value to work. To work was to be able to support oneself, so that one needed to ask alms of no one, but above all, the goods bestowed by successful effort were to be shared with the less fortunate in the Christian community. Riches shared with the poor would bring God's blessing on the giver. In addition, the early Christian community began to view work as necessary to the health of the body and the soul, which without work would become bogged in idleness and fall prey to evil thoughts and habits. It became the duty of Christian brotherhood to give work to the unemployed so that no person needed to remain in idleness. But if a member of the community refused to work, that person was to be expelled from the community. This may well have been a hard economic necessity for the small, poverty-stricken groups of Christians who needed everyone's production in order to survive.

Early Catholicism added something to the dignity of work in that descendants of the wealthy entered monasteries to take on voluntarily the burden of unrewarded work. Work became an instrument of purification, of charity, of expiation. However, from the 11th to the 14th centuries, certain Catholic groups preached the importance of work, not because work was good but because they believed it to be painful, humiliating, a scourge for the pride of the flesh. Poverty was an exalted state (Tilgher, 1962, pp. 11–23).

St. Thomas Aquinas drew up a hierarchy of the professions and trades according to their value to society. From his time through our own, we find the concept of work as a natural right and duty, the sole legitimate base of society, and the sole legitimate foundation of property and profit. For St. Thomas, work becomes an obligation only insofar as it is necessary to maintain the individual and the community. That end lacking, people do not need to work. It is much better for them to pray and contemplate. Thus, high above material work stands contemplation, which takes the spirit into the divine order of things and enables the soul to perceive the purpose of God. Essentially the hierarchy drawn up by St. Thomas followed the social structure of the time and solidified the class divisions of his age.

In the 19th century, certain Christian socialist groups proclaimed labor as the foundation of all human progress; they saw work as a duty imposed by both divine and human laws. Their notions challenged limits that had been set by St. Thomas by holding that within the maximum and minimum set by society, individuals were able to be absolute masters of the rewards of their labor. In affirming that the true source of human prosperity was work, their position harshly condemned the modern capitalism that was developing at the time. They held as sinful the economic system in which money of itself created profits without personal work and of itself automatically and endlessly increased.

The spiritual meaning of work

The Protestant Reformation of the early 16th century and the teachings of Luther (1483–1546) pulled together and sharpened many of the older notions of work as one's duty before God. Work is seen as natural, the base and key of life, the remedy of the fallen, with both a penal and an educational character. Work is a form of serving God. If activity of all kinds is divided, there is no basis for making distinctions between the service of God and one's everyday work, whatever its nature.

From these premises, Luther drew the following conclusions: all who can work, should work; idleness, beggary, and lending money at interest are unnatural and evil; charity should be bestowed only on those who cannot work; the contemplative life is the result of egotism and lack of human affection on the part of monks who enter the cloister to evade their duties to their neighbors. A further important premise of Luther was that people were saved by their faith alone and that there was no spiritual value in good works or charity to others. These notions served to free the developing economic system to go its own way and set up its own laws, free of the authority of the church and the existing religious institutions (Tilgher, 1962, pp. 11–23).

The development of Calvinism (Calvin lived from 1509 to 1564) gave work an added religious value. All persons, even the rich, must work because work is the will of God. But they must not lust after the fruits of their labor. The only worthy use for profit is to finance fresh economic ventures so as to breed new profits that can again be invested to provide further work opportunities, and on to the end of time.

These statements of values from the religious movements of the time combined with changes in the economic system and in the structure of the family and the group to produce a time of crisis and change for society. It was not the new value concepts alone or the development of trade and industry alone that brought this about. Modern society and the modern personality were forged by the combination of these two forces, together with such unforeseen events as the plague and such events in the political system as the imposition of social order by the Tudors and Henry VIII's efforts to obtain spiritual approval for his marital adventures.

The new individual, shaped by this cluster of events and the interaction of these forces, was to be strong-willed, active, austere, hardworking from religious conviction, and individualistic. Idleness, luxury, and anything that might soften the soul was to be shunned as a deadly sin. Inactive contemplation was rejected, as people cannot influence their salvation by taking thought; only work suffices, and, to please God, it must not be casual. It must be methodical, disciplined, rational, uniform, and specialized. Calvinism thus developed as a value system that served to support the discipline of the modern factory founded on the division of labor. In this movement we also see the growth of the distrust of the intellectual, the thinker, in our society, though two other factors have contributed to this: (1) the Catholic hierarchy of the Reformation era, whose members held themselves out as intellectuals, was found to be corrupt and power hungry; and (2) it is the efforts of the thinkers in society that push us toward the changes that we so often resist.

Puritanism, which developed out of Calvinism, goes still further and teaches that it is one's duty to extract the greatest possible gain from labor, not for love of money or to satisfy a thirst for pleasure, but so that more blessings will fall on one's head. Moreover, success is to be proved by profit, and profit is a certain indication that the chosen work is pleasing to God. The greater the profit, the greater is the certainty that one is serving God with one's work. This opens all work to the possibility of great wealth if the effort pleases God. For the first time in history, wealth is reconciled with a good conscience. To be poor becomes a disservice to God as well as to one's neighbors. It is no virtue to remain satisfied with the class or profession to which one is born, but on the contrary, one should seek out the profession that will bring the greatest return.

Deny the world, but live in it, work in it, succeed in making yourself wealthy in order that the earth may reflect the majesty of God. Such is the command of Calvin. Along with the economic, political, and social changes of the 16th and 17th centuries, this command became the foundation of the modern industrial age and shaped much of the policies of the emerging social welfare institution.

Work in today's society

However, with the passing of the years and the growth of the modern economic system, work has lost more and more of its connections with religious values until it stands today almost as a religion of its own. We can hardly say that our present attitude toward work represents the Protestant ethic. Today's value of work for work's sake rather than for the glory of God is a radical departure from, though it may be an outgrowth of, the ethics of the Reformation.

Studies of modern employed persons indicate that for most people having a job serves other functions than earning a living. In fact, even if they had enough money to support themselves, individuals would still want to work. It would appear that in modern times the economic system has taken on certain functions of the family and religious systems in relation to integration, mutual support, socialization, and social control. Working gives today's individual a feeling of being tied into the larger society, of having something to do that matters, of having a purpose in life quite apart from its value as a service to God.

The primary reason for working at a particular job may be money, but that is far from the only reason. For the middle-class person, life without working would be less purposeful, stimulating, and challenging. For many working-class persons, the job concerns activity, so that life without working becomes life without anything to do (Morse and Wiese, 1962, pp. 29–34).

In recent times, certain psychological knowledge has also supported the notion of the importance of work. Asked to define the hallmarks of a well-functioning personality, Freud said that these were the ability "to love and to work." Many personality theorists take the position that all of us need commitment to something beyond ourselves and that this may, in part, be represented by work (Erikson, 1959, p. 127).

And there are those who believe that out of the present-day functioning of the economic system a new value system is beginning to develop, a value system of large buying and amusements, of comfort, of well-being, of convenience, of cleanliness, a religion of the body.

> If this is really true and if this condition lasts and becomes more marked, then the foundations of contemporary civilization have begun to crack. Nor may it be said that this slackening of the will-to-work does not affect the elite who direct affairs—the only persons of real significance in the matter, since the joy of creative work is their monopoly. (Tilgher, 1962, p. 23)

Tilgher also points out that the big industrial systems in our society have a need to create the demand which merchandise is to satisfy, "to create conditions favorable for the ever greater supply of goods which it is continually producing." That need supports installment buying, high wages, short workdays, and all kinds of incitements to spend and enjoy and especially to waste. In other words, Tilgher suggests that a shift is beginning to take

place from an ethic of work to an ethic of leisure and self-indulgence.

It may be that our recent awakening to the problems of resource limitation and our growing knowledge of the importance of an environmental balance to the existence of humanity on this earth will move us to new value systems. But today we are in the midst of a growing questioning of our economic system and our view of work. Over the years, social workers involved with policies of income maintenance, economic security, and work force development have called attention to the adverse effects, on individuals and our society, of viewing people as without value (regardless of the work they do or its contribution to society) if they do not earn a paycheck. The effect of this view on women who may be nonearners, and, thus, whose work and whose very existence may be held as being without value, is only beginning to be understood. And its effect on men, particularly minority men for whom the economic system does not provide a job, has been to blame them personally, as individuals, for a failure in the social system. But we shall see how the values and notions regarding work become operationalized through the policies of the social welfare institution. As we move on, other concepts and values will be identified and discussed, but for now it seemed important to concentrate on the concept of contractual relationships and the values of work and economic independence, since these matters were so basic to the shaping of the initial programs of social welfare.

✑ The control of labor in changing economic institutions

Political and economic regulation of labor

If one is seeking a starting point for the study of modern social welfare, one should perhaps begin a little over 625 years ago, with the establishment of the first Statute of Laborers. It begins the concern of the government (the political system) with the problems of social welfare in modern times. The Statute of Laborers (1349) was not so much an effort of the government to aid the poor as an attempt to support and help English landowners by assuring them of an adequate supply of agricultural workers at a price they could afford (de Schweinitz, 1943, p. 1). Thus, the objective of the first governmental effort in modern social welfare was to aid the producers of agricultural products.

The Statute of Laborers read in part:

> That every man and woman of our realm of England, of what condition he be, free or bond, able in body, and within the age of threescore years, not living in merchandise, . . . nor having of his own whereof he may live, . . . nor proper land . . . , and not serving any other . . . he shall be bounden to him which so shall him require; and take only the wages, livery, meed, or salary, which were accustomed to be given in the places where he oweth to serve. . . . And if any such man or woman, being so required to serve, will not the same do, . . . he shall anon be taken . . . and committed to the next gaol, there to remain under strait keeping, till he find surety to serve in the form aforesaid.
>
> Because that many valiant beggars, as long as they may live of begging, do refuse to labor, giving

themselves to idleness and vice, and sometime to theft and other abominations; none upon the said pain of imprisonment, shall under the color of pity or alms, give anything to such, which may labor, or presume to favor them towards their desires, so that thereby they may be compelled to labor for their necessary living (de Schweinitz, 1943, pp. 1–6)

In that time of change and emergence from feudalism, perhaps the best way for an individual to indicate freedom and ownership of self was to travel. Many individuals chose to leave the land and wander. There were several things that supported this declaration of independence. There was the example of the mendicant friars who went about from village to village begging their daily bread. They were evidence that one could live by begging, together with whatever sustenance one could find in forest and moor. Workers also migrated from one part of the country to another to gather in the ripening crops. The wars in France offered further opportunity for freedom. Men who followed their lord or king to war often did not return to the land. Then as now the city was an attraction that drew many.

Vagrancy and population movement

The movement to the city was accelerated by the introduction of the sheep raising and of the manufacture of wool. The enclosure of state, church, and manorial lands in order to accommodate grazing sheep pushed many off the land. England's population doubled. A commerce between nations began to develop. In the cities there was a growing demand for craftsmen. Prices for agricultural products began to soar, and land became more valuable. The lord of the manor began to permit his serfs to pay rent instead of giving service. He could then use the money to hire the best workers. The rest could be set adrift. He could also turn to raising sheep, which required less labor than did the cultivation of crops. This evolution from a status to a contract society; the growth of a money economy, with its elements of credit, interest, rents, and wages; with the movement of a peo-

ple from serfdom to freedom, often through wandering, marked the period as one of extreme stress. All that was needed to turn these elements of change into a social crisis was a national calamity (de Schweinitz, 1943, pp. 1–30).

From 1315 to 1321 there was famine in England serious enough to reduce the number of laborers significantly. There was a steep rise in wages. Then in August, 1348, the bubonic plague broke out. In a year over one third of the population was dead. The plague was to stay in the country for 300 years, coming in cycles. The population fell by over a million between 1348 and 1377. The result was a reduction in the supply of labor, so that the surviving workers were able to ask what wages they wanted, work when they liked, and observe what holidays they pleased. The need of the landed proprietors for labor was not relieved by the first Statute of Laborers. No one law could really stem the tide of social, religious, and economic change. A second, more punitive statute was enacted (de Schweinitz, 1943, pp. 1–30).

The central notions of the first two Statutes of Laborers were that begging, movement, vagrancy, and the labor shortage were essentially the same problem and were to be dealt with through one law. Thus, begging was not a problem in destitution but a threat to the labor supply. The king and his nobles attempted to solve this problem by fixing a maximum wage, by forcing any unattached person to work for anyone who needed labor, by forbidding alms, and by limiting the right of workers to movement. Although legislation could not stop change, it could influence its direction. In these statutes we find the seeds of the attitude that poverty is a crime, at least for the able-bodied male. The problem of poverty became linked with vagrancy.

The classification of beggars

In 1388 Parliament again tried to deal with the labor shortage by enacting a law that attempted in more specific language to restrict the movement of people. It required that no individual should leave the place of residence unless

he bring a letter patent containing the cause of
his going, and the time of his return, . . . without
such a letter, . . . he shall be . . . put in stocks,
and kept until he hath found surety to return to
his service, or to serve or labor in the town from
whence he came. (de Schweinitz, 1943, p. 11)

Under this law, beggars, the transient, and those
seeking higher wages were all treated the same,
with one exception. The law recognized that there
were beggars who were unable to work. Such "beggars impotent to serve" were to abide in their place
of residence, but they could also continue to beg
and they were not required to work. Thus, for the
first time in modern legislation we see a recognition
that the unemployable person may need different
consideration than the able-bodied. This statute
also approved begging as a way of supporting such
persons (de Schweinitz, 1943, p. 8).

It was more than 100 years later that laws began
to recognize a difference in psychic or social needs
among those who sought to support themselves
by begging. Under Henry VII, over a period of
ten years, laws were passed that provided for special consideration for "women great with child,
and men and women in extreme sickness," as well
as "persons being impotent and above the age of
sixty years" (de Schweinitz, 1943, p. 8). Thus began an attempt to classify the poor and to define
unemployable persons as well as to sanction a
mechanism by which the latter might gain relief
from destitution. But life did not get easier for the
people of England. A different way of life was beginning. True, there were crop failures and plagues,
problems that have troubled people since their existence on this earth, and there were the dislocations in agriculture caused by sheep raising and
enclosure. But there was also a beginning of reliance on world trade that meant England was no
longer a self-contained country and that its laborers
were affected by events in the outside world. With
the beginning of the factory system, industry began
to assemble masses of workers with special skills
in the urban centers. These workers and their families were subject to cyclical and seasonal unemployment. There was something very different
about the problems of unemployment. The serfs

had died in their huts when famine struck and there
was no food, but now the problem was not that
food was unavailable but that one might be unable
to find the work with which one earned the money
to purchase the available food. The problem had
become that human beings were caught in the society of their own making rather than that they had
failed in the struggle against nature (de Schweinitz,
1943, pp. 8–12). In an attempt as futile as earlier
attempts to regulate the movement of individuals,
Henry VII proposed limiting the number of sheep
that one person could own. He saw this as a way
to stop enclosure and promote agriculture.

Perhaps one reason that people were slow to
move toward some relief for the destitute was that
the rapid social change left them with no stable
place from which to view the desolation of others;
but more important may have been the notion that
ample resources were available if people would
only avail themselves of them. This should sound
very familiar to the reader of today because it is
still often advanced as a reason for not instituting
new social welfare measures.

≈§ Responsibility for the relief of the poor

In addition to begging, which has been discussed
above, people could seek relief from destitution
through three other avenues: (1) the ancient institution of the guilds, cooperative, self-help brother-
hoods that, while basically set up to aid their own
members, did seek to aid the town poor in intermittent ways; (2) facilities established through private
foundations of various kinds (at the time of the
Reformation there were at least 460 charitable
foundations in England; and, far more important
than the other two avenues, (3) the aid provided
by the church.

The church

The teaching of the saints of the church gave
a kind of dignity to poverty, in that they saw parting
with one's material possessions and abandoning
one's concern about such things as steps toward

salvation. The giving of alms to those in need was also presented as a way of achieving spiritual grace.

> . . . I give no alms to satisfy the hunger of my brother, but to fulfill and accomplish the will and the command of my God; I draw not my purse for his sake that demands it, but his that enjoined it. (Browne, 1672, as quoted in de Schweinitz, 1943, p. 48)

The heart of the system of church relief was not the monasteries but the local, largely rural parishes which relied on tithing to secure funds that were divided one third for the maintenance of the church, one third to support its clergy, and one third to support the destitute.[2] No social institution is complete, and in feudal England the church filled in gaps in security that had been left by the system of serfdom. The existence of these voluntary patterns of relief for the destitute meant that the government was free to take the punitive stance that it did over the first 300 years of beginning industrialism.

From the perspective of the 20th century and a political culture in which separation of church and state is enjoined, it is probably difficult to recognize the importance of the state church of the Middle Ages. In effect, the church was an arm of government and church law was public law. Thus, the church requirement of tithing could be seen as both a public and a private source of aid. However, no institution of medieval society was to be free of the stress of change, and the church was no exception. The Reformation brought a significant, worldwide challenge to its authority. At the same time, both the parishes and the monasteries began to neglect their duty to the poor, partly because individuals were no longer bound by the injunction to give charity. Ownership was no longer seen as the privilege of stewardship but came to

mean the free use of possessions unencumbered by considerations of communal welfare.

Legislation was enacted which stated that the church had to give one third of its income to the poor. Again, legislation proved ineffective. Then, in 1536, Henry VIII began to appropriate the monasteries. Schweinitz says of this movement:

> . . . A social resource, inadequate at its best was now substantially diminished. What was more, one of the great symbols of charity had been removed, and there was consequently double occasion for public action.
>
> The church, along with the hospitals and other religiously inspired [private] philanthropies, represented the positive approach to human distress. With this resource available to the person in need the government could be negative in attitude and action. It was only when, in the presence of the overwhelming effects of great social change, the church and private charity could manifestly not relieve the vastly increased distress that public provision supported by funds secured through taxation was introduced. (1943, p. 19)

The first positive public responsibility for the poor

The two statutes in which the government assumed the first positive responsibility for dealing with destitution were enacted during the reign of Henry VIII. Taken together, these laws of 1531 and 1536 contained the following provisions.

1. Local officials were to make a search for all residents in need and to register them.

2. The statute of 1531 provided for the licensing of beggars. But in the statute of 1536 for the first time, the proper administration under state supervision of funds collected by voluntary contributions was substituted for begging.

3. The government took the responsibility for stimulating and securing contributions. There was to be a transfer of funds from the wealthier to the poorer parishes. Receipts were to be recorded and accounted for. And the administrators were to be paid for their work. Perhaps one could say that the first public welfare officials were provided for in 1536, about 450 years ago.

---

[2] Authorities differ on this matter. Brian Turney, *Medieval Poor Law: A Sketch of Canonical Theory and Its Application in England* (Berkeley: University of California Press, 1959), and Blanch D. Coll, *Perspectives in Public Welfare* (Washington, D.C.: U. S. Government Printing Office, 1969), support this view. de Schweinitz 1943, p. 18) sees monasteries as most important sources of aid.

4. There was a recognition that those able and willing to work might not be able to find work, and for the first time the government took the responsibility for putting such persons to work, although there was no plan as to how such employment was to be supplied.

5. There was to be severe punishment for the able-bodied who refused to work. The first offense was to be punished by whipping, and the punished persons were to be sent back to their place of residence. They were to supply their own transportation of being required to walk ten miles each day. The second offense was to result in the cutting off of the "upper part of the grissle of the right ear." The third offense was punishable by death.

6. Children under the age of 14 and above the age of 5 who were found in begging or idleness were to be put to work with a master craftsman, or other person, by whom they were to be taught a trade so that they could earn their living.

During the remainder of Henry VIII's reign and after the accession of Elizabeth I, there was an increasing pressure by the state and the use of its police power to secure voluntary giving from the wealthier citizens to support the poor. It was natural that this should develop into a program of taxation. In 1572, previous statutes relating to the poor were repealed and the 14th Elizabeth, chap. 5, was enacted. This legislation marks the first use of the tax powers of the state to provide for the relief of the poor. It also introduces the position of overseer of the poor. The persons appointed to this position was responsible for administering relief and for putting rogues and vagabonds to work. The local officials were to see that there was a stock of wool or hemp or other such raw materials that could be given to the poor for spinning into wool or other materials which the government would then purchase and sell. If people refused to work, they were sent to the House of Correction, where they could be made to work under a regimen of strict diet and punishment. Thus, refusal to work if one was destitute and in need of aid from others became a crime.

England suffered another period of hard times during 1596–97, when many died of starvation in the streets, and as a result another attempt was made to develop a more adequate legislative program for the care of the destitute. The new legislation represented only a clarification of the earlier laws except for two matters: (1) it was made lawful for the officials of the locality to erect "convenient houses of habitation" for the poor who were unable to work; and (2) it established the mutual liability of parents and children for each other's support. Thus, this law established the use of the almshouse for the "impotent" poor and the use of the prison for the able-bodied unemployed who refused work. It also marked the beginning of responsibility for relatives, expressed in individual terms. Relatives were directed to support each other as individuals. There was no recognition under law that the welfare of the family as a whole should be considered.

The Elizabethan Poor Law

The Act of 1601, the 43d Elizabeth, usually referred to as the Poor Law of 1601 and usually cited as the most important law in relation to the care of the poor during England's long march from feudalism to an industrial state, was in reality anticlimactic. It was primarily a pulling together of the earlier laws concerning the poor. What makes it important is that it was the last total reworking of such laws and that it was to influence thought regarding governmental relief in both England and the United States until the present day. Essentially, this law provided for:

1. Public, tax-supported aid to the destitute.
2. Locally financed and locally administered relief, with a publicly appointed overseer of the poor as administrator.
3. A system that included direct aid for those unable to work and work for the able-bodied. Thus there came into existence a system of classification and differential treatment of the poor.
4. Responsibility for relatives.
5. The apprenticeship of children as a way of both caring for them and educating them.

There are some later developments that we should consider. In 1662 the Law of Settlement was enacted. It provided that people who came into a parish at less than ten pounds a year could be forcibly returned to the place from which they came. This law gave officials the authority to forcibly remove a person, not because that person had become a public charge but because officials feared that the person might become one.

The employment of the poor

At about the same time that the negative and punitive Law of Settlement was enacted, there started a movement to employ the unemployed by establishing workhouses as centers of manufacturing throughout the country. It was proposed that at the workhouses materials, supervision, and training would be offered the poor so that they might learn to support themselves and so that the children of the poor would acquire skills and habits of industry. Many prominent people in England endorsed this notion, particularly the employment of children so that they could learn proper discipline and skills early in life. De Schweinitz quotes the comments of Andrew Yarranton, a successful businessman, about the employment of poor children in Germany:

> I will show you the way, method, rule, and order how they are governed. First, there is a large room, and in the middle thereof a little box like a pulpit. Secondly, there are benches built around the room as they are in our playhouses; upon the benches sit about two hundred children spinning, and in the box in the middle of the room sits the grand mistress with a long white wand in her hand. If she observes any of them idle, she reaches them a tap; but if that will not do, she rings a bell which by a little cord is fixed to a box, and out comes a woman; she then points to the offender, and she is taken away into another room and chastised. And all this is done without one word speaking. And I believe this way of ordering the young women in Germany is one great cause that the German women have so little of the twit twat. And I am sure it would be well were it so in England. . . .
>
> Is it not a pity and shame that the young children and maids here in England should be idle

within doors, begging abroad, tearing hedges, or robbing orchards, and worse, when these, and these alone, are the people that may, and must if ever, set up this trade of making fine linen here? And after a young maid hath been three years in the spinning school, that is taken in at six and then continues until nine years, she will get eight pence the day. And in these parts I speak of, a man that has most children lives best; whereas here he that has most is poorest. There the children enrich the father, but here beggar him. (de Schweinitz, 1943, p. 51)

Thomas Firmin, a merchant and a manufacturer, and one of the leaders of the Unitarian movement in England, actually carried through a plan for providing work for the poor. He erected a building in which poor people could spin flax into thread and receive pay for their work. He advocated that this income be an addition to relief granted through pensions. At Bristol, England, under a special act by Parliament, a corporation was established to provide both employment and relief for the poor. The effort was a failure in spite of much initial enthusiasm for it. However, the idea that public employment of the poor can be a profit-making enterprise with the added payoff of moral uplift has continued to surface from time to time.

> The impossibility of making aptitude the basis of employment and the necessity of operating irrespective of the demand for the product—the greatest need coming in bad times when the market for goods was lowest—defeated the hopes of those who believed that England could rise to prosperity through the productivity of her unemployed, as similar hopes have been defeated ever since. (de Schweinitz, 1943, p. 57)

The workhouse

But the poor and the unemployed continued to be a problem, and in 1722 a different philosophy came to the fore. A law was passed "authorizing the overseers and the church wardens to establish workhouses, to contract with private individuals for the employment and maintenance of the poor in these houses and to refuse relief to any person not willing to enter the house" (de Schweinitz, 1943, p. 58). The use of the workhouse was not new, but the plan initiated in 1722 and put into wide use was based on a new attitude toward the poor. Firmin and others like him had believed that the unemployed could be an asset to the nation if they were but given the opportunity. The men responsible for the new plan were cynical, pessimistic, and punitive. De Schweinitz contrasts the views of Firmin with those prevailing after 1722 as follows:

> **Firmin:** . . . there are many thousands whose necessities are very great, and yet they do what they can by their honest labor to help themselves; and many times they would do more than they do, but for want of employment.
>
> **Defoe:** Tis the men that won't work, not the men that can get no work, which makes the numbers of our poor.
>
> **Locke:** The growth of the poor must therefore have some other cause [i.e., than "scarcity of provisions" or "want of employment"] and it can be nothing else but the relaxation of discipline and corruption of manners. (1943, p. 59)
>
> **Maudeville:** . . . Going to school in comparison to working is idleness, and the longer boys continue in this easy sort of life, the more unfit they'll be when grown up for down right labor, both as to strength and inclination. Men who are to remain and end their days in a laborious, tiresome and painful station of life, the sooner they are put upon it at first, the more patiently they'll submit to it for ever after. (1943, p. 60)

As the above quotations imply, Defoe and Locke held that poverty was a defect in the character of the poor. This view not only set the tone for public assistance in England for two centuries, but it is frequently heard in the United States today. It was the basis for the law of 1722, which gave the overseers of the poor the right to refuse relief to a family unless the family was willing to enter the workhouse. Overseers of the poor could also contract with private persons to care for and employ the poor. The result can be imagined if one

recognizes that the contractor wanted to make as much money as possible from caring for the poor and that the parish wanted to spend as little as possible.

The Law of 1722 resulted in a rapid increase in the number of workhouses in England. It was thought that these would reduce costs in three ways: (1) people would be maintained more cheaply in congregate care than in their own homes (this proved to be untrue); (2) people would forgo assistance rather than enter the workhouse; or (3) if people needed help, they would settle for less rather than enter the workhouse. However, promising as the workhouse may have seemed, its horrors brought about significant objections to its use. Studies of children under one year old in workhouses found that their death rates were as high as 82 percent. In one workhouse, of 19 babies only 3 survived; in another not a single child survived; only 7 children in 100 survived three years in workhouses (de Schweinitz, 1943, pp. 65–66).

Thomas Gilbert was one of the many opponents of the Law of 1722. Believing in the classification of those who needed assistance, Gilbert had proposed that the aged and infirm be cared for in almshouses, that the "idle and dissolute" be sent to hard labor in houses of correction, that children be placed with proper persons, and that work be found for the employable. A Member of the House of Commons, after 20 years of work he was finally able to introduce a reform measure into Parliament and to get it enacted into law. The Statute of 1782 (known as the Gilbert Act) repealed the right of the overseers of the poor to contract the poor out to private caretakers and directed the overseers to find suitable employment for employable persons or to maintain such persons in the community until work could be found. Poorhouses rather than workhouses were to be established to care for the aged, the sick, the infirm, and orphaned children or children whose mothers were being cared for in the poorhouses. Although few parishes took advantage of the new law initially, England did begin to turn toward outdoor relief (relief to people in their own homes) following the passage of this act. In 1795 Parliament enacted an enabling amendment to the Poor Law that permitted any "industrious poor person or persons" to ask for and receive relief in their own homes (de Schweinitz, 1943, p. 73).

Speenhamland

The latter part of the 18th century was a time of great suffering among the poor of England, with the agricultural worker suffering more than others. The distress of the agricultural poor was accelerated by two movements. The farm laborer had depended since the beginning of money wages on two important supplements to the inadequate wages received. Each laborer had land around the family cottage that could be used to grow food. In addition, the agricultural family was entitled to use common lands of the village, where it could pasture stock and have a strip assigned to it for cultivation. There the family also found the fuel it needed. The use of the common land to supply needed food and fuel made the amount of wages received less crucial to sheer existence. But in the second half of the 18th century, the large landowners began to introduce law after law in Parliament that permitted them to appropriate these lands to their ownership and use. While the enclosures were depriving the agricultural laborers of subsistence farming that had supplemented their inadequate wages, their families also lost income that had been devised from labor in the home. The spinning and weaving involved in England's woolen industry had been carried on in the home, with the family as the unit of production, and had been performed throughout the agricultural parts of the nation as well as in the towns. With the coming of power machinery that began at this time, the industrial establishment rather than the family became the basis of production. The rural family was faced with the fact that it could no longer support itself in the same way that it had. It must either move to the larger towns or starve. Although rioting and the seizure of food occurred in many places, labor at this time, and for a long time to come, was not conscious of itself as a unit in the industrial equation. The status relationship between laborer

and employer of feudal times was rapidly disappearing, but there were no meaningful ties among the rapidly growing number of laborers that could lead to organization or power. Riots are not systematic opposition. Something may be done to solve the problems that give rise to riots, but without some organization, power, or goals of their own, rioters are rarely allowed a significant input into the solutions that are reached. These solutions tend, therefore, to support the status quo rather than to bring about change.

One solution to the problem of inadequate wages would have been to increase the wages that agricultural workers were paid. Since the first Statute of Laborers, there had been laws fixing the level of wages, though these laws had generally legislated the maximum amount of wages that could be paid rather than setting minimum amounts. However, the Act of James I (1604) had represented an attempt at minimum wage legislation, and under this act a meeting was called at Speenhamland on May 6, 1795, to consider the establishment of minimum wages for agricultural laborers. Two plans were advanced. One called for the fixing of minimum wage levels. The other plan was to establish set levels of need for each family and to order that each family's income be supplemented up to that amount. The second proposal that passed, and a practice was begun of making up the difference between a person's earnings and the minimum that the family was thought to need. A scale was drawn up (very similar to the schedules for relief clients today) which provided that "when the gallon loaf sold for one shilling, enough relief would be added to the laborer's wages to bring his income to three shillings; if he had a wife, to four shillings six pence; if a wife and one child, six shillings, and so on according to the size of the household" (de Schweinitz, 1943, p. 72).

As this plan of supplementing wages was developed at Speenhamland, it became known as the Speenhamland Act. The act assured the poor a minimum income irrespective of the level of wages paid by industry or agriculture. It operated to keep laborers on the land by subsidizing their earned income from public taxes. Although the act un-doubtedly relieved the suffering of individual fami-lies and allowed them the security of their former way of life, it also subsidized the owners of large enterprises by making it unnecessary for them to bargain competitively for labor and it retarded the organization and movement of labor.

For a generation this program of supplementing wages in order to provide employed persons with a living was a primary method of relief. It also supported further programs to provide relief for the nonworking poor in their homes instead of almshouses. This effort failed because, lacking a floor on wages, it led only to a further depression of wages and to further rise in the taxes that were to supplement them.

At this time, three other methods that failed were also tried. One of them called for the parish to sell the services of the poor to the highest bidder. A second method provided that the employers in a locality had to employ certain individuals sent to them or pay an additional tax for failing to do so. The third method, under which the locality was to provide employment on public works, was little used. Eventually all of these programs came to di-saster. The underwriting of the wage system, the small geographic area of administration (the parish), and the low level of the administrative skills of the time all combined to bring them to a disastrous end. And out of the angry reaction to these failures came the punitive Poor Law Reform of 1834.

The Poor Law Reform of 1834

In discussing the various factors underlying the establishment and administration of assistance to the poor in England, de Schweinitz discusses the problems of taxes and the initiative of workers as follows:

The burden fell unequally. The increase in En-gland's wealth from 1760 to 1834 was chiefly in manufacture and related fields, whereas the taxes for relief were paid by householders and other occupiers of property. The system by which each parish was responsible for its own destitute in-

volved an additional inequality. The places where there were many poor were seldom the places where there were many rich, and the communities with the greatest need were often the communities least able to pay the cost of meeting that need.

An additional source of dissatisfaction to the taxpayers was an apparent deterioration in the quality of labor. This deterioration was blamed upon relief, although there were in reality other and more influential factors. What enthusiasm could a man be expected to exhibit in life and in work who had been deprived by enclosure of his use of the commons; who had thereby been obliged to give up his flock of geese and his cow; who no longer had a strip of land which he could cultivate; and who had no access to wood and other sources of fuel which he had been accus-tomed to finding on the wastes, or to the game which had formerly played a part in his diet? Add to this a system of settlement laws that in effect imprisoned him within his parish, giving him little chance to look for better things—and what in the way of initiative could one expect? (1943, pp. 114–15)

At the same time that the poor were being in-creasingly controlled, there was a movement in England to extend the right to vote to the business and industrial classes. In 1832, just after he had acted to ensure electoral reform, the king an-nounced that he had appointed a Royal Commis-sion for Inquiring into the Administration and Prac-tical Operation of the Poor Laws. The commission, spurred by problems with the administration of re-lief and the failure of the Speenhamland Act, en-gaged in "one of the most extensive, effective, and dramatic pieces of social investigation ever to have been carried on in Great Britain" (de Schweinitz, 1943, p. 117). The study took two years, and it culminated in a report that was made in 1834.

The major recommendations of the report were that relief should be refused to persons considered able to work except through their institutionaliza-tion in workhouses and that relief should be admin-istered through a central board with powers to ef-fect combination of parishes and to oversee the operation of the workhouses. The poor were to be classified into: (1) the aged and impotent, (2) children, (3) able-bodied females, and (4) able-bodied males. The report suggested that there should be further study about the apprenticing of children, illegitimacy, and the laws of settlement. It "placed the burden of destitution upon the shoulders of the individual. Poverty was regarded as essentially an indication of moral fault in the person requiring relief" (de Schweinitz, 1943, p. 126). Three years after the passage of the laws based on the report, "Disraeli summed up the program in one sentence, 'It announces to the world that in England poverty is a crime' " (de Schweinitz, 1943, p. 124).

The published report of the study was 13,000 pages long. A book of 400 pages then summarized the findings in ways interesting to the general reader. There was great reliance on direct quotes, dramatic statements, and arresting case examples. The report was one of the most widely read public documents of its time. Its opening statement said that the findings demonstrated that the previous methods of giving relief to the poor were only destructive to their morals and welfare. The report failed to recognize the existence of a whole complex of social conditions that might have adverse effects not only on paupers but on all citizens. The report held that the evil was caused by the way in which relief was given and the effect this had on the character of the persons receiving aid. Having explored the failures of the existing system, the report proposed what it regarded as a promising solution: the establishment of a type of workhouse in which the food, work, and discipline were to be deliberately made so disagreeable that "none would consent to receive it who could possibly do without it" (de Schweinitz, 1943, p. 122). Thus, not only had the commissioners found a way of administering relief, but they had also developed a way of determining eligibility:

> Into such a house none will enter voluntarily; work, confinement, and discipline will deter the indolent and vicious; and nothing but extreme necessity will induce any to accept the comfort which must be obtained by the surrender of their free agency, and the sacrifice of their accustomed habits and gratifications. *Thus the parish officer, being fur-*

> *nished an unerring test of the necessity of applicants, is relieved from his painful and difficult responsibility; while all have the gratification of knowing that while the necessitous are abundantly relieved, the funds of charity are not wasted upon idleness and fraud.* (de Schweinitz, 1943, p. 123; italics in report)

The report also set forth a principle that affected England's approach to relief into the 20th century and is still of concern in American programs of income maintenance. This was the doctrine of *less eligibility*. Under this doctrine, the assistance provided a person in need should always be at such a level that his condition will be less desirable that that of the lowest paid wage earner. The workhouse was to be the deivce through which England could assure that the condition of those in need would be made inferior to that of workers. Another important outcome of the report was that, after 200 years of the most extreme form of local responsibility for social welfare, England was beginning to move in the direction of national responsibility and larger administrative units.

The Reform Act of 1834 was the first major English poor law legislation since 1601, and it is noteworthy that its supporters saw it as a return to the basic principles of the Elizabethan act. The goal was to assure that all able-bodied persons assumed individual responsibility for their own security. The act marked the discarding of the last remnants of a status relationship (Mencher, 1967, pp. 57–58).

With our discussion of the Reform Act of 1834, we have completed our overly brief survey of the early English programs to deal with the economic need of individuals and families. We will now briefly summarize some programs found in other countries, and we will end the chapter with a discussion of social and economic ideas and concerns that had an impact on the development of the English programs. These programs and certain socioeconomic philosophies of their time were to form the basis on which Americans were to establish their programs of income maintenance and the way in which they were to look at the poor.

The care of the poor in Europe

England was not alone in being confronted by the problems of poverty and upheaval nor in struggling to care for the destitute. England's struggle has been detailed here because of the direct influence that English laws and procedures had on the United States. However, during the 13th to 16th centuries the countries of Europe were facing problems similar to those of England, and there is evidence of much correspondence and exchange of information among those countries and England. We will very briefly discuss three developments here.

One of the leading European thinkers of the 1500s was Juan Luis Vives, a native of Spain who was educated in France and lived in Flanders. He proposed that relief be organized, that begging be forbidden, and that the poor be registered. His plan caused much dissension in Europe because of the general social and religious acceptance of begging. His plan, however, also urged that when people fell on hard times, their neighbors should seek to relieve their pain, not only through alms, but also by visiting them—seeking to comfort and sustain them through this demonstration of caring. This notion was proposed three and a half centuries before the Charity Organization Society in the United States began a program of friendly visiting for somewhat similar reasons. The COS program of charity organization and friendly visitors is generally credited with being the beginning of modern social work.

Protestant Germany was a few years ahead of England in plans for relief. In 1520 Martin Luther had urged the abolition of begging and the institution of a "common chest." Money was to be accumulated in the common chest to support three social welfare activities. It was to support religion by paying the salaries of the clergy, to support education by paying a schoolmaster, and to relieve the poor. This notion preceded by 400 years the development of the U.S. Community Chests, through which one gift was to support many voluntary social welfare activities.

Dr. Chalmers in Scotland

In Scotland, a Reverend Dr. Thomas Chalmers developed a theory about the helping of people in need and then proceeded to translate it into a way of working with the poor. This was contrary to the method used in England, which was to try to develop specific projects or approaches to poverty without being concerned about the underlying needs of people. Dr. Chalmers's early experience as an assistant pastor in a semirural area where there were also a large number of industrial laborers led to his concern with poverty. He came to oppose public relief and to support the notion that more meaningful help could be developed through the organization and the personal interaction of the poor themselves, through the kindness of relatives, and through the sympathy of wealthier persons.

On being assigned a new parish, Dr. Chalmers demanded the right to totally control relief within it. He rejected both public assistance and the general church fund, holding that his parish (which was very poor indeed) could take care of its own financial needs. He divided the parish into 25 districts, established the office of deacon to separate the spiritual from the temporal, entrusted the administration of relief to the deacons, and used funds collected at the evening services to support the needs of the parish. The deacons were selected from outside the neighborhood and were wealthier persons than the members of the parish. Chalmers trained his deacons in methods of working with needy people and supplemented these instructions with careful individual supervision and ongoing advice to volunteers. His expectations were that the deacons would not only administer funds but would bring the needy to a new respect, care, and help in terms of good examples and good advice. He substituted the measures of personal care and influence for the punitive measures that were used in England.

Although this effort was far in advance of other efforts of the time, Chalmers, like his contemporaries, completely overlooked the socioeconomic causes of poverty. However, no English experience approached the record of St. John's parish in the reduction of the expenditures for relief. But Chalmers's effort was totally ignored by the members of the 1832 commission (de Schweinitz, 1943, pp. 100–113).

✎§ Social and economic thought

During the 1700s in England, there developed large-scale agricultural and industrial establishments. This shift in the operation of the economic institution resulted in tremendous changes in the lives of individuals and families. The economic system began to depend on a large supply of workers whose worth was evaluated by their individual organization and self-discipline that resulted in the dependable, routinized performance necessary to the operation of the new industrial machinery. The great mass of working people became urban wage earners and thus were completely dependent on the growth of economic markets. So while the individual efforts of the people did not determine their welfare as directly as was possible when they could cultivate their assigned gardens, hunt and fish as they desired, and collect wood for fuel, they were now being held more responsible. In addition, the need for large numbers of laborers in one place resulted in the growth of urban areas and in the displacement of many persons from rural life. During the 18th century, England had more years of war than of peace. Goods and food were consumed by its wars, and prices increased much faster than wages. And despite the unfavorable economic and social conditions, the population increased at a greater rate in that century than during any earlier time.

The changes summarized above also were marked by the drastic curtailment of social supports. The movement from the familiar surroundings of the countryside was disruptive, and the social ties between farmers and the agricultural laborers who remained on the land were replaced by the money economy that was already prominent in industry. This drastic change left individuals and families without a viable pattern of supportive relationships. Determined to prevent the organization of the working classes and frightened by the French Revolution, industrialists in 1799 and 1800 worked to suppress trade unions and restrain all forms of organized working-class activity, including political and industrial activity. However, despite these difficulties the standard of living of laborers rose markedly during the 1700s, so that they could no longer be lumped indiscriminately with paupers and vagabonds, as in previous periods. The poor were sorting themselves out into those who were attached to the work force and those who did not work.

As to ideologies, the 1700s were marked by a gradual destruction of old values, a mourning of their loss, and the problem of substituting some rationale for the confusion and void created by the lack of any organized pattern of social responsibility. But by the 1800s the old values had been replaced by the principle of individual liberty, which was supported by all the major social institutions of society—religious, political, and economic. During the 1800s it came to be believed that society was made up of individuals who were the best judges of their own interests Organized institutions, including the state itself, came to be regarded as fluid conveniences that could be dissolved if they conflicted with the interests of the individuals who created them. In discussing this, Mencher writes:

> The scientific justification of the contract conception of society was to a great extent abandoned by the end of the eighteenth century, and had little practical impact. The welfare of the whole was seen as the function of the activities of the members rather than the welfare of the members being determined by the desires of the whole. Any interference with the freedom of the individual's behavior in his own interests was a blow at both the individual and the social good, which were synonymous. This belief was based on natural law, which effected the natural harmony of the free play of discrete forces. (1967, p. 63)

Although institutions of control, such as government, were seen as evil in that such organized approaches were restrictive to individuals, there was considerable disagreement about their necessity. Philosophers who believed in the humanity and the good impulses of people minimized the need for government, whereas those who saw the basic impulses of people as hostile and aggressive saw strong government as a necessary way of controlling the basic antisocial nature of people. The relative strength of people's concern for the general interests of others and their push toward self-interest was debated by the social thinkers of the time. Efforts were made to define the forces that pulled people together and helped them relate to others. Further, there was a search for a "natural order" or "natural laws" that would harmonize individual interests with the social good.

Adam Smith

In the midst of these arguments, Adam Smith, in 1776, published his *Wealth of Nations,* giving enormous impetus to the doctrine of laissez-faire. Smith believed that the welfare of society was best ensured by the freedom of each person to act in self-interest, that the welfare of society depended on the free flow of market forces unimpeded by social or economic regulation.

Joseph Townsend

In 1786 Joseph Townsend, a clergyman, wrote of the poor laws as follows:

> By establishing a permanent community of goods, and neither increasing the quantity of food, nor limiting the number of those who are to share it, they divert the occasional surplus of national wealth from the industrious to the lazy, they increase the number of unprofitable citizens, and sow the seeds of misery for the whole community; increasing the general distress, and causing more to die for want, than if poverty had been left to find its proper channel. . . .
>
> There is an appetite, which is and should be urgent, but which if left to operate without restraint, would multiply the human species before provision could be made for their support. Some check, some balance is therefore absolutely need-

ful and hunger is the proper balance; hunger not as directly felt, or feared by the individual for himself, but as foreseen and feared for his immediate offspring. Were it not for this the equilibrium would not be preserved so near as it is at present in the world, between the numbers of people and the quantity of food.

> It seems to be a law of nature, that the poor should be to a certain degree improvident, that there may always be some to fulfill the most servile, the most sordid, and the most ignoble offices in the community. The stock of human happiness is thereby much increased, whilst the more delicate are not only relieved from drudgery, and freed from those occasional employments which would make them miserable, but are left at liberty, without interruption, to pursue those callings which are suited to their various dispositions, and most useful to the state. As for the lowest of the poor, by custom they are reconciled to the meanest occupations, to the most laborious works, and to the most hazardous pursuits; whilst the hope of their reward makes them cheerful in the midst of all their dangers and their toils.

> . . . When hunger is either felt or feared, the desire of obtaining bread will quietly dispose the mind to undergo the greatest hardships, and will sweeten the severest labors. The peasant with a sickle in his hand is happier than the prince upon his throne. (de Schweinitz, 1943, pp. 115–16)

Malthus and Ricardo

Townsend was an influential person in England, but Reverend Thomas R. Malthus was an individual of even greater influence. Malthus was concerned that the growth of human population would inevitably outstrip the growth of food supplies unless population was limited by famine, war, and disease. In 1798 he published his *Essay on Population,* which set forth this notion. Given this conviction, Malthus saw relief as having a disastrous impact on the welfare of people in that by attempting to feed the entire pupulation it only increased the numbers of the poor and therefore reduced the welfare of all. Poverty was not to be tampered with, because it was a part of a natural law. Malthus saw the disasters of humanity as God's punishment of human beings for their inability and unwillingness to control their sexual behavior. The only exception to the law of population growth lay in the possibility that through education people could learn sexual restraint.

Another economist of the time, David Ricardo, was concerned with the level of wages. He believed that the level of wages would always move toward a subsistence level; that increases in population would always keep wages at the "natural price of labor" which would be necessary for the subsistence and existence of the laboring population (Mencher, 1967, p. 75).

Hobbes, Locke, and Harrington

Hobbes, Locke, and Harrington were social and political philosophers. Thomas Hobbes was one of the earliest thinkers to advance the theory of the social contract. He assumed that the basic nature of individuals was hostile, aggressive, and competitive and that no harmony could exist among people without a strong central government to control their competitive interests in society. John Locke held that the most important of human rights was the right to property. He argued that such a right exists in nature and is therefore superior to the rights of government. He held that property, and not government, should be absolute and that it is the duty of people to remove from power any government that does not safeguard such rights. Locke's philosophy seems to justify any use to which individuals might desire to put their property. James Harrington advanced the theory that the political power of the state depends on economic power and that economic power depends on the distribution of property (Dillard, 1967, p. 140).

The utilitarians

There were other voices, and among them were those of the utilitarians and the humanists. John Stuart Mill and Jeremy Bentham were leaders of the utilitarian movement, which believed that the goal of all national policy should be directed toward

achieving the greatest happiness of the greatest number of people and that such happiness was an aggregate of the happiness of all the individuals in a nation. The utilitarians believed further that wealth was the primary source of happiness, making it possible for people to promote what they saw as their own happiness through the ways in which they used their resources. Each member of society was the equal of every other member, and all members of society had the right and the potential to fulfill their notions of happiness. Carried to its logical conclusion, the utilitarian position also supported the notion that the suffering of the poor or the handicapped in any society would, by that much, weaken the happiness of all. This represented a very different position from the earlier view that the poverty of the lower classes was the result of natural law and thus of benefit to the national welfare.

Bentham supported univeral suffrage because this would permit all members of society to be represented in the determination of governmental policy, but he believed that in the long run the interests of the greatest number would be best served by giving people the freedom to pursue their individual interests rather than through governmental action. Although Bentham had no doubts about the importance of wealth for happiness, he "concluded that the protection of property was more essential to the welfare of the community than the creation of equality" (Mencher, 1967, p. 76). He took this position because he felt that any scheme for the redistribution of wealth would threaten the entire economic system and thus reduce the amount of wealth that would be available for distribution. Believing in the fundamental equality of all people, the utilitarians had little patience with the notion that individuals possessed innate tendencies. They found the explanation of behavior in the social conditions of people's lives. They stressed the importance of education for the poor as a way of preparing them to safeguard their own interests.

There also were religious reformers. John Wesley, the founder of Methodism, approached the problem of material wealth differently from Bentham but reached essentially the same conclusions. He emphasized the importance of success and satisfactions in this world, holding that the exercise of personal freedom toward these ends demanded security in the use of personal property.

The traditional elite

The position that many wealthy and influential people took toward the poor was rooted in the paternalistic concept of earlier traditional societies and was supported by many religious values. This demanded that the well-to-do take some responsibility for those who were less well off and that the workers be able to rely on the goodwill of "their betters." Individual moral behavior rested on the acceptance of mutual responsibilities. The wealthy had an obligation to serve as the teachers and the uplifters of the poor, and the poor had an obligation to accept such help (Mencher, 1967, pp. 61–92).

The paternalistic concept influenced those who worked to replace the public system of poor relief by self-reliance supplemented by voluntary communal help. This belief system included the notion that public moneys expended to support the poor produced an unhealthy dependence on social support and discouraged the informal loyalty of neighbors and the charitable efforts of the wealthy. A sense of interdependence within and between classes was a means of educating the lower classes toward morality and self-support and of furthering the unity of the nation (Mencher, 1976, pp. 61–92).

The humanitarians

The humanitarian position began to develop in the early 1800s. It favored the readjustment of the balance of social, economic, and political forces so that the disadvantaged might achieve a more equitable distribution of the benefits of society. Humanitarianism was an important factor in the democratic movement, as it conceded the qualities of humanity to the poor as well as the rich, although its advocates were careful to maintain class differences. The humanitarianism of the period was a part of the spread of democratic thinking throughout the Western world. It was supported by the growing rational and scientific spirit, although it was less a reasoned approach than an emotional reaction to the cruelty and degradation of the past.

❧ Summary

In this chapter we sought to lay certain foundations upon which to build our understanding of the development of social welfare in the United States. We discussed three notions that have their roots in 13th to 16th century England: the new concept of economic independence, the values of work, and the change from status to contractual relationships among individuals.

We also discussed the development of the English Poor Laws from the 1300s to the Elizabethan Poor Law of 1601, which was to form the base for much of the thinking about the relief of need in the United States. We saw the development during this time of the classification of the poor, tax-supported aid to the poor, the local financing and administration of relief, responsibility for relatives, the apprenticeship of children, and government-supplied work for the unemployed.

We looked briefly at the developments on the Continent and at the effort to establish a guaranteed income for the poor. We saw how organized work began to be viewed as a source of training for children, the prevention of crime and vagrancy, a test of the good intentions of the poor, and relief from poverty.

It was during this era that the foundations of modern economic security policies were established. Fundamental questions raised during this period are still unsettled issues: (1) the role of the state in the economy; (2) the function of economic security programs in an industrial society; (3) the balance between local and national interests; (4) the influence of economic security programs on the economic, social, and political structures of the nation; and (5) the relationship between programs for the poor and general measures concerned with individual and family welfare in the nation.

In the 13th to 16th centuries the link was forged

between social provision for the people and employment. This link led directly to the concern that the poor and poverty could be a threat to the stability of society and the nation and to the conclusion that the state should play a major role in social welfare planning.

There was a prevailing belief at the beginning of the era that unemployement was socially caused, that the problem was to balance the needs of employers for adequate sources of cheap labor with the needs of employees for adequate work at a living wage. However, toward the end of the period, the impression was gaining ground that the causes of poverty lay in the poor themselves. The notion that the laziness of workers and their preference for idleness was the cause of poverty became more and more prevalent. The Poor Laws themselves were also seen as the cause of poverty in that any assistance to the poor was viewed as an invitation to idleness.

The development of the concept of private property was of primary importance during this time. The new entrepreneurial class had little tolerance for the concept of interdependent relationships. The development of this concept was supported by the increase in the population of England; by the spread of Protestantism with its individualistic values; by the desire of Henry VIII to be free of the Catholic Church and thus the confiscation of church resources and the destruction of the church's pattern of dealing with human need; and by the development of commerce and industry, which rested on the acquisition of new knowledge and on the production of the means of commerce (great sailing ships) and machines.

During the time of Elizabeth I, England rose to greatness, sending its representatives throughout the New World, laying the seeds of empire, growing in stature both economically and spiritually. "This was the age of Shakespeare and Bacon, of intellectual and scholarly probing, a time, in other words, when conscience was stirred by the winds of national pride" (Lens, 1969, p. 16). In this spirit of the times, attempts were made to organize and plan for those who were destitute. But the question of who should benefit from the aid of the nation was a troubling one. Although no one wanted to deny the helpless, the sick, and the aged the benefit of the country's help, idleness was seen as the most flagrant of sins. If a person would not work, that person could be whipped, branded, have an ear lopped off, or be put to death. But if he would work but could not find employment, the government would supply wool, hemp, and iron in workshops for the unemployed. Almshouses were set up for the sick and infirm and as a place where children could receive a certain education.

We need to consider the conditions of life in 16th century England. Life was exceedingly harsh and brief. Many of the things that we take for granted were unavailable. There was no modern plumbing and sewage disposal, for instance. Modern methods of sanitation were yet to come. People did not expect much from life. Life was terribly precarious even for the wealthy. At the beginning of this period it was generally accepted that the world was flat. Most of our knowledge of human beings and the way they develop had not yet been acquired. A question well worth thinking about is why some of our basic assumptions about social welfare policy have changed so little since this period, given the great changes in our knowledge; our notions of social, church, and family relationships; and our economic system.

✑ A look ahead

In the next chapter we shall continue our examination of historical developments with an account of the development of social welfare as an institution in colonial America. As we do so, we shall see how the patterns for the relief of poverty and social philosophies were transported from England. As the readers begin the next chapter, they might want to consider the pace of social change in a new land.

✑ Study questions

1. Go back through the chapter and list ways of dealing with the problems of poverty that it describes that

resemble ways you may have heard suggested in today's world.

2. Develop an outline that shows the effects of the industrial revolution—a change in the economic institution—on the other social institutions (church, family, and political) of England.

3. Make a list of the new needs of individuals or families that were created by the changes in the economic institution during the mercantilist era and the beginning of the industrial revolution.

4. What problems in the functioning of what social institutions brought about the beginning of the institution of social welfare in 15th century England?

5. The last part of the chapter dealt with some aspects of the social and economic thought of the 1700s and the early 1800s. Identify those theories that are still viable and are still utilized in making social welfare decisions today.

6. Develop a dialogue between a laborer of the late 1700s and a wealthy landowner who sees the workhouse as a way of controlling poverty.

৶ Selected readings

Coll, B. D. *Perspectives in public welfare: A history.* Washington, D.C.: U.S. Government Printing Office, 1969.

The first chapter in this monograph—"The English Heritage"—is an excellent reading to accompany our text. It presents the background of the American approach to public welfare.

de Schweinitz, K. *England's Road to Social Security.* New York: A. S. Barnes, 1943.

Chaps. 1 through 12 of this work have been used extensively in developing the material in this chapter. For those classes in which it is possible to spend some time on our English heritage, this material furnishes an excellent extension of the information in the text. The quotes from documents of the time contained in this reading should help students gain a better understanding of our history. Students' reactions to the quoted material might furnish some good material for class discussion.

Jordan, W. K. The English Background of Modern Philanthropy. *American Historical Review,* 66 (1) (1961):401–8.

A good article that deals with the material in this chapter.

Trattner, W. *From Poor Law to Welfare State: A History of Social Welfare in America.* New York: Free Press, 1974.

The first chapter of this book discusses the same material that we cover in our chapter.

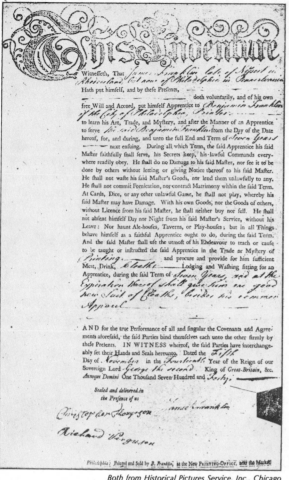

Involuntary servitude in colonial America.

Two types of forced labor are illustrated: Left, an indenture agreement (of James Franklin to his famous uncle, Benjamin Franklin); and, right, a slave auction.

Chapter 10 ತಿ⋟

⋞ಿ Social welfare in colonial times: Influential forces, 1600–1780 ತಿ⋟

⋞ಿ Introduction

In this chapter we shall discuss the forces in colonial society, including the philosophy of the leaders of the time, that affected the development of the early American social welfare programs. In the next chapter we shall discuss the process by which the colonial social welfare programs developed and the structure of the various programs. Together these chapters cover the 180 years during which Americans were moving through the processes of settlement, federation, revolution, and the establishment of a national government. The discussion in these two chapters and in subsequent chapters attempts to follow the broad outlines of the framework for analysis that was developed in Chapter 6. The colonial period is covered in two chapters because of the importance of understanding in some detail the beginnings of American social welfare and because the period is a long one. The division is logical in that the first chapter discusses the influential forces and the second discusses the development of the welfare institution itself.

⋞ಿ Forces toward change

Never were forces for change more powerful and never was the pace of change more dizzying than during the early colonial years in America. One cannot help but wonder about the drives that impelled the early explorers and settlers to undergo an experience in which so much was unknown and uncontrolled. For our purposes, we have identified the following factors as important ones in the development of the social welfare institution in the American colonies:

⋞ಿ 1. Optimism and a positive orientation toward change (beliefs).
2. Geography and climate.
3. Work and the shortage of labor.
4. Contract relationships.

5. Voluntary benevolence and religious values.
6. Social, economic, political, and religious leaders.

Optimism and the orientation toward change

The early immigrants to America came from many walks of life. A mixture of small tradesmen, wealthy businessmen, farmers, criminals, paupers, adventurers, and explorers, they were on the whole a socially mobile group seeking something different from the life they had known. Some came pushed by despair or anger, hoping to escape the control, hopelessness, and frustration of their lives. Some came pulled by individual dreams and looking forward eagerly to making those dreams become reality. Some came simply because they were challenged by the risks of the unknown and to find out what the excitement was all about. But few of those who came had any concept at all of what awaited them in the unexplored vastness of America. This is the spirit of the pioneer, to risk one's all in the challenge of the unknown. Every society has its pioneers, who often are later honored as heroes because of their willingness to risk; but seldom before, and seldom since, have so many people, from so many walks of life, for so many different purposes, put so much faith in the new and unexpected. One of the factors basic to the understanding of American life is that it began to flourish even before it was known and perhaps because it was not yet known in even the roughest outlines (Boorstin, 1965, p. 1).

The first colonists lived in the constant belief that something better might turn up—and probably would if they could just keep things changing and moving. This orientation toward change, this belief that solutions to human problems may lie in the new, the different, and the unexpected, is an important part of American life and institutions (Boorstin, 1965, p. 1).

The heterogeneity of the colonial population, the diversity of individual areas, the size of the country and the great climatic differences, the rich-ness of natural and human resources, the conflicts of diverse interests, and the force of individual leadership all contributed to push the settlers of the new land toward change in the social institutions they were constructing.

There are those who would maintain that the settlement of America was one of the most important social welfare events that the world has known in that it offered an opportunity for the underclasses of England and Europe to find a new life. Perhaps Sidney Lens puts it best when he says, "The first war on poverty, though no one thought to give it a name, was the settlement of America itself" (Lens, 1969, p. 2). But it was not easy. People found that even in the new country, with all its promise, there was tragedy and trouble. Many kinds of human services were needed and systems to offer such services had to be developed. The people who developed the programs and services were people who had come to the colonies with a vision of establishing communities that would be better and would offer more opportunities than the ones they had known at home. Most of the efforts at colonization had articulated the need for changes in the way society dealt with the welfare of its members. Yet these people, for all their push toward change, carried with them the social patterns of the life they had left behind.

Geography and climate

When the colonies were first settled, among the greatest problems that the settlers faced were a lack of equipment and technical knowledge to deal with the forces of weather and climate, the vast geographic spaces, the wilderness that surrounded them, and the need for the unremitting labor of all members of the community. Looking back at that time from the vantage point of a society in which most human effort is assisted by the technology of the machine, it is hard for us to grasp the harsh demands that had to be met by the first Europeans who came to America if they were to subdue the forces of nature sufficiently to support life itself.

Just the difficulties of finding or making shelter (in the way that these Europeans understood shelter) must have been almost unbearable. There were forest trees of every size and variety, but the first settlers had no way to turn trees into lumber; there was plenty of clay and limestone, but the settlers could not make bricks and mortar; huge boulders of granite and other rocks were all around, but the settlers did not have a single facility for cutting, drawing, or using stone. The settlers learned to use caves or learned how to make bark wigwams from the Indians. In 1626 all but one of the 30 homes of Europeans on the island of Manhattan were made of bark (Earle, 1974, pp. 1–10). To move beyond such shelter to a log cabin a settler had to possess, or be able to borrow, a broadax and a pair of strong and willing arms. But, more than this, the settler had to be willing to engage in new and strange activities. If the community was to exist, its members had little time and energy to plan. They had to do—the strange and difficult.

Governor William Bradford reported on the landing of the *Mayflower* passengers on the New England coast in 1620 as follows:

> . . . they had now no friends to welcome them, nor inns to entertain or refresh their weather-beaten bodys, no houese or much less townes to repaire too, to seeke for succoure. . . . What could they see but a hidious and desolate wilderness, full of wild beasts and wild men? (Boorstin, 1958, introduction)

The new environmental forces resulted in the development of a new, secular view of work. Many New England settlers would go on believing in the puritan value of work as one's duty to God, but the new value of work as a necessary contribution to the existence and welfare of one's neighbors, of the group of which one was a part, began to be established. Work became not only a duty owed to God, but a very concrete and important duty owed to others. All persons had an obligation to do everything in their power to provide for and care for themselves both as a moral responsibility of the individual and as a responsibility to the welfare of the group. They had a further obligation to govern their behavior by consideration of the present and future needs of the entire social group.

Beyond individual inclination, the authorities of the community supported a group obligation to preserve the lives of group members. Those who did not carry out their obligations to the group, or who obstructed the group's purpose and development, were punished, compelled to change their behavior, or banished from the group.

The scarcity of labor

In addition to the disparities between the dreams and plans of those who came to the colonies and the realities they found, there were other important forces toward change. The sparseness of the colonial population was in marked contrast to the heavily settled industrial areas of England from which most of the settlers came. Until the first quarter of the 19th century only a relatively small number of people were dependent on wages from employment. There was no real consciousness of a working class or identification with workers' interests. The American settlers did not see themselves as wage earners. They were small businessmen, artisans, craftsmen, and farmers. There was always the fresh opportunity of the frontier. Thus even in the mid 19th century labor leaders opposed a plan for free boarding schools at which children could acquire mechanical and industrial skills. At that time a majority of the labor leaders wanted their children to have the traditional education received by upper-class children in preparation for professional careers (Beard, 1931, p. 42). The influence of the early scarcity and mobility of labor on social thinking had profound effects on the development of social welfare programs. Instead of passing laws to confine the poor and unemployed to a geographic area (such as were enacted in England), the colonies became convinced that it was the obligation of the unemployed to move on to areas where work was available and that such areas could always be found.

Laborers in the American colonies were optimistic about the potential for an increasingly "better" life for their children. In this optimism of the early laborers lay the seeds of the present-day notion that one can always find work if one really wants it and in the lack of an effective consciousness of a "laboring class" that would further a struggle for more effective protection of persons in that group. The social history of other industrial countries reveals an earlier and more progressive movement toward the assurance of income and security for the working classes, but in the United States, where many workers expect by their own efforts to be able to finance a profession for their children, they hardly feel it necessary—in fact, they may find it contradictory—to support higher taxation and greater limitations on profit in order to assure security for the working group.

Contract relationships

Another important force toward change in the colonies was the lack of a system of traditional rights and relationships. There was little in colonial society that would justify the concept of class relationships or allow for the recognition that lower orders existed in the social and economic system. One might owe it to one's neighbors to work, but one did not owe anything either to one's superiors or inferiors simply because they occupied that status. "Contract was the foundation of the social system, and no people had so literally absorbed the notion of the social contract as had the early Americans" (Mencher, 1967, p. 132). Having no obligations to other people other than those willingly assumed in quid pro quo arrangements meant that individuals had a great deal of freedom to develop new ways of relating to one another.

Voluntary benevolence and stewardship

Supported both by their early sense of community (the group would stand together against all perils) and by the mandates of their religion, many of the early colonists were deeply committed to the obligation to care about others and to express neighborly love in their daily lives.

En route to New England in 1630, John Winthrop preached a sermon to the immigrants entitled "A Model of Christian Charity." As used by Winthrop,

the term *charity,* really meant "brotherly love" (Bremner, 1960, pp. 1–4). He was concerned that the company of Christians en route to the new land should understand the obligation to love one another and to be concerned with the burdens of others. The obligation to one's neighbors has continued to be a value in society and is still one of the principal methods of social advance in America. Voluntary benevolence, aimed not only at assisting the poor but at improving the quality of life for everyone, has played a large role in the development of American social welfare (Bremner, 1960, pp. 1–4).

It is true that the thrust toward voluntary giving has aroused mixed emotions in our society, even in those who have been deeply involved in the giving. *Do-gooders* and *bleeding hearts* are not exactly terms of endearment and approval in our society. And as we move farther into our account of the development of social welfare in America, we shall find a constant concern about "unwise giving."

Perhaps the conflict over giving has its roots, at least in part, in religious teachings, particularly those of the Puritans. God required His chosen people to love all persons, but love for one's neighbors meant assuming the responsibility to "make them good." The perfect expression of benevolence was to make others moral. If you cared about others, you wanted to assure them both a good life and salvation after death, and you assumed that you had the answers that would make this possible. Thus, we find that much of the social welfare thinking and much of the private giving in America combined the ideas of benevolence and trusteeship.

These two concepts were then easily tied into a third: that idleness was evil and destroyed people's souls. So we come to the principle that, although the support of others is important, supporting others in idleness is very destructive. Thus, it follows that we must always be cautious not to be destructive rather·than helpful in our benevolence. We should try to make sure that our help furthers the moral welfare of those to whom we give.

This was truly a new concept—that we owe our wealth and our help to the less fortunate *for their sake*. The concept is a very real departure from the notion that we give for our own sake— that salvation is found in the act of giving, without concern for either the object of our charity or the effectiveness of our gift. If God shows His pleasure in our performance on this earth by blessing our activities and giving us an abundance of goods, then we have evidence that we know the good way and we have an obligation to show that way to others, not only through the giving of resources but also through the greater gift of ourselves in advising, teaching, and counseling. This is a value question—how do we help others best? Do we give money and concrete resources, or do we give advice and support for a way of living? When is which type of help important?

Such questions about our responsibility to our neighbor, about how we truly help others, have been with us throughout our history of social welfare development and continue to plague us today.

> We expect rich men to be generous with their wealth, and criticize them when they are not; but when they make benefaction, we question their motives, deplore the methods by which they obtained their abundance, and wonder whether their gifts will do more harm than good. (Bremner, 1960, p. 2)

The revolution

In American history the great force for change was the Revolution itself. The Revolution was fought, not only against the king of England, but against certain injustices in the colonies themselves. By the time of the Revolution, many social welfare issues were facing the colonists—slavery, education, imprisonment for debt, the limited franchise, landlessness on the part of many who wanted land, and great poverty (Lens, 1969, p. 60). These pressures and problems were intensified by a series of religious revivals earlier in the 18th century that encouraged religious humanism and a greater movement toward democracy. Among the important changes brought about by the Revolution were

the following: (1) the freeing of the colonists from the status of colonials and their union in a federation that paved the way for a new national government; (2) the opening of the frontier beyond the Appalachians; and (3) the destruction, for free white males, of the notion that persons inherited the right to rule others. Actually, the leaders of the time could speak of the "rights of all men" because slaves, women, and children were not regarded as persons.

✑ Leaders in social welfare development

Cotton Mather

One of the chief proponents of American philanthropy during the colonial period, Cotton Mather was a native of New England and the grandson of two founders of Massachusetts. The son of a president of Harvard and himself a founder of Yale, Mather published about 450 works, one of which, "Essays to do Good," influenced American philanthropy for many years. Mather proposed that "men and women, acting either as individuals or as members of voluntary associations, should engage in a perpetual endeavor to do good in the world" (Bremner, 1960, p. 12). He wrote: "If any man asks, 'Why is it so necessary to do good?' I must say, it sounds not like the question of a good man" (Bremner, 1960, p. 12).

Mather did not see charity as a means of salvation but as a duty that human being owed God, and he had no doubt that God would punish the individuals who neglected such an important charge. He also thought that doing good was a reward in itself, that being able to help the unfortunate should be considered an honor. Given our present interest in the concept that the social welfare institution operates as a force of social control, it is interesting to note that Mather took care to point out that doing good served as a gentle instrument of social control. He believed that the competing and conflicting interests in society could be brought into harmony through "pious example, moral leadership, voluntary effort and private charity" (Bremner, 1960, p. 13). He also believed that "each man must start his career of doing good by correcting whatever was amiss in his own heart and life" (Bremner, 1960, p. 13).

Believing both in a social gospel and in individual reform, Mather wrote that the poor often needed "admonitions of piety" quite as much as they needed concrete resources, that "charity to the souls of men is the highest form of benevolence" (Bremner, 1960, p. 14). We will see certain variations of this thought in the agencies of the late 1800s. While acting "as a one-man relief and aid society through his own charitable gifts, Mather recognized the need for enlisting the support of others in causes" (Bremner, 1960, p. 14). He called the attention of the wealthy to the spiritual and material needs of the poor, worked tirelessly for the relief of the poor.

However, at the same time that he urged giving, Mather expressed concern about the possibility that benevolence might nourish evil ways in the idle. Predating the Charity Organization Society by 100 years, he urged extreme care in the bestowal of alms. He wrote: "Let us try to do good with as much application of mind as wicked men employ in doing evil" (Bremner, 1960, p. 14). He told the people of Boston: "Instead of exhorting you to augment your charity, I will rather utter an exhortation . . . that you may not abuse your charity by misapplying it." (Bremner, 1960, pp. 14–15). He held that it was even more important to give wisely than to give generously and that it was as helpful to the undeserving to withhold alms as it was to bestow alms on those who deserved them. The poor who could not work should be the object of giving, but the best gift to those who could work was to see that they did so.

Benjamin Franklin

One of the most outstanding leaders in the social thought of the colonial era was Benjamin Franklin. Franklin, the first colonial leader to come from the working class, addressed himself to those of humble origin as well as the wealthy. He conceived of a society in which there "would be no poor and little need for relief" (Bremner, 1960, p. 16). He believed in self-help, desiring that all people be free from dependence on the uncertain charity of the world. He preached the gospel of industry, frugality, and sobriety as a way of *achieving individual freedom* rather than as either a spiritual value or a road to wealth. At 42 Franklin decided to sell his printing establishment and to devote the rest of his life to public service.

In place of the existing emphasis on pious work and personal charity, Franklin introduced a secular spirit into concern with the general welfare. His religion consisted in the belief that people should show their gratitude to God "by the only means in their power, promoting the happiness of his other children" (Bremner, 1960, p. 17). Sounding as though he came from the 19th century rather than the 18th, Franklin advocated the abolition of all public support of the poor on the ground that the public provision for the needy had an even greater tendency to cause dependence than did private almsgiving. Believing in the importance of preventing poverty rather than relieving it, he worked hard to increase the opportunities of people for self-help. He believed that it was the responsibility of everyone to work for the establishment of a society in which all people would be able to take care of themselves.

Among Franklin's efforts to serve the community were the following: (1) starting a club for the mutual improvement of its members that later resulted in the establishment of a library; (2) founding a volunteer fire company; (3) formulating a scheme for paving, cleaning, and lighting the streets of Philadelphia; (4) formulating a plan for policing Philadelphia; (5) leading the effort to establish the Philadelphia Hospital; and (6) founding an academy that later became the University of Pennsylvania. In his will Franklin underwrote the founding of a technical institute in Boston. More than any other American before him, Franklin established the principle of improving social conditions and opportunities for the poor through voluntary associations and worked to apply the principle of self-help to the community as well as the individual (Bremner, 1960, p. 18).

Anthony Benezet

Another leader in social welfare thought at the time was Anthony Benezet. Benezet came to Pennsylvania in 1731 as a schoolmaster and was almost as poor as those he helped. He not only struggled to relieve misfortune but also exposed and fought injustice. He worked hard at improving relationships between the Indian and the white, not to convert the Indians or to make them allies in war and trade, but to obtain consideration for them as fellow human beings and to secure recognition of their rights. He wrote:

> "Is it not notorious that they are generally kinder to us than we are to them? . . . the difference between them and us is cheifly owing to our different ways of life, and different ideas of what is necessary and desirable" (Bremner, 1960, p. 29).

Convinced through his experience as a teacher of both black and white children that there was as much talent in one race as in the other, Benezet regarded the notion of black inferiority as "a vulgar prejudice" (Bremner, 1960, p. 30). His major mission in life came to be combating racial prejudice and showing that white superiority was based on illegal force and unjust laws. During the 1770s Benezet backed up the antislavery views of his friend Benjamin Rush and encouraged the young physician to fight against the slave trade. Benezet's last public act was to urge the first Congress to go to the very limit of its powers to discourage the slave trade.

Benjamin Rush

Benjamin Rush, a generation younger than Franklin and Benezet, was a physician, a teacher, a statesman, and, above all, a reformer. An intense man, he tackled all causes as though the fate of the world hung in the balance. Rush was trained in Calvinistic doctrines, and although he rejected them in later life, he remained a moralist all his life, deploring idleness, the use of tobacco and alcohol, and violations of the Sabbath. After the Revolution, in which he served briefly as the physician-

general for Washington's army, he was fond of saying, "The Revolution has just begun" (Bremner, 1960, p. 30). His life span bridged the colonial period and the early 19th century. During the early 1800s he founded the first free medical clinic in the United States, the Philadelphia Dispensary; was deeply involved in the study of mental disease and in experimentation with the humane treatment of the insane; agitated for moderation of the criminal laws, holding that capital punishment was the punishment of murder by murder; and sought to transform the houses of correction into agencies of repentance and reform. Rush strongly supported public education and argued for milder discipline in the classroom, and pointing out that "schoolmasters were the only despots still tolerated in free countries" (Bremner, 1960, p. 35).

Stephen Girard

In the midst of the terrible crisis of a yellow fever epidemic in Philadelphia, another unlikely social welfare leader came forward. Stephen Girard was 43 and a self-made businessman whose gospel was hard work, laissez-faire, and caveat emptor when he became involved in the effort to help the yellow fever victims. Girard dropped his business interests in order to administer the pesthouse that had been set up in an old mansion. He made the old house a model institution, changing it from "a place of horror to a well-administered haven of mercy where tender care was rendered to the sick and the dying" (Bremner, 1960, p. 39).

Rush and Girard had no love for each other. Rush disliked what he saw as Girard's arrogance, while Girard never tired of railing against doctors as "ignorant jackasses." (Bremner, 1960, p. 40). It was Girard's belief that fear made people ill and that doctors only compounded the problem. Like that of Rush, Girard's career spanned the colonial era and the national era that followed the Revolutionary War.

Perhpas Girard is best remembered for his will, in which, as a childless widower at odds with his relatives, he made tremendous bequests to further the welfare of many social causes in Philadelphia.

He set aside the bulk of his estate for the founding of a boarding school for poor, white, male, orphan children. Girard felt under no obligation to promote social reforms or to prevent social disorders. He believed in economic self-interest and was responsive only to the concrete needs of those who seemed worthy.

Whitefield and the Great Awakening

As we move to consider events in the third and fourth decades of the 18th century, we see threads of developments that began to weave the separate English colonies together and to make them one people. One of these developments has been called the Great Awakening. Although the Great Awakening was a series of religious revivals that encouraged individual religiosity, strengthened the spirit of religious independence, and weakened the authority of the churches, the movement was also very influential in social welfare development because it was humanitarian and because it was concerned with the relationship and responsibility of individuals to one another. The two great preachers of the Great Awakening were George Whitefield and Jonathan Edwards.

Edwards and Whitefield preached a gospel of spiritual rebirth through an individual inner experience quite outside the established forms of worship. Never again would organized religion have the controlling place in American life that it had had earlier in the colonial period. As a result of the Great Awakening, ordinary people developed a tremendous interest in partaking of the pleasures of piety and benevolence. The Great Awakening transformed philanthrophy from a predominantly upper- and middle-class activity into a broadly shared, genuinely popular activity of all (Bremner, 1960, pp. 20–22).

Whitefield made seven visits to the colonies during which he preached a gospel that called for relief of the poor and a generous response to the needs of neighbors as well as spiritual revival. Whitefield's favorite charity was the first orphanage in America, which he founded in 1740 though it never fulfilled his expectations that it would be a

model institution for children. The orphanage was funded by contributions from England and all the colonies, and thus it was one of the first colonial institutions that was not limited to a particular colony or town. Whitefield also took up collections for poor debtors, raised money for victims of disaster, and secured assistance for colonial colleges (Bremner, 1960, pp. 22–23).

❧ Limiting conditions

The natural resources and the climatic conditions of the colonies were critical to the shaping of the colonial social institutions, both in supplying opportunities and in setting limits. Difficult environmental conditions may have forced people to find new ways to do things, but they also limited what could be accomplished. Trying to develop new coping patterns takes energy that cannot be devoted to developmental tasks. Thus, we must place climatic conditions and the lack of tools and knowledge to deal with the possibilities of the environment under limiting conditions as well as under forces for change.

The occupied land

From our perspective, it may be difficult to understand how the Indians who occupied the American continent when the settlers came could have been so effectively ignored as a limiting condition to the settlement of the colonies (Boorstin, 1958, p. 259). Who owned the American continent before the first explorers arrived? How and from whom did the colonists secure title to the land? From the reading of history it becomes obvious that when the first Europeans came to the New World they felt that the continent was not yet possessed by anybody at all. It was theirs to take, to exploit and despoil, or to use to build a new society. By the strict letter of English law, "the Crown (having 'discovered' the territory) had pre-empted North America as a protectorate; title to American lands therefore could be secured only by a grant from the Crown." There was no consideration of the Indians' rights of ownership (Boorstin, 1958, p. 259).

The Pilgrims may have shared their first feast of Thanksgiving with the Indians, but there is no record that they paid the Indians for title to the land on which the feast took place. The Dutch were the first national group to pay the Indians for land they occupied. This episode (the purchase of Manhattan for $24), which has to be regarded as a classic example of how the whites swindled the Indians, was actually remarkable in that anything at all was paid for the land or that the rights of the Indians were recognized. On that day the Dutch set a very dangerous precedent. The Dutch settlers were allowed to hold title to land only if they first purchased it from the Indians and then received a grant from the Dutch authorities. Only after their disputes with the Dutch over title to land did the English begin to buy title from the Indians. At that point, the English undoubtedly purchased the land they obtained from the Indians not so much because this was the moral thing to do as because they could not afford to lose even the slightest advantage in their disputes with the Dutch (Boorstin, 1958, p. 259).

Roger Williams was viewed as a dangerous heretic for insisting that the Indians had a valid title not only to their villages and gardens but to their hunting grounds as well. He acquired his first title to the land for his colony by purchasing it from the Indians. It was only after the land had been occupied for some time that he received title from the crown. William Penn was another colonial leader who recognized the Indians' rights to land, and the treaty that his Quaker colony concluded with the Indians was one of the most scrupulously observed of early American history.

From the typical European viewpoint, however, the Indians were often included with the harsh weather, the great and unknown distances, and the wild animals as the perils of the wilderness that stood in the way of American progress. The fact that the land was not empty but was occupied by peoples of ancient and multiform cultures may have been viewed by the settlers as only one of the limiting conditions of their progress. However,

the clash of cultures between the Indians and the whites was a tragic encounter of greatly unequal opposing forces in which "the growth and development of the American society advanced over the prostrate culture of another people" (Boorstin, 1958, p. 259). The inability of the white settlers to find a way to understand and value the culture of the Indians was a limiting factor in the development of the colonies.

Illness and other hardships

In the harsh new environment, illness and accidents were a constant threat. In considering the devastating threat of illness, accidents, and wounds to the settlers, we must remember the primitive state of medical knowledge and the lack of methods and techniques of caring for the sick that we take for granted today. The principles of contagion and sanitation were not yet known. People were largely helpless before epidemics. There were no hospitals to take care of the sick and wounded. Care was given by the family in the home, or neighbors helped as best they could. Epidemics and conflicts with the Indians that left many sick, wounded, and dead were serious threats to the existence of all members of the group. The devastation that such experiences brought to the colonists set very real limits to the growth and development of the good life they had come to seek and left many persons in desperate need.

Political concepts

By the middle of the 18th century, most of what is now the northern coast of the United States and Canada was viewed as belonging to England. The only obstacle to the effective seizure and colonization of additional lands was the Indians, who were not seen by the English as an important obstacle. There were two visions of America in England at the time: the vision of certain leaders who saw in the new lands an opportunity to build new societies in which people could live more satisfactorily, which we have discussed as a force toward change, and the notion of certain powerful interests that the function of the American colonist was to create profits for the mother country, which was a restrictive force. Many of the wealthy and the powerful in England looked to America to fulfill two purposes:

1. To offer a place to export the poor and thus rid England of the "dangerous classes."
2. To supply raw materials and other resources that could support England's growing industrial development.

The English and Dutch monarchs granted huge tracts of land to wealthy and titled persons, many of whom were not so much landlords as exploiters of the resources of the land, concerned with the profits that could be made from speculation, tenancies, and the transportation of raw materials. The colonies especially affected by this notion were Virginia and the area that later became New York. In these colonies, an attempt was made to repeat the social patterns of England and Europe rather than to establish a new way of life (Boorstin, 1958, pp. 20–22).

As we mentioned earlier, all people bring with them to any new experience their earlier patterns of coping, but there was an additional factor to be considered in the settlers' experience in America. All of the settlers were colonials, and as such no group of settlers considered themselves to be free to construct their social institutions out of whole cloth. Even in New England, the settlers needed ample support in terms of new and local needs before they could effect changes in the English way of doing things.

In discussing the ties of the Massachusetts colonists to England and English institutions, Boorstin writes:

> The lawmakers of the colony, to the extent their knowledge allowed and with only minor exceptions, actually followed English example. Their colonial situation made them wary of trying to create institutions according to their notions. . . . They were hardly more worried that their laws should be "scriptual," that is approved by the Bible, than that they should be sufficiently English; and that

any changes in Enlgish laws should have ample warrant in local needs. (1958, pp. 20–21)

English law and their religious beliefs gave security to the colonists, but they also set the limits within which new policies could be developed. The English colonists brought with them the English welfare law of the time, in which we find the following principles:

1. The focus of economic security was the relationship between unemployment and the able poor.
2. The stability of society was threatened by poverty and the poor.
3. The state should play a major role in welfare planning through its smallest local divisions.
4. The poor were categorized into "the worthy" and "the unworthy" (or "the impotent" and "the ablebodied"), with different treatment assigned to the two groups.
5. Children were cared for through indenture.

Although there were local forces of sufficient strength to make the resulting patterns of welfare uniquely American, the dominant groups in the 13 colonies were of British origin and the emergent social welfare instititution of the new country resembled that of England in many ways.

Orthodoxy

A hallmark of the New England Pilgrims, and of some other colonists as well, was the certainty that they were on the right track. They firmly believed that God was with them and that no one could long stand against them. This served to restrict not only their questioning of their theology but the ways in which they utilized that tehology as a base for social relationships. The Pilgrims came to America determined not so much to have freedom to perfect the truth as to establish a society that would apply the truth as they already knew it to the affairs of everyday living. Thus, in the Massachusetts Bay Colony an orthodoxy was set in place by a self-selected body of conformists.

And the members of the colony were totally opposed to changing this state of things (Boorstin, 1958, p. 5).

Believing that there was but one truth and that they possessed it, the Puritans were intolerant of differences. They had no doubts and they allowed no dissent. While certainty as to their position regarding considerations of political or philosophic theory freed them to focus on building new towns, enforcing the criminal laws, and taming the wilderness, it restricted the range of the alternatives they considered. As communities formed by the free consent of like-thinking members, many of the early settlements, particularly in New England, saw no reason why they should not exclude from their midst those whom they saw as undesirable, dangerous, or subversive of their approach.

The exclusion of dissidents

Thus, several of the early colonies excluded and "warned out" persons who did not fit their definition of acceptability as members of the group. Among the criteria of acceptibility community were that one not be troublesome in behavior or speech and that one believe in the orthodoxy of the community without reservation. Another criterion was that newcomers not become dependent on the group for support. Winthrop records the following in his journal:

> Dec. 11, 1634. One Abigail Gifford, widow, being kept at the charge of the parish of Wilsden in Middlesex, near London, was sent by Mr. Ball's ship into this country, and being found to be somewhat distracted, and a very burdensome woman, the governor and assistants returned her back by warrant, 18, to the same parish, in the ship Rebecca. (Pumphrey and Pumphrey, 1961, p. 20)

The authorities expected to be notified of the presence of strangers and to judge whether they should be allowed to stay. Church leaders carefully examined newcomers. Persons who refused to either leave the community or abide by its religious beliefs were executed. Several Quakers, including women from Pennsylvania, who came into the Puritan settlements of New England to preach and refused to leave were hanged.

Also, in order to control the activities of single persons, they were required to live in families. The Province Laws of Massachusetts Bay for the session of 1692–93 expressed the prevailing attitude toward single persons. They ordered that every single person under 21 must live "under some orderly family government" but added the proviso that "this act shall not be construed to extend to hinder any single woman of good repute from the exercise of any lawful trade or employment for her livelihood, whereunto she shall have the allowance and approbation of the selectment (Abbott, 1909, p. 33).

Social superiority and inferiority

Although the notion of status relationships was never a part of American thinking, there were clear assumptions about social superiority and inferiority that were typical of the thought of the time. Even in the Quaker colony of Pennsylvania, which emphasized equality, freedom of conscience, and the separation of church and state, we find the notion that class distinctions are an essential part of the divine order. Penn wrote that God had not placed men on a level but had arranged them in orders of subordination and dependence. Due respect for these divinely ordered differences required that we love our equals and give our obedience to our superiors and our help and tolerance to our inferiors (Bremner, 1960, pp. 8–10).

In Plymouth, Winthrop likewise felt that disparities in wealth and condition were divinely ordained. He did not hesitate to distinguish between persons who were great and eminent and persons of a poor and inferior sort. He was convinced that such distinctions among individuals were necessary for the preservation of society and that they enhanced the "glory of his creator and the common good of the creator man" (Bremner, 1960, pp. 8–10).

In all 13 colonies, voting and office holding were tied to the ownership of property. Following the Revolution, these rights were extended somewhat, but they were still limited to free, property-owning males. The leap from this system to a franchise for all white males based on citizenship was still too great to contemplate. And certainly the notion of the equality of women, servants, and slaves as members of society was out of the question. "Benjamin Franklin once told the delightful story of a man who by virtue of owning a mule, earned the precious right to cast a ballot. But when the mule died, his right perished with it. 'I wonder,' mused Franklin, 'who had the vote, the man or the mule' '' (Lens, 1969, p. 71).

The unwillingness to accept differences in thought or behavior, the notion of an accepted order of individuals in the social structure, religious orthodoxy, and the need to follow English law set limits to the ways in which the social institutions of the colonies could depart from their previous function and structure. In the next section of this chapter we shall examine some of the mediating forces that were a part of colonial development.

ᴈ§ Mediating forces, processes, and structures

In addition to the forces for change and the limiting conditions that existed to some extent in all the colonies, there were crucial differences among the colonies that served as mediating factors in shaping the development of the various programs within the social welfare institution. Among the principle respects in which the colonies differed were the following: (1) the purpose of settlement and the type of government established; (2) the conditions of settlement; (3) the religious institution brought with the settlers; and (4) given the above, plus the differences in climate and geography, the type of economy that developed.

The purposes of settlement and government

With the exception of the areas of New York and Virginia, the American colonies were settled by persons who came expressly for the purpose of building a new way of life.

New England. The Plymouth and Massachusetts Bay colonies were settled primarily by Puritans who fled the efforts of the Stuart kings and their supporters to enforce a uniformity of religious belief upon all English subjects. The Pilgrims, anxious to escape the restrictive religious climate of England and to build a society of their own that would embody the truth as they knew it, free from the presence of opponents, were able to secure a grant of land from the Virginia Company of London and a capital fund of 7,000 pounds from a group of London merchants. For seven years each colonist was to put everything produced into a common store and was permitted to take from it what was needed for subsistence. At the end of seven years the accumulated surplus was to be divided between the Pilgrims and the English investors in proportion to the number of shares they held (Jernegan, 1929, pp. 110–21).

In the summer of 1623, the common land and labor system of the colony broke down. The members of the colony began to dislike having persons who contributed differential labor receive the same rewards, and husbands disliked having "their wives act as public servants and having them wash and cook for any member of the community" (Jernegan, 1929, p. 121). Besides, it was becoming evident that the English backers would not get their investment back and that there would be no profits. Faced with these problems, the Pilgrims revised their plans and families were given individual grants of land on which they could raise their own corn and other crops without having to place the produce in a common store (Jernegan, 1929, pp. 195–215). At the end of the seven-year period, the London investors got back about one quarter of their investment.

Other Puritans in England, disturbed by the political and religious theories of James I and Charles I, dissatisfied with the low moral standards of the time and with the decline of employment opportunities, and pulled by the possibility of establishing a model social and political system based on the biblical injunctions as they interpreted them, began to consider colonization (Jernegan, 1929, p. 125). The Massachusetts Bay Colony was chartered in 1629 for commercial purposes by men who were for the most part influential Puritan merchants. Among them were some of the wealthiest men in England who, unwilling to conform to the dogma of the Church of England, fled to America. These wealthy and influential men were able to arrange a charter that allowed the Massachusetts Bay Colony to function relatively independently of English supervision. The charter issued to the colony provided for a general court of the "freemen" (male church members owning a certain amount of property). John Winthrop, whose private income was $15,000 to $20,000 a year, was selected as governor of the colony. Through much of the colony's history the right to vote was held by about one fifth of the male citizens, while church attendance and taxation for the support of the church were made compulsory for all persons.

New York, New Jersey, and part of Delaware. The colonies of New York, New Jersey, and Delaware were first settled by the Dutch, who had begun to explore the New World at about the same time as the English. In the spring of 1623, 30 families of Dutch and Wallon Protestants, sponsored by the Dutch West India Company, established two settlements: one near the present site of Camden, New Jersey, and the other near the present site of Albany, New York. In 1626 Peter Minuit, the Director General of New Netherlands, made the famous purchase of the island of Manhattan. A third settlement was then established at the southern end of the island, which the Dutch named New Amsterdam (Jernegan, 1929, pp. 203–8).

The Dutch West India Company, which was originally formed to exploit the lands, furs, and trade of the New World to the profit of its proprietors, moved in 1629 to establish patroonships. Each patroon was given the absolute ownership of a huge tract of land in return for establishing a colony of 50 adults in the area. Under this system the Dutch permitted a monopoly of government, trade, commerce, and land to pass into the hands of a relatively few men who had extensive autonomous powers. The New Netherland colony, which the British renamed New York after they seized it from the Dutch, was governed autocratically and was directed from abroad (Jernegan, 1929 pp. 198–200).

Pennsylvania. While at Oxford University, William Penn, son of the wealthy and influential Admiral William Penn, became interested in Quakerism. He was expelled from the university for his interest, and he later spent several years in three different prisons. Having observed the persecution of other Quakers and experienced persecution himself, Penn dreamed of establishing in the New World a "Holy Experiment" under which virtuous men could build a virtuous society (Lens, 1969, pp. 41–56). He wanted to translate the beliefs and values of the Quakers into everyday life. On October 27, 1682, Penn and about 100 other immigrants arrived in America on the ship *Welcome*. They proceeded up the Delaware River and founded Philadelphia.

By the royal charter that he had been granted, Penn was made the absolute proprietor of Pennsylvania. Penn, however, wrote, "You shall be governed by laws of your own making. . . . I shall not usurp the right of any, or oppress his person" (Boorstin, 1958, p. 62). He proposed that the colony be governed by a governor, deputy-governor, and a council of 72 persons, of whom one third were to be elected each year. He proposed that all males who owned land or paid taxes should also elect an assembly that would assent to or dissent from laws prepared by the council. He also drew up a code of laws which provided for religious freedom and a mild criminal code. Apart from the differences indicated above, there were other important differences between Pennsylvania and other colonies. Pennsylvania opened its doors to all Christians, including non-Englishmen, on a basis of full equality. Though its open-door policy did not apply to Jews or other non-Christians, the colony gave refuge to more "foreigners" than did any other colony of the time. Moreover, it imposed fewer restrictions on the right to vote than did the other colonies. There were no religious qualifications for voting and only small property requirements (Boorstin, 1958, pp. 62–64).

Pennsylvania was not the only colony which paid the Indians for their land, but Penn and his governors were meticulous in avoiding deception or bargains to which they did not adhere. The Quakers believed in pacifism, and no forts, armies, or defenses were included in their plans for the colony.

The Quakers tended to settle in Philadelphia, and did not push into the lands beyond the Allegheny Mountains, as did other Pennsylvania settlers. As a result of the Quakers' refusal to vote for funds to help the outlying settlements protect themselves against the Indians, there was tremendous conflict within the colony and the Quakers lost control of the government of Pennsylvania (Boorstin, 1958, p. 64).

Georgia. Between South Carolina, which belonged to England, Florida, which belonged to Spain, and Louisiana, which was the property of France, was an unoccupied area of land which the English wanted strongly to have settled by British settlers. James Edward Oglethorpe, a member of Parliament, conceived the idea of using this land for the rehabilitation of criminals and small debtors. These people were to be brought to Georgia as freemen, not as servants, and given land and tools to work it. In return, the immigrants needed only to pledge to do military duty in defense of the crown. Georgia was the only colony that was not established as a religious haven or as a means of making money. It was the most liberal of the English colonies in that it accepted non-Christians (Jews) as equals and operated on a nonprofit basis. Slavery was not permitted within its borders, though indenture was practiced on a limited basis.

Hopes ran high as Governor Oglethorpe sailed with 130 carefully screened persons in the fall of 1732. But the initial design of the colony lasted less than 20 years. These forces united to bring disaster to the colony: (1) the potential of the land had been seriously miscalculated, and the crops of silk, grapes, and rice were not appropriate for the climate; (2) the division of the land among the settlers left them with plots too small to eke out even a minimum living, and the plots could be inherited only by the oldest son and not sold; and (3) the colony was ruled by the strong and auto-cratic hand of Governor Oglethorpe, who laid down firm and rigid rules of behavior. The rigid limits that were set did not allow the colonists enough flexibility to adapt to the problems of life in the New World (Boorstin, 1958, p. 56).

Virginia and the Southern colonies. Virginia's experience was very different from that of Georgia. Virginia was the oldest colony in America, and it was originally promoted as an adventure that would lead to riches. Later the leadership of the colony was provided by middle-class people who sought to find space in Virginia that would allow them to become a "new kind of English country gentleman." They sought with a good deal of success to translate the ways of the English manor house into the American milieu. The acquisition of a manor house did not signify a life of wealth and idleness but rather the acceptance of the burden of government and public responsibility—it meant becoming a justice of the peace, overseeing local church matters, being a father confessor to the peasants, serving as an overseer of the poor, and perhaps even serving as a member of the government (Boorstin, 1958, pp. 97–99).

In these Southern colonies there was struggle, tumult, discontent, and rebellion as a result of the conflicts between the settlers and the government imposed by England. The system of local government was patterned after the English system and based on the use of the county and the county court as a unit of government. The counties were divided into parishes, each of which was governed by a vestry, a body of 12 men which had both civil and church duties, including the care of the poor. This government was unlike the New England town in that the officers of government were appointed by the governor or by the county court. Power radiated downward rather than upward.

The conditions of settlement

There were two basic modes of immigration and settlement in the American colonies. In New England and Pennsylvania, the settlers came primarily to establish communities that would give their members a better way of living. With the exception of Georgia, the other colonies were settled to exploit the resources of the new country for the benefit of England or Holland. The differences in purpose resulted in certain differences in family and community life that affected the development of social welfare organizations. In New England and Pennsylvania, the immigrants came in family groups and settled in towns. The composition of the population was remarkably pure (particularly in New England), being largely English middle class. As a result the settlers were interested in developing social welfare organizations that would foster and support family life.

In New England the proportion of educated leaders was higher than in any other colony. Over 100 graduates of Oxford and Cambridge settled in New England before 1650. The migration to New England to 1643 is commonly considered to have been about 20,000 persons, or 4,000 families. Thus, about one person in every 40 families was a university graduate. This may help explain why a public school, a printing press, and a college were established in Massachusetts before 1640 (Jernegan, 1929, pp. 194–208).

In both New England and Pennsylvania a greater number of citizens participated in the government of the colonies because of the religious orientation of the colonies and because the colonies were not governed from England. Even though such colonies as the Massachusetts Bay Colony were governed by a small handful of men, these were men of the colony, neighbors of the governed, and concerned about the welfare of the community of which they were a part (Jernegan, 1929, pp. 194–208).

The middle colonies of New York, New Jersey, and Delaware, settled by the Dutch, were very different from New England in their social, religious, and national characteristics. When those colonies were settled, civil and religious liberty were farther advanced in Holland than in any other country of Europe. The colonies under Dutch rule became the asylum for every religious sect in Europe, and representatives of all races could be found among

the population. As early as 1664 it was reported that 14 languages were spoken on Long Island. Thus we find a very different social and cultural climate in the middle colonies than in the New England colonies. Of all the colonies, these were the most cosmopolitan and diverse, and they suffered from many of the problems of diversity. They were settled for profit, and no strong religious or moral purposes or cultural ties ran through the lives of their inhabitants (Jernegan, 1929, pp. 194–208).

The South was settled quite differently. Virginia was settled largely by adventurers who came to find a fortune and return to England as wealthy gentlemen. Its population increased slowly, partly because there were few families and partly because of a high mortality rate. Eventually, the male immigrants began to establish families and build an organized life. Because of the scarcity of women, at least two shipments of brides were made from England to Virginia. Its organized social life modeled on upper-class English life, with landed estates and an aristocratic government. The estates were largely on rivers, and supplies were brought in from England and Europe by boat. Thus, there were no towns. Since the planters were relatively self-sufficient, they saw no need for the resources of trade and commerce that towns could offer.

The churches and religious life

The colonies that were first established for profit motives show the least impact of organized religion on the day-to-day life of the settlers or on the development of social welfare organizations. Although the Anglican church was recognized as the state church of Virginia and the people were originally required to attend and support it, it was not a dynamic force. Later in the history of the Virginia colony, people were no longer required to attend church but still had to support it. Finally, they were allowed to attend and support any church they desired as long as they supported some religious body. The impact of the state church was even smaller in the culturally diverse New York colony.

However, in Pennsylvania the picture was very

different. Here the deeply devout Quakers brought their religious principles into every area of life. But although the Quakers suffered deeply for their beliefs, and attempted to convince others of the correctness of their approach, their very adherence to religious principles cost them the government of their colony. They believed in religious freedom and practiced it to the extent of admitting any Christian to their colony. This resulted in more religious freedom than one found in New England, for example. They believed very strongly in the individual's right to know what was best; thus there was little push for schools for all children (the parents could educate their children). They showed little concern about having an educated ministry; there was an early movement to limit slavery in the colony; and most important, they were actuated by a belief in pacifism that resulted in gradual loss of control over their own government.

New England was settled by a group of persons who believed in freedom of religion before they came to the new country. However, once here, their efforts to preserve their faith and to develop a particular style of life resulted in great intolerance and in the development of a social life in which the church stood at the center. The concern of the settlers to assure the church of learned leaders was a part of the strong push toward organized education in New England. Unlike the Quakers, the New Englanders adapted their religious beliefs to the world around them (Jernegan, 1929, pp. 110–42; Boorstin, 1958, pp. 35–49).

The place of women

The shortage of male laborers and, in Massachusetts, the puritan attitude toward idleness resulted in new and more diversified roles for women in American life. Women were tavern keepers and shopkeepers, traded and speculated in the seaboard towns, kept "dame schools," engaged in nursing midwifery, and domestic service. There were also instances in which women worked in or headed industrial establishments, for example, sawmills, distilleries, and slaughterhouses. A large number of women were employed as newspaper publishers or printers, and not all of them were widows who took up the husband's work. There were women apothecaries and even medical practitioners, although the jobs women did for pay were generally the same as those they did in their own households without pay. It was not unusual, and not frowned upon, for the daughter of a good family to go into domestic service. It is recorded, for example, that Judge Samuel Sewall's sister planned to become a maid. We should note that the domestic servant was employed for a considerable part of her time in the processes of home manufacture. A servant who was a good spinner or a good tailoress was valued accordingly (Abbott, 1909; Boorstin, 1958; Baxandall, Gordon, and Reverby, 1976).

Because of the scarcity of schools, women assumed much of the responsibility for colonial education. Some of the leading men of the time educated their daughters in other than domestic skills. Mather taught his daughter both Latin and Hebrew. Jefferson (a Virginian whose social and political views we shall discuss later) tutored his daughter. He explained that the subjects he taught her needed to be "considerably different from what I think would be most proper for her sex in any other country than America." He felt that it was necessary to look beyond his daughter's individual welfare and to consider the possibility that in marriage "she will draw a blockhead I calculate at about fourteen to one, and of course that the education of her family will probably rest on her own ideas and direction without assistance. With the best poets and prosewriters I shall therefore combine a certain extent of reading in the graver sciences" (Boorstin, 1958, p. 187).

Certain colonial laws seem to have equated the legal status of men and women. Married women had the right and the power to carry on businesses and to secure divorces. Like the women of England, the women of colonial America lacked the franchise, but otherwise they were protected in ways not even considered in England, and they were probably more prominent in professional and public life than they were to be again until this century (Boorstin, 1958, p. 187).

The place of children

Children, like women, were an integral part of the colonial labor system. In colonial life, the labor of children was a social fact and a social necessity, not a social problem. In 1641 the General Court of Massachusetts ordered: "All masters of families should see that their children and servants should be industriously applied" (Bremner, 1970, p. 322). If necessity justified the labor of young children, religion sanctified it. From an early age children were warned that idleness destroyed the soul and undermined the social system. Women were also warned of the dangers of idleness. It was not uncommon in New England for well-to-do parents to bind their children to other households to serve as servants so that they would experience and profit from the discipline of work. Family, church, and government had a part in keeping everyone employed. Later we shall examine the systems of apprenticeship and indenture that affected children in colonial America. The above material has discussed children as a source of labor for their own families (Bremner, 1970, pp. 103–4).

Indenture

In addition to availing themselves of the labor of women and children, colonial families turned to three other sources of labor: the Indian, the Negro slave, and the indentured servant. The settlers quickly found that the Indians were not easily domesticated. Although Indian slavery survived for a long time—as late as 1708 there are records of natives in bondage—it was not a dependable supply of labor. Thus, in the history of the economic development of America, the immigrants may have utilized and exploited the land of the Indian, but they were unable to exploit the Indian's labor.

One important source of labor, at least until the late 17th century, was the indentured white servant. In order to secure transportation to America, men and women would bind themselves by a written contract, called an indenture, to serve some individual (any individual) who would pay the costs of transportation. They served for a specified period

of time, usually four to seven years, for the food, clothing, and shelter necessary to maintain life. There were three general groups of indentured persons:

1. Persons who entered into a contract with an agent, usually the master of the ship that would take them to the New World, where the master reimbursed himself by selling the services of the person to the highest bidder.

2. Persons who were called "redemptioners" or "free-willers." They signed no contract in advance but were given transportation by the shipmaster with the understanding that when they arrived at their destination they would find someone willing to pay for their passage in return for binding themselves to service. The master would be free to sell them himself if they could not find a buyer.

3. Persons who were forced into service, such as convicts, vagrants, and other "dissolute persons," and persons who were kidnapped or "spirited away." As we shall see, many in this last group were children (Jernegan, 1931, pp. 45–47).

Indenture was also a way of dealing with the ablebodied poor citizens of the colonies. This practice will be discussed in the chapter dealing with the social welfare programs of the colonial era. Another practice that involved contracting for service was apprenticeship. However, apprenticeship was, at least in theory, a method of education in a skilled trade rather than a method of providing for one's expenses and physical needs. It will be discussed in our treatment of colonial education. In contrast, indenture was practiced in America in order to obtain labor or relieve the community of the support of the unemployed or teach good work habits.

It is estimated that more than 250,000 persons were indentured during the colonial period. In 1683 there were 12,000 indentured servants in Virginia (one sixth of the population), while at that time in Pennsylvania they made up two thirds of the immigrants (Jernegan, 1931, p. 45). Indenture seemed to have advantages for everyone involved: the colonists got the labor they needed; England rid itself of the idle, the wretched, and the criminal and relieved itself of their support; the indentured were given transportation to what many of them viewed as a world of opportunity; and the shipping trade had a good source of income.

Although there were times when the colonists questioned certain practices of indenture, in the beginning they were anxious to further it. The middle and southern colonies offered land in order to recruit labor, indentured or otherwise, a practice we will discuss later. In New England a cash bounty was more likely. For example:

> From and after the first day of April . . . any master, merchant, or others, that shall import or bring in and dispose in service within this province any male servants of the Kingdom of Great Britain, being between the age of eight and twenty-five years, there shall be paid unto such master, merchant, or other person, the sum of forty shillings per head, gratis, for every such male servant. (Bremner, 1970, p. 22)

There is the plea that, among other helps, Providence would assist New England

> by stirring up some well-minded to clothe and transport over poor children, boys and girls, which may be a great mercy to the bodies and souls and a help to us, they being super abundant [in London], and we wanting hands to carry on our trades, manufacture and husbandry there. (Bremner, 1970, p. 20)

Many people saw indenture as an opportunity to leave England for a better life in America and voluntarily entered into it. In addition, agents of the transporters traveled throughout England and Europe, speaking of the great fortunes that were to be made in America and persuading people to accept the opportunity to gain free passage to that wealth. Perhaps one of the most troubling sources of indentured labor was kidnapping. The profits to be made from supplying labor to the New World were so great that kidnapping developed as a regular business in London and seaport towns. Agents called spirits would find ways of enticing persons aboard ship and keeping them there until the vessel was under way. Even children were sent to America by this method.

Great Britain was particularly anxious to rid itself of its convicts, and America became a resource of the British correctional system. In 1717 an act of Parliament gave judges the power to order the transportation of convicts; those sentenced to death were to be indentured for 14 years and other felons for 7 years. The persons who took the responsibility for transporting the convicts were free to sell them as servants.

The voyage to the New World for indentured persons ordinarily took 6 to 12 weeks, but it could last much longer. A space of six feet by two feet was allowed for each passenger. Ships often boarded twice as many people as they were supposed to. Food was very short, and there are records of the passengers almost fighting for the bodies of mice and rats. On one ship, six dead humans were eaten before another ship came by and replenished the supplies. On one ship only 13 out of 150 servants survived, and on another only 50 out of 400 were still alive when the ship docked in America. Children under seven rarely survived, and an eyewitness recorded that he saw 32 dead little children thrown into the ocean on one voyage (Jernegan, 1931, p. 50).

When the ship finally made port, no one was permitted to leave unless the passage was paid. The others were put on the auction block. Parents were forced to sell their children and often never saw them again. Husbands and wives were separated. Children under 5 often could not be sold, and they were then given away to serve the family that took them until they were 21. However, indentured servants were protected by the terms of their indentures, and at the end of their service they were provided with "freedom dues," which included clothing, food, a gun, and, sometimes, 50 acres of land. Indentured servants were treated harshly; many were beaten as a regular form of punishment. But unlike the black slaves, they did have certain legal rights and they could sue their master in the courts for breach of contract.

The master controlled all the personal affairs of the indentured servants. They could not buy liquor or make other personal decisions without the master's consent. Usually marriage was forbidden, because sexual relations were likely to result in childbearing, with the consequent interruption of work and impairment of health and stamina. There is at least one record of a married couple being forbidden to cohabit during their term of indenture (Baxandall, Gordon, and Reverley, 1976, p. 28). As a practical matter, the prevention of illicit sexual relationships was difficult. Children were commonly born out of wedlock among the indentured servants. In many colonies a servant guilty of having a child out of wedlock was required to pay a fine as well as to indemnify her master for the loss of services he had suffered through her pregnancy. Since indentured servants had little financial resources of their own, usually the only way they could reimburse the owner was to extend their term of service. Except in Virginia, where the putative father had to post bond for the support of the child, the responsibility for the child and the extra service was imposed on the mother only. The law was concerned only when the putative father happened to be the owner, as he stood to benefit by his own illegal acts if the term of service were increased because a child had been born from his relationship with his servant. In that case, the churchwardens were to sell the woman for her extra term of service. However, they might sell this extra term of service to the original master. No punishment was accorded the master.

In colonial America, free labor on a wage system was impossible because of the scarcity of such labor, high wages, and the availability of free land. The system of indentured labor served to provide the labor needed until the slavery of blacks was extended in the South and laborsaving machinery was developed in the North. Given these developments, by 1831 indenture was no longer an important source of labor. Indentured servants did not become a distinct class in society after they were

freed. Many emigrated to the frontier lands in the West. Few became wealthy or prominent, but we know that two signers of the Declaration of Independence came to America as indentured servants.

Slavery

The terrible story of Negro slavery forms a special chapter in the history of American life and American social welfare. The horror that was slavery in the colonies began in 1619 with the landing at Jamestown, Virginia, of "twenty negars" in August. However, blacks had come to America long before this as servants, explorers, and slaves. Pedro Alonso Nino of Columbus's crew has been identified as a black man by some scholars. Certainly, black people accompanied Balboa, Ponce de Leon, Cortés, Pizarro, and Menéndez. Black slaves were a part of the first settlement in the area now occupied by the United States—a Spanish colony in the area of present-day South Carolina. They revolted and fled to the Indians. William Tucher, the first black child to be born in English America, was baptized at Jamestown in 1624. Every colony except Georgia had black citizens—free men, artisans, and slaves. The history of slavery is usually thought of in connection with the South, but there were slaves in New England. And the shipping industry in New England was deeply involved in the transportation of slaves from Africa to America. Thus, the slave trade was economically important to New England as well as the South. In fact, Massachusetts in 1641 became the first colony to give statutory recognition to slavery, followed by Connecticut in 1650.

It is often assumed that the black people of colonial times were passive and accepting, contributing only unskilled labor to America, but this is far from true. Many free blacks fought long and hard against slavery. In 1723 serious fires in Boston were believed to have been set by slaves and indentured servants. The Massachusetts governor issued a proclamation on the "fires which have been designedly and industriously kindled by some villainous and desperate negroes or other dissolute people as appears by the confession of some of them" (Bennett, 1964, p. 361).

Crispus Attucks, a black hero of the American Revolution, was owned by a Framingham, Massachusetts, man from whom he escaped on September 30, 1750. Twenty years later, he was the first of five persons to be killed in the Boston Massacre, on March 5. He is generally regarded as the first martyr of the Revolution. Black and white minutemen fought side by side at Lexington and Concord. Blacks also fought in most of the battles of the American Revolution. At one time, George Washington issued an order forbidding the enlistment of blacks in the revolutionary forces, but alarmed at the possibility that they might be persuaded to join the British, he rescinded the order in less than a month. It has been estimated that 5,000 black soldiers fought in integrated units during the Revolutionary War (Bennett, 1964, pp. 363–64).

In 1773, slaves in Massachusetts petitioned the legislature for freedom. (This petition was followed by eight others during the Revolutionary War.) In the same year Phillis Wheatley's *Poems on Various Subjects, Religious and Moral,* was published in Massachusetts. It was the second book to be published by an American woman and the first to be published by an American black. Vermont, on July 2, 1777, became the first American state to abolish slavery. In 1783 slavery was prohibited in Massachusetts and New Hampshire. Connecticut and Rhode Island barred slavery in 1784. Thus, soon after the Revolutionary War slavery had been abolished in New England.

Like indenture, slavery grew out of the growing labor requirements of the colonies. In the face of those requirements, white indenture and native labor were inadequate, particularly in the South. Furthermore, the cost of indentured servants was relatively high compared to the cost of black slaves. It is estimated that the cost of buying and maintaining an indentured servant ran to 22 pounds, and at the end of a period of years the servant was free. In the early colonial period, a young black slave could be bought for 18–25 pounds (by 1770 this had increased to 50–80 pounds), and the slave

not only worked for life but provided his or her master with salable or usable children. It is estimated that during the century from 1686 to 1786 approximately 2 million Africans were spirited away from their homes; 250,000 of them ended up in the American colonies (Lens, 1969, p. 27).

Everything that was said about the cruelty and inhumanity of the indenture system could be multiplied many times over in describing the slave trade and slavery.

We may well ask how a people who were as concerned with religion and morality as were the people of America could countenance an institution that violated all religious commands regarding the treatment of other human beings. One of the arguments offered by religious people in defense of the slave trade was that the members of infidel groups (blacks and Indians) could be enslaved by Christians because their infidelity put them outside the pale of spiritual and civil rights and their souls were doomed. Another argument advanced by religious people was that the enslavement of such people was an act of mercy because only through slavery could large numbers of them be brought to Christ.

This religious sanction for slavery raised many troublesome questions, and it led some to believe that a black who had been converted to Christianity was entitled to freedom on the ground that one Christian could not own another. "If proof of heathenism legalized the enslavement of a negro, would his subsequent conversion to Christianity be a reason for enfranchisement?" (Jernegan, 1931, p. 25). The question of the conversion of slaves was argued with much heat throughout the American colonies. Many slave owners were hostile to conversion because they feared that it would lead to increased demands for equality on the part of the slaves and that it would weaken certain practices that the masters found necessary for effective control. To resolve this dilemma, some colonial assemblies based the validity of slavery on race. The Society of Friends was the only religious group that gradually forced members who held slaves to free them or face expulsion from their religious community.

The American Revolution

The history of the American Revolution has been well told by competent historians. We will not dwell on it here, except to point out that it was a movement toward securing the rights of individuals for a voice in their government and in their lives. The increasing difference between the social and economic life of America and that of England made it impossible for the English government to speak for the interests of the colonists. However, in addition to being a revolution against Britain, the American Revolution was a revolution against certain controlling interests in the colonies that were unwilling to share the wealth and power that they had developed.

During colonial days many lower-class Americans were more angry at the native aristocrats than at the king. The great estates and the concentration of wealth in a few hands resulted in rebellious anger among many of the common people and among such leaders as Rush. The Revolution deflected and channeled that anger into a war against England. One of the significant results of the Revolution was that it opened up land west of the Alleghenies for settlement and that it broke the large estates that had been held by the wealthy on grants from the king or English land companies. As with all other times of crisis, there was great suffering by many during the Revolution and a few used the opportunity to amass fortunes.

ᴥᔕ Summary

In this rather lengthy chapter on colonial America, we have examined certain forces that we have identified as contributing directly and indirectly to the development of the institution of social welfare in the United States. We have identified as forces that promoted change the optimistic orientation of American colonial society, the geography and the climate, the shortage of labor, the contractual relationships between individuals, the religious base of benevolence, and certain charismatic leaders of the time. We have identified as forces that limited change the occupied land; illnesses and other hardships of life; political structures and concepts that were imported by the colonists; religious orthodoxy, which pushed some settlers to make a new life but was used to limit other settlers; the exclusion of dissidents; and the notions of social superiority and inferiority. We have identified as mediating forces the variety of purposes for establishing the colonies; the political, religious, and economic conditions under which the colonies were established; the churches and religious life; the place of women and children in the social structure; and the patterns of indenture and slavery that were developed to furnish labor for the new communities.

ᴥᔕ A look ahead

In many ways the next chapter represents a continuation of this chapter. It deals with the development of social welfare policies and programs as they grew out of the needs of people and were shaped by the forces discussed in this chapter.

ᴥᔕ Study questions

1. Given the discussion in this chapter and what you know about American colonial history, what would you view as the primary threats to the security of the early Americans?

2. What would you see as the primary social welfare problems of the various colonies?

3. If by some magic you were to find yourself in trouble in colonial America, what problem would you prefer to have, in which colony would you prefer to be living, and what personal characteristics would you prefer to possess?

4. Make an outline of the sources of economic, political, and religious power in the various colonies. Do these sources overlap? How do you think this affected social welfare programs?

5. What notions about people and their relationships that you find in this chapter do you think exist in America today?

6. List the groups in colonial America that were politically treated as "nonpersons."

✌§ Selected readings

Boorstin, Daniel J. *The Americans: The Colonial Experience.* New York: Random House, 1959.

> This is an excellent account of colonial American life. It is strongly recommended for students with an interest in history.

Bremner, Robert H. *American Philanthropy.* Chicago: University of Chicago Press, 1960.

> The first chapters in this text deal with the early American philanthropists. These chapters should be very interesting to students and are a nice expansion of the material in this chapter.

Lens, Sidney. *Poverty: America's Enduring Paradox.* New York: Thomas Y. Crowell, 1959.

> Lens presents an interesting account of American attitudes toward the poor and American programs for income maintenance. We would recommend that students read the first four chapters of the book as an accompaniment to the material in the text.

Baxandall, Rosalyn; Gordon, Linda; and Reverby, Susan. *America's Working Women: A Documentary History 1600 to the Present.* New York: Vintage Books, 1976.

> The women in the class should enjoy reading pages 1–34 of this book. These deal with the work of women in colonial society.

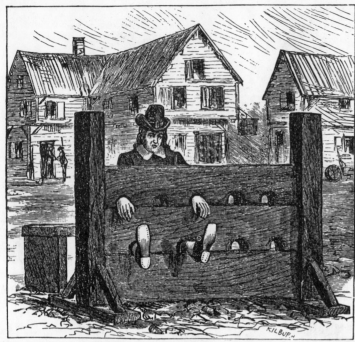

The corrections system of the colonies was primarily local, involving direct punishment as the method of correction.

Both from Historical Pictures Service, Inc., Chicago

Chapter 11 ॐ

ॐ Social welfare in colonial times: Policies and programs,1600–1780 ॐ

ॐ Introduction

In this chapter we will deal with the development of social welfare in the human service systems of income maintenance and social services, education, health and corrections. Because of the close interaction between the problems of income maintenance and the supply of labor in a tight market, these will be treated together under income maintenance. The interaction between the need for an adequate supply of labor and the shape of the income maintenance program should always be kept in mind. We will discuss the care of children as a specialized area within income maintenance and social services.

The reader should be aware that most of the programs discussed are developed and supported at the local level, which we would expect, given the pattern of locality brought from England and the different patterns of settlement and government found in the colonies. However, we will spend some time on programs that were mounted at the level of the colony rather than the community. These programs were the first exceptions to the doctrine of locality, and they set precedents for state actions following the Revolution.

We will also discuss privately supported social welfare programs, because such programs have been an important part of American social welfare.

ॐ Public welfare—Income maintenance and social services

Although the American colonies offered more promise to more people than any other place on earth, there were many threats to the security of the American settlers: (1) The settlers had to clear their land and pray that their crops would not be destroyed by plague, famine, or fire. (2) The Indians stubbornly refused to be cheated of their heritage, Christianized, domesticated, or enslaved, and their resistance reduced many settlers to stark dependence through the destruction of villages and farms;

(3) Illnesses and accidents left many people unable to care for themselves and left many children without parents. (4) Many people were victimized by the economic and political manipulation of the powerful, which resulted in devalued prices, high interest rates, increased rents, and limitations on the availability of the lands beyond the Alleghenies (Lens, 1969, pp. 30–33).

Dealing with income maintenance needs

As we stated earlier, in attempting to develop ways of dealing with destitution, the English colonists brought to their settlements the central concepts of the English Poor Laws: (1) public responsibility; (2) local responsibility; (3) responsibility for relatives; and (4) residency. They followed the English practice of classifying the poor into three groups: (1) the impotent poor who were unable to work; (2) the able-bodied idle; and (3) children. These concepts and this rough classification of persons in need have remained a part of American thought about programs of public welfare to the present day. They have also been a part of public law and legislation from their formal adaption by the colonial legislature of Rhode Island in 1647 until their gradual erosion in the 1960s and 70s.

The primary reasons for the settlers' adoption of the harsh English laws were: (1) the low level of productivity and the high level of need, which meant that no excess of common wealth was available for relief purposes; and (2) the moral underpinnings provided by puritan Calvinism, with its stern beliefs in the necessity for work. However, it is important to remember that, harsh as these laws may seem to be, they also demanded, from the beginning of colonization, that those who were better off should accept a public responsibility to provide maintenance for those who were without provisions. Following English law, and certainly supported by the social organization of the colonies, this public responsibility was assumed by the smallest unit of government—the town, county, or parish.

Warning out. The first method that the colonists used to control poverty was to prevent individual persons from entering the colony or the towns. We discussed earlier the fact that dissidents were not welcome in the towns and that this preserved a unity of belief and action. However, persons who were in danger of being unable to support themselves were also refused the right to settle in the towns. It was the duty of people who received strangers in their homes to notify the selectman so that he could warn the strangers that they could not gain residence in the town and would have to leave if they became dependent. Plymouth made the shipmasters responsible for bringing in persons who might become dependent on the town and required shipmasters to either post bond for such persons or return them to their place of origin. Others who brought into the colony or gave shelter to persons who were likely to become paupers were required to free the town from any responsibility for those persons and to agree to maintain them at their own expense.

A newcomer who was allowed to stay in the town did not immediately become a citizen. Such persons were put on probation for three months to a year. If they became dependent on others for their support before that time, their support was chargeable to the individuals responsible for their entrance to the town (Jernegan, 1931, pp. 192–94).

As New England developed, Boston found itself in a peculiar and unfortunate situation because it was the largest town of the area and a seaport. Thus it was unable to "warn out" all undesirables and it became a place of refuge for persons who were compelled to leave the smaller towns. "The towne is fild with poore idle and profane persons which are greatlie prijuditiall to the inhabitants," complained a petition to the general court which demanded some relief from the burden. In 1715 Boston provided that justices, selectmen, overseers of the poor, constables, and tithingmen should visit families "to Inspect disorderly persons, New-comers And the circumstances of the poor and the education of their children" (Jernegan, 1931, p. 197).

Local responsibility. The first American law relating to the poor was established in Plymouth in 1642. It provided that the people of each town should maintain their poor "according as they fynd most convenyent and suitable for themselves by an order and genall agreement in a publike town meeting." (Jernegan, 1931, p. 196) The first colony-wide poor law in New England was enacted by Rhode Island. It was followed by a Connecticut law of 1673 which ordered every town to maintain its own poor. It provided that after three months' residence relief should be provided for any person who "by sickness, lameness or the like comes to want" (Jernegan, 1931, p. 196). Massachusetts provided in 1692 that towns must relieve those who were unable to work (Jernegan, 1931, p. 196). These laws were the forerunners of our current, challenged, residency requirements found in assistance programs.

Under such laws the situation of each person or family needing help was examined separately at town meetings or by selectmen; and the decision regarding the type of care represented an individual judgment as to what the needy person or family deserved. In Virginia, the unit of government concerned with the poor was the parish and tithes were collected for their support.

Farming out. In the colonial towns it was common practice to place a poor or sick person with a family. The family was then reimbursed by the town for its costs. A not unusual example of such care is provided by a Hadley, Massachusetts, town meeting in 1687, which voted that the Widow Baldwin should be sent from house to house, spending two weeks with each family "able to receive her." Ten pounds a year were allowed by the selectmen of Watertown in 1680 to "Widow Bartlet to diet ould Bright and carry in his diet or send it for his necessary supply" (Jernegan, 1931, p. 196). Under this system of "farming out," the adult poor might well be turned over to the persons who were willing to take care of them at the lowest charge to the community. This might allow poor persons to remain in their own homes, or it might result in what amounted to private almshouses.

Indenture. Besides the impotent poor there were the able-bodied poor who were not self-supporting. On May 28, 1629, the first instructions of the Massachusetts Bay Colony to Governor John Endicott ordered that "noe idel drone bee permitted to live amongst us" (Jernegan, 1931, p. 199). Early laws of the colony provided for the whipping, imprisonment, or binding out to service (indenture) of the able-bodied idle. We discussed the importation of indentured laborers in the preceding chapter. Here it should be noted that the able-bodied poor were also sold into service at public auction.

Almshouse and other indoor care. As the colonial cities grew and the numbers of the able-bodied poor increased, the individual handling of their cases became difficult and group care developed. The poor might be cared for at a privately owned workhouse under contract with the public authorities or at a publicly owned house of correction, a poor farm, or an almshouse.

The first almshouse in the American colonies was established at Rensselaerswyck, New York, in 1657 (Axinn and Levin, 1975, p. 13) Plymouth authorized the erection of a workhouse or house of correction in which the inmates were to "have noe other supply for theire sustainance than what they shall come by their labour all the while that they shall continue there" (Jernegan, 1931, p. 201). Boston constructed an almshouse in 1660, but until 1712 it was little more than a house of correction in which all sorts of persons were herded together. By 1712 the town had become concerned about the conditions in the almshouse and it was ordered that a workhouse be built to put the able-bodied persons to work. However, the workhouse was not constructed until 1739.

By the end of the colonial period the notion of whipping the idle to make them work had been largely given up and the concept of providing some form of work, either by establishing workhouses or by binding offenders out to service, had taken hold.

The workhouse was invariably a combination of penal institution and poorhouse. At the time it was considered a most useful and beneficial institution, fulfilling a number of functions. It served as a penal establishment for vagabonds and rogues, the idle and the vicious; as a means of profitably employing the able-bodied poor; as a deterrent to persons who might easily become dependent were it not for the threat of forced labor; and as an asylum for the insane (Jernegan, 1929, p. 201).

The purposes of the first of these institutions to be built in New York, in 1736, were stated explicitly in its name: "Poor-House, Work-House, and House of Correction of New York City." In that institution, rogues, vagabonds, and petty offenders were grouped with the ill and the insane. The "unruly" insane were confined in special dungeons in the "Western division of the cellar" (Deutsch, 1949, p. 52).

The Dutch and the care of the poor

The Dutch pattern of public relief provided for classification of the poor, as did the English, but there were significant differences between the Dutch and English patterns of care for the impotent. The charter of New Amsterdam gave the patroons extensive powers in dealing with "vagabonds and outcasts who live on alms and in idleness and crime." Such persons could be bound to the service of the patroon for board and clothing only, for life if need be (Jernegan, 1931, p. 204).

However, the impotent poor were to be provided for in their own homes, where they were to be supervised by the clergy. Deacons were given the responsibility of administering poor relief funds derived from Sunday parish collections and from fines assessed for various offenses. The Dutch viewed the poor as neighbors, as belonging to the community. This concept supported mutual aid, with the church functioning as the center of charitable activity and as the monitor of the community's conscience. We see the concept of the poor as needing support and comfort carried out in the establishment of the church office of comforter of the sick. The comforter of the sick, who was charged with seeing that the poor or troubled had psychological support and comfort as well as concrete resources, stands in some contrast to the English overseer of the poor, whose primary responsibilities were to see that the poor were worthy of the aid given them and that the aid was properly used.

When the Dutch lost New Amsterdam to the English, the English Poor Law was substituted for church care of the impotent. The parish became the unit of administration, and in each parish an overseer of the poor administered relief with the aid of two churchwardens. New York, like Boston, was a port of entry for immigrants and a bustling seaport, and as a result it too had special problems in caring for the poor which resulted in unusually harsh measures at times (Jernegan, 1931, pp. 200–210).

The Quakers and the poor

Collective responsibility for reducing inequality and poverty was a central concern of the Quakers. At every monthly meeting of the Philadelphia Quakers, help for the poor was a major point on the agenda. People in difficult straits presented their problems to the group or arranged to have someone speak on their behalf. The meeting then voted sums for food, clothing, shelter, and coal that were to be dispensed by a caretaker. The help provided was not confined to members of the Society of Friends, and it frequently included more than relief. When a person was out of work, efforts were made to find a suitable job. If that were impossible, material was supplied so that the unemployed person might engage in handicrafts at home. Help was given through voluntary subscription rather than public funds, and every effort was made to teach people to become self-reliant.

As Philadelphia developed, the problems of the poor could not be taken care of entirely by the meeting of Friends, so almshouses and houses of correction were built. In addition, "Visitors of the Poor" were employed to seek out and aid those in need. By the time of the Revolution, Philadelphia had established a complex of three buildings that were devoted to the problems of the poor—the Bettering House, the House of Employment, and the Philadelphia Hospital (Jernegan, 1931, p. 210).

Colony-wide income maintenance

Disaster victims. In 1675 we have the first example of a departure from the principle of local relief. A bitter war was being waged with the Indians on the western borders of the New England colonies, and the settlers in that area had suffered terribly in loss of life and homesteads. As a result, the Massachusetts legislature authorized funds to be appropriated for their relief from the colony's treasury. The towns in the area were too overwhelmed by the disaster to be able to help themselves

Veterans. Another departure from the usual relief practices was adopted by Plymouth Colony in 1636, when it enacted legislation stating that any veteran who was injured in the service of the colony was entitled to support. Other colonies followed this example, so that by 1777 all of the American colonies except Connecticut had made special provisions for veterans. This help did not carry the onus of pauperism. It was accepted that the soldier was entitled to it as a partial payment for the service he had given the state (Lens, 1969, pp. 38–39). The aid given to the veteran was provided by the colony rather than the locality because the veteran had served the colony. Special treatment of this type was discussed in Chapter 6 as one way of allocating support to persons assumed to have been damaged for, or to have given special service to, society (compensation for identified disservice). Veterans were being compensated for the disruption of their lives and for their special contributions to their colonies. At the same time, they had demonstrated a special kind of individual worth.

This principle of the right of veterans to aid was so well received that the Continental Congress in 1776 adopted a report of the Committee on Disabled Soldiers and Sailors recommending that the states establish pensions for invalid or disabled veterans.

The unsettled poor. Occasionally the American towns were confronted by poor persons who seemed to have no settlement, or whose settlement was impossible to determine. In cases of this kind in which there was great destitution, it was possible for the unsettled poor to receive a certain amount of help from the colony rather than the town.

These colony-wide programs of help for the veteran, occasional help to the unsettled poor, and help to the settlers of western New England during King Philip's War began to establish certain practices that would later serve as precedents for state and federal participation in public relief activities.

✑ Privately supported income maintenance and personal social service

In addition to the colonies' public system of poor relief, there also grew up certain private ways of helping those in need. As we wrote earlier, there was great emphasis on helping one's neighbor as a religious duty. The New England and Pennsylvania towns were small, and the people knew one another's troubles intimately. Thus, there was undoubtedly much informal sharing.

In 1657 the Scot's Charitable Society was founded in Boston. This was a group of Scots who banded together to aid one another in need. The society was established in the port town of Boston, and it became the forerunner of many such friendly societies, especially in the northern seaport cities. Through these societies, immigrants of a similar background could help one another as they came to the new country. As the friendly societies developed, they became a source of information and support for newcomers. They also served as insurance and funeral associations. Members paid dues, used to care for them in time of sickness and death (Bremner, 1960, p. 187).

One of the first attempts of the settlers in the various colonies to offer help to one another in a disaster was stimulated by the Boston fire of 1760. Individuals in various communities in the middle colonies, led by Pennsylvania, joined together to collect donations and send relief to the sufferers in their neighboring colony.

✑ Child welfare—Personal social services and income maintenance for children

Child labor

As was pointed out earlier, the colonists had a great need in the colonies for labor, so it seemed only natural that they should expect their children to work. In addition to expecting their own children, or the children of their neighbors, to be employed and taught a trade, the colonists imported poor and orphan children from England and Holland to America to be bound out as laborers.

In one example the superintendents of the almshouses in London were directed to "take from the almshouses or orphan asylums 300 to 400 boys and girls of ten, twelve to fifteen years of age" for transport to America (Bremner, 1970, p. 23). In 1654 the burgomasters of Amsterdam sent a cargo of poor children to Peter Stuyvesant at Fort New Amsterdam. In the quotation below, from a letter accompanying the children to the New World, we see clearly the social welfare implications involved. The plan appears to be ideal. It relieves the mother country of the responsibility of caring for the orphans at the same time that it gives the orphans an opportunity to work out their own destiny.

> Being informed by the governors of the almshouses of the vast number of poor people where with they are burdened and charged, we have concluded to relieve them and so do the Company a service, by sending some of them to New Netherland.
>
> We have, therefore, sent over in the ship belonging to the bearer hereof, twenty-seven or twenty-eight boys and girls, requesting you, in a friendly manner, to extend to them your kind advice and assistance, and to advance them if possible; so that they, according to their fitness, may earn their board. If you consider that the populations of that country could be advanced by sending over such persons, we shall, on being informed, lose no time to have some more forwarded. Meanwhile, we shall be much obliged by the aid and assistance you will extend in this instance. (Bremner, 1970, p. 23)

Orphans

In March 1642 the first of many colonial laws relating to orphans was enacted in Virginia. The guardians and overseers of orphans were ordered to furnish an annual account of the handling of the estates of the orphans to the commissioners of the county court. They were also ordered to

educate and instruct their charges "according to their best endeavours in Christian religion and in rudiments of learning." If the guardians or overseers were found to be delinquent in their duties, the commissioners were empowered to see that the orphans were provided for "according to their estates and qualities." The legislation stated that orphans whose estate was not large enough to provide for their education and care were to be apprenticed until 21 to learn a trade. An act of 1705 added that every orphan should be taught to read and write while so apprenticed (Jernegan, 1931, pp. 143–56). In general, this Virginia legislation is a good example of the usual care of colonial orphans. However, institutions for the care of orphaned children began to develop in the late 1700s. These institutions, usually called orphanages, also provided care for classes of children other than orphans.

Institutional care of children

As we have seen, George Whitefield established a church-related orphanage in Georgia in 1840. The first public orphanage in the American colonies was established in the city of Charlestown, South Carolina, in 1790. The institution was to care for and educate both orphan children and children whose parents were destitute and unable to maintain them. The matron of the orphanage was also the schoolteacher, and she was charged with teaching the children as well as watching over their morals and their conduct (Abbott, 1938, pp. 29–31).

Although New Orleans was not a part of the 13 English colonies on the eastern seaboard, it appears important that we discuss briefly the orphanage that the Ursuline nuns founded there in 1729. It was the first children's institution in the country. Mother Marie Tranchepain de St. Augustin was the first of a tiny band of Ursulines who left France in 1727 to create an institution in New Orleans that would care for the "sick poor" and provide for the "education of youth." The planters in the area had asked the nuns to come because there were no schools for their daughters in the area and they were tired of sending them to school in Paris. They had hoped that the nuns would start an academy for the young ladies of New Orleans. In the original plan there was no mention of the need for an orphanage. However, on November 28, 1729, a band of Natchez Indians attacked Fort Rosalie and killed every man in the post. Given this emergency, the Ursulines made room in their charity hospital for the orphans and so was established the first children's institution on the American continent. The Ursulines' hospital was also one of the first charity hospitals in America (Whittaker, 1970, pp. 29–31).

Indigent, dependent, illegitimate, and mulatto children

Between 1646 and 1769, Virginia enacted a series of eight laws dealing with the education of poor, illegitimate, or mulatto children. In general, these laws provided for and regulated the apprenticeship or indenture of these children and required that they be taught to read and write during their indenture.

Illegitimate children. There were special acts of legislation affecting the illegitimate child. In some colonies the father of such a child was obliged to give security or indemnify the parish for the child's support. If the father was an indentured servant who had no resources, the parish was to keep the child until the father could make satisfaction to the parish for expenditures on its behalf. Later, churchwardens were required to bind out the illegitimate children of single white women. If an indentured woman bore an illegitimate child during her term of service, the child was to be maintained by the master and the master was entitled to its service until the age of 21 if the child was a boy and until the age of 18 if the child was a girl (Jernegan, 1931, pp. 164–65).

Dependent and neglected children. In 1727, churchwardens, on the orders of the county court, were given the power to bind out the children of idle and "dissolute" parents who either could not support their children or did not take due care of their instruction in "Christian principles." Children

so apprenticed were entitled to certain legal protections in relation to their education, provided that they could interest someone in seeing that their cases were brought to the attention of the court (Jernegan, 1931, pp. 143–56).

Apprenticeship. Under the laws mentioned above, the parishes were to keep records on apprenticed children. The records of two parishes are interesting as examples of what was happening to four classes of children: orphans, poor children, illegitimate children, and mulatto children. Children without parents constituted just over one third of all the children apprenticed by order of the court. As there was a shortage of artisans in Virginia, the boys were most often apprenticed to carpenters, shoemakers, blacksmiths, or planters. The girls were usually apprenticed as domestic servants, with no particular trade mentioned, though in nine cases there were requirements that they be taught to knit, spin, and sew.

The educational requirements were sharply different for boys and girls. The minimum requirement for every boy was reading and writing, and boys had to have one or two years of formal schooling. Girls, on the other hand, were to be taught both to read and write in only three cases, and in no case was it required that they be sent to school. While there is no way of knowing how well the educational clause in indenture contracts was actually fulfilled, it does appear from the examination of old records that Virginia did establish and develop a real system of compulsory education for the classes of children mentioned above. The system of apprenticeship was an important agency for the elementary education of poor children in colonial Virginia. The system required the separation of children from their families at an early age, but it also provided for their upbringing in other families rather than institutions (Jernegan, 1931, pp. 164–65).

Some children who could not be expected to work, including infants and sick or crippled children, received relief in their own homes or were boarded out at the expense of the town. However, the usual method of providing for destitute, neglected, or orphaned children was to indenture, or bind them out, as early as possible on the best terms available.

✑§ Education

Massachusetts

From the very beginning, the New England colonies, led by Massachusetts, were concerned with education. The settlers of these colonies had immigrated in family groups and thus were immediately confronted with the need to train and educate their children. Also, as noted earlier, Massachusetts had an extremely high ratio of university-trained people, most of whom served as pastors of churches. Given the influence of the church in the life of the people, these pastors had great opportunity to influence their congregations in favor of public education. Both the pastors and the people wanted to continue to have educated religious leaders. Thus, they needed to supply their children with a type of basic education that would support later university education and the development of a university-trained pastorate. Religious values also promoted education in two other ways: (1) children had to be able to read in order to understand the principles of their religion; and (2) education was needed in order to carry the good news of the gospel to the Indians and to assist the Indians in acquiring the learning that they would need to receive the message.

Given the prevailing abhorrence of idleness, there was a desire to have all children taught some definite calling or trade so that they might serve the commonwealth well. There was also a desire to attack pauperism at its source by developing skilled labor as a defense against unemployment, idleness, and poverty. The experience of the Massachusetts colonists with the great unemployment problem in England had made them fearful of the growth of a class or group of unskilled laborers. Finally, the colonists felt that in order to be good citizens people had to have enough education to be able to understand the laws of the community.

The movement toward the establishment of schools was also furthered by the geographic and social conditions of the colonies, in that people lived in towns that were in close proximity to one another. This meant that there was a large enough concentration of children to develop schools.

Public schools. In 1647 the General Court of Massachusetts took the first step in establishing a system of public education. It required that towns of 50 households maintain a schoolmaster capable of instructing children in elementary skills and required that larger towns of 100 households maintain a schoolmaster capable of preparing children for entrance to college. The towns that did not comply were to be fined.

The means of supporting the schools were left to the towns. In some towns the schools were supported by taxes levied on all householders (truly public schools), and in other towns the parents whose children attended the schools were asked to pay fees. Often these fees were not great enough to support the schoolmaster, so that a combination of public and private support was utilized.

It should be noted that this system was not a system of compulsory education. No parent was forced to send a child to school. However, all parents (or masters in the case of indentured or apprenticed children) were required (1642) to teach the boys in their care to read and write and the girls to read. In some instances the courts removed children from the care of parents who failed to educate them properly. In 1648, the town selectmen were charged with investigating how well parents were fulfilling this responsibility (Bremner, 1970, p. 28).

Apprenticeship. Another type of education for the children of New England, and for all colonial children, was provided by the apprenticeship system. Under this system children were bound out to a master craftsman to learn a skilled trade. Apprenticeship differed from indenture in that the primary purpose of indenture was to assure support for a dependent person whereas apprenticeship was primarily educational in purpose. Sometimes families paid the master a fee for accepting their children as apprentices. Benjamin Franklin, born in New England, was apprenticed to his brother to learn to be a printer.

Voluntary apprentices normally served for seven years. Boys were apprenticed at between 10 and 14 years of age and served until they were 21. Girls served until they were 18 or until they were married. Some compulsory apprentices were placed as infants and had to serve until they were 21. Such instances were more indentures than apprenticeships. The mutual obligations between apprentice and master were spelled out in a contract that was witnessed and registered with the court. The apprentice lived in the master's household and saw his own family rarely, and then only with the master's permission. The master assumed responsibility for the apprentice's spiritual and material welfare and was empowered to enforce his rule with the usual means of discipline. The apprentice on his part owed his master service, obedience, and loyalty. Colonial laws required masters to teach their apprentices to read and write. The masters could either do this themselves, or they could arrange to send the apprentices to a private teacher during a part of the day or evening (Jernegan, 1931, pp. 59–116; Bremner, 1970, pp. 72–127).

Schools for Indians. Firmly believing that they possessed "the Truth" and that they were obligated to disseminate it throughout the world, the Puritans were much concerned with the conversion and education of the Indians. Many devout preachers and teachers did missionary work among the Indians, and there were attempts to set up schools for them. With the founding of Harvard, a special college was set up for the Indian youth. However, these substantial efforts were largely ineffective. The Indians did not see the missionaries as having the truth, and considering the behavior of some of the white persons, they were rightly suspicious of the motives of those who attempted to convert them (Jernegan, 1931, pp. 59–116).

Pennsylvania

The Quakers, believing that each person was his own minister, lacked the religious push that moved the Puritans to establish schools in order to assure an educated ministry. However, one of the first laws passed in Pennsylvania subjected parents to a fine if their children had not been taught to read and write by the 12th year. A year after Philadelphia was established, public and private schools, almost all of them coeducational, began to be built there. Both the children of the rich and the children of the poor were required to learn a trade so that they could become self-sustaining.

New York and New Jersey

The middle colonies also utilized apprenticeship as a primary method of vocational training. The Dutch established a system of education quite as liberal as that of New England in this period. The Dutch colonists, supported by the Dutch West India Company, the States General, and the Dutch Reformed Church, established parochial, religiously based, elementary schools in towns and villages. These schools were under the control of the Dutch Reformed Church and were free to poor children but charged fees to others. The charter of the Dutch West India Company provided that it should "maintain good and fit preachers, school masters, and Comforters of the Sick," the latter to act as assistants to the pastor in giving help and solace to persons suffering from troubles, illness, or disability. It was possible to combine the offices of church clerk and church chorister with that of teacher, so that the teacher was often really an official of the church (Jernegan, 1929, pp. 234–35).

In spite of good intentions, however, the establishment of schools in New Amsterdam was delayed by two factors: the weakness of the church in the New World and its inability to furnish strong leadership and the attempts by the Dutch West India Company to shift the burden of education, clearly its responsibility under its charter, to the patroons. By 1664, however, 10 out of the 12 Dutch settlements had established schools. These schools were usually supported by a number of sources—the town through some form of taxation, tuition fees, the company, and the church. Control was exercised by the church and the local court.

Land grants to support schools. In New Jersey, schools were established 20 years after those in New Amsterdam by providing for public support through taxation and through grants of land that could be sold or rented to support the schools. This practice of setting aside certain lands to support schools had been utilized in Europe and England for some time. The Puritans were aware of it when they came to New England, but with land on the frontier so easily available they felt that it would be impossible to rent land for enough money to support education adequately. However, we will see how this way of supporting public education was used later to establish our large public midwestern universities. Also, the reader should note that the colonial schools were supported by a combination of private and public funds.

The education of slaves. New York and New Jersey were the first colonies to move toward the education of slaves. In 1704 Elias Neau, a Frenchman, established a Catechism School for Negroes at Trinity Church in New York City. In 1787, just following the Revolution, the first free school for blacks was established in New York city, and in 1788 a New Jersey law required that blacks be taught to read. In 1760 Jupiter Hammon, a New York slave who was probably the first black American poet, published "Salvation by Christ with Penitential Cries" (Bergman, 1969, pp. 24; 64).

The South

Education lagged in the southern colonies, although there were laws to provide for the apprenticing of children so that they might learn a trade. There were a number of reasons why the provision of education was of less concern in the South than in the North. The first reason might well be related to the church leaders. Here, no strong churchmen served as community leaders and there were few educated persons. In the first 15 years of Virginia's history, only two or three of its settlers had a university education.

A second influence affecting southern education is to be found in the social organization of the southern colonies. The establishment of a sound spiritual family life was not what brought the colonists of the South to the New World. Families were formed slowly in the South. Also, the people of

the South lived on scattered farms and plantations rather than in compact towns. Wealthy planters employed tutors for their children, and some planters had their children educated in England. Schooling in the colonial South was private, scanty, and haphazard.

Although the above is generally true of southern education, it is interesting that the earliest endowment for a free school in the colonies consisted of 200 acres of land and eight cows bequeathed by Benjamin Syms of Virginia in 1634 (Jernegan, 1929, p. 106). In contrast to Sym's interest in free education, an excerpt from the report of Sir William Berkeley, governor of the State of Virginia, on the state of learning in the colony reads:

> . . . but, I thank God, there are no free schools nor printing, and I hope that we shall not have these hundred years; for learning has brought disobedience, and heresy, and sects into the world, and printing has divulged them, and libels against the best government. God keep us from both. (Bremner, 1970, p. 90).

Health

General medical care

The health care and medical practice of the 17th and 18th centuries bore little resemblance to what we think of as medical and health care today. Medical researchers in Europe were beginning to understand such things as the circulation of the blood, but these studies had little effect on practitioners in Europe, let alone colonial America. Although some Scottish physicians did emigrate to the American colonies in quest of a better life than Britain offered, the thin, scattered settlements, the poverty of the inhabitants, and the lack of medical schools were unlikely to attract the skilled physicians of the Old World.

Thus, medical care in colonial America was even poorer than that of Europe. Few of the colonial physicians had earned the academic right to the title of "doctor." Ordinarily these physicians received their training through an apprenticeship and the medical books of the day. Medicine was commonly administered by clergymen, barbers, civil officers, and certain women. The larger almshouses were partly hospitals, partly mental institutions.

Hospitals

One of the most important accomplishments in social welfare in Pennsylvania was the founding of the first general hospital in America—the Pennsylvania Hospital. This hospital was to receive the mentally ill as well as other sick persons. It was the first institution in our history in which cure, rather than custody and repression, was the goal of treatment for the insane.

Among the hospital's founders two men stand out: Thomas Bond, a distinguished physician of his day, and Benjamin Franklin. Encouraged by Franklin's efforts at mobilizing public opinion in support of such a hospital, the Pennsylvania assembly passed an act on May 6, 1751, to "encourage the establishing of a Hospital for the Relief of the Sick Poor of this Province, and for the Reception and Cure of Lunaticks" (Pumphrey and Pumphrey, 1961, p. 42; Grob, 1973, pp. 16–20; Deutsch, 1949, pp. 58–66). The assembly offered a grant of $2,000 for the initial expense of the institution, provided that a like amount could be raised by private subscription. Benjamin Franklin led the successful drive to raise the money.

Pending the erection of a hospital building, a private home was rented to receive patients. Of the first two patients received there, one was a "lunatick" sent for care by the city's visitors of the poor. Insane patients were lodged in crowded damp cells in the basement of the house (Deutsch, 1949, pp. 58–66; Grob, 1973, pp. 16–20).

The care of the mentally ill

When the Pennsylvania Hospital proper was constructed four years later, it seemed natural that the mentally ill should again be confined to the cellar. There they were subjected to treatment which seems cruel to us today but was the best treatment known at the time. Patients were committed with an amazing ease and informality. All that was necessary was that another person apply to a physician for an order of admission. A few words scribbled by the doctor on a scrap of paper, and the deed was done. An attempt was made to offer occupational therapy in the form of light labor to persons who were able to engage in it.

A shocking practice was the exhibiting of the insane patients to curious sightseers for a set admission fee. However, this practice grew up as a way of protecting the patients. When the hospital was first opened, the public was permitted to enter and roam at will about the grounds, which were unprotected by fence or wall. On Sundays and holidays it was customary for the curious to gather about the ground-level cell windows of the insane patients and to tease the patients. In an effort to control the crowds, the hospital authorities started charging admission. Despite efforts to force abandonment of the practice, as late as 1822 there is record of an order raising the admission fee.

In spite of the regimen imposed on the mentally ill and the practice of exposing them to visitors, Pennsylvania Hospital's handling of the mentally ill represented a tremendous step forward in that it was the first public American institution in which mentally ill persons were separated from other troubled persons and admitted for treatment and cure. Moreover, it attempted to apply a humane approach to the treatment of the mentally ill (Deutsch, 1949, pp. 58–66; Grob, 1973, pp. 1–36).

Actually, the problems of mental health and the problems of the economic functioning were intimately related in the colonies. Thus mental illness was treated primarily as an economic and social problem. Only persons who were especially troublesome to family or community were institutionalized as ill. The rest were treated under the poor laws or the criminal laws.

The first law providing special care for the insane was enacted in Massachusetts in 1676. The selectmen in all the towns of the colony were "empowered and enjoined" to provide care and to see that others were not disturbed by the "distracted persons" in their midst. This first statute may have been aimed more at the protection of the community than at the protection of the ill person, but it was the beginning of some kind of special care.

In North Carolina, during the latter part of the

18th century, the first almshouses for the care of the insane were built and the churchwardens were directed to keep the occupants confined as long as necessary. Presumably some of the more violent insane individuals were confined in the local jail and some of the less harmful ones were treated in the same way as other impotent poor.

The first colony-wide public hospital for mental illness. In 1769 Virginia founded the first colony-wide, publicly supported hospital solely for the treatment of mental illness in this country. The preamble to the act establishing the hospital indicates that the legislators wanted it to be, not merely a custodial institution for troublesome persons, but an institution that would treat and cure mental patients. The new institution was named the "public Hospital for Persons of Insane and Disordered Minds. It was located in Williamsburg, and for 60 years it served as the colony's only facility for the mentally ill.

The care of mentally ill blacks. There is little information about the care of mentally disturbed slaves or free blacks. A clause in the 1751 South Carolina poor law provided subsistence for lunatic slaves belonging to persons too poor to care for them. The justices of the peace and the overseers of the poor were required to prevent such slaves from "doing mischief" by securing them in some safe, convenient place, with the cost to be borne by the local treasury. It was not uncommon at the time to keep mentally ill free persons in cages or to incarcerate them under cruel conditions. Certainly the fate of slaves was no better.

The Virginia policy as to the care of blacks is also confusing. One of the earliest patients admitted to the Williamsburg hospital was a free mulatto woman named Charity. Many years later the Virginia legislature provided that insane slaves were to be admitted to this hospital if space was available after all white persons had been accommodated (Wiener, 1970, pp. 54–57).

Maternal and child health

In the American colonies the mortality rate, particularly for children and their mothers, was very high. Cotton Mather (who had 15 children and was preceded in death by 13 of them and their mother) lamented that at least half of the children died before their 20th birthday.

Contagious diseases. There were epidemics of smallpox, diphtheria, and yellow fever. And children who survived such epidemics often found themselves without parents. Many times, epidemics were seen as an expression of the displeasure of God. However, Cotton Mather, although a devout man, supported any measure that gave promise of avoiding unnecessary death. In 1721, during a severe smallpox epidemic, he persuaded Dr. Zabdiel Boylston to inoculate healthy children with material from those ill with the pox as a possible means of preventing fatal cases of the disease. Both Mather's and Boylston's children were inoculated. The practice of inoculation generated a heated controversy on both medical and religious grounds, and it remained a controversial issue until the introduction of vaccination by Benjamin Waterhouse of the Harvard Medical School early in the 19th century.

Obstetrics and birth control. The dismal state of obstetrics contributed to the high rate of both infant and maternal deaths. The average delivery was in the hands of midwives who possessed little knowledge of gestation and delivery. How much knowledge colonial women had of birth control is unknown. It is known that birth control techniques were initially invented by lay women rather than medical men and that they have been in use in most societies from earliest recorded history. A cookbook of old and traditional recipes published in 1844—well after the period of our concern here—contained two recipes for "preventive lotions," or birth control douches. Also published in this little book was a test for the detection of pregnancy (Baxandall, Gordon, and Reverby, 1976, pp. 16–17).

✍§ Crime and delinquency

In general, the colonies controlled crime and delinquency by: (1) driving out people who were troublesome to the community or promised to become so; (2) requiring that all persons live in family groups, which enabled the community to control much nuisance behavior; (3) inflicting capital punishment for serious crimes; and (4) making confinement in the stocks, physical mutilation, whipping, or fines the punishments for lesser crimes. There were local jails, workhouses, and houses of correction in the colonies, but no prison was established in America until after the Revolution.

Children

There were certainly no special facilities in the colonies for the correction or reformation of children and youth. The colonial authorities recognized the problems inherent in putting children in jails with adult criminals, but they could hardly afford to maintain the children who needed care apart from their families, much less be concerned about creating separate institutions for delinquent children. Thus we find children in almshouses and workhouses with all kinds of adults. However, when it came to crimes, courts and juries often acquitted children or refused to prosecute them. Perhaps one of the most common problems presented by the youths of New England was that of runaways—servants or apprentices who sought to escape harsh masters. It will be remembered that Benjamin Franklin came to Pennsylvania as a runaway from his brother in New England (Boorstin, 1958, p. 28).

Institutions

The institutions, workhouses, local jails and houses of correction were used primarily to punish able-bodied persons who would not work and debtors. Individuals could be jailed for owing someone only a few cents, and while in jail they were required to pay for their own upkeep. In Vermont a man was jailed for owing 54 cents to two creditors, and in Philadelphia a man went to prison for being unable to pay a debt of 2 cents. In New York, Philadelphia, and Boston about 1,000 persons a year went to prison for debts, many of which were for less than $25. In practice, debtors were treated worse than murderers, thieves, or other offenders, since debtors had to pay for their own

food, clothing, and medicine and had no cot, bed, table, chair, or bench unless they or their friends were able to furnish such supplies. One might say that at this early period of our history the crime of poverty was the greatest crime.

The Quakers

The approach of Pennsylvania to problems of unacceptable behavior was quite different from that of the other colonies. The Quakers sought to reform rather than to punish, to persuade rather than to imprison. Although in most 17th-century thinking the responsibility for crime was placed on the individual, the Friends placed part of the responsibility on the environment. Penn abolished imprisonment for small debts but not for large ones. The number of crimes for which capital punishment could be inflicted was reduced from 150 in England to just 2 in Pennsylvania—murder and treason.

✑§ Summary

We have now completed our brief account of the social welfare institution in colonial America and the factors that influenced it. We would hope that the reader has noted two trends in this discussion: (1) the past experience with the welfare structure of England influenced all of the colonial developments; and (2) yet the various purposes for founding the individual colonies and the various social structures and value systems of those colonies had tremendous influence on the welfare programs they developed.

Church and state

This discussion should have helped to make clear the role of the church in our early social welfare activities. We see the interaction of church and state, the intermingling of public and private funds, in a way that we will not see in our later history. The utilization of public and private funds in the same programs is an issue that still troubles us.

Issues in social welfare

We also see developing in the colonies concern with caring for the needs of others, but fear that giving will cause idleness and the destruction of the character of the persons who receive help. Thus, although there is a pressure for caring and free giving, it is also believed that one needs to be very sure that these are truly deserved and are well used by the receiver.

An issue in social welfare that emerges during the colonial period is a certain conflict or difference in approach between those who would give only to relieve serious and immediate suffering and those who are interested in the prevention of social problems. This difference between those who would emphasize individual reform and those who would emphasize social reform has affected the shape of social welfare throughout our history. The hostility between Girard and Franklin in their approach to the problems of people is enacted again and again between people who hold two differing approaches.

We see developing on the new continent the same classifications of needs and programs that began in England. We have a continuation of the differences in the treatment of the able-bodied poor and the impotent poor. We see children beginning to be provided for as a special group, and the enactment of legislation to ensure their care in certain ways. We have the beginning of concern with the sick and the insane as newly identified special groups. We also see the emergence of the notion of veterans as a special class whose previous service entitles them to relief without stigma. There is a feeling that veterans have "earned their help," and "deserve the gratitude of the nation."

Children and social welfare

The legislation that permitted children to be removed from their parents and placed with other families is very interesting and important. From the beginning, in all the colonies, children could not be removed from their parents without a court order, although in England the Virginia Company was given the authority to send children to Virginia against their wishes. The agents of the welfare system in America were never given the authority to remove children on the basis of their own judgment.

It is also important to note the reasons for which children could be removed. There is very little evidence that the community was interested in protecting children from hard labor or abusive treatment. Children were removed when the parents seemed unable to bring them up so as to give promise that the children would become independent citizens. Thus, orphans and illegitimate children were often removed from their mothers on the ground that the mothers could not care for them. And children of the poor were removed so that they might be placed in a situation in which they would learn a trade. Children were usually seen as little adults, and there was little concern about depriving them of opportunities for play and self-development activities. As we pointed out earlier, child labor was a necessity, not a social problem. Thus, the right of the state to interfere between parent and child was established. But at this point in our history, that right was exercised only when parents were poor or when the failure to educate was the result of the child's own delinquency.

In the colonial period we also have the beginnings of institutions for children. Late in the period, communities overwhelmed by the large numbers of orphans seemed unable to indenture or apprentice children to families. Thus began a movement toward the children's institution rather than foster families to provide care for children. That movement continued to develop in the next period.

The administration of welfare

Another thing to note is that while laws may be enacted and programs may be set in place, these must all be administered by someone. Thus, offices and positions are created through which selected persons administer the laws and programs. Although modern social work may be reluctant to claim the early overseers of the poor or comforters of the sick as a part of social work, it seems important to recognize that even the infant social welfare institution needed agents to carry out the programs that were established and that the positions occupied by those agents were later claimed by social workers. One should perhaps note that the early agents of the social welfare institution had two functions that are a part of the present social work profession—that of social control and protection and that of "helper of the troubled" and rehabilitator.

This concludes the chapters on the colonial experience. In tracing the development of social welfare in the American colonies, we have seen the emergence of programs that were to be carried on as a part of the welfare system. We have also seen the development of certain philosophic issues that we will be tracing in the next chapter as we present the development of social welfare in the early national period.

₰ Study questions

1. Most of the programs presented in this chapter were developed and supported by local communities. However, there were some colony-wide social welfare programs. List all of the colony-wide programs that are mentioned in the chapter, and state what values, needs, and forces made these colony responsibilities rather than local responsibilities.

2. There are brief discussions dealing with the differences in various social welfare programs from colony to colony. What forces in the separate colonies resulted in the different shapes of programs with similar purposes?

3. List the programs found in most colonies. What needs resulted in these programs that were different in shape but were directed toward a common purpose?

4. Throughout history, society has been concerned with the relationships between parents and children. What safeguards did the colonies develop in common to protect the rights of parents? The rights of children? How did these rights compare to the rights of persons who were to be insane?

5. List the special programs discussed in this chapter that were developed around minority peoples.

₰ Selected readings

Trattner, Walter I. *From Poor Law to Welfare State.* New York: Free Press, 1974. Chaps. 2 and 3.

These two chapters cover the same material that we have presented in our two chapters. They make a good accompaniment to our text.

Axinn, June, and Levin, Herbert. *Social Welfare: A History of American Response to Need.* New York: Harper & Row, 1975.

The introduction and chap. 2, which deals with the colonial period, offer the student some interesting material to supplement the reading in our test.

Pumphrey, Ralph E., and Pumphrey, Muriel. *The Heritage of American Social Work.* New York: Columbia University Press, 1961.

This collection of documents that relate to social work and social welfare can furnish the students with interesting material for class discussion or individual enlightenment. The section containing documents from the colonial period (chaps. 1–8) is recommended as excellent reading to accompany this chapter.

Bremner, Robert H. *Children and Youth in America: A Documentary History.* Cambridge, Mass.: Harvard University Press, 1970.

This three-volume work (five books in all) is an excellent source for historical material relating to the welfare of children in America. The first volume covers the period 1600–1865. Students reading it may want to divide the documents presented into those relating to the colonial experience and the Revolution and those relating to the next two chapters of our text. Interesting term papers might be developed by having students use these documents to assess the trends relating to specific social welfare problems and programs.

One infamous episode in the relationship of the United States with its minorities is illustrated in Robert Lindneux's "Trail of Tears."

In 1838 the Indians of the great Cherokee nation were banished from the Appalachian region, and herded by the U.S. Army to a Western reservation. On that long winter trek—their "Trail of Tears"—one of every four Cherokees died from cold, hunger, or disease.

Chapter 12 ৡ৸

ৡ৸ National development and social issues: Pre–Civil War, 1780–1860 ৡ৸

ৡ৸ Introduction

In April 1783 Congress proclaimed the end of the "war of the Revolution," and the American colonies, having attempted a loose confederation during the war, now faced the question of building a permanent government. A number of issues were highlighted by the need to construct a form of government that would meet the needs of a newly independent people. The most critical of these related to the nature of human beings and how their welfare could be furthered by the government they established; how a government that had as its purpose the welfare of the governed could be brought about; and what the shape and powers of that government should be. If significant changes in the functioning of one or more of the social institutions of a people are a force toward change, then certainly the forces toward change were overwhelming at this time. Americans were faced with the tasks of developing a new political institution made necessary by the Revolutionary War; of developing a new economic institution made necessary by the industrial revolution; and of developing a new set of social relationships and social arrangements made necessary by the movement of people within the country, by the tremendous influx of immigrants from Europe, by relationships with minority groups, by the growth and utilization of industrial technology, by advances of knowledge in many areas of human life and human relationships, and by the interaction and growing complexity of all these factors.

It is perhaps a mark of the growing complexity of the interactions of forces that it becomes increasingly difficult to label large movements clearly as forces toward change or forces toward conservation. Within many of the events of the times we find both types of forces at work. In addition, it becomes increasingly necessary to distinguish between change and forward movement. The pull and tug of many new forces at this time should

211

alert students of social welfare to the fact that change is not necessarily positive progress toward the development of opportunity, equality, or security for all people.

In this chapter we shall examine very briefly the social and economic forces of the time that had impact on the development of the social welfare institution of the United States. The treatment of these forces will be indeed brief, and it is suggested that readers may want to expand their knowledge of the period by studying the readings suggested at the end of the chapter. We will consider the social and economic thought of the Revolutionary era; the framing of the Constitution; the acquisition of land and its use; the changing population, with its ethnic, racial, and sexual minorities; political leaders and political parties; the inequalities of the time; and labor and economic security.

☙ Social and economic thought

We have discussed earlier the role of values and beliefs both as a restrictive force and as a guide to change in the development of social policy. Although such beliefs may not be discussed in the process of decision making, they play a critical part in the social life of a nation. At the point of forming a new government, the people of America and their leaders were faced with the fact that the shape of the future life of the American people depended on the answers to certain philosophic and value questions. These questions could not have been answered by empirical data, even if such data had been available. The national political decisions of a people have to be lived out in the arena of human interaction and human development. At the time of the Revolution, and just preceding it, some of the world's best minds had been raising, and attempting to develop positions on, some of the basic questions about people and their society. The most philosophic and theoretical of these developments took place on the Continent and in England; but the political leaders who were charged with shaping the new American nation were aware of and influenced by them. These questions can be summarized as follows:

1. Is there a natural order of things which people cannot alter and with which they tamper at their peril—a natural order which social scientists may seek to understand but which they should not seek to alter?

2. Are human beings, rich and poor alike, of equal value and worth as human beings? If they are of equal value, how is equality to be established and how are differences to be recognized? On what concept of humanity are equal rights grounded.

3. Do people as individuals generally seek to act in the highest moral way, or are they self-seeking in ways destructive to the fabric of society? Is the primary purpose of government order or justice?

4. What are the basic rights of people? Should property rights be protected so that the rich have capital to invest in creating public facilities and employment for the poor, or should wealth be redistributed so that the poor can be offered a better life? If wealth is to be transferred from one group to another group, how is this to be done?

5. How much government is good for a people? And how are the positions of government to be determined? Is the power of government inevitably repressive? What is the concept of liberty—liberty from interference or liberty to act? What is the purpose of the state?

6. Is the welfare of a people best determined by the desires and needs of the whole, or is the welfare of the whole best determined by the actions of individuals as individuals?

Smith, Malthus, and Ricardo

In Chapter 9 we discussed three important English economists and philosophers whose concepts of natural laws (laws deriving from the innate physical and psychological nature of people and their relationships, and thus immutable and eternal) operated to the detriment of the poor. Adam Smith's work *The Wealth of Nations* had great impact on the American economic thought of his time and down to the present. In this book Smith postulated that natural law supports the principles of the free market system, in which decisions made by individuals in their self-interest presumably coincide with the highest welfare of society at large. People attempt to control free market factors at their peril and must rely on utility and self-interest for the stability of society. The wealth of nations is best promoted when people are free to pursue their own interests without government interference.

With "the nature of society" already settled, "the contributions of Malthus and Ricardo merely confirmed that it could not be otherwise" (Mencher, 1967, p. 67). Those contributions were discussed in Chapter 9 and will not be repeated here.

The humanitarians

In Chapter 10 we discussed the beginnings of the humanitarian movement. One leader of that movement was Thomas Paine, whose pamphlets on liberty during the American Revolution became well known to Americans. Following the Revolution, Paine lived in England, where he urged that the Poor Law be replaced by a system of pensions, family allowances, subsidized education, and guaranteed employment. He believed that such measures would decrease crime, improve relationships between parents and children in poor families, and give everyone a stake in developing good government (Paine, 1942, p. 253).

Mathew Carey, an American humanitarian, took the position that rather than look to the poor as the cause of the rise in public welfare costs, one should look to the workings of the market economy. He believed that low wages were the cause of much of the problem. He felt that many of the things that were commonly believed about the poor were in error, and he listed the following as commonly accepted myths about the poor:

1. That every person willing to work can find employment.
2. That the poor by hard work and careful saving would be able to support themselves without aid from others.

3. That poverty comes from idleness, immorality, and extravagance.
4. That aid to the poor increases poverty (Carey, 1833, pp. 3–34).

In an effort to change the thinking of people about the poor, Carey collected facts related to the gaps between the income of the poor and the income they needed. His work showed that only 549 poor families had been supported by relief in Philadelphia in 1830. The relief granted these people had averaged less than 47 cents a week, or less than 7 cents a day (Carey, 1833, pp. 3–34). In this early effort we have the beginning of the survey method of research, in which empirical findings are used to correct and redefine problems—to help people see problems in a new way.

Jefferson

One of the greatest American political philosophers of the time was Thomas Jefferson, who conceived of society as an "organic whole and of the government as a collective repository for the people's welfare." Where others

> spoke of life, liberty and property, Jefferson wrote, "life, liberty and *the pursuit of happiness.*" There is a subtle difference that is the essence of modern liberalism. . . . Every man is due basic liberties, including that of owning property, but where it impinges on the "happiness" of others the community, through its government, must take action to create a balance between the two. (Lens, 1969, p. 63).

Jefferson proposed many measures to reduce the gap between the haves and the have-nots, including a progressive tax on wealth that would exempt from taxation all property below a certain amount and tax higher accumulations of property "in geometrical progression as they rise" (Lens, 1969, pp. 65–66). This tax on wealth would have been a more extreme measure than our present progressive income tax.

Jefferson also believed that the United States should remain a nation of small farmers. He wanted to provide "by every possible means that as few as possible shall be without a little portion of land" (Lens, 1969, pp. 63–64). To ensure the operation of the democratic process, he proposed a universal, state-financed education for everyone decades that idea was acceptable to the general population. In addition to free education, he worked for prison reform, full male suffrage, and the freeing of the slaves.

The Federalists

The concepts of Jefferson were unacceptable to the early American leaders who were known as Federalists. The Federalists accepted the view that human beings were dominated by economic self-interest. They had little faith "in the socially benevolent nature" of people (Mencher, 1967, p. 139). They did not speak of the rights of people but of the interests of people. Those interests were seen as often being in conflict, and for the Federalists the function of government was to conciliate and police the discordant interests. The Federalists were concerned with the protection of economic interests in property from the encroachment of government. Given their views about the basic nature of human beings and the natural law of property, it is not surprising that the Federalists took the position that the primary duty of government was to protect the property of the few so that they could lead and serve the nation.

✑ The Constitution

The effort to construct a national government by having a written constitution drafted by a convention of elected delegates, adopted by the people, and subject to amendment in some orderly manner was a critically important and courageous undertaking. Given the different histories and life-styles of the 13 independent colonies, as detailed in Chapter 10, it would have been perfectly possible for 13 separate national states to develop and to exist in bitter contention with one another. In addition to the political and economic rivalry and the different life-styles of the colonies, there was the conflict of differing political and economic phi-

losophies that has been detailed above. As a result, the Constitution as finally written emerges as a conservative document that was vague enough not to provoke resistance at the time but also vague enough to cause many problems of interpretation. It may also be that the vagueness of certain constitutional provisions has had the advantage of allowing flexible adaptations in court interpretation through the years.

The division of powers

One of the important questions at the time of the Constitutional Convention was how powers were to be divided between the federal government and the state governments. This question was resolved in such a way that federal authority was restricted to specifically delegated areas and all other powers were reserved to the states. This means that in order for Congress to pass any enforceable law there must either be an express grant of authority provided for in the Constitution or such a law must be necessary to carry out the functions allocated to the federal government. The state governments may do all things not specifically reserved to the federal government. If a question is raised regarding the validity of a federal action, the federal government's power to perform that action must be shown to exist in the Constitution and its amendments. If a similar question is raised in relation to actions of the states, they need only show that the Constitution does not prohibit the exercise of such power.

The power of government lies not only in the making of laws but in the power to enforce whatever laws and regulations are needed in order to protect and promote the general welfare of all people—in the power not only "to prevent unfortunate occurrences, but to compel positive action for the general welfare" (Clarke, 1957, p. 6). This power to protect public rather than private interests is commonly called the police power by social and political scientists. There are two important principles related to this "power to compel": (1) it can never be precisely defined because it must have the capacity of accommodating to changing needs and demands if it is to protect the general welfare; (2) in the United States it is a power that is commonly regarded as being reserved to the states, as it is nowhere mentioned in the Constitution. Most political scientists concede that in the exercise of its listed powers—powers of taxation, interstate commerce, defense, and so on—Congress can exercise police power. However, the federal police power has strong opponents and supporters. The courts—and as a last resort, the U.S. Supreme Court—have to decide whether, in enacting federal laws, Congress is exercising its constitutionally conferred powers or is entering areas of states' rights.

Social welfare and the federal powers

Nowhere in the Constitution is the responsibility for social welfare or the right to exercise police power for enforcement of social legislation conferred upon the federal government. The first paragraph of the Constitution reads: "The Congress shall have the power to lay and collect duties, imports, and excises, to pay debts and provide for the common defense and general welfare of the United States." Over the years there has been extensive debate as to the specific powers conferred upon Congress by this wording. If Congress has the power to collect taxes for the general welfare, what are the limits imposed on that power and when can taxes be levied for this purpose? If Congress has a general welfare power, why does the Constitution list specific powers that relate to the general welfare? Does this mean that the federal government only has the power to collect taxes for the purposes listed but no other police power? When does Congress in imposing taxes and acting for the general welfare deprive the states of the powers reserved to them (Clarke, 1957, p. 7–10). What is the general welfare? How are welfare functions divided between the state governments and the federal government?

Federal-state relationships

Given the loose federation of states when the Constitution was drawn up, it is doubtful whether a stronger and more centralized federal government could have been developed. As it has developed over the years of our existence as a nation, our system of government has resulted in the sharing of most governmental functions by all levels of government. But during the first 150 years of our national existence it left the development and support of most social welfare programs entirely in the hands of the states. This position was confirmed by two presidential vetoes. Thus, while many who see the need for programs in social welfare do not care at what level of government such programs are established, or may, because of resistance at the local level, prefer the federal level, the Constitution demands state participation. When public social programs are developed at the federal level, the states must pass enabling legislation at the very least, and generally federal legislation relating to social welfare is drawn to require state participation or to give the states a choice as to participation. However, ever since the adoption of the federal Constitution two schools of thought—the strict and the liberal constructionists—have existed as to the nature and the boundaries of federal and state rights, though both schools agree that both the state and federal levels of government are necessary and must accommodate to each other.

From the very beginning of our country, Americans have been a people on the move, and as a national economy has developed, more and more people and goods have flowed across state boundaries. Thus, no matter how much states have desired to control their own destinies, they have had to be involved in decisions at the national level. This concept was tested in relation to one national social problem in the Civil War. Although such a time of bitter conflict will not come again, many areas of social and family welfare still need to be resolved as national issues rather than as matters affected by state boundaries.

The rights of people

The important assumption made by the political leaders of the time was that all power, all rights, and all authority reside in the people. The U.S. Constitution and the various state constitutions exist to define and guarantee the rights of people in relation to the state, not to create rights or grant rights. The first ten amendments to the Constitution were added because of the reluctance of some to ratify it without a formal guarantee that fundamental rights would be respected. They are a statement of what government cannot do (Clarke, 1957, pp. 11–13).

Originally the Constitution did not mention the rights or position of women, Indians, or black slaves. However, as a compromise document, in its formula for representation and taxation it provided that each slave should be counted as three fifths of a person. It also banned the importation of slaves after 1808, and it guaranteed that all states would cooperate in returning fugitive slaves to their masters. Many people see these provisions as furthering the problems of the blacks in that the provisions formally recognized slavery and the rights of owners to their property. Others see the provisions as furthering the movement toward freeing the slaves.

Judicial review

One of the most important guarantees of rights in the Constitution is the doctrine of judicial review—the right of the courts to declare legislation contrary to the authority granted to the government. This review is not automatic but occurs only when an action is brought by someone who has been injured by the enforcement of the legislation (Clarke, 1957, p. 14). Judicial review provided for in the Constitution of the United States is unique among the governments of the world. Although used throughout our history to extend and support the rights of people, such reviews have had particular impact since the 1950s.

Due process, equal protection of the law, full faith and credit

Three important constitutional questions in addition to those discussed above are the question of due process, the question of equal protection of the law; and the question of full faith and credit. Due process means that an individual has a right to expect a dispute with the government to be resolved by a proper and fair procedure of enforcement and by an examination of the law itself to determine that it is a proper and fair law. In essence, due process means that people are guaranteed a fair trial in relation to a reasonable government action. Equal protection of the law means that all units of governments are required to give equal protection and security to all persons under like circumstances.

The full faith and credit concept relates to the equal rights of the states as members of a federated union. In our form of government every state is independent within its sphere of government. The laws of a state have no legal effect outside its boundaries. However, the federal Constitution declares that "full faith and credit shall be given in each state to the public acts, records and judicial proceedings of every other state." Under what circumstances the behavior of individuals in one state is bound to be recognized in another is one of the most baffling and confusing parts of the law, but without that constitutional provision, the states would have the same relationships to one another as do nations (Clarke, 1957, p. 16).

The separation of powers

In addition to providing for a division of authority between the state and federal levels of government, the Constitution provides for a division of powers among the federal legislative body, which enacts laws; the federal executive branch, which is charged with carrying them out; and the federal judiciary, which settles controversies arising under the laws, including controversies as to whether the laws are constitutional. The functions of these three branches of the federal government are familiar to all, so they do not need to be discussed further here. As we shall see, however, there are times when social welfare legislation is passed by the legislative branch only to be vetoed by the executive branch or to be held unconstitutional by the courts.

✍ The question of the western lands

In addition to being confronted by questions regarding the nature of its government, the new nation was confronted by the question of how to dispose of the lands beyond the Alleghenies that had been gained by treaty with England. These lands comprised 488,248 square miles in comparison to the 341,752 square miles of the original 13 states.

With this region a U.S. possession, the 13 states might have followed European precedent and designated it a colony or several colonies to be ruled by some federation of the original 13 states indefinitely. But instead it was agreed that three to five states would be carved out of the territory and that when any one of these divisions contained 60,000 eligible voters, it would become a state on "equal footing with all others." Also, the federal government imposed restrictions on the new states that had not been imposed on the original 13. For example, the right to vote was to be granted to any of their residents who owned 50 acres of land. Slavery was to be prohibited in the area north of the Ohio River (Lens, 1969, pp. 46–70).

The distribution of frontier land

How the western lands should be distributed to settlers gave rise to a bitter dispute in the country between those who looked on the lands as a source of revenue for the original states and those who looked on them as a means of spreading agrarian democracy.

The Land Ordinance of 1785 provided that the government was to lay out rectangular townships of 36 square miles, putting aside one section in each to support public schooling. Half of each township was to be sold at auction at a minimum of $1 an acre, and the other half was to be sold in sections. Each section was one mile square, or 640 acres, and cost $1,250, which was far more than an individual settler could possibly afford. This plan gave a great advantage to land speculators (Lens, 1969, pp. 64–70).

Yet the best-laid plans often go awry. This plan was never fully implemented. Families simply moved west, found land, and settled on it without the formality of purchasing it. The government sometimes used force to evict such families, but it often recognized their claims and let them gain title by purchasing the land on which they had settled at $1 to $2 an acre. This method of settling the frontier lifted many families out of poverty and deepened the spirit of equality and democracy in America.

Other land

In addition to the lands in the West, property in the original 13 colonies became available for settlement through the appropriation of the holdings of the Tories. "It was as extensive a land seizure as any in the annals of the Western hemisphere" (Lens, 1969, p. 66). In the process these holdings were divided into small and middle-sized farms. Many of these farms went to reimburse the soldiers of the Revolution. The rights of squatters who had simply occupied some of the Tories' land were also recognized, and they were allowed to buy the parcels they occupied on generous terms (Lens, 1969, pp. 71–78).

The states also moved to divest the country of two feudal carry-overs. One of these allowed individuals to put a "tail" on any land they owned. This stipulated that the person who inherited it could not sell it or give it away but could only pass it to others through inheritance. A second feudal carry-over was the law of primogeniture, under which the property left by a man without a will went exclusively to the eldest son. The two laws promoted a kind of inequality that most Americans wanted to abolish. Laws were soon passed that allowed persons owning property to dispose of it as they wished and that allowed all children to inherit property.

Land acquisitions

During this period the United States moved to acquire lands that had previously been held by other countries. In 1795 the territory lying east of the Mississippi and north of the 31st parallel was ceded to the United States by Spain; in 1803 the United States purchased the Louisiana Territory from France; and in 1820 the United States attempted to purchase parts of Mexico's northern frontier, where the development of irrigated farming, cattle raising, and mining was beginning to attract settlers from both the United States and Mexico. Mexico refused to sell the lands, and in May 1846, following increasingly hostile confrontations on the borders of the countries, the United States declared war against Mexico. In 1848, by the Treaty of Guadalupe Hidalgo, the United States acquired California and the Southwest (Meier and Rivera, 1974, pp. xv–xvii).

✎§ Steps toward democracy

Steps toward equality and democracy were taken by the states in areas that were barred to federal intervention: the liberalization of voters' rights, modifications in the laws governing imprisonment for debt, and a few modest moves against slavery. In no case did these steps reverse the previous policies, but they did ameliorate them. Even given the crisis of the Revolution, "it was probably too much to expect that the founders of the nation would be able to move in one giant step" to abolish slavery, do away with imprisonment for debt, and declare a franchise based on citizenship (Lens, 1969, pp. 71–78).

Imprisonment for debt

Our nation would be over 50 years old before imprisonment for debt was abolished, but during the first 50 years of our national history states began to set minimum limits on the amount of debt for which persons could be imprisoned and passed laws that allowed imprisonment for debt only if debtors failed to use all of their personal resources to satisfy the claims of creditors or if fraud was involved. In 1785 half of the inmates of Philadelphia prisons were there because they had violated the debtor's code, and in 1787–88 the New York

jails housed 1,200 men who had been unable to pay obligations as small as $5.

In 1817 Pennsylvania forbade imprisonment for debts of less than $25, and in the following year New Hampshire prohibited imprisonment for debts of less than $13. In 1821 Kentucky became the first state to abolish imprisonment for debt. Ohio followed in 1828, New Jersey in 1830, and New York in 1834. The pressures of such groups as the Humane Society and the Boston Society for the Relief of the Distressed resulted in the gradual abolition of imprisonment for debt in all states (Lens, 1969, pp. 71–72 and 96).

The franchise and office holding

Under the Constitution and the division of powers, the right to determine who could vote and the laws relating to the exercise of that right belonged to the various states. Each state initially determined what the limits of its franchise were to be. This right was later limited federally in certain ways by the 15th Amendment, which forbade abridgment of the right to vote because of color, race, or a previous condition of servitude; the 19th Amendment, which forbade abridgment of that right because of sex; and the 24th Amendment, which forbade the levying of a poll tax in federal elections.

In the beginning, New York and Massachusetts continued their previous systems, under which the possession of a wealth of $300 was needed in order to vote, $500 to $1,000 in order to run for Congress, $1,500 to $3,000 in order to run for the Senate and $5,000 in order to run for governor. However, many of the new state constitutions made changes for the better. Pennsylvania granted the right to vote to any male who paid taxes. Other states reduced the property requirement for voters. Also, an increasing number of offices were filled by elections rather than by appointment. Pennsylvania again took the decisive step when it declared that all men were eligible to hold public office, regardless of wealth or religion, and Delaware followed Pennsylvania in banning all religious qualifications for office holding.

Universal male suffrage. In 1812 New York legislated universal male suffrage for male whites (free blacks who owned property were also given the right to vote). In 1856, when North Carolina did away with property and religious qualifications, all of the 13 original states had universal suffrage for free male whites. At about this time, property qualifications for holding office began to be removed, and the selection of electors for president was taken away from the state legislators and put in the hands of the voters. The 14 frontier states that joined the union between 1789 and 1840 all adopted constitutions granting the vote to all white males, regardless of land or wealth. These new states brought a newer tradition of democracy to the nation. Women did not achieve legal and political equality with men, but this period marked the formal beginning of a long campaign for women's rights (Lens, 1969, pp. 96–97).

✑ Inequality in wealth, income, opportunity, and power

Although there were significant movements toward granting the common man political power and some economic freedom, this time in our history was marked by a "surprising inequality, whether of condition, opportunity, or status, and a politic seeming deference to the common man by the uncommon man who actually ran things" (Pessen, 1978, p. 327). The second half of the period between 1780 and 1860 was dominated by Andrew Jackson and by the common assumption that a strong bond of identification existed between Jackson and the common man to whom he sought to give power. (We use the word man advisedly, as shall be seen later.) It was a time of the rise of national political parties that sought the vote of the common man and extolled his simplicity and wisdom. However, the leaders who controlled those parties were distinctive "not only in their ability but also in the possession of status and wealth that were unrepresentative of the mass of men" (Pessen, 1978, p. 325). Pessen writes that although reform movements designed to end social injustice and enhance the quality of life flourished,

those movements were led by "unusual men and women whose values were outside of the mainstream of American life" (Pessen, 1978, p. 326). The stronger current was personal enrichment rather than moral uplift, and the persons who struggled to change the conditions of the weak and vulnerable were espousing values different from those held by the majority.

Political power in America began to be closely allied with economic power, and economic power resulted in unusual ability to influence political decisions in such a way that individual economic power and wealth were protected and furthered. Each generation of common Americans lived better than their parents, and average persons were able to exert considerable power, especially when compared to their counterparts in the older societies of Europe, but a small group of wealthy people held an inordinate proportion of the wealth of their communities early in the era and a still greater share, almost twice as large at the end of the era. "In the great cities of the northeast, the top 1 percent of wealthholders owned about one fourth of the wealth in the mid-1820s and about half the property by midcentury" (Pessen, 1978, p. 81). "During the so-called era of the common man, the mass of the nation's inhabitants, white Protestants as well as blacks and recently-arrived Irish Catholics, owned practically none of its wealth" (Pessen, 1978, p. 82). There were those who rose to great wealth and influence from great poverty, but they were few and almost the exception that proved the rule. People who did achieve social mobility usually moved only a step or two upward on the economic and social scale.

✑ Indian-white relationships

The question of the settlers' relationship to the Indians and the question of the *individual states'* claims to the lands west of the Alleghenies were intertwined, since the only way in which settlers could occupy those lands was by displacing the Indians who occupied it. By the time of the Revolution a pattern of Indian-white relationships had developed. First, traders invaded the Indian lands employing the Indians to gather furs and the standard of living rose as the Indians were able to acquire firearms and metal tools. But the traders were followed by settlers who wanted to acquire land on which to establish their homes. In order to do this they had to either persuade or force the Indians to sell their land. Occasionally the use of force would escalate into a war which inevitably crushed the Indian's resistance, and often the subsequent treaty resulted in the cession of even more land to the white settlers. The Indians thus forced from their lands might migrate westward to compete with already established tribes, or they might be absorbed by neighboring bands, or they might be located on a reservation (Hagan, 1961, p. 8–29).

The Revolution

At the beginning of the Revolution, the Continental Congress was concerned with establishing some neutral relationship with the Indians so that the colonies would not be confronted with two wars simultaneously. A report by a committee appointed by Congress to examine the situation resulted in the enactment of the first federal act relating to the Indians. The Continental Congress established northern, middle, and southern departments of Indian affairs to improve relations with the Indians and to protect Indian lands against seizure without treaty. However, fearing the loss of their claims, individual colonies opposed the federal government's efforts to make policy in this area. Throughout the Revolution individual states impaired the American war effort by fighting and negotiating with Indian tribes without consulting Congress. The end of the Revolution brought even greater movement by white settlers into Indian lands, and Congress seemed unable to deal with the problem.

The constitutional convention

At the Constitutional Convention, there had been proposals that the Cherokees be permitted to send a representative to Congress and there was also talk of establishing one or more Indian states. However, the last thing that the pioneer settlers wanted was the creation of Indian states or Indian representation in Congress. They were not interested in a "paternal policy that would civilize the Indian if it also safeguarded the rights to land" (Hagan, 1961, p. 40).

Given the pressures from the states that claimed rights to Indian lands, the framers of the Constitution only mentioned the Indian in connection with Congress's control of commerce. Despite the threats of a number of states to secede from the infant Union if they were deprived of their rights to settle the land to their west and to deal with the Indian as they saw fit, between 1790 and 1799 Washington's and Adams's administrations carefully formulated four temporary trade and intercourse acts that established the federal government as a protector of the Indians' rights in land.

Jefferson's administrations

However, when Jefferson became president he was under severe pressure to satisfy the land hunger of the pioneers and there was still talk of secession. Jefferson saw the Louisiana Territory as a possible answer to the "Indian problem." If the Indians could be persuaded to exchange their lands east of the Mississippi for lands west of it, the problem could be solved. Despite his concern with human rights, Jefferson was blind to the rights of Indians to their homes when the inevitable conflicts between Indians and whites arose.

Under Jefferson's direction there was written into the act organizing the Louisiana Territory in 1804 a provision for exchanging Indian lands in the east for other lands in the west. Following the War of 1812, with the threat of British intervention removed, more and more demands to surrender their lands were made on the Indians by the flood of settlers to the frontier. Between 1816 and 1848, 12 states west of the Alleghenies became populated enough to enter the Union and scores of treaties were negotiated by which Indian tribes were persuaded or forced to relinquish most of their holdings east of the Mississippi and to move west. Two Indian wars were fought in connection with this removal policy (Hagan, 1961, pp. 66–91).

The Bureau of Indian Affairs

In 1824 a Bureau of Indian Affairs was created within the War Department. Under the administrations of Presidents Monroe and Adams pressures to oust the Indians grew even greater, though under these administrations there were presidential attempts to safeguard Indian rights as more and more treaties requiring the Indians to move west were negotiated. However, President Jackson was less sensitive to the rights of the Indians. "Reared on the frontier he had absorbed much of the frontier attitudes toward Indians. He felt that treating the tribes as though they were independent nations was absurd and a farce" (Hagan, 1961, p. 72). Under Jackson, Congress gave legislative sanction to a formal removal policy in the Removal Act of 1830. This act authorized the appropriation of $500,000 to aid the emigration of the Indians and provided for an exchange of lands, compensation for improvements, and aid to the Indians in their removal and in their initial adjustment to their new homes.

We shall not try to generalize about the Indians' actual experience of removal from their tribal lands to the unknown west. A literature is available that provides the details of the various tribal experiences and resistances, of the tragic clash between two cultures, made more tragic by the great inequality of the opposing forces. The time span covers more than half a century. The detailed accounts should be read by all students of social welfare. The treatment of the Cherokee and the Creek led Grant Foreman to use the term *trail of tears*. About half of the Creek nation died during their migration and their first years in the West. But other tribes about whom less has been written suffered as much. The Winnebago, for example, were forced to move six times between 1829 and 1866 (Hagan, 1961, pp. 66–91).

The Indian laws of 1834

In 1834 two laws were enacted that still influence the Indians' relation to the U.S. government. The first, the Indian Trade and Intercourse Act, redefined the Indian territory and strengthened the hand of the federal government in dealing with white intruders into it. The second, the Indian Reorganization Act, was in part an act to reorganize the Bureau of Indian Affairs, but it also provided that money paid the Indians should be paid to the tribal chiefs rather than to individuals. This provision was resisted by many settlers because it emphasized the position of the chiefs and strengthened the tribe as an institution. In 1849 the Bureau of Indian Affairs was transferred to the Department of the Interior and the right of the federal government to deal with the Indian tribes was established (Hagan, 1961, pp. 66–91).

✑ The place of women

The ideal of womanhood that prevailed during this time glorified four great virtues; piety, purity, submissiveness, and domesticity. Women's only worthwhile purpose in life was to marry and to care for home and children. Although the daily activities of wealthy and poor women were very different, the goals and orientations of both wealthy and poor women were essentially similar. The prevalent notion of womanhood was supported by contemporary medical opinion, which held that women were too delicate to be anything other than wives and mothers: reading or thinking to excess, working too hard outside the home, or living too freely could only result in unhealthy children. Women suffered terribly from medical ignorance regarding gynecologic problems, which were often considered matters of morality or "delicacy" rather than proper concerns for clinical investigation (Pessen, 1978, pp. 47–48).

Legally, women's situation was one of dependence and inequality. For all practical purposes they belonged to their husbands. Women could not vote, testify in court, serve on juries, sign papers as witnesses, hold title to property, or establish businesses. As long as the marriage lasted, the husband had absolute control of the wife's property and actions to right any wrongs done to her could only be brought by the husband since he had the sole rights to her person.

Many women, convinced that the situations of American women and blacks were similar, were active workers for the abolition of slavery. In 1840 women delegates were excluded from a world antislavery conference in London because they were women. In response, they determined to "seek freedom for themselves as well as the slave." In 1848 a large national women's rights convention was held at Seneca Falls, New York (Chafe, 1972, p. 4). This early feminist movement was a radical one, aimed at completely eliminating the role differences between men and women. Its long list of demands included the demand that women have the right to engage in all behavior that was accepted for men.

These early feminists addressed themselves to the assumptions underlying discrimination against women as well as to concrete matters. "Hardly an area existed, the feminists concluded, where man had not consciously endeavored to destroy woman's confidence in her own powers, to lessen her self-respect, and to make her willing to lead a dependent and abject life" (Chafe, 1972, p. 5). The declaration passed by the group that met at Seneca Falls advocated a "complete transformation in society's thinking about women" (Chafe, 1975, p. 6) and courageously challenged every social convention relating to "woman's place."

❧ Black people in American society

Although the blacks suffered more than any other group in American society, there were significant internal differences among them. There were black slaves, but there were also free blacks, some of whom achieved considerable wealth. There were urban and rural blacks; and there were southern and northern blacks. It is impossible for a single description or stereotype to cover the range of black experiences in America during the period

from 1780 to 1860. It is true that most of the blacks were slaves who resided in the South. It is also true that although there has been some disagreement among historians about the treatment of slaves, most scholarly investigation appears to support the conclusion that slaves were indeed harshly used—cheaply housed, clothed, and fed; often beaten; and helpless to determine the course of their lives even to the extent, as parents, of protecting their families from punishment or separation.

Antisalvery movements during the Revolutionary era

During the Revolutionary War white Americans in both the North and the South were concerned with the moral issues involved in slavery. Undiminished support for the slave system was found only in South Carolina and Georgia. The antislavery and racially egalitarian tendencies of the Revolutionary era came from four forces: (1) the struggle for independence from England was a political force toward democracy for all; (2) slaves had never been particularly remunerative in the North, and therefore there was an economic push toward an antislavery stance; (3) the Enlightenment and humanitarian movements resulted in a belief in human liberty and natural rights; and (4) certain religious groups opposed slavery.

The need of the Revolutionary army for recruits was also a powerful factor in the movement away from slavery on the part of the northern states, which at this time had little to lose economically by their stand. In general, the northern states promised liberation for the slave at the end of three years of military service. Vermont had never recognized slavery, and in 1777 its constitution prohibited it. Pennsylvania in 1780 and Connecticut and Rhode Island four years later legislated the gradual abolition of slavery within their borders. In Massachusetts slavery was abolished when the Supreme Court of the state, in response to a suit by a black man, ruled that the reference to "free and equal" in the Declaration of Independence applied to all men, regardless of skin color. In 1804 New Jersey became the last northern state to institute a program of emancipation. In 1776 the Quakers decided that all members of the Society of Friends must emancipate their slaves, and even some substantial slaveholders among them freed their slaves rather than leave the Friends.

It should be said that the white antislavery forces were not necessarily believers in equality between the races. Many accepted the notion of black inferiority and advocated the return of the blacks to Africa or their removal to a colony in the West as the only satisfactory solution of the racial differences (Meier and Rudwick, 1976, pp. 48–50). In 1817 the American Colonization Society was founded to transport free blacks to a colony in Liberia. It was never a very successful organization, managing to send only a few hundred settlers to Africa.

In the upper South, Virginia and North Carolina passed laws encouraging owners to free their slaves and in 1783 Jefferson persuaded the Virginia legislature to enact a law enabling an owner to free his slaves by will or other written instruments. Though the law held the former master responsible for the economic maintenance of the freed slaves, many owners did set their slaves free. The high point of the antislavery movement of this period was reached in 1787, when the Northwest Ordinance prohibited slavery in the Northwest Territory.

Blacks in agrarian America

Slavery was the preferred labor system in the agrarian South. At the beginning of the Civil War, there were slightly more than 4 million slaves in the South. Yet only one white southern family in four owned slaves, and only slightly more than 10 percent of the slave owners held more than 20 slaves, while three quarters of the families that owned slaves held less than 10. Nearly half of the slaves belonged to the 25,000 planters who owned 30 or more slaves.

All of the southern states had enacted slave codes, though these were often ignored in practice. After the Revolution the slave codes became more flexible, only to become more stringent later. The codes were primarily provisions for the control and discipline of the slaves. The slaves were not permitted to travel or to attend meetings not overseen by a white man. They could not be taught to read and write, and they were not allowed to serve as ministers. Basically, slaves were regarded as property and they had no civil rights. They could not be parties in lawsuits, offer testimony in court except against other slaves, or make contracts, and their marriages had no legal standing.

The plantation way of life was a complex one, and the owners' relationship to their slaves was equally complex. Cruelty was mixed with sentimental attachment on the part of many masters, and deep resentment was mixed with respect on the part of the many slaves. Slavery in the United States is no longer seen by historians as a history of unmitigated oppression, the harshest system in the New World. "There is evidence that in the very period when the Southern slaveholders were tightening the slave codes so as virtually to prohibit manumission, the diet, housing, and health of the slaves in the United States was actually improving" (Meier and Rudwick, 1976, p. 73). There were slave revolts. Herbert Aptheker indentified 200. Other sources say that the number of revolts was considerably less. The most serious slave revolt was the Nat Turner insurrection of 1831, led by a 31-year-old Baptist slave preacher.

In 1797, with the invention of the cotton gin, slavery became more important in the agrarian South. The effects of the cotton gin were:

1. To make cotton king of southern staples in place of tobacco.
2. To encourage the textile industries that were developing in the North.
3. To dash the hopes of those who were working for emancipation in that both southern and northern capitalists were now interested in the profits of slave labor (the Southerners directly, the Northerners indirectly).
4. To increase the value of land and the price of slaves and to create a push to extend the right to hold slaves to new southern states.

◄§ 5. To hinder the development of manufacturing in the South and thus to discourage
new immigrants from entering that section
of the country, thus lessening the democratic impact of such settlers (Jennings,
1929, pp. 140–43).

Urban free blacks

Although there were urban slaves, many of them
highly skilled artisans, slavery was not an urban
institution. However, free blacks tended to reside
in the cities. A majority of the free blacks were
unskilled laborers. In the skilled trades, if an employer was willing to employ a black, whites were
often unwilling to work with him. Black artisans
faced greater obstacles in the North than in the
South and greater obstacles in the upper South than
in the lower South. Despite the obstacles in finding
and being accepted on a job, a minority of the
urban free blacks made a comfortable living and
a few founded modest fortunes. The most successful of the free black entrepreneurs catered to well-
to-do whites and were concentrated in the service
trades. In 1850 the free blacks of New Orleans
included 1 architect, 5 jewelers, 4 physicians, 11
music teachers, and 53 merchants. The influx of
immigrants into the northern and eastern cities resulted in a sharp deterioration in the wealth and
job distribution of the urban blacks (Meier and Rudwick, 1976, pp. 90–96).

The free blacks suffered from legal restrictions
in voting rights and in court actions. In addition,
other forms of oppression were inflicted on them,
including mob violence. During the 1830s and
1840s, riots directed against blacks occurred in the
large eastern cities and Cincinnati. And patterns
of segregation were widespread. Segregation by
law or custom resulted in separation in jails and
hospitals and in exclusion from public parks and
burial grounds. Traveling by public conveyance
was difficult for blacks. Sometimes they were not
allowed to use public transportation, and they were
segregated everywhere. In 1854 a black woman
sued after having been forcibly ejected from a New

York City streetcar. Although she was awarded
damages, the practice of denying the use of public
transportation to blacks continued (Meier and Rudwick, 1976, p. 97).

Black leadership and the abolitionist movement

In 1826 John Russwurm received a college degree at Bowdoin, the first black to graduate from
college. He joined with Samuel E. Cornish to found
Freedom's Journal, the first black newspaper,
which began publication in New York City on
March 16, 1827. *Walker's Appeal,* a radical antislavery pamphlet, was published in Boston on September 28, 1829, by David Walker, a free black.
The first national convention of black people met
at Philadelphia's Bethel Church in 1830, with Richard Allen in the chair (Bennett, 1964, p. 131).

The American Anti-Slavery Society was organized in 1833 under the leadership of William
Lloyd Garrison and Arthur and Lewis Tappan for
the purpose of educating free blacks for U.S. citizenship (Bremner, 1960, pp. 48–49; Bennett,
1964, p. 133). During the years 1838–41 David
Ruggles, a black, founded the first black magazine—*Mirror of Liberty;* Frederick Douglass and
Charles Lenox Remond became the first black lec-
turers to be hired by the antislavery societies; and
the Liberty Party, the first antislavery political party,
was organized in Warsaw, New York. In 1843 So-
journer Truth, the first black woman to become
an antislavery lecturer, began her work. Harriet
Tubman, another famous black woman who became active in the movement for freedom, escaped
from slavery herself and was able to bring more
than 300 blacks out of slavery through more than
19 trips that she made into the South (Bennett,
1964, pp. 144–45).

From various sources, more and more began
to be written against slavery by black authors and
white abolitionists. William C. Nell published *Services of Colored Americans in the Wars of 1776
and 1812.* In 1852 the first edition of *Uncle Tom's
Cabin* was published. William Wells Brown pub-

lished *Clotel,* the first novel by a black author. Two black colleges were established; Lincoln University, founded as Ashumm Institute, in Pennsylvania and Wilberforce University, founded by the African Methodist Episcopal Church, in Ohio. In 1855 John Mercer Langston, the first black elected to public office, became the clerk of an Ohio township (Bennett, 1964, p. 343).

The struggle over slavery

From the late 1840s until the beginning of the Civil War, slavery and the place of black people in the United States became heated national political issues. There was continual struggle over whether new states admitted to the Union should be "slave" states or "free" states. The details can be found in any good history text, so they will not be set forth here. It does seem important, however, to mention that in 1851 the American Anti-Slavery Society was torn by arguments between Garrison and Douglass and divided into two groups over the issue of moral force versus political participation as ways of bringing change.

The last ship to bring slaves to America landed at Mobile Bay, Alabama, in 1859, the same year that John Brown attacked Harpers Ferry, West Virginia, with 13 white men and 5 black men in an effort to free the blacks. Brown had tried to recruit Douglass to his cause, but Douglass felt that such an open attack was ill advised. However, the issues related to the institution of slavery and the relationships between blacks and whites were escalating rapidly toward armed conflict. We shall consider that conflict in Chapter 14.

❧ Poverty and European immigration

The 19th century in America was a time when thousands of people, native and immigrant, were achieving a standard of living beyond anything they had dreamed of, but at the same time thousands more were living in great poverty knew only despair and misery. Decade by decade, the output of farm, factory, and mine climbed to higher and higher

totals and more and more Americans lived in an ever more comfortable manner.

In discussing this period, Bremner wrote: "Unfortunately, the very economic processes that promised ultimately to free mankind from want had the immediate effect of aggravating, rather than alleviating, the distress of the working class" (1956, pp. 3–7). Bremner points out that at this time all the advantages in bargaining for jobs and wages lay with the employers, who, impelled by the desire for profit and by the necessity for meeting the competition of rivals, drove hard bargains with their employees, altering pay and hours and dismissing workers as they saw fit. Economic panics in 1819 and 1837 were followed by very hard times for the average person. Thousands of Americans sank into a degradation and dependence previously unknown in the brief history of the United States with its reliance on plentiful land and scarce labor. "A poverty problem, novel in kind and alarming in size, was emerging in the United States" (Bremner, 1956, pp. 3–7). Urbanization, industrialization, and an influx of unskilled labor spawned a new kind of poverty.

The housing of the immigrants

One of the most debilitating features of the life of the poor of this time was the slums in which they lived. As immigration increased and people poured into the cities, rental housing became a seller's market. When all possible buildings were filled, people began to occupy cellars. In 1843 it was reported that 7,196 people in New York were living in cellars, and by 1846—only three years later—there were 29,000. The New York chief of police reported in 1850 that one out of every 20 slum dwellers lived in a cellar, the averate number of occupants per room being 6, the maximum 20. Two years later a police report indicated that 10,000 abandoned, orphaned, or runaway youngsters were living on the streets, sleeping haphazardly in privies, hallways, or alleys, anywhere that they could fit. "According to labor historian Norman Ware, the life expectancy of an Irishman after he moved into the Boston slums was fourteen years" (Lens, 1969, pp. 87–91).

Immigration as cause of poverty

For many people, the simplest, most frequently advanced explanation for the problems of the slums, and the one most easily believed, was "immigration." The second- and third-generation citizens of the land of opportunity began to look upon the newcomers with suspicion and anger as the cause of the social problems of the time. In 1819 in its *Second Annual Report* the New York Society for the Prevention of Pauperism listed immigration as a principal cause of poverty, deploring that for years to come "winds and waves will still bring needy thousands to our seaports" and warning that New York was "liable to be devoured by swarms of people" (Bremner, 1956, p. 8). A tendency grew to blame the immigrant for everything from "hives to job stealing" (Lens, 1969, p. 56). Certain Americans professed to see behind this influx of people a sinister design by Old World tyrannies to destroy the United States by overwhelming its economy with a flood of paupers and criminals. Some European cities did, indeed, rid themselves of their poor by paying the passage to America of those who could be induced to emigrate.

Protecting the immigrant

The first move to protect the immigrant came from the federal government. In 1819 Congress set a limit on the number of persons that a vessel could carry. In 1848 and 1855 there were further attempts to legislate standards of immigrant transportation. These laws were generally unobserved, but they did indicate that the federal government was willing to undertake a certain responsibility for protecting those who sought to come to America.

The local governments, however, were more concerned about protecting their residents from the immigrants than about the welfare of the newcomers. New York City bore the heaviest burden of newcomers, and finally, in 1847, New York state established the Board of Commissioners of Emigration, the first permanent state agency for the protection of immigrants. Indeed, this agency is important not only because it marked a concern with the welfare of immigrants but because it was the first *state welfare agency* in our history (Bremner, 1970, pp. 334–98).

The first state welfare agency

The Board of Commissioners of emigration collected taxes and imposed indemnity bonds on immigrants, crews, and ships arriving at New York ports. These funds were used to support the arriving settlers through general relief (or to reimburse local communities for the relief they advanced to immigrants), information, transportation, and job placement. The board acted on the principle that since the immigrants had paid for the help, they were *entitled to it*—it was their right, not charity. In 1848 the board leased Ward's Island in the East River, where it established a hospital and a refuge for unemployable persons. The board also took charge of illegitimate children and orphans and maintained a nursery and school for them on Ward's Island. In 1855, in an effort to offer better protection to the immigrant, the board established a central compulsory landing depot in Castle Garden at the foot of Manhattan. All immigrants seeking admission to the country had to come there for processing. At Castle Garden the board could offer centralized help, including medical care to arrivals suffering from illnesses, especially contagious diseases (Bremner, 1970, pp. 334–98).

ঙ The Chicanos

In 1848, by the Treaty of Guadalgo Hidalgo, the United States acquired a new ethnic group that needs to be considered separately from the European immigrant groups. Not only was the social, political, and economic history of these new citizens markedly different from that of the Europeans, but their experience in becoming part of the nation was also distinctly different. Like the Indians, the Chicanos "were there first," having begun to settle the Southwest as early as 1530. They did not come into the United States voluntarily but as a conquered people.

The Treaty of Guadalupe Hidalgo had guaranteed them citizenship, personal property rights, and religious freedom. However, change took place so rapidly during the years following the treaty, and so many land-hungry Anglos moved into the area ceded to the United States by the treaty, that many rights of the Chicano people were ignored or rejected. In California the Chicanos lost the right to vote in the 1850s as a result of the wave of Anglos that came, lured by the discovery of gold. In New Mexico the Chicanos were disenfranchised in the 1870s with the coming of the railroads. By the beginning of the 20th century, much of their lands, which had been in their families for generations, was in Anglo hands and only their right of religious freedom was left unimpaired (Meier and Rivera, 1974, pp. xiii–xviii).

❧ Labor and economic security

The years from 1819 to the Civil War were difficult years for the industrial laborer. During those years there were times when one third of the labor force was without work. Wages fell 30–50 percent. In the first two years of the 1840s some families starved or froze to death. Most of the New England factories were closed. This was the time when Horace Greeley urged the jobless to "fly, scatter through the country, go to the Great West, anything but stay here" (Bremner, 1956, pp. 14–15).

Early industrial employment

In this new era labor was far more mobile than it had been during the colonial period. However, the freedom from indenture, slavery, or long-term contracts also included the freedom to starve. In the depression periods that seemed to sweep the nation in ten-year cycles during the 19th century, the urban free laborer, unlike the slave, could rely neither on the obligation of the master to provide at least a little food and some kind of shelter nor

on the land to provide enough food to support life.

Although the introduction of machinery created new and great possibilities of national growth and prosperity, the United States was at first confronted with the problem of establishing manufactures in a country where labor was still scarce and where there were strong prejudices against diverting people from agriculture.

The problem was solved initially by employing women and children to operate the new machines. This was a natural solution since the machines were doing work that women and their children had been doing in their own homes. As early as 1656 there had been efforts in Boston to make children useful in the manufacture of cloth by establishing "spinning schools" that would teach them how to spin. Although some individuals worried about what was happening to children in the mills, child labor was generally viewed as beneficial to the child and society. Alexander Hamilton's *Report on Manufacturers* of December 5, 1791, stated:

> The husbandman himself experiences a new source of profit and support, from the increased industry of his wife and daughters. . . .
> . . . .There is . . . the employment of persons who would otherwise be idle (and in many cases a burden on the community). . . . women and children are rendered more useful, and the latter more early useful, by manufacturing establishments than they would otherwise be. (Bremner, 1970, p. 172)

Child labor

At the beginning of the factory system the employment of children in factories did not appear to be drastically different from the child labor that had existed in every colony during colonial history. Advocates of child labor used the prevalent views of the sanctity of work and the evils of idleness as strong arguments for employing children in manufacturing work. They declared that giving children work would not only enable the industries to increase production at minimum expense but would also provide useful employment for poor and potentially vicious elements of society. However, the labor of children in factories was very different from the earlier practices in which children shared in domestic chores and engaged in training and craft work. The factory owners treated children as a distinct labor force, measuring the efficiency of their work against the wages paid them as laborers, and were not responsible for their maintenance or their instruction. The master, on the other hand, had been obligated to teach the apprentice a trade and to accept responsibility for his welfare. Also, whereas both the apprentice and the master were bound by contract, the children who were employed in factories had no legal agreement to protect them against abuse, to set forth their rights. Many of the national leaders who were struggling to secure protection for the development of the infant industries did not see the need to protect the small workers.

General Humphries, a factory owner who had been influenced by the apprentice system, became concerned with the fact that under the new system child laborers were receiving no education. He worked for a law requiring that the children employed in factories be taught to read, write, do sums, and attend a public workshop. In 1813 the Connecticut legislature passed the first compulsory school attendance law in the nation, requiring that manufacturers see that children in their employment were educated in the same way as other children. The law provided that the selectmen and magistrates of the town in which an industry was located should constitute a board of visitors to inquire into the manner in which the employer conformed to this law. However, like much of the later child labor legislation, the law was very poorly enforced (Bremner, 1970, pp. 437–77).

The employment of women

Abbott states that in relation to the employment of women the mill town of the late 1700s and early 1800s was very different from the factory of the 1850s. The early textile mill operatives were daughters of the early settlers of New England. Work in the mills was carefully supervised and was

perfectly acceptable socially. Educational opportunities were provided to the workers.

These conditions lasted, at best, 10 years. Gradually, the working population of the mills came to consist of children, older married immigrant women, and immigrant men. Systems were developed in which whole families were employed in the mills as family units. With the replacement of the young women of the early period, who did not see being mill operative as a lifetime career, by older women and immigrant men, there grew up a fairly permanent body of factory operatives.

In 1831, 18,539 men and 38,927 women worked in the cotton industry. As late as 1850, women accounted for 24 percent of the total number of manufacturing workers. In the next 50 years the proportion dropped to 19 percent (Abbott, 1910, pp. 48–62).

Trade unions

The first trade unions of workingmen in America were formed by skilled craftsmen such as carpenters and masons during the 1790s. By 1837 there were at least five national trade unions in the country: cordwainers, combmakers, carpenters, weavers, and printers. Strikes were common (Jennings, 1926, pp. 295–97). Unskilled as well as skilled workers were joining unions, with two out of every three workers in New York a union member. In the mills, women workers often took the lead in militancy. The Lowell Female Labor Reform Association was one of the most ambitious early efforts to create a union.

The issues that concerned the unions and the workers' associations in the early 1800s were:

1. Universal free education.
2. Free public lands for settlement.
3. The curbing of child labor and apprenticeship abuses.
4. Restrictions on the private use of prison labor.
5. Better working conditions, particularly for women.
6. The establishment of a ten-hour day with no reduction in wages.

7. Governmental control of the currency.
8. The right to organize.
9. Public works programs to employ the unemployed (Jennings, 1926, pp. 295–312; Baxandall, Gordon, Reverby, 1976, pp. 63–66; Axinn and Levin, 1975, p. 33).

In these goals we see an emphasis on political action toward programmatic and policy change. The radicals of the labor movement talked of full economic equality to supplement political equality.

Labor won a victory when President Martin Van Buren by executive order established the ten-hour day for federal employees without any reduction in pay. Van Buren was also active in supporting an adequate wage for all workers. Although it was a long time in coming, free land for settlers became an important step in freeing many workers from poverty. A radical labor group took the lead in urging that union members work to elect representatives who would support legislation to make public land available to people without charge in return for their pledge to live on the land and develop it (Lens, 1969, pp. 122–24). With the passage of the Homestead Act in 1862, this was achieved.

By the beginning of the Civil War, however, the labor movement had collapsed. This disintegration probably stemmed from three sources: (1) the very success of the movement for free land, which had lightened certain unemployment pressures; (2) the organized corporate opposition; and (3) the attitudes of the courts. The courts were not friendly to the interests of the labor unions, often holding the act of organizing to be an unlawful conspiracy (Jennings, 1926, p. 296). Since the Statute of Laborers of 1349, laws had punished efforts of laborers to improve their conditions. The English common law on conspiracy made the act of organizing a union illegal, as a conspiracy to interfere with the natural operations of the market and to "terrorize" other workers and employers (Boorstin, 1965, pp. 46–48).

◄§ Urbanization

The industrial revolution resulted in far-reaching social change that was to touch every aspect of American life. At the beginning of Washington's presidency, only six cities in the United States had more than 8,000 residents. The population of all six totaled only 130,000. When Lincoln became president, there were 5 million people in the nation's 141 largest cities. By 1860, Manhattan had a population of 813,000, Baltimore of 312,000 and Philadelphia of 56,000. In 1810 no city had a population of 100,000 but in 1860 eight—New York, Philadelphia, Baltimore, Boston, New Orleans, Cincinnati, St. Louis, and Chicago—were above that number. In many large cities half or more of the population were foreign born. Both the number and the employment of immigrants changed dramatically over the years from 1790 to 1860. From 1790 to 1800 about 5,000 immigrants a year came to the United States, but 427,833 came in 1854. In the colonial period, almost all of the immigrants were employed in agriculture as servants, tenants, or owners. And the vision of most servants and tenants was to own their own piece of land eventually and to plant, harvest, and market in their own way. But in the 19th century only one third of the newcomers became a part of farm life. Two thirds made their way to the cities, finding work as common laborers in industry or construction (Lens, 1969, pp. 93–99; Jennings, 1926, pp. 225–26).

◄§ Summary

One of the greatest forces affecting change during the period from 1780 to 1860 was the view that most Americans seemed to have of their country and their developing society. As in the preceding period, there was a general optimism in all areas of American life. The Revolution had been won, and Americans seemed to believe that both natural law and Providence were on their side (Boorstin, 1965). That belief tended to limit change. If Providence is one your side and everything in your country is wonderful, what need is there to be seriously concerned about such things as a few economic dislocations, the exploitation of certain groups, or the people who get left behind temporarily in the forward movement.

The immigrants who poured into the United States at this time had broken their previous social ties and had no claim on an established social group when they arrived. They were driven by a mixture of despair with their lives in the countries they came from and of hope that they could achieve in the New World. They sought opportunity, not help, considering themselves as temporarily poor rather than as a dependent class, as on their way to something better, rather than as members of the lower class. And in most instances they found a better and freer way of life than the one they had left. We may view their way of life with horror, but it was better than the life they had left. Thus, the poor, expecting to succeed by their own efforts and feeling that no one owed them a living, were a part of the general assumption that America offered the greatest opportunities in the world and that if one failed there it was one's own problem and not the problem of the society. These views limited the formation of groups to press for change.

Geography

The geographic size of America, the spread of land for the taking if one were willing to assume the risks of the journey, the hard work, and the conflict with the Indian, furthered optimism and ameliorated the effects of commercialism and industrialism. Thus, the properties of the American environment, while offering a wide expanse for change and resulting in the development of a unique way of life and a unique character, also slowed certain basic social changes in the ways individuals related to one another. On the whole, the environment within which American society developed was a force toward optimism, toward individualism in the sense of being responsible to no one and of having no right to expect help from others, and toward the belief that by moving on, people could flee their problems.

The lack of knowledge

Lacks in knowledge and technical understanding also helped shape American life in the first half of the 19th century. Knowledge of the special needs of children had not been developed, and the value system supported work and the economic need for child labor. So it is to be expected that children were treated in ways that we find cruel today and that their needs were neglected in ways we find shameful.

Families were seen as economic and socializing unites only. There was no developed knowledge base about the need of human beings for affection and emotional support that could be utilized to oppose this view and the treatment of families that followed from it. There was little scientific medical knowledge, and a scattered population took care of illness in the home, so there was little need for hospitals until late in the period. Yet medical advances also had to wait on the construction of hospitals, in a kind of circular process.

Technology

In the South, geography, a scattered population, the technological advance represented by the invention of the cotton gin, and the social pattern of rural life and slavery tended to slow any development of new social patterns. But in the North the growth of technology and industry resulted in a great mobility of people and in the rise of the industrial worker. Also, events in Europe had made many of its people desperate, and thus the new industries and the immigrants came together.

Political philosophy and organization

Two important factors affecting social welfare related to views about the organization and functioning of government.

From these came a Constitution which provided for a series of checks and balances among the various units of government. The Constitution also severely limited the use of federal power. There was no mandate for a strong central government. For more than 100 years this was to limit social welfare programs to those that localities were willing and able to support.

✑ A look ahead

In the next chapter we shall discuss the types of social welfare programs that developed during the period from 1780 to 1860. We shall see that despite the individualism that was developing, and despite the optimism which furthered the belief that all people could take care of themselves, there were persons who marched counter to the forward rush, who stopped to care about others.

✑ Study questions

1. Find an example in your local newspapers that relates to the use of judicial review, the problem of due process, or violation or concern with the violation of an article in the Bill of Rights.
2. Find an example in your local newspaper that illustrates either the division of authority between the state and federal levels of government or a program that rests on cooperation between the state and federal levels of government.
3. Find an example of the division of powers among the three branches of the federal government.
4. Make a list of issues that surfaced during the period from 1780 to 1860 and are unresolved today. Keep the list to trace how these issues have changed in later eras of our history.

✑ Selected readings

Pessen, Edward. *Jacksonian America: Society, Personality, and Politics.* Homewood, Ill.: Dorsey Press, 1978

This history text contains many chapters of interest to the social work student who is seeking to understand the issues of this era. If there is time, students could be assigned to report on chapters of particular interest.

Meier, August, and Rudwick, Elliot. *From Plantation to Ghetto.* New York: Hill and Wang, 1976.

The first three chapters of this book will provide students with a very complete discussion of the complexity of black life in America during the period (1780–1860). The book is highly recommended.

Hagan, William T. American Indians. Chicago: University of Chicago Press, 1961.

The first three chapters of this book will give students a perspective on the life of the American Indian during this period.

By the 1860s Social Welfare in America was beginning to divide into specialized systems.

Here are pictured two of the many institutions that evolved to handle problems of illness and deviance. Above is the McLean Asylum for the Insane, at Somerville, Massachusetts. On the right, young boys make ladies' skirt frames at the New York House of Refuge.

Chapter 13

Curative social policy and programs, 1780–1860

Introduction

In this chapter we shall discuss the development of social welfare policies and programs from the establishment of the federal government until the beginning of the Civil War. Our account will be written as an integrated story of processes and programs. As readers move through this chapter, they may want to note the processes by which programs came about. How was the problem defined? What were the underlying value assumptions? Were the actions taken based on collected facts or assumptions?

In the first half of the 19th century most people believed that the poverty of the able-bodied was caused by defects in character. Many of the individuals in positions of power and leadership saw their own experience as testimony to the validity of this position. Given the available knowledge of human motivation and human needs and the principal value systems of the community, most of the philanthropists and political leaders of the time firmly believed not only that the poor were the cause of poverty but that pauperism was promoted by making financial aid too easy to get and not shameful enough to receive. Many of these leaders felt that their own ability to survive early hardships was truly responsible for their later ability to succeed. Thus, they supported efforts for the reform of the individual poor and for wide use of the almshouse, where, under careful guidance and judicious management, paupers could engage in wholesome, productive labor and earn their own keep.

Public welfare—Income maintenance and social services

The methods used for public support of the poor during the period from 1780 to 1860 were similar to those that had been used prior to the Revolution. They involved caring for the poor in their own homes and three other types of indoor care. Of

233

these methods the almshouse became the primary method of care during this period.

The almshouse

The greater use of the almshouse, or the contracting out of the poor, was especially favored in the larger cities because of their growing numbers of poor people. No longer could outdoor relief, or venue, keep up with the need. It was believed that the advantage of the almshouse (or poor farm), or contracting with one person for care for all of the poor, was that it could keep the costs of care down by having paupers perform certain tasks under supervision.

Whatever the original dreams of the reformers, however, the almshouse became a place where the towns could place their poor so that they were out of sight and, for many, out of mind. Over the years, the poor farm was to become a symbol of mismanagement, political corruption, public lack of interest, and human wretchedness, with the trends being toward overcrowding, neglect, and inadequate funds. The buildings were often old and were allowed to deteriorate from lack of care and proper upkeep. The beds were often no more than piles of straw; sanitary facilities were lacking, and the sanitary conditions were terrible. Admitting children under a year of age to some almshouses was the same as signing their death certificates. Between 80 and 90 percent of all the infants sent to the Massachusetts almshouse at Tewksbury died there (Kelso, 1928, pp. 198–204; and Schneider, 1938, p. 84).

Yet almshouses remained a major form of care for dependent children during the first three quarters of the 19th century. In 1834 a Boston almshouse contained 134 sick persons, 132 children (of whom 28 were infants), and 61 insane or idiotic persons. The average number of children in the Boston almshouse was 100–150. In 1823 there were 500 children in the Bellevue Almshouse, and 25 years later there were 1,000. However, not all the children of the poor were in almshouses. In 1834, when there were 500 children in the Bellevue Almshouse, 4,000 more children were in families on outdoor relief. A study of the poor in New York state in 1824 reported that of those receiving "permanent support" 35 percent were unable to work because of age or infirmity, 27 percent were able-bodied, and the remaining 38 percent were children under 14 years of age (Kelso, 1928, pp. 198–202; Schneider, 1938, pp. 80–85).

The increase of the poor

During the period from 1780 to 1860, the rapid growth of immigration and the urbanization and industrialization of society caused the poor to increase rapidly in number. Troubled by the increased taxes for assistance to the poor and the continuing increase in the number of poor, it appeared to many that the practice of giving relief to the poor in their own homes actually increased the need for relief. This notion became so prevalent that the larger cities moved to abolish all outdoor relief. However, the other solutions utilized at the time seemed no better. The abuses of the helpless indentured servant and the inadequacies of the contracting-out system were widely discussed. Even the almshouse became suspect. The fact that the problem seemed to increase with each solution that was tried, combined with a growing faith that solutions could be found for human problems, gave impetus to a growing interest in assessing the public relief programs and in getting at the causes of the difficulties. As a result a number of investigations of the existing public relief programs were launched.

Investigations of poverty

In 1821 Josiah Quincy, the mayor of New York City, headed a committee to study the city's relief laws and practices. The committee concluded that the sole program for the administration of poor relief should be the almshouse. The committee saw outdoor relief as the worst possible way to help the poor, and the most economical method was an institution in which the poor could be provided with some form of work and supervision (Breckinridge, 1935, pp. 30–54).

In 1823 the legislature of New York state directed that J. V. N. Yates, the secretary of state, study and report on the effectiveness of the operation of the poor laws in New York. The Yates report, submitted in February 1824, classified the poor into two groups: (1) the "permanent poor," or those who received relief regularly during the year; and (2) the "occasional poor," or those who received only occasional or brief relief. The number of occasional poor was more than twice as great as the number of permanent poor (15,215 as against 6,896). In investigating the state of the permanent poor, Yates determined that roughly 25 percent could, "although not in the vigor of life," be considered able to earn their own sustenance. Among the permanent poor, Yates listed 2,604 children under 14 years of age. It is interesting that 14 was much older than the age at which it was generally thought that children could be expected to work. It is also interesting that the Yates report found that many of the men receiving care as well as their families had become dependent because of alcoholism (Breckinridge, 1935, pp. 30–54).

The Yates commission made four major findings: (1) that contracting out the poor often resulted in their being treated with abuse and neglect; (2) that under the relief systems used at the time the education and care of poor children were almost totally neglected; (3) that there were no adequate means for providing work or training for persons able to support themselves; and (4) that there was no adequate supervision of the use of the funds provided for the care of the poor. The Yates report recommended the division of the poor into two groups— the worthy poor (those who were unable to care for themselves or to work) and the unworthy poor (those able to work). The report further recommended that each country adopt the almshouse system for the care of the poor. Under this system two connected institutions would be erected in each county of the state (in a populous county there might be more than one pair of institutions in operation). One institution was to be a poorhouse in which paupers would be maintained and supplied with such work as they could do to maintain themselves and in which children would be

cared for, instructed, and placed out as suitable. The other institution was to be a penitentiary in which the *sturdy poor* could be confined and subjected to a routine of strict discipline and hard labor on a minimal diet (Breckinridge, 1935, pp. 30–54).

The Yates report was probably the principal work that led to the widespread use of the almshouse as the major way of caring for the poor. It should be further noted (as almost every careful subsequent investigation of poor relief has resulted in the same findings) that the report's statistical evidence showed that the overwhelming majority of the poor who asked for help did so because of social and physical problems beyond their control. Yet, as we shall see, although certain populations were identified as needing special care because they were obviously unable to care for themselves, the primary concern and the major solutions proposed during this time emphasized deterring the able-bodied from accepting relief and saving them from pauperism.

⇜ Private philanthropy, income maintenance, and social services

In discussing this period, Robert H. Bremner has written: "Throughout the 19th century, the charitable response of the American people was almost as generous as their pursuit of gain was selfish" (Bremner, 1956, p. 31). To the radicals of the time, however, there was nothing particularly admirable about men who gave away a tenth or less of their earnings to charity while retaining the rest of the wealth they had gained, as the radicals saw it, by robbing the poor, in their capacity as landlords or employers. However, there is little in the records left behind to indicate that these men gave out of the feelings of guilt that have been ascribed to them (Bremner, 1960, pp. 1–3 and 44–47). They seem to have been very confident that their good fortune came from God, and they gave to discharge the obligations of stewardship and religious duty, as well as because they enjoyed giving, because they regarded the support of certain causes as a good investment, and often simply because some appeal had touched their hearts. An example of the last is Elias Boudinot's bequest of funds to provide spectacles for the aged poor.

The number of charities

People chose to support a great number and variety of charities. These included the American Female Guardian Society, the Home for the Friendless, the Children Mission to Children of the Destitute (an agency supported by the contribution of children in Unitarian Sunday schools), the Society for the Relief of the Ruptured and Crippled, the Indigent Widows and Single Women's Society, the City Infant School Society, the Association for the Relief of Respectable Aged and Indigent Females, the Home for Little Wanderers, the American Temperance Society, the American Colonization Society, and so on. In the first half of the 19th century, religious societies for the redemption and regeneration of a sinful world and the moral reform of individual sinners grew more rapidly than did religious societies for the income maintenance of the poor (Bremner, 1960, pp. 58–61).

The principle of voluntary association to further the benevolent impulses of individuals was so much a part of American political and economic theory that the larger cities began to have an embarrassment of associations. It is interesting to observe, however, the highly specialized purposes of most of these organizations, and this pattern has remained a problem to the present day. Private benefactors have a need to see that the objects of their beneficence accord with their values and beliefs about who and what should be supported. This is not to say that private philanthropies are not of value to many persons, nor is it to deny the importance of such philanthropies in the total social welfare function of society. But those who seek an understanding of the social welfare institution need to recognize that along with their important benefits to society these specific and competing groups also bring problems in coordination and often leave great gaps in the coverage of need. The very number of these helping agencies may serve to assure the community that it is being generous enough, that there is no need to worry further about

people in trouble or to be concerned about needs that have not been covered or about families and individuals that have fallen into the gaps in the specifically defined services.

Private efforts at rehabilitation and prevention

At the beginning of the 19th century we also find a growing interest on the part of private givers in finding, through careful study, the causes of poverty and in developing constructive remedies for people in economic distress. One of the first organizations that was devoted to these purposes was the New York Society for the Prevention of Pauperism, established in 1817 by Thomas Eddy and John Griscom. It sought to investigate "the circumstances and habits of the poor" in order that they might devise "means for improving their situation, both in a physical and moral point of view" (Bremner, 1960, p. 61). The founders of the society understood the need for relief, especially during periods of high unemployment, but they regarded such remedies as temporary measures and they were interested in finding a way to do away with the need for employing them. They tried to develop means for preventing poverty and for rehabilitating the poor—a beginning of personal social services.

Those of us who are critical of the emphasis on the individual investigation and rehabilitation of the poor find in this view of poverty a "blaming of the victim." However, we need to recognize the importance of the emergence of the belief that want and trouble result from human behavior, not acts of God—that poverty, far from being inevitable, is an abnormal condition. We will see, as we move forward in our account of the development of social welfare in the United States, that we have sometimes acted as though we expected distress to cure itself, as though social ills could be treated by spiritual disciplines, or as though economic ills should respond to individual counseling. But underneath all of this, pushing us constantly toward reform, there has been the belief that if we could just find the proper remedy, the illness of distress and poverty could be cured. This belief, despite its limitations, reflects a hopeful view of human nature and of the possibilities for changing human beings and social systems, a view that grew out of our geography and our natural resources. The hope of the immigrant was strengthened by pride in the economic, technical, and industrial achievements that marked our years of national growth. Thus, though we may be critical of the studies that blame poverty on the poor, we need to recognize the merits of the conviction that poverty and even emotional distress, though shameful are not acts of God and can be eradicated (Bremner, 1956, pp. 16–18).

The Society for the Prevention of Pauperism

In a survey made under the auspices of the Society for the Prevention of Pauperism in the City of New York, the listed "causes of poverty," except for the last one, were a catalog of individual sins and weaknesses supported by such business organizations as pawnbrokers, saloons, and "houses of ill fame."

1st. Ignorance, arising either from inherent dullness, or from want of opportunities for improvement.

2nd. Idleness. A tendency to this evil may be more or less inherent. . . .

3rd. Intemperance in drinking. This most prolific source of mischief and misery drags in its train almost every species of suffering which afflicts the poor. . . .

4th. Want of economy. . . .

5th. Imprudent and hasty marriages.

6th. Lotteries.

7th. Pawnbrokers. The establishment of these offices is considered as very unfavorable to the independence and welfare of the middling and inferior classes.

8th. Houses of ill fame. The direful effects of those sinks of iniquity upon the habits and morals of a numerous class of young men, especially sailors and apprentices, are visible throughout the city. . . .

9th. Is not the partial and temporary good which [the numerous charitable institutions of the city] accomplish . . . more than counter-

balanced, by the evils that flow from the expectations they necessarily excite; by the relaxation of industry, which such a display of benevolence tends to produce. . . ?

Lastly. Your Committee would mention War, during its prevalence, as one of the most abundant sources of poverty and vice, which the list of human corruption comprehends. (Griscom, 1818, pp. 59–60)

Given these ten causes of poverty, the society sought to attack poverty on two levels. It sought to deal with the primary causes of destitution by introducing bills in the city council to prohibit street begging, to "prevent access of paupers . . . not entitled to settlement in the city,"and to restrict saloons (Griscom, 1818, pp. 59–60). The society established an employment bureau and a savings bank and encouraged the founding of mutual aid and mutual life insurance groups that would protect their members against economic hazards. It provided supplies for the home industrial employment of women and worked toward better cooperation among the various charities in the city. In addition to these efforts to bring about modest social reforms and to provide certain opportunities to the poor, the society mounted a vigorous program to rehabilitate individuals living in poverty. It divided the city into districts, and in each district it assigned two or three volunteer "visitors of the indigent" to serve as its agents. These visitors were to work to change the habits of the poor by visits and friendly advice on how to live a life free from drink, the pawnshop, and other temptations (Friedlander and Apte, 1974, p. 82).

Hartley and the AICP

Probably the most important single leader in philanthropy during this period was Robert M. Hartley, who served for over 30 years as secretary of the New York Association for Improving the Condition of the Poor (AICP). He was the first individual to devote all of his efforts to one charity and its daily work over a lifetime.

Earlier than most reformers of the 19th century, Hartley came to believe that the material conditions of the poor had to be improved before their moral health could be restored. So he launched the AICP in 1843 in order to provide a comprehensive service for the poor of New York City and to attempt to *organize the work of more than 30 other charities operating that were at the time.*

The primary function of the AICP was to render service to individual families, but the AICP also undertook to improve social conditions, especially those relating to housing, health, and child welfare. Under Hartley's direction the AICP made two housing surveys that led to the appointment of the first state legislative commission to investigate the tenement problem in the metropolis. The Association founded two dispensaries and a hospital for the treatment of crippled children, campaigned for compulsory school attendance laws, and espoused efforts to promote personal hygiene and public sanitation (Bremner, 1956, pp. 35–38).

The volunteer. The AICP revived volunteer personal service to the poor in order to counter the prevailing trend toward indiscriminate almsgiving. The association believed that almsgiving without an attempt at moral uplift only furthered pauperism. It set a pattern, followed by other private charities, of opposition to public relief, though association agents did refer people to that source of help. The organization built on the methods of the New York Society for the Prevention of Pauperism and divided the city into districts corresponding to the city wards. *Each AICP district set up an advisory committee of local residents who lived in the area served.* These residents were expected to advise and direct a corps of male volunteer visitors.

The volunteers were to: (1) visit applicants for assistance living in their section; (2) ascertain the facts of the case; (3) provide the deserving with aid suited to their particular requirements, which might include referral to another agency for help and grants of coal, food, or other necessities; and (4) provide encouragement and counsel along the path to rehabilitation. The AICP also employed paid staff members whose principal duty was to administer the work of the districts and supervise the volunteer visitors. Hartley urged that the city's tract mis-

sionaries be employed as paid agents of the society to perform the supervisory duties (Becker, 1961, pp. 255–60).

The visitors gave advice, support, and medical care; referred families to sources of financial help; and procured work for family members. Several visitors reported that they had begun a practice of using group meetings to help their families. Once these visitors had become acquainted with their families, they invited those with common problems to attend group counseling sessions at their homes. As time went on, many of the visitors found their work too heavy, especially for a volunteer service. Paid workers took over their functions. However, these workers were charged with giving mechanically without proper investigation or proper counseling.

The contributions of the AICP. After a long record of service to the community, the AICP gradually declined in influence and prestige. The reason for its decline seems to have been the inability of its leaders to give up their preconceived notions about the causes and treatment of poverty. The obsevations and experiences of the volunteer visitors over years of drastic changes in the economic and social climate of the city were never utilized to change the thinking of the society (Bremner, 1956, pp. 51–52).

The contributions of the AICP included the implementation of the belief that philanthropy must be planned, not haphazard; that methods of charity can be defined and transmitted; that certain environmental conditions are a community responsibility; and that personal service is helpful in itself. The district monthly meetings of the AICR's advisory committee was one of the earliest attempts by a charity society in the United States to organize and disseminate knowledge through the natural leaders in a community. The AICP structure served as a model for the Community Organization Society, a society that developed during the 1870s. Although historians generally place the beginning of social work at that time and give the COS credit for founding the social work profession, it would appear that the AICP, 50 years earlier, also used paid agents and hired those agents on the basis of their experience in moral counseling and their knowledge of their clients' life situations. These AICP agents appear to have supervised the volunteers by teaching and advising them. It is also interesting that almost a hundred years before the date commonly assigned to the beginning of group work in social work, the volunteers were reporting the use of group work as a helping method.

Religious charities

In the eyes of many people the greatest need of the poor was the need for moral and religious counseling and guidance. Various religious groups were involved in efforts to help the poor by printing religious literature and biblical tracts and distributing these materials on the docks and in the jails. Missionaries who were employed to visit the poor in their homes often gave temporary economic assistance to poor families and tried to find jobs for the unemployed in addition to seeking to persuade the poor to come to church and to send their children to Sunday school.

The Roman Catholic Church was active in helping the needy at an early date: the Sisters of Charity of Saint Vincent de Paul, which came to this country in 1809, was particularly active in establishing hospitals and orphan homes; the Little Sisters of the Poor, founded in 1840, assumed the task of caring for the aged poor; and members of the Society of Saint Vincent de Paul, a Roman Catholic layman's group that came to America around 1850, visited the destitute of their parishes and attempted to meet the spiritual and other needs of the poor as their resources permitted (Bremner, 1956, p. 34).

A Unitarian clergyman, Joseph Tuckerman, worked with and for the poor in Boston from 1819 to 1833. He was interested in bringing about changes in housing, wages, education, the handling of offenders, and relief (Bremner, 1956, pp. 33–34). He urged the repeal of the existing poor laws and the abolition of all public assistance except that furnished in almshouses under close supervision.

In these early efforts we see the fear that the giving of public money to the poor would increase pauperism, that the principle commodities of value to the poor were advice and opportunity.

Mutual aid societies

As we discussed in the last chapter, groups of people with common interests often banded together to help one another in mutual aid societies. These societies, often built around the church by the members of the congregation rather than by the hierarchy, were a particularly important source of help to urban blacks. The earliest record of black mutual aid organization was the Free African Society, formed at Philadelphia in 1787. Through the society, members pooled their resources to "support one another in sickness, and for the benefit of their widows and fatherless children" (Meier and Rudwick, 1978, p. 106). Black benevolent societies multiplied all over the North. By the 1830s there were 100 such societies, averaging 75 members, in Philadelphia alone. Many other communities, North and South, had similar mutual benefit and burial societies, many of which had to meet in secret. These societies often persuaded influential white leaders to aid them in instituting certain social changes, such as setting aside land for burial of their people.

The benevolent societies and the black church offered to blacks the major—and often the only—aid. Their rules for membership often reflected middle-class moral values, such as one rule denying membership "to those unwilling to lead an orderly and sober life." In addition to these organizations, blacks established chapters of secret fraternal orders such as the Masons and the Odd Fellows, though the charters of these chapters sometimes had to come from groups in Europe (Meier and Rudwick, 1978, p. 106).

✌§ Special populations

During this period we see a growth in the concern for the welfare of certain special populations. Veterans remained a special group that was considered to have earned a special right to compensation. But children, the blind, the retarded, the deaf, and the mentally ill also began to be identified as groups that needed special care. In some instances the care offered was developed under private auspices; in other instances it was publicly supported. In our account of the beginning of these services, we shall classify the programs by the special population rather than by whether the resources developed were public or private. However, it is always important in analyzing a program to note the sources of support.

Children

During the first half of the 1800s the legal relationships between children and parents were beginning to change. Judges' decisions as to the needs of the child in particular cases began to override the rights of parents, particularly fathers, and even the rights of the community. This trend toward concern for the protection of the child was to accelerate in the last half of the 19th century. The trend was perhaps most evident in divorce cases, in which the judges no longer acted solely on the assumption of the father's rights to the child as property and began to be concerned with which parent could best care for the child as a human being. Considering the distribution of tasks in the 19th-century family, it is perhaps understandable that the mother began to be accepted as the parent who was most capable of caring for minor children.

As we have seen, in the colonial and early national periods, children were largely cared for and educated through "binding out" and apprenticeship. In both instances, the child became, in essence, part of another family that assumed the responsibility of caring for it, socializing it, and training it to perform some work role; in return, the family profited from the child's services. However, as industry moved out of the home, as slavery grew, and as the tasks of the frontier no longer demanded the unskilled hands of every available person, taking young children into one's home became more a burden than an aid. As a result, by the 1800s, hundreds of children in large cities were housed in almshouses, with or without their families (Bremner, 1970, p. 266).

By 1830 several things were pushing society toward the rapid development of special institutional care for children; (1) the number of orphans and dependent children was growing; (2) there were graphic reports by respected persons of the terrible conditions of life in the almshouses; (3) an increasing number of women were becoming active in benevolent activities, with a special interest in the welfare of children, particularly girls.

Orphanages. Institutions for children—orphanages—began to develop throughout the United States. These were usually supported by some mixture of public and private funds. Although founded and managed by private associations under private auspices, they were performing a public service and were therefore seen by the state as appropriate objects of at least *some* public support.

Whether they were raised in orphanages, almshouses, or their own homes, on reaching a "suitable age" poor children were "bound out" for the rest of their minority. The practice of forcing poor children to become involuntary servants seems somewhat contrary to other movements of the time, but it was done under the fiction that teaching them to work was a way of preventing future dependence. Gradually laws began to be passed to give protection to such children. The age at which they were bound out was gradually raised until it was higher than the usual age at which most poor parents sent their own children to work (Bremner, 1970, pp. 262–63).

The first *public orphanage* was established at Charleston, South Carolina, in 1790. Groups of women established most of the private orphanages, such as those founded by the Female Charitable Society of Salem, Massachusetts, and the Society for the Relief of Poor Widows with Small Children in New York. Some orphanages were founded by religious organizations, such as the Bethesda orphanage in Georgia and the Ursuline orphanage in New Orleans. The AICP stimulated the founding of the New York Juvenile Asylum to care for vagrant and neglected children. This institution usually kept the children it accepted for a considerable period of time before placing them, usually with farmers in the West. The Asylum was notable for its concern with placement and follow-up. It placed its charges with care, having a committee consider the matter and an indenturing agent to place and follow-up on the children (Abbott, 1938, pp. 22–35).

Foster care. The concept of placing children in the West, as family members rather than indentured servants, is usually thought to have originated with Charles Loring Brace, reformer of the mid-19th century. Brace studied for the ministry and worked as a missionary to prisoners and the poor. This work exposed him to the problem of thousands of vagrant children. These were not the children of poor homes but children who had no homes at all. Brace became desperately concerned about these children. He came to believe that most of the preventable causes of poverty could be avoided by getting such children out of the city and into a rural environment as members of a rural family.

The Children's Aid Society was established in 1853 under Brace's leadership. It was different in that it intended to employ paid agents to work with children. It also intended to cooperate with other groups, such as orphanages. The society planned to provide a complete program of child care, not just to place children in rural homes in the West. The paid agents (the first child welfare workers?) were to make themselves acquainted with the problems of the children in their area, to conduct informal religious exercises for the boys of the neighborhood, and to establish a reading room and an industrial school. Later the society established lodging houses for girls and one for working boys, vacation and convalescent homes for ailing children, and even a sick children's mission employing 12 doctors and 4 nurses to visit sick children in their homes.

Much of the effort to help children in the 19th century did not make a very clear distinction between orphans and dependent children. It seemed to be generally assumed that poor children with families were in need of care because the indolence and immorality of their parents resulted in their living in poverty. Allowing this situation to continue would only cause the children, in turn, to grow up without effective habits of industry and self-discipline. Orphanages, binding out, and apprenticeship were seen as ways of providing necessary discipline and education that such dependent children could not receive in their own homes. However, Brace was concerned primarily with the orphans, or the street children of the time—children without families (Brace, 973, pp. 234–70).

Another important thing to note about Brace's work is that his concept of foster home placement differed from the earlier use of indenture and apprenticeship in putting a certain emphasis on healthy family life and family interaction, rather than work, discipline, and training, as the means for achieving rehabilitation. His approach began the movement toward the foster home programs that we know today.

Illegitimate children and adoption. During our early history, illegitimate children were often ignored by society, except as such children might be seen as orphans. The courts had held that these children had no rights of inheritance from either the mother or the father. However, states gradually passed laws that allowed for legitimizing a child when the father and mother married or when the father wished to do so by declaring that he was the father. An Alabama law also provided for a new type of legal parent-child relationship—the adoption of nonrelated children.

In the adoption procedure a legal relationship identical to that between the biological parent and child is established between the child and another individual. There was no provision for adoption in English common law, and adoption was not authorized by statute in Britain until 1926. Although families had taken in unattached children and raised them as family members from the beginning of our country, such actions established no legally binding parent-child relationship like that between parents and their genetic offspring.

Grace Abbot speaks of the earliest adoption laws as merely providing "evidence of the legal transfer of a child by the natural parents to the adopting parents, and provision for a public record on the transfer, similar to the registration of deeds" (1938, p. 172). These adoption procedures were largely a matter between private citizens in which the only legal issue involved was the right of inheritance and the control of the child. A court clerk took care of the matter. However, as concerns for the protection of children developed, adoption law became somewhat more complex. A Massachusetts law of 1851 made the consent of the natural parent necessary to adoption and stipulated that a probate judge had to determine that the adoption was in the interests of all concerned. Not until well into the 1920s did modern adoption procedures begin to be recognized as a part of child welfare services. However, a persistent characteristic of adoption has been the conflict between the benefit to the adopting parent and the benefit to the child, with the needs of the unwed parents falling far behind (Abbott, 1938, pp. 172–73; Billingsley and Giovannoni, 1972, pp. 35–36).

Black children

Our discussion above has been concerned primarily with the care of white children. Until after 1865, slavery was the major child welfare institution for black children. In a peculiar way slavery as an institution performed many of the functions that the social welfare institution performs in a free society; that is, slaves "must be supported in some fashion when they were too old to work; they must have attention in sickness for they represent capital; and they could never be among the unemployed" (Billingsley and Giovannoni, 1972, p. 22). Thus, in the South there was no identified need for a separate system of child care. However, the black child was almost equally ignored in the North. Black children were found in almshouses, but they were excluded as a matter of policy from most of the orphanages established before the Civil War.

It is not surprising, therefore, that the Quakers, who, as we have seen, were among the leaders in the abolitionist movement, became concerned about the care of black children. In 1822 they established the Philadelphia Association for the Care

of Colored Children to develop and support the first orphanage for black children. This institution was followed by others, in Providence (1835) and New York (1836). The founders of the black orphanages were concerned that these institutions not be connected with the abolitionist movement because of the high feelings that surrounded the issue of slavery. However, despite the efforts of the founders to divorce the care of black children from the conflict of the times, white mobs burned the shelter for colored orphans in Philadelphia in 1838 and the Colored Orphan Asylum in New York was broken into and set afire by 500 white men and women during the Draft Riot of 1863. The founders of the New York orphanage tended to limit its admissions to children under eight because, like those who had established the white orphanages of the time, they saw the institution as preparation for indenture, which would supply care and socialization to older children until adulthood (Billingsley and Giovannoni, 1972, pp. 28–30).

Indian children

Caught between the dying world of tribal culture and the dominant world of white society, Indian parents were in a difficult situation. Increasingly, they were forced by public law to surrender their children to white schools for the larger part of the year, and this caused them to lose trust in themselves and in their ability to pass on to their children the valued ways of their ancestors (Hagan, 1926, pp. 87–91).

The blind

Indigent blind persons were objects of public and private charity, but many blind children and adults were to be found in the almshouses. Drs. John D. Fisher and Samuel G. Howe, both of whom had traveled in Europe and observed the methods of teaching both blind and mentally retarded children, began the institutional care of the blind. Their school soon became too small for the numbers of blind children who came, so it was moved to a mansion donated by Thomas H. Perkins. The institution was later to become the Perkins Institute and Massachusetts School for the Blind (Friedlander and Apte, 1974, pp. 73–74; Farrell, 1956; Bremner, 1970, pp. 768–74).

The retarded

Dr. Howe's interest in the blind led him to a broader interest in the rehabilitation of children with sensory handicaps, especially the conditions of retardation. In 1846, he became chairman of a Massachusetts commission to inquire into the conditions of idiots in the commonwealth and he visited France and Switzerland to learn of their methods of treatment.

As a result of growing interest in the retarded, Dr. Howe was able to establish with *state funds* an experimental school for idiots within the Perkins Institution for the Blind in 1848. Subsequently, this section was expanded to become the Massachusetts School for Idiotic and Feebleminded Youth. It is notable that in this time of local and private financing for most social welfare work, Howe was able to secure state funds to conduct some experimental work with this group of people.

By the beginning of the Civil War there were schools for the retarded in four states—New York, Pennsylvania, Ohio, and Connecticut. The establishment of these schools marked the beginning of state responsibility for certain types of social welfare problems (Adams, 1971; Friedlander and Apte, 1974, pp. 74–75).

The deaf

The deaf first found a champion when Dr. John Stanford, a minister, found a number of deaf children on his visits to the New York almshouse in 1810. Up to this time, deaf children had generally been treated as idiots and either left to their families or placed in almshouses, but Stanford began to offer these children religious instruction, the first attempt to help them understand the world around them.

In Hartford, Connecticut, Dr. Thomas H. Gallau-

det also became interested in the deaf. Friends took up a collection and sent him to Europe to study methods of teaching the deaf. He returned to America with Laurent Clerc, one of the best European teachers of the deaf, to open the first American institution for the deaf at Hartford, in 1817.

This institution was a private one, but it was subsidized by the state and it was intended to serve both charity and tuition students. Massachusetts in 1819, New Hampshire in 1821, and Vermont and Maine in 1825 began to send their deaf students to the school and to pay for their care through state appropriations. The New York Institution for the Instruction of the Deaf and Dumb was established as a private institution in 1818. It was 1822 before a limited number of charity patients were accepted there for three years' instruction at the expense of the state. Pennsylvania established a state institution for the deaf in 1820, and Kentucky established one in 1822. The southern states sent their deaf children to the Kentucky institution (Friedlander and Apte, 1974, pp. 75–78; Bremner, 1960, pp. 66–67; Bremner, 1970, pp. 760–68).

The mentally ill

As we have seen, during the colonial period of our history, mental illness was not seen as either a major medical problem or as a matter of pressing social concern. Except for the efforts that were made in Philadelphia and Virginia, the mentally ill were, for the most part, cared for under the aegis of poor laws or private charity. At that time, the United States was predominantly rural and many informal arrangements could be made for the mentally ill. Knowing little about mental illness and how to treat it, the colonial society was less concerned about treatment than about the economic and social ramifications of the problem and about the threat of mentally ill individuals to public safety. The development of hospital care, both for general medical patients and for the insane, was very slow, and most of the sick and the mentally ill in urban areas, where families could not care for them at home, found their way into almshouses. Even the movement to classify the poor did not help the mentally ill, since they fell into the general class of "the impotent" or the "worthy poor."

The first urban hospitals began to appear just before the Revolutionary War, and their establishment was rapidly accelerated during the period just before the Civil War. In Chapter 11 we discussed the first general hospital, founded in Philadelpia in 1752, which also admitted the "curably insane." The first public hospital for the insane was established at Williamsburg, Virginia, in 1773.

Finally, in 1771, New York chartered a general medical hospital. It did not accept patients until 1791. While the hospital was under construction, it was directed to "appropriate the cellare part of the North Wing or such part of it as they may judge necessary into ward or cells for the reception of Lunatics" (Russell, 1945, p. 10). The number of mentally ill persons who sought admittance to care in the hospital was small until after 1800. Then their number increased rapidly, leading eventually to the establishment of the Bloomingdale Asylum for the Insane in New York, in 1821. In Philadelphia, as a result of similar conditions, the Pennsylvania Hospital established a separate institution for the mentally ill in 1841 (Grob, 1973, pp. 1–34). The Quakers, concerned about the treatment of the members of their faith, established the Friend's Asylum, a private institution for Quakers, at Frankfort, Pennsylvania, in 1817. In 1834 the asylum began to admit persons of other faiths who could pay for care.

Rush. Dr. Benjamin Rush, whom we met in our discussion of colonial health practices and who was connected with the Pennsylvania Hospital for nearly 30 years, remained active as a physician-reformer until the middle of this period. Among his greatest services to the medical profession were his study of mental disease and his experiments in the humane treatment of the insane. He supported attempts to provide occupational therapy, but inadequate staff and facilities hampered significant progress along this line. In addition to being an active physician, Rush was an active teacher of medicine, and in 1812 he wrote *Medical Inquiries and Observations upon the Diseases of the Mind.* In this text he took the position that insanity was an illness and that the insane should be treated as sick persons requiring specialized attention. Since sick persons are ordinarily not held responsible for their illnesses, this definition of the insane as sick removed the moral implications of their behavior. For many years Rush's work was the only American textbook on psychiatry (Deutsch, 1949, pp. 77–94; Bremner, 1960, pp. 31–37).

Moral treatment. While Rush was the outstanding leader in American treatment of the mentally ill, there were two other important pioneers in this field: Phillipe Pinel of France and William Tuke, an English Quaker. Pinel's reforms grew out of his faith in human progress and his push to end suffering. He found the traditional practices of the time seldom brought positive results. Therefore he opposed them and developed what came to be known as "moral treatment" which relied on the creation of a new environment marked by patience, kindness, guidance, and good treatment. In this approach the institution and the therapeutic relationship to the physician, who was seen as occupying a dominant position, were necessary to adequate treatment.

William Tuke founded the York Retreat in England in 1792. It was begun both as a humanitarian act and as an effort to assure that Quakers who were mentally ill were cared for according to the principles of their faith. Tuke was distrustful of contemporary medical practice and felt that much more could be accomplished through efforts to help patients develop self-restraint and self-control. Coercion and physical punishment were virtually eliminated and the "desire for self-esteem" encouraged. Quaker religious beliefs and values were a part of the treatment. It should be noted that these two separate streams of "moral treatment" were more a reflection of social and intellectual notions than an advance in medial theory (Grob, 1973, pp. 39–49).

The early hospitals. As population and urban stresses increased, the mentally ill could no longer be cared for in the homes of families. Thus they were becoming more visible to the general population, which felt threatened by their bizarre behavior. Three new mental hospitals were established between 1811 and 1821: the McLean Asylum, the Friend's Asylum, and the Hartford Retreat. During this time the Bloomingdale Asylum was established as a separate part of the New York Hospital and given its own independent identity (Grob, 1973, pp. 125–30).

These early institutions made several contributions: (1) they gained considerable support for the concept of caring for the mentally ill in their own communities; (2) they were instrumental in spreading and popularizing some of the newer concepts of mental disease and treatment; and (3) they served as training centers for the psychiatric profession. However, the influence of these hospitals as models of care was limited by their goals, which were essentially to develop internal forces of restraint through a system of rewards and punishments; their structure, which was that of a small institution closely supervised by a psychiatrist superintendent who knew all of the patients; and their reliance on the private sector as a source of operating funds. Although the founders of these institutions envisaged accepting all comers, the popularity of the care provided, together with the social problems of the times and the private financing of the institutions, meant that these institutions were soon unable to accept persons who could not pay for their own care. Thus, there was an inevitable and rather rapid shift to a homogeneous, affluent patient body. However, the shift was not altogether a function of economics. The management of the private hospitals recognized the growing differences between their patients and those of the almshouses, but they did not necessarily oppose the trend. Also, psychiatrists, drawn largely from the middle and upper classes, found it more comfortable to work with the patients in the private hospitals, and some took the position that it was more effective and better for the patients to be separated into the two populations (Grob, 1973, pp. 67–83).

Public hospitals. Actually, the beginning of the push toward the public care of the mentally ill as a special group needing special kinds of care really began with the formation of the Boston Prison Discipline Society and its investigation of conditions in the public jails. As a result of the society's report

urging the care of the mentally ill in separate public hospitals, the General Court in 1830 approved a bill authorizing the erection of a state lunatic hospital for 120 patients and appropriated $30,000 for it. The new hospital opened in 1833, and it quickly gained a national reputation. In its national battle to secure better care for offenders the Prison Society pointed to the public mental hospital in Massachusetts as a model that other states should follow.

Dorothea Dix. In the 1840s, when some of the earlier reformers in the area of mental health were growing older and less active, the gap in leadership was filled by Dorothea L. Dix, "who without doubt became the most famous and influential psychiatric reformer of the nineteenth century" (Grob, 1973, p. 103).

Dorothea Dix's work offers one of the best examples in our history of social welfare of sustained, determined, and constructive agitation for reform. She was one of the first women to take leadership in a national reform effort. She was a schoolteacher by profession, not a doctor or a businesswoman. However, a modest bequest from her grandmother was sufficient to support her. Thus, she was able to devote all of her time to reform activities. Her work began when she volunteered to teach a Sunday school class for women in jail and in the course of her teaching became aware of a group of insane women who were locked up in unheated cells and suffering from gross neglect. Deeply touched, she decided to see that these women were moved to better quarters, but also to do something about the existence of such conditions.

Dix began her work by making an exhaustive personal examination of the condition of the mentally ill in Massachusetts. This took her well over a year. It was two years before she was ready to report her findings to the legislature. Combining passion and knowledge, her report cited instance after instance of the mistreatment and neglect of the mentally ill. She insisted that the state had moral and legal obligations to the mentally ill, and she demanded that the legislature fulfill its obligations to them. Dix had not only facts but friends at her disposal. Her friends included Horace Mann and Samuel Gridley Howe (her report was referred to the legislative committee chaired by Howe), with their help she was victorious in securing the passage of a bill enlarging the Worcester Asylum to provide more space for poor patients.

This was the first phase of a 40-year agitation for reform that took Dix over a good part of the world in the interests of the mentally ill. Her work led to a tremendous increase in the number of state hospitals for the care of the insane, though the conditions in the new hospitals were often far from ideal. Not until 1904 did Massachusetts assume financial responsibility for its public mental institutions and relieve local communities of the burden of local support.

Federal financing sought. The most significant attempt to alter the manner in which mental hospitals were financed was undertaken by Dorothea Dix in 1848, when she presented the U.S. Congress with a long memorial requesting legislation to distribute 10 million acres of federal land to the states, whose proceeds would be used to support the indigent insane. (She started by asking for 5 million but raised her request when she met resistance.) Precedents for such a subsidy existed in that federal land grants had already been made to support the public schools, the Hartford and Kentucky institutions for the deaf, and the private railroad industry. Nevertheless, much debate in Congress centered on the constitutional question of whether the federal government had the legal authority to use the federal public lands for such purposes.

Finally, in 1854, after eight years of lobbying, the bill passed both houses only to be vetoed by President Franklin Pierce. Because of the importance of this veto to the issue of federal support of social welfare projects, we will quote it in part:

> It can not be questioned that if Congress has the power to make provision for the indigent insane without the limits of this District it has the same power to provide for the indigent who are not insane, and thus to transfer to the Federal Government the charge of all the poor in all the States. It has the same power to provide hospitals and other local establishments for the care and cure of every species of human infirmity, and thus to assume all that duty of either public philanthropy

> or public necessity to the dependent, the orphan, the sick, or the needy which is not discharged by the states themselves or by corporate institutions or private endowments. . . .
>
> . . . The question presented, therefore, clearly is upon the constitutionality and propriety of the federal Government assuming to enter into a novel and vast field of legislation, namely, that of providing for the care and support of all those among the people of the United States who by any form of calamity become fit objects of public philanthropy.
>
> I cannot but repeat . . . if the several States . . . shall be led to suppose, as should this bill become a law, they will be, that Congress is to make provision for such objects, the fountains of charity will be dried up at home, and the several States, instead of bestowing their own means on the social wants of their own people, may themselves . . . become humble supplicants for the bounty of the Federal Government, reversing their true relations to this Union. (Bremner, 1970, pp. 789–91)

The presidential veto was upheld by a wide margin. Thus the issue of federal support for social welfare programs disappeared as a viable alternative for decades to come, except in relation to specific programs for specific populations that could not easily be considered the charge of the states, such as the Indian, the veteran, and the immigrant. For the remainder of the 19th century and the first part of the 20th century, responsibility for the mentally ill would continue to be borne by state and local communities (Grob, 1973, pp. 121–30; Deutsch, 1949, pp. 178–79).

War veterans

We have already discussed the establishment in the New England colonies of pensions for disabled war veterans and their dependents as a departure from the principle of the responsibility of the states for social welfare matters. Now, with the establishment of the federal government we find this type of relief, medical care and counseling service becoming the responsibility of the federal government.

By 1790 Congress had provided that the federal government would take over the responsibility for disabled veterans, veteran's widows, and orphans of veterans. Pensions for these groups were established for service in the Revolutionary War, the War of 1812, the Seminole Indian wars, and the Mexican War of 1846–48. The pensions and benefits were small, nevertheless a precedent of benefits based on the notion of compensation for an identified inservice rather than economic need was being established (Axinn and Levin, 1975, p. 39).

✑ Health

Public hospitals

The first public hospitals in the United States were the almshouses; the wealthy were cared for at home. In the larger almshouses, sick paupers might be separated from other inmates and placed in an infirmary, where they might receive rare visits from the doctor. However, not until the end of the 1700s were special wards in almshouses set aside for the medical care of the poor. Not until the end of the 18th century did Massachusetts and Rhode Island set up what was called "almshouse hospitals."

But as the population in urban centers increased and as the understanding of contagious diseases and the number of persons suffering from contagious diseases grew, it became necessary to develop an institution to care for the sick, rich or poor. Bellevue Hospital in New York was started in 1794 as a "pesthouse," and a special ward for patients suffering from contagious diseases was added in 1825. The separation of the hospital from the almshouse became increasingly necessary. An important stimulus was a growing awareness of the dangers of contagious diseases to the entire community. Thus, the development of the early hospitals reflected a growing social concern rather than a development in medical theory and practice. However, the radical advances of medical knowledge in the late 19th and early 20th century were made possible, at least in part, because of the clinical data that were supplied by the grouping together

of large numbers of ill people under medical auspices (Duffy, 1953, p. 26; 1961, pp. 101–109).

Medical schools

The first U.S. medical school was founded by Dr. John Morgan in 1765 in Philadelphia in conjunction with the Pennsylvania Hospital. The second medical school was established in New York in 1767 at King's College (later Columbia University) at the suggestion of six physicians, including Dr. Samuel Bard, whose father, also a physician, had been a friend of Franklin and Rush. Young Dr. Bard had had to go abroad to acquire his medical education at Edinburgh University, and he came home acutely aware of the need for both a hospital and a medical school. At the first King's College commencement, in 1769, Bard commented on the absence of a hospital in the city. Such an institution, he pointed out, "would benefit the entire community, rich and poor alike" (Grob, 1973, pp. 29–30). Bard noted that the undertaking would raise the standards of medical practice and permit proper instruction of medical students and that New York City had developed sufficiently to support it. On June 3, 1771, a charter was granted to the Society of the Hospital in the City of New York in America for the "purpose of erecting an Hospital for the reception and relief of sick and diseased persons" (Grob, 1973, pp. 29–30).

Public health

At the beginning of the 19th century, smallpox, yellow fever, diphtheria, malaria, and dysentery resulted in high mortality rates and incapacitated great numbers of people. Diseases were seen as "God's will." There was a lack of knowledge of how to treat them. Summer in the urban areas was viewed as the dangerous season, and those who could fled to the country. It is startling to learn that the 1850 mortality statistics were no better than those of 1790. However, investigations of the various philanthropic associations and societies were slowly accumulating evidence that connected living conditions with public health. In 1800 the smallpox vaccine was developed. In 1842 Edwin L. Chadwick's report, *The Sanitary Condition of the Labouring Population of Great Britain,* appeared. It moved the cities to greater concern with urban sanitary control. The American Medical Association was founded in 1847.

The first *federal* program in public health was the Marine Hospitals Service, established in 1789 to care for seamen. Once again we see federal support for a special population group that could not be defined as the responsibility of any particular states. The first federal concern with immigrants was related to the control of contagious diseases. The Federal Passenger Act of 1819 required medical inspection of arriving immigrants.

Children

The health problems of children were the first health problems to receive concentrated attention from medical practitioners during the first half of the 19th century. In 1825 William P. Dewees, lecturer on midwifery at the University of Pennsylvania Medical School, published the first comprehensive American work on the medical treatment of children. During the 1850s the first two American hospitals to be established exclusively for children were founded in New York and Philadelphia.

✏§ Crime and Delinquency

Prisons

During the years from the Revolution to the Civil War the beginnings of the modern system for treating the offender were furthered by two forces: (1) a rapid increase in the numbers and types of offenses and (2) the influence of a growing humanitarianism which made it less acceptable to punish offenders by severe physical punishment, mutilation, or death. This humanitarianism also turned the attention of reformers to the terrible conditions of the local jails, and a demand grew that the state rather than localities take responsibility for the serious offender as well as the responsibility for improving the conditions under which persons were incarcerated (Lewis, 1922, p. 13).

The movement to improve the conditions of prisons went back to 1776, when a Society for Alleviating the Miseries of Public Prisons had been organized in Philadelphia (Bremner, 1960, p. 64). In 1790, under the influence of this society, the Pennsylvania legislature decided to convert the Walnut Street Jail into a state prison. The legislature was convinced that the best treatment of offenders was isolation and meditation, which would lead, through the divine power within each individual, to their reformation. The prisoners admitted to the Walnut Street Jail were therefore classified into two groups. Older offenders who had been convicted of serious crimes were lodged in solitary cells and deprived of communication with other prisoners. Younger offenders who had been convicted of less serious crimes were lodged in dormitories, where they lived in groups. This method meant a classification of prisoners according to offense, and it also marked a beginning of the belief that rehabilitation rather than punishment for the sake of punishment should be the goal of the system. Further, such practices introduced the notion that cruel punishment for an offense did not necessarily either rehabilitate the offender or deter others from crime.

A second model of the state prison was introduced at Auburn, New York, in 1816. It differed from the Pennsylvania plan in that prisoners were confined to cells only at night, having to work during the day in congregate prison workshops. However, silence was imposed during working hours, with severe punishment for talking. The Auburn prison was built on the model of a Belgian prison. It had a star shape, with cell blocks opening into a gallery which could easily be supervised by one centrally positioned guard. The Auburn system was the more widely accepted of the two systems, with such well-known prisons as Sing Sing in New York, established in 1825, and San Quentin in California, established in 1852, adopting its pattern (Friedlander and Apte, 1974, pp. 77–79).

During the first half of the 19th century each system had staunch advocates. The Pennsylvania plan, as indicated earlier, appealed to humanitarians because of the supposed penitential benefits of meditation in solitary confinement, whereas those who were impressed with the importance of work and the economy of prison labor supported the Auburn plan. Samuel Gridley Howe, Horace Mann, and Dorothea Dix, among others, supported the Walnut Hill model. The influential Boston Prison Discipline Society, founded in 1825 to give prison reformers an organization that backed better care of the offender, supported the Auburn system. The heat of the controversy and the interest it evoked enabled prison administrators to initiate reforms in the construction and management of prisons which "for a brief period made American penitentiaries among the best in the world" (Bremner, 1960, p. 64).

Probation

Because of his concern for offenders and their rehabilitation, Isaac Hopper (1771–1852) began his work of helping discharged prisoners find homes and jobs. Meanwhile, in Boston a new program for offenders began when John Augustus (1785–1859) voluntarily agreed to supervise the behavior of an offender if the offender were returned to the community instead of being sent to prison.

Augustus was a shoemaker by trade, and he had no official standing with the court. His work consisted of persuading the court not to sentence an offender, but to continue the case and allow him to post bail for the offender's good behavior. He would report back to court at stated intervals, and if all went well, the case could eventually be dismissed. He began his work in 1841, and over a period of almost 20 years he devoted the earnings of his shoe shop, and any contributions he could secure from others, to rehabilitate persons who had committed petty crimes (Bremner, 1970, p. 732). Augustus was not a wealthy man, and his account of his work is full of his concern about the costs of providing bail as well as food and clothing for the offenders he accepted.

Juvenile correctional insitutions

In 1823 Thomas Eddy and John Griscom established the Society for the Reformation of Juvenile Delinquents. The society received authority from New York state to establish and manage a school for juvenile offenders, and it obtained an initial subscription of $18,000 from private individuals. The school, the New York City House of Refuge, was opened on January 1, 1825. Each subscriber had a voice in its management and it was to be a community venture divorced as far as possible from state control. The first institution of its kind in the United States, it was to be a "prison, manufactory and school" (Teeters and Reinemann, 1950, pp. 431–32). It was to endure until 1932, when it merged with the New York State Vocational Insitution, which had been established that year, and came under the supervision of the state department of corrections.

Boston opened a House of Reformation in 1836, and Philadelphia opened a House of Refuge in 1828. The Philadelphia House of Refuge grew out of the interest of women who belonged to the Society of Women Friends, an association for visiting women in prison. In 1850, as a result of friction that came with the increasing number of black children among the inmates, new buildings for the black children were erected at some distance from the building that housed the white children. In 1872, separate schools for white boys and white girls were erected.

The New York, Boston, and Philadelphia insitutions, like the orphanages, indentured or "farmed out" children to homes. The first child to be indentured from the New York City House of Refuge was "Diana Williams, Mulatto, aged 13," who had been sent to the school for stealing (Teeters and Reinemann, 1950, p. 433).

In 1847 the first public state reform school for boys was established in Westboro, Massachusetts. The first public institution for girls was an industrial school established in 1854 in Lancaster, Massachusetts. The institution had a farm for outdoor work, but a feature that was new to America at the time was its use of cottages to house small groups of girls. Unlike the houses of refuge, it had no fences and no barred windows. Four years later this same system was used in Lancaster, Ohio, by an institution for boys. From the beginning, children sentenced to the houses of refuge were under an indeterminate sentence, the courts leaving their release up to the managers of the schools. The managers were assumed to have jurisdiction and supervisory authority over the children until they reached their majority (Teeters and Rinemann, 1950, pp. 435–48). The Philadelphia courts in 1838 held that various officials, including justices of the peace, had the right to commit children to houses of refuge, even over the objections of their parents, if charges of vagrancy, incorrigibility, or other crimes were proven against them (Bremner, 1970, pp. 691–93).

It is interesting to note that the concern of the criminal justice reformers at this time was directed exclusively at the treatment of juvenile offenders *after conviction.* On a few occasions, John Augustus intervened in situations involving children before the court hearing, but these were exceptions that seemed to involve clear examples of miscarriages of justice that Augustus could make a strong case with the judge for dismissal.

However, interest gradually shifted to reforms that were needed in the procedure preceding punishment or correction. Massachusetts was one of the first states to gradually relax the strict, technical criminal procedures when dealing with child offenders. Not until 1869, however, was a law enacted that provided for the presence in court of a "state agent" or his deputy when cases were heard involving the possible commitment of a child to an institution. This was the beginning of a movement that culminated in a separate court for children 50 years later (Glueck, 1959, p. 256).

✑ Education

A major achievement of this period was the gradual advance toward a free, compulsory educational system. In conformity with the constitutional provision that all powers not specifically granted to the federal government would remain the domain of the states, the development of education was the responsibility of the various states. By the time of the Civil War the northern and western states had enacted permissive statutes allowing localities to establish public schools, but the South had no statewide system of public education until after the Civil War.

Dr. Benjamin Rush, whom we met earlier, pro-

posed a plan for a public system of education in Pennsylvania in 1786. Among other things, he proposed that 5,000 acres of land be set aside to support each academy and that 60,000 acres of land be set aside for the support of the elementary schools. In addition, he proposed that tax money be used to support a university (Bremner, 1970, pp. 218–23).

Most of the state constitutions were committed to the state support of education, but most of the early state laws regarding education were permissive rather than mandatory, allowing local officials to establish schools but not requiring that they do so. Such laws provided that the support of education be met out of local taxes and fees, lotteries, and fines. Also, particularly in the western states, the land policy of the federal government provided that sections of land in each township be set aside for the support of public schools. In addition to being interested in the financial support of public instruction, the states were interested in establishing some sort of supervision of the schools and some standards of education. In 1812, legislation enacted by New York state provided that schools had to stay open for at least three months of the year in order to qualify for state funds (Bremner, 1970, pp. 218–23).

Poor children

In 1802 Pennsylvania authorized the overseers of the poor to provide for the education of poor children. Washington, D.C., established schools for poor children in 1804, with Jefferson as the first president of the school board. Virginia, Delaware, and New York City also moved toward the free education of poor children. In addition, leading philanthropists of the day contributed to free charity schools for the poor because they feared social chaos and believed that a need existed for social order and discipline.

However, other reformers were not satisfied to limit free schools to the poor. They worked for free, public, tax-supported schools for all children without any stigma of charity attached to their use. Actually, the free schools for the poor that the private philanthropists supported, blocked the development of a universal free educational system. Philanthropists with a vested interest in their free schools for the poor were not interested in surrendering their prerogatives to the public. Thus, the fight to establish public schools is a good example of the difficult problems that are involved in the relationship between private charity and public reform.

Between 1820 and 1865, new social and economic conditions brought new urgency to the cause of free public education. The public schools were expected to help weld a rapidly growing diverse population into one people. They were to increase social stability by molding the young into loyal and useful American citizens as well as help the young to develop themselves as individual democratic citizens. With the expansion of the public school system and the growing interest in the school as an instrument of socialization, there came compulsory school attendance laws. The first of these was the Massachusetts law of 1852, which required that all parents send their children between the ages of 8 and 14 to school during at least 12 weeks of the year. Other states did not enact compulsory attendance laws until after the Civil War (Bremner, 1970, pp. 210–61). At the time of this writing, one state—Mississippi—does not have a compulsory school attendance law.

Black children

In contrast to the growing democratization of public education for whites, education for blacks was becoming less available. After 1831, one southern legislature after another outlawed the education of blacks. In the North education was expected to serve as an agent of socialization, but in the South education was feared as a process that would give blacks the knowledge necessary to organize and communicate, that would teach them about the world outside slavery.

The situation of *free* black children was much the same in the North and in the South. In neither section was there equality before the law. Segregated schools were the rule. Black property owners paid taxes for the support of schools that their children could not attend. The separate black schools were almost uniformly less adequate than the white schools.

There were growing but generally unsuccessful attempts to establish integrated private schools. An academy for black girls in Canterbury, Connecticut, was forcibly closed, and its founder was arrested. The Noyes Academy, an integrated school in Canaan, New Hampshire, was forced to close by mob violence. Only in Massachusetts do we see an effort to change the situation. A black father, whose daughter was forced to attend the black primary school, sued for her admittance into a white school that was much closer to her home. The Supreme Court upheld the school committee's decision to segregate the black children with its famous "separate but equal" decision, holding that there was no discrimination as long as the separate facilities were equal. This doctrine was used until the 1950s to defend discrimination in education. However, the people of Massachusetts were troubled by the decision, and in 1855 there was legislation to do away with separate school systems. This was the only legislative victory that blacks in the North could claim before the Civil War (Bremner, 1970, pp. 513–39).

Indian children

The education of Indian children was considered to be a function of the federal government rather than the state governments. The U.S. government subsidized private, missionary religious agencies as a primary means of educating Indian children. Since colonial times, religious missionary groups had been seeking without great success to bring Indian youth into their schools and to convert the Indian people to Christianity, so they eagerly accepted the responsibility. In 1819 the federal government appropriated $10,000 to help pay the expenses of missionaries and teachers chosen by the religious groups to work in the schools scattered among the Indians. It was soon recognized that the conventional education was not effective for Indian children, so two other models were tried: instruction in manual trades and the use of the boarding school, to which Indian children were removed from their parents and their tribal ways for most of the year in the hope that they would adopt the outlook of whites (Bremner, 1970, pp. 547–58; Hagan, 1961, pp. 87–91).

☙§ Summary

In looking at the process and structure of the welfare programs of the period between 1780 and 1860, we must first look at how the level of knowledge and the value system of the time affected the definition of the welfare problem. Given the belief that individuals were totally responsible for their own welfare unless they were severely ill, old, or very young, it is to be expected that the problem would be defined in terms of individual failure and that the programs developed would focus on individual change. As the beliefs of the time tended to focus on moral behavior rather than on scientific knowledge of human development and behavior, it is to be expected that the change efforts developed would focus on changing moral beliefs and behavior. In this period there were attempts to collect data on the extent and the cause of people's troubles before trying to correct them, but the data collection tended to support already accepted beliefs.

The process of setting up programs seemed to go something like this: one or two concerned persons defined a problem; they got together a group of people who could also be expected to be concerned; that group formed an association to deal with the problem; the association usually proposed a remedy with little data collection, though in some cases it attempted to assess the extent of the problem; the association proceeded to formulate a program, relying largely on its own concepts as to necessary action; money was raised to support the program; and the members of the association, volunteers, or paid staff began to carry out the program.

The programs of the time were financed largely through one or more of four avenues: (1) a wealthy person would assume most of the costs; (2) a group of wealthy people would assume most of the costs; (3) the association would attempt to get local, state, or (in the case of the insane) federal funding; or (4) some combination of the above was utilized. The intermingling of public and private funds with little concern was more prevalent in this period than it was ever to be again.

The social welfare programs operated on the basis of various social allocations:

☙§ The poor on the basis of a means test.
The mentally ill and the handicapped on the basis of crude diagnostic formulations.
The veteran on the basis of identified compensation for disservice.

The social provisions provided by these programs were:

☙§ Money and goods.
Advice and brokerage.
Opportunities, such as educational programs and apprenticeship.
Services in the case of the mentally ill and the sick.

We have now completed our account of the development of the various social welfare programs of the first half of the 19th century. We have noted that some of these programs, such as poor relief, were directed at the maintenance of functioning and that others were directed at individual change (and there were those who felt that both objectives were necessary if programs were to be of help to people). Except for the programs directed at the abolition of slavery and an occasional protest on behalf of the Indians, all the programs of the time were aimed at the maintenance and protection of the known patterns of functioning of society.

☙§ A look ahead

In the next chapter we shall examine the development of social welfare programs during and after the Civil War, employing the same pattern that we have developed in this chapter.

⸎ Study questions

1. Select an individual who was active in the initiation of certain programs of social welfare, and find out all you can about him or her as a person. What accounted for his or her development of interest in particular areas?

2. Go back through the chapter and make a list of the various types of programs that began during the first half of the 19th century.

3. What forces do you think caused a focus on the notion that the poor were responsible for their own troubles?

4. Although the chapter emphasizes the focus on changing the individual, it also mentions programs of social reform. Make a list of those reforms and the people who worked at them.

5. Select a specific program, and find out all you can about the way in which it came about and operated. Use the columns on process and structure in the chart at the end of Chapter 6 as a guide in organizing your material.

⸎ Selected readings

Brace, Charles Loring. *The Dangerous Classes of New York and Twenty Years' Work among Them*. New York: Wynkoop and Hallenbeck, 1872, as reissued by the National Association of Social Workers, 1976.

This reissued work is an excellent introduction to the problems of children in the 19th century and to the thinking about them. It is highly recommended to give students the flavor of the time.

Bremner, Robert H. *Children and Youth in America*. Vol. 1. Cambridge, Mass.: Harvard University Press, 1970.

Selections from this volume may be used to give students an opportunity to read original documents relating to the programs of 1780–1860. The volume contains many colorful and interesting accounts that could not be included in this chapter.

Axinn, June, and Levin, Herman. *Social Welfare: A History of the American Response to Need*. New York: Harper & Row, 1975.

Chap. 3 on the pre–Civil War period is a good supplement to this chapter.

Trattner, Walter I. *From Poor Law to Welfare State*. New York: Free Press, 1974.

Although Trattner does not organize his material as the material in this chapter is organized, chaps. 3–6 are a significant supplement to our material.

Although we seldom read of the role of black troops in the Civil War, black people were an active part of the struggle.

In the picture at right, black recruits board railroad cars to join the Federal (Union) Army fighting in Tennessee.

Civil War histories rarely record the service of women, yet in hospitals, in schools, in offices, in factories, and on farms they took over the jobs previously done by men.

The festive hospital ward pictured here was in the Armory Square Hospital, of Washington, D.C.

Chapter 14 ❧

❧ The Civil War years, 1860–1877 ❧

❧ Introduction

In this chapter we shall discuss some of the social welfare agencies that were founded, or developed during the Civil War. Some of these agencies were short-lived, existing only briefly during the war, but the fact that they existed is important in understanding the response of a people to crisis. We shall also discuss the effect of the war on the Indian tribes and some of the struggles of the black people for security, opportunity, and social recognition. There are many history books on the causes and course of the Civil War, so we shall limit our discussion to the social welfare aspects. The period covered in this chapter overlaps that of the next chapter. This chapter shall be limited to social welfare responses to the Civil War and the freedom of the black people. The next chapter will discuss the social welfare activities of the northern cities, beginning in 1860 and continuing until approximately 1900.

❧ The blacks in the Civil War

The Civil War was fought around two issues: (1) the primary question was whether a group of states had the right to secede from the union of states formed under the Constitution; and (2) the secondary question was that of freedom for the blacks. In the decade before the outbreak of the Civil War, the conflict over the place of the free black had escalated on many fronts. It is important to recognize that most white people in the North were not abolitionists and that they did not welcome blacks to their communities or their social life. Rather, the majority of northern whites, though troubled by the moral aspects of slavery, believed firmly that the slave owner had property rights in the slave that should be protected. In addition, the free blacks of the North were seldom treated as free or equal. They were surrounded by restrictions of every variety.

Before the outbreak of the war

There were at least five major antiblack riots in Philadelphia between 1832 and 1840. During one of them, Pennsylvania Hall, a building erected by abolitionists, was burned. We have discussed in the last chapter how black males could not vote (no women, black or white, could do so); how black males were denied access to training and apprenticeship; and how as a result of competition for jobs with white male immigrants, black males were deprived of opportunities to work. Congress passed a law guaranteeing residents of slaveholding states the perpetual right to own slaves.

In addition, the cause of the blacks as free members of American society suffered a severe blow when the Supreme Court in the Dred Scott decision of March 1857 decided that "people of African descent are not and cannot be citizens of the United States, and cannot sue in any of the United States courts." In rendering its decision, the Court declared that "this unfortunate class have, with the civilized and enlightened portions of the world, for more than a century, been regarded as being of an inferior order, and unfit associates for the white race, whether socially or politically, having no rights which white men are bound to respect" (Aptheker, 1951, p. 392).

Black and white abolitionists. Another dispute that was becoming bitter just before the outbreak of the Civil War was taking place among the abolitionists themselves around two questions: (1) the place of black people in the movement and (2) the methods that should be used to advance the cause. Frederick Douglass, Samuel R. Ward, and Henry H. Garnet, independent black leaders who felt uncomfortable about playing subsidiary roles in a conflict involving their people, were demanding a share in the leadership of the abolitionist movement. Douglass expressed this feeling when he said, "Our oppressed people are wholly ignored, in one sense, in the generalship of the movement. . . . the man who has suffered wrong is the man to demand redress. . . . It is evident that we must be our own representatives and advocates, not exclusively, but peculiarly—not distinct from, but in connection with our white friends" (Bennett, 1964, p. 149).

The abolitionists led by William Lloyd Garrison and Charles Remond condemned separate institutions for blacks and whites and advocated a campaign based on passive resistance and moral force. The abolitionists in New York, led by Ward, Garnet, and Douglass, favored political action, and if this proved impossible, they were willing to resort to violence. They too wanted integrated institutions, but they were willing to settle for separate institutions if integration appeared impossible. The two groups were divided on their view of the Constitution. Those who opposed political action held that the Constitution was a proslavery document and that blacks would never be accepted as citizens under its provisions. Others took the position that although the interpretation of the Constitution had supported slavery the document was not proslavery and that it was both possible and necessary to fight politically within its framework (Aptheker, 1951, pp. 289–90; Bennett, 1964, pp. 149–66).

The black soldier

During the Civil War, the problem of the black soldier was as troublesome for the white leaders of the North as it had been to General Washington during the Revolution, and with the same results. All over the urban North, blacks came forward to volunteer for military service, but the Lincoln administration thanked the volunteers and sent them home with the understanding that this was a "white man's war" (Bennett, 1964, p. 166). The hard-pressed Union generals found it hard to understand the order that slaves who ran away to join their forces were to be returned to their masters. Some of the Union generals began to enlist and train black troops without waiting for official orders that permitted them to do so. By the end of 1863, some 50,000 black soldiers were in the Union ranks. They often fought in segregated regiments, and if they were captured by the southern forces they faced certain torture and death. Originally the black soldier was promised the same pay as the white soldier—$13 a month—but the black soldiers were actually paid $7 a month. Many black regiments refused to accept any pay, saying that they were fighting for freedom and not money. The Massachusetts legislature, moved by the injustice of the pay differential, passed a bill authorizing the black Massachusetts soldiers to be paid an additional $6 a month from state funds, but the black Massachusetts regiments refused it (Bennett, 1962, p. 175).

During the Civil War many black people dared more, sacrificed as much, and fought as hard as the white people. Those who need more specific evidence can find it in the literature, and in the fact that five black men were awarded the Medal of Honor (Bennett, 1962, pp. 162–67).

৵৪ Women in the Civil War

In addition to fighting forces, all armed conflicts demand supplies and programs for the support and succor of the fighting forces. Traditionally, as men have gone to war, women have taken their place in industries and have built on the home front a will to sacrifice and win. Thus, an increase in women's employment out of the home has usually been supported during wartime in the expectation that once the conflict is over, the working women will return to their prewar occupations and status. However, this was not to be the case after the Civil War in at least two areas—nursing and social welfare. After the war, women of genius who had organized much of the welfare efforts of the war and many women who had been widowed during the war were ready to assume leadership positions in social welfare activities. Thus, we can trace the activities and leadership of women in the reform movements of the late 1800s and early 1900s to the developing consciousness of upper-class women in the abolitionist movement and to the "uprising of the women in the land" during the Civil War (Bremner, 1960, p. 77).

Nurses and nursing care

One of the first women to present herself as a volunteer for war duty, and one of the last to leave the field, was Dorothea Dix, who was nearing 60 when the Civil War broke out. She was offered, and accepted, the post of Superintendent of Female Nurses. Her years of service in the battle to improve care of the mentally ill had prepared her well for the battles that followed as her authority was challenged by the Medical Bureau of the Army, which held that nursing soldiers was an improper occupation for women. A letter to the *American Medical Times* setting forth the views of the medical profession on this matter contains so many of the arguments that women hear as they challenge educational and job discrimination today that we shall quote excerpts from it:

> . . . a man who has had experience with women nurses among male surgical cases, cannot shut his eyes to the fact that they, with the best intentions in the world, are frequently a useless annoyance. . . .
>
> Women . . . are utterly and decidedly unfit for such service. They can be used, however, . . . in delicate, soothing attentions which are always so grateful to the sick. . . .
>
> But as hospital nurses for wounded men, they are by nature, education and strength totally unfitted . . . when we consider all the duties surgical nurses are called upon to perform. (Baxandall, Gordon, Reverby, 1976, pp. 75–76)

The Civil War changed the general view of nursing as an occupation improper for women to the view that it was a profession for which they were uniquely suited (Baxandall et al., 1975, pp. 75–77). It is estimated that 3,200 nurses served with the Union forces alone. Most, but not all, of these nurses worked behind the battle lines. The black abolitionist Harriet Tubman followed the Massachusetts regiments to the battlefield. She engaged not only in nursing duties but in scouting and spying behind the enemy lines. Nursing appealed as strongly to southern women as it did to northern women, and following Gettysburg some southern women actually tended their wounded on the battlefield under fire.

Clara Barton and the Red Cross

Clara Barton was a teacher who in 1854 went to work as a clerk in the patent office in Washington. At the beginning of the Civil War, she resigned her civil service post to become a volunteer nurse in army hospitals and camps. She had a genius for obtaining necessary relief supplies and seeing that they got to places of need when they were needed. This brought her to President Lincoln's attention, and in 1865 he appointed her to correspond with the relatives of missing and dead soldiers. She was indefatigable in checking hospital and burial records to obtain information for answering inquiries about missing prisoners, and in identifying and marking the graves of thousands of soldiers.

In 1869 she went to Geneva, Switzerland, to attend a meeting of the International Committee of Relief for the Care of War Wounded. She discovered that this organization, under the name of the Society of the Red Cross, had been doing for several years what she had been doing as an individual.

Barton lived abroad for several years after the Civil War, and she served with the German Red Cross during the Franco-Prussian War of 1870–71. When she returned to the United States in 1873 she was committed to the value of the Red Cross. In 1881 she helped organize the American Committee of the American Association of the Red Cross. In 1882 President Chester Arthur signed a treaty providing for the establishment of an American branch of the International Red Cross. Clara Barton, who was then 61 years of age, accepted the presidency and served until 1904.

Perhaps even more important than Barton's ability to convince Americans of the importance of an international humanitarian undertaking was her conception of the Red Cross as an agency for rendering assistance in all human disasters, not just war. Americans had recently been through the experiences of the Boston and Chicago fires and were certainly aware of the havoc rendered by natural disasters, epidemics, and accidents, so Barton's appeal made great sense to them. In 1884 she secured an amendment to the rules of the international Red Cross society that permitted Red Cross relief in catastrophes other than war. Under her personal direction the American Red Cross was active during the Johnstown flood of 1889 and the Sea Island

hurricane of 1893. In 1900, at age 70, she directed relief activities at Galveston, Texas, for six weeks before suffering a physical breakdown.

Clara Barton did not see the Red Cross as charity but as the temporary giving of aid to normal people who were victims of abnormal misfortune. Her aim was not to institute reforms but to restore the victims of disaster to their previous level of living. She simply met emergencies as they arose without concern as to the causes, or the creation of dependence. She was committed to the Red Cross as a truly neutral agency that was interested in alleviating human suffering, not in people's beliefs, moral behavior, or possible dependence. This lack of regard for reform, or of concern with the causes of poverty, put Clara Barton and the Red Cross outside the usual philanthropies of the late 1800s (Abbott, 1935; Barton, 1922; Bremner, 1960, pp. 78 and 91–95, pp. 20–25; Becker, 1977, pp. 84–85).

✌ Private philanthropy

Women in the North and the South took collections and held fairs, bazaars, and other activities to raise money to meet various war-related needs. Of the funds raised, the largest amounts were used to aid and support the families of servicemen. It is interesting that in this outpouring of aid no one raised questions about the dangers of unwise giving or the morality of the recipients.

Organized religious groups on both sides of the battle lines were deeply involved in the distribution of religious tracts. Lincoln is reported to have said in 1864 that "both read the same Bible, and pray to the same God; and each invokes His aid against the other" (Bremner, 1960, p. 79). An organization of churches, the Christian Commission, sent what material and spiritual aid it could to soldiers and recruited delegates, primarily clergymen, to perform personal helping services for the fighting men, particularly the sick and wounded.

The U.S. Sanitary Commission

However, the most meaningful wartime social welfare activity was that of the U.S. Sanitary Commission. This privately financed and directed organization was founded in June 1861 by a group of men who had been impressed by the work of the British Sanitary Commission during the Crimean War. These men believed that the knowledge gained by the British Sanitary Commission regarding medical and sanitary practices under conditions of war should be utilized to prevent "needless suffering and loss of life through disease" (Bremner, 1960, p. 80). The list of the Sanitary Commission's achievements is a long one:

1. It united local relief societies into a national force that utilized money, influence, and knowledge to prevent needless suffering in camps and hospitals by improving their sanitary conditions and their administration.
2. It carried out inspections of camps and hospitals to correct defects in drainage, water supply, diet, and sanitary arrangements.
3. It secured a much-needed reorganization of the Army Medical Bureau.
4. It developed better ways of transporting the wounded.
5. It collected food, clothing, bandages, and supplies, storing and distributing them as needed.
6. It aided soldiers to obtain back pay, bounties, and pensions and other relief due them.
7. It collected and tabulated vital statistics on military personnel, and it helped relatives of military personnel to locate the missing.
8. It gave people a sense of participation in the war through tremendous charitable campaigns and giant Sanitary fairs that were organized and operated by the women of northern cities.

Aid to blacks

In addition to the problems of aid to the men in the field, the northern forces were confronted with the problem of what to do with slaves who could not join the Army. From the beginning of the war, fugitive slaves had made their way north to the Union lines. As time went on, the Union armies advanced and the planters fled, abandoning their lands and their property, including their slaves. Many of these destitute blacks sought protection within the Union military camps. For the newly freed blacks, emancipation was a catastrophic social crisis. Army commanders struggled to care for the growing wave of refugees, allocating rations, clothing, medical care, and housing to them. Sometimes a military commander designated a member of his staff to serve as supervisor of Negro affairs. Many of these supervisors attempted to develop ways in which blacks could operate abandoned plantations in order to provide themselves with food and shelter. In some regions, federal Treasury agents placed blacks on leased lands and established schools to satisfy the newly freed blacks' hunger for education.

However, there were too many fugitives for the Army to care for, so an appeal was sent to the various northern philanthropic groups to send aid and volunteer help. There was an immediate response from these groups. Freedmen's Aid associations were established in many cities, and food, clothing, medical supplies, and school equipment were sent to the South, along with volunteers to serve as teachers, nurses, and aides.

The Freedmen's Bureau—A public federal program

But the agents of these groups found the conditions of thousands of freedmen to be desperate. Acting for the Freedmen's Inquiry Commission, Dale Owen and Samuel Gridley Howe, with others, undertook an investigation that revealed shocking conditions in the camps and on the plantations that had been taken over by the government and leased to private individuals. Tens of thousands were dying of disease and want. According to the commission's estimate, over one fourth of all blacks had died in some plantation communities. After the report of the commission was issued, the Freedmen's Aid societies redoubled their efforts, but they realized that the problem was too great for voluntary resources, so they urged Lincoln to establish a government bureau, with all the powers of the government behind it, to care for the freed blacks (Olds, 1963, pp. 247–54; Bennett, 1962, pp. 186–90; Bremner, 1960, pp. 85–88).

The establishment of the Freedmen's Bureau

Despite the urgency of the situation, it was March 1865 before Congress passed the legislation that established the Bureau of Refugees, Freedmen, and Abandoned Lands, commonly referred to as the Freedmen's Bureau. Lincoln was assassinated in April, so the appointment of an administrator and the beginning of the work of the bureau were delayed until May, when President Andrew Johnson appointed Major General Otis Howard as administrator. It is fortunate that the legislation establishing the bureau was passed before Johnson came to power, as he was opposed to its activities. Like President Franklin Pierce a decade earlier, Johnson felt that the federal government should not take part in welfare activities. He wanted to restrict the bureau to job placement of the freed blacks.

The act that created the bureau authorized it to assist in the relief and rehabilitation of all destitute persons, regardless of race, and stipulated that it was to be only a wartime measure by attaching it to the War Department and providing that it was to exist only for the duration of the war plus one year. No appropriation for the operation of the bureau was made from the general revenues. The secretary of war was ordered to issue rations, fuel, clothing, and supplies to the bureau for the use of the freedmen. Fortunately, the commissioner was given full authority to deal with all matters relating to refugees and freedmen, and the scope and provisions of the act were unusually broad and flexible. Commissioner Howard was convinced that black people were capable of becoming self-determining and productive and that it was the bureau's job to help them toward a better life. He moved energetically and forcefully to draw freely from the Army what he thought was needed, including school desks, hospital beds, and military vehicles. Later he was able to persuade Congress to pass an appropriation for the bureau. The bureau aided both whites and blacks. In the first three

years of its existence, it issued some 18,300,000 rations, of which about 5,230,000 went to whites (Olds, 1963, pp. 247–54).

The life of the bureau was extended indefinitely by an act of Congress in 1866. President Johnson vetoed the act with an angry message which stated that the war was over and that there was no longer any need for such an agency. Congress passed a two-year extension over his veto. As time went on, however, there was mounting criticism of the bureau as a waste and an extravagance and as creating dependence by giving to those who ought to be supporting themselves. As a result, Howard himself seemed to lose faith in his work. At his recommendation the bureau was officially abolished in 1872 (Olds, 1963, pp. 247–54).

Social welfare implications

Before we leave our account of the Freedmen's Bureau, we need to summarize the implications of its activities. It was an instrument of the federal government that provided welfare for people at a time of stress when private resources and local facilities were insufficient to cope with the prevailing destitution. Its close ties with the private agencies in the field were a model of the cooperation that could be established between public and private welfare. Commissioner Howard was responsible for the scrupulous detailed reporting that his staff presented to Congress and the people, thus setting high standards of accountability years before this became an issue of public welfare.

The program of the Freedmen's Bureau was far ahead of its time in two other central aspects. It was the first public welfare program in the United States to operate without residence requirements for eligibility. Not until the early 1930s, with the institution of a federal program to send unemployed transients to areas where there was work, was there to be another public program without such requirements. And the bureau was far ahead of its time in its ability to offer comprehensive family-centered services. The services provided by the bureau were as follows:

1. Families were provided with food, shelter, and clothing on a temporary basis, pending the employment of their adult able-bodied members.

2. Families and children were protected through efforts to reunite families, analyze marriage relationships, place and educate children whose families could not be located, and provide advocacy for children who were being unlawfully exploited in indenture arrangements.

3. Hospitals and outpatient clinics were established for the sick. At one time the bureau operated 45 hospitals.

4. Jobs were provided through the construction of schools and the improvement of military installations and through the use of leased plantations.

5. Freedmen were supplied with lumber to build their own homes on land acquired at cost.

6. The elderly were cared for in institutions, and black orphanages were established.

7. Employment counseling and job placement were offered under contracts drawn up to meet the standards of the bureau.

8. Advice was given about civil rights, and the bureau protected persons who were exploited and harassed.

9. Schools were established. This was perhaps the most important achievement of the bureau. It provided about half of the money spent on black education between 1865 and 1870. The bureau built and repaired school buildings, and it provided quarters and transportation for teachers (Olds, 1963, pp. 247–54; Bremner, 1960, pp. 85–88; Bennett, 1962, pp. 187–89).

The distribution of land

One of Howard's great disappointments was his inability to implement the authority he had been given to distribute 40 acres of abandoned land to each freedman, to be held for three years at a reasonable annual rent and with an option to buy.

This provision of the legislation setting up the Freedmen's Bureau was never carried out because, under the terms of Johnson's amnesty, forfeited lands were returned to southern landholders. This meant not only that insufficient land would be available for the freedmen but that the land they had been given was abruptly taken away. Howard felt that by this action he had broken faith with those whom he had been pledged to aid. He called a mass meeting of the freedmen who faced eviction to give them an opportunity to vent their anger and frustration. This may have been one of the earliest instances of client participation in social welfare. The move reflected Howard's conviction that public agencies should set an example of fair play, reliability, consistency, and concern for the welfare of those they would serve (Olds, 1963, pp. 247–54; Bennett, 1962, pp. 187–89).

New constitutions in the South

For the first two years after the Civil War, the government of the southern states was in the hands of the former leaders of the Confederacy due to Lincoln's plan of reconstruction, which allowed the Confederate states to be restored to their functioning as states once one tenth of those who had voted in the elections of 1860 had taken the oath of allegiance to the United States. Under this arrangement, all blacks were effectively prevented from voting or holding office. Within a year following the Civil War, Southern states had enacted the "black codes"—a set of laws regulating black-white relationships. While there were differences from state to state, these codes embodied many common features. While recognizing certain legal rights (such as the right to marry) they were designed to maintain the separation of the black citizen from the mainstream of American life, and to continue black subordination (Franklin, 1961, pp. 48–50). These codes restricted the black person's freedom of movement through vagrancy and apprenticeship laws, freedom to work through license requirements, and freedom of behavior through special discriminatory laws (Bennett, 1962, pp. 183–219).

The movements to exclude the black people

from any participation in the life of the South caused concern in Congress. Congress moved to put the South under military control and to authorize new elections in which all males, black or white, could participate. The enfranchisement of blacks and their participation in the affairs of government were radical departures from anything that had ever happened in the South. However, the blacks controlled no state government and they constituted a majority of only one state legislature—that of South Carolina (Franklin, 1961, pp. 218–27).

The new state governments were charged with drawing up new state constitutions under a congressional provision that a Confederate state could not reenter the Union unless its constitution provided for political equality and contained guarantees against flagrant racial discrimination. At the constitutional conventions, many argued with great passion that it was the state's responsibility to establish agencies to deal with the prevailing destitution and some progress toward public welfare measures was made. Slavery was abolished; imprisonment for debt was ended; universal male suffrage authorized; public schools established; and some provisions for economic relief enacted (Bennet, 1962, pp. 198–99).

With the southern states forced to consider the sharing of power with blacks, many wondered whether the blacks would use their new political power to force a redistribution of land at the state level. However, no state enacted such a program. South Carolina came closest to doing so. Its constitutional convention created a commission to purchase land and resell it to blacks who would settle on it and repay to the state the money it cost plus 6 percent interest (Franklin, 1961, pp. 104–26).

✑§ Southern social welfare

Income maintenance

One of the first problems that confronted the southern states at the close of hostilities was the destitution of the people, and one of the first things that the new governments did was to establish relief and welfare programs for the Confederate veterans and their dependents. Some of the southern states tried to provide direct home relief for the suffering white population. However, these efforts were never even minimally adequate and the Freedman's Bureau provided more public welfare for both blacks and whites than did all the southern states.

In these two years the southern states did nothing to relieve the sufferings of black persons. Instead, the southern states enacted the Black Codes, which were intended to reestablish slavery under another name. Black people without "visible means of support" could be imprisoned, placed to work under state overseers, or bound out to work for an unspecified period of time. In general, blacks were forbidden to travel without the permission of their employer.

When work on the new constitutions began, there was great interest in the statewide public assistance measures. However, these proposals met with fierce opposition because of the strong feeling that relief measures should be local concerns. In 1868 Florida authorized the counties of the state to provide care for persons who were unable to fend for themselves because of "age, infirmity, or misfortune" (Franklin, 1961, p. 115). The North Carolina constitution of the same year provided that the General Assembly should appoint a Board of Public Charities which was to have supervision of all "charitable and penal state institutions and . . . annually report to the governor upon their conditions, with suggestions for their improvement" (Franklin, 1961, p. 115). Because of the overwhelming hostility of the state's most influential people to this board, it lapsed into inactivity in 1872. In 1888 it was able to resume some of its duties when urgent problems of poverty forced a reconsideration of public welfare issues.

The Alabama constitutional convention of 1867 passed a resolution incorporating into the new state constitution a provision for the establishment of a poorhouse in each county. Texas required that each county establish a "manual labor poor house, for taking care of, managing, employing and supplying the wants of its indigent and poor inhabitants, under such regulations as the legislature may direct" (Franklin, 1961, p. 115).

Child welfare

The problem of child welfare was a difficult one for the post–Civil War South because of the need to care for black orphans and the large numbers of orphaned children of Confederate soldiers. Orphanages were established for the children of deceased Confederate soldiers, or, if the orphanages seemed inadequate, legislation provided for the apprenticing of such children to other families, with guarantees written into the indentures to deal with matters of food, clothing, and education.

But for black children such guarantees were not seen as necessary, whether orphaned or dependent. Most of the southern states enacted laws which provided that as many black children as possible should be apprenticed as laborers in the fields, shops, and kitchens of whites who were given virtually complete control over their lives. If the former owner of a black child was seen as suitable, he was given preference in acquiring the child. Although this policy was instituted at the state level, the local judge or magistrate carried it out. In Maryland a parent whose daughter had been apprenticed under such a law appealed the matter to the higher courts, and in 1867 won the case and regained the child on the ground that apprenticing children in this way was the same as reenslaving them (Bremner, 1971, p. 611). This may be the first example of parents challenging the right of the courts to remove their children for poverty only.

Health and special populations

Assistance for the physically handicapped was more popular than help for the poor. North Carolina and Georgia established institutions for the deaf and dumb and the blind, though these institutions were segregated by race. There was much illness in the South following the Civil War, and periodic epidemics wrought havoc among the people, particularly the blacks. In 1872, in an attempt to deal with these problems, Virginia established a state board of health composed of seven physicians appointed by the governor. In 1875 Alabama established a state board of health under the supervision of the state medical association. The board was to be concerned with all aspects of public health. The southern states remained concerned about the mentally ill, and Florida and Arkansas were the last of the former Confederate states to establish state mental institutions. Eventually all of these states felt it necessary to construct separate mental institutions for the two races.

Education

One of the first things that the new southern governments did was to establish systems of public education for all the people. However, most of the southern states were opposed to the mixing of whites and blacks in the schools and only in South Carolina and Louisiana did the state constitutions provide for racially mixed schools.

Summary of Southern social welfare

It is hardly to be expected that the southern states would develop a strong system of public welfare, given their welfare system before the Civil War, the chaos and destitution wrought by the war, and their overwhelming preoccupation with the relationship of the races. However, the southern welfare record is stronger than we have usually been led to believe. There was prejudice, and there were mistakes, but the former Confederate states began to lay the foundation upon which future developments could be built. To summarize the southern achievements: universal public education was established; state boards of health were established; special institutions were set up for the handicapped and the mentally ill; some steps were taken toward poor relief, even if mostly at the local level; and some attention was given to the problems of children. In 1868 Florida enacted the first state legislation relating to county care of the aged, and North Carolina established the first state Board of Charities as an overseer of welfare activities (Franklin, 1961, p. 387). Although none of these programs operated equally for blacks and whites, there was at least a beginning of service to both blacks and whites.

ᦕᕽ The national scene

Land

As we have said, of the many matters that the new southern governments faced, none was more critical than that of land. The destitution of the freedmen was overwhelming, and no measure would have been more effective in providing immediate relief than the redistribution of land. Earlier, at the national level, two white men, Charles Sumner a senator from Massachusetts, and Thaddeus Stevens, a congressman from Pennsylvania, had made a bitter fight in Congress to pass legislation authorizing the break up of large plantations and their distribution to the freedmen in 40-acre lots.

Stevens's plan would have left more than nine tenths of the southern whites in possession of their small farms and would have reimbursed the large owners for their loss. Fewer than 70,000 southern families owned more than 200 acres. If the land owned by these families had been confiscated and added to the land already owned by the states, 394 million acres would have been available for distribution to the 1 million black families in 40-acre tracts. Stevens proposed that the land left over from such a distribution be sold to provide each black family with a cash grant of $50 to buy seed and tools, to provide pensions for the soldiers of the Union, to reimburse the owners for the land taken, and to pay off the national debt that the war had brought (Lens, 1969, pp. 140–42). The plan was rejected. Commenting on this action, Lens states:

> At a time when millions of acres of land were being given away in the West, under the Homestead Act and grants of millions of acres to railroads, Congress refused to vote forty acres to the million black families. To cede virgin land that belonged to no one but possibly the Indians was one thing, but to make grants that involved already established property rights was . . . something entirely different. (Lens, 1969, p. 144)

Constitutional amendments

In December 1865 the 13th Amendment, which abolished slavery in the United States, became a part of the federal Constitution. The 14th Amendment, which became effective in 1868, gave all citizens of the nation equal protection of the laws and due process before the courts; the 15th Amendment, effective in 1870, provided that no citizen could be deprived of the right to vote on account of "race, color, or previous condition of servitude"; and the Civil Rights Bill of 1875 provided that all persons should be entitled to "equal enjoyment of accommodations, advantages, facilities, and privileges of inns," transportation, theaters, and the like, regardless of race, color, or previous condition of servitude. These provisions all applied to males. However, women were still denied many of these rights.

But gradually through political maneuvering and terrorists tactics (amply recorded in the literature) the former southern leaders regained their political dominance. In 1883 the Supreme Court held the Civil Rights Act unconstitutional on the ground that the 14th Amendment forbade *states,* not *individuals,* to discriminate. In 1896, in the case of *Plessy* v. *Ferguson,* the Supreme Court held that the provision of "separate but equal" accommodations for blacks was a reasonable exercise of state power. After this, "Jim Crow" laws came in "spurts and waves," until blacks and whites were "forcibly separated in public transportation, sports, hospitals, orphanages, prisons, asylums, funeral homes, morgues, cemeteries." Through various devices, measures to discourage blacks from voting were taken without exciting nationwide concern (Bennett, 1962, p. 233).

Thus, although steps toward social welfare programs of benefit to the freedmen in the South were being taken between 1867 and 1877, the passion for reform was cooling. Many of the white reform leaders were gradually passing from the scene. Although there had been concern for black persons as slaves, there seemed to be little concern about black people as human beings "without a hut to shelter them or a cent in their pockets," without an education or any understanding "of the common laws of contract, or of managing the ordinary business of life" (Stevens, as quoted in Lens, 1969, p. 140). So there was no overwhelming support for social equality of blacks in the North. In the South, blacks who tried to vote became the victims of terrorism: in the 1878 elections in Louisiana, for example, 30 blacks were murdered. Between 1889 and 1918, some 2,522 blacks were lynched. In 1887 in Arkansas 32 percent of all blacks sent to prisons either died there or on the "work gangs"; 16 percent of such offenders died in Mississippi. At the beginning of the 20th century, there were fewer skilled black craftsmen in America than there had been in 1865. Half the blacks of the nation were still illiterate, and three quarters of them were living as sharecroppers in the South (Lens, 1969, pp. 140–44).

Soldiers and veterans—National legislation for a special group

At the beginning of the Civil War, Congress had passed an act to encourage enlistment in the Union forces. This act stated that it was the citizen's duty to serve his country and the government's right to enforce that duty. But this right was seen as imposing a responsibility on the government to care for those who had served. Thus, Congress enacted a pension system covering individuals who had been disabled in the line of duty, as well as the widows, children, and other dependents of those who had been killed. The number of dead and wounded in the Civil War was high. In the Union forces, 719,000 died and 280,000 were wounded out of a total of 2.3 million men. In the Confederate forces, 307,000 died and 280,000 were wounded out of a total of 781,000 men. However, the legislation passed by Congress for the relief of veterans was limited to Union soldiers and veterans. The southern veteran returned to face his devastated land and his disrupted life with what local or state aid could be found. Certainly, the people of the South regarded their veterans as brave and worthy men, but they had little to give them (Axinn and Levin, 1975, pp. 81–83).

The U.S. Sanitary Commission, which we discussed earlier, was active in overseeing the welfare of the military. As a result of its recommendations, an act was passed (signed by President Lincoln, March 3, 1865) to establish a national military and naval hospital for the relief of totally disabled officers and men. Later this legislation was expanded to establish a group of national homes for Union veterans suffering from wartime disabilities, and still later it was again expanded to include economically distressed veterans whose disabilities were not service connected. A Pension Act passed in 1890 provided pensions for veterans and their dependents on the basis of need alone. Neither disability nor death in service was a criterion for receiving this income maintenance support. By 1900 federal and state responsibility for the care of needy and disabled veterans had been established as a special obligation of society as a whole.

In 1866 the Grand Army of the Republic was founded by Union veterans. This provided an organized interest group to work for veterans' benefits (Axinn and Levin, 1975, pp. 81–83).

It is important to note that the various programs for aid to veterans were developed in ways that avoided the stigma of "relief." The allocation of income maintenance and health benefits was seen as an earned right, and great efforts were made to separate these benefits from other local and state programs of aid.

✑ Black philanthropy

W. E. B. Du Bois, in his research on black life in the United States, documented five major sources of social welfare aid that were available to blacks. The first, and perhaps the most important for many blacks, was the black churches and the black mutual aid societies. Du Bois wrote: "The Negro church is the only social institution of the Negroes which started in the forest and survived slavery; . . . the church preserved in itself the remnants of African tribal life and became after emancipation the center of Negro social life" (Billingsley and Giovannoni, 1972, p. 47).

Schools also provided a "multiplicity of social

welfare and child welfare functions." It has been estimated that from 1844 to 1898 black people contributed through their churches more than $15 million annually to the support of their own education. Nevertheless the black students and their families still had to bear a great part of the costs of their education. "It is probably true that the Negroes pay possibly a larger percentage of the costs of their schools than any other group of poor people in America" (Billingsley and Giovannoni, 1972, p. 48). Even though Lens estimates that at the beginning of the 20th century half the blacks were still illiterate, we must recognize that there is no other instance in which a wholly illiterate race has reduced its illiteracy by half in a single generation. In addition to providing education, the black schools often took on the following social welfare functions: (1) recreation; (2) "friendly visiting" of the poor, the institutionalized, and the incarcerated; (3) educational activities, such as conferences, meetings, and the dissemination of agricultural knowledge; and (4) free kindergartens and day care (Billingsley and Giovannoni, 1972, p. 48).

In addition to the social welfare work done by the black churches and schools, much social welfare work was done by black lodges and other secret black organizations, such as the Masons, the Odd Fellows, and the Knights of Pythias. Many of these organizations paid sick benefits and a small death claim to their members besides doing many other things for the good of the black community. In the North, black women's clubs also engaged in philanthropic work. The National Association of Colored Women was founded in Washington, D.C., in 1896, and in its early years it held its national conferences in northern cities. The last source of social welfare aid to the black people came from their own individual philanthropies. Du Bois described the work that 17 wealthy black men had done to aid their people.

✑§ The Indians and the Civil War

Neither the South nor the North "considered the area west of the Mississippi an important theater of war or made much use of Indian troops except

as scouts and skirmishers" (Hagan, 1961, p. 101). Certainly the Indians as a group allied themselves to neither side of the conflict. However, there were tribes that had entered into treaties with the Confederacy, and in so doing they afforded the government a "favorable opportunity" to rule that they "had compromised their rights under existing treaties" and thus to negotiate for their removal from Kansas. This was the beginning of 20 years of constant conflict, on one front or another, between the Indians and the advancing settlers. The federal government attempted to contain the settlers, but as the settlers continued to push into Indian lands, the government felt obliged to offer them military protection.

The various secretaries of the interior and certain presidents made many attempts to upgrade the quality of the Indian agents so that the Indians might get better service and better support in their efforts to preserve their way of life. But the amounts appropriated by Congress for the Bureau of Indian Affairs was always so pitiably small that it was impossible to recruit competent persons for the job. By 1885, the buffalo herds were gone from the plains and the Indians had realized that the march of the whites could not be halted. Thus, by the beginning of the 20th century, after nearly three centuries of conflict, the wars between the Indians and the whites came to an end. Although these wars had brought untold suffering to the Indians and the settlers, they had also furthered the political careers of such men as Andrew Jackson and William Henry Harrison and in some ways had they been an economic boon to the frontier (Hagan, 1961, pp. 72–75).

✑§ Summary

This completes our account of the social welfare activities of the United States during the Civil War and our brief survey of the struggles of two minorities after the war. It is interesting that so many of the achievements of federal social welfare at that time were ended and forgotten with little impact on the mainstream of social welfare development. It is also troubling that the people whose enslavement had been fought for 50 years by the abolitionists were now so often forgotten and bypassed as a special interest by the leaders of private philanthropy. It would be almost a hundred years before the blacks were again of concern to the mainstream of national social welfare. The Civil War also marked the beginning of the end of Indian resistance to the westward movement of the whites.

The major achievements of the social welfare institution during and after the Civil War were as follows: the blacks were freed, and three new amendments to the Constitution offered some minimal protection to them; the South moved forward on certain social welfare fronts, including voting rights, imprisonment for debt, and public (though segregated) education; the foundation of the Red Cross was laid in the work of the Sanitary Commission and the dynamic leadership of Clara Barton; and the role of women in social welfare activities increased dramatically.

A look ahead

In the next chapter we shall discuss the issues that were basic to the development of social welfare thinking in the nation as a whole from the Civil War to 1900.

Study questions

1. In this chapter we discussed two national publicly funded programs: the Freedmen's Bureau, which did not last, and veterans' legislation, which did last. Go back to Chapter 6, and consult the chart at the end of the chapter. Analyze these two programs in light of the material related to program development. Pay particular attention to the basis of the social allocation of the two programs.

2. What was the Civil War about? Were the issues that gave rise to the Civil War settled? What problems were left in the wake of the settlement?

3. Find the ratio of the dead to the total number in service and the ratio of the wounded to the dead for both forces in the Civil War. Find the rates of the dead and wounded in the wars in which the United States has fought since that time. What do you think accounts for the differences in these rates?

Selected readings

Axinn, June, and Levin, Herman. *Social Welfare: A History of the American Response to Need.* New York: Harper & Row, 1975.

The chapter "The Civil War and After" complements and expands some of the material found in this chapter. In particular, students might be encouraged to read the Franklin Pierce and Andrew Johnson vetoes and to compare the two messages.

Olds, Victoria. The Freedmen's Bureau: A Nineteenth Century Federal Welfare Agency. *Social Casework,* 44 (5) (May 1963): 247–54.

A very interesting account of the Freedmen's Bureau from the perspective of social welfare.

Social Work Year Book or *Encyclopedia of Social Work.* New York: Columbia University Press, any year of issue.

It is suggested that the articles on the Veterans Administration or on services to veterans found in most issues of these two publications would be interesting as a focus of discussion about the underlying values and beliefs about the allocation of resources.

Workers of the late 1800s endured poor living conditions (as shown in the picture of New York's first large tenement, "The Big Flat"), and poor working conditions. The Great Labor Demonstration of 1887, here filling New York's Union Square Plaza, was an outpouring of frustration, not triumph.

Chapter 15 &

& Scientific and industrial development, 1860–1900 &

&§ Introduction

In the next two chapters we will be primarily interested in tracing the development of social welfare thought and social welfare programs during the latter half of the 19th century. As in our previous discussions, we will examine the conditions and forces that interacted with the problems and needs of people to shape such development in this chapter and the development of the welfare programs themselves in the next. We shall use an order of discussion different from the one we used in the last chapter, presenting the material on social and economic thought last, as such material may have more meaning after one understands other movements and forces.

The Civil War and the constitutional amendments that followed it could be said to have laid the base for modern social welfare in that they "reversed the traditional relationship" of citizens to their government "by throwing the protection of the Federal Government around the rights [of citizens] that might be invaded by the states" (Commager, 1951, p. 292). The reconstruction programs and the constitutional amendments that followed the Civil War, represented the efforts of a victorious majority, but they also represented the "first major effort on the part of government to protect the rights and raise the standards for a deprived segment of citizens" (Cohn, 1958, pp. 47–48). As such, they were the beginning of two important ideas: (1) that government can and should use its powers on a large scale for the public welfare and (2) that individual citizens may be faced with social forces before which they, as individuals, are helpless without the intervention of government.

In addition to these political developments, for the North the Civil War had meant prosperity and a stimulus toward industrialization. The increased demand for goods to supply the demands of the military forces and the home front had produced new jobs and economic growth. Newly created jobs and the demand for labor to fill the jobs left vacant by the men who were at war resulted in the continuing encouragement of immigration and the steady expansion of the cities. For the South, too, the Civil War saw a beginning of a new way of life in the breakup of some plantations and in a trend toward the decentralization of landownership. For the South, however, the war had devastated land and property, transportation and communication facilities, and the economic base in general. Although the changes we will discuss in this and the next chapter had an impact on the South, they were essentially changes of the North and West, as the South remained heavily agricultural, with trends toward smaller farms, some diversification of crops, and tenant farming, and great rural poverty.

Urbanization and industrialization

The 40 years between 1860 and 1900 were actually a time of revolution in America—of an economic and social revolution in which the nation changed from a predominantly rural and agricultural society to an urban and industrial society. In the four decades from 1860 to 1900 America became a mighty industrial nation with a standard of living and affluence unknown in the previous history of the world.

Science, invention, and industrial development proceeded with great strides to produce a new wealth and a new life-style for the American people. Methods of transportation changed radically with the development of the steam engine and the internal-combustion engine; the development of the telephone and wireless telegraphy not only radically changed the means of communication but the entire relationship of communication to time; railroads began to span the country, tying the farthest reaches of the West to the industrial centers of the East in a manner not dreamed of earlier; thousands of new industries appeared, marked by new forms of business and commercial organization and the sustained growth of new credit institutions. The discovery of new natural resources and of ways to use and exploit them through new inventions led to the acquisition of major fortunes (Axinn and Levin, 1975, pp. 75–79).

In 1897, about a dozen corporations plus the railroad companies had a capital investment of over $10 million. Five years later the number of such corporations had risen to 300. Of these, 17 were capitalized at almost $100 million and one, U.S. Steel, was capitalized at almost $1.5 billion. Some of America's largest supercorporations in iron, steel, oil, railroads, tobacco, and public utilities were being formed at this time (Axinn and Levin, 1975, pp. 75–79). The growth of these great business organizations limited the sphere of individual action. The merchant adventurer, the individual businessman, was being rapidly replaced by corporations run by a professional managerial class responsible to a board of directors and often controlled by a small and powerful group of investors. The barriers of passing from laborer to employer or individual entrepreneur became ever higher and more fixed.

After the Civil War, free land for homesteading, dissatisfaction with the urbanization and industrialization of the Northeast and with the tenant farming of the South, and the need of returning veterans for jobs intensified the westward movement of population. In 1860 the five states just west of the Mississippi—Texas, Arkansas, Missouri, Iowa, and Minnesota—had only 15.3 million acres of improved farmland. By 1880, these states had 50 million acres under cultivation. The number of states west of the Mississippi increased from 7 in 1860 to 18 in 1900, so that by 1900, there were 45 states in the United States (Axinn and Levin, 1975, p. 77). Thus, the frontier, which had long been considered an endless source of opportunity, no longer existed by the end of the century. The ideal of Jeffersonian democracy was no longer a force on the American scene, and Jefferson's prediction that the West would furnish America with homesteads for 1,000 years had proven wrong by 900 years. "Vigor and ambition alone no longer made the difference between success and failure. In the future, circumstances would limit the opportunity of both the enterprising and their less venturesome neighbors" (Mencher, 1967, p. 234).

In the years from 1860 to 1900, the population of the United States "increased from 31.5 million to 76 million. Of the 44.5 million persons represented in the increase, 13.7 were immigrants" (Coll, 1969, pp. 40–41). In 1860 one fifth of the U.S. population lived in towns and cities, but by 1900 this proportion had grown to 40 percent. Even more striking was the movement away from farm and farm-related occupations. In 1860, of a total of 10.5 million gainfully employed workers, 6.2 million were on farms and 4.3 million were employed in nonfarm occupations. By 1900, of a labor force of 29 million persons, 18 million were employed in nonfarm occupations and only 11 million were in farm or agriculturally related occupations (Coll, 1969, pp. 40–41). From 1860 to 1900, the U.S. gross national product rose about 2½ times, which meant that even though the four decades had been marked by two serious depressions, all groups were better off in 1900 than they had been in 1860 (Axinn and Levin, 1975, pp. 75–80).

However, although working-class incomes were rising, there was an increasing concentration of wealth and income among a small group of multi-millionaires. It has been estimated, for example, that Andrew Carnegie had an average annual income of over $10 million at the turn of the century, a time when there was no income tax. In 1899 the richest 1.6 percent of the U.S. population received 10.8 percent of the national income. Ten years later, their share had risen to 19 percent. Although this was a time of progress and economic expansion for all, a time when the base of America's phenomenal productive capacity was being developed, it was also a time of ruthless competition characterized by the exploitation of people and resources. Crass materialism and sharp business practices were admired, and open illegality was often winked at. The businessman became the American hero (Coll, 1969, pp. 40–41).

Perhaps because of the worship of money to the neglect of many other aspects of life, there was widespread inefficiency and corruption in American government. Scandals were commonplace at all levels of government. Public officials expected to be paid for the many public services they rendered, and businessmen expected to pay them. Bribes and favors made a mockery of the free competitive market, but what little concern was expressed regarding such corruption was expressed as a belief that since government was corrupt, we needed less of it. A reaction against monopolies resulted in the enactment of the Sherman Anti-Trust Act in 1890, but the provisions of this act were too weak for it to have any real effectiveness in retarding the development of larger and larger trusts (Coll, 1969, pp. 42–44).

✑§ Migration and immigration

During this period, there was a steady flow of immigrants into the United States, with almost a third of the nation's population growth accounted for by newcomers. The immigrants and their children settled in the eastern and midwestern cities, in which the foreign born and their children often outnumbered native-born citizens. Without question, this steady (and constantly increasing) flow of laborers made it possible for employers to keep wages at or below subsistence levels.

In addition to the movement of the foreign born into the cities, by the end of the century Mexican-Americans in the Southwest were beginning to move from farm to nonfarm urban jobs. And there was an increasing flow of white, native-born young people from farms to cities. However, at this time there was little migration of blacks from the South to the urban North in spite of the bitter poverty and discrimination that most southern black families endured. In 1860 about 300,000 blacks lived in the North; by 1900 their number had grown to just over 700,000. During the same period the number of blacks in the South increased from 4 million to 8 million (Coll, 1969, pp. 66–68).

As noted in the last chapter, the tendency to blame the immigrant for whatever was wrong with American economic life was widespread. By 1850, there were growing movements not only to limit the number of immigrants who could enter the country but to limit the political rights of those who had already made their homes here. Many U.S.

leaders felt that there was significant misuse of the vote by immigrants who gave their loyalty to political bosses in exchange for kindnesses and favors. As the 19th century drew to an end, there was a general feeling that uncontrolled immigration added greatly to poverty in the United States by constantly increasing the numbers of the very poor. Many workers felt that industry's policy of flooding the labor market with aliens was the major cause of unemployment and low wages. Some people thought that each group of immigrants admitted to the country increased the danger of anarchism, communism, or other doctrines subversive to American institutions (Bremner, 1956, pp. 7–10).

⊷§ Labor

Although the availability of immigrant labor may have added to the difficulties of workers who were struggling for decent wages and working conditions during this period, immigration tended to provide such a convenient rationalization for all the nation's ills that other central issues escaped the attention they deserved. Throughout the 19th century, students of industrial problems generally thought that if only employers would deal kindly with their employees, labor would respond by offering faithful and competent service. Capital, holding the superior position, should act as a guardian of the interests of labor. Thus, labor strife would disappear, unions and strikes would be unnecessary, and labor would support capital. "There were undoubtedly employers who attempted to build a mutually supportive and helpful relationship with their employees, but there were also many instances of employers who regarded their machinery with more tenderness than their workers" (Bremner, 1956, pp. 7–10).

Industrial injuries and working conditions

The problems of industrial accidents and occupational diseases were largely ignored by both industry and government during the decades from 1860 to 1900. Aside from the victims and their families, social workers were among the first persons to recognize the tremendous cost of industrial accidents to workers and the community. Railroad accidents were especially numerous. In each of his annual messages to Congress, President Benjamin Harrison called attention to this problem, recommending the passage of legislation requiring the gradual installation of air brakes and automatic couplers on the railway cars that were used in interstate transportation. Finally, in 1893, after more than half the states had enacted laws providing for the use of railway safety devices within their boundaries, the federal government passed the recommended legislation. By the end of the 19th century, one out of seven railway workers was protected against injury or death at work by insurance schemes that employers had established voluntarily. However, the great mass of the workers in industry or transportation had no protection against loss of income or provision for medical care in case of industrial accidents.

In cases of occupational injury or death that came to court, the employer had several defenses that were generally upheld. One defense, used especially in cases involving children, was that the children, or their parents acting for them, had willingly and knowingly assumed the risks of the job when they accepted employment. Another defense was that the accident had resulted either from the worker's own carelessness or from the carelessness of other workers and that the employer could not be held guilty of negligence in such a situation.

Despite efforts to reduce the workday and despite the insistence that fewer hours would promote the intellectual and physical development of the worker as well as increase the hourly output, little success was attained. In opposing shorter hours, many persons were convinced that less time at work would only mean that workers would have more time to waste in idleness and intemperance. When the Civil War ended, the average workday was about 11 hours. Not until after 1880 was the workday brought below 14 hours in some industries, and as late as 1900 the average was still close to 10 hours. Several eight-hour laws were found unconstitutional as an illegal interference with the rights of the employer, but the Supreme Court in

1898 upheld the eight-hour law in mines and smelters as a reasonable exercise of the police power of the state (Jennings, 1926, pp. 468–89).

Organizations

Over the earlier years of U.S. history, the availability of free land and the paternalism of employers in small businesses and industries had held down interest in labor organizations. As we pointed out earlier, the attempt to organize that followed the depressions at the beginning of the 1800s had been largely ineffective. However, as free land disappeared and the factory system increased in scope, laborers found themselves increasingly dependent on employer actions. Printers, bricklayers, cigar makers, and railway conductors, among others, quickly organized after the Civil War, so that by 1870 there were about 40 national trade unions in the United States. Efforts to form one national organization of all laboring groups were made as early as 1861 by the leaders of the machinists and the blacksmiths. In 1866 a National Labor Congress was held at Baltimore. It was followed by annual meetings until 1872, when only seven delegates attended. The demands of this congress were: the eight-hour day, land grants to actual settlers only, a national bureau of labor, restriction on immigration, the reductions of tariffs on the necessities of life, the abolition of prison labor, and the establishment of such supports as cooperative stores and workshops and reading rooms (Jennings, 1926, pp. 469 and 476).

The Knights of Labor was formed in 1868, but it was no longer in action after the recovery from the Panic of 1873. The Knights of Labor preferred cooperative action and the arbitration of disputes to the use of the strike. It used political action and education to the needs of labor rather than economic pressure. Although it was interested in most of the demands of the earlier labor organizations, the Knights of Labor also sought the prohibition of child labor, graduated income and inheritance taxes, a postal savings bank system, government ownership of railroads, and public utilities. The Knights of Labor was too centralized in administration and too idealistic for the most practical and independent unionists, who were less concerned about social changes than about improving their working conditions, increasing their wages, and decreasing their working hours.

Thus, in 1881 came the second major effort to unite all wage earners in a single organization— the American Federation of Labor—which differed from the Knights of Labor in several respects. First, the federation was based on the notion that each trade should be independently organized and that each local organization should retain control of its own internal affairs. In addition, the federation was opposed to political activity. The AFL had no desire to reform society, but it was interested in achieving the greatest gains possible for labor within the existing system. It believed that those gains could be made by direct negotiations between the unions and the employers. The AFL's emphasis on organizing skilled labor meant that the interests of the unskilled and the most poorly paid workers were not represented by unions (Jennings, 1926, pp. 472–85).

There were groups that expressed more fundamental dissatisfactions with the conditions of the working poor. These groups included the Populists, a political party; the Industrial Worker of the World, an international labor association; and the early Socialist Party of Eugene Debs. However, they received only limited support, indicating that labor was not seriously interested in economic reform.

Women

During the 19th century, the employment of women in industry increased steadily. In fact, the number of female wage earners increased more rapidly than did the population as a whole, the male population, or the female population. In 1870 a little over an eighth of the nation's women were gainfully employed, but by 1900 nearly one fifth were employed. In every age group except that from 16 to 20, the percentage of gainfully employed women was highest among blacks. In the 16–20 age group, it was highest among foreign white women (Jennings, 1926, pp. 478–79). Many of these women worked in the "sweated" industries of the textile trades. In this type of work the industrialist contracted out piecework to a secondary contractor who then recruited women to work in attics, lofts, or the tenement home of the contractor, sewing or doing handwork on garments. The women had no protection,worked under incredible conditions, and were paid on a piecework basis. The amounts they earned were extremely low. Throughout the period from 1860 to 1900, the wages of women were significantly lower than those of men and the question of their right to be represented in unions remained open. The problem was often settled by forming women's locals (Jennings, 1926, pp. 478–79).

Children

Even more problematic in its effects than the low wages of women workers was the employment of child labor on an extensive scale. The Census of 1870 reported that over 700,000 children between the ages of 10 and 15 were engaged in gainful occupations and that nearly a sixth of these children were employed in industry. The conditions under which they worked varied from industry to industry, but at best the employment of children stunted their growth and development (Jennings, 1926, pp. 429–80).

John Spargo, a New York labor investigator, writes in his book, *The Bitter Cry of Children,* of finding children of six and seven canning vegetables at two in the morning. On June 1, 1900, in Augusta, Georgia, an investigator wrote of finding 556 children under 12 years of age at work in eight cotton mills at midnight. These children were offered no more protection, and often less, than adult workers. One physician said that he had amputated the fingers of more than 100 children whose hands had been caught by the rapidly running machinery in a cotton mill. In 1895 a report of an Illinois inspector stated that in several places he found boys at work at dangerous machines because their fathers had been disabled by the very machines the boys were operating. The boys were keeping the job for the fathers, pending the fathers' recovery. The

fathers' jobs depended on the sons' doing their work during their absence (Bremner, 1971, pp. 612–47; Jennings, 1926, pp. 429–80).

Immigrants and blacks

In certain occupational groups, from 76.3 percent to 50.4 percent of the male workers were foreign born in 1900. Of all gainful workers, 38.4 were foreign born in that year.

During the 40-year period from 1860 to 1900, black laborers achieved some improvement in their conditions, along with the gains made by other workers, but their hours of labor were long, their wages were small, and they were continually discriminated against. Blacks were decidedly unwelcome in most labor organizations, and the most disagreeable work was uniformly reserved for blacks. Competition with immigrant workers contributed to the decline in the blacks' position in society, as we pointed out in the last chapter. The refusal of many white laborers to work side by side with blacks created a desperate situation. Sometimes by their poverty and the promises of employers drove blacks to engage in strikebreaking, which increased the antagonism of organized labor toward them. Enforced residential segregation confined many blacks to living in alleys, cellars, garrets, and other unsuitable quarters at noncompetitive rentals. This resulted in the isolation of blacks in the community as well as in work life. The low wages and hard conditions of the blacks are further illustrated by the fact that in the youngest age group, from 10 to 15, and in the highest, over 65, the percentage of gainfully employed males was considerably higher among blacks than among any of the white groups (Jennings, 1926, 480–82).

Industrial conflict

From 1870 until the end of the 19th century, industrial conflict grew. During the years 1880–1900, there were 23,798 strikes and lockouts involving over 6 million workers. In every year of those two decades, there were at least 1,000 strikes. The first important railroad strike, in 1877, was caused, among other things, by a 10 percent reduction in wages. When the strike broke out, the strikers tried to destroy railroad property. The state militia was sent out to quell the strike, but it joined the strikers. President Rutherford Hayes sent federal troops to restore order. In the fighting that followed, several people were killed (Jennings, 1926, pp. 484–85).

An incident that set back the cause of labor was the Haymarket Square bombing. May 1, 1886, had been set for general strikes and demonstrations throughout the country. In the gathering of 30,000 strikers in Chicago, police fired, killing a striker. A mass protest of this killing was called for May 4 in Haymarket Square. During the protest a bomb was thrown, no one knows by whom, and 60 policemen were wounded and 7 killed. In the panic and demand for justice that followed, eight anarchists were arrested and found guilty, even though one of them was not in Chicago at the time of the bombing. Of the eight, four were hanged, one committed suicide, and three went to prison (Jennings, 1926, pp. 485–87).

The Pullman strike of 1894 was a violent and far-reaching one. It was brought about by the dismissal of some workers and the cutting of the wages of others. When a committee of men called on George Pullman to protest the action, three of them were discharged by Pullman, who resented their protest. Twenty-seven states and territories, and railroads across the country, were affected. Governor John Altgeld of Illinois refused to do anything to protect the railroads and their property, so President Grover Cleveland sent 2,000 troops to Chicago. In the meantime the strikers, disregarding their leaders' pleas to avoid violence, burned and looted buildings and destroyed trains. Federal troops fired on the rioters. Some of the strike leaders were imprisoned as a result of the violence (Jennings, 1926, pp. 486–87).

Labor legislation

Gradually the states enacted laws to offer workers certain protections and appointed inspectors

to see that the laws were enforced. However, enforcement was very lax during these years. In general, the laws related to the protection of health by establishing regulations concerning ventilation, heating, sanitation, and so forth; to the prevention of accidents by forbidding the employment of women and children in dangerous work; and to the regulation of the hours of labor. Ordinarily, the courts had declared laws regulating hours of work to be unconstitutional, holding that they violated the 14th Amendment (thus the amendment passed to protect the rights of individual citizens was used to protect corporations). But when the Supreme Court upheld an eight-hour law in 1898, some state legislators tried again to regulate working hours.

During this period, Massachusetts took the lead in labor legislation. In 1866 it enacted the first child labor law (apart from the earlier laws relating to indenture and apprenticeship). Three years later it established a state bureau of labor, and soon after that it enacted a ten-hour law for women and children along with a factory inspection act. By 1900, several states had established eight hours as the legal workday and the average workweek was six days, as most states prohibited the employment of labor on Sunday. The age below which children could not be legally employed varied from 10 to 16 under the new laws that began to be enacted to protect women and children (Jennings, 1926, pp. 488–89).

The farmers

The Homestead Act of 1862 and the bills that supplemented it were among the most generous pieces of legislation on behalf of the average person that Congress has ever passed. One might have thought that the western farmer would be affluent indeed, given the right of any citizen to purchase land for the price of $1.25 to $2.50 an acre by living on it and improving it in certain ways; the invention of the reaper, the binder, the combine, the cultivator, and other machines; and the development of barbed wire as a fencing material and the windmill to provide water. Yet, the western farmer, too, faced formidable forces. First, there were the forces of nature, including periodic grasshopper plagues. But other things that contributed to the poverty of farmers were the amount of land controlled by railroads and speculators; exploitation by mortage holders, grain elevator owners, and merchants; the lower prices they received for their crops and the need to pay back earlier loans with more expensive money because the federal government withdrew millions of dollars of unsecured paper money that had been issued to finance the Civil War; and exorbitant railroad fees. Most of the railroads held monopolies of transportation in the rural areas they served, and thus the farmers were almost totally in their power in terms of the rates paid for the transportation of products. At a time in 1869 when corn was selling for 70 cents a bushel in the East, shipping charges from the West were 52½ cents, leaving the farmer 17½ cents for his product (Lens, 1969, pp. 148–67).

During the last third of the 19th century many farmers were suffering severely, and their poverty was a poverty of native-born whites who had truly exemplified all the virtues of initiative and hard work. Because of their independence and their feeling that they had earned a right to share some of the prosperity of America, this was the first poverty experience of a group to provoke a sizable and conscious reaction against laissez-faire and opposition to the thesis that the best government governs least. That reaction was furthered in 1887 when President Cleveland vetoed a bill to distribute seed to drought-stricken farmers with a message acknowledging that "there existed a condition calling for relief" and that a donation of seed "would serve to avert a continuance or return of an unfortunate blight." Nevertheless, President Cleveland felt "obliged to withhold approval of the plan." On the grounds that *"I can find no warrant for such an appropriation in the Constitution, and I do not believe that the power and duty of the General Government ought to be extended to the relief of individual suffering,"* he urged that such programs should "be steadfastly resisted, to the end that the lesson should be constantly enforced that *though the people support the government,*

the government should not support the people" [italics added] (Lens, 1969, p. 250).

Political activity

Farmers

In the last 30 years of the 1800s, farmers joined forces with a variety of movements that aimed at change in the economic and political climate. Among these groups were the Grange, the Greenback Party, the Alliance, the Wheels, and the Populists. In 1880 a novel means of redistributing income—the graduated income tax—was advocated by a combination of the Greenbackers, the Marxist Socialist Labor Party, and Susan B. Anthony, the suffragist leader (Lens, 1969, p. 177).

The Populists charged that the corporations and other special interests had grown rich and powerful, not because of freedom of enterprise but because of class legislation and favoritism. They held that the first duty of government was to protect the weak, rather than permitting the strong to control. They argued that the federal government "had the responsibility to regulate commerce, issue money, and take other actions so that the natural rights of the many were protected from the few" (Lens, 1968, p. 177). The overriding significance of Populism was that it "initiated a national dialogue over government intervention, and was the first step toward a controlled capitalism and the welfare state" (Lens, 1968, p. 185). The Populists eventually developed three main organizational bases— the Farmers' Mutual Benefit Association, located largely in the West; the Southern Alliance; and the Colored Farmers Alliance.

Blacks

With the support of the Colored Farmers Alliance, black cotton-pickers engaged in strikes in 1891. During this period, other black unions, such as that of 2,000 black longshoremen in St. Louis in 1892, attempted strikes, most of which were unsuccessful. From 1894 until 1898, a coalition formed by the fusion of the Populist groups in the

South with the black Republicans gained control of the political process in North Carolina (Aptheker, 1951, pp. 805–11).

Populist programs

In a meeting at Omaha on July 4, 1892, the Populists called for a graduated income tax, postal savings banks, government ownership of utilities, and the appropriation of railroad lands other than those the railroads needed for their operation. As the new century approached, there was a "beginning recognition on the part of a number of groups that economic life was interdependent," that even on the prairies rugged individualism was not enough for survival, and that "in the cities no person's future" was entirely dependent on fitness or unfitness, virtue or immorality (Lens, 1969, pp. 182–83).

Coxey and the Commonweal of Christ

One more general force toward reform and the welfare state should be discussed before we go on to the development of social and political thought and of social welfare in the period from 1860 to 1900. This force, called "Commonweal of Christ," was a bedraggled band of unemployed, led by Jacob S. Coxey, which "marched out of Massillon, Ohio, on a chilly Easter Sunday in 1894" to demand that work be made for them, and for all in similar circumstances, by the federal government (Lens, 1969, pp. 192–94). Coxey had been a member of the Populist Party and had drawn up previous bills that in one form or another called for the government to make jobs by having the unemployed pave city streets, build courthouses or schools, and so on. The effort to secure federally financed jobs for the unemployed failed, but it was one more step toward the idea of federal aid for the unemployed (Lens, 1969, pp. 192–94).

Social and economic thought

It was estimated in 1890 that the average family required an income of $700 for the year in order to purchase the barest essentials. At that time, 79 percent of the heads of families earned less than $700. This meant that even for the fully employed, poverty stalked not far away unless more than one member of the family worked. Poor health, depressions, large families, industrial factors, lack of job security, and long days at hard labor for most family members threatened the way of life of the marginal wage earners. By the end of the 19th century, the United States could no longer avoid giving serious attention to the problems of poverty and economic insecurity of large numbers of its people. The American attitude toward poverty at that time might be summed up as follows:

1. Poverty is unnecessary, and it is the result of the varying ability of people to care for themselves rather than divine action.
2. Far from being a state blessed by God, poverty is evidence of sloth, laziness, or other personal defect.
3. Given the inherent laziness of people, the threat of poverty is probably inevitable and not necessarily undesirable.
4. Poverty goads people to work and strive, thus contributing to their development.
5. It is the responsibility of all people to look out for their own individual interests.
6. Work is of value for its own sake, not as a duty to God.

Bremner points out that "for almost the first time in history, work is not viewed as an onerous duty attaching to the lowborn but is highly regarded and prized for its own sake," that "the founding fathers may have intended the United States to be an asylum for the distressed people of the Old World; but it was a workhouse that they had prepared, not a refuge for idlers" (Bremner, 1956, pp. 17–18). He highlights the incongruous American attitude toward poverty by pointing out that it left uncertain whether poverty was to be regarded as "the soil from which Lincoln and Carnegie had sprung, or the breeding ground of the dangerous classes" (Bremner, 1956, p. 17).

Certainly, from the founding of the United States the twin notions of the importance of work as a social virtue (not a religious one) and the importance of individualism were two outstanding values of American society. Both of these values coalesced in the idea that public intervention to alleviate the effects of poverty was actually harmful to the development of people; that the way to benefit the poor was to guide them toward morality and self-discipline, as all persons could purge themselves of the bad habits that led to indigence if they possessed the will to do so. When this interpretation of poverty came into being, it was essentially a radical and hopeful doctrine that preached the triumph of the individual over nature and stood for the perfectibility of the individual. However, it came to represent a defense of conservatism.

Romanticism

In the mid-19th century there was a heightened sense of individualism stemming from the teachings of romanticism and transcendentalism. This movement emphasized the unique aspects of the individual and demanded that the independence and separateness of people be obtained at all costs. Emerson and Thoreau, leaders of this school of thought, did not visualize a society of interdependent members but a society of separate individuals. They were reformers, but they did not have any fundamental philosophy about social change. They neither concentrated on constructive social action nor shared a spiritual concern for the social good. Although they rejected the materialism of the American society of the time, they provided little to replace it but a sensitive and refined individualism. The individual became the center of the picture, and the social scene remained a shadowy background (Mencher, 1967, p. 242).

Social Darwinism

The name of this doctrine gives the mistaken impression that it relates to Darwin's work in biology. In fact, the doctrine that later became known as social Darwinism predated the work of Darwin by nine years, and the phrase "survival of the fittest" was first used by Herbert Spencer, an English philosopher. This view held that the characteristics of individuals, including those that seem to have been acquired through experience, were genetic in origin. Nature had decreed that some people were fit to advance the cause of life and should survive, but that others were unfit and that the misfortune of poverty for the unfit was to be expected. Meddling by the state in the regulation of industry, subsidies to the poor, public education, and even the improvement of sanitation was a conspiracy against the natural order. *Such actions not only deprived people of their inherent right to fulfill themselves but were contrary to the laws of nature and a crime against the gradual advancement of the human race.*

Social advancement required freedom of individual action, for social evolution toward a better society was hampered by any attempt to support the less able. As a social doctrine, social Darwinism summed up and gave scientific approval to many of the beliefs already present in American society. By holding that the currently successful people were in effect the most capable, the social Darwinists reinforced the values and beliefs of the contemporary society (Mencher, 1967, pp. 237–45).

During the latter half of the 19th century, one of the strongest proponents of faith in America's continued growth and in competition founded on individual self-interest was William Graham Sumner. On most social questions, Sumner held views similar to but more extreme than Spencer's. For Sumner, the ideal was laissez-faire, which stood for the abandonment of false sentimentality. Reliance on help from others was a form of primitive behavior, and in the contemporary world it generally resulted in depriving the energetic of their just earnings. Democracy depended on having people accept complete responsibility for themselves (Mencher, 1967, pp. 237–45).

Henry George

Henry George's contribution to the thought of the time was to direct the attention of people from the individual benefits to the social consequences of private profit in land. George asserted that land values *were created by the growth and needs of the community rather than by the efforts of the owner.* These views were set forth in *Progress and Poverty,* published in 1879, in which he supported a single tax on increasing land values. He held that allowing landlords to take for their own use the socially created value of land meant allowing them to appropriate wealth that properly belonged to the community as a whole. However, George did not depart far from the laissez-faire notions of his time in that he believed that the evils of society could be remedied by free and unhampered individual competition (Bremner, 1956, pp. 23–25).

Edward Bellamy

Except for their common emphasis on social change, Edward Bellamy differed strongly from George. His *Looking Backward,* published in 1888, compared what he saw as a cruel and competitive way of life with an efficient, cooperative society. The other members of the group believed that the material wealth in the world would be great enough for all to have and enjoy abundance if there were but a system for the equitable distribution of that abundance. They preached that not only moral values but the realities of industrial society proved that society was a whole, an organism, in which the hurt and pain of any person had a negative influence on all people (Bremner, 1956, p. 25).

The Social Gospel

The gradual recognition of the unwholesome results of individualism in economics was accompanied by a lessening emphasis upon individualism in religion. The Social Gospel doctrine of the late 19th century cut across all denominations, with roots in the religious and humanitarian movements of a half century earlier. This doctrine was to influence the development of the settlement house movement, which we will discuss in the next chapter. The YMCAs and the Salvation Army were also part of the movement. They led the way in interesting other religious goups in moving into the slums

of the country and establishing domestic missions to serve the poor. Certainly the writings of General William Booth of the Salvation Army *(In Darkest England)* did much to popularize the idea that one could not expect moral improvement of the poor until their economic situation was improved. This view was the exact opposite of much of the social philosophy of the time, calling as it did for social rather than individual reform (Bremner, 1956, p. 29).

The Roman Catholic Church of the time, although adhering to the traditional religious interpretation of poverty, was frankly critical of individualism in both religion and society. Although believing that much of people's ills was the will of God, the Roman Catholic Church was much more accepting than many Protestant churches of the failures of people to live up to the highest ideals. In 1891 Pope Leo XIII issued an encyclical on the condition of the working class. This encyclical condemned socialism and defended private property, but it upheld the right of workers to unionize and it sanctioned moderate legislation to support social reform. The encyclical also denounced the tendency of laissez-faire to treat workers as commodities and not as human beings (Bremner, 1956, p. 28).

Other social reformers

Another development during this period was the work of Karl Marx. Marx was the founder of modern theories of socialism. It was his thesis that economic factors were the determinants of all history, that the building of a better society necessitated ownership and control of all the tools of production by the state rather than by individuals. Many social reformers in the United States took their stand somewhere between the extremes represented by laissez-faire and Marx.

Certain institutional economists, among them John R. Commons, held that, at the very least, society was responsible for providing its members with minimal subsistence. Commons held more radical views than many of his colleagues in economics, and his views were often confused with socialism.

But he favored the existing economic system, believing however that all members of the system had the right to subsistence.

Pragmatism and the scientific method

An important developing force during the late 19th century was a growing knowledge of human functioning based on a developing scientific method. This scientific method, which did not believe that anything was "self-evident," supported the development of pragmatism. For the pragmatist, all ideas had to be evaluated by how they worked rather than by how they looked or sounded. Life experience was the laboratory for testing hypotheses about people and their environment. Truth and good were not to be dealt with abstractly but in terms of their impact on the existing life situation.

The gospel of wealth

Probably one of the most influential statements in the development of American philanthropy was an article by Andrew Carnegie entitled "Wealth," which was published in the *North American Review* in June 1889 (Bremner, 1956, p. 271). In this article, Carnegie proposed that instead of passing on vast fortunes to their relatives, the wealthy should administer their wealth as a public trust during their lifetime. Bremner writes:

> His view resembled that of John Winthrop and William Penn, except in one important respect. Carnegie did not say, as those men had, that the great ones owed their distinction to peculiar arrangements ordained of God. He attributed the eminence of the millionaire class to fitness to survive and triumph in the competitive struggle. The trusteeship Carnegie proposed thus differed from the traditional doctrines of stewardship. The millionaire, a product of natural selection, was an agent of the public, of the forces of civilization, rather than a servant of God. Trusteeship devolved on the man of wealth because he was fittest to exercise. In the exercise of his trust he was responsible only to his own conscience and judgement

of what was best for the community. (1956, p. 106)

According to this view, *philanthropy was a substitute for social reform.* Recognizing the obligation of the state to care for the destitute and the helpless, Carnegie urged the wealthy to concentrate their giving on the able and the industrious. He was not interested in reforming either society or the individual. Rather, he supported the notion of providing opportunities for the aspiring. His establishment of libraries throughout the nation fitted in with this belief.

✌§ Summary

The years following the Civil War, from 1865 to 1900, marked the growth and development of the United States as a nation and as an international power. These were years of rapid economic growth, of the development of industries unheard of in earlier years, of the development of the scientific method and an explosion of knowledge in many areas of life, of tremendous growth in the population and the gross national product. But they were also years in which the problems of poverty intensified, in which the frontier came to an end, in which the problems of minorities seemed to grow greater, in which workers were often caught in the economic crises of society. This was a time when the problems of an urban, industrial society were becoming more visible. It was also a time when the concept of the government's responsibility to intervene in the economic and social sphere to protect the vulnerable and effect redistribution of income and wealth in favor of the poor first began to be heard.

Commager has commented that "the great issues of the nineties still commanded popular attention half a century later," that the problems which monopolized public interest in the 1890s seemed "no less urgent in the 1930s and 1940s" (Commager, 1950, p. 4). Thus, the problems that have been discussed in this chapter were to be the problems with which the 20th century would continue to struggle.

ᴖ§ A look ahead

Much of our discussion in the rest of this text will be an account of the various ways of defining these social problems, various philosophies as to their causes, and plans to solve them. We shall begin in the next chapter with a discussion of the way in which philanthropists approached many of these issues in the years from 1860 to 1900.

ᴖ§ Study questions

1. In this chapter it was stated that one of the two largest groups of employed blacks included teenagers. Today, the greatest amount of unemployment is found among black teenagers. What are possible explanations of this difference? How do you evaluate these explanations in terms of human welfare?

2. The quotation from President Cleveland's veto message contains a statement that is very similar to a statement in a modern presidential message. Can you identify it?

3. How was the poverty of the farmers different from the poverty of the immigrants and the blacks?

4. Farmers suffered in the late 19th century because the railroads monopolized the transportation of grain. In what ways does the present problem of transporting grain over long distances differ from the problems that existed at that time?

5. List the various notions discussed in this chapter about people's relationship to their government and about the relationships of people to one another.

ᴖ§ Selected readings

Lens, Sidney. Poverty: *America's Enduring Paradox.* New York: Thomas Y. Crowell, 1969.

Chaps. 8 through 12 offer students a very interesting expansion of the material presented in this chapter.

Bremner, Robert H. *American Philanthropy.* Chicago: University of Chicago Press, 1960.

This book is an excellent one for increasing the student's understanding of the development of U.S. social and economic thought from the beginning of the nation through the 19th century. Although it might be worthwhile to use some of its chapters as a review of earlier material, the chapters dealing with the gospel of wealth and other notions of the latter half of the 19th century should be of special interest to students at this point.

Axinn, June, and Levin, Herman. *Social Welfare: A History of the American Response to Need.* New York: Harper & Row, 1975.

Chap. 4 relates both to our last chapter and to the material in this chapter. Chap. 4 has been recommended earlier.

The advancement of public health and child care programs in the late 1800s is illustrated by these pictures of, *above,* scenes from The New York Infant Asylum, and, *on the right,* compulsory vaccination in Jersey City (after a smallpox scare in 1881).

Chapter 16 ൙

൙ Scientific philanthropy, 1860–1900 ൙

൙ Introduction

With this chapter we begin the study of what might be considered the development of the modern welfare institution. The problems and issues identified in the 1890s remain the focus of our attention today. The questions of the responsibility of society to guarantee minimal standards of living and access to opportunity for all, of the right of individual ownership and the free disposal of property in a democratic society, of the existence of wealth created by and rightly belonging to the whole of society, of the nature of human beings and the limits of their perfectibility, of the relationship between democracy and social security, are central questions of our age just as they were central questions a century ago.

The shape of the institution of social welfare depends in part on the answers we develop to these questions. But in addition the actual programs developed depend not only on the answers to the questions but on the values, knowledge, wisdom, and skill of the persons charged with constructing the program—on the answers to the issues outlined in the right-hand column of the chart at the end of chapter 6. In the period 1860–1900, people struggled with how social needs should be defined; they also began to develop knowledge, wisdom, and skill that allowed for more sophisticated definitions and a wider range of solutions. Social science knowledge based on observation and research rather than values began to develop. Such knowledge stimulated the growth of human service professions. Thus, by the end of the 19th century we were moving in the direction that we have continued to pursue even unto today.

Some of the problems in program construction that presented themselves with new force during this period were: What should be the basis of social allocations? Do we construct programs with the notion that social welfare organizations should be residual, serving only those who cannot help themselves? Do we continue to think in terms of relief and charity to ameliorate poverty, or do we see programs of public works and social insurance as a prevention of poverty and the ultimate expression of a modern industrial state's responsibility for the economic security of its citizens? And do we classify persons as worthy and unworthy (separating special programs for children, the handicapped, and the ill from general programs to support all people and all families), or do we classify problems as acceptable (blindness, handicaps, aging) or immoral (unemployment, mental illness, delinquency, crime)? What is the nature of the social provisions offered? What kind of assistance do we offer, and at what level? (Should a family "on welfare" always have less than a family whose head is employed?) What is the structure of the delivery system and the source of support? Should social welfare be built primarily on public agencies or on private ones? Do we put our primary resources into programs offering indoor assistance or into programs offering outdoor assistance? Which is more important: personal social services or material aid? Which is of primary value: individual help or social reform? What is the relationship between knowledge and values? And what is the appropriate division of responsibility between the lay citizen and the professional? Although not always clearly defined, these questions of modern social welfare development began to be at least dimly perceived by at least the last two decades of the 19th century. By the beginning of the 20th century, this was clearly discernible through major concerns of social welfare leaders: (1) a search for improved methods of serving special groups; (2) a search for the causes of poverty in the individual; and (3) a search for the causes of poverty and human trouble in the social system.

≈§ Public income maintenance and personal social services

As the consequences of industrialization were beginning to be recognized in the 1870s and 1880s, America was still trying to develop a social welfare structure based on the philosophy of laissez-faire

and personal responsibility for one's economic security. Or, perhaps it would be more accurate to say that America was still trying to avoid developing a social welfare structure, still struggling to limit economic security measures to intermittent programs of private charity and local public relief. Although the charitable response of the American people was generous and every large city in the Northeast had long lists of charities, these efforts added nothing to the understanding of poverty in an industrial society and developed no solution to the problem other than the familiar one of moral improvement of the poor. In general, there was no recognition that the "suffering society generously relieved with one hand was, in many instances, but the product of the ills that it casually sowed with the other" (Bremner, 1956, p. 32).

Just as the officials in the Northeast were questioning the adequacy of almshouses as the base of economic assistance, the rest of the country was beginning to move from binding out the needy and auctioning off the destitute to the lowest bidder to the construction of almshouses.

Although, as we discussed in the last chapter, this was a time of tremendous mobility, the concept of local responsibility for poor relief remained dominant. Local areas were careful about providing assistance to the able-bodied resident unemployed poor, but they were unbelievably cautious about giving aid to migrants who came to their attention. Particularly during periods of depression, able-bodied laborers were treated as vagrants and sent back to their communities of settlement. For example, New Yorkers complained bitterly that they were expected to assume the support of some 7,000 paupers who had been sent into their state by Massachusetts, although many of those paupers had not been former residents of New York (Schneider and Deutsch, 1941, pp. 107–10).

The extent of local public assistance programs is difficult to calculate because accurate records of either persons in institutions or persons receiving outdoor relief in the community were not kept. The available reports of efforts to deal with the unemployment that followed depressions indicate the limited capacity of the public agencies and the helter-skelter measures that were developed by private charities. Outdoor public relief in times of depression usually consisted of temporary relief in kind: food, lodging, and clothing. Sometimes work relief was initiated by either public or private agencies. In 1894, New York had a public works program that employed some 2,000 laborers at a weekly payroll cost of $30,000. At that time, at least 17 other cities were using programs of subsistence gardening for the unemployed (Mencher, 1967, p. 281).

While the development of a consistent program of either economic aid or economic security under public auspices was resisted by the general population of the country, the development of outdoor public relief programs was under constant attack by the private charities of the community. In other words, because of conflict between welfare authorities the public received mixed and confused messages about the type of program that would be most effective.

The political corruption that was rife during this period placed a very "potent weapon in the hands of the opponents of public outdoor relief" (Coll, 1969, p. 43). Investigations which began in 1873 of the activities of the Boss Tweed ring in New York revealed the misuse of $100 million of public funds, part of which were funds of the Department of Public Charities and Correction. The general belief that public aid corrupts the client was now easily translated into the concept that public aid corrupts all who deal with it, which was easily expanded into the notion that all of the people involved in the administration of public relief are inept, if not dishonest. No public sphere suffers more from revelations of unethical or inadequate behavior than that of public assistance. Corruption and dishonesty in the police department results in sympathy for the victims and a call for reform in administration, not in doing away with the police. However, the response to the revelation of dishonesty in the administration of public relief in New York was followed by a complete suspension of public outdoor relief from mid-July 1874 to January 1875, and then the resumption only allowed for aid to the blind and the distribution of coal. Finally,

in 1876 and again in 1877, the city voted a large sum of money for outdoor relief, but it stipulated that the distribution should be made by voluntary agencies (Coll, 1969, pp. 43–44).

Corruption was also discovered in the distribution of outdoor relief in Brooklyn. This discovery resulted in the abrupt cessation of outdoor assistance in the middle of the winter of 1878. Boston, too, had its problems. However, despite the problems, Boston clung stubbornly to public outdoor relief. Its firm stand could be attributed to the position taken by Samuel Gridley Howe. In 1879 Philadelphia followed New York City and Brooklyn in suspending relief. Among other large cities, Baltimore and San Francisco gave no outdoor relief and St. Louis had only a small contingency fund to take care of emergencies. However, such large midwestern cities as Chicago, Cleveland, Milwaukee, Minneapolis, and Detroit utilized both outdoor relief and almshouses (Coll, 1969, p. 59). Confronted by the example of its sister cities, in 1888 Boston sent a committee to study the situation in Brooklyn and Philadelphia. Noting the large number of children in institutions, the committee concluded "with alarm that Brooklyn must be breaking up families for no other cause than poverty" (Coll, 1969, p. 60).

◂§ Income maintenance and personal social services—The Charity Organization Societies

It seemed to concerned people that the greater the increase in philanthropic efforts, the greater grew destitution and poverty. A possible explanation that occurred to a group of young men in Buffalo, New York, was that the large number of charities was actually causing the problem. They reasoned that the control of poverty rested on the control and careful organization of charity. The Reverend S. Humphreys Gurteen, a minister who had recently come from England to Buffalo, was familiar with the work of the London Charity Organization Society, which had been established in England in 1869 to remedy conditions similar to those found in Buffalo. Based on his knowledge, a Charity Organization Society was founded in Buffalo in 1877 (Rich. 1956, pp. 3–10).

The COS approach

In many ways, the aspirations and practices of this new organization were not greatly different from those of the earlier AICP (discussed in Chapter 13). Perhaps one of the most significant differences between the two organizations was that the AICP had relied exclusively on men to do the work, whereas the new organization encouraged qualified women to join, both as paid agents and as volunteers. By 1892, women far outnumbered men among the 4,000 volunteers who were enrolled in COS work (Bremner, 1956, p. 52). From this point through the reform efforts of the first quarter of the 20th century, the leadership in philanthropic work and the development of the new profession of social work were largely in the hands of women.

"Whether male or female, friendly visitors were expected to be combination detectives and moral influencers." They were to make a careful and objective study to ascertain the reason for the applicants' need and to work with them "to overcome it." Their function was, by advice and example, to help the poor to become self-supporting and to help them obtain assistance from the appropriate agencies if there were no other resources. The basic concept of the COS work was that some personal weakness of character, intellect, or body was ordinarily the real cause of the distress of the poor, and that the only effective way to really help suffering people was to discover such weaknesses and correct them (Bremner, 1956, p. 52).

In most places where a COS was organized, it attempted to institute a threefold approach: (1) the provision of new facilities, such as day nurseries and sewing rooms, to encourage thrift, the promotion of health practices, and the provision of better and humane care; the enactment of (2) legislation to limit and control the quality of public services and to discourage vagrancy and vice; and (3) the perfection of methods of personal treatment. Paid agents made investigations; committees of volunteers determined what approach should be attempted in each situation; and a volunteer "friendly visitor" used personal influence to bring about the desired changes in family circumstances (Rich, 1956, p. 11).

The philanthropy of the COS

The name Charity Organization Society was not the best name for the new effort, but it did convey the idea of order and system. The name did not, however, convey that the societies were concerned with the family as the "civic unit" and that all their undertakings were related, directly or indirectly, to protecting and strengthening the home. Years later, the term family service came into being to describe this focus. The private "family agencies" of today are the most direct descendants of the early COS agencies.

The new agencies were a strong protest against the lack of factual knowledge about poverty which had characterized so much of the philanthropic work of the time. "In addition to having a strong belief in the need for order and for system and kindliness in meeting human need, the men and women who started the charity organization movement were convinced that there was a science of charity," that poverty could be cured and prevented if its causes could be discovered and removed (Rich, 1956, p. 13). But the movement was more than a protest. It was concerned not only with knowledge and an orderly system, but also with bringing about a more abundant life for the individual—better wages, better housing, better working conditions, and some of the pleasures of living. Although each local society was expected to subscribe to the general principles of the COS movement, it was free to carry out its program in whatever way was best. Where to begin and what activities to undertake were to be determined by the individual situation as long as the general principles were adhered to.

The COS emphasized the separation of relief from personal service. Relief, though a necessity, was an obstacle to the independence of clients, which was to be achieved through personal service. The leaders of the COS believed firmly that giving relief contributed to the continuance of dependence and that public assistance should be granted only in ways that would most discourage people from seeking it. As we try to evaluate this position, we must remember that its apparent harshness was the result of a sincere effort to really help people, "to do a difficult task in a competent manner" (Bremner, 1958, p. 55). It was an advance in social thought "to recognize that poverty was an abnormal condition, that it was unnecessary, that it was curable, and that its treatment required more fundamental changes than an increase in generosity on the part of the rich" (Bremner, 1958, p. 55).

The causes and cure of poverty

Actually, the work of the COS agents undermined much of the social thought of the day regarding the cause and cure of poverty. In carrying out their duty to get the facts about the condition of persons who asked for help, the caseworkers uncovered significant information about unemployment, industrial accidents, sickness, wages, and family expenditures. "Through their work they compiled a fund of more reliable and comprehensive data on the economic and social problems of the very poor than had been available since the days of the close knit village economy" (Bremner, 1956, p. 55).

The COS agents also began to develop the case method of social research. This method called for the treatment of each individual or family as a unique situation. The case method forced the COS agents to reject preconceived notions about poverty. "From the beginning, the aim of the charity organization movement had been, not to expand, but to restrict, the charitable impulse. Increasingly, the agents of organized charity came to look upon the attainment of social justice as a more important field of endeavor than the administration of private benevolence" (Bremner, 1956, p. 57).

✑ Personal social services—Youth agencies and missions

Many of the youth-serving agencies that we know today began their work in the mid-1800s.

The first of these was the Young Men's Christian Association. As with so many of our other private philanthropic organizations, the roots of this movement lay in England. In an effort to bring the young drapers of London back to the Christian way of life, George Williams, a draper, established the first YMCA. A retired sea captain from Boston, impressed by the success of the London society in improving the condition of young men who came to the city to seek work, established the first American YMCA in 1851.

YMCAs and the YWCAs

The purpose of the Ys was to protect new urban citizens from the dangers of irreligion, intemperance, and immorality. Although the early Ys offered living quarters with decent, sanitary facilities at a low price, and friendly and familiar moral influences, their activities were diverse indeed. Most of them had relief committees which gave help to poor families in their neighborhood. Until the COS was strong enough to take over the work, the Ys in Washington and Chicago coordinated relief and welfare resources in those cities.

The Ys also contributed to the development of the survey technique that was later to be so widely used in social work. Believing that they needed to know about the factors that affected young men in urban areas if they were to offer adequate and improving services to their communities, the Ys gathered data on the many factors that seemed to relate to the problem. When a YMCA secretary assumed the direction of a new agency, the first program initiated was often that of surveying the actual needs of the neighborhood. Students at the YMCA college in Massachusetts were trained in gathering and interpreting survey data. It is important to realize that the Ys were pioneer agencies in compiling factual information on urban social conditions and that "the purpose of such work was not of academic interest only, but was to serve as a foundation for corrective action" (Bremner, 1956, pp. 41–46). The first Young Women's Christian Association was founded in Boston in 1866, followed by one in New York in 1867. The YWCAs followed the pattern that had been established by the YMCAs.

The Boys' Clubs and the Jewish Centers

In 1860 the first Boys' Club was founded in Hartford, Connecticut, by a church women's group for the purpose of giving boys an opportunity to participate in various sport and social activities in a Christian atmosphere. These clubs quickly spread over the country. The Jewish Center movement traces its roots back to the 1840s, when groups of Jewish young people began to establish literary societies. Jewish Centers served both boys and girls, and their programs were usually not segregated by sex.

The Salvation Army

The Salvation Army, an international evangelical and charitable organization, was established by William Booth in 1865. Later, his son founded a similar organization, the Volunteers of America. The Army was formed to "uplift the outcast and the distressed." Its activities and its successes in working with the very poor helped convince more respectable people that even the most desperate and vicious persons might be saved. No place was shunned by the Army, and no men or women were considered to have sunk so low that they should be excluded from "God's bounty."

The Army's dramatic and apparently successful methods of dealing with the dangerous classes aroused new support for slum evangelization in the old-line churches (Bremner, 1956, p. 29). No less important than its evangelical crusades was the interest that the Army aroused in social reform. In 1890 General Booth published a book, ghostwritten by the journalist William T. Snead, which set forth the concept that the moral improvement of the poor was dependent on the improvement of their economic condition.

Missions

Partly stimulated by the example of the Salvation Army, during the 1890s many middle-class

churches conducted discussions on the question of the church's responsibility in relation to the welfare of the urban workers. Many of the pastors of such churches felt that the condition of the working class should be of no concern to the church, which dealt with spiritual rather than social matters. However, concern over the growth of Roman Catholicism, worry about the growing antagonism between capital and labor, the development of a Social Gospel, and the example of the Salvation Army persuaded many Protestant groups of the need for "missionary labor in the roaring wilderness of American cities" (Bremner, 1956, pp. 28–29). By 1880, there were at least 30 undenominational missions in the slums of cities. In addition to conducting gospel meetings for the residents of the slum neighborhoods, these missions attempted to help improve the material condition of the poor by engaging in limited relief work, providing facilities for training children in trades and domestic occupations, equipping libraries and reading rooms, and sometimes building and operating rooming houses and tenements.

The Church of Holy Communion in New York City was active in establishing St. Luke's Hospital to serve the community. Russell H. Conwell's Baptist Temple in Philadelphia instituted a night school for working people in 1884 that later became Temple University, and it also founded a hospital and instituted visiting nurse services. Many churches engaged in surveys of the type initiated by the YMCA, and in the last years of the 19th century the Federation of Churches and the Christian Workers took over this work in New York, acting as resources for the knowledge they accumulated on the social conditions of the city (Bremner, 1956, p. 59).

✒§ Personal social services—The settlement movement

The settlement, like the COS movement, was brought to the United States from England. In 1884, with the help of his wife, Samuel A. Barnett, vicar of St. Jude's, Whitechapel, a parish acknowledged to be one of the worst in London, converted the rectory into a social center for the neighborhood. They named the center Toynbee Hall, and they invited university men to settle in the hall, participate in its educational and recreational programs, and become friends and neighbors of the poverty-stricken people of the community as a way of overcoming the dangers of social and spiritual disorganization.

The first American settlement was founded in New York by Dr. Stanton Coit, following experience with settlement work in England. Returning from England, Coit rented an apartment on New York' East Side. Initially it was difficult for police and neighbors to believe that a person of Coit's social standing would voluntarily take up residence in the area. Coit began by cultivating people in the neighborhood, organizing picnics, and offering his apartment as a meeting place for groups. Eventually his work resulted in the establishment of the first American settlement, known as the University Settlement.

The second U.S. settlement grew out of the experiences of Dr. Jane E. Robbins and Jean Fine with Coit. They rented quarters not far from his and opened a club for girls. The police were even more suspicious of these two unattached girls for being in the neighborhood than they had been of Coit, and they offered Robbins and Fine suitable protection for their "business" for a fee. The settlement established by Robbins and Fine came to be known as the College Settlement.

One of the better known settlements in New York was the Henry Street Settlement, or the Nurses' Settlement. Lillian Wald, its founder, was a nurse who began her work by teaching nursing to immigrant women in the hope of being able to select appropriate candidates for nursing education. The unique contribution of the Henry Street Settlement was the vast variety of public health efforts that developed after 1900 from the work of the nurses who lived there. Confronted by the overwhelming amount of disease and illness in the slums, along with the lack of care, Wald founded the visiting nurse service (Levine and Levine, 1963, pp. 96–97).

Jane Addams and Hull House

Perhaps the most noted settlement in America was Hull House, founded by Jane Addams and Ellen Gates Starr in 1889, following a visit to Toynbee Hall. Hull House started with no planned program, but as Jane Addams once confessed, the movement "was based on emotion as much as conviction," and on the desire to learn from the life of the neighborhood, to collect facts as a basis for public improvement, to devise means for gaining insight into the needs underlying the facts, and to work with, not for, the people of the neighborhood, and others, to promote justice and human welfare (Bremner, 1960, p. 114).

The settlement was not a charitable or relief-giving agency, and the leaders of the settlement movement tried to distinguish the laborers with whom they interacted from the clients of the charity agencies. They concentrated on the needs of labor rather than of the destitute, and by so doing they played a role in raising the standards of all. In discussing the differences in the problems of the two groups, Jane Addams once wrote, "To confound the two problems is to render the solutions of both impossible. . . . Working people live in the same streets with those in need of charity, but they themselves, so long as they have health and good wages, require and want none of it" (Addams, 1935, p. 21). The settlement leaders hoped to provide the poor with facilities for recreation, enjoyment, friendship, and self-development; but they were just as eager to have the settlement serve as a sort of graduate school at which young men and women of the upper classes could become acquainted with a life-style very different from their own and could learn from people and situations that they would never have encountered otherwise.

The settlements were thus directed toward the so-called normal people and toward programs to support a good life, rather than toward people who were antisocial or sick or toward the solution of individual problems. The settlements were based on the interests and abilities of their beneficiaries rather than on a pattern of behavior prescribed for them. Each settlement concentrated on the total problems of a single geographic neighborhood and saw the individual as a member of a group through which joint activities could be conducted. In fact, few clients came to the settlements as individuals. They came in twos and threes with their neighbors and friends. The founders of the settlements believed that broad social and economic reforms would result from the experience, the thinking, and the joint action of the whole population of a neighborhood. Though this was not enunciated at the time, the settlements, in their effort to divorce poverty from pauperism, were raising the view of the "employed poor."

Clubs were the heart of the settlement program, and originally many of the settlement houses were little more than meeting places for different neighborhood organizations. Other features were added as the need for them became apparent or in response to the interests of the community or of the house residents. Most settlements operated playgrounds, kindergartens, day nurseries, and baths and offered classes in music, art, and domestic science. Particularly important were the socialization and acculturation classes that the settlements offered to immigrants to help them become Americanized. Settlement workers tended to place greater emphasis on social reform than on individual improvement. Their relationships with the people in their neighborhoods led them to become more aware of problems as social rather than individual and enabled them to make detailed and realistic investigations of various social problems. In general, the settlement leaders did not believe in making moral judgments, and they had great faith that a simple statement of the facts was a powerful weapon for social change.

Life in the settlements

The settlements generally occupied large houses that had been owned by the wealthy before the character of the neighborhood changed. The early living arrangements of the settlements were much like those of families. Most of the early houses were run on cooperative principles, with the members doing much of the work necessary to maintain the house and its living arrangements. Many of the settlements had family councils which discussed problems and difficult situations. In addition, there were periodic meetings or seminars on settlement work and the intellectual exchange and debate of the dining table. Many young intellectuals other than the residents were regulars at the dining table, partly because of the stimulating debate and, no doubt, partly because the meals tended to be nourishing and cheap (Levine and Levine, 1963, pp. 96–123).

The financial base of the early settlements

The financial situation of the settlements changed as the residents changed. Most of the earlier houses were founded and financed by a group of unsalaried residents who rented their own quarters and paid for their own expenses. However, the settlements gradually recruited people who needed to earn an income from their labors. As people without independent incomes were attracted to the settlements, it became necessary to find money for the salaries of full-time residents and other employees and for student scholarships. Although some people felt that the neighborhoods should support their own settlements, the poor, whom the settlements were established to serve, could hardly be expected to contribute the necessary funds. The two most important early sources of settlement funds were probably wealthy individuals and such organizations as the Junior League. However, this type of support was not without problems in that funds were often given for specific projects and thus could not be freely used in the ways the settlements might desire, and the settlement workers soon learned that the displeasure of a patron could cost them a program. In addition, at one time or another almost all of the active settlements or their residents took stands on controversial issues that cost them support. Thus, the settlements began to understand that any group bent on social reform needs independent sources of funds.

The settlements and women in social welfare

The majority of settlement residents and workers were women, many of them well-educated women who had to make extraordinary efforts to secure their higher degrees because of the discrimination of the universities. For instance, Florence Kelley, a resident at Hull House and a leader in social reform in the early 1900s, was unable to find an American law school that would admit women. After searching throughout Europe with the same results, she was finally admitted to the University of Zurich, the first European university to open its doors to women. For such women the challenge of social change was perhaps a channel for expressing their own struggle for emancipation.

These women had grown up in secure and privileged families and amid wealth only to find, as young adults, that further self-development in a chosen way was cut off by the social, legal, and cultural concepts of society. They knew the feelings of anger, frustration, and helplessness that this raised. In a sense, they were a minority group that took on the battle of other minority groups, in the belief that the solution of any minority problem lies with community and social change. Just as the early philanthropists knew from their own experience that any industrious and moral person could succeed, as they had succeeded, these women knew from their own experience that no matter how competent people are, they cannot achieve certain goals if society prevents them from doing so.

COS-settlement rivalries

By 1899 the COS and the settlement movement had become rivals for the financial support, the allegiance, and the voluntary service of the community. Each group had an eloquent professional spokeswoman. Mary Richmond, a leader of the COS, and Jane Addams were born only a few months apart, and both began to participate in philanthropic activities at about the same time. Both contributed invaluable leadership to the develop-

ment of a common profession of social work, though each spoke to a different way of working.

Mary Richmond wrote and taught about methods of social casework (working with individuals and families), while Jane Addams was a founder of group work (working with small groups) and of community organization and social action. There were interesting points of difference and similarity between the two women. Both were well aware of the possibilities of helpfulness on the part of sincerely concerned and caring persons of privilege. Both recognized the possible dangers of unnaturalness, superficiality, and condescension in paid neighborliness. Addams and the settlement movement generally doubted the wisdom or the efficacy of the formal methodology and the careful investigations of the COS staff. On the other hand, Richmond and the COS leaders were suspicious of what appeared to them to be the fuzzy and opportunistic thinking of the settlement workers who sought to become a genuine part of neighborhoods that they could leave at any time for a very different life.

Still, many of the young men and women who lived and worked in the settlements during the 1890s developed knowledge about the poor and an understanding of the daily life and trials of the urban worker which they later carried into careers in social work, business, government service, and other spheres. This was one of the great contributions of the settlement house movement, and it was destined to exert a great influence on the development of social work and the shape of social reform in the 20th century.

✑ Social services for special groups—Children

Up to the middle of the 19th century, there was little consideration of childhood as a special time of growth and development. Instead, children were treated as small adults, though without adult rights. The father was considered to have an absolute right to their custody and control. Not only dependent children, but most children, were set to work very early, with little concern about childhood as a special stage of human development. However, in the late 1800s the rights of children began to get increasing attention as the result of three forces: (1) the proportion of children in the population began to decrease, so that more adults were available, both to do the work of society and to care for children; (2) more knowledge about the needs of children as a special group became available through the infant sciences of psychology and human learning; and (3) there was a general growth of concern for the rights of all persons and for the reform of situations that oppressed people.

The needs and rights of children

Thus, toward the end of the 19th century we find two movements developing in child welfare: (1) a growing concern with the needs of childhood as a special period of life and (2) an enlargement of the rights of children in relation to parents or to persons standing in the place of parents. In these movements the tendency has been for society as *parens patriae* to intervene so that the "presumably fair and uniform treatment" at the hands of professional authorities and agencies can be substituted for the "ignorance, neglect, and exploitation of some parents." This transfer of responsibilities required the development of administrative, judicial, and professional techniques of investigation, decision, supervision, and care (Bremner, 1971, p. 117). As a result, from the late 19th century to the present there has been an increasing substitution of public norms for the appropriate care, custody, control, and behavior of children in place of the private standards of the family in such matters. The rights of children that began to be of concern to the public were the right to an education; to protection against being sent to work too early or in certain types of industries; to protection against immoral influences; to adequate food, clothing, shelter, and medical care (the lack of which has generally been defined as neglect); and to protection against physical (and later emotional) abuse.

The challenge to the rights of the father

A part of this movement to uphold the rights of children to adequate care was a growing challenge to the exclusive right of fathers to control and obtain custody of their children. Under common law, the mother of a child had no voice in the welfare of her children, being entitled "only to reverence and respect" (Abbott, 1938, p. 7). As the public became aware of the injustice of this position to the mother, and of the threat that this position could well pose to the welfare of children, there was a movement in many states to formulate a new series of laws and policies that recognized the equality of the mother and the father in the control and the custody of children and that made the welfare of the children the controlling consideration in any case of disagreement over parental rights. As a result of these new laws and policies, over the years the custody of children has been awarded to the mother more frequently than to the father in custody disputes, when both were considered equally good parents, based on the concept that the mother was more important to the welfare of the child and more skilled in child care. Today this concept is being strongly challenged by men who believe that it is fathers who are now being deprived of their rights, not by common law, as was the case for mothers, but by certain assumptions as to the needs of children and stereotyped sex roles.

The growing rights of the mother

Independent ownership of property and earnings, the responsibility to society for their own acts, and the right to the care and custody of their children came to married women only by legislative enactments after long struggles. It is interesting that the rights of the mother were not established as early as the rights of the wife. Except for a few southwestern states with community property laws that affected husband and wife alike, before the end of the 19th century all of the states had passed legislation giving married women the right to make a will and to own property separate from that of the husband. However, only 14 states had passed laws making the mother equal with the father as a guardian of her children. Kansas became the first state to move in this direction when it established a constitutional provision for joint guardianship in 1859.

As an example of the general 19th-century tendency to limit the rights of the mother, we have the decision of the Supreme Court of New Jersey in 1857 that

> the rights of parents result from their duties, their duties being the same, their rights must be the same also. While the father is living, the authority of the mother, for obvious reasons, is in abeyance. As the mother herself . . . owes obedience to the father, her authority must submit to his. In a competition, therefore, of commands, the father is to be obeyed. In the case of the death of either, the authority, as well as the duty of both parents, devolves upon the survivor. (Abbott, 1938, p. 63)

The welfare of the child in custody disputes

In a Kansas court decision of 1881, we see an example of the movement toward giving the welfare of the child priority over the rights of parents. In a custody case in which the father had left his child with relatives for several years and then sought to reclaim her, the court held that the child had formed ties with the people who had cared for her over the years and that these ties could not be severed without damage. Thus, the rights of the father and the rights of the people who had offered the child a home were both held to be less important than the welfare of the child. In that same year, and in the same spirit, another judge decided that a court might deny custody to both parents in a divorce matter. In this situation, the maternal grandmother was awarded custody. Further cases involving the custody and support of the children of divorced parents established the principle that the father might be required to support his children even though he had been deprived

of their custody. A court in Iowa, in 1870, held that the father was obligated to support his child even though he had been denied the services of the child. The father's obligation to support the child came from "the inability of the child to support itself. *It is not only a duty to the child but to the public*" [italics added] (Bremner, 1971, p. 126).

Child protection

In addition to such instances of governmental intervention in custody and support disputes, there was a growing movement, as we have said, to protect the child from abuse, neglect, and immoral influences. It should be recognized that this movement did not begin until very late in the 19th century, and that until the 1860s there was no legal precedent for removing children from their parents on the basis of the parents' care and treatment of the children. Protecting children from physical abuse by their parents, or by other persons who have control over them, has been a very difficult issue because of the widespread belief that physical punishment is a necessary part of the effective discipline of children and that parents have the duty to control their children. As an example of this belief, we have had the Supreme Court decision of 1977 which holds that teachers have the right to use reasonable physical punishment to control children in school.

If we believe that physical punishment is a necessary and appropriate method of discipline, then the appropriate degree of severity of physical punishment is certainly a matter of judgment, and this raises the issue of who makes this judgment. The teacher? The parents? The state? And who represents the state in this matter? Social workers? The judge? In the final analysis, in a dispute over the appropriate use of physical punishment or other attacks on a child, Americans have determined that children cannot be removed from the custody and control of their parents without a court hearing to determine that the reasons for such removal are truly significant to the welfare of the child. This poses a difficult decision for a judge who is confronted with the conflict between the rights of parents and the rights of children. Another often unvoiced problem is the issue of what will be done with children once they are removed. The removal from a poor home does not automatically assure that children's needs for care will be met.

As an example of an early decision relating to neglect, in 1869 an Illinois court held that parental authority must "be exercised within the bounds of reason and humanity" (Bremner, 1971, p. 119). In this situation a father and a stepmother had kept a blind boy in a cold, damp cellar without fire. But the Supreme Court of North Carolina set very extreme standards of determining abuse when, in 1886, it reversed a lower court's conviction of a father for assault and battery on the basis that there had been *no permanent physical injury* inflicted and that to leave the correct exercise of the authority of parents in the correction and discipline of their children to a jury decision would "tend, if not to subvert family government, greatly to impair its efficiency, and remove restraints upon the control of children" (Bremner, 1971, p. 121).

The first organized work aimed at the welfare of abused and neglected children was that of the New York Society for the Prevention of Cruelty to Children, established in 1875. The New York Society for the Prevention of Cruelty to Animals had been established for eight years when a mission worker discovered that a child named Mary Ellen was being cruelly beaten, and otherwise mistreated, by a family that had taken her from a children's institution in infancy. Unable to obtain court removal of the child from this situation through her own efforts, the worker appealed to the SPCA, which, holding that the child was an animal, took Mary Ellen's guardians to court under the laws relating to cruelty to animals. The child was removed, and her guardians were sent to prison for one year. As a result of this case, a Society for the Prevention of Cruelty to Children was established in New York in 1874. From this beginning, such societies developed rapidly until there were more than 250 of them by 1900. Following this demonstration of the need of children for protection, the Humane societies, groups that had been created in a number of cities for the protection of animals, decided in 1887 to add the prevention of cruelty to children to their activities.

The SPCCs

The New York SPCC became a powerful and influential organization. Although it was a private corporation, its agents wore police badges and were duly constituted officers of the law. During its early years the society was primarily interested in the removal of children from improper homes, the enforcement of child welfare laws, and the punishment of offenders against children. Thus, there was a rapid movement from refusing to interfere in family life to giving the SPCCs great powers in the protection of children from their parents. The SPCC usually supported the institutional care of children that were adjudged abused or neglected, and, as critics pointed out, it had little interest in what happened to the children once they were removed or in the return of institutionalized children to the community (see Folks, 1902).

However, the New York society did work for the passage of many laws for the protection of children. Legislation was passed to prevent "baby farming," the business of boarding unwanted infants in private homes or in institutions until their death, adoption, or other disposition. This legislation allowed the society to inspect such homes, limited the number of children that could be accepted, and required the homes that accepted such children to be licensed by the society. Here again, we see the society, a private group, acting as an arm of the state with licensing powers. The society was also able to secure the passage of federal legislation forbidding the importation of poor Italian children by padrones, who bought the services of such children from their parents in Italy for an agreed term of years and brought them to the United States to work as beggars or street musicians. The padrones confiscated the earnings of the children during the term of service. The societies also worked to prevent abuse in the employment of children in the performing arts. Young children were often secured from parents and used as performers in traveling acrobatic acts. In 1887 the societies caused the cancellation of the American debut of the pianist Josef Hofmann, who was 11 at the time and was scheduled to play 80 concerts in the United States. His tour was canceled after 42 concerts.

The early SPCCs assumed differing forms of organization and took differing positions on the best response to the abuse of children. In general, the "cruelty" agencies were supported by private funds, but one form or another of public subsidy helped support the work of most of them. In Massachusetts and Rhode Island the societies were statewide almost from their beginning. In New York there was a regional organization of the societies operating in large cities, but the activities of the SPCCs and the Humane societies have generally been confined to one city. There have been two fundamental differences among these groups. One question has been whether the protection of animals should be combined with the protection of children on the model of the Humane Society, which has its national headquarters at Denver and still operates in this way. The other question relates to the focus of the societies.

The conflict over the focus of child protection work

The New York SPCC continued to act in a law-enforcement capacity, assisting the police and prosecuting officers in bringing to justice adults responsible for crimes against children and in removing children from dangerous conditions. However, the Massachusetts SPCC thought that the tendency to become agents of law enforcement was a dangerous one for the societies. This group was more interested in preventive and remedial measures. Many societies, among them those of Philadelphia, Newark, Cleveland, Detroit, and Minneapolis, adopted this approach instead of concentrating on the punishment of parents and the removal of children. The societies that employed this family approach, as opposed to a "child-saving" approach, began to use social workers to work with parents

toward the development of greater parenting skills. As we shall see in the next chapter, the most important advances in the protection of children came with the development of public agencies charged with this function and with improvements in the administration of child welfare agencies.

Child neglect

The concern for the welfare of neglected children and the movement to protect children against immoral influences developed concurrently with, and along lines similar to, the concern for abused children. The New York Society for the Suppression of Vice was established in 1872 by Anthony Comstock, with the backing of certain Christian businessmen and the YMCA. Like the SPCC, this society was a private corporation that utilized delegated police powers. A federal obscenity act, which became known as the Comstock Law, was passed in 1873. This law prohibited the use of the U.S. Postal Service for the transmission of contraceptives and birth control information, as well as "obscene, lewd, or lascivious" printed material or art. During the last decade of his life, Comstock became concerned with the regulation of the rapidly developing motion-picture theaters.

The problem of defining what constitutes neglect of children has always been a difficult one for the courts. Is it neglect if the parent is unable to support a child because there is no employment or income? In the 19th century many children were removed from parents, particularly widowed mothers, because the parents had no way to support them. Not until the early 1900s did social workers take the position that children should not be removed from their parents because of poverty alone. And it may be that in society in general there is still dispute about this concept. Although the neglect laws vary from state to state, the elements commonly found today in the state laws covering neglect are: (1) inadequate physical care, (2) the absence of or inadequate medical care, (3) cruel or abusive treatment, (4) improper supervision and control, (5) exploiting the child for monetary purposes, (6) unlawfully keeping the child out of school, and (7) exposing the child to criminal or immoral influences that might endanger morals.

The conflict between the SPCC and the COS

Being agencies that were concerned with the importance of the family to the development of children, the COSs were generally opposed to the "easy" removal of children from their parents. In an address to COS workers in 1879, Josephine Shaw Lowell expressed concern about the number of children being removed from their families for neglect, raising the question of how these children were to be cared for once they were removed from their own parents and recommending that children not be removed from families only because of the death or incapacity of the breadwinner or from families in which "the deficiencies are moral."

In situations involving a widowed mother, Lowell recommended that a regular monthly pension be paid from the time of the father's death until "all children are over ten years of age" and that supportive help also be offered to the mothers who needed it. She said, "It ought to be considered cruel and wicked to take children away from a decent mother just for want of money to support them and friends to look after them." For parents with moral deficiencies, Lowell recommended "a wise and patient friend" who would see that the children were properly trained. "The whole problem is one of human weakness and human vice. What is needed is education of every kind" (Bremner, 1971, pp. 349–52).

Children of unmarried parents

From ancient times until the 20th century, children born out of wedlock have been placed under considerable legal handicaps. The only duty recognized by the state in the first half of the 19th century was that of preventing or reducing illegitimacy and the dependence it created. Under the double standard of morals of the time, mothers were held to be the offenders and the major question was as-

sumed to be how women could be kept from transgressing the moral and statutory law. Harsh punishment for the mother and denial of legal rights to the child were relied upon to reduce illegitimacy, without concern for the needs of the illegitimate child.

During the latter half of the 19th century a few advances were made in the rights and care of the child born of unmarried parents. Fathers began to be held responsible to support their children born out of wedlock. Also, the legal handicaps relative to the rights of illegitimate children to inheritance began to change. The common law, which considered the illegitimate child to have no right to support or inheritance from either the father or the mother, began to give way to consideration of the rights of the child. A movement was made toward allowing such children to inherit not only from the mother and father but from other relatives as well.

Birth control and abortion

The problems of birth control and use of birth control procedures were of some concern at this time. In 1826 Dr. Charles Knowlton, a Boston physician, had been prosecuted for publishing a book that advocated mechanical and chemical means of contraception. In England, 1876–1877, groups organized to further the knowledge of birth control distributed Knowlton's book. However, in the United States general public concern with birth control did not develop until after the beginning of the 20th century.

Although there may have been differences among the states, at this time the state laws on abortion generally distinguished between aborting the fetus during the first stage of pregnancy and aborting after the fetus had "quickened in the womb," which usually occurred about four months after conception. Since it was generally assumed that life did not begin until after this point, earlier abortion was only immoral, not criminal. In some states it was possible to prosecute those who were involved in early abortions for having committed "an offense against morality and decency," a minor charge. As an example of the treatment of earlier abortions, we have a decision of the Kentucky Supreme Court in 1879. The court stated that although it felt that all abortions willfully produced at any stage after conception should be punished, since its duty was to pronounce what the law was rather than what it should be, it found "that it never was a punishable offense at common law to produce, with the consent of the mother, an abortion prior to the time when the mother became quick with child" (Bremner, 1971, p. 168).

Dependent children

During the latter part of the 1800s, three ways of caring for dependent children were generally utilized: specialized children's institutions, foster homes, and adoption. During this period, adoption probably developed more slowly than the two other ways. Adoption procedures changed little from those discussed earlier. Perhaps the major change was a growing recognition of the interests of the state in seeing that adoptions were sound decisions.

This recognition was first expressed in a Michigan law of 1891 which required that the judge investigate the fitness of the plan for all concerned before entering a decree of adoption. It was soon discovered that the judge alone was unable to make such investigations, and the law was amended to require the employment of court agents for this work.

Public institutional care and foster homes. Early in this period, concern was aroused by the growing number of children in almshouses. Actually, the number of children in almshouses doubled during the 12 years after 1856. The states adopted various programs for dealing with the problem, but almost all of these programs involved removing children from the almshouses and substituting some combination of institutional care and foster home placement. Some of the states established statewide public institutions, with active placement efforts a part of their program. Other states enacted legislation which required that the county or some other local unit develop placement programs. In most of these programs agents were hired to find foster homes, make placements, and supervise the children in the foster homes. These agents might be considered the first public child welfare social workers (Abbott, 1934, pp. 8–9).

Charles Loring Brace, as secretary of the New York Children's Aid Society, offered to accept all dependent children in New York and to place them in homes in the Midwest. But as the Midwesterners were generally Protestants and the children in the New York almshouses were usually Catholics, there was much objection to this plan (Abbott, 1934, p. 10). A law was passed requiring that children be placed in institutions of the same religious faith as that of their parents. Thus we see another concern entering into the care of children—the concern of the church that they not be separated from the religious beliefs of their parents.

In some areas the effect of this concern was to create a subsidy system, with per capita payments from public funds for children committed to the private religious institutions of the community. With public support of the private institutions thus assured, the number of children placed in such institutions grew by leaps and bounds. It was fatally easy to place children in private institutions and forget them. This system did, however, get children out of the almshouses.

Private institutions and foster homes. During this period the number of subsidized private institutions and the number of children in their care increased rapidly. The growth of the private institutions was supported both by subsidies and by the backing of religious groups which saw such care as the best way to socialize children from families of their faith into their religious beliefs. Although the care in these institutions was far better than the undifferentiated care of the almshouses, in many ways the private institutions were discouragingly similar to the almshouses. Their buildings were usually of a forbidding congregate type in which there was little privacy for individual children and in which individual attention was a scarce commodity. The programs of the private institutions often involved a rigid schedule of both activities and behavior, with severe punishment for violations. Most of the programs involved long hours of work, with little time devoted to school and even less to recreation.

Foster care of children was also developing rapidly at this time. In theory, foster care was complementary to the institution, since as a rule the institutions had some system of eventually placing out the children in their care. In practice, however, the two systems began to be regarded as rivals in the field of child care. Gradually, however, reform and child welfare leaders began to take the position that children were generally better off in foster homes than in institutions, even though these leaders deplored the often haphazard placement standards, the lack of supervision of the foster homes once children were placed in them, and the difficulties in finding and maintaining good foster homes.

One of the first professional approaches to the use of foster homes for the care of children was developed by Charles W. Birtwell, who came to direct the work of the Boston Children's Aid Society sometime after its founding in 1864. He was convinced that there was more to placing children than simply moving them from their own homes to foster homes and, further, that the unique needs of children required more than fresh air, country living, industry, and religious training. Birtwell developed three important innovations in the child-placing process: (1) there should be extensive knowledge of the child and its needs before placement; (2) an adequate and comprehensive study of potential foster homes should be undertaken, so that the best could be chosen; and (3) consistent supervision of the child and the foster home should be undertaken after placement. Birtwell believed that separation from their own families had a distressful effect on children, no matter how necessary it might be, thus every means should be explored to keep child and parent together (Lundberg, 1947, p. 20).

Birtwell's belief that the rehabilitation of children's own homes should have priority over any foster home placement was undoubtedly his most important contribution to the welfare of children and undoubtedly entitled him to be considered the father of protective services to children. Certainly the effect of this emphasis on the importance of keeping children in their own homes was to change the focus of work in the area of child abuse and child neglect from a focus on "saving children" from their parents to a focus on helping the parents to develop ways of coping more productively with the tasks of child care and family life. Birtwell also made the "child savers" more aware that one had to be as concerned with seeing that children received proper care after removal as with rescuing them from cruel parents and inadequate situations. In such a position lay the seeds of the social worker's present-day involvement with the maintenance of the family as a primary concern of society.

One other pioneer needs to be mentioned here. In 1883 the Reverend M. Van Buren Van Arsdale, a pioneer in the home-finding movement in Illinois, founded an organization for the purpose of combining child placing with helping young women get an education. He called it the American Aid Association. Later this organization became involved primarily in statewide recruiting and supervision of foster homes. It changed its name to the Illinois Children's Home Society, and later it became the parent agency for the National Children's Home Society, a federation of 28 statewide children's home societies that are active today (Lundberg, 1947, pp. 20 and 85).

Day care of children. Before we leave this account of the development of child welfare services we must briefly introduce another service that is of growing concern in today's society—programs for children's daytime care and development. Day care of preschool children has developed in two parts that despite certain common elements have served different groups and classes of children and have developed under different auspices. Organized day-care programs have existed as philanthropic undertakings to serve the children of working mothers, these are called day nurseries and are usually under social work auspices, and as nursery schools, usually under educational supervision, which serve as a form of preschool education and child development. These latter programs have usually served the upper middle classes and professional groups.

Day care began in the United States in 1854, with the establishment in New York City of a congregate care facility called the Nursery for Children of Poor Women. This program was developed to offer care to the children of poor working mothers. Gradually, other such programs developed. Usually they were sponsored by a church or a settlement house such as the Hull House day nursery, and sometimes by other child-caring agencies. The primary purpose of such programs was to prevent the neglect of children during the mother's working hours and to help the poor mother to care for her child in her own home rather than placing it in an institution. The day nurseries served a group of families that were often very poor, in which the mother was often heavily burdened by the need to work (often at very exhausting jobs) and to care for her children by herself.

A National Federation of Day Nurseries was founded in 1898, and other associations were also formed to encourage the development of day care and the maintenance of adequate standards of care (Lundberg, 1947, pp. 283–90).

✐ The mentally ill

Although by the end of the Civil War most states had accepted the principle that the *state* had some responsibility for the care of the mentally ill, and most states had established two or three state institutions in the years between 1833 and 1875, it was becoming apparent to the social reformers of the late 19th century that the care of the mentally ill was far from adequate. The early reformers had seen the public mental hospital as a therapeutic institution that would care for all mentally ill persons, irrespective of class, ethnicity, or color. These reformers firmly believed that early treatment, properly administered, would result in a relatively quick cure of mental illness. Their notion of treatment was largely that of "moral treatment," for which small institutions with close ties between psychiatrist and patient were essential. So effective

was the work that these reformers did to win others to their beliefs that within two decades most states had established mental hospitals. The opening of such institutions also resulted in the emergence of psychiatry as a profession and in the establishment of a national professional association by the psychiatrists to represent their interests and outlook (Grob, 1973, pp. 132–73).

The overcrowding of the mental hospitals

Yet, as with so many reform movements, the institutional system that developed during the 19th century did not much resemble the dreams of those who worked for its development. From the very beginning, mental institutions that were designed to remain small found themselves overcrowded and understaffed. The institutions were forced to accept an increasingly large number of chronically insane persons, so that eventually a significant proportion of their population came to be older, poor, longtime public charges who had been sent to the mental institutions from almshouses or other vehicles of public care. This resulted in a significant change in the role of the superintendents, who found their therapeutic concerns rapidly taking second place to managerial problems and considerations of order and efficiency. In theory all patients in the public mental institution received the same quality of care, but in practice class, ethnicity, and race played a significant role in the types of treatment that patients received. Decentralized and relatively isolated from one another and from effective interaction with the general public, the superintendents of the early mental hospitals found nevertheless that this autonomy was limited in significant ways by legal, administrative, and financial constraints. Even though the psychiatrist might regard the mental hospital as a self-contained medical institution, it could not exist in isolation from public concern, values, or support.

Criticism of the mental hospitals

Investigations of the mental hospitals became common, and exposés of neglect and abuse in the

mental hospitals began to be written by former patients, some of whom held that they had been perfectly sane when they were committed to mental
institutions. One of the most spectacular of these
exposés was that of Mrs. E. P. W. Packard, who
charged that, though sane, she had been committed for three years to the state mental hospital by
her husband. This type of charge led to charges
of poor administration and to the publication of
reports highly critical of some superintendents for
their administration of the hospitals. There seemed
to be a great wave of public criticism of and loss
of confidence in the mental hospitals of the time.

The Jarvis study

Perhaps the most famous legislative study of
mental illness was that conducted by Edward Jarvis
in 1854 at the request of the legislature, which,
dismayed by the problems of adequate care of the
insane at the two existing state mental institutions,
decided to appoint an impartial commission to
study the problem and to recommend the adoption
of a "general and uniform system" of care (Grob,
1973, p. 275). Besides completing the most authoritative statistical study of mental illness that had
been done up to that time, Jarvis developed an
analytic framework which related mental disease
to class and ethnicity. The report showed the incidence of insanity, idiocy, and crime to be greater
among poor and pauper groups than among other
population groups. Jarvis took the position that
most insane persons could not be cured, holding
that both poverty and insanity were the result of
an "imperfectly organized brain and feeble mental
constitution" which led to both poverty and insanity (Grob, 1973, pp. 239–40; 259–61). He recommended that the state establish separate institutions
for native and foreign-born patients. As a result
of his report, a third hospital was established in
the state.

Four years earlier, Thomas R. Hazard had presented a report on Rhode Island's mental hospitals
to the Rhode Island legislature. Like Jarvis, he was
concerned with the link between poverty and mental illness, but he did not see poverty in terms of

character problems. His analysis was sympathetic
with the plight of the poor. He was interested in
protecting the poor from long hospitalizations, and
he suggested care in the community for the chronic
mentally ill. However, his report had little effect
on the thinking about the problem (Grob, 1966,
pp. 276–80).

In New York the state legislature appointed a
committee to study and report on the situation.
The committee's report recommended the appointment of a state commission, much like the later
State Board of Charities, to supervise all public
mental institutions.

The New York report is an example of the movement of states to rationalize their welfare systems,
both to protect the users of welfare services by
seeing that the services offered met certain standards and to ensure the most efficient use of public
expenditures by instituting effective controls and
thus establishing a system of greater accountability
and efficiency. Although, as the reader will remember, there were earlier efforts to collect data on
social problems, the reformers of the last few decades of the 19th century used the collection of
data as information on which to base policy and
determine public priorities. This new use of social
statistics was the hallmark of the "scientific reformers" of the time, and eventually it resulted in the
establishment of the State Boards of Charities. Most
of the state boards were sympathetic toward the
mental hospitals and placed the responsibility for
their identified shortcomings on overcrowding and
the high percentage of chronic cases. The state
boards made proposals to improve the situation
by expanding existing facilities, constructing new
mental hospitals, and establishing a dual system
of mental hospitals for the curable and incurable
insane.

Conflict over control

Both the concern over commitment procedures
and the establishment of state boards with certain
investigatory powers were moves toward central
lay control of what had been previously seen as
autonomous medical institutions. Most of the state

mental hospitals had a high degree of autonomy, functioning under the authority of an independent board of trustees appointed by the governor. Accustomed to such autonomy in the management of their internal affairs, the individual hospitals resisted any attempts to impose controls by external authorities. At the same time, the Association of Medical Superintendents of American Institutions for the Insane (AMSAII) assumed the role of the preeminent authority on mental illness and its treatment. It, too, resisted this new movement. The result was several decades of conflict. During the beginning of the controversy over commitment procedures, the AMSAII took the position that any form of government supervision of mental hospitals was "not only wholly unnecessary, but injurious and subversive of the present efficient system of control" (Grob, 1973, pp. 293–96).

Basic issues

In the acrimony of the conflict that raged, two deeper issues were hidden from view. These issues are basic, and they are still the source of controversy. The first of these issues was the problem posed by the claims of a profession for autonomy against the claims of the society that established and supported the profession and its practice. The second issue was the problem that was posed for psychiatrists by the growing tendency to relate poverty and mental illness. Many members of state boards tended to see poverty as the cause of mental illness, whereas the members of the AMSAII tended to see mental illness as the cause of poverty. In any case, the AMSAII resisted the absorption of the mental hospital into the general welfare structure. This is an interesting and disturbing issue. If one is concerned about the distribution of society's ability to care for troubled people, one cannot help but wonder at the tendency of those representing special groups to attempt to separate those groups from the poor. Are the mentally ill, or the crippled, or the blind, or the aged, more deserving than the poor child? How do we divide our resources?

Two other conflicts over the care of the mentally ill took place during this period. One centered on the proposal of some state boards to have separate institutions for the incurable and the treatable insane, and the other centered on the questioning of the large congregate institution as a helpful institution for treating the mentally ill. The AMSAII remained unalterably opposed to separate institutions for the incurable insane. In its eyes, all mental illness was curable. Many never lost their faith in moral management and saw the issue in terms of the size of the mental institutions and the availability of adequate resources for the job. This argument was carried on in a "bitter and acrimonious manner," with both sides defining the issue in terms of "unyielding moral principles" (Grob, 1973). Given the emotional tone of the controversy, it is probably not surprising that its only effect on public policy was to accelerate the end of local responsibility for the mentally ill. Both sides could agree that, bad as the state hospitals might be, the local institutions were invariably far worse. When given an option, the local citizens inevitably voted to lower taxes rather than to maintain service to dependent groups such as the mentally ill.

Between 1840 and 1860 there had been certain suggestions about using a model other than the large congregate institution for the care of the mentally ill. William M. Awl, superintendent of the Ohio Lunatic Asylum, thought that detached cottages would be highly appropriate for private institutions. John M. Gault, aware of the developments at Bicêtre, a famous French hospital, and the system of caring for the mentally ill at Gheel in Belgium, proposed a series of innovations that would have greatly modified the mental hospitals of the time. He proposed that farms with cottages be attached to mental institutions to serve both chronic and convalescent patients, and he recommended the initiation of a system for boarding out suitable patients with families in the community. He felt that chronic cases might be particularly appropriate for boarding out. Galt and his proposals came under sharp criticism. The type of hospital that Galt proposed clearly minimized the role of the physician, and as a loose and decentralized system, it was viewed as a step backward. This controversy was as bitter as the one over the institutions for the incurable insane. By the end of the century, it was evident that the hopes and aspirations of those who had struggled to improve the care of the mentally ill had fallen short of what they had hoped to achieve (Grob, 1973, pp. 303–39).

✍ Other special groups

The deaf

In 1860 Gardiner Greene Hubbard, whose daughter had lost her hearing through illness at the age of four, established the Clarke Institution for Deaf Mutes, the first institution to employ the articulation system of teaching the deaf to speak. This method of educating the deaf was strongly supported by Samuel Gridley Howe. Howe wanted to discourage the use of sign language by the deaf, feeling that lipreading and artificial speech were much less likely to isolate the deaf from their contemporaries. Howe also opposed segregation in large institutions for the deaf. Helen Keller began her instruction with Anne Sullivan, a graduate of the Perkins Institution for the Blind, in 1887 and commenced her instruction in articulation at the Horace Mann School for the Deaf in Boston in 1890 (Lundberg, 1947, pp. 49–74; Bremner, 1971, pp. 845–67).

The blind

One of the important advances in the prevention of blindness was the development, in 1881, of silver nitrate prophylaxis for the eyes of the newborn. However, silver nitrate prophylaxis was not in general use until the 20th century. In the meantime, state schools for the blind continued to develop (Lundberg, 1947, pp. 49–74; Bremner, 1971, pp. 845–67).

The retarded and the epileptic

During the period 1860–1900, schools for the retarded child began to develop on the state level. A practice used at several of these institutions was to remove the testicles of boys or the ovaries of

girls whose aggressive or sexual behavior was not controlled by the usual disciplinary measures. There are reports on the good results of such surgical asexualization.

Sometimes these institutions for the retarded also accepted epileptic children. Before 1900, epileptics of all ages were usually confined in either county hospitals or institutions for the feebleminded. However, a beginning was made on special treatment for these children toward the end of the 19th century, when a private institution for epileptic children under the age of 14 was founded at Baldwinville, Massachusetts. In 1891 Ohio was first in establishing state public care for epileptics with the founding of the first state institution for their exclusive care (Lundberg, 1947, pp. 49–74; Bremner, 1971, pp. 845–67).

✍ State Boards of Charities

As we have seen, by the 1850s many states had established state institutions to care for particular groups, such as offenders and the mentally ill. Thus, by the 1860s there were township, county, city, and state officials administering institutions, outdoor relief, and indenture programs without any supervision except when their activities became so corrupt or questionable that they were investigated by legislative commissions or brought before grand juries.

Beginning in 1863, the more progressive states began to be concerned about the situation and established permanent boards to inspect, report on, and suggest improvements in public charities, particularly the institutions. By 1897, 16 states had established State Boards of Charities. In Massachusetts, where the first such board was established (1863), the board was given the authority to reorganize the programs of the state institutions and to redistribute the inmates according to a statewide classification plan, but it was not given authority over the business operations of the separate institutions. In most of the eastern states, the early boards were totally investigatory and advisory, depending on moral persuasion and influence to bring about necessary changes. The states that set up state boards after the 1870s often set up administrative boards with authority to supervise. There was often struggle between the agencies, the institutions and the state boards over the balance of control in the operation of the state charities (Pumphrey and Pumphrey, 1961, pp. 142–46; Frattner, 1974, pp. 79–86; Bruno, 1957, pp. 31–42).

In general, the states that set up administrative boards were seeking something different from those that set up supervisory boards. Supervisory boards were usually established in states that had already developed charitable agencies whose operations were generally accepted. In such states it was more practical to try to assure competent programs and competent administration by establishing an advisory agency to influence general improvement than by abolishing the agencies and beginning all over again. The states that established administrative boards of control were usually more recently settled western states that had few agencies or organizations and wanted to assure as adequate a state program as possible (Bruno, 1948, pp. 31–42).

The establishment of the state boards is an extremely important milestone in social welfare history in that the assumption of responsibility by the states for overseeing the operation of social welfare organizations has never been reversed. In some states, new boards have been established for the oversight of particular types of institutions, such as institutions for the insane or institutions for offenders, leaving to the original state board the responsibility for the dependent wards of the state. Some states have abolished the state boards in favor of a single commissioner of public welfare. At present, about half of the annual expenditures of most states is devoted to services performed under the supervision or administration of state boards of welfare, health, insanity, and correction.

The organization and work of the state boards

The state boards were usually given the authority to require uniform reports from welfare officials and to inspect the state institutions and agencies. The boards were made up of prominent citizens who donated their services, a salaried executive, and several administrative assistants. Two qualities of the boards led many of them to play influential roles in the development and reform of public welfare activities. One key to the success of the state boards was the establishment of the position of secretary (or chairperson) apart from that of the agent (or salaried executive). By dividing the executive responsibilities, the state recognized the need for two types of leadership: leadership in the analysis of needs, the planning of new methods, and the exercise of political influence; and leadership in the responsibility for the ongoing work of the organization. The second key to the success of the state boards lay in the quality of the persons appointed to them, especially the person selected to offer leadership (Pumphrey and Pumphrey, 1961, pp. 142–46).

As an example of the operation of the state boards, we cite the work of the New York board, which was established in 1867. In the same year, it began to collect statistics on the number of children in almshouses. It found 2,300 children in these local institutions, in contrast to the Yates report of 1856, which had stated that 1,300 children were being cared for in this way. Lacking the authority to close almshouses to children, the board sought to induce the counties to make other provisions for children. However, the local authorities were opposed to this proposal. Concluding that persuasion would never accomplish the desired result, William Pryor Letchworth, a leading member of the board, began to generate support for state legislation that would prohibit superintendents of almshouses from accepting children. Eventually, Letchworth was responsible for the passage of just such an act by the state legislature in 1875 (Abbott, 1938, p. 6).

As an example of the conflict between the board's authority and the private agencies' sense of autonomy, the New York Society for the Prevention of Cruelty to Children challenged the board's supervisory powers by refusing to let the board inspect the quarters in which it provided temporary shelter for children. In the court action that followed, the courts ruled that the jurisdiction of the boards was limited to charities receiving public funds. Thus, the SPCC was not subject to visitation. A statement from the chairperson of the board reports that as of the close of the year 1899 it would discontinue inspection of the 663 private institutions that were entirely supported by private funds. These institutions included 47 day nurseries, 74 homes for the aged, 3 institutions for the blind, 35 children's institutions, 6 homes for women and children, 14 homes for women and girls, 63 general hospitals, 8 convalescent hospitals, 1 reformatory for children, and 8 reformatories for women and girls. The report further stated that during the year 1899 the board had inspected about 1,200 charitable charities caring for 540,000 indigent persons (Bremner, 1971, p. 337). The New York board's authority to visit and inspect private charities not receiving public funds partly restored in 1931, and it was finally fully established by a constitutional amendment in 1938.

It is easy to see from the above figures that the work of the State Boards was very heavy. In several states, boards sought to recruit "the better class of citizens" to form voluntary societies for the purpose of conducting monthly investigations of jails and almshouses. Visiting committees for public hospitals were also established. Eventually State Charities Aid associations were established in several states. The purpose of these associations was to organize local visiting committees which would make more frequent inspections of local institutions than the state boards could manage (Bremner, 1956, pp. 48–50).

❦ The National Conference of Charities and Corrections

The Massachusetts State Board of Charities was only a year old when it launched a national movement by issuing an invitation to a meeting of a "Social Science League." The American Social Science Association, founded by this meeting, brought together persons who were interested in social welfare and social welfare institutions, and there was a tendency for special groups to form around specific issues. Many of these groups ultimately devel-

oped into learned or professional organizations of their own and left the parent association. The American Social Science Association was dissolved in the early 1900s (Pumphrey and Pumphrey, 1961, p. 166). The members of state boards who belonged to the American Social Science Association found that they had mutual interests and shared problems. Thus, in 1874 the representatives of four state boards met under the auspices of the American Social Science Association and formed permanent committees to study their more urgent problems.

The Conference of Charities and Corrections

The Conference of Charities, as the representatives of the State Boards called itself, continued to meet with the American Social Science Association until 1878, when the conference voted to separate from the parent association and to meet separately in 1879 as a conference of professional practitioners under the name Conference of Charities and Corrections. The Conference has met annually from that time to the present for the purpose of presenting papers and discussing social welfare and social work practice. The major papers presented at these annual conferences have been published each year in Conference *Proceedings.* These collections of papers constitute a rich source of historical material regarding social work and social welfare (Bruno, 1957, pp. 10–30).

The growth of the Conference

The Conference invited to the annual meetings all persons interested in problems of "pauperism," charity, and philanthropy, and extended an especial welcome to persons who were engaged in religious and private philanthropy. By 1880, the Conference was attended by 125 persons, most of whom were representatives of public institutions or private social welfare. Today these annual meetings may be attended by 10,000 persons. The leading private philanthropic movement at the time was that of the Charity Organization societies, and delegates from these societies at once took an important place in the Conference. The rapid growth of the representation of the COSs, with their radically different philosophy concerning the role of the state and with their criticisms of public relief, led to a good deal of conflict within the Conference and to a concern on the part of the state Boards that the interests of public welfare groups were being ignored. With the election of a COS leader as president of the Conference in 1895, the control of the Conference did pass to the voluntary agencies. However, during recent years the Conference has once again become a rallying ground for those social welfare interests that are seeking economic and social reform. As the interests of the members of the Conference have changed, the name of the organization has also changed. In 1884 "National" was added to the name, so that it became the *National* Conference of Charities and Corrections. In 1917, with the emphasis on methods and techniques of practice holding center stage, it became the *National Conference of Social Work.* In 1957, with a renewed interest in public welfare and reform, it became the *National Conference on Social Welfare* (Bruno, 1957, pp. 10–30).

☙ Public subsidies and public control

Many states, particularly those on the eastern seaboard, drifted into the policy of subsidizing private institutions because this seemed to be cheaper than having the state open and operate its own institutions. In states whose constitutions prohibited such grants to private institutions, programs of local payments were developed. There were two systems of subsidy payments. In one system the institutions were annually paid a lump sum for children committed to their care. Some states used a contract system, with specific payments to institutions for their care of specific children over specific periods of time. There were many problems with both systems, with the question of applying publicly developed and enforced standards to private agencies operated under private board of directors being at the heart of the difficulties.

At the meetings of the National Conference of Charities and Corrections which took place in the 1890s, there were many discussions of the responsibility of the state to know how its dependent children were cared for. Gradually, progress was made in bringing the private child-caring agencies under state supervision. The devices developed to ensure that all private agencies provided reasonable care for children were: the requiring of reports to the state welfare agency, the right of inspection and investigation, the necessity for state approval before the incorporation of an agency, and the annual licensing system. Not all states adopted all of these devices. In fact, most states adopted only one or two of them. The most useful of the devices was found to be the annual licensing system. When an agency seeks a renewal of its license at the end of the year, it is easily possible to make a routine review of its work, and the refusal to renew a license is not nearly so difficult as the revocation of a charter.

In general, the first groups of institutions to come under the licensing system were the boarding homes for children under two or three years of age. But the system spread. A continuing demand for some type of regulation of those who would care for children and other vulnerable populations began to be heard, though there was resistance from the administrators and boards of both private and public agencies and from religious bodies that resisted encroachments on their authority. By 1937, 37 states had adopted a licensing system for child-placing agencies, and all but 6 of these states required that the licenses be renewed annually (Abbott, 1938, pp. 18–19). Today all states have some kind of statutory provision for licensing in the field of child care. This type of regulation is a state function, and therefore the laws differ from state to state, reflecting local conditions and interests at the time of their enactment. For a licensing law to be effective, the law must have public approval and support and must provide for some type of administrative staff and process; the administrative staff must be large enough to do an adequate job of inspection and must have the knowledge and skill needed to explain standards and to work with institutions toward an ever-increasing excellence of service; and finally, the community must possess sufficient resources to allow for the closing of unsatisfactory agencies and still give clients the necessary care.

✍ Health

During the 19th century a foundation was being laid for developments in medical knowledge, sanitation, and public health practice that were to occur with increasing rapidity in the 20th century. There was the work of Robert Koch in advancing the germ theory of disease, which made possible advances in the prevention, control, and cure of some of the most dreaded diseases of the time. Paul Ehrlich made significant contributions to the understanding of chemotherapy. Crawford Long's and William Morton's discovery of the use of ether as an anesthestic, allowed surgery to become a more effective way of treating certain illnesses. Joseph Lister's advances in antiseptics made all types of medical treatment, but particularly surgery, safer. In the middle 1800s Frédéric Le Play established the importance of the case method for studying illness. And last, but of critical importance to the protection of city children, was the work of Pasteur in discovering the necessity for the pasteurization of milk that was sold in cities.

Milk stations

Beginning in 1885 with the publication of medical and scientific papers on the relationship between the health of children and bad milk, two general approaches adopted to assure that the milk sold was not pathogenic. One was pasteurization to kill the unwanted bacteria, and the other was the certification of milk distributed by dairies which maintained sanitary standards. With the discovery of the relationship of milk to infant sickness and death, philanthropic individuals and groups undertook programs to save the lives of children. Milk stations and depots were established at which safe milk was sold below cost and in many instances was given away. At first, these milk depots were

privately financed and supported, but in 1897 Rochester, New York, established the first municipally operated milk station, and other cities soon followed. This saved the lives of many infants. Beginning in 1880, infant mortality in New York City steadily decreased. These discoveries in the area of health care and medicine vividly illustrate the fact that advances in social welfare must often wait on the growth of knowledge (Bremner, 1971, pp. 817–1003).

Public health

In addition to the advances in knowledge mentioned above, there was growing attention to public health matters. Less than a year after the Civil War, New York passed a law creating a Metropolitan Sanitary District and a Board of Health to help preserve "life and health and to prevent the spread of disease" (Bremner, 1971, pp. 817–1003). In 1869 Massachusetts established the State Board of Health and Vital Statistics, the first permanent state health department. By 1877, 14 more states had established state health departments. These state agencies served both as educational forums in matters of health, working to secure the adoption of health legislation, and as repositories of facts on the health of state citizens.

In 1892 Herman M. Biggs organized the first municipal department of pathology and bacteriology, in the New York City Health Department. Biggs waged an active war against tuberculosis, attempting to help people understand that the disease was contagious and not hereditary, as was generally thought. Tuberculosis was a plague of the city tenements that was to continue unabated into the 20th century. Tubercular people lived in close proximity with their families, crowded together in small rooms, so the disease spread. Members of families with tubercular people were often employed in the needle trades, making clothes for sale in other parts of the city, or in food markets. These types of employment led to spread of the disease as the tuberculosis bacilli moved from host to victim on the materials. Social workers were the first professionals to become involved in tuberculosis prevention.

Health societies

The period from 1860 to 1900 was marked by a growth of special organizations and societies interested in health care. The American Public Health Association was founded in 1872; the American Association for the Study of the Feeble-minded, in 1876; and the National Association for the Deaf, in 1880. The first journal dealing specifically with the medical problems of children, the *Archives of Pediatrics,* was established in 1884, following Dr. Abraham Jacobi's establishment of the Pediatric Section of the American Medical Association in 1880. Jacobi had been appointed the first professor of children's diseases in the United States in 1860 (Bremner, 1971, pp. 811–16).

The health of children

This period was also marked by concern with the health of children. By the mid-90s most large cities had at least one children's hospital. The first state to become interested specifically in the welfare of crippled children was Minnesota, in 1897. It was followed by Massachusetts and New York. Voluntary groups found the notion of helping crippled children to be appealing.

By the end of the 19th century, public schools were beginning to be involved in the attempt to detect and control the illnesses of children and were beginning to be concerned about the safety and sanitation of the school building itself. Actually, occasional medical inspection of schoolchildren had started in the 1870s, but it was not until 1894 that organized medical examinations were begun on a regular basis. Beginning in 1895, school physicians and nurses began to be appointed to the school systems. The New York City Health Department established compulsory vaccination of schoolchildren in 1897. The health programs in the schools had three primary aims: (1) to exclude children with contagious diseases as soon as possible; (2) to detect various physical defects of schoolchildren; and (3) to correct such defects where possible (Bremner, 1971, pp. 813–15).

✑ Education

There were four major concerns in U.S. education during the latter half of the 19th century: (1) concern with the role of the federal government in education, (2) concern with the development of the American high school, (3) concern with the progressive school movement, and (4) concern with the education of the black, the immigrant, and the Indian child. Americans have always had a love-hate relationship with their public schools. Although we have been the only nation in the world that aspired to educate all children equally, we have never been able, as a people, to settle the issue of what the primary mission of the public school should be. Given the wide diversity in the backgrounds and life-styles of our people, there have always been those who would put the primary focus on the socialization role of the schools. In their view, the purpose of the public school should be to develop "one people" and a sense of national unity. But others have argued that the purpose of the schools is to train the leaders of a professional and technical society in order to operate an industrial society and assure leadership for the nation. And yet others have claimed that the schools should be a means of social advancement for the gifted and ambitious children of the poorer families in society. All of these notions relate to social values.

The progressive movement

The progressive movement in education which began at the turn of the century was a protest against the use of the schools to implant social values apart from concern with the actual individual needs of the children who attended them. According to progressive philosophy, every child had instincts for constructive, creative activity that needed to be released by the educational experience in order to assure the child's best development as an individual and its commitment to a common way of life. The progressive movement asked that teachers leave behind the crude methods of rote instruction and the demand for verbal agreement and acquiescence and attempt instead to "engage the deepest emotional forces within the child" (Bremner, 1971, p. 1095). In the progressive movement in the schools we see the beginning of the same trend that we have discussed in relation to child welfare services—a trend toward a growing consideration of the needs of the child as a developing individual and toward concern with the child as a person rather than the treatment of the child as a little adult. The progressive notion of education as human development rather than training is still heatedly argued in many school districts of our country.

Federal participation in education

We have discussed in a previous chapter the development of schools in the South under the auspices of the Freedmen's Bureau. This was the first federal agency in the area of education. Educators had been interested for some time in the possibility of the establishment of a federal office of education which would serve as collector and disseminator of information and ideas about school systems and methods of education. Given the prevailing interest in the development of the school systems of the South, it was possible to establish a national office of education soon after the Civil War. On March 2, 1867, an act establishing a federal Department of Education was passed by Congress. Henry Barnard was appointed the first commissioner of the department.

Despite the interest in education and the establishment of the Department of Education in 1867 (not given Cabinet rank until 1979, and, indeed, merely a part of the Department of Health, Education, and Welfare until 1979), between 1870 and 1890 Congress failed to pass bills proposing federal support for education. The federal government had in the past supported specific educational measures for specific groups, and would continue to do so in the future, but no national educational policy was formulated, nor was any direct federal influence exercised on educational policy. The Ordinance of 1785 had set the precedent for making federal lands available for the establishment of

schools in the territories, and the Morrill Act of 1862 had aided the northern states in establishing colleges. Federal funds were utilized to support the education of Indian children and were later made available for agricultural and vocational education. But the control of the various state and local bodies over the common public schools was to remain intact (Bremner, 1971, p. 1260).

The public high school

The need to provide a more immediately useful training to the majority of American teenagers than was supplied by the private academies led to the establishment of public high schools within the structure of public education between 1866 and 1932. The first public school for boys only had been established in Boston in 1820. By 1850 about half the Massachusetts towns were providing for such schools. In Michigan the legal right of school districts to levy taxes for the support of high schools was upheld by the Michigan Supreme Court. Thus, slowly, was the public high school open to both sexes developed. It must be remembered, however, that attendance at the public high schools was not compulsory. A study done after the turn of the century by George S. Counts of Columbia showed that there was a close relationship between parental occupation and attendance in secondary schools.

The education of black children

In both the North and the South we find problems in admitting black children to equal educational experiences with white children. Among the problems were the following: (1) a large majority of teachers were white and did not understand the culture or aspirations of the blacks, though thousands of concerned white persons, selfless and dedicated for the most part, were committed to free and equal education for blacks; (2) there was resistance to the integration of the schools in both the North and the South; and (3) there was disagreement about the type of education that should be offered to black children. Should blacks be offered the same range of education as was offered to middle-class white children (lower-class whites were often given more limited educational choices), or should their education be confined to vocational training? The black leader Booker T. Washington, president of Tuskegee Institute in Alabama and influential among white groups, strongly advocated industrial and domestic training for blacks, believing that this would prepare them for immediate entry into the job market and thus for economic progress on which social progress could be built (Bennett, 1964, pp. 274–77).

Integrated schools in the South were largely abandoned during the last half of the 19th century, though many of the southern state constitutions called for such schools. Massachusetts had abolished legal segregation of its schools before the Civil War, but other northern states were in no haste to follow suit. By the beginning of the 20th century no state constitution required that the state offer separate educational experiences to blacks and whites, but in many states the question school integration was left to the localities. And even in states whose laws prohibited discrimination, the segregation of blacks in ghetto areas in many cities resulted in substantially separate and unequal education for blacks and whites. There are records of black parents suing, usually unsuccessfully, for the admission of their children to white schools (Bremner, 1971, pp. 1292–1317).

In 1896, in the case of *Plessy* v. *Ferguson,* the Supreme Court upheld the doctrine of racial separation and classification, declaring that the establishment of separate but equal accommodations of blacks was a reasonable exercise of state power. Thus, we have today a heritage of over 125 years of separate but unequal opportunities in education for blacks.

The education of immigrants

For most of the immigrants who came to America, the schools were the gateway to the opportunities and rewards of American life. Yet the immigrants themselves had little input into what their children should be learning or what the school pro-

grams should be. The question that concerned school authorities was whether schools should operate to teach a conformity to the American way of life, even though that way of life was but poorly defined, or whether schools should seek to preserve independent cultures, teaching a broadened tolerance for all. Most educators believed in unity, and most schools operated to socialize all of their students to the American way.

The American Indians and their schools

When it came to the Indian child, the government "conceived of its task as that of civilizing savages" (Bremner, 1971, p. 1238). Officials did not show respect for the culture of the Indian and were insensitive to the conflicts and frustrations of Indian life. Certainly there was no consultation with Indian leaders as to the needs of their children. Instead, it was assumed that Indian children could and should be taught the same things in the same way as white children even though this often represented a denial of the needs and the past of the Indian children. As with blacks, there was a tendency to emphasize industrial and domestic training for Indian children in the hope of giving these children useful skills while saving the government money.

One of the cruelest practices in the education of Indian children was the requirment that they leave their homes and families and spend most of the year at a far-off boarding school. Often, police had to be sent to Indian homes to round up children and take them to school. By the close of the 19th century, many educators involved in the education of Indian children were beginning to recognize the failure of this type of education and were urging the establishment of a greater number of day schools for Indian children.

With the recognition of the need for education of three groups of children—the blacks, the immigrants, and the Indians—American schools confronted the issue of whether American culture should be pluralistic or unitary and what voice parents should have in the education of their children.

The issue was generally resolved in the direction of a unitary culture, with the shape of education determined by the educator. The only difference between the education offered the children of blacks, immigrants, and Indians, and the children of middle-class white Americans was that the education of the former was less adequate and "more practical" in that it presumably led to early employment. Today we are still struggling with some of these questions.

✎§ Adult corrections

During the second half of the 19th century, the number and variety of the institutions developed to deal with offenders of various ages increased greatly, but so did the problems faced by such institutions. Except in the deep South, state governments established separate reform schools for boys and girls and separate reformatories for young men and women (ages 16 to 30) who were first offenders, apart from the state prison system. Beginning with the Elmira, New York, Reformatory in 1869, many of these institutions began to use the indeterminate sentence. The basic concept of this type of sentence was that the convict's behavior would determine the length of his or her stay in prison. Some of these institutions also used the system of rewarding good behavior within the prison.

In 1876 Zebulon R. Brockway assumed the administration of the New York State Reformatory at Elmira. Upon becoming superintendent, Brockway sought to rehabilitate the inmates by a system that rewarded good behavior by tangible benefits and a reduced stay in the institution. Brockway explained that the rehabilitation of prisoners should be judged solely by their behavior and should not "trespass on the mystical field of the soul's moral relations" (Brockway, 1912). This emphasis on the observable behavior rather than the spiritual reformation of the offender through silence and penitence was a major change in correctional philosophy. Brockway contended that his method was "scientific" (Hawes, 1971, pp. 146–49).

Developments in criminology

The primary papers relating to social problems in America were those given at the National Conference of Charities and Corrections by philanthropists and social workers who remained essentially practical rather than theoretical in their orientation (Bruno, 1948, pp. 7–8). At the 1885 meeting of the Conference, William T. Harris, who later became the U.S. commissioner of education, presented a paper in which he held that crime was the result of the failure of society to effectively socialize the individual (National Conference of Charities and Corrections, 1885, pp. 228–40). In 1886 J. C. Hite, the superintendent of the Ohio Boys' Industrial School, presented a paper in which he told the delegates to the Conference that delinquent children were those whose characters were weakened by the influence of poor and evil surroundings (NCCC, 1886, p. 59).

Hite had taken a position on a theme that generated many arguments in the late 1800s—which was more important in determining human character, heredity or environment? Although at times the delegates to the Conference stressed the importance of heredity, in general, seeing no way to overcome the effects of heredity, they preferred to consider envirnomental factors the deciding ones in human development. Most of the delegates seemed to agree with Peter Caldell when he said: "Every delinquent child is a living indictment of society's neglect and indifference; and when he becomes old enough to realize the full consequence of his neglect, it cannot be surprising that he should feel justified in . . . getting even" (NCCC, 1898, pp. 407–13).

However, there were those who stressed the importance of heredity as a cause of crime and pauperism. One of the earliest and most well known of these was Richard Dugdale, a member of the executive committee of the New York Prison Association, who published a study of the Jukes family, a family with an unusually large number of members who became insane, criminals, or prostitutes. Dugdale's work was an important contribution to American sociology, and though imma-ture, it marked the beginning of the application of the scientific method to the study of criminology in the United States.

⊰§ Juvenile corrections

During the years between the Civil War and the turn of the century, there was considerable public debate about the increasing problem of juve-nile delinquency. The number and variety of reform schools increased greatly, but the rapidly develop-ing institutions were not without their problems. The need for heavy taxes to pay off the costs of the war, plus the need for increased funds for other rapidly growing state social services, meant that the reform schools were subject to increasing pres-sure to earn part of their own income by contracting out the labor of inmates to local manufacturers (Bremner, 1971, p. 439). As a rule, manufacturers had complete control of the children during the working hours, and instances of exploitation and brutality were not uncommon. Occasionally the children retaliated.

Rioting, arson, and even murder were far from unknown in the juvenile reform schools. In May 1872 the boys working in one of the shoe shops at the New York House of Refuge revolted and stabbed the foreman and his assistant. It took two companies of police to put down the riot that fol-lowed. In 1877 the superintendent of the Massa-chusetts girls' reform school reported that one of the oldest buildings on the grounds had been set on fire by two of the girls (Hawes, 1971, pp. 42–55).

Increasingly, concerned citizens and officials recognized the failure of the reform schools and efforts were mounted to improve the life led inside the schools and to find better ways of treating delin-quent children so that less of them would be sent to the reform schools. Two groups were specifically concerned about the contract system—the unions, which feared the competition of the inmates' labor, and the reformers, who were concerned about the children's welfare. Special legislative committees

were appointed to investigate the abuses in the contract labor system in New York (1871) and Pennsylvania (1876). With the establishment of the State Boards of Charities some improvements were made, as the reform schools came under the yearly inspection of these boards in the various states.

Investigation of the reform schools

William Pryor Letchworth, appointed to the New York State Board of Charities in 1872, decided to devote his work to the investigation and better-ment of children's institutions. We have already discussed his efforts to get children out of the alms-houses. Once that was accomplished, he turned his attention to the reform schools. In 1879 he began investigating the New York House of Refuge and similar institutions. In an effort to learn more about the care of delinquent children, he took a trip to Europe. He returned full of admiration for the cottage or family system of managing reforma-tories. He had two primary concerns about Ameri-can children's reformatories. One was the use of the contract system, and the other was the failure of the institution to make proper arrangements to provide follow-up services for those discharged. In 1884, as president of the State Board of Charities, Letchworth was able to influence the legislature to outlaw contract labor in the reform schools, and the next year he was one of the leaders in the establishment of the Western House of Refuge at Rochester, New York, the first reform institution to offer a comprehensive plan of vocational educa-tion (Bremner, 1971, pp. 439–40).

Private agencies for delinquent children

The slow rate at which improvements in the public reform schools were effected was often dis-couraging to even the strongest of the reformers. Consequently, private institutions designed to save children from the reform schools as well as from crime began to appear.

One of the earliest of these institutions was the New York Catholic Protectory, founded in 1863 to care for children from 7 to 14 who might be sent to it by the courts or by their parents. The protectory became the largest institution for delinquent and paradelinquent or neglected children in the United States.

In 1890 William R. George, a New York businessman, took a group of city slum children to his country farm for the summer. This led to the establishment of the George Junior Republic. Boys coming to the farm lived in cottages whose accommodations varied in quality from the very Spartan to relative luxury. The boys paid for their food and lodging with "Republic" money earned by work at the institution. Even school lessons were done by contract. George gradually came to believe that the solution to delinquency was to create a microcosm of American society in which boys were responsible to one another and in which the values of self-help were strongly reinforced. At the Republic, proper behavior and hard work led to tangible rewards. The goal was to have the "citizens" learn a more acceptable social behavior pattern than they had demonstrated previously (Hawes, 1971, pp. 154–56).

Another private institution was the Burnham Industrial Farm, established in 1887. Burnham, a wealthy New York lawyer, established what was later to be known as the Berkshire Industrial Farm for delinquent and neglected boys. Women's organizations in several states, starting with Illinois in 1879, established industrial schools for girls who were on the verge of delinquency and needed a year or so of residential training. A somewhat similar institution serving boys from a class of families that could afford to pay its charges was the private military school, which was established to help relieve families of the burden of bringing up difficult boys.

Before we leave the discussion of reform schools we need to mention the establishment of the Virginia Manual Labor School. The South had progressed little in developing institutions for children in trouble with the law. Most such children were blacks, and the only institutions to which they could be sent were the local jails or the prisons. Conditions in the prisons were so bad that juveniles were often pardoned to avoid sending them there (Bremner, 1971, pp. 443–45). However, in 1897 the Virginia Manual Labor School, a private institution, was established to serve delinquent black boys. It came about as the result of efforts by John Henry Smyth, a freeborn black who held a law degree from Howard University. Smyth had taught in the Pennsylvania public schools and had served under President Hayes as our minister to Liberia. After his return from diplomatic service he became editor of the *Reformer,* a newspaper in Richmond, Virginia, and he began to devote much of his time to getting black children out of the Virginia jails. The first private reform institution in the South was the result of this effort.

Probation

As we have seen, the use of probation began in Massachusetts with the efforts of John Augustus in 1841. By the time of his death, in 1859, Augustus had demonstrated the worth of his system of probation. Other volunteers carried on his work for another ten years until the state brought the practice under its control and supervision. In 1869 the Massachusetts General Court passed an act which established the office of state visiting agent. This person, appointed by the governor, was to act as the supervisor for all children who became "wards of the state." He (the first state agents were men) was responsible for supervising the care and welfare of all children who were placed in charge of any individual by the state institutions and all indentured or adopted children. He was also to serve the delinquent child by appearing "in behalf of the child" at all hearings "held for the purpose of committing children to the state reform schools," and he was to act as the probation officer for delinquent children who were allowed to remain in the community (Hawes, 1971, p. 176).

Separate court hearings for children

In 1870 the Massachusetts General Court changed the accountability of the state visiting agent, placing him under the supervision of the

State Board of Charities. This act was very important because of provision which provided for separate hearings for children accused of delinquent acts. Outside Boston, children under 16 were to be tried before probate judges, and in the city their cases were to be heard separately from the other business of the court. This system of separate trials and probation for juvenile offenders worked very well. Most of the cases concerning children were heard in the afternoon, after the judge had disposed of adult criminal cases. The judge usually heard these cases "in chambers," with only the state visiting agent or his deputy present, and he usually accepted the agent's recommendation as to the disposition of the child. In 1871 the agent or his deputy appeared in 1,463 cases involving children under 17. Of these children, 1,169 "were found guilty and the agent arranged to have 584 of them placed out in families on probation" (Hawes, 1971, p. 176). Although the Massachusetts treatment of juveniles appeared to be successful, the system had spread to only two other states—Michigan and California—by 1899, when the first juvenile court was established in Chicago.

The juvenile court

With the movement from concern with the punishment of wrongdoers to concern with their reform and their return to society as productive members, with the growth in understanding of the needs of children as distinct from those of adults, and with the new humanism that was beginning to develop in many groups, it was probably inevitable that the time would come for a fundamental change in the treatment of children by the courts. That change came in Chicago on July 1, 1899, when the first juvenile court met.

Authority, structure, and function. The "Ladies of Chicago" (Hawes, 1971, p. 158), who could be considered the founders of the juvenile court, began their efforts, as did many reformers of the time, with a concern for keeping juvenile delinquents away from adult criminals. However, these "Ladies of Chicago" secured the passage of a law that did a great deal more than that. "It

provided for a new and unique institution . . . clearly the most important agency to deal with juvenile delinquents created in the nineteenth century" (Hawes, 1971, p. 159). On the surface, the Illinois juvenile court law appeared to combine the Massachusetts concept of probation with several New York laws providing for special detention plans and trials for juveniles. In fact, however, the juvenile court concept was a radical departure from these earlier developments in that it established an entirely new type of court. The new court was explicitly designated a chancery, or noncriminal court of equity. Thus, by its very nature the juvenile court was assumed to be acting in the best interests of the child. The court acquired its right to intervene in children's lives from the right of the state to exercise parental power over children *(parens patriae)* Acting as a good parent within a child-parent relationship, the new court did not need to be as concerned with due process or the child's legal rights as did the criminal courts, which had been established primarily to protect the public, rather than to protect the individual before the court.

The legality of the new court was upheld in a number of challenges to its constitutionality, and the chancery nature of its proceedings rendered it impregnable, in its first half century of existence, to the charge that it denied children of their legal rights. The concept known as *parens patriae* was originally developed in law for the purposes of dealing with matters of property and wardship—to protect the property rights of incompetents. By adopting this concept in relationship to the delinquent child, the founders of the juvenile court were hoping to move the emphasis of the courts from what the child had done to what should be done to aid the child (Rosenheim, 1974). "Thus, from the outset, the child welfare and the crime control functions of the juvenile court were intertwined" (Rosenehim, 1974, p. 166).

Critics of today's juvenile court suggest the possibility that children's vulnerability is being used to justify the imposition of plans which have the underlying purpose, not of child protection, but of enforcing court-approved standards of juvenile behavior. It is certainly desperately important for social workers employed by the juvenile court to recognize that acts which they perceive as benevolent and rehabilitative may, and perhaps most often are, perceived by the child as punitive. And, further, it is possible that the notion of presumed benevolence and protection of the child is being used to hide underlying invasions of the rights of the child.

We need to recognize that *every child in our society* is subject to the jurisdiction of the juvenile court. The juvenile court, which began as a humanitarian reform, can well be perceived as the most powerful agent of behavior control that our society has constructed. The principal features of the juvenile court are: (1) nonadversarial, informal proceedings replace adversarial trials to determine guilt; (2) indictments are replaced by petitions; (3) the rules of evidence are suspended and are largely replaced by experts' reports; (4) the concept of the child's "need" replaces the use of narrowly defined laws of evidence; and (5) a "fatherly judge and concerned probation officers" replace the usual lawyers, clerks, and bailiffs of the traditional court (Rosenheim, 1974, pp. 169–70).

The founding of the juvenile court. In the last half of the 1800s, there were, for all practical purposes, no institutions especially set up to deal with juvenile delinquents in the city of Chicago. Young offenders were taken to the same courts, subjected to the same procedures, and confined in the same cells as adult criminals of all types. Or else, faced with a minor offense, committed by a very young child, police simply let the child go rather than subject it to what they saw as an inhuman experience. However, some Chicagoans were trying to halt the increase in juvenile delinquency and at the same time to protect the children of the city from negative experiences. The Waif's Mission sought to eliminate vagrancy; the Chicago Visitation and Aid Society (a Catholic charity) offered help to "street children"; and the Visitation and Aid Society worked hard, but unsuccessfully, to pass "a bill for an act to authorize corporations not for pecuniary profit to manage, care and provide for children who may be abandoned, neglected, destitute or subjected to perverted training," which would have provided for the commitment of neglected or delinquent children to private agency care under court supervision, rather than sending them to jail (Bremner, 1971, p. 505).

In 1888 the Chicago Women's Club became interested in doing something about delinquent children. The club started its effort by calling for a strict enforcement of the Illinois act of 1883 making school attendance compulsory. It persuaded the authorities to add jail matrons who would serve women and children. It also maintained a school for children in the jails. In 1892 the club supported the creation of a separate court for children, but it could not arouse support for the proposal. However, it did secure the establishment of a manual training school for boys within the adult penal institution who had been sentenced to the House of Correction (Bremner, 1971, pp. 504–24).

This only marked the beginning of the organized effort to reform the treatment of juvenile offenders. The efforts of the Chicago Bar Association were enlisted, and an investigation of the Cook County grand jury urged improvement in the treatment of children. The 1898 meeting of the Illinois State Conference of Charities devoted its entire proceedings to the problem. "From this Conference emerged the committee which drafted the Illinois Juvenile Court Act" (Lathrop, 1925, pp. 290–95). On July 1, 1899, the first juvenile court of the nation was established by action of the Illinois legislature as a result of the hard work of the members of the Chicago Women's Club, the State Conference of Charities and Corrections, the Chicago Bar Association, Hull House, and the Visitation and Aid Society. It was hoped by the bill's supporters that this action would mark the end of the penal approach to juvenile delinquency and the beginning of a flexible, scientific, and preventive approach.

The operation of the first juvenile court. When the first juvenile court began to operate in 1899, with Judge Richard S. Tuthill presiding, there were many details to work out. One of the first was the problem of housing children who needed shelter while awaiting court hearings. The Illinois Industrial Association, a children's charity, offered to house such children for 20 cents a day. This plan was agreed to. Not until the beginning of the 20th century did the court have its own detention facility.

In disposing of the children before his court, Judge Tuthill had a number of options open to him, but he much preferred to use probation. However, probation obviously required probation officers. The juvenile court law had provided for probation officers, but it had specifically stipulated that these officers must be volunteers. Thus, the court that had to depend on private charity for a detention facility also had to depend on volunteers to do what was perhaps its most important work.

There were probably several reasons for the requirement that probation officers be volunteers: social work was just beginning to be recognized as a profession; the use of volunteers for philanthropic work had a long history in American society; and the supporters of the act probably wanted to ease the legislators' fears about the cost of the new court. But the notion that volunteers would be able to give the effort, time, and thought demanded by children on probation proved to be totally inoperable. Alzina P. Stevens, a member of the Hull House staff, had for some time been acting informally as a probation officer through an arrangement under which the police in the Hull House district released selected children to her care. Judge Tuthill now appointed her the city's first probation officer, and Lucy L. Flower of the Chicago Women's Club arranged to have some of her friends pay Stevens's salary. But more probation officers were needed. The Chicago Women's Club agreed to pay the necessary salaries, and the next year six probation officers were serving the court. Timothy D. Hurley of the Visitation and Aid Society became the chief probation officer, and the police department was prevailed upon to assign some of its officers to the juvenile court to function as probation officers (Hawes, 1971, pp. 167–88).

It is interesting to note that the first probation officer in the juvenile court was both a social worker and a woman. The first chief probation officer was also a social worker. In the development of the juvenile court since its founding, many questions have been raised about the use of social workers as probation officers and women became a distinct minority of juvenile court workers.

One may think of the criminal justice process as a continuum with the offense at one end and the societal action relating to the convicted offender at the other end. Along this continuum one finds the reporting of the offense, the investigation of the offense, the arrest of a suspected offender, the disposition of the offender while awaiting trial, the trial, and the disposition of the offender following the trial in whatever manner was called for by the trial. During the 19th century, as we have seen, intervention to help or reform children occurred at several points on the continuum. Through his program of placing the children he saw a vulnerable to becoming offenders, Charles Loring Brace sought to prevent offenses. The various agencies that set up the early Houses of Refuge sought to modify the punishments imposed after offenses had been committed. John Augustus also tried to modify the final step by substituting a new experience for the usual imprisonment. Then came a series of efforts to modify the middle of the process by establishing separate detention facilities and separate trials for child offenders. Now we have a major reform in the court itself.

❧ Summary

We have finished tracing the development of social welfare services and institutions during the last half of the 19th century. The 30 or so years between the end of the Civil War and the turn of the century were a period in which the foundation for the reform movements of the early 20th century was being laid rapidly. The young women and men who were active in bringing change in the late 1880s lived into the 20th century and were to become even more influential and effective as time went on.

These were years in which knowledge of the growth, development, and needs of individuals began to grow rapidly. During these years we also learned much about the social, economic, psychological, and health needs of all people. The use of the case method of study and the inductive method of reasoning was introduced into study of health and human behavior. Critical health knowledge on such matters as pasteurization, antiseptics, and the germ theory of disease began to be disseminated through the news professional associations and the new professional journals that were developing.

During this period, women were active in the social services and in nursing. Much of the active reform leadership in the last decades of the 19th century came from women, and their work was to become even more important in the early years of the 20th century. The notion of "scientific charity," generally meaning a new managerial and organizational system, offered hope of controlling the spread of delinquency throughout the United States. However, there was also a growing concern for people whose lives were different from those of the philanthropists. There was a beginning realization that those who would help others need first to learn about the dreams, hopes, and troubles of those others. With the growth of both public and private aid, there began to be some conflict between the individuals working in the two systems. Members of private agency staffs held most of the leadership positions and were often skeptical of public assistance.

Social work has its professional roots in this period. Although scattered individuals had been paid agents of charities before this time, it became evident at this time that the development of knowledge and skill in the social services could not be left to volunteers but needed full-time attention. The National Conference of Charities and Corrections, the first national social work organization, had great impact on many of the social developments of the time. A beginning was made in professional education for social workers.

An important social work development of the period was the establishment of the State Boards of Charities. This set certain patterns of state organization and control. The boards became powerful advocates for reform. They demonstrated the importance of the social investigation as a method of collecting data that could be used as the foundation for social change. Perhaps the institutions lagged behind other areas of social welfare during the last decades of the 19th century. Established earlier, with the best of intentions, many institutions were not fulfilling the dreams and hopes of their founders. They were often overcrowded and poorly funded. Our growing understanding of the needs of people was also leading us to question the continued development of institutional care.

✑§ A look ahead

We are now ready to move into the 20th century, the century of the welfare state. At the beginning of this century, reform proceeds more rapidly than it did during the period we have just studied. But before we move on, it might be well to pause and consider where we are. Much of the knowledge and technology that makes our life relatively secure, comfortable, disease-free, and long began to be developed during this period—less than 100 years ago. Sometimes we think that change comes slowly, and in terms of the needs of any individual it does, but considering the social welfare programs and policies of 100 years ago and those of today should make us aware of the rapid pace of change.

✑§ Study questions

1. Select a book relating to a specific movement or to the development of an agency program from the reading list, and outline the material, using the Framework for Analysis at the end of Chapter 6 as much as possible

2. How did the concept of *parens patriae* in the juvenile court affect the procedures of the court? Find out how the juvenile court in your community operates.

3. The National Conference on Charities and Corrections has always published its official proceedings. Find the earliest issue of these proceedings available to you, preferably one for a year before 1900, and compare the types of problems discussed in that issue with the types discussed in the official proceedings of the last two or three years. Today's proceedings are published under the title *The Social Welfare Forum.*

4. The early settlement leaders, as well as other reformers, strongly favored compulsory education. What institutional functions did they see education as performing in our society? Go back to Chapters 3 and 4 and review the functions of institutions in our society.

5. Many of the early social welfare reforms have not seemed to fulfill the promise that their advocates thought they had. Why do you think that some of these reforms failed to achieve their promise.

⧓ Selected readings

Bremner, Robert H.   *Children and Youth in America: A Documentary History* Vol. 2:*1866–1932.* Cambridge, Mass.: Harvard University Press, 1971.

Vol. 1 of this book has been recommended in earlier chapters. As was done for earlier chapters, we recommend that students read a selection of the original documents collected here that deal with the programs we have discussed in this chapter.

Pumphrey, Ralph E., and Pumphrey, Muriel W.   *The Heritage of American Social Work.* New York: Columbia University Press, 1961.

This book, like the one mentioned above, is a collection of documents from the past. We recommend that students read selected materials found in this book, especially those found in chap. 17–26. The manual for visitors to the poor found on pages 176–78 is especially interesting as a base for class discussion.

Rich, Margaret E.   *A Belief in People: A History of Family Social Work.* New York: Family Service Association of America, 1956.

An excellent source on the development of family agencies. We recommend the reading of the first four chapters as an expansion of our present chapter.

Bruno, Frank J.   *Trends in Social Work, 1875–1956.* New York: Columbia University Press, 1957.

The material in the first 12 chapters of this book furnishes students with a good overview of the late 19th century through its analysis of the proceedings of the Conference on Charities and Corrections.

Schorr, Alvin L.   *Children and Decent People.* New York: Columbia University Press and Basic Books, 1974.

We recommend that students read chaps. 1–3 and chap. 7. These chapters raise many questions about the programs that began to develop during this period of our social welfare history. The chapters recommended should sharpen the students' analytic power as they read this chapter and those to come.

Chapter 17 ❧

❧ Reform and reaction, 1900–1930 ❧

The first two decades of the 20th century were marked by growth and change. Two components of this growth and change were the influx of immigrants to the big cities of America, and the increasing militancy of women—against both employment and socio-legal discrimination.

The photo., *top left,* shows an Italian immigrant family at Ellis Island, New York. *Top right,* young women meet at Union Headquarters during the New York City Shirtwaist Workers' Strike of 1910. Suffragettes and their supporters converge on the White House in the *bottom photo.*

❧ Introduction

In the last two chapters we traced the development of the social welfare programs and policies, and the social forces that supported those programs and policies, from the Civil War until the beginning of the 20th century. Actually, the time division that we made at the century mark is an artificial one, as the atmosphere that led to the reform movements of the first two decades of the 20th century really began with the Progressivism of the 1890s. And the period that we are treating in the present chapter could well be divided into two parts—the reform movements of the years from 1900 to 1920 and the reaction that followed World War I.

The most critical belief that guided the reforms of this era was the growing conviction that poverty and other social ills within American society could actually be abolished. This conviction flowed naturally from the belief that the social causes of poverty could be discovered through the use of the scientific method and rooted out; and the individual causes of poverty were to be dealt with by providing an environment that supported the development of good character in people. Most of the Progressive reform movements that we will be tracing were dedicated to these ends. Campaigns for better housing, public health, stricter child labor laws, compulsory education laws, more adequate protection for women working in industry, compensation for accidents at work, and even the Prohibition Amendment were parts of a concentrated attack on poverty and the causes of human misery (Bremner, 1956, p. 201).

❧ Forces for reform

Why did this abrupt movement forward occur at this particular time in our history? What factors coalesced to produce 30 years of development that in retrospect appear to have been one of the most fruitful epochs of our national life?

Prosperity and peace

One reason is that the two decades preceding our entry into World War I were relatively, though not uninterruptedly, prosperous. For an increasing proportion of our population, these were happy years marked by a rapid rise in the standard of living that led to a growing confidence on the part of all people that old evils could be abolished, that an abundant and more wholesome society would be developed, and that the *price of such a society could be borne by the country without demanding significant sacrifice of anyone.* Another reason was that the energies of our nation were no longer tied up in the arguments over the right of states to leave the Union. Although the role of the various levels of government, and even of government itself, in protecting the average citizen was far from settled, the federal government's right to govern had been significantly strengthened.

Scientific method, knowledge, and technology

In addition, the growth of methods of scientific inquiry added significantly to our knowledge about the developmental needs of human beings and to our knowledge about the interaction of social factors to produce good or evil in human life. Further, the movement toward inductive thinking and experimentation led to a rapidly developing technology, so that human labor was able to produce processed goods far beyond anything dreamed of 25 years earlier. There was a rapid growth in the belief that scientific inquiry could reveal the sources of human misery to us and that we could then construct the technology to deal with them. During the period from 1900 to 1930, we did not recognize that the social values and philosophies of the past still had a strong grip on our emotions as distinct from our knowledge, that international events would influence domestic advancement, and that our economic system as it was then constructed was more fragile than we thought.

Women's leadership

Women of education and social position played leading roles in the development of the institution of social welfare in these first decades of the 20th century. They brought to their efforts the conviction that no matter what the moral strengths and the coping skills of the individual, barriers were often constructed by the attitudes and decrees of social groups that could not be breached by an individual alone. As a minority group in society which had discovered that the gates of opportunity were closed against them as a group, no matter what their individual qualities and characteristics, they were aware of the invincibility of such barriers. Their position was different from that of the male social welfare leaders of 50 years before. These male leaders came to the human service area after marked achievements in other areas of life, achievements that had convinced them that since they had made a successful life from an original start in poverty, anyone could do likewise.

Social work and reform

And the last, and critical, force toward social reform came from the new profession of social work, a profession that was largely begun and nourished by the women referred to above. "Labor unions, women's clubs, religious and academic organizations, and various civic associations all made vitally important contributions to the reform movement, but none of these groups was more consistently active" and more effective than the social workers (Bremner, 1956, p. 202). Charity agents and settlement residents were regularly to be found in the forefront of social welfare movements (toward reform), not so much because they believed in radical philosophies as because they were so keenly aware of the necessity for improving the social conditions in which their clients or their neighbors lived.

The social workers were better informed, not only intellectually but emotionally, than most persons about the actual situation of the poor in this land of opportunity. In the early years of the 19th century the "friendly visitors" of the charitable associations sought to uplift the poor by teaching them the ways of temperance and frugality. In the middle years of the 19th century the Charity Organization societies attempted to educate the well-to-do away from indiscriminate almsgiving to satisfy their own impulses and toward more scientific philanthropic practices in the interests of the receivers of aid. Now, at the beginning of the 20th century, without giving up their efforts to develop better methods in serving the individual in need, many social workers became propagandists of high living standards for all and crusaders for social justice. They were no longer exclusively "preceptors of the poor and advisors of the rich and became, instead, teachers of a more wholesome way of life to the entire community" (Bremner, 1956, p. 202).

The fact that social workers were so often found in the leadership positions of reform movements and that so many reform movements were begun by leaders of the National Conference of Charities and Corrections probably helps explain the pragmatic character of early 20th-century liberalism. The aim of the social work profession was well expressed in a slogan carried on the cover of a philanthropic journal, "Charity today may be justice tomorrow." These aims might be visionary, but the methods by which the social work profession moved to implement them were neither utopian nor radical.

By temperament and experience, caseworkers and settlement residents were convinced that persuasion and education were the most effective methods for obtaining improvements in social institutions. They tended to emphasize the harmony rather than the conflict of class interests, seeking to bridge the chasm between righ and poor. And these efforts led to two decades of some of the greatest social advances that America has ever known—not that utopian goals were achieved but that real changes were initiated.

The social workers held "the greatest good for the greatest number" to be too vague an ideal to serve as a guide to programs of action. "Their approach was just the opposite. Abolish the misery of the most miserable, they counseled, and repeat the process as long as want and suffering persist" (Bremner, 1956, p. 203). Individual social workers represented many different shades of political opinion, including socialism. In their professional capacity, however, they were practicing humanitarians,

not doctrinaire advocates of any particular economic system. Hence their appeal was to altruism rather than to ideology. They were content with piecemeal pragmatic progress.

Population, immigration, and urbanization

Between 1900 and 1930 the population of the United States increased by 46.8 million persons to reach 123 million. During these same years the total number of persons living in urban areas increased by 38 million persons, to a total of 69 million. By 1900, 40 percent of the U.S. population lived in urban areas; by 1930, this proportion had grown to 56 percent. Part of the shift from an agricultural to a predominantly urban society was brought about by a steady migration of young people from the farm areas to the cities. This was true for both the black and the white population. For the United States as a whole, 27 percent of the black population and 49 percent of the white population lived in urban areas in 1910; by 1930, 44 percent of the black population and 58 percent of the white population lived in urban areas. In 1900, there was a heavy concentration of black population in the rural areas of the South. In the northern and western parts of the country, blacks, though a smaller part of the population, lived largely in the cities. After 1915, as blacks were increasingly forced off the farms of the South by the growth of agricultural mechanization, they moved increasingly into the cities of the North (Jennings, 1926). This movement increased during the war years, when jobs were plentiful in northern industries.

During the period 1900–1930 the United States absorbed almost 20 million immigrants. By far, the bulk of this movement of people into the country took place in the first 15 years of the century, when 14.5 million people came, many from southern and eastern Europe. In the peak year, 1907, 1,285,000 newcomers arrived at Ellis Island (Jennings, 1926, p. 554). Approximately 75 percent of the immigrants to America stayed in the cities. This rapid population growth in the cities meant a booming construction industry, but it also meant many other

things to America. The balance of power was shifting rapidly from rural areas to the cities; the great
fortunes were to be made in the cities; as the free
land available for agriculture came to an end, the
cities seemed to offer better chances for the young;
the sense of growth and adventure shifted from
the frontier to the cities. Between 1920 and 1930
some 6 million people moved from farms to cities,
resulting for the first time in a net loss—1.2 million—in farm population. The agricultural frontier
was indeed closing (Axinn and Levin, 1975, pp.
115–21; Coll, 1969, pp. 63–69; Jennings, 1926,
pp. 547–65).

Immigration

The causes for the heavy immigration prior to
the outbreak of World War I were basically the
same as the causes of immigration in earlier periods. Tired of the heavy taxation, compulsory military service, unequal opportunities, and the barriers
of class distinctions, the immigrants sought better
opportunities in a new land. They tended to move
into the cities of the North and to avoid the southern states. Nearly three fourths of all the immigrants
who came to America in the first two decades of
the 20th century remained in the Middle Atlantic
and the East North Central states, and only about
one half of 1 percent of the total population of
the southern states was foreign born (Jennings,
1926, pp. 547–65).

One of the most significant movements in the
period from 1900 to 1930 was the shift in the
source of immigrants. In 1907, over 75 percent
of our immigrants came from southern and eastern
Europe, as compared with 10.5 percent in 1882.

Before we leave the discussion of immigration,
mention must be made of the Japanese and Chinese
who came to the West Coast. There was much
opposition on the part of the Westerners to this
immigration, and in 1882 the first immigration law
was passed to restrict the immigration of Chinese.
In 1907 a "gentleman's agreement" with Japan
stopped the immigration of the Japanese (Jennings,
1926, p. 556).

Immigration legislation

Most of the immigrants who came during this
period were unskilled, illiterate, non-English-speak-
ing people from southeastern Europe. The influx
of these persons resulted in a demand for literacy
tests and other restrictive legislation. Much of this
demand came from organized labor, worried because foreigners were willing to take jobs for less
than were native workers. In response to such concerns, Congress passed an immigration act in 1907,
amended in 1910, providing for a head tax of $4
on each immigrant and carefully listing certain
classes of people who were excluded, such as idiots, imbeciles, the feebleminded, the insane, paupers and those likely to become such, persons with
contagious diseases, criminals, anarchists, children
under 16 except if accompanied by an adult, and
laborers who came to this country with contracts
to work for specific industries.

At the time this law was passed, the Immigration
Commission recommended that other laws be considered, among them the exclusion of all illiterates,
limitations on the numbers of certain races or na-
tionalities, and an increase in the amount of money
that the immigrant had to have in order to be admitted to the country. Laws were passed allowing for
the deportation of aliens who after arrival were
found guilty of a crime or of belonging to one of
the excluded groups on arrival. Finally, in 1921
and 1924 definitely restrictive measures was
passed. The 1924 laws set quotas for admission
limiting the number of admissible immigrants from
nations other than Mexico and Canada to 2 percent
of the given nationality living in the United States
in 1890. The laws operated to favor immigrants
from the British Isles and northern Europe and to
limit the new immigrants from southern and eastern
Europe and the Mediterranean (Jennings, 1926, pp.
557–560).

City growth and urban problems

As the growth of the industrial society accelerated, the city assumed an increasingly important
role in the ecology of America. The growth of man-

ufactures, the development of transportation facilities, the growth of urban wealth, high wages, steady employment, shorter hours, better religious and educational opportunities, and the lure of companionship and amusements drew increased numbers of people to the cities. The declining importance of agriculture, improved laborsaving farm machinery, the ambition of farm youth who began to see that the wealth was now in the cities, the superior comforts and conveniences of city life, and the system of taxation all favored city development. The American taxation system of the time operated unfavorably for the farmer, for in the city much personal property, securities, and income escaped taxation, while the farmer's personal and real property could not escape such duties. However, pauperism was far more marked in the cities than in the rural areas, though the residents of the rural areas, particularly in the South, did not escape poverty (Jennings, 1926, pp. 560–62).

In 1910, less than one fifth of New York City's population was native born. Russia, Italy, and Ireland were each the birthplace of more than 250,000 of the city's inhabitants, and Germany, Poland, and Austria were each the birthplace of more than 100,000. Immigrants to the cities, both native born and foreign born, faced several problems of adjustment and living.

In the case of the foreign-born immigrant, the move to the city meant a change in language and culture, in a whole way of living. As we have mentioned, most immigrants were forced here by the poor conditions in their own land. They were generally unskilled and from rural areas, so they were faced with the problem of adapting to city life as well as factory labor. Industrialization, with its tendency toward specialization of function, removed workers from their households, subjected them to the external discipline of the factory, made them dependent on the labor market for their existence, and tended to take away their sense of pride in individual workmanship.

Workers in the cities were no longer individuals in a community of individuals, with many and diffuse ties to meaningful others. Relationships in the urban situation tended to be more impersonal, utili-

tarian, and transitory than they had been in the rural areas from which many of these workers came. Primary group control became less effective, and both integration and social control were maintained increasingly by agencies that fell within the social welfare institution, such as the police, social agencies, and correctional institutions. These bureaucratic agencies operating by explicit and impersonal rules were difficult to understand or utilize effectively. The newly arrived city dwellers were used to having the controlling and helping functions of society maintained by internalized folkways and mores and governed by close personal relationships.

The strain on families was severe. In place of the extended family in which parents of both sexes and their children worked together for the survival of the unit and in which the labor of children also contributed to the children's education for competence in adulthood, family members now worked separately as individuals. The employer no longer had any responsibility for the well-being of workers, and, even while poverty pulled children from home and school into spending most of their waking hours in hard, dangerous, and exhausting work, the factories increasingly required education as a base for advancement. Irrelevant and inadequate school programs, geared to the wealthier, older American groups, often had curricula and teaching methods that forced children out of school and contributed to the alienation of the young. Jane Addams says that she became a member of the school board precisely because she hoped to be able to influence school programs and thus reduce a cause of delinquency (Addams, 1910). Children tended to assimilate much faster to the new and different life than did their parents, making for intergenerational conflict and a reduction in the authority and influence of the family.

The politics of the time

During the period from 1900 to 1930 the balance of political power shifted from the countryside to the urban center. It was inevitable that the center of political power would follow the movement of financial power and population. The large number of voters in the cities became important to any political leader who wanted to maintain his position. However, the social and economic vulnerability of the newcomers made them subject to political exploitation. Thus, the "big city bosses" were able to set up and control political machines that operated in the interests of certain groups while more pressing needs for housing, sanitation, fire protection, and educational facilities were ignored.

The new residents from rural communities were patterned to look for the personal response to need that the bosses provided. To secure trust and votes, the political bosses became masters at giving families direct assistance with some of their immediate problems in the complex and impersonal city. These private systems of public favors served some important functions that could not be served by impartially administered laws. The bosses got people jobs, got husbands out of jail, and did other favors, such as providing treats for children. The ward boss was often the first person at the scene of a fire, getting food, clothing, and shelter for the burned-out families without the delay and questions that would have been imposed by an investigation of the Charity Organization Society. To the people receiving such help, it was not important that the boss was able to do such favors because he offered protection to the owner of the slum firetrap in which the family had lived or that the same landlord would also provide their new and equally inadequate shelter. Immediate response to expressed small daily needs of the oppressed, rather than working toward a just administration or toward larger social reforms, was what bought power for the political bosses of the time (Riordan, 1946, pp. 46–53).

Through the boss system many state governments came to be controlled by city political machines. At the state level many economic benefits could be conferred on corporations or other interests that could reward the bosses. It was probably inevitable that settlement house workers would come into conflict with the ward boss in their area as they worked for reform. In their crusade for

better streets, or more frequent garbage service, or against vice and prostitution in their area, they discovered that a powerful combine of property owners, bankers, churchmen, and journalists was in league with the local political boss (Levine and Levine, 1970, pp. 112–15).

Settlement workers learned some other interesting things in their attempts to bring about reform through political activity. They discovered that the adolescent street gang was often both a source of support for the present bosses and a source of training and support for later political leaders. Through their gang activities, potential political leaders became streetwise and skilled in the organization and manipulation of people. They also made their reputation as successful managers among their peers who later could be counted on to join the ward clubs and offer uncritical support. They discovered that a political candidate who dressed in work clothes and acted as a representative of the people was *not likely* to be elected. People were more favorably inclined toward leaders who drank champagne and wore elegant clothes, who acted like success. People were also not greatly worried when their leaders accepted money from business leaders in the form of campaign contributions. They thought that such money was used to buy the favors they needed (Levine and Levine, 1970, pp. 112–15).

◄§ Industrial growth

The industrial explosion that followed the Civil War came to a climax during this period with the rise of the self-made entrepreneur and the national corporation. Before the last quarter of the 19th century a broader diffusion of wealth, power, and status and the smaller size of communities made it possible for men of only moderate means to be leaders in their communities. But in the early years of the 20th century the locally important small manufacturer, lawyer, and minister found themselves far overshadowed by the chief officers of great national corporations. Local persons of power and importance may not have been any poorer in terms of income and the respect of their peers, but they were far less important in determining the fate of the state or nation, or even the large city.

The new organization of industry also produced a changed relationship between employers and employees. When a little capital and a new idea were sufficient to start persons in businesses of their own, workers could feel relatively independent in their relationships with their employers. But as small businesses with small amounts of capital began to give way to huge corporations with great amounts of capital and beginning a new business began to take even larger amounts of capital, the workers of America found it increasingly difficult to influence their own financial welfare.

By the end of World War I, the United States had become the richest country on earth, a world leader in both industrial and agricultural output. The entire continent had been spanned by the railroads and the automobile, and the telephone and telegraph had become an important fact of daily living. Communication was furthered by the development of federally supported airmail routes, and radio and motion pictures were moving the nation toward cultural as well as economic unification. In the early years of the 20th century, the advancement of technology and the development of innovative managerial skills revolutionized agriculture and industry. Living standards rose rapidly. In the first 20 years of the century, the total output of manufacturing increased 273 percent. Despite brief recessions, the GNP climbed from $17 billion in 1900 to $104 billion in 1929. Allowing for price changes, the per capita GNP rose by 73 percent in the first three decades of the 20th century (Coll, 1969, p. 63).

Growth and change occurred in the organization of industry as well as in its output. These were the years when some of the largest trusts in America were formed: U.S. Steel, Standard Oil, Consolidated Tobacco, and American Smelting, among others. In spite of the government's efforts to slow down the growth of monopolies, supercorporation came to dominate anthracite coal, agricultural machinery, sugar, telephone and telegraph, iron and

steel, oil, railroads, tobacco, and copper. Also, the control of American industry shifted from individual owners to boards of directors that were often controlled by a powerful group of investment bankers. In addition, the daily operation of industry was no longer the responsibility of the individual owners but shifted to professional managers who were responsible to the boards.

In 1919, less than 4 percent of U.S. industrial establishments produced more than $1 million worth of goods, but these establishments employed more than half of the wage earners in the United States and contributed more than two thirds of the gross national product. During the period from 1900 to 1930 there was a rapid increase in productivity. For example, in 1913 it took 14 hours to assemble a car; in 1914 the job was done in 93 minutes; and by 1925 the Ford Motor Company was able to assemble an automobile every ten seconds. This was the era of the multimillionaire, as the concentration of corporate power was paralleled by a concentration of wealth and income. The growth of wealth at the top of the social structure far exceeded the growth of wealth among either the middle class or the working class. (Axinn and Levin, 1975, pp. 115–16; Coll, 1969, pp. 63–65; Jennings, 1926).

A report of the Commission on Industrial Relations for the period 1890–1912 pointed out that although personal wealth had increased 188 percent during this time, the wage earner's share of the Gross National Product had actually declined. The commission estimated that the average urban family had 5.6 members and needed an income of $700 a year to meet basic subsistence needs. However, the census data of the time showed that 79 percent of the nation's fathers earned less than this amount, so that earnings from other family members were necessary to sustain many families. In spite of the labor of wives and children, 50 to 66 percent of working-class families were poor and a third lived in "abject poverty," according to the commission. It is small wonder that the Census of 1900 showed 1,750,000 children between the ages of 10 and 15 as regularly employed and that in the following ten years this number had dropped by only 175,000. Robert Hunter, a social worker writing in 1904, estimated that 10 million urban workers were living in poverty. "Between the newly rich, with its extreme wealth, and the working class, with its extreme poverty, lay the large middle class—a group with adequate income but little to spare, a group that was increasingly dissatisfied because it could not keep pace with the rapidly rising standard of living of those on top" (Axinn and Levin, 1975, p. 118; Hunter, 1904, pp. 2–7, 56–65, 76–88, and 96–97).

Tariff and tax policy

The attitude of government during this time directly encouraged the growth of manufactures. There was no income tax. Throughout the period, the tariff laws gave protection to manufactures, and thus the government guaranteed that the continued investment of capital in industry would yield significant returns. Tariff laws that protected American goods against foreign competition by taxing goods produced outside the United States were strongly urged during the first two decades of the 20th century.

In 1909 Congress imposed a 1 percent tax on the incomes over $5,000 of all corporations formed for profit. This measure aroused considerable argument. Those who opposed the measure saw it as unduly burdensome to industries upon whose health many of the country's jobs rested, as unjustly discriminatory against business, as double taxation, as of doubtful constitutionality, and as un-American. A proposal for a general income tax amendment to the Constitution passed Congress and was submitted to the states. This amendment, the 16th, declared effective by the secretary of state on February 15, 1913, reads: "Congress shall have the power to lay and collect taxes on incomes from whatever source derived, without apportionment among the states, and without regard to any census or enumeration." Although an income tax had been used during the Civil War and attempted as part of an earlier tariff law, and although the amendment had been discussed long before its final adoption,

its imposition was not without difficulty. Many saw the income tax as an unfair tax on wealth, and the eastern section of the country believed that the new tax was the result of class and sectional discrimination (Jennings, 1926, pp. 623–24).

The trust and antitrust movement

In the last years of the 19th century and the first years of the 20th century, a new form of business organization was initiated. Groups of businessmen began to form *trusts* as a way of controlling the market and assuring profits. Eventually, some 40 companies controlled 90 to 95 percent of the country's oil-refining capacity through the use of trusts. A trust generally required that stock in any member company be held in a joint account under the control of a board of trustees that determined policies and generally held enough shares of the trust's stock to appoint the trust's officers and the directors of the trust's member companies. The Census of 1900 reported 185 industrial combinations which, though comprising less than one half of 1 percent of the country's industrial establishments, owned 15 percent of the capital, employed 8 percent of the workers, and turned out 14 percent of the manufactured product (Jennings, 1926, pp. 631–48).

Trusts came under much criticism because of their political influence, their ability to secure raw materials and transportation at lower prices than were paid by other concerns, their restraint of trade, and their monopolistic ability to control consumer prices in particular areas. After two years of congressional debate, the first of the federal statutes curbing trusts, the Sherman Anti-Trust Act, became law in July 1890. In 1902 President Theodore Roosevelt instructed the attorney general to bring suit under the Sherman Anti-Trust Act against the Northern Securities Company, a consolidation of railroads, thus blocking its efforts to bring all important railroads under one control. Regulation of big business was begun in 1906, with the passage of the Hepburn Act, which permitted the Interstate Commerce Commission to fix the rates of railroads and certain facilities necessary for the movement and distribution of goods and people, such as terminal facilities, sleeping cars, and pipelines. In 1910, the ICC was given authority to regulate telephone and telegraph companies. The Clayton Act, passed in 1914, declared that price discrimination in interstate commerce was unlawful. Violations of the antitrust acts by a corporation were considered to be violations committed by its individual directors, officers, and agents, and such persons were declared liable as individuals to prosecution under the penalties of the Sherman Act. Among the most famous cases heard under this law were the *Standard Oil Company, Tobacco Trust, Powder Trust, Shoe Machinery Trust, Cash Register Trust, Harvester Trust,* and *Steel Trust* cases (Jennings, 1925, pp. 631–48).

◄§ Agriculture

Along with the labor unrest and dissatisfaction of the middle class in urban centers, a farm crisis was developing. Farm machinery and new power sources together with improved means of transportation were bringing a revolution in farming that was no less far-reaching than that of industry. The value of agricultural production rose steadily due almost entirely to the increase in crop yields per acre. However, the closing of the frontier meant higher and higher land prices. For marginal or small farmers, farming became an increasingly precarious way to make a living. In terms of the purchasing power of their production efforts, farmers were worse off than workers in other industries during much of the period from 1900 to 1930 (Jennings, 1925, pp. 566–70).

Agricultural aid through education

The federal government, beginning with the Morrill Act of 1862 and through subsequent amendments, attempted to aid farmers by *helping the states* to support the establishment of agricultural experiment stations and agricultural colleges. Located in every state and usually connected with agricultural colleges, the agricultural experiment stations served farmers by disseminating information about the best methods of farming, thus saving farmers millions of dollars annually. In 1914 the scope of agricultural education was increased by the Smith-Lever Extension Act, whose object was to spread useful knowledge related to agriculture and home economics. In 1923 the amount appropriated by the federal government for these purposes had grown to $4,580,000, the money being allotted to the states in proportion to their rural population on condition that the states contribute an equal amount. In these acts we see a pattern of *federal participation with the states to support the welfare of a particular population group engaged in production believed valuable to the welfare of the country.* This pattern was to be used more extensively in the 1930s in relation to "welfare legislation."

The Smith-Hughes Act of 1917 followed a similar pattern. It provided for national aid for vocational education on condition that the states contribute sums equal to those furnished by the federal government. For the year ending June 30, 1919, 2,039 schools of all types were reported as receiving money from federal funds. Of these schools, 42 percent were agricultural schools, 28 percent were trade or industrial schools, 23 percent were home economics schools, and 7 percent were general continuation schools. Through public funds, half provided by the federal government and half by the states, many high schools have thus taken up the study of agriculture and have been provided with teachers trained under the earlier acts. In 1923, there were 68 U.S. land-grant colleges and universities that had been established under the Morrill Act. These included 24 state universities and 17 colleges for blacks.

The county agents, one of whom was found in every county, were still another potent factor in helping farmers. Supported by state and federal funds, the county agent was responsible for traveling throughout the county to advise farmers and help them in the use of the best agricultural methods. These efforts at education included such matters as fertilization; improved methods of breeding horses, cattle, and poultry; equipment; and, in short, everything else that would make farm life better, happier, and more remunerative (Jennings, 1926, pp. 571–73).

Agricultural cooperatives

In discussing the agriculture of the time, one should not overlook the further development of the cooperative movement that began in the last decade of the 19th century. Among the organizations of this type, many of which have survived and are active today, were the milk producers' associations, the farmers' grain dealers' associations, and the National Federation of Live Stock Shippers.

Another agency which brought farmers together and promoted the diffusion of knowledge among them was the American Farm Bureau Federation, which was organized in November 1919. The organization was built on state federations, which, in turn, rested on county organizations. In addition to serving as an instrument through which farmers could make their concerns felt by the government and by industrial interests, the Farm Bureau cooperated with agricultural colleges in introducing improved practices on the farm and supplied leadership and advice in setting up boys' and girls' clubs made up of farm children. Still another movement which had an educative effect on farmers was the Non-Partisan League, which was founded in North Dakota in 1915 with a view to remedying unfair marketing methods. The basic idea of this group, which had political control of North Dakota for five years and was strong in Minnesota, Idaho, Nebraska, and Colorado, was to control agricultural marketing facilities by state action. In time, this broadened into the support of state control or ownership of natural resources, banks, and marketing facilities. The Non-Partisan League was fought bitterly by various vested interests and was labeled Bolshevist and pro-German. The state officials who supported the movement were not reelected, but the people of North Dakota refused to give up their state-controlled bank and their state-owned mills and elevators (Jennings, 1926, pp. 581–83).

Government aid to farmers

At this time government in addition to aiding agricultural education, irrigation projects, and so forth, helped farmers through the Federal Farm Loan System, the War Finance Corporation, and the Federal Reserve banks. The Federal Farm Loan System was intended primarily for farmers who had special problems in borrowing from commercial banks because their income for repayment generally came only once a year, at harvesttime. The Federal Farm Loan banks advanced money to farmers for long periods at low interest rates. The War Finance Corporation aided farmers in financing domestic exports of agricultural products. Two other acts to help farmers might be briefly referred to here, partly because of the constitutional issue they raise. These were the Packers and Stockyards Act, approved August 21, 1921, and the Future Trading Act, approved nine days later.

The first act prohibited packers engaged in interstate commerce from using unfair, unjust, or deceptive practices or from manipulating or controlling prices. Thus we have legislation which attempts to deal with certain issues of farmers' welfare through the use of the federal government's constitutional powers to regulate interstate commerce. The federal government does not have the power to regulate state actions within state boundaries, but it does have the power to forbid certain goods to move in interstate commerce or to set rules for the operation of the interstate distribution of goods.

The second act was based on the power of Congress to tax, imposing a prohibitive tax of 20 cents a bushel on grain sold for "future delivery." The next year this act was declared unconstitutional as exceeding the power of Congress to tax. However, another act placing grain exchanges under the supervision of the Department of Agriculture was found constitutional in 1923 on the basis of the power of Congress to regulate interstate commerce. Among other things, this act gave the federal government, the power to inspect agricultural products (Jennings, 1926, pp. 583–85).

►§ Labor

The well-being of workers is influenced by (1) the level of the wages they receive; (2) the cost of living in relation to wages; (3) the hours of work that are required to earn the wages; (4) the conditions of work, such as sanitation facilities and proper protection from dangerous working conditions; and (5) the level of unemployment. During this period the general tendency was for both wages and the cost of living to rise steadily. Despite the rise in the cost of living, it has been estimated that in 1920 labor's purchasing power was about one third greater than it had been in 1913 (Jennings, 1926). One of the greatest struggles of labor and labor organizations of the time was toward a shorter workday. It is probably difficult for people living in the last quarter of the 20th century to really comprehend the working conditions that existed in our country during the first quarter of the century. The 40-hour week and the two-day weekend is so standard in modern life that it is difficult to realize that in 1900 the average standard workweek was slightly over 57 hours (Douglas, 1930, p. 28). In unorganized industries, as might be expected, the hours were longer. For example, employees in the steel mills normally worked a 12-hour day and an 84-hour week, whereas the organized building trades workers had achieved a 48-hour week, working 8 hours a day, 6 days a week. By 1920, hours of work in unionized manufacturing had declined to 46 per week and in non-unionized manufacturing to 54. In many cases, decreased hours of work were accompanied by increases in efficiency and higher wages. The eight-hour day began to be supported by the unions not only as a necessary condition for employed workers but as a way to spread jobs, as the unions became fearful that technology and increased productivity of workers would lead to fewer jobs unless the time each person spent on the job was reduced.

Organized labor and many reformers, including social workers, were concerned about the health hazards in industry. Workers were virtually without protection against the unsafe conditions that marked many jobs. There was no federal agency to regulate the use of dangerous substances used in manufacturing processes, such as tetraethyl lead and radium. Railroad employees regularly suffered mutilating accidents. Mining involved great dangers from mine damp, explosions, cave-ins, and other disasters. There was no recourse for workers who became ill as the result of the health hazards of

their jobs, and there were no laws to regulate working conditions. Employers regularly and firmly denied any responsibility for the work-related illnesses of their employees.

For those injured on the job, the only recourse was to sue the employer for damages. This required an investment of time and money that few workers had. To win such a suit, the worker had to prove that the employer had been negligent, a fact to which other employees were understandably reluctant to testify, considering that there was no job security at the time. The law, moreover, gave employers three defenses. They could plead (1) that the worker's injury had been due to the negligence of another worker, (2) that the worker's own actions were a factor in causing the injury, or (3) that the worker had knowingly and voluntarily assumed the risk of injury in taking a job and in accepting the wages paid for doing it. In the face of these defenses, nine plaintiffs out of ten lost their suits (Wilcox, 1969, p. 103).

At the beginning of the 20th century, there was no program to ease the burden of unemployment for workers who lost their jobs. In fact, any worker who was unable to keep up with the demands of the job, or who missed time for illness or accident, could well expect to be fired. Although the economy was expanding and times were good through the end of World War I, there was significant unemployment and little concern for the unemployed (Jennings, 1926, p. 662).

The organization of labor

Membership in labor organizations grew during this period. The most powerful of these organizations, and the one with the most members, was the American Federation of Labor, a national confederation of local unions that were organized on craft lines. There were, however, also company unions and such independent unions as the Amalgamated Clothing Workers of America. The Industrial Workers of the World was organized in 1905, but it failed. Unlike the American Federation of Labor, which fully accepted the labor-management structure of the society and was primarily interested in making better bargains for labor so that the worker's share in the country's wealth was increased as much as possible and working conditions were made as safe and comfortable as possible, the IWW urged the complete abolition of the wage system and the employing class. It strongly favored strikes of all workers in any one industry or a general strike of workers in all industries if necessary to gain its ends (Jennings, 1926, pp. 649–54).

Labor disputes

The first quarter of the 20th century was marked by great labor-management conflict. Strikes occurred by the thousands of lockouts by the hundreds. In the first five years of the century, there were 13,964 strikes and 541 lockouts. There were steel strikes, mining strikes, agricultural strikes in California, two textile strikes, and the railroad strike of 1922. Many strikes were brought about by the action of employers in cutting wages without reason. Early in 1921, wages in the textile industry were reduced by 22.5 percent. A year later they were again reduced, this time by 20 percent, and the weekly hours of work were increased from 48 to 54. About 100,000 workers left their jobs, and by fall labor had won the strike. The railroad strike likewise followed wage reductions (Jennings, 1926, pp. 663–65).

In the winter of 1909–10 the "first great women's strike" took place in New York City. About 30,000 women in the shirtwaist trades struck because their employers refused to meet with them to arbitrate certain points of dispute. Women in this industry were then earning as little as $4.50 per week, and they were required to buy their own needles and thread and to pay for the electricity their machines used. Aided by the Women's Trade Union League and women reform leaders, they won a 52-hour week, limited overtime, and the more even spread of work through the year. This strike demonstrated the ability of women to organize (Jennings, 1926, pp. 663–64).

During World War I, there was a rapid increase in the demand for workers on the home front at the same time that there was a heavy conscription

of men for duty at the front lines. When the war was over, however, the demobilization of the troops proceeded helter-skelter, with little direction or planning. Prices shot up, but wages, salaries, and farm income did not increase. Labor went out on strike. In Seattle, a walkout became a general strike and the general strike almost became a class struggle. The Boston police struck, and the city was close to anarchy. Workers in coal, railroads, and steel walked out and were defeated by the combined power of employers, the press, and often police action.

Employers' associations

To combat unionism, employers formed various employers' associations. Among the employer organizations that were most bitterly hostile to union labor was the National Association of Manufacturers. Encouraged by the open hostility between many labor unions and the employers' groups, organizations were formed for the express purpose of breaking strikes.

Labor arbitration

With labor organized and growing increasingly militant, and capital equally well organized and militant, methods had to be developed to preserve some sort of industrial peace. As early as 1888, the federal government tried to set up machinery to arbitrate strikes. The first arbitration act was passed in 1898. It allowed either the employer or the striking union to ask for the mediation of the chairman of the Interstate Commerce Commission and the U.S. commissioner of labor.

In spite of laws, regulations, and investigations, over the next 20 years tension increased and in 1919 the president called a conference attended by representatives of labor, management, and the public. The conference was frustratingly inconclusive because the management representatives would not accept the principle that workers had the right of collective bargaining or the right to deal with employers through agents of their own choice. Unable to reach agreement, the labor representatives walked out of the conference. In 1925 the Supreme Court held that the compulsory arbitration of labor disputes and the fixing of maximum hours of work by state industrial commissions violated the 14th Amendment and were therefore unconstitutional. It became very evident during the first three decades of the 1900s that labor was less well protected in securing good working hours than capital was in acquiring wealth.

✍§ Child labor

As we have pointed out earlier, children in America have always worked, their labor serving two functions: support of the developing economy (and sometimes their families) and preparation for adult roles in the community. With the coming of the industrial revolution, the growth of a new humanism, and growing knowledge about child development, there were changes both in the types of work done by children and in the way child labor was regarded by reform leaders. Although being a bound child was an unenviable state, and being an apprentice was, in many instances, only slightly better, there was a close personal interaction, harsh and depriving as it may have been, between child and master. In accepting the child, the master accepted certain minimal responsibilities toward the child.

The majority of children, of course, were neither bound or apprenticed, but worked hard at home under their parents' direction and supervision. But with the move from rural to urban life, the work of large numbers of children moved from the home to the factory, or if work was brought into the tenements, the children were under the supervision of a foreman rather than the parents. And the relationship between the child and the employer changed radically. It changed from a status relationship to a contract relationship in which the employer had no responsibility for the welfare of the child and provided no training other than socialization to a hard, unskilled, insecure future. During the 19th century the children's issue had been

schools for all children; now the reformers began to focus on protecting children from industrial hazards and exploitation.

Industrialization and child labor

Rapid industrialization following the Civil War increased child labor, introduced new occupations in which children were useful, and spread child labor into new parts of the nation, especially the South. The extent of child labor first became visible on a national scale when the Census Bureau began to record the number of children who were gainfully employed between the ages of 10 and 15. According to the census records, by 1900 about 1,750,000 children, or one out of six, were gainfully employed. Half of the children were from immigrant families. Sixty percent of them worked in agriculture for persons other than their parents, and 40 percent worked in industry (Jennings, 1926, pp. 656–58). However, the census figures probably underestimate the actual amount of child labor in that many children were employed before the age of ten and many others worked in the street trades, which were difficult to count. In a book about child labor, John Spargo (1906) estimated the number of working children in the United States at 2¼ million. He held that children were employed mainly because it was cheap to use them than to install and maintain machinery or to hire adults.

During the 1890s and on into the early years of the 20th century, the manufacturers of cotton textiles began to move South. In New England, the cotton textile industry had been notorious as a user and abuser of boys and girls for more than a century. New England's experience now began to be repeated in the South, but the situation there was further complicated by the poverty of the region. Local thinking tended to regard rapid industrialization as necessary to the welfare of the South, regardless of the human costs, and that cheap labor was necessary to such industrialization. During the last decade of the 19th century, the number of children employed in southern mills increased 160 percent. Persons under 16 years of age comprised nearly 30 percent of the workers in the textile industry in the South (Bremner, 1971, p. 601).

The new view of child labor

Although it is true that many industrialists benefited financially from the work of children and that consumers paid less for goods produced by child labor, it must also be recognized that opinions regarding child labor were tied very closely to attitudes toward poverty and the poor. As long as poverty was regarded as a blessing in disguise, the employment of boys and girls in industry could be regarded as a positive experience of discipline and training. As long as poverty was regarded as inevitable, it could be argued that it was necessary for the children of the poor to help support their families. Thus, groups concerned with the welfare of children might stand mute while children were burned, crushed, or otherwise injured and killed by industrial accidents (Bremner, 1956, pp. 76–77).

However, with the coming of the new view of poverty, and with gradually growing knowledge about child development and the needs of children, child labor came to seem absurd and reprehensible. Jane Addams wrote that the child laborers of today would be the paupers of tomorrow. Growing up without either formal schooling or the knowledge of a trade, they would become dull, shiftless drifters (Addams, 1903, pp. 114–21). S. W. Woodward, a prominent Washington merchant, wrote, "For every dollar earned by a child under fourteen years of age tenfold will be taken from its earning capacity in later years" (Woodward, 1905, pp. 800–801). G. Stanley Hall defined distinct periods of growth in a child's life, each with its own needs. He warned that depriving children of certain needs and experiences could seriously damage their future development. The "new psychology" stressed that play and freedom from certain responsibilities were needed by children for physical and psychological development (Bremner, 1971, p. 602).

Those interested in limiting child labor were motivated by concern over its bad economic and social consequences as well as by humanitarianism.

They pointed out that children were competing with adults for the available jobs. Taking advantage of the prevailing concern for the conservation of natural resources, Jane Addams, among others, argued that the employment of children robbed the community of assets that should be husbanded if for no other reason than self-interest (Addams, 1903, pp. 114–21). Fundamentally, however, the reformers' concern was motivated by humanitarian rather than economic considerations. Spargo wrote: "This great nation in its commercial madness devours its babes" (1906, p. 147) Addams summed up her case against child labor as follows: "It confuses our sense of value, so that we come to think that a bolt of cheap cotton is more to be prized than a child properly nourished, educated, and prepared to take his place in life" (1903, pp. 114–21).

Child labor committees

Concern for the welfare of working children began in the 1880s and had become an organized crusade by the opening of the 20th century. In 1902 Lillian Wald, founder and director of the Henry Street Settlement in New York City, and Florence Kelley, a social worker formerly employed at Hull House as a counselor for girls, called a meeting of representatives of 32 settlement houses in New York City to consider action against child labor. This group formed a committee which launched the first investigation into the working conditions of the city's children. A year after its founding it was able to secure the passage of a stronger child labor law which included regulation of the street trades, and in 1909 it obtained the passage of the dangerous trades act. Under Kelley's leadership, a "White List" of manufacturers was prepared in an attempt to persuade buyers to limit their purchases of goods to those produced under approved working conditions.

At the 1903 Conference of Charities and Corrections a determined effort was made to build the opposition to child labor on national lines, and in 1904 the National Child Labor Committee was organized. The board of the committee was headed by Felix Adler, and it included the social workers Jane Addams, Florence Kelley, Edward T. Devine, Robert W. D. DeForest, and Homer Folks, Lillian Wald and Edgar Gardner Murphy.

A National campaign. The National Child Labor Committee mounted a national campaign to accomplish its goals, organizing local committees in every state that had a significant number of employed children. The committee cooperated with any state committees that were already in existence, and it became a propaganda agency and a clearinghouse for child labor campaigns. Not only did it publish its own pamphlets, but it was active in seeing that material about child labor appeared in other publications. Staff members of the committee put together traveling exhibits and became the first organized reform movement to make wide use of photographic propaganda (Bremner, 1971, pp. 651–61). Although a national organization, basically the committee directed its activities toward reform activities at the state level. It developed standards for child labor legislation which included a minimum age of 14 in manufacturing and 16 in mining, a maximum of eight hours of work a day and a prohibition of all night work, and documentary proof of age. Although 34 states passed new child labor laws, exceptions to the laws made them far less effective than the reformers would have wished (Bremner, 1971, pp. 651–61). Despite having achieved unprecedented gains in the area of child labor, the committee was discouraged, as it was beginning to realize the magnitude of the problem. The greater the advances made, the more the problem seemed to grow.

In 1907 Senator Albert J. Beveridge presented a paper at the Conference of Charities and Corrections arguing that the way to handle the problem of child labor was to enact a federal law based on the power of Congress to regulate commerce. The Supreme Court had just held that Congress had the power to prohibit the interstate distribution of lottery tickets in the interests of the national welfare. In 27 cases the Supreme Court had approved the exercise of power by Congress to prohibit the transfer across state boundaries of goods deemed in some way injurious to the general welfare of

the nation. Beveridge believed that child labor could be stopped only by a federal law because states in advance of their neighbors in social legislation often suffered a handicap in attracting and keeping industries, and he believed that such a law would be found constitutional (Chambers, 1963, pp. 29–30).

Child labor legislation and the Supreme Court

By 1914 the Committee was convinced that it should work for a national child labor law. And in 1916 came the greatest victory that the reformers had won in the area of child labor—Congress passed the Keating-Owen Act, which applied standards relating to child labor across the whole nation. However, joy of the reformers was dashed when in 1918 the Supreme Court, by a margin of one vote, found such enforcement to be an invasion of the police power reserved to the states and forbidden to the federal government. The response to this setback was immediate. Congress attempted to control child labor by passing a law which imposed a 10 percent tax on the interstate commerce of mining firms employing children under 16 and manufacturing firms employing children under 14 (Chambers, 1963, pp. 29–41).

Then, in 1922, in the case of *Bailey* v. *Drexel Furniture Company,* the Supreme Court handed down a decision, without any recorded dissenting opinion, declaring the 1919 law unconstitutional, chiefly because it was an attempt in violation of the federal Constitution and the 10th Amendment to regulate an exclusively state function by extension of the taxing power. Owen Lovejoy of the National Child Labor Committee field staff immediately suggested another attack. He asked the board of the committee to consider the possibility of working for a constitutional amendment.

Every social movement involves some supporters who insist on total change and see anything else as betrayal and other supporters who will compromise in order to achieve some immediate tangible gain. So it was now with those who had worked for child labor legislation. The AFL and the National Labor Committee, probably more aware than others of the difficulties of passing a constitutional amendment, urged that such a bill had to have explicit guarantees of local action and responsibility, that the states had to be considered. On the other hand, Florence Kelley, who had invested so much of her life and energy in the fight, had no patience with what she felt were sellouts to "reactionary politicians and selfish employers" (Chambers, 1963, pp. 35–36). She was unable to tolerate the notion of moderate action involving both the federal and state fronts.

In the meantime, World War I had ended and people who had suffered from the crisis of war seemed oriented toward finding ways and means to win a larger share of the material abundance that America promised. People were frightened, suspicious, resentful, and restless. John A. Fitch reported that never before had he witnessed such fear and suspicion of organized labor, with most people wanting "suppression rather than understanding" (Fitch, 1920, p. 61). The Red Scare, coming on the heels of wartime hysteria, damaged any reform proposals. Such proposals were labeled pro-German or pro-Russian, and this was often enough to assure their defeat. Teachers were required to take loyalty oaths, and aliens suspected of disloyalty were rounded up and deported. Evidence began to accumulate that the Progressive movements of the first decade of the 20th century were encountering unexpected difficulty in the second.

Efforts for a child labor amendment

Finally, in 1924, with everyone weary of fruitless debate, Congress agreed upon an amendment giving the federal government the right to regulate the labor of children under the age of 18, an increase in the usually accepted age. Once the amendment had been approved by Congress and submitted to the states for ratification, serious opposition mounted. Manufacturers' associations testified that hard labor was character building and that both states' rights and personal liberty to work as one wanted was at stake. Groups such as the Sentinels of the Republic, the Women Patriots, the

Citizens' Committee to Protect Our Homes and Children, and the Moderation League of Pennsylvania viewed the Child Labor Amendment as a Bolshevik plot to nationalize the nation's children, to destroy the home, and to destroy democracy by centralizing the government. But the opposition of the American Farm Bureau Federation was the most difficult for the committee, which had labored hard to allay the fears of rural America that the Child Labor Amendment would make it impossible for rural parents to require their children to do farm chores (Chambers, 1963, pp. 33–40).

The proposed amendment was considered first in Massachusetts, in which several reform groups had considerable strength and which had long had one of the stronger state child labor acts. However, it was not approved. Manufacturing associations were extremely vocal in charging that the amendment was Bolshevik-inspired. The Citizens Committee for Protection of Our Homes and Children, which is said to have been financed by the textile industries, warned that the amendment would allow governmental invasion of the privacy and sanctity of the home. When William Cardinal O'Connell saw a threat to parental discipline in the amendment, the Roman Catholic hierarchy in Massachusetts threw its strength against the amendment. An even more serious threat than that to the home was the perceived threat that the hierarchy saw to the Catholic educational system. To many Roman Catholic leaders, any expansion of the powers of the government, especially in relation to children, represented a threat to the church.

However, all the Catholic leaders were not united on the issue. Father John A. Ryan had long been working actively for the measure. He was able to recruit a number of important Catholic groups to its support, including the National Conference of Catholic Women. Edward Keating, the author of the first national child labor law, was a Roman Catholic. But Cardinal O'Connell's pastoral letter of October 1924 doomed the amendment in Massachusetts, and Father Ryan admitted to defeat in the national effort (Chambers, 1963, pp. 40–42).

✍ Women in industry, politics, and economic life

Readers will remember the earlier discussion of the feminists who met at Seneca Falls, New York, in 1848 and their *Declaration of Sentiments and Resolutions*. The *Declaration* courageously challenged the 19th-century notions of woman's "proper place," implicitly holding that as long as society prescribed separate areas of responsibility for men and women, women could not be free. For much of the rest of the 19th-century, women's rights leaders continued to press for sweeping social change. But after Congress failed to recognize women's right to vote in the 14th and 15th amendments, which granted civil rights to the freedmen, suffrage for women began to surface as the primary "women's issue," although there remained those, such as Elizabeth Cady Stanton and Charlotte Perkins Gilman, who felt that women's greatest problem was to achieve equality with men in the church and the home rather than in the state and the labor market.

By the end of the 19th century, however, the more radical group had encountered such a hostile political climate that its position seemed untenable and it was willing to accept a "more respectable and limited feminist demand" (Chafe, 1972, pp. 12). Thus, a new group, the National American Woman's Suffrage Association (NAWSA), was founded (1890) as a coalition which accepted as its primary purpose the winning of women's suffrage as an expedient and achievable goal.

The battle for women's suffrage

Rather than arguing that men and women were alike in their humanity, the "suffragettes" argued that women deserved the vote precisely because they were different from men. They held that because women were more spiritual and moral creatures than men, giving them the ballot could "elevate the moral level of government." Thus, the feminist position moved from one of demanding justice and "emphasizing the inalienable rights of females as individuals" to one of emphasizing the "utility of the ballot as an agent for reforming society" (Chafe, 1972, p. 13).

In a time marked by fear of anarchism and social disorder (remember the arguments that defeated the child labor amendment), it made sense for women to de-emphasize positions that were often associated in the public mind with divorce, free love, and threat to the sanctity of the home. This was one reason for the change in the feminist position, but another reason was that the leadership of the women's movements was changing. By the beginning of the 20th century, most of the early feminists had died or had retired from active participation in the cause. Their places were taken by such leaders as Carrie Chapman Catt, Jane Addams, and Florence Kelley. These new leaders shared many of the ideals of the first feminist generation, but they tended to accept the opposition's premise on the sanctity of the home and the conventional notion of woman's place.

Many of the new leaders, observing the suffering of poor women and their vulnerability to exploitation by those holding economic power, were interested in achieving a *special protection* of women in society because *women were different* rather than a recognition of the equality of women. And many feminists who were social workers had learned from other battles that victory often comes to socially concerned women who maintain a low profile and recruit men of power to support them. They had further learned that the poor and the vulnerable in society may live better as a result of piecemeal concrete gains rather than as a result of boldly taken radical positions that arouse hostility in major groups of society and thus result in the denial of all advance.

Women's clubs

As the middle class grew during the 1890s through the 1900s, it developed a self-consciousness that contributed to the development of women's clubs. In 1890 the General Federation of Women's Clubs (GFWC) was founded with

500,000 members. Originally the purpose of women's clubs had been to offer women an opportunity for recreation and social interaction and to encourage their intellectual growth. However, by the 1900s such clubs were turning their attention to the social order and providing a constant force for Progressive legislation.

Once these women became involved in reform movements they began to recognize the importance of the franchise, and in 1914 the GFWC formally endorsed the suffrage campaign. For the first time in history, the women's movement had a strong base of support among women themselves. And equally important, an interlocking directorate linked the women's movement to other groups in the Progressive coalition. Florence Kelley was vice president and executive secretary of the National Consumers League, a resident of the Henry Street Settlement and a former member of the Hull House staff, a board member of the National Child Labor Committee, and chairperson of the child labor committee of the GFWC. Jane Addams, founder of Hull House, served as a national officer of NAWSA and was a board member of the Women's Trade Union League, a member of the National Child Labor Committee, and an adviser to Theodore Roosevelt. Male reformers worked beside and often under the direction of women in the same organizations and came to believe that the vote for women represented a step toward a better society (Chafe, 1972, pp. 16–17).

By 1914, 11 states had enacted legislation giving women the right to vote. In 1915 the NAWSA reorganized its national office and asked Carrie Chapman Catt to take charge of an overall suffrage campaign. Catt brought an overwhelming amount of energy and efficiency to the movement. She mobilized crucial local affiliates to work toward state victories, carefully selected a group of lobbyists to cultivate members of Congress, and herself concentrated on President Woodrow Wilson. "She solicited his advice, invited him to address suffrage conventions, and in every way possible associated him with the suffrage cause" (Chafe, 1972, p. 18). The president became an active supporter of women's suffrage after the women's groups took a position supporting his war policies.

Congress passed the Women's Suffrage Amendment in 1919, with such a good majority (304 to 90 in the House and 56 to 25 in the Senate) that one would have thought that no controversy had ever existed. Fourteen months later, Tennessee became the 36th state to ratify the amendment and thus made it a part of the Constitution. Women had won the right to vote.

Women and politics

Assuming that female citizens would act together as a cohesive force, female leaders believed that the way was now clear to work for the passage of forward-looking welfare legislation, to improve consumer protection measures, and to clean up the political problems of the cities. In selected cities there was evidence that women were voting in a block for reform and were rejecting the regular party apparatus. The head of the Illinois Republican Women's Committee bolted her party and led the effort to unseat the Republican mayor. Mary Garrett Hay, national vice chairman of Republican Women, opposed the reelection of James Wadsworth the Republican senator from New York. Faced with the horrible specter of female opposition, politicians moved quickly to win the support of the powerful new voters.

The state legislatures moved rapidly. Twenty states granted women the right to serve on juries. Night work and wage and hour laws were passed by other states. Michigan and Montana passed equal pay laws, and Wisconsin approved a far-reaching equal rights bill. The Virginia legislature granted reform leaders 18 to 24 requests, including a children's code, a child placement bill, and a vocational education law.

Congress demonstrated its concern about the new voters by acting on the demand of female reform organizations for passage of the Sheppard-Towner Bill, which will be discussed later. Congress would have preferred not to pass the bill but did not dare to turn it down. Other important legislation was enacted under the pressure of women reformers: the Packers and Stockyards Bill to increase consumer protection, an act reforming the citizenship requirements of married women, and an act upgrading the civil service. And as we have said earlier, the Child Labor Amendment was sent to the states for ratification, where it failed.

Just at the time that the Child Labor Amendment came before the states, there was an abrupt reversal of the politicians' concern with women's groups. This reaction could be attributed in part to the changing climate of the times: reform was much less popular, and many women's organizations had been smeared as Communist front groups. The Supreme Court added to the change of climate by ruling against the child labor legislation and minimum wage laws. However, the principal reason for the reversal was that it was becoming increasingly clear that women, if they voted at all, tended to vote as their husbands did and that women as a group gave only limited support to reform measures. An attempt in 1923 to determine why women did not vote found a number of causes, but the most important specific cause cited was the belief of women that they should stay home and leave the voting to men. Eleanor Roosevelt and other female liberals were ignored when they attempted to get a hearing on welfare measures before the Platform Committee of the Democratic Party at its 1924 national convention. So deeply was discrimination involved in the very structure of society, so strong was the idea of woman's place as primarily limited to the domestic arena, that suffrage could not alter it (Chafe, 1972, p. 29).

Women and economic equality

Although some changes occurred in the composition of the labor force and in the distribution of the jobs that women performed, in the first three decades of the 20th century aspiring career women were still limited to positions that had traditionally been set aside for women. The drive to abolish economic discrimination received very little support, and the overwhelming majority of working women continued to be employed in menial occupations for inadequate pay. And most important, whatever positive impact World War I had had on women's opportunities was surprisingly short-lived. By 1920, women's participation in the labor force had actually declined from the 1910 level. Neither the labor movement nor the government was prepared to accept any permanent change in women's status.

In 1919 the Central Federated Union of New York City proclaimed that "the same patriotism which induced women to enter industry during the war should induce them to vacate their positions after the war" (Chafe, 1972, p. 53). Male workers went on strike in Cleveland in order to force women streetcar conductors off their jobs, and other women were dismissed in spite of any seniority that they might have acquired. Twenty women judges in New York were forced to resign on the ground that their appointments were only for the duration of the war. Females were barred from taking examinations for civil service positions in 60 percent of federal government jobs. A Treasury official decreed that no woman in his department could earn more than $1,200 yearly.

Important changes also took place in the age and the marital status of employed women. In the 1890s the average woman worker was single and less than 25 years of age. She left her job at marriage after six or eight years of work. From 1900 to 1910 the percentage of working women rose from 20.4 percent to 25.2 percent of all women. From 1900 to 1940, however, the average age of the female employee rose to over 30, with the number of older women seeking work almost doubling. In 1940, married women comprised 35 percent of all employed women—in contrast to 15 percent in 1900—and joined the labor force at a rate five times as fast as single, widowed, or divorced women. White-collar work provided employment opportunities for middle- and upper-class women, and the teenage girl who entered the labor market in the 1920s had a larger number of vocational choices and a greater amount of freedom than her mother did. However, none of these changes signified the emancipation of the woman worker. It is important to recognize that the increase in the number of married women workers had little to do with the freedom of women to pursue life outside the home on an equal basis with men. Work outside the home was definitely undertaken so that families could survive economically (Chafe, 1972, pp. 48–65).

People who saw this shift as a movement toward economic independence for women also overlook the types of positions held by working women and the kinds of women who entered the labor force. As late as 1930, over 57 percent of all the women who were employed outside their homes were either blacks or immigrants. Both of these groups worked primarily in domestic service or the textile industries. They worked 10 or 12 hours a day for wages that often failed to average $1 a day. They enjoyed neither the freedom nor the independence usually associated with the "new women" of the 1920s, yet their story describes the economic situation of women in the early years of the 20th century just as much as does the emergence of the typist or the stenographer (Chafe, 1972, pp. 40–65).

Even in the case of the professions, the small numerical gains made by women did not signify any expansion of opportunities or represent inroads into fields previously dominated by men. Women's portion of total college enrollments actually declined from 1920 to 1930, and women college graduates tended to concentrate in careers that had customarily been set aside for females.

In 1920 only 40 of the 482 general hospitals listed in the *American Medical Association Directory* accepted women as interns, and from 1925 to 1945 American medical schools placed a quota of 5 percent on the number of women they admitted. During the 1920s both Harvard and Columbia refused to consider women applicants to their law schools, and as late as 1937 the New York City Bar Association excluded female members.

Whether the woman worker was employed in industry or in the professions, discrimination also placed a ceiling on possible job advancement. Women industrial workers rarely became supervisors or forepersons. Although women constituted over 80 percent of the nation's teachers, they served as superintendents of schools in only 45 of 2,853 cities. Although women received about one third of all graduate degrees, they comprised only 7.9 percent of the professors in the country's colleges.

Unequal and inadequate pay constituted the most blatant evidence of the inferior economic position of women. Throughout the industrial world, women earned at best only 50 to 65 percent of what men were paid. In 1937, women workers took home an average of $525 a year in contrast to the $1,027 earned by men. Probably the greatest problem of institutionalized discrimination faced by women was that they regularly received less pay than men even when they did exactly the same work. For example, the annual income of male and female teachers averaged $1,953 and $1,394, respectively; earned $1,718, and $1,442 respectively; a male finisher in the New York City paper box industry earned $35.50 a week when women doing exactly the same work earned $17.83.

A serious public misunderstanding that has led to dismissing women as casual members of the labor force with no serious grievances was the notion that many women joined the labor force solely in order to earn pocket money or to indulge frivolous desires while they received primary support from the home or the husband. This theory by implication justified the unequal treatment of women workers. If women were subsidized by their families, or wanted to earn money only for "extra" things or to gain independence, there was no compelling reason to treat them in the same way as men who had, by definition, to support families were treated.

The Women's Bureau conducted a series of investigations of employed women in the 1920s and 1930s. These studies revealed that 90 percent of women went to work because of economic need and used their income to support themselves and their dependents. One out of every four working women was the principal wage earner for her family, and as many as 95 percent of working wives *contributed all of their earnings to support their families.* Even among single women living at home, *two out of three contributed all of their income to the households* of which they were a part.

Yet authorities and leaders of public opinion continued to insist that women belonged in the home and that the working woman could be tolerated only if work were a temporary occupation before marriage. Working wives were disapproved, and working mothers came in for special attacks. The wife of the labor leader Samuel Gompers declared that women's employment took jobs and bread away from men; and in 1923 the secretary of labor declared that the employment of mothers would sooner or later bring the economic system "crashing down around our heads" (Chafe, 1972, p. 64). Even the women's Bureau, established to educate the public on women's economic role and to protect women workers, stated that wives who worked menaced the health and happiness of the home. An almost unbelievable gap separated the reality of women's economic situation from public opinion about it. In 1929 Alice Rogers Hagar, a labor expert, wrote: "The woman is nearly always the cheap or marginal worker, and . . . she is expected by the public and employer to remain one" (1929, p. 65).

Women in industry

In an earlier section we briefly discussed the strike of the garment workers in 1909. If the example set by the garment workers had been followed by women in other industries, perhaps the poor treatment of women industrial workers would have been alleviated. However, few women outside the garment industry had union representation.

Certainly, at this time the AFL, then the dominant labor organization, did almost nothing to unionize women. The AFL leaders seemed to believe that women should be obedient and should not compete with men. Both Gompers and William Green, who succeeded Gompers as president of the federation, attacked the presence of married women in the work force, asserting that women should direct their efforts toward getting married and raising a family. The International Moulders Union adopted as a goal the ending of employment for

women in any job "recognized as men's employment."

When women organized themselves they were denied recognition. Female printers who worked side by side with male union members applied for membership in the International Typographical Union, only to be turned down on the ground that they were unskilled workers.

While organized labor was resisting the efforts of women to assure themselves of a living wage and minimum working conditions, middle-class reformers were pressing vigorously for state regulation of wages and hours as a solution to the problem. In 1908 the regulation of hours and working conditions for women came before the Supreme Court in *Muller* v. *Oregon,* a case involving a challenge to Oregon's legislation limiting the number of hours that women could work and setting certain conditions of work for women. Under the aegis of the Consumer's League, Florence Kelley and another social worker, Josephine Goldmark, did the research for the arguments used by Louis Brandeis in upholding the constitutionality of laws limiting women a ten-hours workday. The Court found that such laws were an entirely reasonable exercise of the state's police power to promote the health, morality, and welfare of the community.

Then in 1922 came a hard blow. The U.S. Supreme Court by a vote of three to five found the minimum wage act of the District of Columbia null and void. A majority of the Court held that the minimum wage legislation constituted arbitrary *interference of the state in the private affairs of citizens competent to make their own decisions about the conditions under which they would accept a job.* Minimum wage laws violated the rights of women to bargain directly with employers as to the price of their services. Justice George Sutherland, who wrote the majority decision, stated that the premises of the *Oregon* decision no longer applied in that women, by the passage of the 19th Amendment, had reached equality with men and thus needed no special protection.

There was much angry response from reformers, but it was Florence Kelley who commented that no woman had participated in the judicial process at any stage. The decision throughly discouraged the reform groups, as it removed the principal ground on which they had sought legislative help—that women needed special protection. There were proposals for an amendment to the Constitution that would allow Congress to reenact by a two-thirds majority any law found unconstitutional by the Supreme Court. Florence Kelley proposed enlarging the Court to 15 or 18 members in order to change the balance. Angry though they were, however, the reformers recognized that there was no way to restrict the Court's powers without jeopardizing the equilibrium of government or the security of individual rights. It was not until 1937 that the ruling of the Court was overridden.

Professional and college women

Women entered colleges and universities in record numbers during the first two decades of the 20th century. The number of women increased 1,000 percent in public colleges and 482 percent in private colleges. Since educated women had traditionally furnished the leadership for the feminist struggle, women's rights leaders optimistically expected that an enlarged new generation would carry forward the fight for equality. However, not only was there an absence of startling advances by women into new professions, but the number of women in some professions actually diminished. In 1902–3 there were 1,280 women in medical schools, but by 1926 this number had dropped to 992. Even in occupations which they dominated, women were seldom found in the top positions. For example, although Bryn Mawr had graduated 1,088 PhDs by 1927, most of whom went into teaching, only 21 of those graduates held professorships in women's colleges and only 4 in coeducational institutions.

Although the resistance of males to the influx of females into what they saw as their areas certainly had something to do with women's lack of progress following World War I, the problem could be attributed, at least in part, to the indifference of the young college woman. At an earlier time, the very act of going to college set the young

woman apart. A woman who chose this path had to be dedicated to an overriding goal and willing to pay the price of her success by careful preparation and discipline. Such women felt "on trial before the world" and dedicated themselves to proving that women had the brains and the endurance to achieve. Furthermore, in order to prove their point, their achievement had to be significantly better in quality than that of the average professional male. But the new generation of college women lacked the sense of purpose that had infused the female pioneers in higher education. Many people blamed the war for the change in women, but whatever the cause, it was the "carefree flapper rather than the dedicated career woman" who symbolized the new woman of the 1920s (Chafe, 1972, pp. 89–91).

However, the above does not tell the whole story of women's activities in the 20s. A new freedom in women's manners and morals substantially increased the liberation that women enjoyed in the sexual areas of male-female relationships. Artificial contraceptive devices were becoming more reliable, and they were becoming more available to educated women. These women could exercise some control on family size, and they could express their sexual desires with somewhat less fear of becoming pregnant. Although we cannot know with any accuracy how individual women behaved, the stereotype of the young woman of the 1920s was of someone who went from one adventure to another, interested primarily in accumulating experience for its own sake. Certainly, popular discussion of sex reached an unprecedented level during the years 1910–30. The number of articles in popular magazines on birth control, prostitution, divorce, and sexual morality increased tremendously, and it appeared that the new morality was being translated into action. There was evidence that a critical change occurred in the generation of women who came to maturity in the early 1920s, including an overwhelming increase in premarital and extramarital sex among women (Chafe, 1972, pp. 90–95).

The new spokeswomen for "freedom," such as Ellen Key and Margaret Sanger, defined this concept very differently from the way in which the concept of equality had been defined by the older generation of feminists. The new leaders urged women to "become as distinctly feminine as they could," developing their own sphere of love and motherhood. The women of the 1920s concentrated on the right of women to control their own bodies; the earlier feminists had concentrated on the need of women to achieve equality in the nation's social, political, and economic institutions. The focus changed from the responsibility of women to advance the equality and opportunity of women everywhere to the right of women to freedom for self-development and sexual experience (Chafe, 1972, pp. 89–132).

Such an increase in sexual freedom actually operated to perpetuate the traditional sexual division of labor, in which women assumed responsibility for the home and men went out into the world to earn a living. Marriage, sexual experience, and child rearing were to be the goals of female existence, and material success in the outside world was to be the goal of males. On the other hand, the concept of women's liberation as meaning that women should have an opportunity to pursue a career equal to that of men and should be active on the political, social, and economic scene involved drastically modifying women's status, altering the basic distribution of roles between men and women, and challenging the structure of society. Instead of being helpmates to men, women who chose a serious commitment to careers were seen as competitive with men. Such women violated the most deeply held conceptions of their proper role and began an uncharted journey with few guideposts to direct them. The literature of the time supported the women who deviated least from the role of supportive and nurturing wife and mother, often attacking career women as traitors to their womanhood. Opinion and evidence cited in that literature suggested that women could not successfully engage both in a career and a satisfying relationship with a husband and children.

After all, most of the early feminists had been single women—never married, divorced, or widowed. Only 12.2 percent of all professional women were married in 1920, and 75 percent of all the women who earned PhDs between 1907 and 1925 remained single (Chafe, 1972, p. 100). These women may have remained single because their commitment to an uncharted life-style left them with little time to pursue "the dating game" or because men were fearful and threatened by achieving women. But the most important reason was that most employers of the time flatly refused to hire married women or fired them when they married. No one thought it strange that the dean of a midwestern college was dismissed when she married. When she had the temerity to protest the firing she was told that marriage was an adequate career for a woman.

An interesting change that occurred between the beginning of the 20th century and the second decade of the century was the change in the curriculum of women's colleges. The founders of these institutions had been determined to offer the same courses as those available at the best men's colleges. However, by 1915 the women's colleges were developing courses in home economics, domestic science, hygiene, family relationships, and the family. Thus, these institutions of higher education followed the overwhelming trend which viewed the purpose of women's education as that of fitting women to be better wives and mothers.

The Equal Rights Amendment

In 1923 the National Women's Party, the more radical arm of the feminists, proposed the first Equal Rights Amendment to the Constitution. The amendment read: "Men and women shall have equal rights throughout the United States and every place subject to its jurisdiction." The radical women's group hoped that making the principle of feminine equality a visible part of the highest law of the land would end the distinctions between men and women in all areas of life, including divorce, the ownership of property, and employment opportunities. The group felt that discrimination against women could be eliminated effectively only by writing the rule of equality into the basic law of the land.

United States courts had ruled that any interpretation of the Constitution, including the 14th and 15th amendments, had to take into account the English common-law doctrine that a woman's legal existence merged with that of her husband upon marriage, so that in effect she ceased to be a person in her own right. As a result, women were often denied legal standing as persons before the courts. An Illinois court had ruled that married women could not practice law in Illinois as they were not covered by the equal protection clause of the 14th Amendment. In making this ruling, the judge stated that "the idea of a woman adopting a distinct and independent career from that of her husband" would be destructive to the family. In 1912 the highest court in Massachusetts had ruled that women could not serve on juries as they were not persons "in the eyes of the law" (Chafe, 1972, p. 122).

The National Women's Party believed that suffrage was only one step on the journey of women's equality; that the whole structure of society and the fundamental relationship between men and women needed to be changed in order to eliminate discrimination against women; and that this could be done only by writing the rule of equality into law.

The radical women employed such tactics as picketing without permits and picketing in forbidden areas. They also chained themselves to the White House fence and engaged in other provocative behavior. These tactics led to arrests. In jail the arrested women engaged in hunger strikes and were often force-fed by their jailers.

The radical group was in serious conflict with the women "reformers." The women reformers were interested in using the women's vote to attack specific inequalities and social problems one by one, thus gradually winning social reform for all people. The reformers felt that most discrimination against women was rooted in custom, not law. What bothered the reformers above all else was the potentially destructive effect of the Equal Rights Amendment on protective legislation for women. Wage and hour laws for women, support laws for wives and children, and special penalties for rape and sex offenses against women would all be endangered by the amendment. This question of whether protective legislation helped or hindered the quest for the equality of women was at the root of the conflict between the reformers and the radicals.

The radicals believed that protective legislation was a way of assuring that women did not compete with men for jobs. The group brought together evidence which showed that after the passage of special hour legislation women were denied the higher-paying night jobs and were limited to day jobs only. Laws that prevented women from working overtime to fill rush jobs or from working on split shifts might result in their being fired. Minimum wage laws invited men to undercut women by offering to work for less than women could under such laws. Basically, such legislation set women apart as a special class and assigned them a place inferior to that of men. The radicals agreed with the Supreme Court decision in the *Adkins* case that such protective legislation violated women's freedom of contract and treated them as weak and dependent beings, unable to make their own decisions (Chafe, 1972, p. 127).

The reformers rejected these arguments. They felt that protective legislation was a way of bringing the standards under which women worked up to greater equality with those of men. They pointed out that the radicals were interested in liberating the individual woman, with special emphasis on individual accomplishment and personal freedom—a position that appealed to the professional career woman who was in individual competition with men. However, this position did not take into consideration that the factory was a collective institution and that the women working in industry were more interested in economic security and adequacy than in personal liberty. *The reformers felt that for the sake of individual freedom a small women's elite was undercutting the only protection which the poor and unskilled woman might have.* Basic to many of the reformers' positions on women's legislation was the fundamental assumption that women *did differ significantly from men.* The reformers placed special emphasis on women's role within the family and saw full-time permanent work as the role of men. They pointed out that women who sought the same pay and hours as men might be putting their husbands or their brothers out of jobs.

The Equal Rights Amendment did not pass Congress, but the disagreement over its passage left the women's groups hopelessly split. Had the groups been willing to compromise, they might have gotten together to back an amendment along the lines of the 1921 Wisconsin law which provided that "women shall have the same rights, privileges and immunities under the law as men" but declared that nothing in the law should deny women "the special protections and privileges which they now enjoy for the national welfare" (Chafe, 1972, p. 118). But the conflict was too great, too basic to the notion of woman's place in society to allow for compromise. Consequently, the issue of women's equality—what it is and how it should be assured—ceased to be an important national issue.

⊰§ The blacks

During the critical years of social reform in America—1895 to 1915—Booker T. Washington was the most prominent black in the country. Washington was a conservative man who supported a program of conciliation and gradual change. Although he commanded enormous financial resources and had the support of some of the most important white men in America, including the president and industrial giants, he consistently refused to make an attack on segregation. His conservativism brought him into conflict with two other outstanding black leaders, William Edward Burghardt Du Bois and William Monroe Trotter, both of whom were Harvard graduates.

In 1903 Du Bois attacked Washington in *The Souls of Black Folk,* a book which had a tremendous impact on the black community. Du Bois assumed command of the groups of black people who opposed Washington's program of conciliation and separation. As Du Bois's words were heard more clearly, almost every literate black person had to choose between Washington and Du Bois.

In the 12 or 14 years after 1903, there was tremendous bitterness and antagonism between two black groups—one standing for moderation and submission and the gradual economic betterment of black people's lives by education; the other standing for black activism on the political scene and for the right of blacks to justice and equality, including the right of black youths to attend the leading universities and colleges of the nation instead of being limited to vocational schools.

The Niagara Movement

Aided by William Monroe Trotter, in 1905 W. E. B. Du Bois organized black intellectuals and professionals into a protest group, the Niagara Movement. In that year, at a secret meeting near Niagara Falls, Canada, this group demanded the abolition of all distinctions based on race and color. At its first national meeting, at Harpers Ferry, West Virginia, in 1906, the Niagara Movement, as the group had come to be called, issued a challenge to the nation, claiming for blacks all the political, civil, and social rights that had been given to other Americans and demanding "full manhood suffrage . . . now, henceforth, and forever." The Niagara Movement made a lot of people uneasy. It laid the foundation for the National Association for the Advancement of Colored People, which merged the forces of white reformers and black militants.

The NAACP

It was a race riot in Springfield, Illinois, in 1908 that led directly to the founding of the NAACP. As a result of the riot, a white woman, Mary W. Ovington, became concerned about what was happening in interracial relationships. She conceived the idea of a national conference on "the Negro question." The conference convened on May 30, 1909, in the United Charities Building in New York City.

It was attended by whites and blacks with a wide range of beliefs. There were Jane Addams, Florence Kelley, and Sophonisba Breckinridge, among other white liberals, and there were such

Niagara militants as William Trotter and Ida B. Wells Barnett, both of whom were more militant than Du Bois, who also attended. After long and earnest debate the major disagreements were smoothed over in a way that allowed for the founding of an ongoing organization. The NAACP opened for business in a room at 20 Vesey Street, and Du Bois resigned his position as professor at Atlanta University and joined the organization as director of research and publicity. Earlier, while at the University of Pennsylvania, Du Bois had made the pioneer sociological study of a black community, *The Philadelphia Negro.* He had then gone to Atlanta University, where he had organized one of the most important studies ever done on the U.S. black population. Although Du Bois was the only black officer of the organization, he gave tone and direction to the struggling new group.

To the surprise of many, the NAACP survived and grew. Branches were established in other urban centers, and *The Crisis,* published under Du Bois's editorship, stirred blacks as they had never been stirred before. The association moved into the arena of civil rights for blacks, taking battles for black rights to the courts and beginning to win these legal battles.

The Urban League

The National Urban League, was organized in April 1901 in New York City. This group was also an interracial organization. It concentrated on the social problems of urban blacks. Quieter in its methods than the NAACP, the league utilized techniques of persuasion, conciliation, and economic opportunity. George Edmund Haynes, the first black to receive a degree from the New York School of Social Work, and Eugene Kinckle Jones were the first executive officers of the league.

The National Equal Rights League and the black press

An organization that stood to the left of the NAACP and the National Urban League was the National Equal Rights League, an all-black organiza-

tion founded by Trotter. Trotter held fast to one idea, the importance of the complete integration and equality of blacks in every facet of American life. Perhaps his most important achievement was reestablishing of the black press as a dominant force in the black protest movement. Before the Civil War the black press had played a leading role in voicing the aspirations of black people. Now, as black Americans were becoming convinced that they were not going to be integrated into the total fabric of American life, they began to turn to the black press for an interpretation of the world in which they lived and the black press began to play a different and increasingly crucial role in the black community. There were 10 black newspapers in 1870, 31 in 1880, and 154 in 1890.

In 1913, 50 years after the Emancipation Proclamation, black Americans counted their achievements. In that year blacks owned 550,000 homes, operated 937,000 farms, and managed some 40,000 businesses. They held $700 million in funds. More than 70 percent of the black population was literate, a remarkable gain in 50 years. There were 40,000 black churches, 35,000, black teachers and 1.7 million black students in public schools. Yet in this year of celebration a wave of segregation laws was sweeping the South. In June 1913 Atlanta passed a law forbidding blacks and whites to live in the same neighborhoods. And in the summer of 1913 Woodrow Wilson ordered the segregation of government employees in federal bureaus. In the South there was a wave of brutal murders—the NAACP reported that 79 blacks had been lynched in that year of celebration (Bennett, 1954, p. 287).

The Great Migration

However, a new force was entering black life in the South. Letters from the North to families back home were reporting that the air was freer and the jobs better in the northern cities, and suddenly there was the phenomenon of the Great Migration. This was one of the greatest migrations of a people in history—a great movement of people who were not seeking to leave a country but to find a better life within it. The personal letters to families back home were supplemented by the need for labor in the defense industries and by the welcome given to the newcomers by the black press, especially Robert Abbott's *Chicago Defender.*

Like the immigrants, these American migrants settled in the cities of the North, and for the first time large numbers of blacks sought employment in urban industries. Here they were not welcomed with open arms. White workers, particularly the immigrants, objected to working side by side with black workers. Labor unions were unwilling to receive blacks as brothers, but gradually separately organized black unions were allowed to join the AFL.

Blacks in the armed services

During World War I, not only were thousands of blacks employed in industries for the first time, but thousands more, both in the North and in the South, entered military service. It is estimated that there were 370,000 black enlisted men and 1,400 black commissioned officers. A little more than half of these saw service in France, where they made an enviable record. Two black men, Henry Johnson and Needham Roberts, were the first two American soldiers to be cited for bravery in service abroad. For black Americans, however, World War I was a traumatic experience in which they were repeatedly humiliated. There were often conflicts between black soldiers and white soldiers and between black soldiers and white civilians. Many black men who had been trained to fight were assigned to menial duties as orderlies. Black regiments were often assigned as French complements. There were attempts to keep black officers from getting to know and associate with French officers. And there was the inevitable concern about black soldiers becoming friendly with French women.

Social conflict

At home, as abroad, black Americans faced troubled days. There were 54 lynchings in 1916 and 38 in 1917. On July 12, 1917, white workers in East St. Louis attacked black workers in one of the bloodiest race riots in American history. Nearly 6,000 blacks were driven from their homes, and estimates of the number killed ranged from 40 to 200. The NAACP organized a parade in New York City to protect this atrocity. However, the horror went on. There were 64 lynchings in 1918 and 83 in 1919. The violence of the mobs grew worse. Eleven blacks were burned alive in six different states. America erupted in the Red Summer of 1919, when 26 race riots occurred. During that summer, 170 blacks were killed and 537 blacks were injured in riots in Washington, Chicago, Omaha, and Knoxville. There was, however, a new dimension to these riots in that they were not all one-way massacres. Some were, in fact, wars in which blacks fought back and whites as well as blacks were killed.

The pessimism, despair, and cynicism among the blacks was exploited by Marcus Moziah Garvey who built up the first mass movement to urge the return of the blacks to Africa. Urging blacks to glory in their blackness, Garvey taught that God and the angels were black and that Satan and the imps were white. He collected more money—an estimated $10 million—than any other black organization had ever dreamed of raising. In 1925 he was arrested for using the mails to defraud and deported to his native Jamaica. He died in London in 1940.

Following World War I there was a change in the attitude of the white intellectuals toward the black artist and entertainer. This was the time of the black Renaissance—a period of exceptional creativity on the part of black artists and of great receptivity on the part of the white public. It was a time when every season at least one Broadway play was acted by a black cast. The black was in vogue. One of the outstanding black poets of the time was Langston Hughes.

✑ The Indians

By the beginning of the 20th century, the armed conflict, with the Indians over the land had been resolved by the greater strength of the white settlers and the conflict now moved to the political and economic areas. Indians still found it difficult to enforce their treaty rights, which were increasingly ignored. Basically, society made less and less room for the Native American.

Although the battles may have been over, the settlers' hunger for land remained unsatiated. The first modern political attack on Indian lands and rights was mounted with the passage of the General Allotment Act of 1887, commonly called the Dawes Act. It authorized the individual distribution of reservation lands among the members of tribes whenever the U.S. president believed that the lands might be used advantageously by whites for agricultural and grazing purposes. The Indians would thus become like the homesteaders and would obtain individual economic independence and adopt the life-style of the family farmer. In addition to thus breaking up tribal lands and allowing individual Indians to sell or otherwise use them, this act provided that such lands could then be subject to state property taxation, as the tribal lands were not.

The Dawes Act was an attempt to impose a uniform legal pattern for Indians without regard to cultural differences, and it was passed over the strenuous opposition of most Indians. It completely disregarded mutual agreements that had been a part of U.S. treaty-making with the Indians before this time. Following this new pattern, the U.S. government began bypassing the tribal organizations of the Indian people to deal directly with individual Indians. The Dawes Act did allow the Indians to gain U.S. citizenship through separating themselves from their tribes in this way.

In 1919 a law was passed allowing certain Indian War veterans to gain citizenship. In 1917, 1922, and 1923 additional attempts to fragment Indian lands further alienated the Indian people who persisted in their tribal ways. However, these attempts were unsuccessful or were declared unconstitutional by the Supreme Court. Not until the election of Franklin Roosevelt were attempts made to recognize the importance of the tribal rights and the tribal cultures of the Indian people (Hass, 1957, pp. 12–15).

✍ The Chicanos—Mexican-Americans

But a new group of immigrants were now flowing into the United States—a very different group from the groups which had crossed the ocean to reach American shores. By 1900 the Mexicans in the United States who had become citizens as a result of the settlement of the Mexican-American war were rapidly being absorbed into the Anglo culture. However, a number of forces in both the United States and Mexico were to swiftly alter this development. In Mexico, escalating social and economic strife from 1900 to 1920 uprooted thousands of people from their usual way of life. At the same time, in the southwestern United States there was a rapidly increasing demand for unskilled labor. These growing demands for labor were the result of a number of coinciding factors (Meier and Rivera, 1974, pp. 1–31; Reisler, 1976, pp. 1–48).

Federal land reclamation and irrigation projects in the arid Southwest greatly increased the value of the land and greatly expanded the land under cultivation, resulting in the development of cotton cultivation and in greatly increased vegetable cultivation. These crops required large numbers of people willing to work at what has come to be known as "stoop labor." Vegetable crops were becoming more and more important as the completion of railroads enabled the growers to supply the hungry cities with fresh vegetables.

The rush to complete the railroads in order to support the agriculture of the Southwest resulted in a desperate need for unskilled laborers who were willing to work hard on the land in the difficult climatic conditions of the region and were willing to maintain the railroad beds. These forces, plus increasing mining activities, were a pull that combined with the push of poverty and political chaos to set in motion a massive 20th century movement of people. This migration, in turn, created economic pressures in the Mexican communities of the Southwest that resulted in a secondary wave of migration from those communities into American communities farther north. Moving north in a fanlike pattern, Mexican-Americans inaugurated their own patterns of migration from south-central Texas. "Using railroads as their chief mode of transportation, sixable numbers of Chicanos soon appeared in almost every part of the United States except the South" (Meier and Rivera, 1974, p. 4). Industries in the North, as well as such agricultural interests as the growers of sugar beets, began to see economic advantages in using tractable and cheap Mexican labor. From the beginning of their work in the United States, Mexicans have paid less than native labor, have been housed more poorly, and have contributed greatly to the economic development of the United States.

The unique qualities of Mexican immigration

There were, and are, significant differences between the Mexican immigrants and other immigrants who came to the United States. The first difference has been the difficulty of appropriately controlling Mexican immigration. When the original restrictive immigration acts of 1921–24 were passed, immigrants from Mexico and Canada were specifically exempted, and thus no attempt was made to either study or control the flow of people from Mexico. Although there have been sporadic efforts to control Mexican immigration, the policing of the border has always been a problem for both Mexico and the United States and hundreds of people have crossed and recrossed the border illegally. At some times this has been easier to do than at other times, and thus there have been recurring waves of immigration rather than a continuous increase.

In addition, the employers of Mexican laborers have profited enormously from the willingness of these laborers to work at stoop labor and other difficult unskilled work for the lowest pay of any laborers in America. In fact, such employers maintain even today that it is impossible to recruit native American labor to do the jobs that Mexicans will accept. At times, these employers have openly recruited persons to enter the United States illegally. The use of both Mexican and American agents to recruit exploited laborers at a profit to themselves has been a constant factor in Mexican immigration.

In addition, unlike the other immigrants, few of the Mexican immigrants intended to make the United States their home. Their home remained in their communities in Mexico, and in difficult times they returned there. This also presented employers with an economic advantage. They had no responsibility to aid these workers, or to continue to employ them, when the need for their labor had passed. As a result, thousands of the immigrants were stranded without food, clothing, or shelter, particularly in the communities of the North. Several times over these years, confronted with the absolute refusal of the U.S. government to assume any responsibility for the Mexican laborers, even that of seeing that they were paid by their American employers as originally agreed, the Mexican government appropriated money for the relief of its nationals.

However, as the years have passed and crossing the border has become more and more difficult, increasing numbers of Mexicans have come as families with the notion of staying in the United States. Still, such people have not broken their ties to their first home, as did the European immigrants. And comparatively few Mexicans have become naturalized citizens. The years of heaviest immigration occurred after the peak of European immigration had ceased. Not until 1965 was a quota of permanent visas set for Mexican immigrants. It was set at 120,000 per year. Being recruited as temporary laborers to fill an immediate need and not as settlers, the Mexicans fitted well with the seasonal needs of agriculture and became migrant laborers, following the crops in a North-South pattern across the country year after year (Reisler, 1976, pp. 111–13 and 169).

Racism and the limitation of Mexican immigration

The immigration of Mexicans was greeted with approval by many employers and with indifference by most other people until the brief depression of 1921 that followed World War I. As the demand for Mexican laborers evaporated, they moved to the cities, where their story was one of joblessness, misery, and starvation. Many of the laborers were sustained only by food provided by the Mexican government. In Kansas City, 1,700 Mexicans had to sleep outdoors and to exist on food provided by the Swift and Armour companies. The economic slump was difficult for Americans as well as Mexicans, and the frustration of Americans resulted in anger against these new immigrants, who were charged with taking American jobs. The fact that Mexican laborers were often imported as strike-breakers during times of labor conflict did not help the situation. Unemployed Americans, both black and white, marched on city halls to protest the employment of Mexicans, and cities were threatened with riots unless they got rid of the unwelcome immigrants. In some cases there were brutal attacks on Mexican communities, and in many cities near panic was caused by the influx of unemployed Mexicans as the communities feared violence from the suffering newcomers. Police arrested and subjected to harsh treatment hundreds of immigrants whose only crime was that they sought work. Some cities resorted to chartering trains and shipping all unemployed Mexicans back to their homeland. In 1923, when industry began to expand again, new efforts were made to increase immigration only to have the whole scenario repeated when the Great Depression came.

The Mexicans suffered seriously from racism. Their mixture of Spanish and Indian blood caused them to be regarded as "mongrels." Although officially classified as whites, they were believed to be of a different race. Many persons lumped them with blacks, and they were denied access to white institutions. In the Southwest their children could not attend Anglo schools and had none of their own. Studies of the conditions under which they lived in the cities of America have indicated that their living conditions were poorer than those of any other group.

Given their housing and other living conditions, it is not surprising that the health of the Mexican immigrants became a major problem. Tuberculosis was perhaps the most widespread of their many diseases. In Chicago the Tuberculosis Institute, through its Christmas Seal Fund, established a Mexican Health Center in 1930. Dating from the 1920s, the mutualista became the principal source of aid to the Mexican families. These mutualista were like the mutual aid societies of other immigrant and black groups. Their membership usually consisted of 20 to 120 families, and their benefits included support and sickness and burial payments (Reisler, 1976, p. 107).

Mexican consuls actively supported and frequently organized the *comisiones honoríficas* which celebrated national Mexican holidays in most Mexican settlements in the United States. Mexicans continued to suffer from arbitrary police harassment. Many policemen coming from first- or second-generation European immigrant families were strongly prejudiced against the Mexicans. In Gary, Indiana, in 1924, Mexicans founded La Sociadad Protectora Mexicana (the Mexican Protection Society), which attempted to protect the immigrants' legal rights. The society provided bail and legal advice for arrested Mexicans.

The churches and the Mexican immigrants

The established Roman Catholic Church played a much less significant and active part in the life of the Mexican immigrants than it did in the lives of the earlier immigrants. The Catholicism brought North by the Mexicans was very different from that of the Europeans who dominated the local parishes. Gradually, separate Mexican churches developed in storefronts, but it was 1927 before a Mexican community had a parish of its own. Our Lady of Guadalupe was established in East Chicago at that time (Reisler, 1976, p. 108).

✒ Social work and minorities

As one reads the social work literature of the early 1900s, it is interesting how little one finds that is related specifically to the black, Chicano, or Indian problems of the time. Social work had always been dedicated to radical equality, but the social work professionals, accustomed to dealing with the problems of immigrants from western Europe, tended to assume that the new migrants needed the same kind of help and service. The case records of the time speak of the struggle to find housing and employment for the new clients, but they give no hint that the social workers recognized that the discrimination which confronted the blacks and the Mexicans was of a quality different from the discrimination which was met by the European immigrant. In the first decade of the century, this attitude could perhaps be explained by the fact that few blacks or Mexicans sought help from organized agencies. At that time, the blacks were a small part of the population and they tended to turn to their own churches or societies in times of trouble. The Mexicans tended to turn to their extended families or to their friends, or to return to Mexico if that was possible. In the debates over Mexican immigration, social workers supported the restriction of immigration because they felt that life in the United States was too harsh and brutal. They felt that ways to help those already here had to precede further admissions.

The settlements and race

The prosperity and economic opportunity that came with the war years brought changes to the neighborhoods served by the settlements. The immigrants who had been the early "neighbors" of the settlements began to move away, and new neighbors moved in. These newcomers were of a different race and culture than the earlier immigrants. Southern blacks, Latin Americans, and other minority groups began to move into the neighborhoods, and tensions began to develop between and among these different groups of newcomers. A group of Italian-Americans threatened to withdraw from Hull House if Mexican-Americans were allowed to use its facilities. Moreover, raising funds to work with blacks or Mexicans was much more difficult than had been raising funds to help the European immigrants.

Some settlements tried to follow their neighbors into new neighborhoods. This was particularly true of the Jewish centers. One such center moved four

times in ten years before it gave up the chase (Chambers, 1963, pp. 119–20). Other settlements began to experiment with separation of groups. The Henry Street settlement experimented with separate clubs, but this did not seem to work any better than had the attempt to maintain no distinction or discrimination. The Godman Guild Association of Columbus, Ohio, set up separate days for blacks and whites to use the settlement. The director of the center justified his policy by stating that both blacks and whites would stay away from the settlement if he tried to integrate it (Peterson, 1965, 191–208).

Some settlements became all black, and some new settlements were developed to serve black groups. There were two all-black settlements in Chicago: the Frederick Douglass Center and the Trinity Mission Settlement. It has been pointed out by black writers (Du Bois, 1909; Billingsley, 1968) that the overwhelming burden of social help for black families fell upon the black people themselves. Few proposals for action, programs or plans were advanced by the settlement leaders of the 1920s and 1930s to guarantee the political, economic, or social rights of the black people or to deal with their special circumstances. Significantly missing from the discussions in the social work and social welfare literature was talk of "assimilating" these new neighbors, though assimilation had represented a priority goal of the settlements in relation to other immigrants.

The National Conference and minorities

To Philip C. Garrett belongs the credit for having organized the only two programs of the National Conference of Social Work to deal with racial minorities in the century between 1850 and 1950, and these programs dealt only with Indians and blacks. Garrett, who retired from business at 42 to devote his life to social work, involved himself primarily with the Indians and served as a member of the Federal Board of Indian Commissioners (Bruno, 1957, pp. 331–40). In the program that dealt with the Indians, the Indian point of view was presented by an Indian, James M. Stuart.

After this conference program the fate of Indians was discussed occasionally in specific papers at the annual meetings. In 1923 Henrietta J. Lund presented a paper on "Casework with the Indians," and in 1929 Meriam presented a paper on the future of the Indian in the Committee on the Immigrant. In this paper Meriam laid down the basic social work principles of self-determination and individuality, holding that the Indians should be consulted about what they wanted for their future and that it was important to recognize differences among tribes. Assimilation might be the answer for some tribes, but there were other tribes with a precious heritage of tribal culture that had no desire to become a part of the white way of life. In 1930 the Conference set up a special program committee on the American Indian with Meriam as chairman. Some scattered papers came from this committee during the 30s.

The program devoted to the blacks was more realistic than that devoted to the Indians. One theme of the Conference papers was the health problems of blacks. The blacks had a death rate that was practically twice as high as the death rate of whites, and there were predictions that the blacks' death rate would increase and that the black race would eventually be eliminated in America. However, Eugene Kinkle Jones of the National Urban League pointed out in 1928 that the death rate among blacks was then about the same as the death rate for whites 15 years earlier, that the differences in the death rates among various socioeconomic levels of blacks were frequently greater than the mean differences between whites and blacks, and that his studies suggested that the influences on the health of black people were largely environmental and therefore controllable.

There was a good deal of discussion of the difficulties faced by blacks when they migrated to the North. It was pointed out that they met segregation and that the unions were closed to them. Black males usually had to work as scabs or in unskilled and unorganized jobs. Many black women found only domestic work available to them. Despite the fact that as blacks continued to move north, there were new problems and new disturbances, including race riots, this was the last time that the Conference dealt with the problems of black migration.

In several addresses at the Conference, blacks stated what they wanted of American democracy. These "wants" consisted mostly of a more adequate part in the political processes of the nation, better justice in the courts, better opportunities for education and jobs, and better protection by government. There was not a word about social equality (Bruno, 1957, p. 399).

ᴥ§ Social, political, and economic thought

As we have discussed, in the 19th century there were two lines of thought about social welfare. The first was the notion of charity as it had developed over the hundreds of years of religious thought. The second was associated with the "liberal thought" of the 1800s, which sought to identify and act in accord with the "natural laws" of politics and economics. These two notions reinforced each other in that an acceptance of the liberal political philosophy was added to the notion that the affluent had a moral responsibility to help the unfortunate. The scientific spirit that became prevalent in social welfare during the late 1800s questioned the means and ends of helping but not these basic economic and political doctrines.

However, as the 20th century began, research in the infant social sciences was leading to the questioning of earlier thought. William James and John Dewey were particularly critical of the assumptions that individuals naturally pursued pleasure and avoided work unless forced or bribed to do so. At the same time, the new Social Gospel was preaching that it was the duty of people to advance the kingdom of God by shaping a new and juster society. As the century brought an increasing rise in the standard of living of more and more people and as the industrial economy seemed to promise an ever greater abundance, the persistence of need and suffering among large groups of people came to seem wrong, and many of the new social scientists puzzled over the paradox of progress and poverty (Leiby, 1978, pp. 136–140).

For those who were actually engaged in charity

work, there began to be a concern with the reciprocal influences of heredity and environment on human behavior and problems. In addition, the notions of technical competence and service began to assume a critical importance. Inductive reasoning began to replace deductive reasoning among the social and economic thinkers; empirical facts became important for what they could reveal about general principles rather than merely for use as evidence supporting an already developed line of argument. By 1912 a bold new concept of social welfare was beginning to emerge, a concept which addressed itself to the impersonal causes of poverty and injustice and looked toward a more equal and just society. The social studies of the time, many of them directed by social workers, began to draw attention to and to detail the way of life of large groups of people who were living in poverty. These studies brought out environmental as distinct from personal causes of dependence and so pointed inevitably to social and environmental reforms.

The definition of poverty

One of the first of these studies was begun by Charles Booth in 1885, when he undertook a careful description of the working classes of London. In his observations Booth was able to group families into eight classes according to their standard of living. Taking the bulk of the families as a normal standard class, he found that, relative to the standard of living of these families, 30.7 percent of London families lived in poverty and 69.3 percent lived in comfort (Leiby, 1978, p. 139). This was a significant contribution to thinking about social welfare in that it introduced the concept of the poverty line and gave that concept empirical content in the form of a descriptive standard of living.

Poverty as threat

The notion of a normal standard of living was significant for economists. In 1890 Alfred Marshall, an economist, published a text in which he developed the concept of a normal standard of living

as "the necessaries for the efficiency of an ordinary agricultural or unskilled town labourer and his family" (Leiby, 1978, p. 140). Marshall believed that the normal standard of living was subjective and changed over time, but he also believed that it was reasonably definite at any particular time. He held that deprivation below this standard would threaten the efficiency of the worker's performance. Jacob Hollander, a professor of political economy at Johns Hopkins and the author of *Abolition of Poverty,* defined the poor as the part of the population that was "inadequately fed, clad, and sheltered" (Bremner, 1956, p. 125). In 1904 Edward Devine, the general secretary of the New York COS, developed a book, *Principles of Relief,* around the formulation of a normal standard of living as a help in defining the amount of need and the adequacy of relief.

In the same year, Robert Hunter, the head worker at the University Settlement of New York, published *Poverty,* which might be called the first version of the welfare state in America. Hunter held that poverty consisted simply of receiving "too little of the common necessities" essential to a state of physical well-being (Bremner, 1956, p. 125) and that much more numerous than the paupers were the poor, who, though they worked hard and long, were simply unable to secure the common necessities of life for themselves. Hunter's principal themes were: (1) look beyond individual pauperism to the more basic problem of poverty; (2) define a poverty line that is related to minimal decency of living and to physical efficiency; and (3) enforce the minimum by positive governmental action. Hunter argued that such governmental action would not destroy but, on the contrary, would increase initiative by equalizing opportunity and increasing security. This sensational and influential statement of the new view of poverty as a threat to the nation's welfare held that the government should: (1) establish and enforce minimum standards of safe housing and safe working conditions; (2) regulate hours of work; (3) supervise the dangerous occupations; (4) prohibit child labor; (5) take steps to eradicate threats to health; (6) provide educational and recreational opportunities; (7) compensate workers for involuntary idleness due to sickness, old age, or unemployment; and (8) restrict immigration.

In 1906 Father John Ryan published his doctoral dissertation, *A Living Wage,* which advocated that a *living* wage be established as the legal minimum wage. He defined this as a wage that would allow individuals a degree of self-respect and spiritual culture.

The surveys of poverty

In 1906 the New York State Conference of Charities employed Robert Chapin, a doctoral student at Columbia, to investigate the actual standards of living in New York City. And in 1907 Paul Kellog, managing editor of *Charities and Commons,* a social work journal, undertook to direct the Pittsburgh Survey. This study, supported in part by the New York and Pittsburgh COSs and the Russell Sage Foundation, undertook to make a broad social analysis of the conditions of life and labor in an industrial city. Kellog sought to assemble and organize a vast array of facts in an effort to find a "human measure" by which to analyze and judge contemporary society (Chambers, 1971, p. 38). His study was the first inductive investigation of the causes of work accidents and of their economic impact on families. It is difficult to assess the complete impact of the study, but it appears to have affected the slum housing of the city, to have helped in the movement toward shortening the 12-hour day, to have promoted safety campaigns in industry, and to have given an impetus toward workers' compensation.

For perhaps a hundred years it had been "an article of faith with dime novelists, Sunday-school teachers, and millionaires that poverty strengthened character, stimulated incentive and punished sloth." Now it appeared that instead of strengthening character and incentive, poverty was a negative experience, debilitating to body, mind, and character. A childhood in poverty was seen as destroying the possibilities for normal development. In *Applied Sociology,* written in 1906, Lester Ward wrote, "Indigence is an effective bar to opportu-

nity." And in 1914, for the first time, two monographs published by the Russell Sage Foundation examined the effects of deprivation on children. William Dean Howells, a well-known novelist of the period, held that the curse of want and destitution was less debilitating to people than was the fear of want. The lack of security in industrial society remained a stressful undercurrent for which the society of the time provided no answer. These definitions were generally accepted, so that in 1921, in his widely adopted text *Poverty and Dependency: Their Relief and Prevention,* John Lewis Gillin, defined poverty as the "inability to maintain a decent standard of living" (Bremner, 1956, p. 128).

Attitudes toward wealth

Along with this change in thought regarding poverty came a parallel shift in attitudes toward wealth. Americans, particularly American Protestants, had seen the possession of wealth as an indication of virtue and special ability. Men who started life with nothing but their own ability and amassed large fortunes were symbols of the optimism and the opportunity that was America. But with the closing of the frontier and with the growing complexity of industrial society, in which wealth was clearly made through the exploitation of others, a strong current of criticism began to supplant the earlier admiration of wealth. Individuals who had been admired for the very bigness of their fortunes were now shown by the muckrakers of the early 20th century to have acquired them in ways that were not only dangerously close to being illegal but had also imposed burdens and disadvantages upon the rest of the community. There was a growing willingness to apply a common standard of morality to all people, whether rich or poor. Louis Brandeis, in the *Oregon* case discussed earlier, argued that low-paying industries (and the persons who controlled them) were parasitic in nature, as they were subsidized by employees, the families of employees, and society as a whole.

The causes and cure of poverty

The reformers, though not denying that individual problems and frailties could contribute to want and insecurity, held that social weaknesses rather than individual weaknesses were the causes of poverty. In 1910 Henry R. Seager of Columbia University listed five great misfortunes that were at the root of most poverty—illness, accident, premature death of the family wage earner, unemployment, and old age. This emphasis on economic rather than moral causes of poverty caused reformers to shift their concern from the morality and uplift of the poor to the rights and grievances of the working class. Believing that society could correct these injustices if it chose to do so, the new reformers were convinced that by callous inaction society countenanced cruelties that few men as individuals would perpetrate, let alone approve.

Believing that the cure for poverty was the correction of unjust and degrading conditions of work and living, the Progressive reformers enrolled in political battle to pass legislation establishing and maintaining fair standards of wages, hours, and housing; prohibiting child labor; regulating the dangerous trades; compensating labor for unemployment, accidents, sickness, and old age; organizing a more vigorous and more effective public health program; establishing playgrounds and more abundant recreational facilities; introducing a more practical system of public education; and restricting immigration. The important thing about these measures was that they all involved the restriction and limitation of private property and the extension of the powers of government into areas that before the 1900s had been considered areas of individual rights. Social justice began to assume an important place among individual rights. Individuals began to have the right to require from their society certain protections and supports that added up to a right to social security. At the time, the formulation and the work to secure the necessary legislation was called "preventive social work," but today, when most of the legislation is in place, we recognize it as the foundation of the "welfare state."

After the war

The 1920s are often seen as an interlude of reaction and conservatism. This view focuses on the political defeats of the reformers as they tried to effect changes through legislation. The various events of the 1920s fostered disillusion about the use of political processes to solve problems. This disillusion was especially marked among the young people of the business and professional class. They seemed to immerse themselves in a search for liberation and individualism, or they became a part of some religious or agrarian order or of some movement supporting a socialist revolution. However, alongside the frivolous quality and the skepticism of the Jazz Age, there were positive strengths: the success of the unprecedented wartime efforts, the remarkable peacetime prosperity, and the steady technical progress of American agriculture, commerce, and industry.

A deep belief in technology appeared in schools of medicine and education and strongly marked the rationale and the organization of the social services. It came to be believed that the political questions of democracy could be resolved by techniques of rational inquiry and experimentation borrowed from science. Thorstein Veblen held that the radical element in society would be the engineers, not the workers. Certainly the newly developing industries created a strong demand for engineers and for the professional experts in scientific management (Leiby, 1978, p. 140). These efforts to be rational and scientific resulted in two fundamental ideas: (1) that to achieve maximum production with a minimum of friction the well-being of the workers had to be taken into account; and (2) that mass production was of no benefit without mass consumption, which in turn rested on wages adequate to elective spending by the mass of workers. These insights led employers to be concerned with various reforms that would support the welfare of their workers and to support the notion of linking a living wage to the worker's rising productivity (Lauck, 1929, chaps. 7–8). These notions were central to the thinking of such leaders as Herbert Hoover, who believed that social advancement had little to do with the intervention of government and put a fundamental faith in improvements in economic technology and attitudes.

The effects of mass production

In these years, the mass production principle brought about by the new industrial order changed the distribution of goods and services and the roles and status of individual workers, became a general principle for organizing people at work, and separated workers from both the product and the means of production. For the first time in human history, the organization rather than the individual became the producer of goods. Most workers no longer had an opportunity to produce economic goods independently with their own hands; in order to be productive in society, they had to have access to a complex organization called a plant.

For the average worker, social status, prestige and social power began to be attached to the job—to membership, status, prestige, and power within the organization—rather than to the work done or to the possession of personal competence. The skill demanded of workers in such a society tended to continually increase, and the skills demanded tended to be social and intellectual skills rather than skills in the manipulating of tools and materials. Thus, in many ways—not just in the early 1900s but in today's world as well—the changes in the production and distribution of goods in the industrial society constantly worked to devalue traditional behavior and values. Because few people in the industrial society can be productive without access to an organization of production, unemployed people found themselves outcasts from society. Their welfare and that of their families depended on their ability to find a point of access, not on their individual ability to be productive. With their membership in society suspended, the unemployed were faced with loss of self-respect, with loss of initiative, and with loss of place, power, and influence in the social fabric.

In the new industrial society, the place of business moved away from the family residence and the family members no longer worked as a unit. This had a tremendous impact on the socialization of children. Children could no longer learn meaningful patterns of work or social skills from close association with their parents. As we pointed out in the last chapter, children had always worked but now they did not work as children within the family but as stunted adults. Even if all the members of a family worked side by side in the same plant, they did not work as a family unit. Thus, production in the outside world, involving, as it did, a new social order, became a tremendous threat to the place of women and children in society and acted to destroy rather than support the cohesion and integration of the family unit.

৺ Summary

In this chapter we have discussed the development of industrialization and urbanization. We have looked at the problems of some of the vulnerable populations: children, women, immigrants, and minorities. We have discussed the efforts of the Progressives and looked at some of the forces of the first three decades of the 20th century. To give a summary account of those forces:

৺ 1. The limiting conditions of knowledge and the technical ability to manipulate and control environmental and individual factors were changing in significant ways. People were pushing hard at the earlier limits of knowledge, and the ability to control factors affecting human life was growing too rapidly to permit people to totally understand its impact.
2. Society was becoming increasingly complex, and there was a growing differentiation among the various parts of an individual's life as well as among the various institutions of society and the subsystems that made up those institutions.
3. The influx of immigrants brought different beliefs, values, ideologies, customs, and traditions into American life.

4. The rapid movement of people and the rapid industrialization of work led to new and more severe conflicts of interest groups.

5. A new group of leaders in social reform came to the fore. They were influential, partly because of the above factors, and their leadership affected the other factors.

6. World War I represented an extrasocietal force that interrupted the movement toward the political reform of social organizations and moved us toward technology as reform.

7. The mass production principle changed the functioning of the economic institution so as to pave the way for severe changes in the allocation of roles, statuses and individual security in society. These changes had severe effects on other institutions and on individuals.

8. The increasing knowledge of human needs, the increasing control over the environment, and the mass production technology interacted to result in a new recognition of human needs and to create new ways for meeting those needs.

9. Increases in knowledge and improvements in the technologies of communication made people (especially the leaders of society) more consciously aware of the wider dimensions of human life and of human needs, beyond those of the immediate group.

10. New methods of inquiry and the use of inductive reasoning led to new views of poverty.

None of these changes sprang up full-blown with the 20th century, but the changes seemed to come together at this time and the pace of change increased during the first two decades of the 1900s.

A look ahead

If we were to follow our usual pattern in developing this portion of the text, we would now offer the reader a chapter describing the social welfare policies and programs that developed during the period discussed in this chapter. However, we are going to depart from this pattern and we shall discuss the social welfare policies and programs of this period in two chapters, for two reasons: (1) the number and complexity of the new ways of thinking about human needs and of taking action to meet them would make for an overly long and difficult chapter; and (2) the foundation of our present social welfare programs and our present social work profession were laid during this period, and it is therefore important to discuss the period in enough detail for students of today to understand how that foundation affected the shape of the framework erected on it later.

Because of the overlapping development and the interaction of the programs of the time, it is extremely difficult to separate them in a rational way. We have decided to describe the efforts toward reform and social welfare in wartime in the first chapter (these are also mostly public income maintenance programs and programs relating to children) and to detail the growth of organization and professionalization as well as other programs in the second chapter. This division follows a rough time approximation, in that reform efforts peaked before the war and organization grew more rapidly afterward.

Study questions

1. In this chapter we have discussed several struggles for change. Outline the interests that opposed restrictions on child labor. Outline the arguments that were used against the constitutional amendment which would have outlawed child labor. What values did these arguments appeal to?

2. What forces opposed the movement of women toward equal rights? What arguments were used against women's suffrage? What were the differences and likenesses of the interests involved and the arguments used in the child labor and women's suffrage battles?

3. Do you favor working for small concrete gains, or do you think it more important to work for radical change? What are the advantages and disadvantages of these positions?

4. List the various conflicts of this time and the groups involved.

5. What was the role of the Supreme Court in the reforms of this time?

✌ Selected readings

Meier, Matt S., and Rivera, Feliciano, eds. *Readings on La Raza: The Twentieth Century.* New York: Hill and Wang, 1974.

This book is a selection of documents that have been collected to illuminate and illustrate salient aspects of what has happened to Chicanos in the United States since 1900. The documents collected here give students a feel for what was really happening in relation to a largely ignored minority.

Reisler, Mark. *By the Sweat of Their Brow: Mexican Immigrant Labor in the United States, 1900–1940.* Westport, Conn.: Greenwood Press.

This history of the experiences of Mexican labor in the United States should be of interest to students.

Meier, August, and Rudwick, Elliott. *From Plantation to Ghetto.* 3 ed. New York: Hill and Wang, 1976.

Chaps. 5 and 6 of this book tell the story of the black people following the Civil War. The book serves to enlarge the discussion in our chapter.

Meier, August. *Negro Thought in America: 1880–1915.* Ann Arbor: University of Michigan Press, 1966.

This book is strongly recommended to students who plan to become social workers as a text that will help them to develop some understanding of the work of black people in our society. It is an excellent supplement to our chapter.

Abbott, Edith. *Women in Industry.* New York: D. Appleton, 1910; reprinted by Arno Press, 1969.

Students should find this book of interest for two reasons. The book itself is interesting as a revelation of early social work thought, and women students should appreciate something of the early history of women and work.

Chafe, William H. *The American Woman: Her Changing Social, Economic, and Political Roles, 1920–1970.* (New York: Oxford University Press, 1972).

A good historical analysis of the women's movement in the United States.

Baxandall, Rosalyn; Gordon, Linda; and Reverby, Susan. *America's Working Women.* New York: Vintage Books, 1976.

Like some of the other books we recommend, this book is a collection of documents. These documents reveal, as nothing else can, the life of women in the first three decades of the 20th century and earlier.

ST LOUIS POST-DISPATCH

FIREPROOF!

NEW YORK EVE. JOURNAL

FIRE PROOF—NOT DEATH PROOF CONSTRUCTION

BOSTON HERALD

Shall There Be Another?

FIRE PROOF BUILDING
HORROR!
141 LIVES
SACRIFICED.

BROOKLYN EAGLE

THE DEMAND

NEW YORK AMERICAN

EXIT

CRIMINAL NEGLIGENCE

CLEVELAND PLAIN DEALER

WARNED

BOSTON POST

One of the 145

NEW YORK EV. JOURNAL

KNICKERBOCKER
NEW YORK

150 LIVES
WASHINGTON
PLACE
FIRE

I WONDER. COULD IT HAPPEN TO ME?.

PHILADELPHIA ENQUIRER

Chapter 18 ❧

❧ Reform and public social welfare programs, 1900–1930 ❧

Child labor and industrial safety were serious concerns for the social workers of the Progressive Era.

The New York Triangle Factory fire prompted the editorial cartoons *(opposite)* in contemporary newspapers.

Early in the 20th century the telegraph and messenger companies were the largest single employers of children in the United States—*above* is a typical messenger boy.

359

✑ Introduction

In this chapter we shall discuss the attempts of the social workers of the Progressive years to utilize political processes to implement a bold new notion of social welfare addressing the social causes of poverty, insecurity, and injustice. In addition, we shall discuss the work of social workers during World War I and their disappointment afterward as they discovered that, somewhere on the road to reform, society appeared to have lost its way.

In the last chapter we addressed the broad issues of the struggles to regulate child labor and to win the franchise for women. The franchise was won, but the struggle to establish the right of the federal government to regulate child labor was lost for the time being through a Supreme Court decision. In this chapter we shall discuss the continued attempt to make the social welfare institution more responsive to human need through political action: the establishment of the Children's Bureau, the passage of the Maternal and Child Health Act, and the struggle for social security through social insurance and for income maintenance through public assistance. We shall also take up the wartime work of the Red Cross.

✑ The White House Conference on Child Welfare

It was the historic White House Conference on Child Welfare in 1909 that first brought the subject of dependent children before the entire nation. That conference also gave social work a place on the national scene that it had never had before. There are a number of stories about how the conference originated. One of the most colorful is given by Bruno (1959, p. 152). He relates that

> Lillian Wald happened to read in the morning paper one day in 1906 about a special session of the President's Cabinet being called to consider the menace of the boll weevil. She turned to her breakfast companion, Mrs. Florence Kelley, and said, "This is interesting. Nothing in the interest of children could or would bring about a special Cabinet meeting, or fix the attention of our legisla-

tors. We count the boll weevil, or the lobster, or a fish, or a pig as more important than a child."

During the discussion between the two social workers that followed, the hope was expressed that someday a federal agency would be established that might be as concerned with the welfare of the nation's children as the agricultural agency was with the welfare of the cotton crop. Florence Kelley later discussed the conversation with Edward Devine, secretary of the New York COS, who sent a telegram to President Theodore Roosevelt expressing concern about the lack of a bureau to protect the nation's children. According to the story, Roosevelt immediately wired back, "It's a bully idea. Come to Washington, and let's see." In an effort to generate public support for such a bureau, the President called the White House Conference on Child Welfare in 1909. Other literature traces the conference to a proposal by James E. West, a Boy Scout executive and a friend of President Roosevelt. An orphan who was reared in an institution, West was concerned about the welfare of dependent children.

However it came about, the president invited some 200 prominent men and women from all parts of the country to attend a two-day conference on the needs of children in late January 1909. The conference was designed to provide for an exchange of ideas about the needs of the country's dependent children and to recommend a plan for their care. The report of this conference, which was unanimously adopted by the persons present, was to have far-reaching effects on the welfare of families and children throughout the nation.

The report

The report stated: "Home life is the highest and finest product of civilization . . . . children should not be deprived of it except for urgent and compelling reasons." It continued by saying that for children "who for sufficient reasons must be removed from their own homes, or who have no homes . . . it is desirable that they should be cared for in families whenever practicable. The carefully selected foster home is for the normal child the best substitute for the natural home" (Trattner, 1974, p. 181). This recommendation became critical to the movement to establish programs for assisting mothers to care for their children in their own homes, to efforts to keep delinquent and dependent children in their own homes, to the development of adoption as a method for providing homes for homeless children, to the increased use of the foster home rather than the institution for the care of children, and to the development of a cottage type of institution for children instead of the large congregate-type of institution.

An interesting outcome of this conference was the precedent it established. Every ten years since 1909, there has been a White House conference on children's problems and needs. And each conference in turn has had important effects on the concepts of child care and on progressive child welfare programs. The conference of 1919 formulated four specific charges for the next decade: to support programs designed to promote and protect the health of mothers and children; to advance knowledge of child life and promote sound programs through study and research; to establish minimum standards for children in industry; and to develop programs designed to meet the needs of children in special jeopardy, such as delinquents.

◄§ The Children's Bureau

However, the most important achievement of the first White House conference was its support for the creation of the Children's Bureau and the inauguration of programs to assist mothers. The idea of creating a federal agency concerned with the problems of children may have been the reason that the conference was originally convened, as our earlier story implies. The bill creating the Children's Bureau was introduced by Senator William Borah of Idaho and followed a special message to Congress from President Roosevelt calling for its adoption. The bill's supporters pointed out that the government spent far more money each year on animal research than the bill would call for (an appropriation of $1,250,000 versus one of $50,000

and a staff of 1,000 versus one of 14) and that as a result the mortality rate of young animals was less than that of young children. In five days of bitter floor debate, the bill's opponents in Congress argued that its supporters were working under orders from European socialists and communists who intended to use the agency to regulate the nation's youth. Finally, however, the bill passed the Senate on January 31, 1912, and two months later it passed the House, and in April 1912 it was signed into law by President William Howard Taft. By the time of its passage, Roosevelt, who had supported it so firmly, was no longer in office so that the bill was signed by his successor.

While the proposed bureau was still being discussed, Homer Folks, a social worker who later became known for his work in the public health movement, gave, in 1910, what could be considered a classic outline of the arguments of its opponents. Some opponents claimed that the proposal did not go far enough, and others claimed that it attempted to accomplish too much at one step. Some opponents claimed that the purposes of the proposal were already being accomplished by existing statutes; others said that the objectives of the proposal were good but that they should be achieved under other auspices. Then the three final arguments (always brought out when other arguments fail) were that the bureau would cost more than the country could afford, that it would destroy our form of government, and that in any event it was unconstitutional. The important thing about such arguments is that none of them are based on the actual faults or merits of the proposal. The tragedy of such tactics is that they work well, even today, without ever dealing with the merits of the issue (Bruno, 1957, pp. 153–154).

The creation of the U.S. Children's Bureau was the first occasion on which the federal government entered the field of social services as distinguished from public health and education. The bureau received an initial appropriation of $25,640 and was located within the Department of Commerce and Labor. A year later it was transferred to the newly created Department of Labor, and in 1953 it was moved again to another newly created department—the Department of Health, Education, and Welfare. In 1967 the Children's Bureau became a part of the General Services Administration. Over the years of the 1960s and 1970s the Children's Bureau gradually lost its central influence in public child welfare. But at the time of its creation it was said to have ushered in a new era in services to children. The bureau was charged with the duty of investigating and reporting on all matters pertaining to the welfare of children and on the lives of children in all groups and classes of Americans. It had no administrative power, and it was to perform no services. It was originally "wholly a research organization and information center, as were the scientific bureaus in the departments of Agriculture, the Interior and Commerce and Labor" (Abbott, 1938, p. 612). It was to serve and evaluate agencies concerned with any aspect of child health, child labor, and child welfare. "The whole child was made the subject of its research" (Abbott, 1938, p. 613). Some of its publications on children and their development have been among the best-selling books in the country.

Julia Lathrop, the first chief of the Children's Bureau, was cofounder of the University of Chicago School of Social Work and had had long years of experience in public welfare as well as private social agencies. She recognized the inevitable limitations of private child welfare and "was convinced that the state had only just begun to accept the responsibility it must finally assume for insuring minimum standards of care for all children. Democracy in her opinion must seek continually new ways of insuring the optimum growth and development of all American children" (Abbott, 1938, p. 613). Lathrop thought that social programs needed to build upon a careful accumulation of facts, and she was prepared to go wherever investigations led her.

Beginning in 1908, some stirrings of interest in the new notion that child health was worthy of some attention had begun to appear in the New York City Department of Health and the American Academy of Medicine. Thus, there was some precedent when the newly established Children's Bureau undertook as its first project a study to de-

termine how many babies died in a year and the causes of their deaths. This was difficult to establish, as many states did not register births and deaths. To the surprise and dismay of many people, it was found that there was not only a terribly high infant mortality rate but a shockingly high mortality rate for mothers as well. It was a startling revelation that in the second decade of the 20th century in America more women died unnecessarily each year during childbirth (or lived on afterward in chronic invalidism) than from any other cause except tuberculosis, that the maternal death rate was higher in the United States than in any other leading nation in the world, and that the large number of orphaned American children was in part the result of the high maternal death rate.

✒ The Sheppard-Towner Act

Determined that something had to be done about this, Julia Lathrop drew up a plan in 1917 for the "public protection of maternity and infancy" and published it in her *Annual Report* to Congress. The plan was that the government would offer grants-in-aid, on a matching basis, to those states promising to establish facilities and services such as outpatient clinics, hospitals, and public health nursing in accordance with standards established by the Children's Bureau. The grants would be administered by the state health departments.

Lathrop was able to gain sponsorship for a bill embodying these notions in 1918, and the Infancy and Maternity, or Sheppard-Towner, Bill was introduced into Congress. During the Campaign for its enactment the same arguments were heard that had been used earlier against the Children's Bureau. However, because of the recent Russian Revolution the references to socialism, communism, and the nationalization of the nation's youth were even stronger and more influential. In addition, the supporters of the measure had to combat a highly organized and well-financed campaign by the leaders of the nation's doctors, who charged that the measure was designed to interfere with the private practice of medicine and that it represented "state medicine." A typical example of the doctors' attack on the bill was a pamphlet titled *Shall the Children of America Become the Property of the State?*, written and circulated by the Legislative Committee of the Illinois State Medical Society.

The *Illinois Medical Journal* stated, "This bill is a menace and represents another piece of destructive legislation sponsored by *endocrine perverts, derailed menopausics* and a lot of other men and women who have been bitten by that fatal parasite, the *uplifticus putrifaciens,* in the guise of uplifters, all of whom are working overtime to devise means to destroy the country" (italics those of author). The *Journal* of the American Medical Association stated, "The Sheppard-Towner law is an imported socialistic scheme unsuited to our form of government" (Bremner, 1971, p. 1020).

The arguments on the floor of Congress were very bitter. They involved appeals to the worst fears and prejudices abroad in the land (many of which are still with us) and very little of the facts of the situation. The bill's opponents invoked the fear of federal control, the fear of socialism and foreign ideas, the fear of racial equality, and all the discrimination against women that could be found in the all-male group representing the highest governing body in our nation.

It is a sad commentary on the regard in which women were held in the second decade of the 20th century in America that the opponents of a bill to further their welfare, and the welfare of their children, should have thought that it could be defeated by speeches which sought to make jokes of women who, by holding administrative offices and by not marrying, had dared to violate the common notions of the place of women in American life. At the same time, these speeches sought to develop fear of knowledgeable, professional women by painting them as seeking to interfere with and control family life.

In support of the statements just made, we shall quote briefly from a speech delivered on the floor of the Senate by James Reed, a Democrat from Missouri, who began by expressing his fears of the vast powers that the bill would vest in the chief of the Children's Bureau. He continued:

As these immense powers are conferred upon the chief and exercised through her associates in the bureau and her chosen assistants, the question of personality becomes important.

The senator then listed the names of the staff of the bureau and continued:

Observe that the entire bureau is composed of unmarried women, except Mrs. Helen Woodbury and her husband, who both hold jobs in the same department.

It seems to be the established doctrine of this bureau that the only people capable of caring for babies and the mothers of babies are ladies who have never had babies (laughter from his colleagues). . . .

. . . All the medical doctors who have been concerned in the preparation of literature or the work of the bureau are women and are, I believe, with one exception unmarried.

At the very threshold, therefore, we are confronted by the remarkable and amusing fact that we are asked to turn over questions of infant bearing and infant care to an aggregation composed almost exclusively of spinsters. It is enough to arouse "the laughter of the gods.". . .

. . . when we employ female celibates to instruct mothers how to raise babies they have brought into the earth, do we indulge in a rare bit of irony? . . . I cast no reflection on unmarried ladies. Perhaps some of them are too good to have husbands. But any woman who is too refined to have a husband should not undertake the care of another woman's baby when that other woman wants to take care of it herself. . . .

. . . the fundamental doctrines on which the bill is founded were drawn chiefly from the radical, socialistic, and bolshevistic philosophy of Germany and Russia. . . .

Before this band of devoted spinsters, who do not have babies, assayed the task of teaching women who do have babies how to raise babies billions of babies were born and managed to survive with no help than the care of a loving mother and the attention of "the old family doctor". . . .

Common sense is, after all, the best guide. The people, living according to common sense, have reared all the races of men who have ever passed across this earth. It is now proposed to turn the control of the mothers of the land over to a few single ladies holding Government jobs at Washington. I question whether one out of ten of these delightful reformers could make a bowl of buttermilk gruel that would not give a baby colic in five minutes (laughter). We would better reverse the proposition and provide for a committee of mothers to take charge of the old maids and teach them how to acquire a husband and have babies of their own (laughter). (Bremner, 1971, p. 1021)

Reed went on to say that "there is not a hamlet or a village that is not blest with its family doctor" and that "what they cannot accomplish will not be brought about by a society of spinsters." Perhaps at this point it would be appropriate to introduce the story of another hostile male critic of the work of the Children's Bureau. Seeking to discredit Julia Lathrop's authority to speak on behalf of the naiton's children, he asked her whether she had ever been a mother. Her response was, "No, sir, have you?" (Social Service Reveiw, 1951, p. 384).

Reed also discussed how the bill would treat the issue of race, pointing out that under the bill's provisions the facilities provided by any state agency were to be available to all residents of the state. He continued, "That means available to all alike, and how it could be conducted without an intermingling of the races, if they are ever called together in any schools of instruction, or in any community matter, is something I do not undertake to say" (Bremner, 1971, pp. 1012–13).

In spite of such attacks, after three years of struggle and days of bitter floor debate in Congress, the Sheppard-Towner Bill was passed on November 19, 1921, and President Warren G. Harding signed it into law four days later. However, Julia Lathrop was not the social worker who administered this act. She retired just before its passage, and Grace Abbott was appointed the second chief of the bureau. Abbott, a former colleague of Lathrop's on the staff of the University of Chicago School of Social Service Administration, had joined the Children's Bureau in 1916.

Under the Sheppard-Towner Act, nearly 3,000 child and maternal health centers, most of them in rural areas, were established in 45 states. The act strengthened state health departments and helped develop better services at the local and county level. The nation's infant and maternal mortality rates dropped significantly during the life of the act. When the act was passed, it authorized an annual appropriation of $1,252,000 for a five-year period. This was later extended to seven years. Each year the Children's Bureau could use $50,000 of the appropriation to administer the act, and the remainder was to be divided among the participating states. In 1927 the Appropriations Committee of the House expressed its unwillingness to continue providing the money necessary to support the administration of the act. However, after a struggle the Appropriations Committee consented to allocate money for the next biennium with the statement that the work was to be completed by 1929. And so Grace Abbott's hopes for the Sheppard-Towner Act came to defeat, not by the process of debate in Congress on its merits, but by a congressional committee's decision that the act could not be afforded in the most prosperous years that the country had ever known. It was the agony of the Great Depression that was to bring back the Sheppard-Towner Act as a part of the Social Security Act of 1935.

The Achievements of Sheppard-Towner

The Sheppard-Towner Act was important for several reasons. It aroused the public's interest in a subject that had long been considered the exclusive domain of the medical profession; it brought the federal government to the field of child welfare; and it furthered the influence of social work in health care. It also laid the foundation for federal grants-in-aid to the states for welfare programs other than education, and thus it laid the groundwork for the Social Security Act of 1935. Alben W. Barkley argued for federal support of the Sheppard-Towner Act on the basis of the general welfare clause of the Constitution, saying, "Its legality . . . is surely based upon the preamble of the Constitution which gives Congress the power to provide for the general welfare of the people of the United States" (Bremner, 1971, p. 1010).

Public child welfare administration

By directing national attention to the defects in the old systems of administration and to new types of organization that promised to improve the services for children greatly, the Children's Bureau helped develop public appreciation of the importance of effective organization in administering services for children. The states established commissions to examine the state laws relating to children with a view to suggesting amendments and additions. It was inevitable that these commissions should discover that state and local machinery was ill suited to provide the needed services. It was clear that a larger unit for local administration than the township was necessary, and a county system or a system combining two or more counties was urged. This movement for the county organization of social and health services made progress first in the Midwest and the Far West partly because in those areas of the United States the county was the unit of local government. Among the states, Minnesota and North Carolina led a new attack on the problem of administration in 1917, the former by adopting the principle of a state countywide system in the administration of its child welfare services and the latter by providing a similar system for its general public welfare services.

Although organization for administration is important, the success or failure of programs is determined by the personnel employed. These years saw a growing appreciation of the value of trained social workers in the public social services. This interest in trained social workers grew out of and was supported by the experience of the private child-caring agencies, which were convinced of the importance of exploring each child's needs and of having a social worker supervise the care of children in placement. Certainly this trend was accelerated by the Children's Bureau, which in its first acts of organization had hired the first 15 social workers ever employed by the federal government.

The adoption of merit systems and the inclusion of social service personnel in civil service classifications marked a movement away from placing political appointees in social service jobs and toward hiring trained workers instead.

Children's codes

In earlier chapters we traced the beginnings of concern with children and discussed how this led to the establishment of many organizations that provided for their care and protection. Every large urban center had agencies for giving service and protection to delinquent, handicapped, ill, and dependent children. These agencies often offered institutionalized services only. When the juvenile court was added to the child welfare scene, it sought to avail itself of these diverse agencies as treatment resources but found that there were problems in how to use these "unrelated and conflicting child welfare resources." In 1910 Judge George S. Addams, of the Juvenile Court of Cleveland suggested that all child welfare agencies get together to codify the laws in their field. "If there is a code of evidence and commercial paper and of Insurance Laws, why not a Children's Code?" Judge Addams went on to say:

> A Judge can commit [a child] to a State institution . . . but . . . cannot compel the institution to receive it. If [it] is suffering from two defects . . . the probabilities are no institution will receive it. . . . Children can quit school at fourteen if they can read, but . . . cannot work until sixteen. . . . All our public institutions are footballs of politics, and a woman cannot superintend even [a correctional] school for girls. (Bruno, 1959, p. 216)

At its next session, the Ohio legislature authorized the governor to appoint a commission to frame a children's code. The commission completed its work by the summer of 1912, and in 1913 the Ohio legislature adopted the first children's code in the United States. By 1930, 29 states and the District of Columbia had appointed commissions to codify their laws relating to children. The work was stimulated and supported by the establishment of the Children's Bureau and by the bureau's help and support. A paper given at the National Conference on Social Work in 1915 suggested the development of a National Children's Charter covering services in behalf of children. The charter was not to contain rules or statutes but only principles to be observed in drafting state laws relating to children.

✌§ Income maintenance—Social insurance

In this period social workers began to work toward the adoption of social insurance to promote security in the face of unemployment, old age, industrial accidents, and disease. Social insurance is a public means of meeting certain defined social risks. It operates to spread among a large statistical population the risks of certain hazards of life, and it is financed by various combinations of taxes that are paid by the beneficiary or by the employer on the beneficiary's behalf or, sometimes, by contributions from general revenues.

Social insurance differs from both private insurance and public charity. Like private insurance, it pools deniable risks in a large statistical population. It is financed by contributions made by or for prospective beneficiaries. Eligibility for its benefits and the amounts of such benefits are determined by a formula based on various objective criteria, such as length of time worked and wages earned, and are not related to need. In American social insurance programs, coverage is related to attachment to the work force.

However, there are great differences between private insurance and social insurance. Participation is voluntary in private insurance, compulsory in social insurance. In a private insurance contract, the contributions and the benefits are stipulated and cannot be legally changed. The contributions and the benefits of social insurance can be altered by legislative action. Private insurance is financed exclusively by the prospective beneficiary's premiums. Social insurance is financed in various combinations by taxes paid by the beneficiary or by the employer on behalf of the insured or by contributions from general taxation. Under private insurance, individuals, or others acting in their behalf, purchase their own benefits with their own payments. Under social insurance, the benefits are financed not by the current beneficiaries but by persons who are currently employed and making contributions. Private insurance does not redistribute income; social insurance does.

The beneficiaries of social insurance usually feel that they have bought and paid for their benefits. This is not true, but it appears to be because contributions and benefits are both related to earnings and thus to each other. The amounts of benefits and their duration are not a matter of administrative discretion—beneficiaries can expect their payments as a matter or right. The benefits of social insurance are predictable, guaranteed, and thus dependable, though they are not a matter of legal right, as are the benefits of private insurance. The right is moral rather than legal (Wilcox, 1969, pp. 86–89).

Industrial nations other than the United States had established well-developed systems of social insurance by the beginning of the 20th century. The United States did not move toward social insurance earlier than it did for significant reasons in addition to selfishness and the resistance of industrial interests. From its beginnings, America has been an individualistic culture without a sense of collectivism. Laborers have seen their future in upward mobility, and thus no class-conscious labor movement of the kind that one finds in other industrial countries has developed in the United States. Moreover, at this time labor in the United States enjoyed a better standard of living than did labor in other countries. Labor leaders were not favorable to the establishment of social insurance. They were not interested in redistributing wealth in order to satisfy a sense of social justice, which is the aim of social insurance. They were also concerned that distributing wealth to the poor would prove so expensive that the contributors' standard of living would be lowered. The leaders of union labor have never stood for significant social change, but rather have thought in terms of power to win favorable labor contracts for their members. Thus, in the

United States the impetus for social insurance came from the middle and upper classes—the reformers and the social workers.

In 1902 the National Conference of Charities and Corrections entertained a suggestion by Charles R. Henderson of the University of Chicago that a commission be appointed to study the matter. The commission was appointed in 1903, and the first scattered, and contradictory, pieces of a report were presented to the Conference in 1904 and 1905. In 1909 the National Conference established a Committee on Occupational Standards, whose task was to identify the most pressing social problems of the time. Among these was social insurance.

Henry R. Seager, in 1910, and Isaac M. Rubinow, two years later, gave a series of lectures on social insurance at the New York School of Philanthropy. Rubinow wrote a textbook on the subject that was published in 1913 and was recognized as an authoritative work on the subject for more than 20 years. Rubinow's statistical evidence showed that 80 to 90 percent of all wage earners earned less than enough to cover the costs of maintaining a decent level of living for their families. At least half of all wage earners earned substantially less than they needed. The only alternative to social insurance was the increased use of charity. In 1916 Rubinow published a pioneering study of health needs. His conclusion was that illness was an insurable risk whose costs could be borne by workers only if the costs of treatment were distributed over a large number of wage earners. Wage and cost-of-living levels in America simply did not permit workers to save enough from their own earnings to cover medical care.

In 1912 the delegates to the National Conference on Social Work, meeting as individuals, endorsed a reform platform which included the insurance principle as a means to promote security in the face of the common hazards of industrial life—unemployment, old age, industrial accident, and disease. Through the influence of Jane Addams or Paul Kellog, this statement was adopted by the Progressive Party and its presidential candidate, Theodore Roosevelt, in 1912 as a "Social and In-dustrial Justice" plank (Bruno, 1957, pp. 214–30 and 25–70; Chambers, 1963, pp. 157–82).

Workers' compensation

Worker's compensation was the first type of social insurance to receive considered attention in the United States. As industrial accidents increased, and as the inadequacy of liability laws under which recovery of damages was dependent on proof of the employer's negligence became more and more evident, criticism became more forceful. No one knew the actual number of industrial accidents that occurred in the United States at the time because many states did not require such accidents to be reported. Enough was known, however, to convince interested persons that the rate of fatal accidents was higher than in other industrial countries and that one third to one half of American fatalities were preventable.

Between 1909 and 1913, 30 states appointed commissions to investigate industrial accidents and the employer's liability. All recommended a system of assured workers' compensation. This system would disregard the concept of negligence. An employer would be required to compensate all employees injured in work accidents without regard to the cause; and the payments made to the injured persons would be determined by (and limited to) a uniform scale of benefits, figured on the basis of a fixed proportion of the economic loss resulting from the injury. The central principles underlying this approach to industrial accidents are: (1) accidents, whatever their cause, are an inevitable accompaniment of the industrial process; (2) thus the costs of accidents should be considered a regular part of the costs of production; (3) like other costs, these should be borne by the producer and ultimately by the consumer of the good produced; and (4) such a system would reward employers who attempted to reduce the number of accidents.

National interest in workers' compensation was high, as evidenced by the appointment of many state commissions to investigate the matter. The movement made such headway that in the years between 1910 and 1920 all but six states and the

District of Columbia passed compensation laws. These laws did not bring about any quick reduction in the frequency of industrial injuries. Given the growth of industry and the increasing complexity of the manufacturing operations, it was probably too much to expect sudden changes. The laws did, however, require the reporting of industrial accidents, and thus they provided the first specific knowledge of the types and number of such accidents (Bremner, 1956, pp. 249–59).

The major defects of the early workers' compensation laws were: (1) they all excluded certain types of employees, and most of them left a substantial number of people outside coverage; (2) only a few states included industrial diseases in coverage; (3) the schedule of benefits in all states were grossly inadequate; (4) being time-limited, the benefits often ran out before employees were able to return to work; (5) there was no control over the quality of medical care; and (6) most states allowed employers to remain outside the system if they were willing to take the risk. However, in most states the employers could not use the old legal defenses if workers should sue, and in some states such employers were required to post a bond. Employers who entered the program were required to insure against risks of occupational injury. In some states this insurance was obtained through the state; in others, through private carriers. In all cases, employers were to pay the total cost of the program.

Health insurance

Meeting in 1915, a group of social workers asked what should be next in reform. The unanimous reply was "health insurance." Assigning the first priority to health insurance could be justified because: (1) illnesses were a more important cause of poverty than even industrial accidents; (2) insurance would provide incentive for preventive medicine and thus improve the general health of the population; (3) health insurance in no way increased the costs of medical care—it merely redistributed them more equitably; (4) the need for medical care was greatest among those who were least able to pay for it and who consequently often went without it; and (5) even for those who were able to escape charity during illness, the costs of illness often resulted in the deterioration of living standards and the sacrifice of necessary food, clothing, shelter, and education.

The group supporting health insurance contained some very powerful social workers and social reformers: Jane Addams, recognized as a national leader; Paul Kellog; Edward T. Devine, perhaps the best-known administrator and educator in social work; I. M. Rubinow, recognized as the outstanding authority on social insurance; and John B. Andrews, secretary of the American Association for Labor Legislation, who had furnished the initial leadership for the passage of workers' compensation. In addition, the precedents of interest in industrial accidents, in maternal and child health, and in the rapidly developing public health movement were seen as supporting the movement toward health insurance.

But these very experienced social reformers, all people who well understood the methods of social change, failed to recognize the variety and strength of the opposition interests. These interests included employers' associations, taxpayers' associations, insurance firms, the AFL and other wings of organized labor, members of the medical and dental professions, druggists, producers of patent medicines, and Christian Scientists (Bremner, 1964, p. 259). Only one state legislature showed any interest at all. Bills were introduced into the New York state legislature in 1916, 1917, 1918, and 1919. In 1919 labels of "Bolshevism" and "made in Germany" were attached to the bill, and by the next year health insurance was dead (Chambers, 1963, pp. 157–58). It is instructive to consider the comments of Isaac Rubinow after the defeat. He stated that the proponents of the measure had erred because of "over-confidence, based upon the implicit faith in the justice and social value of the measure" (Chambers, 1963, p. 158).

Unemployment insurance

In the mid-1920s, all impetus toward the further development of social insurance slowed down.

There was a brief slump in economic activity during 1920–21 that brought about talk of unemployment compensation, including employment services and public works. As things improved, however, the talk of such insurance became less urgent. Despite a general lack of interest, in the mid-20s scattered papers on family allowances or a guaranteed minimum income were appearing here and there. Such efforts received little support. It is true that the nation was enjoying great prosperity. However, the period was also characterized by a growing social service case load, an increasing number of industrial accidents, and no great increases in job or health insurance accompanying the increases in wages.

Interested people continued to point out that "unemployment together with the fear of unemployment had a disastrous impact on worker morale and on industrial efficiency; its sources lay far beyond the control of the individual worker" (Chambers, 1963, p. 173). The supporters of unemployment compensation differed as to how an unemployment compensation system could be insurance paid for by contributions of employers and employees and from general revenue. This system was to be combined with a federal employment service and with a program of public works that would employ persons who could not find other employment after a period of time. Others proposed industry-wide systems guided and administered by the state governments, with industry accepting the burden of the costs. Still others favored a system of taxation on industries, determined by the employment experience of each industry; limitation of benefits to a maximum of $10 a week for 13 weeks; eligibility based on a work test; and a denial of compensation during strikes.

However, not until the Great Depression created an unbearable burden of unemployment did Wisconsin, in January 1932, pass the nation's first unemployment compensation bill. The bill was to go into effect on June 1, 1933. It had a voluntary clause that gave employers the opportunity to voluntarily create a system of reserve funds. If they did not, the state would initiate compulsory action. However, when, as of June 1933, many firms had

not created a voluntary system and no other state had passed similar legislation, Wisconsin became worried at the notion that it might be the only state imposing such a burden on its employers. Therefore, the date was moved forward to July 1, 1934. When, as of that date, many employers had still not acted, the compulsory feature of the law went into effect.

Before 1929, other states, including California, Massachusetts, Oregon, and New York, had all explored the possibility of unemployment compensation without results. Pending state and federal action, during the 1920s a number of industries had, on their own initiative, set up experimental unemployment reserve funds. The Amalgamated Clothing Workers and the Chicago clothing industry had set up a fund financed by contributions of both workers and employers. The Wisconsin effort is of particular importance because it trained Edwin E. Witte and Arthur J. Altmeyer to understand the complexities and the technicalities of unemployment insurance. Both men joined the federal government during the New Deal and had profound impact on one of the most important issues of that time (Chambers, 1963, pp. 174–75).

✑ Public relief becomes public welfare

During the first two decades of the 1900s, as a part of political reform, strong drives developed for efficiency, economy, and honesty in the administration of local government. The shifts in government structure that followed, plus the emphasis on efficiency and economy in public matters, inevitably affected the structure and function of the public social services, especially the administration of relief.

There was at the time, and there would continue to be, a feeling on the part of many leading social workers that public relief was bound to be corrupt and that only the private agency could properly administer financial assistance. An aspect of this stand was the belief that people who needed financial assistance inevitably needed personal social services as well. Thus, in order to be productive, financial assistance should be accompanied by counseling services. In this way, clients could be "rehabilitated," so that they would no longer need assistance. It was thought by many that giving money unaccompanied by private social service would only lead to increasing dependence. It was also feared that those who did not need relief would get it (Frankel, 1925, pp. 65–66). Indiana was the first state in which an attempt was made to apply the principles of the private services to the giving of public relief. Amos W. Butler, secretary of the State Board of Charities (1897–1923), was primarily responsible for the effort to change the politically dominated handling of outdoor relief by thousands of township trustees to a well-organized, state-supervised distribution of assistance built upon the model of the private urban Charity Organization societies. Butler was an interesting man who exemplified the wide interests of the early social leaders. He was secretary of the State Board of Charities for 26 years. He was president of the National Conference of Social Work, vice president of the International Prison Congress during its meetings of 1925 and 1930, and the founder of the International Committee on Mental Health. But his most important service was to demonstrate that the philosophy of charity organization could be as well applied to public outdoor relief throughout a rural state as to an urban center and that this statewide reform could be effected without any basic change in the authority of the local responsibility to administer the service.

In 1910 a group of liberal and forward-looking citizens of Kansas City organized the city's first Board of Public Welfare. The board was founded on the belief that dependence and delinquency were caused, not by the moral weakness of the poor and the offender, but by economic conditions. The factors that produced dependence and delinquency were believed to be: poor housing, the hours and conditions of labor, and the inadequacy of the recreational opportunities that were available to children. In its original charter the board was "given broad powers to devise and execute plans to fulfill the duties of the city toward all the poor, the delinquent, the unemployed, the deserted and unfortunate classes, and to supervise the private

agencies which solicited money from the public." Under this authority the board established a legal aid bureau, an employment bureau, and a loan agency. It did not concern itself with the administration of outdoor relief or with child welfare matters. The function of outdoor relief was left to the strongly entrenched private agencies (Bruno, 1959, p. 208).

Strong opposition to the board's activities in the areas of housing inspection and the enforcement of labor conditions resulted in a gradual reduction of the appropriations to support its activities, and the board failed to fulfill its initial promise. However, the use of the name Board of Public Welfare and the recognition that governmental social services could be an instrument for the promotion of the general welfare were important achievements. Despite its failure, this first board represented the beginning of an enlarged concept of the state's responsibility for the welfare of its citizens.

Denver was the next city to demonstrate the possibility of nonpolitical, humane, and honest administration of public social services. In 1912 Gertrude Vail, a social work graduate of the Chicago School of Civics and Philanthropy, was asked to return to her home city of Denver and serve on the Board of Charities and Corrections. Within a year she was appointed executive director of the board, and by the time she left, in 1917, she had so strongly established the principles of humane and honest administration that her innovations remained in effect. During her tenure Vail was under constant political attack, but she was able to weather the storms and to retain the authority to handle the affairs of public assistance and corrections as she saw fit. One of her successful battles involved the confidentiality of client records. Vail was able to establish that the law required the disclosure only of certain routine data and that to disclose anything else would put her in jeopardy of a client suit (Bruno, 1959, pp. 211–13).

Chicago established the Cook County Bureau of Public Welfare in 1913. St. Joseph, Missouri, established a county-city department of welfare in the same year. In 1916 Westchester County, New

York, established a department of welfare. A year later a State Department of Welfare was established in Illinois. The new director of welfare in Illinois was responsible for administering the state's assistance (relief), services, and institutional programs. This meant that in the states which followed Illinois's example, public welfare services were consolidated into statewide systems administered by appointed heads of state departments of welfare. The two critical elements in this development were the statewide scope of the departments and the removal of the department executives from current political activity, except as their appointment by the governor with the approval of the state legislature might reflect political positions. This move toward public state support of the needs of people was not made without ambivalence and opposition, however. It is interesting that the first efforts in this direction were concerned, not with the needs of all people, but with the needs of groups that might be seen as "the worthy poor": the aged, the blind, and children.

✒ Income maintenance—The development of public assistance

It is probably difficult for those of us who did not live in the first decades of this century, some 60 or so years ago, to understand the economic insecurities that existed at the time. If we were unable to work for any physical reason, we could get some aid in the form of rent payments to our landlord or grocery orders at a nearby store if we lived in an urban area. We could not expect any actual money aid. If we lost our job, through accident or illness, or because of a lack of work, or because the employer just did not like us, there was little recourse or assistance. It was necessary to find some other work immediately or to face the possibility that our family would be broken up and institutionalized. Some private agencies might help us temporarily, but there was no real security in this aid. Indeed, until the 1900s security was not considered desirable, as it was thought to discourage relatives and friends from giving help and the poor from seeking work. Certainly there was

no aid for people deemed able to work, no matter what their other responsibilities. Many widows and many wives of men who had been incapacitated by industrial injuries were forced to give up their children solely because they could not care for them and work.

Some women placed their children in institutions or foster homes or gave them up for adoption. Others attempted to keep the children home while they went to work. But low wages forced women to work long hours, which meant they were usually too exhausted to provide any companionship for their children. The result was that many women broke down and became ill or died. In the end, both the women and their children required aid—in institutions or hospitals. In New York state *alone,* approximately 4,000 children were placed in public institutions in 1913. Of these, 3,000 were placed because their parents could not support them and 1,000 were placed because their mothers had become ill. In the latter cases, many of the mothers were institutionalized in hospitals for the care of physical illness or in mental institutions (Lundberg, 1947, pp. 128–29).

Two groups in our society bore a very heavy burden of the economic insecurity of the time: families composed of parents and young children, and the aged. Wages in American industry were not high enough, or work secure enough, to allow a worker to set aside savings for old age, and the aged were totally dependent on whatever they could save or whatever support their children or other relatives could give. Most older workers lived in fear that when they could no longer work they would be sent to "the poor farm." The poor farms in which the aged poor were institutionalized were both inhumane and expensive. The root causes of dependence were sickness, accident, and illness.

In spite of slow progress and much disappointment on the part of reformers, certain public, outdoor, tax-supported programs to protect certain groups began to appear in some states. These programs were important in that they laid part of the foundation for the more comprehensive federal Social Security Act of 1935. The public assistances were programs of financial aid established by the state or county from general tax funds to furnish a basic financial support in their own homes for certain population groups upon proof of financial need. These aids are usually referred to as categorical assistance because they are available only to people who fall within certain categories. The categories generally followed the older notion of the worthy poor.

Aid to the needy blind

The first public assistance program to be established was aid to the blind. Because the blind were demonstrably handicapped in the labor market of the time and less likely than other groups to earn sufficient money for self-support, the movement for some type of public assistance to this category of the population appeared much earlier than did other forms of public welfare. Care of the blind involved voluntary agencies in some places and public agencies in other places. In some states it involved institutional care, and in others it involved educational and vocational opportunities. As early as 1840, Indiana passed a law to provide for the needy blind. Before the turn of the century, one state, Ohio, had enacted a law providing for public state relief of the blind. However, in 1898 this law was declared unconstitutional, as was a similar law passed in 1904. However, in 1908 an Ohio statute to aid the blind was passed that stood the test of constitutionality. But in the meantime the Illinois and Wisconsin legislatures, in 1903 and 1907, respectively, had acted to grant public assistance to the blind. Thus, before 1911, when the first mothers' aid laws were passed, three states were granting public aid to this group of citizens. By 1929, 16 states had enacted similar laws.

Public assistance to children in their own homes

The first resolution adopted by the White House Conference on Dependent Children laid great stress on the importance of providing some means of keeping children in their own homes. The resolution that "homes should not be broken up for rea-

sons of poverty," but, reflecting much of the opinion of the times the resolution, it added that such assistance should be given "preferably in the form of private charity, rather than public relief" (Abbott, 1938, p. 230). However, as we have stated earlier, the private agencies could not commit themselves to provide security over the long years of children's dependence to all the mothers who needed such help.

Mothers' aid, also known as mothers' pensions or mothers' allowances, originated during a time marked by reaction against the old methods of public relief and the institutional care of dependent children. This form of aid appears to have begun in California, where as early as 1906 the juvenile courts of some counties granted county aid to children in their own homes. In 1911 the state began to reimburse the counties for such aid. An Oklahoma law of 1908 specified that upon the recommendation of the school authorities, the counties would provide for school scholarships to enable the children of widowed mothers to stay in school. A Michigan law of 1911 authorized payment from school funds to enable the children of indigent parents to attend school. Through a resolution passed by the County Board of Milwaukee County, Wisconsin, in 1912, such aid was given through the juvenile court. In New Jersey, some aid to dependent children in their homes had been paid from county funds before 1913 by boarding the children with their own mothers. Some private family welfare agencies, such as the Buffalo Charity Organization Society, adopted this principle, providing regular grants for a selected group of widowed mothers and developing budgetary methods which were later adopted in the administration of mothers' aid (Abbott, 1938, pp. 229–47).

In 1911 the Missouri legislature passed the first definite legal provision for aid from public funds to mothers of dependent children. It applied only to Jackson County (Kansas City). The first statewide mothers' aid law was enacted in Illinois in the same year. The Illinois Funds to Parents Act had its origin in the experience of the Juvenile Court of Chicago in dealing with dependent families. The court was troubled by the number of children who were committed to institutions because there was no other way by which they could be assisted from public funds.

The Illinois law and its administration by the Juvenile Court of Chicago aroused the interest of states and localities throughout the country. In 1912 a session of the National Conference of Charities and Corrections was devoted to discussion of the Chicago experiment and the pros and cons of public pensions to widows. Private versus public relief was the principal question discussed.

The conditions that led to the establishment of this new form of public relief and the arguments marshaled for and against the proposal were brought out in comprehensive inquiries made by a Massachusetts commission appointed by the state legislature in 1912 "to study the question of the support of dependent minor children of widowed mothers" and by a similar state commission established in New York in 1913 "to inquire into the subject of pensions or other relief for widowed mothers" (Abbott, 1938, pp. 229–47).

The Massachusetts study dealt mainly with two situations—the separation of children from mothers because of poverty, and the relief-giving policies of the town overseers of the poor (Commonwealth of Massachusetts, 1913: House Document No. 2075). In order to learn more about the economic causes of removal, the commission sought information from institutions and child-placing agencies. A statistical study of this problem showed that insufficient income of the mother and the mother's absence from home while at work were the two largest causes for the separation of children from widowed mothers.

The New York commission investigated the records of the large public and private agencies in the state, conducted firsthand inquiries into the operations of laws under which communities had been granting aid to widowed mothers for more than a year, and extended its studies to certain European countries (State of New York, 1914). Much of the commission's work was concerned with the question of the ability of private relief agencies to give the aid needed. The report of the commission set forth the following "Basic Principles":

1. The mother is the best guardian of her children.
2. Poverty is too big a problem for private philanthropy.
3. No woman, save in exceptional circumstances, can be both the homemaker and the breadwinner of her family.
4. Preventive work to be successful must concern itself with the child and the home.
5. Normal family life is the foundation of the state, and its conservation an inherent duty of government. (Lundberg, 1947, p. 130)

Given its findings the New York Commission took the position that state aid was the only possible method of meeting the urgent need and recommended the immediate enactment into law of legislation supporting aid to the dependent children of widows.

Legislation and administration

There was a wave of sentiment in favor of such public provision as would make it unnecessary to remove children from their own homes because of poverty. In 1913 and 1914, bills were introduced in the legislatures of 32 states, and a bill was before Congress proposing aid for all mothers in the United States coming within its provisions. The Congress of Mothers and Parent-Teacher Associations and other organizations and fraternal orders fostered the ever-growing movement. In 1913, 18 states enacted laws; 8 states were added to the list in 1915; and 1 was added in 1916. Six states and the Territory of Alaska passed such laws in 1917, and one state in 1918. Four states were added in 1919, and one in 1920. Thus, ten years after the first laws were enacted, 40 states, Alaska, and Hawaii had enacted laws authorizing aid from public funds for children in their own homes. In the ten following years, six states were added and a home care law was passed by Congress for the District of Columbia. Only three states (Alabama, Georgia, and South Carolina) remained without such legislation until 1935 and 1937 (Lundberg, 1947, pp. 113–44).

The enactment of laws, however, did not always mean that the measures actually benefited dependent children. With the impetus of public sentiment for such an ideal, it was comparatively easy to add laws to the statute books, but securing appropriations permitting adequate administration and aid was often another matter. In several states the laws were inoperative; in some states only two or three localities made any provision for aid; and in other states the large cities and some smaller communities made excellent progress, but provision was very inadequate elsewhere. Many of the leaders in social welfare were very fearful that the new form of public aid might become but another form of poor relief and that such an extension of public assistance would "dry up the wellsprings of charity" and cultivate the "pauper spirit." The mothers' pension movement, however, was built upon the foundation of public responsibility for providing aid to needy children and upon the hopeful assurance that honest and effective public administration could be created (Lundberg, 1947, pp. 129–33).

Administrative arrangements. Although it was always recognized as essentially a form of family relief, mothers' aid was fostered mainly as a child welfare measure. Juvenile courts were the agencies which were thought to have the most knowledge of those conditions that mothers' aid was designed to correct. In the midwestern and northwest states the juvenile courts commonly had jurisdiction over dependent as well as delinquent children, and in these states and in southern that followed their example no other local public agencies existed which could be entrusted with this new venture in child welfare. One reason for selecting the juvenile courts as the administrative agency was that, at least in large cities, these courts already had staffs of probation officers who were experienced in social investigation and supervision. In states with different traditions of child care or with less well developed juvenile court systems, other types of agencies were designated (Lundberg, 1947, pp. 129–33).

An important feature of mothers' aid was the introduction of state responsibility for supervision of and assistance to the local units. Types of state control or financial aid, like the types of local ad-

ministrative agencies, differed among states. In 1931, aid to children was provided from state funds in 2 states; 17 states shared the costs with the local units in some measure; and in one state, investigation and supervision were provided by state staff, while the counties financed the grants. The supervisory functions of state agencies varied from complete responsibility or shared responsibility for local administration to activities by the state welfare department designed to raise the standards of local administration.

Eligibility. By 1935 the laws of only two states restricted aid to widows. In 15 states the language was general, or might be so interpreted, permitting aid to any dependent mother, and in several other states the specified types of cases included all or most of the following: mother whose husband is dead; deserting; divorced; totally incapacitated, physically or mentally; imprisoned; in an institution for the insane, feebleminded, or epileptic; suffering from tuberculosis. In a number of states the word *mother* was given a broad interpretation, including any woman standing *in loco parentis,* a guardian or other person having the care and custody of an orphan child, or a relative who assumed the care of a child. Under certain conditions expectant mothers could be given aid in five states, and unmarried mothers were specifically included in the laws of four states. The actual application of the legal provisions was brought out in the study by the U.S. Children's Bureau on mothers' aid administration in 1931. The study showed that 82 percent of the children granted aid were the children of widows (Lundberg, 1947, pp. 132–33).

The legal limitations on the ages of children in whose behalf aid might be granted were expanded during the years in which mothers' aid was in operation. In only nine states was the age limit 14 years by 1935. Four states could grant aid for children up to the age of 15; 28 states, to 16; 2, to 17; and 1, to 18. In general, the age restrictions corresponded to the lower limits of the education and child labor laws in the various states, but some laws made specific provision for extending aid beyond the legal limit if a child was ill, incapacitated, or unable to secure an employment permit.

But permissive legislation and administrative practice were sometimes quite divergent. In one state, as late as 1934, it was the practice in many localities to give aid only for children of school age during school terms. In this same state, which had a large black population, aid to black children was practically nonexistent. In another state, aid was limited arbitrarily to include not more than three children in a family, though the law did not set such a restriction. Because of inadequate funds, the practice in many localities was more limited than the law required, and aid was given only to children under 14. Increasingly, however, the better administrative agencies secured scholarship or other special funds from private sources for children who remained in school.

The level of grants. With the pension idea in mind, the legislatures of most states placed a maximum limit on the grants which could be made to families or to children. The laws of six states placed no limit on the allowance which might be granted to a family or a child. Two of these provided that the amount must be sufficient to care properly for the child at home. One state provided that the amount granted could not exceed the cost of caring for a child in an institution, which, except in unusual cases, was probably adequate for care in its own home.

Following the lead of private family relief and service agencies, it was the theory (and, insofar as funds permitted, the practice) of the better-financed mothers' aid agencies that assistance should be determined for each family on the basis of a budget showing needs and resources, with consideration of family composition, health conditions, and other special factors. "Because of inadequacy of funds, practice often fell short of theory even in the best agencies, but acceptance of this principle of giving aid in accordance with the actual needs of individual families raised mothers' aid administration far above the status of public relief, not only in the larger cities but throughout certain states. A committee of mothers' pension administrators in 1922 recommended that the following items be accepted as requirements of a sound administrative policy":

1. That constructive work with families is conditional upon adequate relief.
2. That adequate aid can be determined only by accurate knowledge of the necessary expenses and income.
3. That the expenditures necessary to health and wholesome living can be determined, especially at the outset, only by the use of a standard budget schedule subject to individual and family variations and other variables.
4. That even when the relief is not adequate the agency should know *how* inadequate it is.
5. That itemized household expense accounts should be required from families receiving assistance. (Lundberg, 1947, p. 136)

Old-age pensions

Americans were gradually beginning to recognize the responsibility of the community to care for its needy aged men and women. The segregation of needy old people in local institutions was being recognized as both expensive and inhumane. A study done by Lucile Eaves with the support of the Women's Educational and Industrial Union of Boston indicated that "dependency in old age was the normal expectancy not only of the poor but also of families" that lived at middle-income levels. The study pointed out that private agency funds were always insufficient in amount and "debasing to the recipient; private insurance schemes were too expensive for the greatest number of the citizenry; to require children to support their parents" was only to deprive their children, in turn, of an adequate life (Chambers, 1963, p. 161). It was a terrible distortion of family affection to force people to choose between their parents' and their children's welfare.

In 1905 the Massachusetts Bureau of Statistics of Labor produced a report that traced the European precedents of old-age assistance and set forth the proposal that public pensions were the only humane alternative to uncertain private charity or institutional care for the aged of the nation. As a consequence of the interest and controversy that followed, the state established a commission in 1907 to thoroughly investigate the care of the aged.

In 1910 this commission recommended strongly against the inauguration of a pension system and thus stopped any further consideration of such a program not only in Massachusetts but in many other states. However, the need to provide acceptable resources for the needy aged grew with each passing year as life expectancy increased, and thus the percentage of older people in the population increased, and as urban, industrialized living became more widespread (Chambers, 1963, p. 163).

The first state to enact a law providing public assistance to the aged was Arizona. However, the law was promptly challenged in the courts and was declared unconstitutional. In 1915 Alaska, then a territory, passed the first old-age law that withstood the test of constitutionality. The first state to pass a law that withstood testing in the courts was Montana, in 1923. By the time of the depression, nine states and one territory had departed from the poor law principle of relief for the aged and had adopted a publicly supported, needs-based public welfare (or pension) system. However, the depression served to greatly increase these programs. Thirteen states were added between the panic and the inauguration of New Deal legislation.

New York had first considered an old-age pension bill in 1927. However, the bill failed in 1927, 1928, and 1929. The new governor, Franklin D. Roosevelt, then appointed a committee to study the matter, and in 1930 he brought a true contributory pension proposal before the legislature. When he recognized that it would be impossible to pass such legislation, he accepted an old-age assistance measure like that of other states. Although the effort to institute a true pension system failed, it was important in that it educated Roosevelt to the principle of social insurance (Chambers, 1963, p. 167).

Administration and eligibility. However, the state laws merely *permitted* rather than required the counties to establish old-age pension systems at their own expense. The only exceptions were California and Wyoming, which just before the depression made such pensions mandatory on counties, with state supervision and state contributions. In no case was any state willing to provide state

moneys. As might be expected, few counties were anxious to take up the programs when doing so meant an increase in the local tax rate. In other aspects the laws differed from state to state, but generally the conditions of eligibility were: 70 years of age, 15 years residency in the state, no more than $3,000 in property, children or other close relatives to assist the applicant if possible, and a ceiling of $1 per day on the grant. Believing that a pension, awarded as right, was the only satisfactory way to support the elderly person and that the eligibility requirements of the old-age assistance rules could not but undermine the self-respect of the applicants, reformers were discouraged indeed at the slow progress in this area of social welfare.

The war years

No social workers supported the things that were happening in Europe, but they were severely divided over what America's position should be. Some felt that England and France were in the right, but many were pacifists who opposed war on any grounds. Jane Addams, Lillian Wald, and Paul Kellog were among those who opposed American "preparedness." However, when Wilson led the United States into war as a way of "making the world safe for democracy," social workers were willing to be of what service they could. To the social workers' surprise, there was support for continued social reform, as the nation considered social justice important because it was the base of good morale and patriotism. The conservation of national resources became important, and due to labor shortages, industry was anxious to attract and hold workers through welfare measures (Chambers, 1963, p. 18).

The government began to build new housing for workers. The prohibition of child labor was made a part of the defense contracts that the government awarded, and later a child labor law was passed that stood the test of constitutionality. Minimum "living" wages were set by the National War Labor Board in 1918, based on a careful survey of actual living costs (Leiby, 1978, p. 156).

⊷§ The Red Cross

More than any other organization, the Red Cross was the vehicle of wartime social service. The organization was engaged in four kinds of helping: (1) canteens and clubs for servicemen, (2) social services in military hospitals, (3) traditional disaster relief for all persons, and (4) "home service" to the families of servicemen. "Home service" was a new development that undoubtedly came from the Civil War efforts to see that families at home had information about their men at the front. Now it attempted to apply the principles of casework to help the families of servicemen cope with the problem of wartime separation. The service was available on request to the serviceman and his family. For the first time in our history, social work help was offered to "those above the poverty line" (Watts, 1964, pp. 303–15). This gave a powerful push to the development of social casework as a professional service of benefit to all persons, and to the education necessary for such service. We will discuss this development in the next chapter (Leiby, 1978, pp. 159–60).

The veterans and social welfare

Two major welfare programs were developed for military personnel; war risk insurance and training camp programs. The training camp programs aimed at making the camps and the experiences of the men who were stationed there as productive as possible. The programs involved the idea of the settlements that proper recreational activities would be powerful deterrents to demoralization and delinquency. War risk insurance, a major venture into social insurance, was established in 1914 to offer insurance on ships and cargoes that were otherwise unprotected because of the costs of private insurance. In 1917 this protection was extended first to ship crews and later to all members of the armed services. In 1917 President Wilson appointed a Council of National Defense to review veterans' benefits and make recommendations. For the first time, the concept of readjustment and re-

habilitation services, along with monetary benefits, was introduced. The new benefits were to include: (1) compulsory allotments and allowances to the families of soldiers, jointly paid for by the soldier and the government; (2) voluntary insurance against death and disability; (3) hospital treatment; and (4) vocational rehabilitation services.

However, the close of the war and the needs of the wounded and the families of the dead forced further consideration of veterans' problems. At the time, veterans' benefits were fragmented among four different bureaus, including the armed services themselves. President Warren G. Harding appointed a committee to consider veterans' services. The committee reported to Congress when it convened on April 11, 1921. Its recommendations were incorporated into Public Law No. 47, which was passed four months later. The most important provision of the law was the establishment of the Veterans Administration as a single authority to administer veterans' affairs. A further extension of veterans' benefits was made available for all honorably discharged veterans with nonservice-connected disabilities. This represented a movement toward public medical care for a "worthy" group, supported by a strong constituency of veterans' groups (Leiby, 1978, pp. 156–62).

Reconstruction

As the war came to an end, hopes were high for a new era of social justice. Social work leaders hoped that the lessons of the war years on the rehabilitation of the handicapped, progressive taxation, collective bargaining in labor relations, worker benefits, the advancement of women and blacks, and the general notion that the nation could afford a decent standard of living for everyone would be advanced in peacetime. Progress at home constituted only one aspect of the aims of many social workers. These social workers were equally hopeful that self-determination and democracy for the peoples of the world would come with peace. But neither of these hopes was to be realized in the harsh light of the postwar world.

᪥ Summary

This chapter has been an account of the attempt of reformers to use the political process to bring social justice and assure the welfare of all people through governmental action. The chapter covers three subdivisions of the period 1900–1930: the Progressive era of the years 1900–1917, the war years, and the conservative reaction of the 1920s. During the progressive years there were exciting advances in social welfare, particularly public welfare, in which the social work leaders of the time could rejoice and from which they could take hope. Even during the war years the reformers believed it possible to establish a decent existence for everyone through the political process. They were certain that the nation could afford it.

However, by 1920 it was painfully evident to even the most hopeful reformer that there had been a significant change in the attitude of the nation. The war had uprooted people from their usual environments and their established ways of life. The sentiment now was for "suppression rather than understanding" (Chambers, 1963, p. 25), with each person oriented only to seeking ways to achieve a piece of the abundance that America had promised. People were frightened, suspicious, and resentful. It appeared to many that all their hopes had been dashed and that their work had been without any gains. However, many others kept the faith and worked on in spite of discouragement, to lay the foundation for the reforms of the depression years.

᪥ A look ahead

In the next chapter we shall discuss the developments in social welfare that took place during the same time period covered in this chapter, but were essentially outside the political process. Many of the developments we shall discuss took place following World War I. Although the 1920s were conservative and reflected disillusion with political solutions to social welfare problems, constructive things were happening that were to have significant effects on the present shape of our social welfare

institution. Increasing attention was devoted to the rationale and the organization of the personal social services, and attention focused on the development of a new profession—social work—and on the development of a growing professional competence within that profession. The National Conference of Charities and Corrections changed its name to the National Conference of Social Work in 1917.

᪥ Study questions

1. This was indeed a time of great leaders in social welfare matters. Select a social welfare or social work leader of the time, and learn all you can about his/her life. Identify the forces which pushed the persons toward concern for others.

2. This chapter has detailed some efforts that were made to secure reform through the political process. Go through the chapter and make a list of the arguments that were used to oppose the reform proposals.

3. Using current newspapers, find some arguments against present reform proposals. Discuss how the arguments have changed or how they have remained the same.

4. The beginnings of public assistance were discussed in this chapter. The discussion was brief, but given what is found in the chapter, make a list of the requirements that had to be met in order to receive aid under these programs.

᪥ Selected readings

Chambers, Clarke, A. *Seedtime of Reform: American Social Service and Social Action, 1918–1933.* Minneapolis: University of Minnesota Press, 1963.

This book is perhaps the most detailed study of the time covered by this chapter in the text. We highly recommend it as supplemental reading.

Chambers, Clarke A. *Paul Kellog and the Survey: Voices for Social Welfare and Social Justice.* Minneapolis: University of Minnesota Press, 1971.

For those interested in a more detailed study of the time, this book offers a fascinating account of the life of a man, Paul U. Kellog, and of the development of a journal of social work, social welfare, social policy, and social reform.

Leiby, James. *A History of Social Welfare and Social Work in the United States.* New York: Columbia University Press, 1978.

Chaps. 9 and 10 in this volume were the foundation of many of the materials used in this chapter. They may be used to expand the student's knowledge of the time.

Abbott, Edith. *Some American Pioneers in Social Welfare*. New York: Russell and Russell, 1963.

First published in 1937, this book is fascinating reading for those who would learn more about the lives and activities of the reformers from the writing of one who was deeply involved with them and their struggles.

Addams, Jane. *Forty Years at Hull House*. New York: Macmillan, 1935.

Jane Addams wrote many articles and several interesting books. We have listed here only her latest and most general work. It is excellent reading for those who would understand the settlement movement and the times in which Addams and the settlements developed.

Goldmark, Josephine. *Impatient Crusader: Florence Kelley's Life Story*. Urbana: University of Illinois Press, 1953.

Florence Kelley was one of the most militant and dedicated of the reformers of these times. This book is the story of her life and work as told by a fellow social worker and friend. It is strongly recommended for those interested in social change.

The quality of family life, and the healthy development of children, were greatly enhanced by better access to medical care, and the outlawing of child labor.

In the picture at left, a Board of Health Doctor visits a New York tenement.

The 1913 cartoon, *below,* shows that as late as the presidency of Woodrow Wilson there was still need for child-labor reform.

"Mr. President, we don't want anything. We just want to grow up."

Chapter 19 ❧

❧ Reform and personal social services, 1900–1930 ❧

❧ Introduction

As we discussed in Chapter 15, the 1920s marked the growth of rational technology. A belief developed that the movement toward social justice came more from competent function than from righteous cause. The reformers of the early 1900s were convinced that political questions could be resolved by rational inquiry and experimentation and by dissemination of the facts and findings of such scientific inquiry. This was not to be, but the movement toward a rational technology had important effects on the development of social welfare and the movement's effects on the profession of social work became central to the profession's system of personal social services. In this chapter we will discuss the rapid development of the personal social services and of the professionalization and organization of social work.

The efforts to be rational and scientific about all aspects of life resulted in strong movements toward the rational organization and administration of the social welfare systems. The importance of appropriate organization of charities had been a part of social welfare efforts since the very early 1800s, but it was only as knowledge of organization and administration developed that such notions could be operationalized. It is in the 1920s that we have, through the Council of Social Agencies and the United Fund movements, the organization of agencies that have lasted until the present time. We need to recognize that as the organization of philanthropy grew and developed, the structure of the actual delivery of services became specialized and organized and the competence of the practitioner who delivered such services became an important question.

❧ The development of a social work profession

In tracing the development of the social work profession during the first three decades of the

1900s, we shall deal with three central aspects: (1) the growth and development of professional education, (2) the growth of professional organizations, and (3) the growth of the literature of the profession.

For those who would comprehend the development of the social work profession, it is very important to understand that the profession was established and grew, not out of the support of the individual clients who needed its services (indeed, the clients social workers served could not have afforded to support such services), but out of the concerns of an elite group whose members came to this work from many differing and complex motivations. One thing that the founders of many social welfare organizations had in common was little acquaintance with or understanding of the lives of the people who would use the services they established. The founders' view of necessary services came from their own values and experiences and, increasingly, from the positions of the professional staff they hired to carry out their programs. The social work profession grew up and its development was supported by the delivery systems in which its members worked and on which they depended for financial support. The organizational structure of social services deeply marked the profession and the way it grew; but the delivery systems were in their turn strongly affected by the activities of the profession's leaders and of the professional staff they hired. Thus it is almost impossible to consider the development of one aspect of this symbiotic relationship without taking the other into account. We shall try to help the reader toward some grasp of this. For this we shall start with a discussion of the development of professional education.

◄§ The development of professional education in social work

One feature that differentiated the new Charity Organization movement from the older AICP of Robert M. Hartley's time was the insistence of COS leaders that effective "scientific charity" demanded knowledge and skill as well as good intentions and

the COS's use of case conferences or staff meetings as opportunities for training its workers, both volunteer and paid. At these meetings the "friendly visitors" gave reports about their work with families and there was discussion as to what was helpful and what was not. Through these discussions of the needs of the individual applicants, "the nebulous mass of the poor resolves itself into individual units each capable of pain and pleasure" (Rich, 1956, p. 39). In 1891 the COS in Boston established the first organized learning experience for social workers. Workers-in-training, usually no more than five in any one year, were accepted into training which, in a remarkable way, embodied the central elements of our social work education of today, consisting as it did of assigned reading, attending case conferences and discussion sessions, and working with people under the careful supervision of more experienced workers. These experienced people, in turn, met periodically to discuss the methods and content of their training efforts.

Toward professionalization

This venture stimulated similar attempts in other COS cities, and in 1893 Mary E. Richmond (who was to be a strong force in the movement toward professionalism and at this time had just begun her career by accepting the leadership of the Baltimore COS) started a series of educational conferences for friendly visitors. The critical contribution she made to such meetings was the publication, circulation, and study of records of actual work with actual families. She believed that workers could learn skills in working with clients through analyzing the work of colleagues. This study of actual cases proved very helpful to the new workers, and it began to be widely used in the seminars planned by agencies. Later it was to become a significant method of more formal teaching and learning in the universities, and the publication and circulation of case records continued to be a function of the Family Service Association until recent times (Rich, 1956, p. 41).

In addition to being interested in increasing the skills of their own workers, the executives of the

COS agencies were interested in encouraging the development of the skills of social workers wherever they were found. Thus they began inviting the staffs of other agencies to join the COS training programs. As a result, the COS staff attained a greater understanding of the range of services in the community, which was important to the staff's work of referral, and the COS agency became a central agency in the structure of the social service programs in many communities—a position that its descendants occupy in today's world. In addition, the staff of these agencies came to be viewed both by themselves and by other workers as among the most skilled professional workers in the community, a status that they still cherish.

University education in social work

At this time, courses on charity organizations and social problems began to develop in perhaps a dozen colleges and universities as well as in some divinity schools. In many instances, university faculties questioned the suitability of material on charities and corrections, usually taught by sociology departments, for a university curriculum. Certain sociologists were not sure that the practical, day-to-day work of the charity societies had any relationship to their effort to discover the general laws and principles governing human relationships. However, the COS agencies did much to support university courses and it was assumed that the new courses in sociology were the best university preparation for social work. This relationship between sociology and the social work has had a checkered history. In the 40s and 50s, the relationship was resisted by both groups as sociologists struggled to disassociate research and theory development from individualized practice skills and use of self. Sociologists in an attempt to be scientific tried to be value free while social workers proclaimed values as the base of much of their activity. Social workers began to realize that professional practice is an application of knowledge drawn from many basic sciences and to turn away from exclusive reliance on sociology. However, in the struggle of the professional schools to find recognition in the

university, with its emphasis on basic science, and in the movement in the 1960s and 1970s to increase the social worker's knowledge of social forces and organized groups, social work has again found knowledge obtained from the social sciences to be important.

The early courses were of great value in stimulating an interest in social conditions among the young college students. Many of these students were carefully selected and were counseled by the faculty members who taught the courses to seek employment in the social agencies, where they found an eager welcome. These young college sociology students were to provide progressive leadership to the young profession, preserving the unity between social services and social reform in the critical years 1918–30 (Rich, 1956, pp. 37–54; Bruno, 1957, pp. 133–44).

In 1893 a two-year course in "philanthropic training" was established in England by the settlements and the English COS. That same year, Anna L. Dawes of Massachusetts delivered a paper at the International Conference of Charities and Corrections in which she urged that a similar school be established in the United States. In 1897 Mary Richmond took up Dawes's thesis but carried it further in that her paper defined the content and method of professional education and set forth the conditions under which the school should be established, the staff it would need, and its cost. Richmond saw the first step in the establishment of this "training school in applied philanthropy" as being the selection of the right *university-trained man* to head it. Such a man would seek a "connection with some institution of learning." She suggested that the school be established in a large city. Its emphasis was to be on "practical work rather than academic" matters, with close connections with the city's social agencies, so that students would have an opportunity to learn methods of practice under supervision while they were learning the principles governing social work in the classroom (Rich, 1956, pp. 42–44; Bruno, 1957, pp. 138–39). It is interesting that Mary Richmond, one of a number of strong women leaders in social work, specified that a man should be sought to head the first school. Perhaps she recognized that, given the discrimination against women, a new professional effort had to be headed by a man in order to be accepted into the male-dominated university setting.

Richmond's paper received a mixed reception. One objection was that the young men and women who emerged from such a school might feel "that they knew all that could be learned." Some thought that social workers were not paid enough to justify a professional education. Others thought that a professional standard for social work needed to be established before it was possible to educate for the profession. But Richmond believed strongly that a professional standard could not be set until there was a school. Her views were supported by Edward T. Devine, executive secretary of the New York COS, and Robert W. deForest, president of the COS board. In 1898, that society with the strong support of its board established the first school of social work in the United States. It was called the New York School of Philanthropy, and it later became the Columbia University School of Social Work, although it continued its connection with the New York COS until 1950 (Rich, 1956, pp. 45–46).

The first schools of social work

From the perspective of present-day notions of professional education, the New York School of Philanthropy may seem more like a workshop or an institute than like a school of social work. Its initial program consisted of a six-week summer course. Not until 1904 was the summer work expanded to a full-year course, and later this was expanded to a full two-year course. In 1940, when it affiliated with Columbia University, this first school of social work became one of the last schools of social work to give up its independent status.

The University of Chicago School of Social Service Administration developed from the efforts of two settlement leaders: Julia Lathrop of Hull House and Graham Taylor of the Chicago Commons. They took the leadership in establishing the Institute of

Social Science in 1903–4 under the auspices of the Extension Division of the University of Chicago. In 1906 the Chicago Commons (a university settlement) assumed responsibility for the Institute and in 1908 it became an independent corporation called the Chicago School of Civics and Philanthropy, affiliating with the University of Chicago in 1920 as the School of Social Service Administration. Chicago's focus was somewhat different from that of the eastern schools of social work. Breckinridge and Abbott wanted preparation in broad principles as well as practice methods—to create social workers who were not only prepared to deal with clients but to conduct research, to understand and shape the policies and structure of public welfare, and to participate actively in social planning (Wright, 1954, pp. 50–51).

Other schools of social work came into existence at Boston, Philadelphia, Baltimore, and St. Louis. Each was organized by practicing social workers with the support of their communities and sometimes with loose connections with local colleges and universities. In the middlewest, by 1915, departments or series of courses were established for college students who were working on their bachelor's degree within the sociology department, for example at Ohio State University, Indiana University, and the University of Minnesota. In contrast, to the independent schools, which were established primarily to furnish the older worker already in the field with professional education, these institutions incorporated social welfare material as an undergraduate major (Bruno, 1957, pp. 138–44; Rich, 1956, pp. 42–45; Lubane, 1965, pp. 18–19).

The founders and supporters of the early schools of social work had long felt that apprenticeship training by agencies was too limited in scope and too specialized, being focused on training for specific agency practice. But the new schools were also closely tied to the social agencies of the cities in which they were established, because the agencies supplied the instructors, the opportunities for field instruction (required practice experience), and the jobs for the new graduates. Thus the new curriculum did not move out ahead with a broad education based on principles and concepts but was closely tied to the demand of the agencies for trained workers, being very specialized, concrete, and practical and subordinating theory and research to technique.

The social work curriculum

Although social work educators agreed that if the education in the new schools was to be superior to apprentice training it had to combine a theoretical understanding and a research base with the practical work, the students in the schools, and the agencies that hired them, were far more interested in field experience than in academic knowledge and were primarily focused on specific techniques of practice. This conflict between the concept of a school of social work as offering a broad professional education, committed to expanding the boundaries of social work theory and research, and the agencies' perceived needs for staff who could move into practice positions and give immediate service to clients within the agencies' parameters of methods and techniques, persists down until today. Most students coming into schools of social work still want to learn "to do," and down through the years field instruction experience has been the most meaningful part of the curriculum for most social work students.

In 1919, at a meeting of representatives from the schools of social work, it was voted that the curriculum of the schools should consist of courses in casework, statistics, and community service. This statement emphasizes another force in the development of the early curriculum, the focus on casework as the primary methodology of social work practice. That focus is easily understood in that the greatest number of jobs and of field placement opportunities was in this area. In addition, casework methodology was much further advanced in its use of clearly defined techniques than were other methods.

The settlement movement could have offered the early schools some knowledge of how to work with the community or to bring about large-scale social reform, but it was not ready to consciously observe and conceptualize its approaches so that these could be transmitted in an organized way. It believed that one learned by a "living experience" that allowed for a gradual absorption of attitudes and values. It resisted the notion of "professional expertise," believing instead that workers were neighbors who were no more expert than those they lived among. This philosophic attitude persisted, even though it was also obvious that the settlement staff increasingly saw themselves as leaders and teachers of the neighborhood residents.

The social science knowledge of the time was not as well conceptualized and ordered as the psychological knowledge that casework began to find increasingly useful. So in many ways the schools of social work took positions and offered learning experiences that established casework as the primary method of social work practice. These two trends—the founding of schools which taught casework as the primary method of social work and the growth of an organized theory of human development and motivation—reinforced each other (Bruno, 1957, p. 135; Lubane, 1965, pp. 85–87).

There were those, however, who saw the mission of the schools of social work somewhat differently, who believed that professional education should offer the student a philosophic and conceptual view of the social processes and of social problems, leaving the training in techniques and special tasks to agency efforts. One of the most vocal critics of the specialization found in the schools was Grace Abbott, a founder of the Chicago school. She resented both the vocational training that the agencies demanded of the schools and the fact that new workers were often advanced to responsible agency positions before they had had appropriate experience.

Professional education had other problems. Perhaps one of the greatest of these was that the new schools could not educate workers rapidly enough to keep up with the demand.

Entry into social work

Thus people did not have to graduate from a professional school in order to find employment, but could find jobs in agencies as social workers directly from high school, college, or even another profession. This meant that during the early decades of the development of the social work profession, and even today, it was not the educational institutions, or even the professional association, that determined entrance into the field or into practice. Entry into the field was by way of the agency and its hiring criteria. It is inevitable that individuals who fill social work jobs without full preparation, and without the socialization to the professional values that professional education provides, are more likely to be more closely tied to the agency, to internalize the bureaucratic structure more easily, and to be less willing to take unpopular stands. Thus the rapid expansion of personal social services and the hiring of large numbers of variously prepared people was probably one of the most important factors in slowing reform and creating a demand for "techniques that work." One often reads articles criticizing the social work profession for its unwillingness to take leadership in certain critical areas, or one sees critical studies of social work practice which fail to differentiate workers by educational preparation and/or show no understanding that the larger number of those who call themselves social workers have never been exposed to the professional education.

Is social work a profession?

The second challenge to the social work schools (and to the profession) came from a paper which Abraham Flexner presented at the National Conference. In it he set forth the criteria of a profession and his findings that the social worker had no unique professional skills but mobilized the skills of other professions and the resources of others to help the client. In discussing Flexner's paper, Bruno says that he cannot see how, if one applied Flexner's criteria, the law or the ministry could be considered professions, since that "they have no unique techniques communicable by educational process or otherwise" (Bruno, 1957, p. 140). Flexner did not view liaison, brokerage, and resource mobilization in a complex urban society as functions that required considerable professional knowledge and skill and specialized training (Bruno, 1957, pp. 140–41; Lubane, 1965, p. 106).

Flexner's paper had a far-reaching effect on social work. Casework had always focused on the individual and the problem, but it had also accepted a liaison and mobilization function which related it closely to social reform. Now, in search of something that could be called a professional method, it was to devalue these skills so essential in a complex urban society and to build a method that came closer to the model of medicine, which, of all the older professions, had the greatest repertoire of specific skills to teach its practitioners. The understanding of what the social work profession was all about and what its ultimate goals and relationships should be got lost in the search for method. Bruno considers it tragic that an impetus in the direction of method "was given social work at the very inception of its professional consciousness" (Bruno, 1957, p. 141). This push toward the perfection of method, which is still reflected in the demands of students and agencies, endangers theory building, on which method should rest, and consideration of what a profession's ethical responsibility is to its time and to notions of justice, equality, and security within society.

Standards of social work education

A third problem facing professional social work education was to standardize admission policy and curricula in order to achieve some consistency of education from school to school. New, unorganized curricula were sprouting up all over. A profession reproduces itself by educating and socializing new members in such a way that by their activities they are recognized as members of the profession. It began to be recognized that some sort of criteria for student selection and educational experiences needed to be established. Representatives of the schools met informally at the National Conference in 1917 and appointed a committee to draft a plan for a national association of schools of social work.

In 1919, under the leadership of Portor Lee, the Association of Training Schools for Professional Social Work (renamed the Association of Professional Schools of Social Work in the 1920s) was established. By 1929 the original 17 schools had increased to 29. Initially the membership requirement was a full-year program, including classwork and fieldwork, but in December 1932 the association adopted its minimum curriculum for the first graduate year of professional education. We will discuss these developments further in the next chapter (Bruno, 1957, pp. 142–44; Lubane, 1965, pp. 151–52).

≈§ The development of a professional social work organization

In an earlier chapter we saw how the common interests of social welfare leaders and their need to share their thoughts and feelings resulted in the establishment of the National Conference. At the beginning of the 20th century, this yearly assembly offered the only opportunity for the paid staff of social agencies to exchange experiences about their everyday work. Although over the years the Conference had attracted fewer and fewer volunteer workers or board members, it still did not consist entirely of professionals, nor was it intended to. Such a change would have altered the whole nature of the Conference. However, increasingly, the paid social workers felt a need to confer with other paid workers. Some states, and even some cities, established local conferences modeled on the National Conference but these tended to be, on the model of the National Conference, forums on social welfare rather than discussions of professional problems.

Social work clubs

The first places at which professional workers could discuss their own concerns were the social workers' clubs that began to meet in some cities. These clubs were organized to fill a local need, and many communities had them, but there was no formal communication among them, and few records were made of their activities. Among the first of these clubs was the Monday Club of Boston, and Zilpha D. Smith of the Boston COS discussed the value of such clubs at the National Conference in 1911. She urged all communities with 12 or more social workers to organize clubs that would be limited to the paid professional staff of agencies, would include representatives of all the fields of practice found in the community, would establish membership fees low enough so that all could join, and would have programs determined by the participation of the members. However, in spite of a growing community of interests, so far as is known, these clubs were not the forerunners of the professional organization. There was no movement to form a national body from the various clubs (Bruno, 1957, pp. 145–46).

Specialization

One of the problems in creating a national body that would include representatives of all the fields of practice, as urged by Zilpha Smith, was the growing specialization among social workers. For example, social workers were beginning to be found in considerable numbers in the health system (medical social work and psychiatric social work) and in the educational system (school social work or visiting teachers). Many of these workers, pushed by the professionals in the host system to define their function and defend their special competence, were rapidly becoming a self-conscious group deeply concerned with the development of technical competence. These social workers moved more rapidly toward national professional associations with restrictive standards of membership than did the social workers within the general social service delivery systems. We shall discuss these special organizations when we discuss those social welfare systems. For now, we shall give an account of the development of the general professional association, which absorbed these special groups in the 60s. However, in the initial efforts to develop a formal professional organization, these special organizations may have served to divide social workers.

The National Social Workers Exchange

As nearly as can be determined, the Intercollegiate Bureau of Occupations was the parent of the national professional association of social workers. The bureau had been founded in 1911 by the New York alumni of the eastern women's colleges in order to offer vocational counseling to women college graduates in search of career opportunities. The bureau was overwhelmed by the applicants for social work positions and found it necessary in 1913 to establish a separate department, with a social worker in charge, to handle these applicants. It was perhaps very logical that, given its broadened activities, the department should separate itself from the bureau. In 1917 it became the National Social Workers Exchange, the first national organization related to the social work professional. The experience of the three years between 1917 and 1920 convinced the leaders of the Exchange of the need for a professional association (Bruno, 1957, pp. 146–47; Lubane, 1965, pp. 130–32).

In those years, the National Exchange did not get involved with trying to define who was a social worker. Rather, it quite freely accepted into membership any persons who defined themselves as eligible. But gradually there was built up a small group of persons who defined themselves as social workers, who tended to characterize social work in terms of the functions in which they were engaged. Thus there formed at the national level a group of practitioners who stated that they were social workers and invited others to join them, who were interested in broad professional issues, who saw the importance of a professional association, and who had at their disposal the organizational machinery necessary to such an association. In 1920 the Exchange even started a journal, *The Compass.*

On June 27, 1921, at Milwaukee, in connection with the annual meeting of the National Conference, the professional association for social workers was launched when it was voted to change the name of the Exchange to the American Association of Social Workers. The Exchange had been financed from three sources: fees for vocational services, dues from members, and gifts from foundations. The new organization's leaders felt that as a professional association serving only the interests of the profession, it should be able to depend entirely on members' dues. This goal was reached in 1927. It is interesting that the *Proceedings* of the National Conference of 1921 makes no mention whatever of the development of the professional association.

A professional association

The new organization faced a huge task in attempting to create a national professional association from the diversity that marked social workers in the second decade of the 20th century. There was a wide range of training, all the way from high school only to graduation from the professional schools or training in another profession. Salaries varied widely, but they generally compared unfavorably with those for teaching, at least for women. And the new AASW had no way of controlling the hiring practices of the agencies. Its only means for advancing the profession were that it could exclude from the professional association those who did not meet its standards and that it provided an institutional channel through which the leaders of the profession could exercise their influence.

The initial requirement for membership in AASW was four years of experience, bypassing entirely the requirement of education, though academic and professional training could substitute for experience. The AASW requirements were revised in 1929, when the principle was established that professional education was essential for social work practice. The new regulations established two categories of membership, junior and full, each requiring courses, supervised fieldwork, and work experiences, but neither requiring a social work degree.

The shape of the profession

It is interesting to consider a description of the movement toward the professionalization of social work that was written by Stuart Alfred Queen in 1922. He identified these factors as hindering social work in its attempts to become a profession: (1) its activities were not sufficiently differentiated from those of the "general public"; (2) it overlapped the field of other recognized professions, such as medicine, law, teaching, and the ministry; (3) it included such a variety of services that it was difficult to set the limits of its work; (4) further development of the social sciences as a knowledge base was needed; and (5) the apprenticeship system under which people were trained for particular jobs in agencies was still in existence. After discussing these factors, McQueen continued:

> Finally, among the causes of failure to attain professional standing, we must note the undemocratic character of social work as implied in the word charity. The physician, lawyer, minister, and teacher are supported by their clients or by the community as a whole, while the social worker has usually been the emissary of one social class to another. . . . The professional folk are engaged in doing things which people need to have done and which in this era of specialization they are not able to do for themselves. There is no assumption of social or economic superiority. There is simply a task to be performed which requires a special kind of ability and training. The social worker, on the other hand, has not escaped the stigma of doing things that "normal" people ought to do for themselves. He is looked upon as handing down to the inferior class some of the surplus of the superior.
>
> Now it is a revulsion against just this sort of thing that is providing one of the most powerful impulses for the professionalization of social work. Charity has sometimes been presented as a device for quieting unrest and avoiding important social or economic readjustment. . . . There is a marked effort to shake off the past and make a new start, not only in name but in character of work as well . . . the gradually increasing use of social agencies by the well-to-do, sometimes with the payment

of a fee for the service, and by the extension of governmental participation in social work. (Queen, 1922, pp. 46–47).

As Queen's statement indicates, in its quest for professionalism social work had to be concerned not only with the definition of a special skill but also with the development of a community of members who shared a common sense of identity and values. This was to be a difficult task because social work was divided in two ways. First, there were the various divisions of work, such as settlement work, social reform, institutional work, administration, and casework. Second, social workers, particularly caseworkers, began to be identified by the field of practice in which they were involved. Thus, we had the child welfare worker, the psychiatric social worker, the medical social worker, the family worker, the probation officer, the visiting teacher, and so on.

The Milford Conference

In the search for professional identification a group of executives and board members of casework agencies met regularly after 1923. In 1929 they issued a report of their deliberations which became known as the Report of the Milford Conference. This report held that *social casework* was generic in its basic purposes and methodology, regardless of where it was practiced. However, the report did recognize that social caseworkers practiced in settings that were administratively different and that often required specialized knowledge and techniques. The report considered only social casework, not social work as a whole.

Casework as a helping technique had always focused on helping the individual, and yet it had always focused on understanding the individual in terms of the social situation and environment. Caseworkers had accepted a liaison and mobilization function as a primary method, considering the coordination of community services and the creation of new welfare resources indispensable to the helping process in which they were engaged. The caseworker's contact with the poverty of the time, as seen in the daily lives of individual clients, furnished the data and the impulse for much early reform. But in the 1920s a significant shift in emphasis began to take place as social caseworkers became aware of the fields of psychiatry and psychology. Caseworkers began to minimize the integrating and coordinating functions of their job and to favor working for personality growth and change through a psychological therapy based on a dynamic relationship between client and worker.

This trend in casework, which was to accelerate through the 1930s and 1940s, was brought about by several forces. First, Flexner's paper set caseworkers on a search for an identifiable method that could be labeled professional. Social workers began to be influenced by their association with psychiatrists in clinics and hospitals (we will discuss this later) and by their work on interdisciplinary teams. During and after World War I, they became involved with clients who were suffering from various stresses and living above the poverty line. Psychiatry also gave social workers new insight into the administration of relief. It taught that the caseworker needed to determine whether economic dependence reflected a more basic personality disturbance that needed treatment or whether clients needed a helping relationship to assure that they did not surrender their self-esteem and independence as a part of the psychological burden of having to accept help in our society, which equated relief with inferiority.

With the acceptance of the psychoanalytic concepts by social workers, it seemed that they had finally achieved a scientific base and a way of understanding and changing human behavior. Given the importance of this new knowledge and the fact that it was in the possession of psychiatrists, the social workers who worked in psychiatric settings began to achieve a certain status within their own profession. This new learning brought a new problem in the identification of social work as a profession. The new psychological knowledge had created an awareness of the complexity and inwardness of many of the problems of the human condition and had taught that it was desirable for individual clients to find their own way to the solution of their own problems. This approach put emphasis on technical skill in helping the individual to change, and it moved social work away from concern with changing the environment.

In his presidential address to the National Conference of Social Welfare in 1929, Porter Lee, dean of the New York School of Social Work, considered this problem. He spoke of "cause and function," saying that the campaigns for social reform represented a cause, but that a cause would never carry over adequately to the "methodological organized effort to make its fruits permanent," that society needed an "embattled host for the cause, an efficient personnel for the function" (Lee, 1937, pp. 4–5). However, the division between cause and function, between reform of society and change of the individual, was to continue, and it would be the 1960s before social work was so involved again with cause as in the years 1900 to 1920.

And when, 40 years later, the interest in reform became dominant once again, it was easy to dismiss this emphasis on the individual as both ineffective and politically conservative. At the time, however, the notion that behavior was not a moral lapse but a symptom of a human response to common human needs, problems, and life experiences was, as the quotation from Queen illustrates, a liberating movement from charity to professional help.

ᴥ§ Professional literature

One criterion of a profession is the creation and sharing of knowledge. Trial and error and personal communication become too costly to both the professional and the client. A written analysis of what is done becomes necessary. Social work as a profession, personal social services, and social work reform efforts each have a literature. It is not always clear how one divides the literature of the profession from the literature of the institution of social welfare or from that of the personal social services system. In this discussion we shall touch on both briefly as we seek to account for the literature that social workers were producing and reading.

The development of schools made the question of social work literature particularly important at this time. There was urgent and continuing need in the early 1900s for material that could be used in teaching. Some books became valuable additions to such material: Amos G. Warner's *American Charities; How the Other Half Lives,* by Jacob Riis; and the writings of Jane Addams, such as *Hull House Maps and Papers*. However, much of the most valuable social work literature was found in the periodicals that were beginning to develop. The journals of a profession detail the cutting edge of practice and thus are critical both to developing the thinking of members and to pointing the way on issues before the profession.

The staff of COS agencies were, from the beginning, anxious to share their problems and their programs with others, and a number of agencies began to sponsor local journals describing their work. Among the first of these was *Lend a Hand,* established by the Boston COS in 1886 and addressed to the whole field of social welfare. The New York COS began a journal called *Charities Review* in 1891. In March 1901 a less well known magazine was published by the Baltimore COS under the name *The Charities Record*. In March 1920 the national association of COS agencies began to publish *The Family*. This journal has continued to the present day, under the name *Social Casework,* and it is still published by the national association, which is now known as the Family Association of America. This development will be discussed later under the section of this chapter dealing with private family services.

National periodicals

In 1896 the settlement movement began to publish a national journal called *The Commons*. In the beginning this journal carried primarily articles from workers in the settlements. As time went on, however, it began to carry material addressed to the difficult social issues of the time. It explored the problems of the immigrant, and it carried articles on the new juvenile court movement, on problems in the public schools, and on the need for

participatory democracy (Chambers, 1971, p. 26).

Charities experimented with devoting special issues to, and examination in depth of, a particular social issue. In February 1904 a special number was devoted to the problems of immigration. In May 1904 an issue was devoted to the Italian immigrant. This issue, in contrast to the earlier one, featured articles written by Italian-Americans who detailed, for the first time in this type of publication, the role of the ethnic groups in caring for their own through their benevolent and fraternal societies. The following year, in October 1905, in the largest issue published up to that time, *Charities* dedicated an issue to "The Negro and the Cities of the North." The issue included articles by both Booker T. Washington and W. E. B. Du Bois (Chambers, 1971, p. 21). In June 1905 the journal attacked the taboo against open discussion of venereal disease with an issue focused on the "great black plague" of syphilis. In discussing this issue, Chambers writes that the subject "was treated impassively and objectively, as a part of the public health movement" and "its tone was not in the least moralistic or sentimental" (Chambers, 1971, p. 22). In a discussion of the themes of the 1904 National Conference, *Charities* reported approvingly that social workers, while still concerned with the need to understand and serve individuals and families in trouble, were concentrating more on the social, searching within society for the causes of problems. "The family had to be considered as an organic whole, related to the particular community and the particular environment within which it dwelt" (Chambers, 1971, p. 23).

In the fall of 1905 *Charities* and *The Commons* merged to create a new journal called *Charities and Commons*. A few months later this journal also absorbed *Jewish Charity,* the official paper of the United Hebrew Charities of New York. By 1908 the board members and staff of the magazine began to feel uncomfortable with the word *charities* in the name of a periodical such as the magazine had become, and in 1909 the name was changed to *The Survey*. In 1923 the *Survey* was divided into two publications, a division which lasted for 16 years. The *Graphic* was to be a high-quality periodical dealing with the facts of social issues by gathering and testing evidence from many different points of view. The *Survey Midmonthly* was to be oriented to professional methods and problems of practice.

In addition to the journals mentioned above, by the 1940s there were the *Social Service Review,* the *Catholic Charities Review,* both published monthly, and the *Jewish Quarterly.* The *Social Service Review* was published by the faculty of the School of Social Service Administration of the University of Chicago beginning in 1929, and it is today one of the leading social work journals. In its second year the *Review* devoted some of its pages to a discussion of the Mexicans living in Chicago. The *Review* has consistently maintained a balance between articles dealing with social issues and reform and articles dealing with the more technical concerns of practice. It has consistently given special consideration to the findings of various kinds of research efforts. Outstanding among the journals devoted to special types of problems and their treatment were *Mental Hygiene,* issued by the National Committee for Mental Hygiene; the *Family,* which was discussed earlier; the monthly *Bulletin* of the Child Welfare League of America, now called *Child Welfare;* and *Probation,* issued monthly by the National Probation Association. Almost every field of social work practice established a medium for transmitting information regarding its activities and its range of interests. A rich body of social work literature began to develop.

Case records as teaching literature

In addition to the periodical literature discussed above, other types of literature were important to the developing social work profession and the schools of social work. In 1905 a group of Charity Organization societies set up a plan for exchanging forms, records, and so forth, to be carried on by the Field Department of *Charities* and *The Commons.* A committee collected carefully disguised case records from 45 Charity Organization societies. These records, together with other materials,

were placed on display at the 1908 session of the National Conference. This case record exhibit continued down until recent years (Rich, 1956, p. 49).

An even more important undertaking was the preparation of selected case records, mimeographed or printed, for use in training students and workers. In 1905, when Mary Richmond became the editor of the Field Department of *Charities* and *The Commons,* her duties included encouraging the exchange of publicity, publications and case records among agencies. The records were carefully disguised, and as a further protection to the clients involved, their distribution was limited to agencies and teachers known to the Field Department. Later, other types of agencies became involved in such record development (Rich, 1956, pp. 80–81; Lubane, 1965, p. 120; Pumphrey, 1961, pp. 350–60).

Books

The early 1900s saw the publication of a number of books based on the work of the COS. In 1900 Mary Richmond published *Friendly Visiting among the Poor; A Handbook for Charity Workers.* In this publication Richmond made it very clear that she saw a considerable difference between the "friendly visiting" of the volunteer and the professional activities of the paid agent. Among the books published in the next few years were *The Practice of Charity* (1901), *The Principles of Relief* (1904), and *Misery and Its Causes* (1909), all of which were written by Edward T. Devine, the executive director of the New York COS, who also served as editor of *Charities* and *The Commons* in his spare time. Richmond wrote *The Good Neighbor in the Modern City* (1907), and Amelia Sears wrote *The Charity Visitor.* In the 1920s books by such social workers as Jane Addams, Grace Abbott, Edith Abbott, and Sophonisba Breckinridge were published. Beginning in 1929 and published biennially by the Russell Sage Foundation and later by the National Association of Social Workers, the *Social Work Yearbook* (later the *Encyclopedia of Social Work*) dealt in brief form with material related to social work.

But perhaps the greatest and most influential works of the time were two books by Mary Richmond herself: *Social Diagnosis* (1917) and *What Is Social Casework?* (1921).

In *What Is Social Casework?*, Richmond defined social casework as "those processes which develop personality through adjustments consciously effected, individual by individual, between men and their social environment" (Richmond, 1922, pp. 98–99). She saw four processes as constituting the heart of casework activities: insight into individuality and personal characteristics; insight into the resources, dangers, and influence of the social environment; the direct action of mind upon mind; and indirect action through the social environment (Richmond, 1922, pp. 100–105).

She wrote: "Affection and kindness unlock many doors, straighten out many complications. But when to affection and kindness we are able to add that knowledge of the workings of the human mind and that knowledge of social resources . . . we have a new power in the world added to the older power of just loving one another" (Richmond, 1922, p. 167). The social worker's unique skill lay in the ability to collect all pertinent data and expertly interpret the social evidence, planning action, or differential social treatment, the basis of that evidence. Skilled, differential casework, emphasizing client participation, was to eliminate once and for all the patronizing overtones associated with philanthrophy. Social work was to offer, not alms, or even a friend, but a skilled service doing differen things for different people and including client participation as a vital part of the process. Each person was the sum of his individuality, his will, his purpose, and his social environment, and was to be so understood.

Just as the United States was beginning to experience the devastation of the depression in 1930, Virginia Robinson published *A Changing Psychology in Social Work*. This book both summed up the trend in social casework and set the direction of the profession for the next 30 years. Richmond had been interested in the collection of objective facts about the client as a way of individualizing the client. However, Robinson introduced the no-

tion that it was not the objective facts but what the client made of the facts and the client's feelings about them that mattered. People responded differently to situations, and it was these inner feelings, with roots in the crises of personality development, that accounted for that difference.

✒§ The organization and federation of charity

Beginning during World War I and continuing afterward, efforts toward centralized fund raising and coordination among the privately supported welfare agencies began to develop in large cities. Often this resulted in the establishment of two city-wide organizations: the Community Fund, to collect in one community-wide drive moneys for all the private social agencies in the city and to allocate the funds contributed to the support of the member agencies; and the Council of Social Agencies, to coordinate and integrate existing agencies and to improve the health and social resources of the city. Actually, the second of these two organizations resulted from a division of the functions of the old COSs. The reader will remember that these societies came into being as a way of creating order and integration among the many and various charities that sprang up during the difficult times following the Civil War. The reader will also remember these societies gradually developed their own division of direct services to people. Often, other agencies in the community deeply resented this move, complaining that the societies could not very well serve in a sort of overseer role when they were in competition with the very agencies that they were attempting to organize.

Other agencies resented being criticized by a group which had arbitrarily assumed the responsibility for being the community commentator and critic in relation to their work. It was Francis H. McLean, associate director of the Charity Organization Department of the Russell Sage Foundation, who suggested a way out of this dilemma. He proposed that the two functions be separated—that the COS concentrate its efforts on service to families and children and that a new organization be developed to carry the responsibility for organizing the charities of the community. This new organization was to be composed of representative of all the social agencies in the community that wished to unite in the common project of establishing and improving standards. McLean's plan differed from the earlier efforts of the COS to organize charities in that it proposed that the new body be made up of representatives of the agencies of the community whose only purpose would be to improve community standards of social service through joint decision making in a democratic process (Bruno, 1957, pp. 192–207).

Councils of social agencies

In 1908, in Pittsburgh, this new form of agency was established, along with the Associated Charities of Pittsburgh, which as the direct service arm of COS was to concentrate on service to families. Other cities were experimenting with a similar form of organization at about the same time. It is very interesting, however, that this movement, which was to affect the shape of social services in the community from the beginning of the 1900s until the present, received no mention in the *Proceedings* of the social welfare conferences of the time. The movement made slow headway for two reasons: (1) If progress was to be made by common agreement in such functions as passing on the establishment of new agencies, the reorganization of old agencies, the combining of existing agencies, or the closing of inadequate agencies, or in the improvement of cooperation among agencies, much time had to be spent in conferences and leading staff and board members had to be willing to give their time to this purpose rather than to direct service. (2) The financing of a strong council staffed by persons whose judgment would be respected required considerable money for adequate salaries, but it was almost impossible to obtain money to support an organization that by definition performed no direct services to individuals (Bruno, 1957, pp. 193–206).

Thus, the growth of the councils of social agencies was slow and difficult, and they might not have lived at all had it not been for another important movement. One of the most important and characteristic developments in social services in America has been the "community chest" movement, through which the joint financing of private agencies is assured. Denver should probably be given the credit for originating the movement when, in 1888, more than a dozen relief-giving societies in that city united their appeals for funds through the Community Organization Society. However, this society did not assume the responsibility for raising all the money needed by its member agencies. Thus, over the years the member agencies gradually increased their independent solicitations, so that by the early 1900s the plan appeared to have lost its usefulness.

United appeals-Federated funding

In 1900, however, the Cleveland Chamber of Commerce organized a Committee on Benevolent Institutions to act as an accrediting agency for community charities. As part of its activities the committee attempted to evaluate the methods of collecting and accounting for money. From such supervision of the ways in which agencies collected and accounted for their money, it was only a short step to proposing a plan for the joint financing of all agencies through a joint appeal. Edward M. Williams reported to the Welfare Conference of 1913 that the "Cleveland Federation" was a success in that the usual givers had increased their donations by 57 percent and more than 10,000 new givers had been secured. Other communities followed Cleveland's example. Although these early projects differed from city to city, they had in common the preparation of a total budget covering the anticipated needs of member agencies, the pledge of member agencies that they would not solicit money from anybody who contributed to the federated fund, and the use of large numbers of volunteers to solicit money from citizens on behalf of the agencies in the group (Bruno, 1957, pp. 204–6).

The promoters of joint financing were faced not only with the problem of raising money but with the problem of how to distribute it fairly. The chests needed advice from a body representing the specialists in the field. The developing councils of agencies seemed the ideal place to turn for such advice. Thus a close association between the chests and the councils developed which assured the councils of an ongoing purpose and of the ongoing financing that they needed. The chest movement was profoundly influenced by World Wars I and II. Wars tend to promote an outpouring of help for their victims out of all proportion to any other appeals. Many communities organized "war chests," and the experience of thousands in combining all of their individual contributions into one pledge was a powerful influence on the continued development of the chests after the war.

Another important long-term influence was the Hollis Amendment to the income tax law, passed just before World War I, which permitted people to deduct from their taxable income contributions to church and charity of up to 15 percent of their total income. With surtaxes rising to 60 percent of income in the highest brackets in World War I, and to 90 percent in World War II, gifts to the chests might represent very little actual money to the wealthy giver. The amendment had other effects. It also meant that the wealthy could choose the beneficiaries of their giving and that large givers could thus influence the welfare of many at little cost to themselves. In addition, because of the amendment public funds for public services might well be smaller, as giving by the wealthy to private organizations decreased the tax base and thus avoided support for public services

The chest movement had both advocates and critics among the professional social workers. Those who supported it felt that it would lead to better accountability in the use of funds, that it would give the agencies better assurance of being able to meet expanding needs, that larger amounts could be secured and more people involved in the funding of agencies, and that joint decision making relative to the collection and distribution of funds would better serve the needs of the whole community. Those who opposed the movement were fearful that the individual agencies would lose autonomy when their funds depended on the authority

of the chest, that social work would find itself controlled by financial interests "whose major concern would be to keep down costs and suppress troublesome movements," and that the chest would "promote mediocrity" by leveling all agencies down to an average standard (Bruno, 1959, p. 203). There has continued to be controversy over whether the council should be a member of the chest. In many cities they are joint organizations.

In discussing the development of the chest, Bruno points out that the task of raising contributions from individuals to finance the rapidly expanding needs of private social services had outgrown the earlier methods in which a few wealthy people might identify a need and organize a small group of believers to support and run a "charity." The chest was able to tap the industrial field. It presented a picture of the total community's need "that makes a valid claim at once upon the national corporation and upon the individual working man" (Bruno, 1959, p. 204). As a result of the chest movement, almost every employed person and many others in the community have become contributors, and it has promoted the notion that since everyone gives, everyone has a right to service. It is neighbor giving to neighbor. In its emphasis on local private giving to support locally determined needs, the chest movement has furthered the notion that private, local service is always best and more responsive to need.

The great contribution of the chest movement has probably been its development of the methods of distribution. It has established budgetary control, requiring agencies to budget expenses and account for services given. Budgeting obviously has great implications for program, and the need developed to look at each agency in relation to the whole community system of service. Thus the agency which wishes to secure funding through the chest (and few others can survive) must submit its program, its plans, its pattern of staffing, and so forth, to the scrutiny of its peers and abide by their judgment. The chests' demand for reports of expenditures and accounts of services rendered, the enhanced power of central bodies to sit in some judgment on the development of new services, obviously resulted in a loss of autonomy for the agencies that joined the movement and increased difficulty in raising adequate funds for those that did not.

The notion that clients and supporters alike (and through the chest movement clients increasingly became contributors) were entitled to accountability on the part of the helpers, that helping people were responsible for giving adequate and competent service to *all clients* equally, imposed certain limits both on individual unilateral actions and on quick and impulsive responses to requests for help. Increasingly, clients had to fit within designated eligibility categories and to come to the agencies by designated access routes. How else could the community, as the supporter of services, be sure that money and staff were being used properly in a complex urban community of heterogeneous population where one was unable, as was the parish priest of old, to know all people's troubles intimately? And what about the judgment of that priest? Did he really know how to help in the most productive way? Given the growing knowledge of human behavior and social environment, how could one be sure that the client had the best help possible if the helper did not have certain knowledge and skills that came with professional education? These questions were to have a particularly serious impact on the settlements and their philosophy of neighbor helping neighbor.

The settlements

By the beginning of the 1900s the settlement movement was growing rapidly. In 1911 the National Federation of Settlements was founded to coordinate the settlements' programs. At that time more than 400 settlements were scattered across the country, and they were interested in working together to advance their programs. The settlements were important in the social reform movements of the time. Much of the reform legislation regulating child labor and women's work, the tenement laws, sanitation codes, regulations promoting health and welfare, improvements in the schools, and the juvenile court movement developed di-

rectly or indirectly from the activities of people who had been a part of the settlement movement. The early founders and teachers in the School of Social Service Administration in Chicago were residents of Hull House. Julia Lathrop, Florence Kelley, Lillian Wald, Grace and Edith Abbott, Mary McDowell, and Graham Taylor were some of the people who lived in the settlements.

The development of the settlements during the early 1900s had important effects in five ways: (1) settlement workers struggled to develop the participation of neighborhoods in working for the betterment of the local community and in assuring the access of slum dwellers to helping services and opportunities; (2) the settlement movement had important effects on the larger society through the surveys and research carried on by the settlement residents and through the writing these residents did; (3) attempts to work through the local government, usually under the control of corrupt bosses, discouraged early settlement workers so that they began to look to the state and federal levels of government and to see the importance of legislation at those levels; (4) the settlements were an educational experience for persons who later took leadership positions in the developing social welfare programs of government; and (5) the work of the early settlement leaders formed the base of many of today's programs.

The early settlement workers were concerned with the quality of life for all people, and they acted to improve this as they understood it at the time. It is possible to argue that the settlement workers were too involved in the effort to socialize the immigrant to American values and morality to be concerned with the issues of the fate of the poor caught between big business and big government, that they did not really develop local and neighborhood leaders who could speak for the poor from the perspective of the poor. The settlements have been criticized for not supporting revolutionary action. It is certainly true that the early settlement workers were uplifters who, seeing their own culture as superior, consciously represented the best of their own social and cultural traditions. But they were deeply committed to the welfare of others and to social justice as well. This was demonstrated over and over again during World War I, when many of the settlement leaders were outspoken pacifists, and after the war, when the settlement leaders strongly supported the "Bolshevik" and "German" ideas of social insurance. During postwar years the settlements also had to face their changing neighborhoods and to try, in a stumbling way, to bridge their programs to cultures that they did not, and were unprepared to, understand. Those were difficult years for the settlements as they responded to changing neighborhoods, a changing national scene, and a changing professional climate.

Issues of controversy and support

Jane Addams and Lillian Wald were not people to back away from controversy, and Florence Kelley was certainly a fighter of great determination. For example, at Jane Addams's insistence Hull House entertained a group of black women delegates to a national meeting for lunch. As a result, Addams found that she could no longer speak in parts of the South, where her speeches had been an important source of income for the settlement. Both Lillian Wald and Jane Addams found their programs threatened by their pacifism during World War I.

Later, after the war, when the political climate was such that reform programs were labeled Bolshevik and controversy was unpopular, the settlements were considered hotbeds of radicalism and had great difficulty in securing support. Hull House once turned down a gift of $50,000 which was dependent on having its residents cease their work for a factory inspection law in Illinois.

The settlements and their residents were also deeply concerned about the way in which wealthy patrons earned their money. Should a charity be concerned about the way in which its would-be contributors have accumulated their wealth? Jane Addams refused a contribution to support a program for working girls from an employer notorious for underpaying his female workers. There were some independently wealthy supporters who were morally committed to the reform efforts of the set-

tlements and had no fear of the consequences of their support. These people were critically important to the ongoing work of the settlements during the 1920s.

Problems related to the issue of support also affected the governance of the settlements. Initially, an effort was made to have neighborhood representation on the settlement boards and to interest wealthy board members in playing an active part in the settlement programs. However, it was difficult to interest wealthy board members in the day-to-day work of the settlement, and it was difficult to recruit the poor to attend board meetings, especially when the board had to accept the financial responsibility for the programs. The problem of control by boards was closely related to the force and commitment of the settlement leaders. Although the more politically active settlements were always involved in financial struggles, it seemed that they could recruit admirers to support their efforts (Chambers, 1963, pp. 119–24; Levine and Levine, 1963, pp. 119–21).

The later financial base of the settlements

A development that affected the support and the programs of the settlements was the gradual transformation of the settlements into social agencies. With the growth of the settlements, the leaders had programs, buildings, and payrolls to worry about. More formal organization and division of labor began to creep into the settlements. The trend toward centralized fund raising and coordination among the privately supported welfare agencies of the city and the interest in the professional development of staff and in systematic financial planning began to reduce the autonomy of the social agencies of the community, the settlements among them.

The community funds' demand for reports of expenditures and accounts of services rendered, the enhanced power of the central agencies to sit in some judgment on the development of new services, resulted in a loss of autonomy for the settlements that joined the movement, and for those that did not there was increased difficulty in raising the necessary funds for adequate support. The notion that clients and supporters alike were entitled to accountability on the part of the helpers, that helping people were responsible for giving adequate and competent service to *all clients,* imposed certain limits on impulsive and quick response to requests for help. The function of the settlements as social centers with a virtual monopoly over the educational, recreational, and welfare services offered in the slum areas began to be reduced as the efforts of the settlement workers toward reform and social justice resulted in the growth of other organizations offering services to the neighborhood residents, as well as to a broader clientele, in a more organized and planned way. Thus we see a contradiction between the settlement movement's pioneering ethos and its community-centered philosophy. With the coming of the depression of the 1930s, the settlements as well as other philanthropic effectors became a part of the transformation from "social reform" and "charity" to social welfare and professional services (Peterson, 1965, pp. 191–208).

Professionalism and the settlements

During the early 1950s Maryal Knox, who had been active in settlement work in New York for over 50 years, remarked that she would not be hired by any settlement of that time because she was unable to communicate in the language of abnormal psychology. She went on to say in what was a somewhat defensive statement that children would come out all right if one made them feel happy and secure and loved even though one might not know "the names of all the complexes they might have" (Chambers, 1963, p. 121). This statement effectively illustrates the movement away from the friendliness of amateurs toward the professional services that began in the settlements, as well as in other philanthropic movements, in the first decades of the 1900s. The earlier flow of untrained and inexperienced young men and women, eager for adventure and looking for opportunities to learn, began to be replaced by a flow of professional specialists who were interested in the effec-

tive operation of service programs. Head residents were recruited largely from graduates of schools of social work, and the settlements began to prefer to hire specialists with proper educational preparation for their work. The informality of settlement life declined as the settlements became organizations with separate departments and programs.

One of the last attacks on the older model of the settlement was the abandonment of the practice of residency. The notion of residency in the neighborhood had been central to the establishment of the early settlements. But the new settlement workers no longer saw this as having an important bearing on the effectiveness of their service to the community. The staff no longer lived at the settlement or in the neighborhood. The older settlement leaders were passing from the scene, and they were replaced by the daughters or sons of immigrants, who had secured training and education in social work and were not interested in living in the slums they had recently left. The slums were not a new learning experience for them; they were the stuff of a painful and tragic struggle toward security and a better life. These sons and daughters knew the slums; the problems of the slums were part of their life experiences. They did not want to learn about them; they wanted to escape from them and to help others to do so by offering the best programs of development possible. We have an example of this from the Columbus settlement we discussed earlier (Peterson, 1965, pp. 191–208).

In 1949 (some time after the end of our present period) the last of the older leaders of the Columbus settlement retired. The new director, Anthony J. Salvatore, son of an Italian immigrant and neighborhood shoe repairman, had known the Columbus settlement and its programs from birth. His life was an object lesson in the value of the settlements. It would have been difficult for him to alter the settlement's programs if he had relied only on his own experience with them. However, he had graduated from the Ohio State University School of Social Administration and he had been the director of the Boys' Department of the Franklin County Juvenile Court. While preserving certain older programs of the Columbus settlement, Salvatore chose to work in terms of his professional training and experience. Residency was abandoned. Salvatore had already left the neighborhood of the settlement, and he was reluctant to resume residency among the poor (Peterson, 1965, pp. 191–208).

Some of the articles that discuss the changes in the settlements at this time speak of the fact that the growing professionalism of the staff, as in Salvatore's case, tended to dampen the fires of reform. The authors of these articles see professionalization as having a conservatizing effect. However, it is difficult to separate the effects of professionalization from those of the bureaucratization and central organization that were occurring in social welfare at the same time. It may well be possible that, because professionalization and bureaucratization occurred together, the separate effects of each on social work and social welfare have not been well understood. At least one study of social workers tends to show that professionalization actually inhibits the conservatizing effects of the bureaucratic agency structure within which the social work profession is lodged (Epstein, 1970, pp. 123–31). This study indicates that an orientation to a professional reference group mitigates the conservatizing effects of promotion to supervisory and administrative positions. However that may be, the settlement experience demonstrates the joint effects of the professionalization and bureaucratization that developed during the 1940s, about which we shall have more to say later.

Another trend that affected the settlements, and all other social agencies, was in many ways the result of the settlements' activities. This was the movement toward what may be called "social justice." The settlements might work to see that certain of their neighbors secured relief and help in time of trouble, but they also wanted to make the right to such help and relief available to all people. They worked to create public services in which fair procedures and benefits were administered with an even hand. But this very move toward a social justice, as opposed to an individualized help (concerned with the unique needs of individuals), resulted in the establishment of rules, regulations, and bureaucratic structures. This operated to put

certain barriers in the way of the "neighbor" concept of the earliest settlement workers.

We are not saying that social justice is wrong or that bureaucratic structures are to be abhorred. We are asking the student to understand that "the same" as determined by law, legislation, or rule is not always "equal." The question of the competence of professional judgment and intent as a way of assuring equality is an important one. However that may be, we must recognize that the growth of legislation began the movement toward establishing the right of all citizens to certain protections and benefits and that it was the development of the bureaucratic structure which made possible certain kinds of regular procedures for assuring that every person received equality of treatment and equal access to rights. Without an organized bureaucratic structure, we would have been unable to move as far as we have toward the advancement of the welfare of all Americans. But the questions of the optimal mix between professional judgment about equality of individual entitlement and formal legal rights assuring the same entitlement remain unsolved.

Community organization

A central purpose of the early settlements was to help neighborhoods become organized for their own development. Stanton Coit saw the first step in the improvement of human living to be that of the "conscious organization of the intellectual and moral life of the people" (Coit, 1891, pp. 4–5). From these beginnings, after much refinement and development, grew the social work method known as community organization, the process by which a community may be helped to identify its problems or objectives, rank its problems, develop a plan for solving these identified problems, and take some action toward carrying out the plan.

Group work

The club, or organized group, was the unit of organization within the settlements. The club was a group of persons who were usually formally organized, with a leader who was a member of the settlement staff or a volunteer but not a member of the club. These clubs were usually laboratories in which members learned to participate in the democratic process, places of self-development through the group's use of programs of activities or task achievement, and places of social learning opportunities for those who were willing to participate in the settlement programs. John Dewey's work on progressive education was an important base for the work with these clubs. Later these experiences were to become the foundation for another method of social work practice—social group work.

✑ From the Charity Organization Society to private family agency

The years from the turn of the century until the beginning of the depression were years of change and challenge for the COSs. The societies began the 20th century as Charity Organization societies, and 20 years later they had been transformed into Agencies for Family Social Work. The change in the name was far more than semantic. During those years three strong currents of change were buffeting the COSs: (1) the beginnings of the chest and council movement and the division of social welfare work into two parts, allocating the organization and funding of charity in the community to organizations of the community; (2) the beginnings of public assistance and social security over the objections of many COS leaders who believed that only private agencies or institutions could effectively administer relief; and (3) World War I and the rapid expansion of the Red Cross, plus the rapid expansion of the desire for social work services in many other areas, and the consequent great pressure to educate social workers and to keep the staff that had been trained and to differentiate their work from other types of social work. Twenty years is not a long time. The leaders of the COSs in the 1890s and the leaders of the Agencies for Family Social Work in 1920 were often the same people, albeit considerably older. One must respect the strength of these leaders and their ability to follow

where the new currents of thought and their own investigations led them.

The public relief question

As we have discussed earlier, the political climate of the cities at the beginning of the 20th century was incredibly corrupt and many efforts to change it seemed to be ineffectual. The votes of the poor in the slums could be so easily bought for a beer, or a city job, or even a bauble given to a child, while the voices of the reformers who could promise only protracted struggles to secure better garbage collection, or better housing, or pure milk and water, fell on ears made deaf by an inability to understand the importance of such services and by the terrible immediacy of other needs. Thus, many social work leaders of the time felt that an increase in public funds for any purpose, no matter how worthy and important that purpose, would only cause more money to flow into the coffers of those bent on increasing their own power and making their own lives more comfortable. Many social work leaders were equally opposed to placing the management of public funds in the hands of private agencies. It was as though money coming from the public coffers was tainted by its source.

However, this was changing. In 1900 Frederic Almy of the Buffalo COS, who had been among the most uncompromising opponents of public outdoor relief, came forward with what was, for him, a new point of view:

> Private charity can be just as vicious and pauperizing, just as wasteful, just as corrupt and profligate, as public charity. If public almsgiving with no investigation or with no intelligence is bad, why not reform it instead of doing away with it? To acquiesce supinely in a debauching city government, and to attempt to organize a private agency to do the city's work is a surrender of manhood. . . . If well-administered city relief is best, reform your civil service and make such relief your goal. (Rich, 1956, p. 64)

There were other such calls for the COSs to accept the responsibility "of using their efforts to bring about the best possible administration of the system [public relief]" rather than to oppose it. The general trend grew for the private agencies to cooperate with the public departments of welfare rather than to seek their abolition, and state after state began to turn to social workers recruited primarily from COS agencies as the professionals who had the knowledge and the competences most needed to administer social service programs and serve families. Many workers with Charity Organization training began to recognize the challenge of this new work and to accept employment in the programs.

Francis H. McLean was one of the social workers whose work had a significant influence on the new public programs. McLean had had a wide acquaintance with both public and private welfare. He had been an executive of the COS of Montreal, a city which had neither public outdoor relief nor almshouses. Here he had found that

> absence [of taxes] has not in any way increased the generosity of the community at large. . . . the simple absence of governmental responsibility works toward an unjust squandering of private charitable resources. . . . [private charity] has possessed itself of some of the worst features of public outdoor relief as administered elsewhere; namely, stereotyped amounts of relief, . . . doles, officialism, and methods of work which mean degradation and humiliation to applicants." (Rich, 1954, p. 71)

In McLean's studies of public agencies he recommended: (1) unpaid advisory committees; (2) case committees to review decisions; (3) qualified staff with as high a degree of training and ability as that found in the private agencies; (4) the keeping of case records to assure accountability and to use in learning and teaching; and (5) agreements between the public and private agencies as to division of work which should be reviewed constantly and revised from time to time. As a result of McLean's work, the American Association for Organizing Charity adopted a resolution in 1918 putting the COS agencies over the nation on record as believing in the interdependence of public and private programs. Although this resolution led to very little

action, some of the opposition to public welfare had been laid to rest.

The development of a national COS association

Since the late 1890s, whenever COS workers came together at the National Conference of Social Work they had discussed the need for a national organization of the agencies and for some mechanism by which the agencies could share policies, programs, and experiences. Earlier in this chapter, we have seen how, in 1905, *Charities* established a Field Department with an exchange branch. This was an attempt to meet the need of new and far-flung agencies for consultation and for an exchange among members of pamphlets, reprints, and so on. The constituent societies were to subscribe $30 a year for the service, and they were asked to pay half in advance so that the new work could start immediately.

But there continued to be pressure for a national association, on June 8, 1911, the National Association of Societies for Organizing Charity was launched. In 1912 the word *American* was substituted for the word *National* so as to include Canadian agencies. The name was changed to American Association for Organizing Charity in 1917, to American Association for Organizing Family Social work in 1919, to Family Welfare Association of America in 1930, and to Family Service Association of America in 1946. The association still functions as the national parent body of such local family agencies as Family Service, Family and Children's Service, Jewish Family Service, Lutheran Social Services, and Catholic Social Services. Most of the sectarian family agencies that belong to this national body also belong to a national body within their own sectarian identification. It is interesting that the first agencies beyond the privately supported nonsectarian ones that were admitted to membership in the association were public welfare departments, in 1921, and units of mothers' aid funds, in 1928. The Jewish agencies joined in 1929, and the Catholic agencies in 1930. These changes could lead the secretary of the association to speak in 1923 of a "united program for the protection of family life"—to be focused and facilitated through the association (Rich, 1954, p. 91).

The original member societies were immediately confronted with the question of the basis on which new societies could be admitted to the association without lowering its level of competence. To ensure the maintenance of standards, the association's first constitution listed five requirements for affiliation and provided for the establishment of a committee, drawn from the member societies, to examine and act on applications. All actions of the committee were subject to the approval of the association board and of the annual meeting, thus assuring full participation of the member in shaping the character of their national body.

The first requirements to be set were:

1. Maintaining a paid agent or secretary on full time (this provision did not apply to cities with a population of less than 10,000).
2. Keeping individual records and exchanging information.
3. Signing rules governing the issuance of transportation by charitable societies and public officials as promulgated by the National Conference of Charities and Correction.
4. Agreeing to answer inquiries from the members of the association.

Rule three refers to the common practice (steming from the English Poor Laws) of returning nonresidents who were unable to care for themselves back to their original place of residence, or even sending them on to another city. In 1902 the National Conference considered this problem and developed an agreement that agencies would not send applicants for aid to other cities without assurance that doing so would benefit the applicants. From its inception in 1911 until 1933, the association required the signing of this agreement as a condition for membership and for inclusion in the yearly directory of agencies. In its second year the association amended the first point to read:

1. The agency shall have a paid secretary or agent who has had at least one year's training in a charity organization society of good standards or any agency having similar methods and

standards of case work employed full time, except in cities of less than 10,000.

It also added an amendment that the directors of the local agencies "must be elected by their own membership which shall be open to all persons in the community."

In 1918 the annual meeting of the association decided that a study should be made as to what the future scope and plan of the COSs should be. The report of the committee suggested that the societies accept the family as their unit of service and that they underline this emphasis by calling themselves Family Social Work agencies instead of COSs. It was voted to change the name of the national organization to American Association for Organizing Family Social Work and to have local agencies use the words *family social work* as they adopted new names. As we have noted earlier, the disruption of the war years brought troubles and disorganization to all families and social workers became involved with clients "above the poverty line." So perhaps at the annual meeting in 1925 the recommendation made "the private society doing family case work of a high order may extend its services to clients who can pay" was not unexpected (Rich, 1954, p. 100).

✎§ Services to children

In its early years the 19th century was heralded as the century of the child. Just as the 19th century came to a close, the first juvenile court was established, and the early years of the 1900s saw a rapid expansion of these courts throughout the country. The resolution of the first White House Conference that no child should be removed from its home for reasons of poverty alone was a major landmark in social welfare. Throughout the country there began to develop programs of mothers' aid to support women who were left alone with their children, so that fewer children would need placement because of poverty alone. States began to adopt children's codes and to assume increasing responsibility for the regulation of services to children. Increasingly, the agencies concerned with children separated from their own parents utilized supervised and paid foster homes rather than institutions. Increasingly, the states and counties were assuming responsibility for foster care of children. We have discussed all of these programs and movements earlier, so we will simply content ourselves with saying that they continued to develop throughout this period. We will emphasize here some of the new issues in the care and protection of children.

Day care

Day care for children who required care for all or part of a day while their mothers worked was first provided in this country in the middle of the 1800s. By the end of this period there were about 900 day nurseries in the United States (Lundberg, 1947, p. 287). All of them were operated under the auspices of settlements, family agencies, or churches. A small number were operated by industries that employed large numbers of children. There were no public funds for such care of children. The day nursery was seen by the social workers involved as serving both the welfare of the families and the welfare of the children entrusted to it.

During these years the more progressive day nurseries steadily improved their care of children and showed increasing concern for parents. Many of them had competent social service staffs and gave much attention to the welfare of the mothers who used their services. Federations of day nurseries in the larger urban centers accomplished a great deal in raising standards. The National Federation of Day Nurseries and the Association of Catholic Day Nurseries offered their members an opportunity to share experiences and develop practice. However, this resource of help to the working poor in their struggle to avoid either neglecting or placing their children was never accorded its full place as a positive force in the prevention of family disintegration. It may be that the ambivalence with which society has often regarded the working mother contributed to the problem of inadequate support of day care.

Homemaker service

When homemaker service is provided, the agency places an agency staff member called a homemaker in the home to care for the home and the children during the temporary absence of the mother for illness or during the incapacity of the mother if she remains in the home. Such service is an important factor in preventing the placement of children for temporary periods. Homemaker service as a definite plan for the care of children in their own homes was developed almost simultaneously, though independently, by Jewish welfare agencies in Baltimore, Philadelphia, and Chicago in 1923 and 1924. As the service grew, it was sometimes located in family agencies and sometimes in child-caring agencies. The service required careful selection of the women who were to act as homemakers and the training and supervision of such women by social workers. The service has always been scarce, and it has usually been necessary for agencies to severely limit the families that they can accept for such help.

The Child Welfare League of America

The delegates at the first White House Conference had discussed the need for a national organization concerned with the welfare of children. In 1915 Carl Christian gave a paper setting out in the strongest terms the need to develop standards for work with children. Influenced by this statement, 18 delegates from 14 child welfare organizations established the Bureau for the Exchange of Information among Child Helping Agencies. The organization met annually between 1916 and 1920. There was a constant pressure to establish a national organization similar to that established by the family agencies. Finally, in 1920, with a grant of $25,000 from the Commonwealth Fund, the executive committee of BEI agreed to organize its 65 members into a new national agency to be called the Child Welfare League of America.

The league exists today as the strongest organized voice for child welfare. It publishes the monthly periodical *Child Welfare,* and it circulates other literature relating to the problems of children. Adoption and foster care have been its primary concerns, but it has also been active in the areas of day care and homemaker service and, more recently, child abuse and neglect. The league has set standards for the operation of agencies in the above areas, has done significant research on child care, and has played an important role in the development of federal legislation in the interests of children (Romanofsky, 1978, pp. 224–30).

☙ Health

The investigations into the causes of poverty conducted by the social workers of this period began to lead to an understanding of the relationship between poverty and ill health. They began to see the illness, invalidism, and premature death of the family breadwinner as a major cause of poverty and poverty as the major cause of family disintegration. Also, in their studies of poverty social workers very quickly discovered a link between poverty and ill health, in that the poor were found to suffer a greater incidence of illness and to live shorter lives. Thus, in the early 1900s we find social workers developing both personal social services and social reform activities within the health system. During the early 1900s social workers became involved in three aspects of health care: public health, medical social work and mental health institutions and clinics. We will discuss these activities briefly.

Public health

From their beginning in the middle of the 1800s, public health activities were characterized by the principle of preventing disease and disability and promoting positive health. Every society tries to explain and control such catastrophes as plagues, and following the Civil War and the lessons learned by the Sanitary Commission, cities tried to control contagion by sanitary measures. However, the breakthroughs in scientific knowledge and the development of technology during the 19th century led to the discovery of specific causes of the major communicable diseases. Public health workers investigating the distribution and the causes of diseases among the population met social workers who were investigating poverty, and the two groups found that they had much in common. Unlike social work, public health work is not a single, distinct profession, but encompasses many disciplines and professions. It was natural that public health workers should join the social work team.

At this time social workers and public health workers were active in efforts to curb tuberculosis, diphtheria, and venereal diseases. Tuberculosis was perhaps the most feared disease of the time. This illness was regarded as a disgrace and a public menace, so that those infected with it often went unattended rather than face the dreaded diagnosis. Many doctors failed to report the disease. Some doctors claimed that patients would commit suicide if they knew that they were tubercular; other doctors did not report cases because they refused to do paperwork for which they were not paid. There was an appalling lack of facilities for the hospitalization of tubercular patients, so they remained at home as continued sources of contagion. Public education, community organization efforts, and the establishment of clinics eventually resulted in earlier identification, better treatment, and the adoption of preventive measures. New York City led the country with laws requiring that tuberculosis hospitals be established in every county in the state. In general, the states were beginning to pass public health laws and to create better-organized public health departments.

Social workers' contributed to the early struggles toward better health for all citizens by establishing clinics in various settlements, often over the bitter objections of doctors; by working toward physical examinations for all schoolchildren; by applying their skills to public educational campaigns; by organizing lay groups to support health activities; and by it working with legislators. The activities of social workers in public health were good examples of the development and the use of techniques that later contributed to the social work method of community organization. Today, through personal social services and development and reform activities, social workers remain a part of and contribute to public health work.

Medical social services

In 1903 Dr. Richard C. Cabot at the Massachusetts General Hospital in Boston became interested in the idea of social adjustment as a part of medical treatment. In 1905 he employed a social worker, and the hospital provided space for the worker in the Out-Patient Department, but it was not until many years later that the hospital assumed any part of the responsibility for the department.

Social service was established at Johns Hopkins Hospital in October 1907 (Brogden, 1964, pp. 88–89). The intent of this new concept in medical care was to treat the patient as an individual and to help patients to deal better with the problems of their illnesses and to make better use of what the doctor and the hospital had to offer.

At that time there were no courses in medical social work and there was considerable controversy over whether medical social workers should be nurses. Initially, social workers who did not have nurse's training were sometimes denied admission to the hospital wards. When Margaret Brogden took charge of the Johns Hopkins Hospital social service department in 1909, she found that no department in the hospital was willing to take responsibility for the expenses of her department. She then discovered that Helen S. Wilmer, the first social worker, had paid the expenses of the department out of her own pocket. Social workers were gradually added to the social service department, and these social workers were instrumental in establishing many outpatient clinics. In time, considering that Johns Hopkins was a teaching hospital, the social service department established a training course for new medical social workers as well as for medical staff. In 1921 the Johns Hopkins Hospital offered a two-year graduate program for social work students. The program later had to be discontinued, but the pattern had been set.

"Between 1905 and 1917, more than a hundred hospitals in 35 cities hired hospital social workers whose backgrounds were most often in nursing, education or social work" (Romanofsky, 1978, p. 19). The war created a new demand for such workers, and in 1918, meeting during the National Conference of Social Work, 30 women created a new social work organization, the American Association of Hospital Social Workers. Its purpose was to facilitate communication among hospital social workers and to improve the standards of and support the development hospital social work. Initially the organization included social workers working in both medical and psychiatric settings. But in 1926 the workers in psychiatric settings formed a separate organization. In 1934 the American Association of Hospital Social Workers was renamed the American Association of Medical Social Workers. In 1955 it merged with six other professional social work organizations to form the National Association of Social Workers.

Initially, anyone who had worked at least one year as a paid medical social worker was eligible for membership, regardless of training. Later the requirements for membership included two years of graduate education in a school of social work combined with either a special sequence while in school or supervised experience in a medical setting after graduation. The organization was primarily supported by dues. Today, personal social services are an important part of the health system.

◆§ Mental health

Just as in other areas of human life, the trend of psychiatric thought had by this time begun to shift from an emphasis on "moral" causes to an exploration of physical causes. The first important step toward organized psychiatric research in this country was taken in 1895 with the establishment of the Pathological Institute of the New York State Hospital Service. In 1905 Dr. Adolf Meyer became chief of the institute. He changed its name to the Psychiatric Institute and moved it into the Manhattan State Hospital, where there was opportunity for clinical observation of patients and for laboratory work.

Social work joins mental health

Dr. Meyer saw mental illness as a maladjustment of the whole personality rather than a disease of the brain. He insisted on complete case records, including data on the life history of patients. He felt that visits had to be made to the patient's family, employer, and friends in order to secure an account of the patient's life that was as complete as possible. In 1904 his wife, a social worker, took over the task of obtaining such information on her husband's patients. Gradually institutional psychiatrists came to appreciate the value of having trained social workers obtain the information necessary for appropriate decision making and participate in the care and treatment of patients and their families, and the social worker became a recognized member of the mental health treatment team.

In the meantime, social workers had been concerned from their own perspective with the problems of the mentally ill. They had been involved with (1) the care of the indigent mentally ill, (2) the care of the families of ill patients, and (3) the provision of aftercare for hospitalized patients when they left the hospital. There was no agency that offered the released mental patient help in readjustment to the community. After a good deal of hard work and at least one formal attempt that failed, the Charities Aid Association of New York was able to establish privately supported aftercare programs in each state hospital in New York in 1906. The work involved in developing such programs had been under the direction of Louisa Lee Schuyler, a social worker, and she engaged E. H. Hostsa, a professionally educated social worker, as the aftercare agent of the association.

In 1902 Albany Hospital, of Albany, New York, became the first general hospital to establish a ward for the actual treatment of the insane. A ward for the insane had been established earlier at Bellevue Hospital in New York City, but it had been used primarily for custody situations. Gradually other general hospitals established wards that were used largely to accommodate mentally ill patients pending commitment proceedings. University medical schools were becoming concerned about the need for adequate research and education in the diagnosis and care of mental illness, and hospitals or wards for the mentally ill began to be established by universities. The first of these was at the University of Michigan in 1901. Gradually four major types of psychiatric hospitals developed: (1) those connected with universities, (2) those connected with a general hospital, (3) those connected with an institution for the long-term care of the mentally ill, and (4) private hospitals for the treatment of mental disorders (Deutsch, 1949, p. 291).

In 1910 the State Board of Insanity of Massachusetts presented a report in which it outlined the functions of a model "psychopathic hospital." The last paragraph of the report called for the establishment of a free clinic to serve persons suffering from "incipient mental disease" (Deutsch, 1949, p. 296). Thus began the outpatient clinics which were to become such an important feature of mental health care and were the ancestors of our present mental health centers.

The mental hygiene movement

Involved as they were with the social problems of people on all fronts and believing in the elimination of human ills as an achievable goal, social workers at meetings of the National Conference of Social Work were expressing their concern over the causes and treatment of mental illness. Under the auspices of the Conference a meeting was held in 1879 to discuss the problems of mental illness. At that meeting it was decided to organize the National Association for the Protection of the Insane and the Prevention of Insanity. The association hoped to accomplish its goals by engaging in research and education, initiating better policies, and working for better hospital conditions. Although it accomplished many reforms, it only lasted about seven years. It appears to have failed because: (1) it was totally unable to interest the public in its cause; (2) from the very beginning it was strongly opposed by the medical superintendents of the state hospitals, who deeply resented its criticisms of the hospitals and their level of care; and (3) it could not resolve the internal conflict between the neurologists and psychiatrists among its members (Deutsch, 1949, pp. 313–14).

The first national group in mental health to survive until today was founded in 1908 by Clifford Beers, who had been a mental patient in three different hospitals and had written a book about his experiences, *A Mind that Found Itself*. Other exposés of the mental hospitals had preceded Beers's work, and in the early 1900s the time was right for reform. The National Committee for Mental Hygiene adopted much the same goals as had the National Association for the Protection of the Insane, with two exceptions: (1) it saw itself as a national movement, and it provided for state chapters; and (2) it hoped to enlist the aid of the federal government. The committee hoped to change the general view that mental illness was incurable and to do away with the stigma of mental illness. It, too, had difficulty in securing support for its work. Beers himself went heavily into debt to support the committee. Finally, in 1912, Henry Phipps gave $50,000 to the organization, and it was able to begin its surveys of the care of the mentally ill and the mentally retarded throughout the United States (Deutsch, 1949, pp. 316–17).

The entrance of the United States into World War I resulted in greater recognition of and concern with mental health, as the federal government, unconcerned with the problems of health during peacetime, turned its attention to problems regarding the physical and mental health of the military forces.

World War I, social work, and mental hygiene

One of the first acts of the federal government on entering the war was to create a division of neurology and psychiatry within the Surgeon General's Office. The functions of this division were to examine recruits for possible mental illness, to observe and treat persons who became mentally ill while in military service, and to provide for the aftercare of those who were invalided at home.

The mental hygiene movement impacted various fields: education, public health, general medicine, industry, and the treatment of criminals. But it was to have its greatest effect on social workers. Forces within both social work and psychiatry brought the two professions together and moved both of them toward the "individualization" of treatment. This had an extremely important effect on social work. Social workers already had an approach to the social problems of people. Their primary unit of work was the family, and their primary focus was on relieving environmental stress and on providing support. Now the individual began to replace the family as the interest and focus of concern became the study and treatment of the personality. This thrust was supported (as discussed earlier) by social work's search for a "technique," which was considered the necessary base for a profession.

As the war progressed, the value of social workers in the treatment and aftercare of military personnel became intense and the demand for "trained" social workers escalated. This demand was not to level off until the present, and it is still very high outside urban areas. In 1914 Mary C. Jarrett, chief of social services at the Boston Psychopathic Hospital, with the support of Dr. E. E. Southard, began conducting training courses in psychiatric social work for six or seven students at a time. In 1918, as a result of her work and the heavy demand, the Training School for Psychiatric Social Work was opened at Smith College. The psychiatric approach (individualization and character change) to social casework gained ground with amazing rapidity, outgrowing the speciality of psychiatric social work and becoming a part of general social work practice. Mental hygiene and psychiatry had become a major focus of the National Conference by 1923.

The psychological clinic

Lightner Witmer developed the first psychological clinic in the United States at the University of Pennsylvania in 1896. It was an effort to introduce scientific knowledge about children into the school system. Witmer had been made director of the psychology laboratory at the University of Pennsyl-

vania. He became interested in working out a relationship between the university and the public
schools as the result of a challenge by one of his
students, an elementary school principal, to apply
his scientific knowledge to the cure of a spelling
deficiency. Witmer's goal in establishing the clinic
was to train teachers, social workers, and psychiatrists and to educate students for a new profession,
that of clinical psychologist. The clinical psychologist was to be a psychological expert interested
in the individual child who would examine and
propose treatment to promote the child's growth
and development (Levine and Levine, 1914, pp.
49–72).

Witmer's original concept of the psychological
clinic was that it would be closely related to medicine, sociology, and pedagogy and that it would
work closely with the schools and the courts. His
ideas were "surprisingly relevant to the contemporary mental health movement" (Levine and Levine,
1974, p. 58).

In 1907 Witmer established the hospital school
for the residential treatment of children with learning disabilities at the University of Pennsylvania.
It supplied medical, nursing, and educational care
to children who were admitted as private, fee-for-
service patients. Witmer started with the assumption that all children could learn if proper ways
of teaching could be found. He did not see people
as sick or inferior because they did not respond
to the teaching methods of the time, but believed
in the perfectibility of human beings and in the
ability of all people to learn if science could find
the proper teaching methods.

The Juvenile Psychopathic Institute

The Juvenile Psychopathic Institute, now the Institute of Juvenile Research, was established in Chicago in April 1909 by an advisory committee on
which Jane Addams and Julia Lathrop served. It
was subsidized by a five-year endowment from
Ethel Drummer. Drummer had been actively involved with the juvenile court of Chicago, and she
was concerned about the number of children
whose disturbances defied understanding by the

people who wished to help them. She called for
scientific research into the causes of behavior and
promised five years' support for such a project
(Levine and Levine, 1974, pp. 165–66).

Dr. William Healy, who had practiced in Chicago as a neurologist and had developed a reputation for his ability to treat children referred by the
juvenile court, was selected as the director of the
institute. Professional social workers from other
agencies and trained probation officers accepted
the responsibility for providing case histories and
family treatment. By the time psychiatric social
workers joined the staff, in 1917, Dr. Herman Adler
had succeeded Healy, who had left to establish
the Judge Baker Guidance Center in Boston.

Healy was interested in studying delinquency,
but he was also interested in providing a service.
Environmental manipulation with the help of
church, school, and social agencies was one part
of his treatment of children. Healy also worked
psychotherapeutically with individuals in what he
called the reeducation of families. He recognized
the importance of creating personality change by
permitting individuals to live out their problems in
a new environment. Running through all of his work
were a strong emphasis on what a person might
become and a lesser emphasis on the person's pathology (Levine and Levine, 1974, pp. 162–83).

The child guidance movement

It is difficult to organize some of the material
regarding social welfare development in a logical
and clear way because so much was happening
so rapidly and so many movements interacted with
one another. The leaders in social work were not
involved in just one thing—they were active in
whatever promised to make the life of all people
more satisfying. Such people as Florence Kelley,
Jane Addams, and Edith and Grace Abbott were
active in the settlement movement and child welfare administration, served on school boards and
supported educational changes, fought for child labor laws and the rights of women, served as probation officers, started public health clinics, and struggled with the establishment of juvenile courts.

These movements and the social service systems that developed from them did not develop in a vacuum. They developed together from the efforts of common leaders. Thus, the beginnings of the child guidance clinics could be discussed under the rubric of child welfare, juvenile delinquency, or children's mental health. The child guidance clinics obviously brought together all of those concerns, and they developed out of the desire to prevent juvenile delinquency. However, since these clinics are usually viewed as a part of the health system, we shall discuss them here.

In 1921 the Commonwealth Fund launched the child guidance clinics as a program that was meant to be a vital force in the community, closely related to other agencies and to the schools and designed to influence those agencies and the schools toward preventive service supporting mental health in children. Today such programs would be called community mental health programs. Once established, the clinics rather quickly adopted their modern form, changing from agencies to provide preventive service and lead efforts for community reform to agencies that dealt with individual children and their mothers who came seeking "treatment." We have already discussed the era of the 1920s as a time of social and political conservatism and of emphasis on individual freedom and self-development. "Given the marked change in manners and morals it is no wonder that parents felt uncertain about what was right" (Levine and Levine, 1974, pp. 234–35). The advice overwhelming parents from all sides was as conflicting then as it is now. The gross attack on traditions and religious values, the shifts in sexual mores and the role of women impelled a frantic search on the part of individuals for new organizing principles of human life. Science became the new god; the psychoanalytic view of people and their troubles became central; and the professions of social work, psychology, and psychiatry became the exponents of this new view of life. In this societal context of emphasis on the individual and the psychoanalytic view of human behavior as it was interpreted by its exponents of the time, the child guidance clinics developed.

The Commonwealth Fund supported the development of only seven child guidance clinics, but these set the pattern for other clinics which developed with surprising rapidity. Essentially the child guidance clinics were privately supported; were staffed by teams of social workers, psychologists, and psychiatrists; and served as important training centers for the professionals they employed. Although these clinics were originally established as part of a program to prevent juvenile delinquency, by enabling other agencies to handle the problems of children more effectively, the clinics moved in the direction of providing treatment services almost exclusively. As this happened, their contacts with other community agencies were minimized and the population they served changed from a predominantly lower-class population to a predominantly middle-class population (Levine and Levine, 1968, pp. 231–77).

৶ Education

These were the years of progressive education and of the influence of such men as John Dewey, who believed in the potential of each child and in the importance of developing that potential. From the perspective of this book, the important educational development of this period was the establishment of personal social services within the educational system through the visiting teacher programs. Today these services are called school social work.

School social work

The visiting teacher service began about 1906 in several cities in a somewhat similar fashion. The urban schools were becoming increasingly isolated from their communities. Classes were large, often with over 60 students, with a rapid turnover of both children and teachers, so the opportunities of teachers to get to know their students were severely limited. Also, most teachers lived outside the neighborhoods of the schools in which they taught, so they did not know the community. Once the students in the schools had been self-selected, but now all children were compelled to attend school and many of these children, including the immigrant children, brought attitudes to school that were different from those of earlier students. The visiting teacher program originated as a way of providing students with a link between school, family, and community (Levine and Levine, 1974, p. 126).

The visiting teacher program originated out of settlement house work with children. Located as they were in the community, the settlement house workers could use their relationship to the child and the family to bridge the gap between them. The settlement worker brought a different view of the child into the school and helped teachers to better understand the child in a new dimension. As a result of this experience, several settlement houses took on the assignment of working with the families of schoolchildren who presented special problems of an educational, social, or medical nature.

The spread of the visiting teacher program was encouraged when the Commonwealth Fund, working through the Public Education Association, placed 30 visiting teachers in 30 communities under a three-year demonstration program. The New York School of Social Work through its connections with the New York school system helped support the program and undertook the training of the visiting teachers. It was not long before the school system took over the demonstration program, and the social workers involved were faced with the problems and conflicts of finding their place within the organizational structure of the school system. The early literature of school social work makes reference to problems, but these do not seem to have been specifically spelled out. Certainly it was critical that the visiting teacher give help in such a way that the host system would view it as assistance and not as a hindrance.

The visiting teacher program focused primarily on: (1) dealing with general problems in the school and the community which might require changes in the approach of the schools; (2) dealing with the needs of individual schoolchildren; and (3) interpreting the individual schoolchild to the school in order to modify the school's response to the

child. Many leaders felt that the school social work system was a logical extension of the school as a child welfare agency (Levine and Levine, 1974, pp. 125–27).

In 1916 the visiting teachers formed the National Association of Visiting Teachers, which was later absorbed into the National Association of Social Workers as the School Social Work Section. By 1921 the association had established standards for its work as follows: graduation from a four-year college with a background in education, one year's training in social work, and two years of grade school teaching experience. Salaries in most systems were based on those of grade school teachers, so recruitment was a problem. Thus, many were recruited to the work from classroom teaching. The workers who were selected from within the system were less oriented to its reform than were the workers who were brought in from outside the system.

Summary

In this chapter we have discussed how the personal social services developed into a freestanding system and into special services within other social welfare systems. We have seen how the social reform thrust faltered and lost momentum when the movement no longer had the significance of the earlier years.

A look ahead

Helping services arise in response to urgent social need, and urgent social need is a product of rapid social changes. When a whole population faces such changes, attempts are made to alter the shape of helping services so that they provide better for human need. In the next chapter we will examine an economic crisis that resulted in radical change in the social welfare institution.

Study questions

1. In the last two chapters we have discussed a number of social reform movements. Generally these efforts

followed a common pattern of action. Outline the pattern usually followed by such efforts.

2. Make a list of the problems and issues involved in the establishment of schools of social work.

3. Select one of the reformers named in the chapter, and make a study of that person's life.

4. Write a brief biography of the person you have studied. Identify as fully as possible the factors in the person's life that may have influenced his/her passion for reform.

5. Select a minority population (including women), and make a careful study of its history during this period of time.

6. Find out whether there is a private agency in your community that was established during this period of time or earlier. Find out what you can about the circumstances in which the agency was established.

✍ Selected readings

Reisler, Mark. *By the Sweat of Their Brow: Mexican Immigrant Labor in the United States, 1900–1940.* Westport, Conn.: Greenwood Press, 1976.

An excellent study that concentrates on those Mexicans who entered the United States in the early decades of the 20th century and on the reception they received in American society.

Meier, August. *Negro Thought in America, 1880–1915.* Ann Arbor: University of Michigan Press, 1978.

An excellent account of black thought and its relationship to the social forces and social philosophy of the time.

Cabot, Richard. *Social Service and the Art of Healing.* New York: National Association of Social Workers, 1973.

This book was originally written in 1915 by Dr. Cabot to discuss the work of social workers in hospitals and the operation of the team of doctor and social worker.

Folks, Homer. *The Care of the Destitute, Neglected, and Delinquent Children.* New York: National Association of Social Workers, 1973.

This book was written in 1902 by Homer Folks, a leading figure in child welfare and public health. It has been reprinted by NASW.

Kelley, Nicholas. The Early Years at Hull House. *Social Service Review,* 38:4 (December 1954): 424–29.

An interesting discussion of Hull House that expands some of the material in this chapter.

Channing, Alice. The Early Years of a Pioneer School. *Social Service Review,* 38:4 (December 1954): 430–40.

A very interesting account of the establishment and early development of the Simmons School of Social Work. It is strongly recommended as reading to expand the material in this chapter on the development of the profession of social work and on the early schools of social work.

For millions of Americans the Depression was marked by unemployment, hunger, eviction, fear, and despair.

The human tradegy is illustrated in these photographs from those years. *Opposite, above,* unemployed men line up for the free soup, coffee, and doughnuts promised at this Chicago "soup kitchen," operated by Al Capone! The black sharecropper families pictured *opposite, below,* have just been evicted from their land and homes in Arkansas because they dared to join the Southern Tenant Farmers' Union. The misery of the unemployed man shown *above* needs no further caption . . .

Chapter 20 🙿

🙾 Crises and Response: Social forces and social welfare programs, 🙿 1930–1940

❧ Introduction

In this chapter we will discuss the social welfare response to the crises of the Great Depression and World War II. In a period of slightly over 15 years, America was confronted first with the near collapse of its economy and then, before recovering from this shock, it faced involvement with a world conflict which was to end the economic crisis at a terrible cost in human suffering the world over. The crisis of the depression was heralded by signs of economic problems, but few people in the preceding decade of extravagance were willing to heed these signs. Speculation and fraud in stock market investments were widespread before the depression, but there were other indicators of trouble. A Brookings study found that in 1929 a family required $2,000 to supply itself with only basic necessities and that an income of $2,500 would supply a family with only a moderate standard of living. Yet at the time 60 percent of all families had incomes below $1,000 and spent more than they earned. Forty percent of all families had no savings. It is easy to understand the heavy use of credit by these families. The welfare and security of such families were completely dependent on regular employment (Levin, Moulton, and Warburton, 1934).

❧ The crash of 1929

In the last months of 1928, as Herbert Hoover prepared to succeed Calvin Coolidge as president, both men exulted in the prosperity of the American people. Coolidge said, "We have seen the people of America create a new heaven and a new earth." Taking the oath of office in March 1929, a proud and confident Hoover said, "We are a happy people—the statistics prove it. We have more cars, more bathtubs, oil furnaces, silk stockings, bank accounts than any other people on earth." But this statement ignored the many depressed areas in the country, the heavy credit load carried by low-income people, the increasing numbers of the unemployed, and the sufferings of many minorities (Carroll and Noble, 1977, p. 335). Then, in October 1929, came the stock market crash, and the Ameri-

can people entered four of the bitterest years that the country had experienced. Before Hoover left office, unemployment in major cities approached 40 percent. Suffering, fear, and insecurity stalked the land. However, the crisis was seen as a result of excessive speculation in securities and not as a sign of trouble in the basic economic functioning of the country. At first, it was thought that business would right itself if only its confidence could be restored. Both the history of self-limiting boom-and-bust cycles of the economy and the economic theory of the time led to confidence that the depression would eventually lead to recovery. But the panic, desperation, and suffering continued.

Believing in business cycles, balanced budgets, laissez-faire, and states' rights, Hoover was reluctant to have the federal government assume new responsibilities and powers. He had worked in emergency relief efforts of the Red Cross, and he believed in voluntary efforts in social welfare aid. He thought that public aid efforts should be limited to the states and local units. Believing that falling prices caused pessimism and delayed recovery, Hoover urged industrialists to keep their prices steady. In 1932 Congress instituted the Reconstruction Finance Corporation to make financing available to banks for loans to farmers, businessmen, and industry, hoping to maintain the stability of financial, industrial, and agricultural groups. In August, 1931, Hoover established the President's Organization for Unemployment Relief, which through local community chests helped arrange a great national fund-raising drive for the support of needy individuals. As the crisis continued to grow, Congress, with the president's acquiescence enacted the Emergency Relief and Reconstruction Act, the only federal relief action of the Hoover administration. The act authorized a program of 3 percent loans to the states for use in relief operations (Salamon, 1978, pp. 71–73; Leiby, 1978, pp. 217–20).

❧ FDR and the New Deal

In March 1933, when Franklin D. Roosevelt became president, there was a better understanding of the depths of the crisis and of the need for new action. Roosevelt accepted three rather contradictory economic beliefs: (1) a basic belief in the efficacy of the market system if only prices could be started upward; (2) a traditional belief in the importance of a balanced governmental budget; and (3) a belief in the new Keynesian theory of "effective demand" as the key to economic health. The Keynesian theory held that the key to sound economic progress was consumer spending. It was not keeping prices up, or the budget balanced, that supported our economy, but rather the ability of the average person to purchase freely. This theory supported government spending and government moves to increase the purchasing power of individuals as necessary to recovery. In addition, although basically conservative, the new president had inherited the Progressives' concern for social justice and was not afraid to use the powers of government to serve that end (Salamon, 1978, pp. 71–73).

The regulation of banks

When Roosevelt came into office, bank failures were almost epidemic and panic was everywhere. The new president acted quickly to preserve the private banking system through reforms and through government regulation of banking, stock exchanges, and holding companies. In addition, he established programs offering increased security to investors and depositors. There was a thrust to induce inflation through experimental monetary policies. Governmental budget deficits continued to be seen as a problem, and there was continued concern with governmental overspending. In spite of Keynesian economics, during the entire period there was no understanding or use of governmental fiscal policy as a way of maintaining consumer spending and thus increasing consumption and raising prices through effective consumer demand which would reduce the oversupply of goods.

Housing

One of the disasters of the depression was the loss of homes through inability to meet mortgage payments because of the unemployment of family members. In June 1933 homeowners threatened with the loss of their homes were helped to refinance their mortgages through the Home Owners Loan Corporation. The Federal Housing Administration was established to insure loans for home repairs and mortgages for new homes. The home construction industry, which had been at a standstill, began to revive. Later in the New Deal (1937) the Housing Act provided the first federal subsidy for housing. With federal support of locally initiated plans, public construction and administration of low-cost housing got under way. During this period New York City provided housing for 500,000 persons—"an entire city, produced with federal help, but planned, built and managed by the local housing authority" (Morris, 1979, p. 100).

The inactivity of the construction industry during the depression, the diversion of labor to war industry, and the return of discharged veterans resulted in a critical shortage of adequate housing after World War II. In 1940, amendments to the Housing Act of 1937 authorized the construction of 135,000 public housing units every year for six years. The Federal Housing Act of 1949 went further in its stated goal of "the provision of a decent home and a suitable living environment for every American family." This ambitious objective has been accepted by every succeeding administration. However, the practical policies in housing have been marked by a reliance on the private market, with government acting in a subsidiary or supplementary role. But since the depression there has continued to be some concern about the adequacy of housing for the most disadvantaged groups in our society (Morris, 1979, p. 100). Thus a new social welfare system—housing—has been developed.

Agricultural policies

Since the end of World War I, farmers had been suffering terribly from low prices for their commodities and high prices for the products they had to purchase. They had gone heavily into debt, buying land in the years of prosperity when costs were high. Many had no way to make mortgage payments and were losing their farms and their way of life. They viewed the horrors of the depression as simply an extension of the economic troubles that had plagued them for a decade.

The New Deal administration's plans to aid the farmers included the restriction of output in order to raise prices; the consolidation of all federal agricultural credit agencies into the Farm Credit Administration; and the authorization of loans to save farmers from the immediate danger of foreclosure, to underwrite the costs of agricultural production, and to help farmers regain their lost farms on easy credit terms (Axinn and Levin, 1975, pp. 167–69). However, the actions of the New Deal were not helpful to the neediest group of farmers—the New Deal's agricultural policies spelled disaster for many tenant farmers. The New Deal legislation not only allowed farmers to retain their farms but encouraged the larger farmers to buy more land and machinery to cultivate it. Thus, this legislation gave a good deal of governmental support to large farmers but gave little support to small farmers. Tenant farmers were actually damaged by the New Deal legislation. As small farms became a part of larger farms and as machinery, bought with government loans, displaced agricultural workers, tenant farmers were evicted from land they had farmed for years and they and their family were set adrift. Belated recognition of this problem resulted in a requirement, in 1935, that farmers applying for government loans keep the same number of tenants that they had had previously.

In the ten years between 1930 and 1940 the number of tenant farmers decreased by 303,000. Blacks accounted for 56 percent of the displaced tenant farmers. The total number of black tenant farmers was reduced by 28 percent. There was a 14 percent decrease in the number of white tenant farmers. The agricultural depression fell hardest on the most marginal group among the farm population, and tenant farmers joined other homeless and jobless people who wandered the country trying to find a new place to build a new life (Axinn and Levin, 1975, pp. 169–71).

In an effort to support farm prices, the federal government also began to buy surplus farm commodities and to distribute them to the needy and to public institutions. This program was generally viewed as a welfare program, and there was tremendous criticism of the welfare clients' waste of this food and of their lack of appreciation for what they were given. However, the selection of foods for distribution was tailored to what the farmer needed to get rid of, not what the welfare clients needed to eat or knew how to prepare. This was a program to support farmers, not welfare clients.

Industry

"In industry, as in agriculture, recovery was to be achieved through regulation of prices and output, and large firms tended to dominate the policy" (Axinn and Levin, 1975, p. 170). The major legislation relating to industry was the National Industrial Recovery Act (NIRA), which was signed into law by President Roosevelt on June 16, 1933. Title I of this act provided for the establishment of a set of industrial codes that would regulate competition, prices, and output. The act also aimed at providing labor with some protection by setting standards of minimum wages and maximum hours of work and by providing for the right of workers to form unions and bargain collectively.

Initially, the act was greeted with great enthusiasm. It certainly broke new ground in that it gave a governmental agency, the National Recovery Administration (NRA), the power to regulate industry and to sharply limit competition. However, such regulations tended to favor the large industrial concern at the expense of the smaller ones, and by May 1935, when the Supreme Court declared the act unconstitutional, it was under severe attack.

Title II of the NIRA provided for a Public Works Administration (PWA). The money available under this part of the act could have been a stimulant toward recovery. However, the PWA, which was under the direction of Harold Ickes, focused more on making carefully planned and important public improvements than on relieving unemployment generally. A program to give employment to the unemployed is constructed very differently from a program to produce valuable public projects, in that a program to employ the unemployed does not focus on economic efficiency in terms of tasks accomplished. It hires those who need work rather than those who have the best skills. It locates projects where the unemployed are rather than where the projects are needed. A project to employ the unemployed expects and supports the movement of its best and most skillful workers out into better-paying jobs. This was not what Ickes had in mind, however. He supported using the PWA funds to build well-developed and well-thought-out public projects. As a result, this legislation did little to provide jobs for the large numbers who needed them.

Labor

The social legislation it enacted in the interests of the worker was one of the most important achievements of the New Deal. When the depression burst on the American people, labor was largely unorganized and it had been the victim of increasing political repression. Our earlier chapters have outlined the unsuccessful struggle for protective labor legislation that occurred just before World War I. The AFL, the most important and the only significant labor organization, represented only skilled workers, and it was primarily interested in protecting the share acquired by this group of workers. It was not interested in measures of social legislation, and it often opposed such measures if they appeared to threaten the welfare of its members. Certainly the unskilled workers in the basic industries of the country were ignored and largely unprotected.

During the depression years, labor gradually began to achieve the right to bargain collectively and to strike. The Norris–La Guardia Act, passed in 1932, barred the federal courts from issuing injunctions against peaceful strikes and prevented the enforcement of "yellow-dog" contracts. The National Recovery Administration established a 44-hour week in covered employment, set a minimum wage, outlawed child labor, and upheld the right to collective bargaining. These provisions were all

aimed at spreading the work among adult workers and maintaining a fair level of wages. President Roosevelt established the National Labor Board to mediate labor disputes. However, due to the resistance of employers, the board was given no legal authority to enforce its decisions and thus was ineffective. A new board, the National Labor Relations Board, replaced the earlier one. Its function was to hold elections among workers to establish a union's right to represent workers in collective bargaining activities. But management was determined to maintain the open shop and to prevent the organization of workers, except in company unions. Without adequate authority, the board could not enforce the regulations.

Although these efforts were ineffective, they laid the foundation for two measures that were to offer the first real protection ever developed for the workers of the country. The National Labor Relations Act (1935)—better known as the Wagner Act—outlawed company-dominated unions and gave the new board authority to supervise elections, to determine the appropriate bargaining agent, and to hear complaints of unfair labor practices. The Fair Labor Standards Act (1938) established a minimum wage and a 44-hour week (to be reduced to 40 hours in three years), and set 16 as the minimum age for employment in industries whose products moved through interstate commerce. It may seem unbelievable to us, as people of our time (less than 50 years later), that the minimum wage was set at 25 cents an hour and resulted in raises for 300,000 workers. The workweek of 44 hours shortened the work hours of 2,382,000 people (Axinn and Levin, 1975, pp. 172–73).

The right of workers to organize and bargain collectively led directly to the unionization of large numbers of unskilled industrial workers for the first time in our history. The new industrial unions (in contrast to the craft unions of the AFL) organized into the Congress of Industrial Organizations (CIO). By 1937 the CIO was achieving major victories in the steel and automotive industries.

At the close of World War II, Congress passed the Employment Act of 1946, which gave the president and Congress the mandate to make and administer policies that would sustain employment and guide the business cycle. In addition, this act established the Council of Economic Advisers to consider the proper course of governmental action in the economy (Axinn and Levin, 1975, pp. 171–78).

✑§ Income maintenance

Federal funds for cash relief

In May 1933 Congress authorized $500 million for relief and Roosevelt set up the Federal Emergency Relief Administration (FERA) and appointed a social worker, Harry Hopkins, to run it. Hopkin's first critical decision was that federal funds should be spent by *public agencies.* He held that relief should be a matter of right, not dependent on anyone's voluntary generosity, and that the people who administered relief should be responsible employees, paid for their service and held accountable for offering it. Because many states did not have local welfare agencies that could work with them, the FERA tended to favor a separate, parallel relief agency that would be concerned with the unemployed, leaving the regular relief cases to the local agencies. These State Emergency Relief associations had strong central direction from Washington, standardized administration procedures, set higher standards of relief, and gave cash grants. This way of operating contrasted with the dispensing of minimum grocery orders, often capriciously, by the local relief agencies (Leiby, 1978, p. 226). Here we see developed a treatment for persons who were considered unemployed through no fault of their own that was different from the treatment of persons who were unable to be a part of the labor market—a differentiation between the old poor and the new poor.

Work relief

Throughout welfare history, work relief had been associated with deterring people from applying for relief. Applicants for assistance were put to work to test their real need for help. However, Hopkins saw it differently. He believed that people would feel better about themselves if they were paid for work done rather than given a handout. He felt that a job could mean a feeling of usefulness, dignity, and competence above the money earned. Therefore, Hopkins was anxious to establish *work relief* for the unemployed. He was anxious to take money from the FERA and to transfer it to the PWA, which had been set up to employ people on public works.

However, as we have discussed, under Harold Ickes the PWA focused more on making carefully planned and important public improvements than on putting people to work. So Hopkins created a new agency, the Civil Works Administration, which was charged with quickly developing programs to put large numbers of people to work. Also, two very successful programs were designed to aid young people: the Civilian Conservation Corps (CCC), which employed young men whose families were on relief in various projects planned by the Department of the Interior, and the NRA, which gave part-time paid work to youth in order to enable them to stay in school or to attend college.

Permanent public employment

In January 1935 Roosevelt proposed that the federal government disband the FERA and replace it with a permanent work program for the unemployed, once again leaving other types of income maintenance to the localities. This plan would not totally abandon relief in that it would provide the states and localities with some subsidies with which they could provide aid for certain groups. The permanent employment program was to be under the Works Progress Administration (WPA).

From that start there were problems with work relief in that it was designed, not so much to accomplish public works, as to give help to the unemployed. Therefore, as we have said, the jobs had to be tailored to the needs of the unemployed and to be located where the unemployed lived. However, work developed merely to fill time would not supply the worker with feelings of usefulness and dignity. The WPA was the focus of everyone's suspicion, yet it was free of serious political abuse. It simply could not supply enough useful jobs. It was not designed for economic efficiency in terms of tasks accomplished. The better-skilled workers left for private jobs, and large numbers of marginal workers were left. In 1943 the WPA was phased out as war-related jobs became plentiful.

The Committee on Economic Security

Actually, although the WPA withered away, it was a part of Roosevelt's plan for long-term federal involvement in public assistance. He had been concerned with the appropriate role of the federal government in on going programs, not just emergency programs. The principles which guided his thinking in this matter were: (1) federal assistance should focus primarily on the long-neglected problems of the able-bodied, leaving to the states, as in the past, the burden of caring for the impotent poor; and (2) this federal assistance should be work related in some fashion. Although Roosevelt's thinking might well be seen as moving toward a reform effort of providing public protection to a group in need, it did not challenge the basis on which deservingness was to be defined.

In June 1934, Roosevelt appointed a Committee on Economic Security and named Frances Perkins, a social worker, as chairperson. The committee met through the summer and fall of 1934 and fashioned "a grand design" for economic security. With some important changes, this plan resulted in the Social Security Act of 1935, which is the foundation of our social welfare policy of today and intimately affects every one of us.

The committee's grand design

The plan that was developed by the committee consisted of two separate programs: one for employables and one for persons who were considered as being out of the labor market. The program for the employables consisted of four parts, designed to work as a unit: (1) unemployment insurance, which would provide financial assistance to newly unemployed workers as a matter of contracted right while they sought new jobs; (2) public employment, which would be available to those who had not found work when their unemployment compensation was exhausted; (3) old-age insurance to provide support for the older worker who was no longer in the labor market through a straight insurance program funded jointly by the employer and the employee from contributions during the employee's working years; and (4) old-age assistance, a relief program which would fill in gaps in social insurance.

The plans for persons considered unemployable were less elaborate, less thought through, and less generous. In fact, these plans were included almost by accident as a result of special pleadings by representatives of two or three agencies who got the president's ear (Salamon, 1978, pp. 72–75). These "unemployables were never considered as a whole by the committee as presenting a problem of economic security to be dealt with by the Federal Government." Instead, certain groups from this category were specifically selected to receive federal assistance through grants-in-aid to the states (Salamon, 1978, p. 75). It was in this rather accidental way that Aid to Dependent Children (AFDC) and Old-Age Assistance (OAA), two programs that we discussed in the first chapter, and Aid to the Blind (AB) came into existence. Although this categorizing of people followed the old notions of the worthy poor, it represented a major step in suggesting federal involvement with the unemployed and federal support of relief.

Although the committee's plan was a bold new step, it represented a retreat from the program of the FERA, which had conditioned assistance totally and simply on human need. The new system proposed to repeat the old practice of classifying persons in need into categories related to work or worthiness. In fact, the plan would expand the categorizing of those in need in two ways. First, the unemployables were to be aided only if they fell into the categories of (1) the aged, (2) the blind, and (3) dependent children. Second, the new unemployment insurance and old-age protection programs were to be work-tested, and thus they would be unavailable to persons without a regular attachment to the work force. Therefore, the economic penalty for not being a part of the regular work force was actually greatly increased. In fact, the plan was even more stringent, since it specified that in order to secure benefits one had to be engaged in "covered employment"—specific types of work defined and covered by the Social Security Act—for a specified period of time. At the time, only 45 percent of jobs came under the proposed definition (Salamon, 1978, pp. 75–79).

Another significant limitation of the plan translated very directly into economic penalties on the working poor—those with low wages and intermittent work. The level of the insurance payments would relate to the level of wages. This meant that large groups of our population—blacks, Chicanos, Indians, and women—would suffer a double economic blow. They did not earn an adequate wage, so they would never receive adequate support from the insurance program. The committee's "grand design" upheld the tradition of the Elizabethan Poor Law, discussed in our first chapter, even to avoiding any interference with prevailing wage rates and working conditions. Later developments built on these principles would further assume the prevailing middle-income pattern by severely and actively penalizing families in which the husband and wife both worked and neglecting married women who did not work. In addition, the returns for the working poor would continue to be meager.

Impelled by a politically motivated desire to give contributors a sense of their legal, moral, and political right to collect their benefits, Roosevelt insisted that the social insurance programs be self-financing. Other industrial countries had financed such social insurance measures in varying ways: some through a combination of worker and employer contributions and general revenues; some through larger taxes on employers and lesser taxes on workers. However, the new plan for America was to be financed by taxes on employers in the case of unemployment insurance and by taxes on employees and employers jointly in the case of social insurance. This type of tax meant that gross inequities in regional and industrial wage rates and discrimination patterns in pay levels would be translated di-

rectly into serious inequities in social insurance and that those subject to poverty-level wages would suffer because of this during their retirement years. Thus, the social welfare package proposed by the committee would not only require the able-bodied to work but would require them to accept whatever job was available at whatever rate of pay prevailed, without offering any assistance in alleviating the continual poverty that existed.

The committee's proposal also responded to pressures to decentralize the control of the assistance program in order to allow the assistance given to adjust to local economic interests. This meant that the traditional pattern of local control of public assistance reasserted itself and that the coverage of the program was grossly limited. For example, important to the rural South and Southwest were the proposals to limit coverage under employment compensation to employers of eight or more people and to exclude farm and domestic workers from old-age insurance. Since in the South and the Southwest these were largely black or Chicano workers, the latter proposal effectively barred most minority workers in these areas from the social insurance program.

Local pressures were even more apparent in the proposed unemployment compensation program than in the old-age programs, and such pressures resulted in the proposal to place this part of the program in the hands of the states. This avoided the possible disruption of local labor practices that might have resulted from a national program.

Minority positions on the committee's approach

However, not all who were involved agreed with the committee's approach. Some urged a broad program of aid to the states for a general assistance program that would cover all who were in need. Failing to influence the community, the professional staff of FERA almost managed to get their broader approach into the bill that was sent to Congress in 1935. In drafting the public assistance part of the bill, FERA staffers included a definition of a dependent child so broad that it would have encompassed almost every family in need with a child under 16 years of age. The definition provided that a child be considered dependent if in his/her family there was "no adult person . . . who is able to work and provide the family with a reasonable subsistence compatible with health" (Brown, 1960, pp. 304–5). This definition meant that any parents, employed or unemployed, could have been given assistance if they did not earn enough to support their families.

✑§ The Social Security Act of 1935

Federal responsibility for income maintenance

Although the Social Security Act, as finally introduced, represented the single most important piece of legislation in the development of the social welfare institution in the United States to date, it also accommodated to, and supported, many of the implicit social welfare principles of the past: reliance on the marketplace, the categorization of the poor, federal sharing but local control, and attachment to the work force. On the other hand, it represented an advance in several ways. It provided, by use of the federal police powers, for compulsory participation. The old-age insurance part of the act provided for administration by the federal government, and it sought to move the income floor somewhat above the base minimum. There was considerable concern about the constitutionality of the act. Did the act fall under the limited powers of Congress? Actuaries said that it would be impractical to have the states administer old-age insurance, so that part of the act could be justified under the powers of Congress to spend and tax for the general welfare. The constitutionality of the act was tested by a suit in 1937, and the act was upheld by the Supreme Court.

Public jobs

In framing the Social Security Act, the administration itself urged the separation of the legislation providing for public jobs for the unemployed from the rest of the act. It was thought that public works were more appealing than the other parts of the Social Security Act and would pass more readily.

However, the result was that the proposal for public jobs was an easy target for congressional conservatives. Thus the act was severely restricted, and when the war brought increased employment, both the relief and the public works acts were terminated. Thus, one important aspect of the New Deal legislation was eliminated. The proposal to make the federal government the "employer of last resort" through public employment of the unemployed is still debated in Congress.

Unemployment insurance

The Social Security Act imposed on certain employers who employed eight or more individuals for 20 weeks or more in a year a tax of 3 percent on the wages of such employees. Workers in agriculture, in domestic service, in private homes, in government service, and in nonprofit organizations were excluded from the coverage. Federal government employees were brought under the system in 1954, with the costs borne by the federal government, and railroad employees were covered by a special system established for the railroads in 1938. In 1956 the Social Security Act amended to cover employers having four or more employees. The proposed program was a very complex one, requiring the cooperation of the federal government, state government, and private industry, and carefully drawn to deal with the problem of constitutionality and with the opposition of industry and of those who opposed "federal interference" with the states. Readers should note that this program is completely financed by employer contributions and requires no taxes directly on employees except in two states. It has changed less than any other program of the Social Security Act, probably partly because it is financed by employers. The primary changes have been increases in the level of weekly benefits to adjust for inflation, from an average of $11.04 a week to an average of $50.45 a week.

The Social Security Act provided for voluntary participation by the states. However, a strong incentive was given to states to adopt unemployment insurance laws by a provision that contributions paid by covered employees under a state unemployment insurance law which met very general standards could be credited against the federal tax on employees up to 90 percent of the tax. The state laws had to meet .the following conditions: (1) benefits must be payable through public employment offices; (2) all contributions must be paid into a trust fund in the U.S. Treasury, where it is maintained to the credit of the state; (3) all money withdrawn from the trust fund must be used solely for the payment of benefits; (4) benefits cannot be denied an eligible individual for refusing to accept work if the position is vacant because of a strike, if wages or working conditions are less favorable than those generally prevailing in the community, or if there is a prohibition against joining a union or a requirement to join a company union; and (5) reduced payroll taxes may be permitted an employer who has a stable employment record for three years (Cohen, 1957, pp. 540–43).

Another incentive to the states to adopt unemployment insurance laws was the provision for grants to the states to cover the entire cost of administering their programs. To receive this aid, states must: (1) provide for the hiring of employees by merit; (2) establish reasonably sound administrative procedures; (3) provide a fair hearing for anyone denied benefits; and (4) keep records and share reports with other states and the federal government. Because the programs are state programs, coverage and benefits are slightly different from state to state. However, all states relate benefits paid to wages earned, in contrast to most foreign systems, which pay uniform benefits to all unemployed.

Workers are disqualified from receiving unemployment benefits if they are unable to work and unavailable for work in the week in which claims are paid. They may be disqualified for other reasons, such as voluntarily leaving work without good cause. The reasons differ from state to state, but in general they have become more restrictive and severe over the years (Cohen, 1957, pp. 540–43).

Old-age and survivors insurance (OASI)

Originally planned only to pay benefits to persons over 65 years of age who were no longer in the work force, the Social Security Act was amended in 1939 to cover dependents. The act is now administered by the Social Security Administration, one of the constituent units of the Department of Health, Education, and Welfare. Monthly benefits are payable under this system to persons who have worked a certain number of quarters (fourths of a year) in covered employment, and benefit levels are related to wages earned in such employment. Those who are defined as dependents under the law may receive a certain percentage of the basic rate of the employed person. The level of benefits, the types of work covered, and the coverage of dependents have changed greatly over the years. The concept of retirement following attachment to the work forces has been expanded to include the permanently and totally disabled worker. We will discuss the present operation of the program in Chapter 23. However, some basic issues need to be outlined here. Perhaps we should start by considering the fact that this old-age and survivors insurance (and now disability insurance) has come to be known to most people as "social security." We shall follow this popular usage and will use social security to mean OASI or OASDI.

The original concept of OASI was that it would act as a buffer against destitution in old age. It was never meant to completely replace a worker's previous income or to assure continuity of the same standard of living to persons when they retired. It was originally developed on the model of insurance based on the accumulation of a trust fund from which benefits would be paid. Most beneficiaries believe that they are receiving benefits from the investment of taxes that they have paid in during their working years. Nothing could be farther from the truth. Social security is as much a social welfare program as it is an insurance program, and in no way have the present recipients "paid for" the benefits they receive. The present work force pays taxes to support already retired workers and their dependents. Social security taxes have escalated rapidly in the past years as benefits to retired workers have increased. These taxes do not represent a base of benefits for present workers, who have no legal call upon the system to pay them a certain level of benefits as a result of their payments.

One of the difficult problems of the system is that it has been supported entirely by taxes on the employee and the employer and that the tax rate has been applied to a set amount of wages, regardless of the total wages earned. For example, in 1957 each worker paid 2¼ percent of the first $4,200 in wages earned that year and the employer contributed a like amount. This means that a person with six children who earned $4,200 in that year paid exactly the same amount as a person with one child who earned $25,000. This feature makes the social security tax one of the most regressive taxes we have in this country, bearing the most heavily on the low-paid worker.

The relationship of benefits to amount paid in has long been a subject of debate around two basic issues: adequacy and equity. How much income is needed for minimally adequate subsistence after retirement (adequacy)? And should benefits be directly proportioned to the amount paid in, so that each person receives equal treatment (equity)? However, if equity becomes a guiding principle, the person who earned the lowest wages might not receive a benefit large enough to provide even a minimally adequate subsistence. As a result of this consideration the amount of benefits is not directly proportioned to the amount paid in. The lowest-paid workers receive a greater return on the amounts paid in than do higher-paid workers. For example, when the program began to make its first payments in 1939, the monthly benefit for a retired person was computed at 40 percent of the first $50 of the monthly wages plus 10 percent of the next $200 of the monthly wages. This formula has been changed over the years as benefits have been raised, but the heavier weighting of the first part of the covered salary has continued as a way to give lower-paid workers a proportionally better return. However, given the generally accepted idea that old-age and survivors insurance is a form of public group insurance, the benefits do relate to earnings and workers who never earned enough to support their families in any adequate way when they were in the work force will never receive benefits large enough to support them in comfort when they leave the work force.

Another problem with the program has been the treatment of the married woman, particularly the married woman who works in covered employment. Old-age and survivors insurance is not a family program. Because it considers only attachment to the work force or dependence on someone attached to the work force, it does violence to married women and to the family as an economic unit. In the first place, married women (or married men) who do not work outside the home make no payments and accumulate no benefit records of their own. They may contribute significantly to the earning ability of the working member of the family, but they can only secure benefits as a dependent of this member. This was particularly difficult for women who were divorced after less than 20 years of marriage. They had no claim for benefits although their minor and handicapped children had such a claim. (Divorced women can now claim benefits if the marriage has endured ten years.)

But the family with two earners is also treated harshly. During their working life this couple may pay twice the taxes of a family with one wage earner. Yet upon retirement, if the family still consists of the two wage earners, they will receive 2 benefits, while the other family will receive 1½ benefits. Or they may select 1½ benefits of one earner if this is larger than the 2 individual benefits. As more benefits are added and become available to the worker and to the dependent spouse on the basis of the worker's record, the family in which both the husband and the wife work is forced to contribute more for proportionally less benefits. Robert M. Ball, former commissioner of social security, has stated that the employed married woman does not get additional benefits that are worth the payments she is forced to make (Ball, 1978, p. 319).

Public assistance

As we said earlier, the committee report on income maintenance proposed a plan of assistance payments based on economic need to certain population groups that are normally considered as outside the work force: the aged, dependent children, and the blind. The plan thus established certain categories of persons who could be considered worthy poor. To aid such people the Social Security Act provided for a program based on federal-state participation. Given the division of powers in the Constitution and the strong principle of locality in the administration of relief, it seemed impossible to take the long step to a complete federal assistance program for all needy people. The act provided that the federal government would give matching grants-in-aid to the states that established programs for these special groups which met federal standards. The states were free to participate or not in the program. The states which did participate had to meet the following conditions:

1. Statewide operation.
2. State financial participation.
3. A single state agency to administer the plan or to supervise its administration by local agencies upon which state rules, regulations and standards were mandatory.
4. Methods of administration as necessary for proper and efficient operation of the plan, including the establishment and maintenance of personnel standards on a merit basis.
5. Restriction of information about applicants and recipients of assistance to purposes directly connected with the administration of the program. Later a provision enacted as part of the Revenue Act of 1951 permitted exceptions to this prohibition under appropriate state legislation. The names of recipients and the amounts of their assistance payments were to be a matter of public record and open to interested persons if the state legislation included safeguards against the commercial or political use of information so obtained.
6. Opportunity for any persons wishing to do so to apply for assistance and to have their applications acted upon with reasonable promptness.
7. Opportunity for a fair hearing before the state agency for any claimant for assistance whose claim was denied or was not acted upon within a reasonable time.
8. Submittal to the Social Security Administration of such reports as required.
9. Consideration of any and all income and resources that the applicant might have when determining need for assistance.
10. Designation of a state authority or authorities responsible for establishing and maintaining standards for all types of public and private institutions in the state in which, under the state plan, a needy person may receive assistance (applicable to all programs except Aid to Dependent Children).
11. Prohibition of the concurrent receipt of more than one form of public assistance under the state plan (Roney, 1957, pp. 440–41).

In the original proposal for these programs, the states were prohibited from using criteria for eligibility for Old Age Assistance (OAA, now SSI) other than age or need and the benefit levels in all programs had to be sufficient to provide for a "reasonable subsistence compatible with decency and health." However, congressmen representing states with significant minority groups and with average wages below this standard of need strongly objected to the proposal. Accordingly, the bill was rewritten to allow states to impose practically any eligibility criteria they wished and to set benefit levels as low as they wanted without losing their federal matching funds. Thus, public assistance came to be marked by state-by-state disparities and inequities that have been with us ever since.

The plan was administered differently in different states. Some states set up a state-administered system in which those administering aid and service in the counties were directly responsible to state administrators. Other states set up a county-administered system under which the counties assumed administrative responsibility with state supervision.

Congress also added 18 words to the definition of "dependent children" which changed the whole meaning of the act, specifying that only children deprived of adequate support "by reason of death, continued absence from the home, or physical or mental incapacity of a parent" would be eligible for aid (Salamon, 1978, pp. 78–80). This definition limited the program to children who were deprived of parental support by reason of the absence or incapacity of one parent. It meant that many needy children would be denied aid because their parents continued to try to maintain the family. It led to many charges that AFDC contributed to family breakdown in that fathers who were unemployed or underemployed might feel that the family would be better off without them because their families would then be eligible for AFDC.

Other titles in the Social Security Act

The sponsors of the Social Security Act had given some consideration to covering health and disability insurance, but the resistance of the American Medical Association was strong enough to discourage such efforts. Readers should remember that work-related accidents and illnesses were provided for by the worker's compensation programs at the state level. The act did include three other aspects of welfare, however. It provided for federal funds for public child welfare services on a matching basis. It included substantial aid for certain public health tasks, especially for maternal and child health and for the care of crippled children. It also included funds for vocational studies (Leiby, 1978, p. 235).

With the enactment of the Social Security Act we thus had in place the foundation of our present income maintenance program. Far from a comprehensive, integrated program of income maintenance, it is a work-enforcing insurance system providing retirement and temporary unemployment protection only to those actively attached to the work force and selected dependents as well as a series of unconnected cash assistance provisions

offering limited benefits to selected groups of the dependent poor on terms decided by each state. However, the social workers and other groups that had worked very hard for a more liberal and complete program were less depressed about the program than one might think, because they held two assumptions that have since proved to be myths. They believed that once the depression was over, the American economy would supply all who wanted work with jobs paying enough to enable families to maintain an adequate standard of living. They also believed that as the economy offered work and adequate income, and as these programs were expanded, all people would increasingly be covered by the social insurance programs and the assistance programs would not be needed. As we shall see in succeeding chapters, these hopes never materialized (Salamon, 1978, pp. 78–80).

✑ General assistance

It is important to remember that the federally supported *public assistance programs* aided only selected groups whose members were further reduced by the restrictive eligibility requirements adopted by the states. Thus there developed a large group of individuals and families, often in desperate need, that had no access to the *public assistance programs*. These families and individuals had to seek whatever help might be available under the local, or local and state, *general assistance programs,* general assistance being simply another term for the old public relief programs.

It is difficult to discuss these programs because they vary so much from state to state and from locality to locality within a state. In general, the benefits under such programs are inadequate and are based on the notion that they are temporary, as people should immediately seek and find work. Thus such items as household upkeep or clothing maintenance may seldom be included as needs.

Support to needy families was often given "in kind" through grocery orders sent to the grocer or through rent vouchers sent to the landlord. The persons relying on such programs often had absolutely no cash available for their use. Access to the general assistance programs has always been, and remains, extremely restrictive and variable. Thus, in some areas all single adults were arbitrarily "cut off' general assistance "rolls" on May 1 and not reinstated until November 1 under the assumption that in the summer anyone could find work. No one inquired how they supported themselves during those months. .

The administration of the general assistance programs varies from place to place. In some states the state helps with some funding and imposes some consistent standards. In other states the county is the unit of funding and the administrative unit. In many states the township, or smallest unit of government, is responsible for meeting the needs of the children, parents, and other individuals who are eligible for general assistance.

Given the way in which the Social Security Act developed, three groups of poor were established within our patterns of income maintenance. One group was developed by setting up separate programs for those who had had a connection with the work force for at least a part of their lives, and a second group was developed from special groups among those considered to be outside the labor market. These groups were the worthy poor (those who presumably suffered from troubles not of their own making, such as the blind, children, and the aged). The third group consisted of those who were left out of the other two groups and by exclusion became the unworthy poor. For this group only local assistance was available.

The differing requirements and the differing administrative structure resulted in complex programs marked by complicated eligibility requirements and rules of access. In addition, dividing common needs into artificial groups caused applicants to have differing feelings about themselves because of the varying social acceptibility of the programs. For example, children living in their own home could now look for help and suppot under the survivors program of OASI, could be helped under AFDC, could receive aid under general assistance, or could be cared for under the Veterans Administration programs. Aged persons could receive aid under the Veterans Administration programs, OASI, or OAA.

Veterans and the depression

Veterans, like all other groups, suffered from the depression. They were, however, a more visible group that was generally able to elicit special consideration. There were marches by veterans on Washington, D.C., in 1932, 1933, and 1934. However, the largest march was the first one, which ended when President Hoover sent troops to clear the veterans out of Washington. Congress passed a bill allowing veterans to obtain, in cash, one half the value of their "adjustment compensation certificates," issued to them after World War I and payable in 1945. Veterans were given special attention in relation to the various relief programs and work programs that were established. In addition, Congress passed legislation increasing their monetary, medical, and hospital benefits. These actions laid the foundation for the treatment of veterans after World War II.

Social work and the Social Security Act

With the passing of the Social Security Act, the various systems within the social welfare institution began to take a modern shape. The foundation was laid for a system of public concern with housing; vocational rehabilitation, which was first legislated in the 1920s, was further advanced by this act; a work force system was formed by the unemployment compensation program and the U.S. Employment Service. Child welfare legislation developed the outlines of a large part of the system of personal social services. In addition, personal social services for the clients of public assistance began a rapid development, although in this aspect of social welfare activities, income maintenance and personal social services were operated as undifferentiated functions for the first decade.

By 1940, three huge new bureaucracies had been created by the Social Security Act. One related to the manpower system in that it administered the unemployment compensation system together with the U.S. Employment Service; a second administered the social insurance program; and a third comprised the public assistance agencies, sometimes including general assistance as well.

The OASI and the UI programs were new, and they embodied the notion of insurance in which clients had certain rights. These programs were under central direction, and their benefits were established by formula and not open to the judgment of the administrators. These two systems were roughly equivalent in size and cost to the schools and the health services, but they were not yet an established part of the social welfare institution, so the pattern of their development was yet to be established (Leiby, 1978, pp. 245–65).

There was considerable misunderstanding and doubt about the whole concept of social insurance, and many questions are still with us. In general, liberals were unhappy with the program because they felt that the benefits were far too inadequate, that the taxation supporting the social security program was too regressive, and that the whole plan was far too limited. Conservatives, however, held to the conventional notion of insurance. They favored the use of private carriers and strict equity. They were suspicious of the compulsory features of social insurance and of what they saw as an inappropriate mixture of welfare and insurance. The conservatives saw social insurance designed to replace a substantial part of the wages that workers lost under certain risks of industrial life. They wanted benefits to be work-related and wage-related. In addition, they wanted benefits to be based entirely on contributions by the worker, or on the worker's behalf by employers. Workers should have a right to benefits because they had earned them and had paid a defined amount into the system. There needed to be a rational, defined formula which assured that the more workers paid in, the more they took out.

Liberals, on the other hand, looked upon social insurance as a means to certain valued objectives rather than as an end in itself. Liberals were far less likely than conservatives to be interested in a rationally developed social insurance program or to be concerned with the careful, detailed consideration of adequacy or equity. Some liberal economists believed that the continuity of funds for consumer use provided by social insurance would serve to stabilize the business cycle and that adequate income maintenance programs would establish a floor of consumer spending. Many social workers and other reformers were concerned with providing adequate income supports for lower-paid workers, and they saw no need to limit benefits to amounts that such workers could provide with their own contributions, but rather wanted general taxes to support the benefit levels of the lower-paid workers. This would result in a redistribution of income from the wealthy to the poorer citizens.

Arthur Altmeyer and Ernest Witte, the men who were responsible for the technical development of the Social Security Act, did not think of themselves as social workers dealing with the problems of the poor but as "experts working with capital and labor to devise a program that was conceived . . . as being in the interests of both employers and employed, and as a rationalization of the economic system" (Leiby, 1978, p. 247). Altmeyer wrote, "The origin . . . of social security will be found more largely in our labor legislation than in our poor relief laws. This is in sharp contrast to Great Britain where the development of social security was largely influenced by dissatisfaction with the poor law" (Altmeyer, 1966, p. vii). President Roosevelt also wanted a broad program of social insurance that would eventually guarantee economic security to all workers as a norm. These men did not think of themselves as social workers concerned with the welfare of individuals or as utopians out to change the system but "as practical men dealing with practical men, negotiating and compromising among substantial interests" (Leiby, 1978, p. 247). They were experts in negotiation, policy, and administration, technicians interested in the careful development of the details of a part of the economic system rather than reformers with a larger view.

Public assistance agencies

The third large bureaucracy comprised the public assistance agencies. Central to this bureaucracy were the county and state welfare departments. They carried on the historic work of poor relief, and as state and local agencies, they were always affected by the attitudes of the state political powers and by the local climate. Access and eligibility to the public assistance programs were often complicated, and might well depend on the interpretation of need made by the worker. Applicants for public assistance were regarded by the general public as having failed in the business of maintaining themselves, and they often regarded themselves as failures. They were likely to be ashamed, defensive, uncooperative, and even hostile. It took skillful interviewing to bring out the facts and to put those facts together to support the client's application so that budgets and eligibility could be accurately determined. All of this seemed to point to the need of social workers to help clients. It was also believed that social workers, as a profession historically concerned with the poor, were needed to administer relief payments, to formulate policy and plans, and to carry through on action. Jane Hoey, a social worker who headed the Bureau of Public Assistance, was firmly committed to adequate money payments and to adequate personal social services, staffed by professional workers, to the recipients of public assistance.

One of the problems of this commitment was the problem of staffing the public social services with persons who had even a minimum of training in social work. In 1939 the schools of social work had decided that only a two-year program leading to the Master of Social Work degree would be accredited. The number of social workers with this level of preparation who were employed in the public welfare system was infinitesimal. The attempt to staff the public assistance programs with social workers and the labeling of the direct service positions as social work positions may have been critically important to the development of both the profession of social work and the system of personal social services. However, the large number of heterogeneous individuals who were recruited into the system to fill these positions may have damaged the view of the profession held by the average American, not because of the association with "relief," but because these people who called themselves "social workers" did not act toward clients or social issues in a way consistent with the values and basic practice principles of the profession. The behavior of many of these recruits, not all by any means, violated many of the basic values and principles of social work, but there was no way in which the profession could control that behavior. These people were recruited into a large bureaucracy in which they were called social workers, but many did not see themselves as members of, or seek to identify themselves with, the profession that they were hired to represent. In many cases these workers were hired by local boards which made it very clear that they preferred a "hardheaded practical person" to the "softheaded do-gooders" represented by persons identified with or educated in the profession. In an attempt to deal with this, the federal Bureau of Public Assistance worked hard for appropriations of federal funds for the in-service training of social workers. But these efforts were hardly adequate to deal with the problems in the delivery of adequate personal social services to the populations that used the public assistance system (Leiby, 1978, pp. 262–66).

This created a division in social work that is still unbridged. There grew up two groups of social workers who made sharp distinctions among themselves but were generally undifferentiated by the public. The social workers hired by private agencies to offer personal social services and those working in personal social services in the health and mental health systems were largely MSWs who had been educated in the graduate schools of the universities. The workers hired in the public assistance agencies and in the corrections system often had not completed their undergraduate college work, had no special preparation for their difficult jobs, and often openly rejected the notion that they were social workers, although that was the position that they were paid to fill.

Many of these "untrained" workers, however, were strongly identified with the people they served, and many of them, when exposed to the knowledge and skills of social work, eagerly accepted at considerable personal sacrifice the opportunities provided by federal funds from the Bureau of Public Assistance, or provided under child welfare legislation, to enter schools of social work and complete the MSW degree. Some of these workers returned to the public assistance system, but many gradually moved into the private child and family agencies or the health system. Thus, the hopes of Jane Hoey and others like her that public assistance and personal social services would be offered by professional social workers were never realized.

At any level in the local and state agencies, professional social workers were very scarce, and given their numbers and their positions in the bureaucracy, they had relatively little impact on the direction of the public assistance system. In fact, the system was usually controlled by elected lay persons whose attitudes toward "welfare" were often punitive and restrictive. Many public assistance clients (not all by any means) and many of the families that were channeled into the child welfare system were struggling with some of the most complex and painful of problems. Yet these clients were often offered, in the name of social work, the poorest of professional services. And the workers who worked with these families often suffered the fate of the families—they were rejected by lay people as do-gooders and by their profession as untrained or second class. Many professional workers who remained in the public system did so out of a real commitment to the welfare of their clients. But the situation only furthered the earlier notions that private agency work was somehow better than public work.

The effect on the profession was to divide it into two groups and to further the concern of the schools of social work and the professionally trained worker with personal social service above the poverty line. The social work roles of broker, mediator, teacher, and advocate received little attention in the schools or in practice. The profession was deprived of the insights and developments that came from daily work with the very poor and with those labeled deviant in our society. Although schools of social work became interested in training some professional workers for leadership positions in public services (as we shall see in a later section of this chapter) by adding certain courses in policy and administration, the central interest continued

to be a direct service to clients and these courses were deprived of the stimulation of knowledge from the personal social services.

Personal social services

The private agencies

The depression and the Social Security Act that followed were forces that deeply stressed the private agencies. Readers will remember the earlier conflicts over whether public agencies should be established to administer public assistance funds or whether those funds should be funneled to the private agencies for allocation to individual families. As the depression broke upon the nation, both systems were in common use throughout the country, and certainly the private agencies were concerned about the disaster that was destroying families before their eyes. The private agencies were very aware of the economic troubles of the country before the crash. Articles appearing in *The Family* during 1927 and 1928 suggested that unemployment was becoming a national calamity and asked how the private agency could deal with the overwhelming need. In 1929, Linton B. Swift, executive secretary of the national association of family agencies, urged agencies not to wait until a full-scale disaster was at hand but to start immediately to develop community committees on unemployment that would begin thinking and planning (Rich, 1956, pp. 107–24).

In June 1933, Hopkins's ruling that FERA funds would be available only to public agencies forced private social agencies to reevaluate their work. At the time of this announcement, 47 out of 67 agencies that responded to a survey were using public funds in some way. Twenty-eight of these agencies had some arrangement whereby public and private agencies shared the responsibility for individual families. In some communities the family societies requisitioned relief from the public department, much as did the department's own staff. The ruling of the FERA meant that those private agencies which had formed some joint financial arrangement with public agencies must lose their share of public federal funds or themselves become public agencies.

Various patterns emerged. In some communities the private agency continued to offer personal social services to the families that received public relief. Many private agencies loaned their administrative and direct service staffs to the public agency. Other private agencies simply transferred their trained staff to the public agency. In at least three cases the private agency transferred its entire social work staff to the public agency. All of these actions were taken in the expectation that the public federal assistance programs would be temporary (Rich, 1956, pp. 107–24).

With the passage of the Social Security Act, the private agencies faced a number of issues: the definition and clarification of the roles of private and public agencies; the unscrambling of some agencies that were trying to be both public and private agencies; the strengthening of the personal social services activities and of the professional competence of the social workers who would deliver the services; the recruiting and training of professional social workers. The private family agencies engaged in community, regional, and national roundtables to consider what the function of the private agency should be. It is interesting, from our perspective, to consider how deeply shaken the private agency was with the proposal that it give up "the relief business." The notion of developing a personal social services system separate from income maintenance programs seemed to be inconceivable. Linton Swift finally published a pamphlet entitled *New Alignments between Public and Private Agencies in a Community Family Welfare and Relief Program*. He suggested that the public agency be regarded as the official instrument of society in mitigating social and economic inequalities which society had not yet corrected, while the private agency was to be concerned with meeting needs not yet recognized by the whole community, and its particular contribution was qualitative and experimental. Agencies began to change their names to Family Service Agencies or Family Welfare, which were considered more descriptive of their new work than Family Charities.

This problem of change of function, and the separation of personal social services from income maintenance, was to be an important consideration of the private family agencies until well into the 60s. Thus we will continue to allude to it in the next chapters.

Child welfare services

During the depression many agencies were developing further programs in the interests of children. This work began in the 1920s and continued into the 1950s. Therefore, we shall take up these efforts in the next chapter. In this chapter we shall discuss very briefly the child welfare services that were to be supported through federal funds provided for by the Social Security Act. Just as the act forced considerable change in family personal social services, so personal social services to and for children were gradually changed by Title V. This title made provision for several grants to the states through the Children's Bureau for the purpose of establishing, extending, and strengthening public personal social services for children, particularly in rural areas. The services provided for were the protection and care of homeless, dependent, and neglected children as well as children in danger of becoming delinquent.

The programs were to be established in all 48 states, the District of Columbia, Alaska, Hawaii, Puerto Rico, and the Virgin Islands, and they were usually lodged in the county welfare agencies. Each state was to receive a flat grant of $40,000 annually and to share in the balance of the appropriated funds on the basis of the proportion of its rural population under 18 years of age to the total rural population under that age. Because of the limited funds, the states initially used the money to hire personnel rather than for direct grants. However, following World War II some states began to use some of the allocations to pay for foster care. Of great importance was the use of some of the money to educate personnel in social work in order to raise the level of service. Over the years immediately following the passage of the act, public personal social services in relation to children began to include:

1. Giving services to children, in their own homes or the homes of relatives, in meeting problems arising from physical, mental, or emotional handicaps, from economic or social disadvantages, or from unsatisfactory relationships.
2. Investigating complaints and requests for services which appeared to involve the welfare of children.
3. General protective casework service in behalf of children who were neglected or mistreated.
4. Preventive services for children who were in danger of becoming delinquent, with the emphasis on assisting communities to make studies to identify needs for children and youth as well as on promoting the development of advisory committees, community councils, and citizen and youth participation in community activities.
5. Foster-home-finding programs to help children who needed to be removed from their own homes temporarily or for long periods.
6. Carrying on an adoption program for children who needed to be removed from their homes permanently.
7. Cooperating with schools and juvenile courts in behalf of children presenting conduct problems.
8. Rendering social service in connection with community and child guidance clinics.
9. Providing foster care in needed situations.
10. Providing service to unwed mothers and safeguarding the welfare of children born to them.
11. Carrying on a public relations and interpretation program relative to children who needed welfare services (Delli Quadri, 1957, pp. 154–55).

The social work profession

As we discussed in the last chapter, social workers in specialized settings began to develop their own professional groups. These actually developed earlier than the formation of the general association of the profession. By 1930 four professional organizations of social workers were showing increasing strength: AAMSW (American Association of Medical Social Workers) had a membership of approximately 1,700; NASSW (National Association of School Social Workers), approximately 270; AAPSW (American Association of Psychiatric Social Workers), approximately 365; and AASW (American Association of Social Workers), approximately 5,030. This was less than 25 percent of the social work force, in spite of the fact that the qualifications for membership in NASSW were based only on length of service until 1933. It was evident that a small nucleus of social workers was pushing the field toward higher professional standards and toward membership requirements that had an educational component.

Between the depression and World War II three new associations were added to the profession: the American Association of Group Workers (AAGW), which began as a professional study group in 1936 and adopted a professional structure in 1946; the Association for the Study of Community Organization (ASCO), launched in 1946; and the Social Work Research Group (SWRG), founded in 1949 (Cohen, 1957, pp. 554–55). When the depression began, the main emphasis of the professional was on family or individual casework service. As social workers became involved in depression programs of a scale and importance that were entirely new, there were new reflections about the nature and role of the profession and education for professional service. Once again, the profession began to be concerned with reform and organization, though the strong push toward individual service continued. As the schools of social work came into being somewhat late in the Progressive movement, they had generally developed curricula that focused on casework activities. Now it became apparent that the professional needed skill and knowledge in group work, community organization, administration, and research. In 1944 the schools agreed to include in their curricula the following eight basic areas: social casework, social group work, community organization, public welfare, social administration, social research, medical information, and psychiatric information.

As we have mentioned earlier, the public assistance agencies attracted a host of new workers who, in filling social work positions, were more likely to see themselves as line workers in a bureaucracy than as professionals. Many of these workers felt close to their clients, as did their professional colleagues, but they were more likely to be interested in better working conditions and job security than were the professional workers, who could easily find positions in the private sector. In 1931 an organization arose spontaneously in several cities among these new social workers. It has come to be known as the rank-and-file movement to distinguish its membership and its interests from the supervisors and administrators. The rank-and-file movement developed in an adversary relationship to the administrators of the public agencies. Marxism had a strong appeal to many members, and most members identified with the labor movement and developed a union mentality. The movement published a journal, *Social Work Today*, from 1934 to 1941. With the coming of World War II, the movement lost its drive and enthusiasm. However, some facets of the movement persisted in the efforts of the American Federation of State, County, and Municipal Employees (AFL) and the United Office and Professional Workers and United Public Workers of America (CIO) to organize social workers (Leiby, 1948, pp. 242–43).

Other social welfare systems

We will pick up the discussion of the development of personal social services as part of other social welfare systems in the next chapter. For now, we would simply point out that there was a further development of the rehabilitation system and that a limited amount of public money was appropriated that could be used to offer heath services to mothers and children.

✑ Minorities

Although all minorities suffered greatly during the depression, and the Social Security Act in some ways institutionalized the problems of discrimination, it was the black tenant farmer and the Mexican agricultural worker who suffered the most. Blacks were evicted from farms on which they had lived for generations as loans enabled the large farmers to industrialize their farming. Mexicans suffered a double jeopardy. Not only did they lose their jobs, or find themselves forced to work for pittances, but they often faced deportation if they applied for financial aid. There were strong movements to deport all Mexicans who applied for aid and to cut off immigration from Mexico entirely. Driven to desperation by the low pay and long hours, the Mexican laborers in the fields of the Southwest engaged in bitter strikes during the depression years. The employers attempted to deal with these strikes in two ways: by mounting programs of violence against the workers and by setting up rival unions. The Mexican unions made sporadic progress and were not very successful. The final end came as the farms in the Southwest were overrun by Americans seeking work, and the Mexicans found themselves with no income and no jobs.

The Indians. Aware of the suffering of the Indians during the depression, Roosevelt was interested in offering them active help. He was supported in this by the competent administrators whom Hoover had appointed to the Indian Service and by a Senate study of the conditions of the Indian reservations that had been made before Roosevelt took office. Roosevelt made the funneling of relief funds into the reservations one of the first orders of business, and he established Civilian Conservation Corps camps for Indians. In June 1934, Roosevelt signed the Wheeler-Howard Act which gave legislative sanction to new policies relating to the Indian people. The act provided for tribal constitutions and tribal business corporations. It discontinued a former land policy that had divided the reservations among individual Indians, allowing them to sell the reservation lands as they pleased, and returned the unsold lands to the tribe. In addition, under the act the government purchased over 1 million acres of new land for the tribes. A fund was created to provide credit for Indian agricultural and industrial projects. Educational opportunities were extended to Indian youth through the improvement of facilities and the establishment of a loan program. Job qualifications were altered so that Indians were given preference for positions in the Indian Service. New policies encouraged native religions, ceremonials, and crafts. Improvement in medical services resulted in a steadily declining death rate that resulted in a slow growth in the number of Indian people (Hagan, 1961, pp. 151–58).

❧ Summary

An understanding of the social welfare developments that occurred during the Progressive era and the depression is crucial to an understanding of the nature of social welfare in American society. The changes that occurred during the depression should be thought of as changes that are possible in crisis situations when society sees its very existence as threatened. However, a careful evaluation of the changes should also help students of social welfare to comprehend how, even in a crisis that disorganizes the basic patterns of our lives, we still find it hard to completely abandon earlier ways of meeting needs. Many of the more important changes that occurred during the depression came about because of the earlier work that had been done by the Progressive reformers. If these plans for reform had not been developed and supported by the social workers of the time, the changes that occurred during the depression might have been more restrictive. But having certain plans already available made change easier, in that completely new concepts did not need to be developed in the midst of crisis. Thus, although many of the earlier reformers felt that their work had been for naught and many did not live to see the changes, the Progressive era did indeed have strong influence on the reforms of the depression era.

❧ A look ahead

In the next chapter we shall continue our discussion of the rapid development of the federally funded income maintenance programs. We shall look in more detail at the development of the personal social services and the social work profession. In addition, we shall once again examine in some detail the happenings in the other five social service systems.

❧ Study questions

1. Why was the Social Security Act of 1935 so important? List the gains that this act represented. What were the limitations to the act? Why were such limitations enacted?
2. Why were the private agencies so opposed to the use of public agencies for administering income maintenance programs? Why do you think the private agencies did not move to completely give up the income maintenance function of their work? Identify the beliefs and patterns that were important here.
3. Outline the significant differences between public assistance and OASI. What is the mistaken notion that most recipients have about OASI? Do you think that this incorrect idea has an important impact on the system? What is that impact?
4. Evaluate the roles that various social workers played in the federal government's involvement in public income maintenance.
5. Why was the inclusion of the states in many of the programs of the time so important? Discuss the constitutional question that was involved in planning programs.

❧ Selected readings

Leiby, James. *History of Social Welfare and Social Work in the United States.* New York: Columbia University Press, 1978.

Chaps. 11 and 12 dealing with social insurance and social security are an excellent expansion of the material in this chapter.

Axinn, June, and Levin, Herman. *Social Welfare: A History of American Response to Need.* New York: Harper & Row, 1975.

Chap. 6 of this text is an excellent supplement for the material in our chapters.

Chambers, Clarke A. *The New Deal at Home and Abroad, 1929–1945.* New York: Free Press, 1965.

This book contains selections of speeches and articles that appeared during the depression. They make very good reading for students who would like to get a better view of this crisis in American life.

Library of Congress photo by Russell Lee

Photograph by U.S. Information Agency, in the National Archives

America's history from 1940 through the 1960s was marked with both shame and victory in the ongoing struggle for equality of human rights—from the internment of Japanese-Americans in World War II, to the passage of the Civil Rights Act of 1964 and the Voting Rights Act of 1965.

The bewildered small boy, and the eloquent Rev. Dr. Martin Luther King, Jr., are powerful symbols of those years.

Chapter 21 ~

~ Toward the Great Society: Social issues ~ and income maintenance advances, 1940–1967

~ Introduction

The period that we shall discuss in this chapter was a period of conflicts and contradictions, covering the administrations, or parts of the administrations, of five presidents. During this period the United States was engaged in warfare, first in Europe and the Pacific and later in Korea and Indochina. Supported by military and civilian demand, these years were prosperous ones. They can be divided into three periods. Until World War II ended in 1945 and during the years immediately following the war, people were caught up in war—both World War II and the cold war and disillusion over Stalinist socialism. High expenditures for defense tended to hold down spending for social welfare. Liberals found themselves divided over relationships abroad and thus less involved in internal problems. The Eisenhower years were marked by prosperity, peace, and a lack of interest in social welfare. Then under the Kennedy-Johnson administrations there was a dramatic acceleration of governmental efforts to assure the well-being of all citizens. Johnson said in June 1964:

> This nation, this people, has man's first chance to create a Great Society; a society of success without squalor, beauty without barrenness, works of genius without the wretchedness of poverty. We can open the doors of learning. We can open the doors of fruitful labor and rewarding leisure, of open opportunity and close community—not just to the privileged few, but to everyone. (Levitan and Taggart, 1976, p. 1)

But the four years from 1964 and 1968 were marked by conflict—armed conflict abroad and domestic conflict over the attempts to deal with poverty and race and sex discrimination and over the meaning of the Vietnam War and the American experience. The vision of the Great Society gave way to doubt over the government's capacity to change institutions, to design and operate effective programs, or to solve the basic and persistent questions of social living. In this chapter we shall deal very briefly with the 1940s and 1950s, concentrating most of our discussion on the developments in social welfare in the 1960s.

⇜ Social forces

In our last chapter we discussed the efforts, in the midst of the Great Depression, to provide some minimum economic security for individuals. However, other forces were to shift the concern of the American people for the next two decades. We became involved in World War II, and when the war ended in 1945, the country had achieved an unprecedented prosperity based on government spending for war. So government spending, as had been suggested by Keynes, was to form the base of prosperity. But it was spending for different purposes than those suggested in the 1930s. Between 1945 and 1970, the federal government spent $1,000 billion, 60 percent of its total budget, on defense. The bulk of the defense spending had gone to the largest corporations and to the organized workers who were employed by those corporations. Thus, military defense was a convenient rationale for massive government spending that was acceptable and approved by business, organized labor, and the average American (Carroll and Noble, 1977, p. 348).

Population shifts

There were huge changes in population size and distribution during this period. The total U.S. population grew from 132.1 million in 1940 to 204.8 million in 1970, largely from natural population increase. The birthrate had fallen during the depression, but the end of World War II brought a large increase in the birth rate, and the birthrate remained high until the mid-1960s, when it began to fall again. The increase in the birthrate was accompanied by an increase in longevity and a decline in the death rate. Life expectancy for whites rose from 62.9 years in 1940 to 70.8 years in 1970. For nonwhites it rose from 52 years to 63.7 years. Thus, over these years the population grew both

younger and older, with a decline in the number of people in the middle, or productive, years (Axinn and Levin, 1975, p. 222).

These changing patterns of population growth were accompanied by an increased population mobility. Not only were industrialization and mechanization accelerated by the war, but wartime needs resulted in the spread of industry across the country. Where industry went, there also went people in search of jobs. In addition, as a result of the movement of people necessitated by military training, families packed up and migrated across the country, often not once but many times. The fact that the war was fought on two fronts resulted in the rapid population growth of the Pacific states, as both industry and training facilities developed on the West Coast. Another important reason for the movement of people, especially among blacks, was the change in agriculture. The increased mechanization of agriculture resulted both in fewer farm jobs and in fewer small farms, as larger farms were necessary to the effective use of the new technology. Although the real value of farm output increased by $6.4 billion during these years, the relative share of employment in agriculture fell from 15 percent of the labor force to 4 percent. Average farm size increased from 167 acres in 1940 to 373 acres in 1970. For 150 years the cities had been growing as the result both of immigration and of migration from rural to urban areas. Although immigration was now only a trickle, the factors mentioned above accelerated the movement from rural to urban areas. From 1940 to 1970, 20 million people, of whom 4 million were black, moved from rural to urban areas. By 1970, 72 percent of the whites and 81 percent of the blacks in America were living in urban areas (Axinn and Levin, 1975, pp. 223–24).

These years of mobility seem to have created an even greater trend toward migration among the American people. However, even if moving was no longer unusual or frightening in a world of the automobile, the airplane, and television, it carried certain social risks. Families moving far from home also moved away from the support and help of relatives and friends, and family life and the family units were severely stressed. There was a growing increase in divorce, in juvenile delinquency, in school dropouts, and in illegitimate births, which approximately doubled for both white and black women between the ages of 15 and 44 between 1940–1970.

Economic advances

The most rapid economic changes of the period 1940–70 took place during the war years. World War II gave a major boost to the development of new products, especially in the chemical, aircraft and aviation, and space technology industries. New industrial processes were further enhanced by the development of computer technology and advanced information systems. Industrial and technological change resulted in an increase in the gross national product and in worker output, a decrease in working hours, and a different occupational distribution of workers. Growing wealth and increasing societal complexity resulted in a rapid development of service industries, and there was a significant growth in the number of public employees. In the postwar period, Americans acquired a renewed faith in the economy and in the ability of government to control the business cycle.

Beginning with the New Deal, as we discussed in the last chapter, labor's demands began to be recognized as valid. The right to bargain collectively, to minimum wages and limitations on hours, and to the prohibition of injunctions against strikes, along with the governmental programs of unemployment compensation and OASI, all advanced the cause of labor. Through the use of these new rights, especially the right to bargain collectively, unions were able to raise and control wages relative to prices and to secure a whole series of fringe benefits that, in effect, comprised a private health and welfare system. Organized labor became a part of the establishment, identified itself with the status quo, and separated itself increasingly from the poor. Real income increased for all people, but it rose proportionately more for poor families than for rich ones (41.6 percent for those in the lowest one fifth and 18.3 percent for the highest one fifth

of the nation's families) (Axinn and Levin, 1975, pp. 223–35).

During the Eisenhower administration economic growth slowed perceptibly, and unemployment rose to 8 percent in 1960. When Kennedy became president he was determined to follow the Keynesian theories of economic development. He asked for a tax cut, but it was not enacted until 1964, after Johnson had become president. However, the budget for national defense was increased dramatically, and another $25 billion was budgeted for the National Aeronautics and Space Administration. Given such governmental spending, the gross national product grew in the 1960s at twice the rate of the 1950s. Average income increased by 18 percent, and corporate profits grew by 65 percent. During World War II, defense contracts were not competitive and allowances were made for cost increases. The same was true for the new defense contracts. By the end of the 1960s the jobs of one out of every ten Americans were tied to the defense budget (Carroll and Noble, 1977, pp. 387–88).

Civil rights

In times of crisis and threat, governments often ignore or suspend the civil rights of their citizens. This happened in America during World War II, when Americans of Japanese ancestry were placed in concentration camps for no other reason than their national origin. The problems with Stalinist Russia at the end of the war resulted in a prolonged "Red Scare" that frightened many people and resulted in serious violations of civil rights. Earlier, Truman had initiated a Federal Employee Loyalty Program because "subversive elements must be removed from the employ of the government." As a result of the investigations of the House Un-American Activities Committee, many persons who were suspected of Communist sympathies, particularly writers, actors, and directors in Hollywood, lost their jobs and were unable to find new ones. Many prominent members of Congress, including John F. Kennedy, Richard M. Nixon, and Lyndon B. Johnson, helped pass the McCarran Act in 1950, which provided for the establishment of six concentration camps which were to house political prisoners. Senator Joseph McCarthy's investigations of possible Communist influences and his accusations of long lists of people climaxed this hysteria and eventually resulted, by its very excesses, in a reaction against this irresponsible activity (Carroll and Noble, 1977, p. 357).

Minorities

When Roosevelt came to office he was conscious of the growing political importance of Roman Catholics and Jews, two groups that had suffered from discrimination, especially in political and academic life. Until World War II, it was almost impossible for Jews to gain tenure at a major university and they continued to be barred from leadership positions in major corporations. Roosevelt brought both Roman Catholics and Jews into his administration, and it was partly the political strength of these groups that encouraged him to support labor unions and social security. In 1919 the Catholic Bishops Program for Social Reconstruction had supported minimum wage laws, social insurance, and public housing for the poor. Father John A. Ryan, a leader in social welfare, took a position in Roosevelt's administration, where he continued his lobbying for social security and rights for labor. As we have stated earlier, Roosevelt appointed Frances Perkins, a social worker, to his cabinet. She was the first woman cabinet member in our history (Carroll and Noble, 1977, pp. 360–62).

The blacks. Under Roosevelt, blacks were appointed to important positions in the federal government for the first time in U.S. history: Robert C. Weaver and William Hastie in the Department of the Interior, E. K. Jones in the Department of Commerce, Laurence Oxley in the Department of Labor, Ira D. Reid in the Social Security Administration, and Mary Bethune in the National Youth Administration. However, the principal impact of the Roosevelt administration on blacks probably came, not from such well-publicized appointments, but

from the relief and welfare measures established by the New Deal. The blacks and other minorities were the hardest hit by the depression, and although the administering of aid was often influenced by racial considerations, especially in the South, a higher proportion of blacks than whites received aid under New Deal programs. Although the housing and agricultural assistance programs of the New Deal definitely discriminated against blacks, this period represented a real turning point in the trends of race relationships. Of great importance was the genuine interest of prominent New Dealers in the problems of blacks. This interest found leadership and support in the activities and attitudes of Eleanor Roosevelt, wife of the president, who was openly and actively supportive of blacks.

Early in his administration, Roosevelt himself had refused to support the antilynching bill before Congress because he was afraid of alienating his southern white supporters. In 1941, blacks threatened a massive march on the capital to protest the failure of the government to support the equal employment of blacks in war industries. Under this pressure Roosevelt appointed a Committee on Fair Employment Practices to require corporations doing government work to hire black workers. The war experience of black people was a mixed picture. For the first time, blacks were admitted into the Army Air Corps and the Marines. And for the first time, blacks were accepted in naval grades above that of messman. The first black naval officers and the first black brigadier general were commissioned. Blacks were sent to integrated officers' training camps. Yet at army posts there was segregation in living quarters and in training and recreational facilities (Meier and Rudwick, 1976, pp. 232–70).

During this time the formation of the CIO and the rise of industrial unionism were of immense value to blacks. Although complete racial egalitarianism was certainly lacking in the interracial trade unions, these unions gave white and black workers a sense of common interests and solidarity for the first time in U.S. history. The movement also benefited from changes in labor management relations that accompanied the New Deal. Finally, in 1937, after years of struggle, the Brotherhood of Sleeping Car Porters received recognition as the porters' bargaining unit.

The Truman administration accelerated the movement of blacks toward political equality. In 1948 Adam Clayton Powell became the second black to be elected to Congress from a northern city. Two decades later there were six blacks in the House of Representatives. Under Truman's leadership, the Democratic National Convention adopted a strong civil rights platform in 1948. This split the Democratic Party, yet Truman won the election, demonstrating for the first time in history the power of the black vote in the northern cities. The proposed Civil Rights Act was not passed by Congress. Nevertheless, the Truman administration was marked by some advances. Truman appointed William H. Hastie to the Third U.S. Circuit Court, making Hastie the highest black judicial appointee up to that time. He also issued an order that the armed forces were to be fully integrated. As a result of this order, millions of young men, black and white, lived and fought together in Korea and white men often served under black officers. The president also ordered that discrimination should cease in firms doing business with the government and appointed a commission to study race relations in the nation. The report of this commission, *To Secure These Rights,* called for the full integration of blacks into national life. Although such commissions were relatively ineffectual, they were important in that they suggested that the right to employment be considered a civil right. Many of the advances of the black people were brought about by the political power of the black ghettos of the northern cities. "Without the urban base, the Negro protest movement would have remained small, and without political leverage the urban masses provided, it would have remained impotent" (Meier and Rudwick, 1976, p. 270).

In 1944 the Supreme Court ruled that blacks could not be barred from primaries in southern states on racial grounds. A small but growing number of blacks began to vote in the southern states during the 1950s. Then, in 1954, as a result of a suit brought by the NAACP, the Court again reversed an earlier decision and ruled that segregation in the public schools was unconstitutional. It took the presence of federal troops to enforce some measure of compliance with the Court's decision. In 1957 Eisenhower was forced to send troops to Little Rock, Arkansas, to desegregate a high school.

The rising use of direct action against discrimination by blacks and white liberals began when Rosa Parks, an elderly black woman in Montgomery, Alabama, refused to obey the law that required blacks to sit in the back of the bus. Her arrest captured the imagination of the nation and led to a spontaneous protest of Montgomery blacks in which a Baptist minister, Martin Luther King, Jr., became a leader. King established the Southern Christian Leadership Conference (SCLC), which was dedicated to the goal of overthrowing discrimination by nonviolent direct action. This new group expressed a position similar to that of the Congress of Racial Equality (CORE), an earlier movement. CORE had been established in 1942 to further the use of nonviolent direct action as a tool for changing race relationships, but it only became important following Rosa Parks's action. Black high school and college students were challenged by the possibilities of such movements and formed the Student Non-Violent Coordinating Committee (SNCC), which initiated sit-ins at lunch counters and other segregated facilities. Arrests of these students numbered in the thousands and set in motion forces that shook both the black and white communities. SNCC made direct action the primary civil rights technique and ended NAACP dominance in the civil rights movements.

Nonviolent sit-ins, freedom marches, freedom rides, and efforts to register black voters in the South resulted in violence between the participants in such actions and the police and whites who disapproved racial integration. Some demonstrators were illegally imprisoned, beaten, and even killed. President Kennedy and his brother Robert, the attorney general of the United States, were forced to offer federal protection to the demonstrators. In 1963 President Kennedy called unsuccessfully for civil rights legislation. In 1964 President Johnson was finally able to get a Civil Rights Act through Congress. This act barred racial, religious, and sexual discrimination in public accommodations and employment. Congress also passed a Voting Rights Act which authorized the sending of federal registrars into counties in which the majority of persons were not registered to vote. By 1970 nearly 70 percent of blacks were registered to vote (Carroll and Noble, 1977, p. 407).

However, blacks were becoming increasingly aware that political victories did not necessarily ensure economic and social power. It was the college generation of the 1960s that turned the black protest organizations toward a deep concern with the economic and social problems of all blacks.

> Involved was a steady radicalization of tactics and goals: from legalism to direct action, and ultimately to Black Power; from participation by the middle and upper classes to mass action by all classes; from guaranteeing the protection of the Negro's constitutional rights to securing economic policies that would ensure the welfare of the culturally deprived in a technologically changing society; from appeals to white America's sense of fair play to demands based upon the power in the black ghetto. (Meier and Rudwick, 1976, p. 278)

A further factor leading to the radicalization of the civil rights movement was the rise of the Black Muslims to national notice. The Black Muslims had been in existence since the 1930s, but their spurt in membership came during the 1950s in the face of rising black unemployment due to technological change and automation. By 1952 the median income of black families was 57 percent of the median income, of white families, and ten years later, in spite of occupational breakthroughs, the median income of black families had fallen to 53 percent of that of white families. By 1962 unemployment among blacks was 2½ times that of whites. Appealing primarily to the lowest social class of blacks, the Black Muslim movement was an expression of the blacks' quest for recognition of their human dignity and of the blacks' impatience with the philosophy of gradualism. The movement demanded a rigid self-discipline of its members, offered them an explanation of their troubles as caused by the

"white devils," and gave them a sense of self-esteem and pride in being black, a vision of a future in which blacks would prevail, and a very practical program of immediate change in their situation (Meier and Rudwick, 1976, pp. 270–90).

The triumph of civil rights legislation in 1964 was followed by spontaneous riots of young blacks in the cities. These riots spotlighted the desperate plight of the black community, caught between rising expectations and rising unemployment. The riots were different from earlier race riots in our history in that they were directed against property rather than against persons.

The Indians. The impact of World War II caused some Indians to develop individual interests that separated them from tribe and family. About 25,000 Indians entered the armed services, for the most part as draftees, and nearly twice as many left the reservations to work in war industries. The returning veterans were less amenable to the influence of tribal officials and more concerned with their rights as citizens. They lodged bitter complaints against laws prohibiting the sale of liquor to Indians and against the discrimination of some western states against Indian voters. Indians gradually became aware of the value of the vote, and in 1959 the annual meeting of the National Congress of American Indians had political action as its theme. Indians became candidates for public office. Equality in the use of alcoholic beverages was achieved in 1953, when an act of Congress removed the ban on off-reservation liquor sales to Indians and approved local option for the reservations (Hagan, 1961, pp. 158–60).

By 1940 the budget for Indian services began to be slashed. There was talk of abolishing the Bureau of Indian Affairs and of repealing the Wheeler-Howard Act. These actions were caused by the heavy expenditures for war and by the fact that an "Indian problem" still remained. The Hoover commission on governmental organization recommended in 1949 that the federal government transfer the responsibility for Indian programs to the state governments and that it enact policies that would encourage and assist Indians to leave the reservation and enter the mainstream of American life. In the early 1950s, the Wheeler-Howard Act was ignored and whenever possible health and education responsibilities were shifted from the federal government to the states. The Eisenhower administration was committed to a lessening of the federal role in social welfare activities. The Indians were relatively inarticulate in the face of this threat, so they were singled out for attention. Congress passed an act which transferred to five states the responsibility for law and order among their Indian populations and opened the door to similar actions by other states. The act ignored any wishes that the Indians may have had, and it eviscerated any law-enforcement programs that the Indians had evolved under the Wheeler-Howard Act. In 1955 Congress transferred the health programs of the Indian Bureau to the U.S. Public Health Service. It furthered the policy of ending governmental responsibility for Indians by removing their health programs from a special category and merging those programs with the health programs of the general population (Hagan, 1961, pp. 162–65).

The Red Power movement among young Indians developed during the 1960s, aimed at developing a sense of cultural pride among their people. The American Indian Movement (AIM) was formed by young Indian radicals such as Dennis Banks, Russell Means, and Clyde and Vernon Bellecourt to pressure the government to provide social and economic justice for their people. During the late 1960s the average income of Indians was $1,500 a year, 40 percent of the Indian work force was unemployed, the Indian infant mortality rate was three times the national average, and the Indian teenage suicide rate was 100 times that of whites (Carroll and Noble, 1977, p. 409).

The Chicanos. Chicanos, too, began a struggle for economic and political rights in the 1960s. Their income was less than half that of the whites among whom they lived, and they received a minimum of social and public services. There were efforts to unionize farm workers by Cesar Chavez, and Chicanos organized the La Raza Unida party in Texas in an effort to win political power in areas in which they were in a majority. Chicano newspa-

pers urged young Chicanos to reject Anglo-American culture in favor of a revival of their own heritage. Rudolfo Gonzales of the Denver Chicano community led his people to work to take over the schools and to see that Spanish was taught as a language along with Spanish-American culture. The paramilitary Brown Berets, formed to offer their people defense against police brutality, represented the most militant part of the Chicano movement (Carroll and Nobel, 1977, pp. 409–10).

The women's movement

World War II had a sharp impact on the employment of women. Although defense industries had been growing for several years, women had not been welcome as employees and it was certainly not accepted policy that they should have access to equal work at equal wages. Within a few months after the declaration of war, however, women became the only available labor reserve, and both government and industry abandoned the reluctance to use females in war industries. Women responded to this crisis with an unprecedented display of skill and ingenuity, and they demonstrated that they could fill almost any job, no matter how difficult or arduous.

This movement of women into the work force was marked by several factors. The industries directly connected to the war hired the largest number of women workers. Many of the women who took these jobs were not new to the work force but had left lower-paid "women's work" to take these higher-paying jobs. It was difficult, if not impossible, to find waitresses, laundry workers, and domestic workers now that better-paying jobs were available to women. This was of particular benefit to black women, who had previously found employment opportunities limited to domestic work or to work in the laundries or the fields. The assimilation of these women into industrial work came slowly and reluctantly, but it came. Many of the industries that employed women were unionized, and for the first time large numbers of women became members of unions. Although women still might suffer some discrimination within certain unions, they benefited substantially from being a part of organized labor. Along with the war industries, the government actively recruited women into employment. As men and women worked together on the same jobs, a new working relationship was established between them. Perhaps the most important change brought by these new employment opportunities involved the age and the marital status of the new employees. The proportion of married women over 35 who were employed rose rapidly. No longer was gainful employment for women confined to the young and single.

Public opinion highly approved the move of women out of the home. All of this had some effect on the opportunities for professional women. Industries began to look for women chemists; women lawyers found new openings in government; and even the Washington Press Corps opened its ranks to women, though it excluded them from its annual White House dinner. Many people felt that all this marked a revolution in women's lives. However, there were signs that "such optimism was both premature and exaggerated" (Chafe, 1972, p. 149). A permanent change in women's economic status required a redistribution of sex roles, a considerable improvement in employment opportunities, and a shift in public opinion that approved the change as a permanent one and not as a temporary expedient.

The war resulted in a critical disruption of family life. Not only were the husbands in battle, but the wives found that they needed to be both mother and father to their children and to work outside the home as well. In an effort to be near husbands in military service, women moved families back and forth across the country, seeking what living and working accommodations they could find. The migration caused unavoidable social problems. Social agencies found their resources tested to the utmost as they sought to help the newcomers that poured into cities near military training centers or into cities that were centers of war work. Delinquency increased, and the number of teenage runaways grew rapidly. Many people blamed women's employment for the increase in domestic ills. For many people, women working represented a threat to the well-being of the family and social life. Some

leading women demanded that women return home and care for their families, and "the Children's Bureau called the growing employment of mothers a hazard to the security of the child in his family" (Chafe, 1972, p. 150).

Although there were some opportunities for professional women, relatively few positions were available to them. The Army, despite an overwhelming need, refused to commission women doctors until an act of Congress in 1943 forced the issue. Women were excluded from executive or decision-making positions in industry and in the governmental bodies concerned with running the war. Some women complained bitterly that they were valued as workers but not as leaders. Although the War Manpower Commission had urged equal pay for equal work, and some industries complied, a multitude of loopholes were used to evade the requirement. In many industries, women and men were assigned to separate labor categories on the basis of sex rather than skill and it was assumed that women deserved less pay than men.

It was, however, around the issue of establishing community services to help the working woman handle the dual jobs of working outside the home and caring for her family that the most resistance was provoked. In contrast to Great Britain, where the difficulties of working wives led to the creation of special community services for their benefit, the United States did little to provide special services for female workers. In order to shop when stores were open or to transact necessary business, women often had to take time off from work. But difficult as these lacks were, it was the question of whether or not to build child care centers that crystallized the conflicts involved in the community services issue. Money represented only one of the obstacles to developing a solution. The central issue was whether the government or community "should sanction the employment of mothers by providing public facilities for the care of children" (Chafe, 1972, p. 164).

When World War II ended, a substantial number of people—men and women alike—believed that the time had come for women to return home. There was concern that women in the labor market represented a threat to the home and the welfare of children; there was the notion that women in the labor force would take jobs from the returning veterans; and perhaps more important than either of these, there was a persistence of hostility toward the idea of women participating as equals in the economic world. Margaret Pickel, dean of Barnard, "claimed that employers found women workers more demanding, more emotional, and less reliable" and that, by middle age, women tended "to degenerate into fussiness or worse" (Chafe, 1972, p. 177). In a conflict over the continuation of wartime day care in New York the *New York World Telegram* charged in 1947 that child care was conceived by leftists operating out of Communist "social work cells" (Chafe, 1972, p. 187). Despite all the disagreements over woman's place, there was no question but that the decade of the 1940s represented a turning point for women.

During the 1950s the debate on woman's place continued from many different perspectives. There was the discovery that inductees into the military had had an unusually high rate of nervous disorders, and the blame was placed on the mothers who had overprotected their sons and created such emotional dependence that the sons did not want to grow up. There were those who held that feminism "represented a neurotic reaction to male dominance and a deep illness which encouraged women to reject their natural sex-based instincts" (Chafe, 1971, p. 203). Women's colleges were urged to devise curricula that prepared women for being wives and mothers rather than exposing them to the same learning as men. Women's magazines took up the cry that women should return to and take care of their families and homes. However, although the traditional values seemed to gain new strength during the 1950s, there were other approaches. Various social scientists began to find evidence that personality was as much a response to cultural norms and social circumstances as it was inborn. Anthropologists arrived at the conclusion that some of the confusion of women came from the strain of trying to handle a confusing number of roles.

In the 1960s the women's movement once again emerged as a crucial issue. Articulate women presented a cogent indictment of society's treatment of women. Large numbers of women had already experienced the difficulties of discrimination and were responsive to the attempt to end it. And the movements of the time among minorities and the young had established a climate that was conducive to the attempt to establish equality for all people.

The leaders of the new feminist movement made some mistaken assumptions. They assumed that, given a chance, all women would choose a career. However, many women in no way considered themselves oppressed, but were quite satisfied with their lives. The feminist movement revealed a middle-class bias in assuming that all women had the necessary training and experience to consider the possibility of an alternative life. In assuming that the "feminine mystique represented a recent phenomenon," contemporary feminists also showed that they were terribly ignorant of history. The most important condition for the resurgence of the women's movement was the amount of change that had already occurred in women's lives. The revolution came not because of severity of oppression but as a response to the rising expectations of women who had glimpsed the possibility of change. And after more than four decades of neglect, feminist demands began to receive political attention. "After having been bottled up in committee for forty-seven years, the Equal Rights Amendment to the Constitution was brought before the House of Representatives once again" (Chafe, 1972, p. 240). Congress passed it and sent it to the states for ratification. There it met with great opposition.

Under the Civil Rights Act of 1964, the attorney general initiated federal suits to end discrimination in employment. Employers were informed that they would be expected to employ certain numbers of women. Like other movements for equality, the women's movement demanded change in the economic, social and political areas of life (Chafe, 1972, pp. 191–241).

The youth movement

In the 1960s, children and youth were deeply involved in struggles to end racial segregation in the schools and to secure civil rights and decent treatment of the poor and the oppressed. Many young men and women took an active part in efforts to stop the Vietnam War. The young of the country came to regard themselves as "the conscience of the nation" (Bremner, 1974, p. 1). The youth culture undoubtedly developed in the way it did as a result of the rapidity of social changes, and within a public climate that accepted the right of people to active protests. The youth movement sought to replace materialism and a striving for achievement with an emphasis on the expressive, the free, the creative. Actually the youth movement's emphasis on liberty and equality was very much in the American tradition. What was different was that the young doubted whether America would ever be willing to live up to their understanding of the meaning of these values. Given these disturbing doubts, the youth culture became increasingly opposed to the adult society. There was a strong belief that one way for the country to find its way toward the values was to make life as simple and natural as possible. As a part of the general youth movement, the voting age was reduced to 18 years by constitutional amendment and the states acted to lower the age of majority.

Summary of social forces

We have now completed our summary of some of the forces that were active in America over the years 1940–67. In the next section we shall begin our discussion of social welfare developments with a consideration of income maintenance programs as they developed during the same years.

✎§ The veterans

Before we discuss the other income maintenance efforts of the United States between 1940 and 1967, we will deal with the benefits that were established for the armed services and for the veterans of those services. This was the major social welfare legislation of the 1940s. Benefits for servicemen and servicewomen did not have to wait

until the end of World War II, as had so often been the case in past conflicts. Dependents of servicemen were protected by the National Life Insurance Act of 1940, which, with later amendments, insured against death or total disability for service-connected or non-service-connected causes. The extent of this program can be grasped if one realizes that combat deaths numbered 292,000, that deaths from non-service-connected causes totaled 114,000, and that 671,000 persons were wounded (Axinn and Levin, 1975, pp. 232–33).

Given the salary levels of servicemen, there was considerable concern for the welfare of wives, children, and other dependents. The Dependent's Allowance of 1942 provided for a program of allotments for the families of the six lowest-paid grades of servicemen. These allowances were available to all such families without a means test, as, given the level of pay, need was assumed. The allotments were financed jointly by the individual soldier and the federal government. The allotments were voluntary, and the servicemen or servicewomen had to indicate that they wished to participate in the program.

The effects of the war on women and children introduced an experiment in the federal control of health care. The low army pay left servicemen unable to provide for the medical costs of childbearing and child rearing. A wartime emergency program, the Emergency Maternal and Infant Care Program was introduced to assure that the medical costs of childbirth and the care of those born would be covered. This was the first program of medical care through the marketplace of private medicine that was administered as a national program under strict regulations.

Veterans' organizations, led by the American Legion, had long been critical of the fact that veterans without some kind of disability were left to their own resources in readjusting to civilian life. The first attempt to deal with such problems was the Selective Training and Service Act of 1940. This provided that persons leaving employment for military service had a right to be reemployed in their old jobs or in jobs that were similar in terms of seniority, status, and pay. In 1944 the famous GI

Bill of Rights was passed. It was formally entitled the Servicemen's Readjustment Act, and it provided that the veteran's adjustment to civilian status was to be facilitated through provisions for education and training; loans for the purchase of a home, a business, or a farm; special unemployment insurance payments; and a veterans' employment service. Memories of the depression and fears that the labor force could not easily absorb all the veterans that would be seeking jobs were undoubtedly major stimuli for the act. Its major purposes were to provide for the veterans' orderly entry into the labor force and, through educational opportunities, to delay the entry of some veterans. The federal government's expenditures for veterans' services and benefits reached a peak of $9.3 billion in 1950. This amount constituted 23 percent of the total federal expenditures. Such benefits are the indirect costs of war and defense, but they are usually listed in the welfare budget rather than in the defense budget. Thus they artificially inflate the welfare budget and result in further anger at what appear to be excessive welfare expenditures (Axinn and Levin, 1975, pp. 232–33).

✑§ Income maintenance—Social insurance

The progress in public assistance and social insurance in the years from 1940 to 1962 was disappointing. Unforeseen events affected the development of the programs in ways that could not have been predicted by the early planners. First came World War II, during which the need for income supports was buried by the general prosperity and the high level of employment. During the administration of Harry Truman the cold war kept levels of defense spending high. In addition, the Red Scare tended to make social programs suspect as un-American and to divide the groups that usually supported such programs. President Dwight D. Eisenhower, popular and conservative, was opposed to any strong federal welfare initiatives, and his administration fitted the tenor of the times, during which there was generally a continued prosperity. In general, the advances in the programs of these years came from the steady improvement in the

administrative methods by which the policies of the social welfare agencies were translated into programs. The expansion, and there were both new programs and some expansion of the old, largely came about through some legislative changes that broadened eligibility requirements or improved benefit levels.

By the 1960s things did not seem so good. There was a renewed and growing concern with unemployment. The minorities in the central cities seemed to share less and less in the general prosperity. President John F. Kennedy came to office with a pledge to get the nation moving again. If there were conscious goals for the social policy of the 1960s, they were to help the victims of poverty and racism to become a part of the general affluence of society. These goals expressed an inclination toward equality of opportunity for all people, toward developing support for a common life, as well as a renewed confidence in the ability of government to bring about social change. When Lyndon Johnson came to the presidency he gave a bolder leadership to the notion that it was now possible for Americans, through the use of government, to create a "great society."

Old-age and survivors insurance

The prosperity of the late 1940s and the 1950s reduced the general interest in social security. In addition, inflation eroded the benefits so that they no longer seemed adequate as a floor against insecurity. In an attempt to deal with the adequacy of benefits, both the wage base on which taxes were paid and the rate of taxes were increased several times.

Tax changes. The income subjected to social security taxes rose to $3,600 in 1951, and by 1967 it had been increased to $7,800. Over the same period of time the tax rate increased from 2 percent to 6.65 percent of the worker's wage. One half of the tax continued to be paid by the employer, and one half by the wage earner. The level of benefits was also raised steadily. In 1940 a single worker who retired after earning $300 per month (the maximum covered) drew $40 per month; in 1951, $80;

in 1955, $98.50; in 1959, $105; in 1966, $112; and in 1968, $127 (Wilcox, 1969, pp. 124–25).

Coverage. The coverage of the program was steadily increased. Amendments to the law eventually extended coverage to virtually all gainful employment—employers and employees; the self-employed, including professionals; and farm workers and farm operators. About nine tenths of all the employed, including those in the armed forces, were covered by the end of this period. The only major exceptions to coverage were federal government employees, who had their own retirement system; railroad employees, who had theirs; domestic and farm workers who were irregularly employed or who had earnings that did not meet the minimum requirements for coverage; and self-employed persons with less than $400 in annual net earnings. In addition, the employees of non profit organizations and of state and local governments were given the option of electing to participate. In 1950 the need to provide benefits for permanently and totally disabled workers was recognized, and benefits for such workers and their dependents were added to the system in 1950. In 1965 insurance of medical care for the elderly was added. This will be discussed more fully later in this section. The system now became OASDI-HI (Cohen, 1971, p. 1278).

Benefits. Coverage was increased. Benefits were established for survivors in case of the worker's death. Benefits were paid not only to workers who retired at age 65, but reduced-rate benefits could be paid to men and women as early as age 62 if they retired. Payments were also made for the retired worker's wife or dependent husband aged 65 or over (or reduced benefits were paid at 62); for the worker's children under age 18, or 18–21 for children who were full-time students; for a worker's child who became disabled before the age of 18; and for a wife of any age caring for a child under 18 who was entitled to benefits. Should an insured worker die, survivors benefits became payable upon the death of the worker to the widow at age 60, or at age 50 if she were disabled, or at any age if she had a child under 18 in her care; to the worker's children under the age of 18, or age 18–21 if they were in school, and to disabled children who were disabled before 18; to aged parents who were dependent; and to a surviving spouse at 62. A small lump-sum benefit was also paid at death (Cohen, 1971, p. 1278).

Although most people who discuss social security are concerned about the retirement benefits of the worker, the extension of benefits to the survivors of deceased workers has also made social security a very valuable form of insurance for young families.

All of the benefits paid under the program are related to the insured worker's monthly earnings. Until 1977 (as will be discussed in the next chapter), the average monthly wage of the worker was computed on the basis of all taxable wages credited to the worker's account since 1950, or since the worker was 21 years old if that date was later than 1950, after dropping out up to five years of the worker's lowest earnings. In 1971 the worker's monthly benefit amount ranged from a minimum of $70 to a maximum of $275. All benefits paid to wives, children, or survivors are percentages of the worker's primary benefit. The highest monthly family benefit in 1971 was $477. The monthly family payments of the disabled or retired worker were 50 percent of the primary benefit for the dependent spouse and for each other eligible dependent. Benefits equal to 82.5 percent of the deceased worker's entitlement were payable in 1971 to the dependent spouse at the age of 62. Payments amounting to 75 percent of the deceased worker's benefit, plus an equal amount for the children, may be made to the young widowed mother or the dependent father (Cohen, 1971, p. 1278).

Health insurance

As we discussed in Chapter 18, health insurance was a plank in the platform of the Progressive Party in 1912. It was kept out by opposition from a number of groups, including the AMA and labor unions. Bills to set up a health insurance system were introduced without success in every Congress from 1929 to 1945. Harry S. Truman strongly advocated health insurance in his 1948 presidential campaign.

A bill to require health insurance was introduced into Congress in 1949, but it failed to pass. During this period, health insurance was available to a growing number of people through the growth of private programs, as we shall discuss in the following section of this chapter. Those who supported health insurance therefore turned their attention to care for the aged. The aged seemed to present a special case in that their need for medical care was greater than that of other groups and they usually had less income with which to pay for such care (Wilcox, 1969, pp. 150–51).

In order to avoid the possibility of health insurance, those who opposed it now advocated meeting the health needs of the aged through a means-tested public assistance program. This program was advertised as being better than a limited insurance program because under it all *who needed* medical care could get all the medical care they needed. The meaning of the word *need* was seldom discussed as involving the application of a public assistance means test. However, an act providing for such a program passed Congress in 1960. Under this Kerr-Mills Act the federal government paid 50 to 80 percent of the cost of medical assistance given to aged persons who were on relief and to others who might be found by the states to be medically needy. By the end of 1964, 39 states had established such programs, 5 other states were in the process of establishing them, and 6 states had decided not to establish them. These programs are commonly known as medicaid programs. It was under such a program that Mr. Olds in Chapter 1 received help (Wilcox, 1969, pp. 150–51).

Not discouraged by the experience of his predecessors, every year of his presidency John F. Kennedy supported the introduction of a bill to provide for compulsory medical insurance for the aged. However, each year the bill was defeated. In the national campaign of 1964, such insurance became an active issue, with Lyndon Johnson favoring it and Barry Goldwater against it. Following Johnson's landslide victory, health insurance for those over 65 was finally enacted into law.

In every industrialized country save the United States, beginning with Germany in 1883, governments have taken some responsibility for financing medical care. The forms of medical care covered differ from country to country. All of the programs cover workers, and some cover dependents; the programs usually cover general practitioner care, some hospitalization, and essential drugs. Some of the programs include specialist and dental care and the cost of appliances. Such programs usually fall into one of these three types: (1) medical personnel are salaried by the government and render services directly to their patients through facilities owned and operated by the government; (2) medical services are provided by independent personnel who are then paid under contract with the government; and (3) medical care is paid for by the patient, who then applies to the government for a refund of the costs (Wilcox, 1969, pp. 150–51).

Attacks on health insurance. Compulsory health insurance has come under heavy attack from a number of interests in the United States. Many oppose it because they equate it with state socialism. Although socialist countries do have a form of government-organized and -controlled health care, there is a tremendous difference between such medical care and the proposed health insurance plans which do not change the organization of medical practice. They do not turn the physician into a government employee. There are other criticisms. One familiar argument is that health insurance destroys the traditional relationship between doctor and patient. This relationship is pictured as involving intimate knowledge and confidence that are necessary for accurate diagnosis and successful treatment. However, such a relationship has never existed for the majority of people, and today one of the most common complaints of patients involves the impersonal and perfunctory character of the service rendered by private practitioners who are uninvolved with the government. Another criticism is that under health insurance doctors will no longer do their best and will allow the quality of service to decline, as there will be no incentive to do their best. Such comments ignore the fact that all major advances in medicine have been made by personnel working within bureaucratic structures and not as private practitioners, that in

Great Britain only 3 percent of people using their system report dissatisfaction with the care, and that such statements would appear to constitute a libel on the medical profession, which certainly does not present itself as a profession engaged in only for monetary gain (Wilcox, 1969, pp. 148–49).

There are other reasons for concern. Medical personnel in our country are not distributed according to need. They are distributed according to economic factors. Under compulsory health insurance the government might attempt to set criteria for the distribution of medical care in accordance with need. Certainly, the experience we have had with our medical care would lead us to expect the profession and the government to differ concerning the amount of the doctor's fee and the manner of payment. Seeking to balance expenses, the government could well attempt to hold down the charges for health care. In the next chapter we will see how this problem has developed. Another problem is the concern that patients may overuse medical care if they do not pay for care privately and that doctors may prescribe a larger amount or a higher quality of medical care than is necessary. If patients paid for this, so the argument goes, the lack of ability to pay would limit the amount and the quality of the medical services consumed. This could be brought under control (and indeed we are now using such procedures) by having the doctor's diagnosis and treatment reviewed by a group of peers. Doctors have traditionally strongly resisted such peer review as they have traditionally held that such an interposition of a third party between them and their patients calls their judgment into question. This argument also raises another significant concern. What does it mean to the welfare of people if their access to quality medical care is limited by their ability to pay? Is this the way we would seek to limit the costs of good health in our country?

Compulsory hospital insurance. In discussing the 1964 effort to enact a medical insurance plan for the aged, Wilcox wrote:

> Two bills were introduced in Congress, one by the administration, and the other by the Republi-

cans. The administration bill made health insurance compulsory, financing benefits for aged persons who were under the federal insurance system by increasing the tax rates on wages and payrolls, and financing benefits for those not so covered by drawing on general revenues. The Republican bill made coverage voluntary, with the government matching contributions made by those who chose to be insured. The final act, popularly known as Medicare, was a compromise, embodying both approaches. It applied the administration plan to hospital insurance and the Republican plan to other medical benefits. This bifurcation is administratively awkward, but it facilitated the enactment of the law. The law also provided for further grants to states to support their programs of medical assistance to the indigent. (1969, p. 151)

The compulsory hospital insurance program as established in medicare covers all persons who are over 65 and are covered by OASDI or the Railroad Retirement System, and it is extended to another 2 million persons who are over 65 and not covered by social security. These benefits are financed by an increase in wage and payroll social security taxes which was set at 0.35 percent in 1966 and reached 1.45 percent in 1968 (Ball, 1978, p. 48). As originally established, the hospital part of the program paid for the following care:

- All services rendered during 60 days in a hospital except for the first $40 and all but $10 per day for another 30 days.

- All services rendered in a nursing home for 20 days following hospitalization and all but $5 per day for another 80 days.

- Up to 100 health visits by nurses in the year following release from the hospital.

- Four fifths of the cost of outpatient diagnostic tests.

Medical insurance. The benefits of medicare's voluntary medical insurance program were originally purchased by a payment of $3 per month by persons over 65 and matched by contributions from the general revenues of the government. Medicare is not a compulsory program. Those who are eligible and want to participate must enroll for its benefits and pay the necessary fees. Most people who are eligible for this program have enrolled in it. The enrollee must pay the first $50 of charges in each year. Following that, medicare pays 80 percent of the charges for the following services:

1. physicians' and surgeons' services.
2. up to 100 home health visits by nurses in a year not following hospitalization.
3. half of the costs of mental illness up to $250 per year.
4. a number of items, such as medical appliances and diagnostic tests.

In its administration, medicare does not deal directly with hospitals or physicians, but operates through intermediaries chosen by them. For this purpose, the hospitals in a region usually choose Blue Cross and the doctors usually choose Blue Shield. These agencies pay the hospitals, and the doctors are reimbursed by the government. Medicare pays each hospital the "reasonable" costs of the services it renders plus 2 percent. It is thus faced with the problem of determining what costs are reasonable. This problem, plus the fact that such criteria offer no inducement to cut the costs of hospitalization, has been a problem over the decade since the program was initiated. Increasingly, there has been concern with hospital charges and proposals and efforts to regulate them.

Doctors may use one of two methods of collecting their bills. They may collect 20 percent of a bill from the patient and 80 percent from the carrier, provided that the charges do not exceed the reasonable or customary fees in the area in which the doctor practices. Or they may collect the entire bill from the patient, who must then collect 80 percent from the insurance carrier. Regardless of what the doctor charges, the patient can only collect 80 percent of the usual and reasonable fees as scheduled. Under this method, doctors charge what they please and patients bear whatever costs are not reimbursed. This method is preferred by many doctors and supported by the AMA.

An evaluation of medicare. In discussing medicare, Robert Ball, who served as commissioner of social security from 1962 to 1973, points

out that while the most burdensome expense of hospital costs are now taken care of, the expenses of long-term care and the costs of prescription drugs furnished outside institutions are a very heavy burden for the elderly. His position is that the full costs of hospital care could be met by medicare at very small additional cost. However, he feels that the greatest problem with the coverage lies in the Supplemental Medical Insurance program. Under the plan in which the physician can charge the patient any amount he chooses, he estimates that most elderly persons are paying, not the 20 percent deductible provided, but 30 or 40 percent of the doctor's bill. He writes:

> This procedure should be changed so that Medicare, like Blue Shield, would have participating and nonparticipating physicians. Participating physicians would be paid directly by the plan in all cases. In return, a participating physician would agree to abide by the "reasonable charge" determination of the plan in all cases and would not be allowed to bill Medicare patients more than a coinsurance of 20 percent of the reasonable charge.
>
> Physician participation would be on an all-or-nothing basis. Those physicians who remained outside the plan—i.e., did not agree to accept the allowable charge of the plan as full payment in all cases—would not have the alternative, as they do today, to take bill assignments from some patients and get the advantage of direct payment from the government when bills are large or when dealing with low-income patients, and in other situations bill the patients directly and charge what they wish. (1978, p. 17)

Ball goes on to recommend an annual limit of possibly around $350 on the total amount that anyone would have to pay in deductibles and coinsurance under the plan. He also proposes that Supplementary Medical Insurance be combined with hospital insurance and that the combined protection be financed partly by a contribution from the employer and the employee during working years and partly by the government, so that the worker would not have to pay the physician coverage during retirement years as at present.

Private benefit plans

Before the depression, some employers had begun providing "industrial welfare" benefits for their employees. They saw this as good business practice. However, these plans had many problems, and with the depression most of them were dropped. During World War II, however, wages and prices were regulated. This was frustrating to the employer who had little bargaining power to attract scarce labor if he could not offer higher wages. At the same time, unions were in a position of strength but they could not strike for higher wages. The War Labor Board compromised by allowing non-wage, or "fringe," benefits but no increase in wages. In this situation industrial welfare came back with a new focus. Paid holidays and vacations, paid sick leave, severance pay, and overtime pay were no longer enough. There was a new interest in insurance. In 1946 Inland Steel challenged the right of labor to bargain for fringe benefits, holding that such benefits were part of its employee personnel policy. But in 1949 the Supreme Court decided that employers had a duty to negotiate with unions about employee plans.

It was estimated that at the beginning of 1969 private pension plans covered over 28 million employees or retirees, almost all of whom were also covered by OASDI. Benefits paid under private pension plans in 1968 totaled $4.8 billion. Besides bargaining for the usual retirement pensions, unions now bargain for an increasingly broad range of benefits, including special disability benefits, early retirement benefits, and payments for survivors. Perhaps the most important of these benefits have been the medical and hospital insurances (Cohen, 1971, pp. 1280–1281). The private insurance plans, while offering those covered an increased security, have, in a larger view, divided the members of society into three classes. At the top of the pyramid are those persons who receive the private employee benefits, which are highly selective in that they are job-, wage-, company-, and union-related. In the middle of the pyramid are the persons who receive social insurances and their benefits. These are job- and wage-related, so that,

though broad, they are still selective. At the bottom of the pyramid are the persons who are on public assistance programs. One of the things that needs to be recognized in evaluating private pension plans is that all members of society, not the companies, pay for them. They are a part of the price we pay for goods, and they are tax deductible under most conditions.

The people who designed the Social Security Act believed that social security and public assistance were alternative ways of maintaining income, and that social insurance was the preferred way. They thought that as social insurance expanded, the number of people depending on public assistance would gradually shrink. In the next section we shall examine what really happened in public assistance in the years from 1940 to 1967.

❧ Income maintenance—Public assistance

The passage of the income maintenance and child welfare titles of the Social Security Act had clearly established public programs in personal social services and income maintenance for those in need. Social workers were now faced with the challenge of properly administering the public programs. Believing strongly that all people deeply needed economic, social, and emotional security, the social work administrators at the federal level were concerned about the adequacy of the programs they administered, but there was no way that Jane Hoey and her staff at the Bureau of Public Assistance could dictate to state legislators about the adequacy of what was a state-controlled system. However, there were some things that could be done at the federal administrative level.

Levels of federal participation

First, Congress could make changes in the levels and conditions of federal participation. Federal administrators could support congressional action to increase the federal share of the costs of state programs under certain conditions. (From 1946 to

1962 Congress increased federal participation every even-numbered year except 1954, and in 1961.) They could then point out to the states that low grant levels and restrictive eligibility standards meant that they were losing matching federal funds while having to care for needy families out of their own general assistance funds. Such arguments were more productive with the states that already had higher levels of payments. For the states that gave little or no general assistance and had a very low tax base, the arguments might have little force. In fact, the federal grant-in-aid program had the effect of "giving to those that have," in that states with high standards of care of their poor expanded those standards to the federal ceiling, while states with low standards, and in which poor citizens had the greatest need, received the least in federal support and had the least to lose in failing to conform to federal standards. There were attempts to remedy this by developing the federal matching formula in such a way that there was some better equalization among the states.

Changes in coverage

Another way to raise the adequacy of the program was through incremental congressional changes that added new populations to the program or gave some new or increased benefits to those already receiving help. In 1950 the program was expanded to include children with parents who were unable to work because they were totally disabled. Also, in the AFDC program federal participation in the grants made to the caretakers of AFDC children was begun. Earlier, although there had been federal participation in the grants to the children, there had been none in the money budgeted for the maintenance of the person who cared for the children. In 1956 federal funding was added for states offering personal social services to welfare families as well as for the actual money payments and administration. In 1958 child welfare grants were extended to urban areas as well as rural counties. Increasing coverage and larger benefits in OASI helped remove some families from AFDC and OAA. Under the Kerr-Mills Bill, federal aid

for medical expenses of families receiving public assistance was begun.

Administrative efforts of the Bureau of Public Assistance

In order for states to get a federal grant, they had to present to the Bureau of Public Assistance all material related to conformance to the federal criteria. The social workers who were employed to make judgments as to the states' conformance with federal conditions were interested in evidences of community responsibility, of the giving of aid as a democratic right, and of the availability of social services in addition to money. They were not just concerned with an audit of how much money was allocated according to what rules of the Social Security Act. The requirements for the state plan were that the program be in operation throughout the state, that there be hearings in which clients could put forward complaints that they had not been fairly treated, that the payments be in money, and that the clients' use of the money be unrestricted. All of these requirements applied both to a state's regulations and to the way in which the state administered those regulations. The requirements could be monitored to attempt to eliminate prejudice toward particular persons, groups, or areas in a state. They could be used to eliminate extreme variations in administration or unusually restrictive county requirements.

Efficiency in administration at the state level was judged by the quality of state supervision of the program operations throughout the counties and by the quality of the staff, state and local, that were employed. As we have indicated earlier, the Bureau was particularly interested in seeing that staff not only were competent to administer money but were committed to meeting the needs of people as fully as possible and were capable of giving competent personal social services. In 1939, when the Social Security Administration established the criterion that the merit system was to be used in appointing staff, the Bureau was able to oversee job classification and appointment and promotion procedures. The Bureau, the American Public Welfare

Association, and the private social work agencies all joined together to encourage a professional social work approach both to the administration of the public assistance programs and to the interaction of staff with the clients of such programs. This approach helped to balance and perhaps to overcome the moralistic and punitive view of families that could not take care of themselves often found in the local communities and in politically appointed administrators. It helped to support those individual workers whose identification with social work put them in conflict with their administration and their community.

Local attacks on welfare clients

However, as these pressures to aid the poor were gaining momentum among professional social workers, workers in public welfare, and liberals, opposition to such aid was growing in other quarters. In the early 1950s the battle over the adequacy of aid to the poor began to warm up. During these years, roughly 2 million persons were unemployed and only 800,000 were on public assistance. However, other factors were assuming importance. The total expenditures for relief were rising, though they in no way kept pace with the actual rise in living costs. In addition, the nature of the people receiving public assistance was changing. The numbers on OAA were decreasing, and the families on AFDC were increasing. The Eisenhower administration's belief in local control resulted in the lessening of the Bureau's authority over state administrative policies. Punitive administrative policies aimed at removing recipients from the assistance rolls and at preventing new applications were given wide and approving publicity in newspapers and magazines, and thus spread from state to state. State residency requirements were strictly enforced, so that newcomers in a state were prevented from receiving assistance. This was aimed particularly at blacks who moved from the rural South to the urban North in search of jobs. There were drives to regularly publicize the names of welfare recipients. Entire case loads were closed, and people were required to apply all over again. The thought behind the

recommended publicity and forcing people to again prove eligibility was that "frauds and cheats" would thus be forced off welfare rolls. The fact that such persons would probably be more willing to undergo these tests than would the proud individuals for whom starvation for themselves and their families was less painful than such public humiliation was never considered. In North Carolina in 1959 legislation was introduced that would have made sterilization a condition for the continued eligibility of a woman who had had illegitimate children while on ADC (Hoshino, 1977, p. 1157).

Two other methods were used in closing relief rolls: the "suitable home provision" and the "man in the house" rule. The presence of a man, related or unrelated to the family, in the home was considered evidence that financial need did not exist. In many states, social workers were required to make midnight raids on the homes of AFDC mothers to determine whether there was a man in the home. Many social workers were fired when they refused to make such visits. In California, social workers sued on the basis that they could not be fired for refusing to participate in an unconstitutional invasion of privacy. A March 1967 decision of the Supreme Court of California effectively halted this practice.

The suitable home provision rested on the federal requirement that parents should maintain a suitable home for children receiving AFDC. In many states it was assumed that an unrelated man living in the home constituted evidence that the home was unsuitable. In other states it was decided that if the mother gave birth to a third illegitimate child the home that she maintained for her children was unsuitable. Thousands of children were denied aid on this basis. In the summer of 1960 Louisiana used this provision to close 6,218 cases involving 23,549 children. No effort was made to find other living arrangements or other support for these children. They were simply deprived of public assistance support because it was felt that their mother's home, in which they would continue to live, was unsuitable. This practice was finally halted in 1961 by an administrative ruling of Arthur Fleming, the secretary of health, education, and welfare. He ruled that cases could no longer be closed on the basis of unsuitable home findings unless other, suitable living arrangements could be made for the children (Hoshino, 1977, p. 1151).

Sources of growing need

Why were public assistance case loads growing despite high levels of prosperity and despite the increase in coverage and the rise in the benefit levels of social security? The answer is probably to be found in unforeseen demographic and economic changes and in a variety of defects in the basic plan for public assistance. These defects were rather clearly seen by the professional planners, but there was no way to deal with them because of entrenched political opposition. The attempts of the professional planners to handle these basic defects by incremental congressional action and by strong administrative leadership were inadequate.

Structural weaknesses in the economy. To assume that OASDI, no matter how complete the coverage, would eliminate the need for an adequate income assistance program overlooked the situation of millions of southern blacks "trapped in agrarian peonage, stranded populations in Appalachia and elsewhere," and populations adversely affected by large-scale changes in the industrial sphere and by "widespread patterns of discrimination in urban labor markets." Effectively meeting the needs of such populations would have required, at a minimum, "a system of wage supplementation for those confined to seasonal or low-wage jobs, and, at best, a comprehensive program of public training, public jobs, and equal employment opportunity" (Salamon, 1978, p. 82). The planners of the time knew well that by rejecting federally aided programs for the working poor, tying OASDI benefits to earnings, and scuttling a public employment program, Congress had assured that the working poor and the longtime unemployed would continue to suffer.

The slowness of the extension of coverage. Coverage in the insurance programs grew more slowly than had been visualized, and benefits re-

mained at a level which assured that even those covered would know considerable insecurity and would have to turn to public assistance programs for help. Not until 1961 was 90 percent of the potential population covered by OASDI, and not until 1977 did benefits approach even minimal adequacy. The growth of the unemployment compensation program was even slower. As of 1960, 34 percent of the nation's workers were not covered by this program.

The rise in the number of AFDC recipients. As readers will remember from the last chapter, it was the hope of planners that OAA and AFDC rolls would gradually decrease to nothing as people were covered by OASDI workers', dependents' and survivors' benefits. Although this trend had begun to be visible in the OAA program by the mid-1950s, quite the opposite happened in AFDC. The number of AFDC recipients rose sharply, from 0.9 million in 1950, to 1.7 million in 1955, and to 2.4 million in 1960. The new recipients were not mothers who turned to AFDC because of the death or the incapacity of their husbands but women who either had no husbands or were separated from them. The extent of change was striking. In 1940, 42 percent of the families on AFDC were on it because of the death or incapacity of the husband or the mother of the dependent children. By 1967 such cases had declined to 17.5 percent, while the proportion of cases attributable to the father's absence from the home for reasons of divorce, separation, illegitimacy, or desertion had increased to 74 percent. A basic change in the family patterns of the poor resulting from urbanization, the disappearance of low-skill jobs for the minorities migrating into urban areas, a rise in illegitimacy, and better welfare benefits and more flexibility in eligibility requirements all probably contributed to this growth (Salamon, 1978, pp. 82–84).

The AFDC program had provoked little serious discussion prior to the mid-1950s, but now whole sectors of society began to raise serious moral questions about the AFDC mother. Public opinion turned against the welfare mother and against the programs that supported her. Some of the factors that might have accounted for the change, such as that young minority males lacked the employment opportunities upon which a secure family life could have been built, or that the father's departure was required in order to be eligible for help, or that divorce and illegitimate births were rising among middle-class families, were ignored in the rush to blame the welfare mother. This movement significantly altered the traditional concept of who was deserving of public aid. Mothers alone were no longer "worthy widows"—they were immoral and undeserving, and furthermore, they were employable. In the 1960s the traditional moral outrage over the undeserving poor converged "with long-standing attitudes of racial biogotry to produce a highly volatile political brew" (Salamon, 1978, p. 84). Although a clear majority of the AFDC recipients were white (54 percent in 1961), the black recipients were far more visible in that they were highly concentrated in the central urban areas.

Problems of state discretion. In spite of the efforts of federal authorities, states increasingly found ways to limit their AFDC programs. The establishment of eligibility was made a complicated and lengthy process, and in many states the assistance provided was well below family needs.

Reforms of the 1960s

By the 1960s four other factors were added to those just discussed: (1) the massive in-migration of southern blacks to northern cities, combined with the out-migration of the middle class and industries, had trapped large numbers of the inner-city poor in poverty; (2) public assistance rolls were growing even more rapidly, increasing the anguish of hard-pressed taxpayers; (3) through the civil rights movement and a series of urban riots, the minority poor had spoken for themselves and their needs in a way that had shocked and alarmed the nation; and (4) a new national leadership had been elected on the pledge to get things moving again with a more active federal policy. Given the opposition of the legislative powers to any expansion of direct aid to "welfare" recipients, there appeared to be only two ways to make headway in aid to the poor: (1) by labeling any new proposals as ways

to reduce AFDC rolls and (2) by designing new in-kind benefit programs that would have emotional appeal to supporters. In-kind programs give the recipients concrete things or specified benefits, valued opportunities rather than cash (see Chapter 4). They appeal to those who do not believe that the poor can be trusted with cash, and they also appeal to those who provide the benefits and thus profit from changing the cash into specific benefits (Salamon, 1978, pp. 85–86). The rich mix of in-kind programs that were developed from 1961 to 1967 offered aid and opportunity in all areas of social welfare: housing, medical care, education, and so on. We will discuss these in the section of this chapter dealing with the Great Society. For now, we shall stay with our discussion of public assistance payments.

The federal government proposed three changes in the AFDC program: one allowing the states to add unemployed fathers to the AFDC program; another greatly increasing the federal participation in social services aimed at client rehabilitation; and a third providing for a system of work requirements, work incentives, and work training, supplemented by day-care services, for AFDC mothers. Each of these changes would add significant costs to the program, but the new costs were presented as investments that would reduce the assistance rolls over the long term.

Coverage to unemployed fathers. There was some concern that the AFDC program actually offered incentives that encouraged men who could not find stable employment at adequate wages to absent themselves from the home so that their families would be eligible for assistance. Responding to this argument, President Kennedy proposed in 1961 to extend aid to children who were dependent by virtue of the unemployment—not just the absence or incapacitation—of the primary breadwinner. Legislation embodying such a plan was passed as a temporary measure in 1961 and then extended for five years in 1962. However, certain restrictions were attached to the program in order to secure its passage. First, the program was to be wholly optional. No state had to adopt it in order to participate in the rest of the AFDC aid.

It is probably not surprising that only half of the states chose to adopt the program. In addition, certain restrictions on the program have kept it small. For example, any family whose breadwinner worked more than 100 hours in any month was abruptly dropped from the AFDC program (Salamon, 1978, pp. 86–87).

The services strategy. In May 1961, Abraham Ribicoff, President Kennedy's appointment as secretary of health, education, and welfare, appointed an Ad Hoc Committee on Public Welfare to study public assistance and to make recommendations for its future. The committee was made up of 25 social work leaders, mostly social workers. Three members of the committee were deans of schools of social work, and a fourth dean was appointed as a consultant to the committee. In September the Ad Hoc Committee released its report, which dealt with four basic recommendations: (1) adequate financial assistance to needy persons; (2) the efficient administration and improved organization of public welfare programs; (3) research into family breakdown and causes of dependence; and (4) the provision of rehabilitation services (personal social services) to public assistance families by professionally trained social workers (Axinn and Levin, 1975, p. 240).

On December 6, 1961, Secretary Ribicoff, in a memorandum to the commissioner of social security, set forth the changes to be recommended in the public assistance program: (1) the location of deserting fathers and the improved detection of fraud; (2) the development of rehabilitation services and a family-centered approach; (3) the development of a plan for statewide training of staff; and (4) changing the name of the Bureau of Public Assistance to the Bureau of Family Services. The report of the Ad Hoc Committee and the secretary's memorandum, among other things, formed the basis of President Kennedy's message to Congress on February 1, 1962. This message, the first ever delivered by an American president that dealt entirely with the subject of public welfare, had considerable influence on the Social Security Act's Public Welfare Amendments of 1962. On July 25, 1962, President Kennedy signed into law the Public Welfare Amendments of 1962, which came to be known as the Service Amendments because they encouraged the states to provide social services leading to self-care and self-support. The amendments brought about changes in all categories of public assistance and in the child welfare provisions of the Social Security Act. The Aid to Dependent Children program became the Aid and Services to Needy Families with Children program and was now known as AFDC.

The 1962 amendments required that a service plan be developed and applied for each child recipient in light of that child's individual situation. The plans could include the use of protective payments if the parents mismanaged the assistance grant, funds for day care for working parents, and the purchase of services for public assistance clients that were not provided by public welfare. Funds for the extension of public child welfare services to all political subdivisions of the separate states were authorized, and it was stipulated that services were to be provided, if possible, by trained staff.

> The 1962 amendments . . . introduced the services strategy in public assistance by making formal provisions for rehabilitative social services to former and potential, as well as current, recipients of assistance. Individualized social casework was assumed to be the principal service method and the formula of sixty assistance cases per worker was adopted. Other activities made eligible for federal financial participation were research, demonstration, and experimentation with services in public assistance. Thus the policy of tieing a program of social work and other personal social services to the administration of financial aid was enacted into federal legislation. Social services were clearly viewed as a means of combating poverty. (Hoshino, 1977, p. 1152)

> . . . Various forms and degrees of service had always been provided to public assistance recipients under the 50 percent federal matching of administrative costs. . . . These amendments authorized the federal government to pay 75 percent of the costs for specified social services and for the training of public assistance staff. (Hoshino, 1977, pp. 1151–52)

Many social work leaders were jubilant, perceiving the amendments as supporting social work efforts to strengthen family life. However, social workers overlooked two critical variables: (1) that the test for strengthening family life was the family's success in achieving financial independence and (2) that Congress had taken seriously the implied promise that social services would move recipients toward work and independence and that public welfare rolls would be reduced. When the rolls increased rapidly instead of declining, social services came under suspicion as a service of value to public assistance recipients.

The purpose of social work is to help people to achieve something they want, and one of the basic principles of social work practice is that help must be given to assist clients toward goals of their choosing. It is recognized that one must start with the problem as the client defines it and with the goals that he/she has. Accepting the imposed goal of getting people off welfare inevitably distorted the social work process in a way that almost assured failure in the helping process. The support of social workers for the Service Amendments came from three primary beliefs: (1) The professional social workers who were involved with shaping the public assistances believed in their profession and believed that social workers had skills capable of helping people to cope with life stresses, of which being without financial resources is one. (2) These social workers believed that such difficulties as delinquency, unemployment, and poverty may be in substantial part the outward manifestation of deep personal malajustment and in any case represent the inability of individuals to cope with the stresses that life presents to them, and they believed that social workers are able to help people to overcome personal maladjustments and to develop more effective coping mechanisms. (3) They believed that by providing a variety of social services offered by competent social workers, it would be possible to break the cycle of apathy and despair that traps people who are longtime assistance recipients in a culture of poverty.

These beliefs rested on several unspoken assumptions: (1) that it would be possible to offer public assistance clients competent social work services, (2) that it would be possible to secure the concrete resources and cooperation of the community toward the end of making available the aids that clients needed to assist them in coping better, (3) that the alleviation of stress and the development of adequate coping mechanisms could be accomplished within a relatively brief time, (4) that the goal of getting off welfare would be a primary goal of the public assistance clients, and (5) that the central core of helpful individual casework service for public assistance clients would be found in the roles of enabling, education, and therapy.

As was pointed out earlier, there were never enough social workers with the assessment ability and the practice skills to offer a competent level of service to people facing the stress that confronts many public assistance clients. The public assistance family's problems of coping may be caused by internal psychological maladjustments, but these problems are far more likely to be caused by a lack of immediate environmental supports and by long-range problems, both of which are beyond the ability of either the worker or the client to ameliorate. An example of an immediate environmental support is an available job that pays adequate wages. An example of a long-range problem that requires significant societal change if the client is to cope adequately with stress is discrimination and its operation in our society. Workers working with vulnerable client populations must have significant ability in making differential assessments as to whether what needs to be changed is the client or the environment or the interaction between the client and the environment, and they must also have great skill in the roles of advocate, broker, and mediator.

It was extremely naive to expect that communities which were persuaded to accept the Service Amendments as a way of getting immoral people off welfare would be willing to make available to social workers the needed types and amounts of concrete resources, under conditions usable by public assistance families. And without such resources it was beyond belief to expect that clients would develop better ways of coping with life stresses. The numbers of clients that workers were expected to work with and the amount of time that was allocated for such work also made effective service impossible. Thus the social service strategy did not produce the results that had been held forth for it. Without any real understanding of what adequate social services would involve, Congress was ready to move on to something else.

The work approach. In 1967, when Lyndon Johnson proposed a series of major amendments to the Social Security Act, conservatives grasped the initiative and passed legislation that would require adults in AFDC families to work or accept training. This legislation established the WIN program. Under this program, all parents in AFDC families were required to work, or accept training, unless they were incapacitated or needed in the home because of the illness of another family member. Local welfare agencies were to make arrangements with the local Labor Department affiliates to develop the necessary training programs. Funds were provided so that the local agencies could cover the costs of day care for the mothers in training. Work-related expenses were treated generously. Finally, the recipient who worked was allowed to deduct the first $30 earned plus one third of the remainder when computing income which would be subtracted from the amount of the grant. The requirement that parents in AFDC families be put to work "officially reclassified mothers of dependent children from the deserving category of the poor to the nondeserving category of the poor" (Salamon, 1978, p. 89).

The belief that large numbers of AFDC mothers could be put to work overlooked a number of critical facts: many of these parents already worked but did not earn enough to care for their children even at the minimum standards of AFDC; many others were not physically able to work; the costs of child care for many of these mothers canceled out the largest part of their earnings; and many, even when trained, could not find jobs.

In addition to the carrot and stick approach of rewarding AFDC parents who had been forced to work, a freeze was imposed—using 1967 as a base—on the number of children under 21 who could receive aid for parental absence from the home, except if the absence was caused by death. President Johnson and President Nixon delayed implementing this legislation, and it was repealed in 1969.

The in-kind approach. In the face of further congressional hostility to the AFDC program, the attempt to further the adequacy of the program through additional cash grants was given up and the attempt to offer more to recipients turned to the in-kind strategy. We have discussed this approach earlier. It had its roots in the 1930s, when the federal government had utilized two in-kind programs: surplus commodities and public housing (both of which were discussed in the last chapter). These programs were continued, and in the 1950s two other in-kind programs were developed: loans to college students and limited medical care benefits for public assistance recipients. In the 1960s, under Kennedy and Johnson, in-kind assistance programs grew with great rapidity: food stamps, interest subsidies for the construction of housing, preschool education, better medical care coverage, and so on. These will be discussed in the next section.

✑ The discovery of poverty

The efforts to deal with the AFDC program that we have outlined above define the problem of income maintenance as one of employability rather than of poverty per se. It was not until the 1960s that the United States rediscovered poverty as a social problem, and even then the problem was poorly understood. One factor in the discovery of poverty was the development by the Social Security Administration of a poverty index with which, for the first time, it was possible to measure the number of individuals in poverty. This measure, which has been widely criticized, is based on the estimated cost of an economy food budget for families of various sizes. It is assumed that if a family on the economy level spends one third of its income for food, multiplying the food budget by three gives the amount of money necessary to maintain the family at just above the poverty line. Over the years this measure has been refined to accommodate different sizes of households and to differentiate farm from nonfarm families. However, it remains a measure that places a family among the poverty population if it lacks the *real income* needed to enjoy some fixed minimum standard of living.

Some of the problems associated with the poverty index are generally identified as follows: it does not assess the impact of direct taxes on spendable income (a two-worker family may pay twice the social security taxes that are paid by a one-worker family with the same income); it omits consideration of in-kind benefits that a family may enjoy (such as employer-furnished medical care); it does not account for the benefit of government services received by families (such as education); it does not take into consideration the possession of wealth or other assets; and it does not take into consideration expected or long-run income (for example, students may be very poor for a number of years while they are accumulating the skills to earn a much higher income in the future). Even given these problems, with this index of poverty we can, in principle, determine the total number of poor families and identify their characteristics. However, merely counting the families below the poverty line does not distinguish degrees of poverty. If the average income of poor families amounts to 80 percent of the poverty line, that is very different than if it amounts to only 40 percent (Plotnick and Skidmore, 1975, pp. 32–41).

In addition to the studies of poverty that confronted the American people, other publications forced the problems of poverty on their attention with an insistency that could hardly be avoided. Michael Harrington's *The Other America: Poverty in the United States,* which was published in 1962, and Dwight Maconald's "Our Invisible Poor," published in 1963, were hard-hitting descriptions of poverty that, for a time, raised the consciousness of the American people. These considerations of the problem of poverty, especially the statistical count of the poor that was now possible, made the special risks of the minority populations very clear. The concerns of the civil rights movement, joined with this discovery of the rate of poverty

in minority groups, resulted in the inclusion of a prohibition of discrimination in employment in the Civil Rights Act of 1964. In addition, the establishment of the Employment Equal Opportunity Commission to enforce this provision of the act served notice that the provision was meant to have an impact on employment. It is interesting that Congress exempted itself from the provisions of this act.

In addition to concern about identifying individuals who were poor throughout our society, there was now concern about the fact that in certain areas of the country, such as Appalachia, everyone was poor. This concern led to the Area Redevelopment Act of 1961, which focused on problems of region-wide unemployment. This act was gradually expanded until the passage in 1965 of the Economic Development Act, which provided federal grants and loans to build industry in identified depressed areas.

Following the discovery of poverty, Americans discovered hunger. Hunger was a unique public issue, not only because it was newly recognized, but because at a time of prosperity it was an attack on Americans' notion of themselves and their country. The efforts to eliminate hunger have always been in-kind programs in which food rather than money to buy food was distributed. The problem of hunger and the battle over ways to eliminate it were to continue throughout the 1960s. Two primary issues kept the battle going: (1) the reports of waste and fraud in the food programs have caused the public to view them as simply one more instance of the misuse of welfare; and (2) since their beginning in the depression, the food programs of America have been created to help the American farmer maintain prices and get rid of surplus crops. The hungry poor have been the avenue of disposal. Although the anger of the American people around what they believe is wasteful administration of food programs has been focused on the Department of Health, Education, and Welfare, food programs have always been administered by the Department of Agriculture.

Since the beginning of the food programs, there have been four major programs, each managed by the Department of Agriculture to help the larger commercial farmer and shaped to respond to the regional biases of the congressmen who controlled the department's pursestrings and its legislation. The four major programs have been: the Commodity Distribution Program, which began during the depression and helped support farm prices by purchasing surplus crops that were then delivered to the poor through the county welfare agencies; the Food Stamp Program (used in 1939–43, discontinued, then authorized again in 1959 by President Eisenhower but never implemented by him, and finally put in operation by President Kennedy), which allows the poor to purchase stamps with a face value greater than the purchase price, and redeemable at face value for food at grocery stores; the National School Lunch Program, which gives the states money and commodities for nutritious lunches for schoolchildren, including free lunches for poor children; and the Special Milk Program, which subsidized the cost of an extra half pint of milk that was sold to children in school at reduced prices.

On his first day in office, President Kennedy doubled the commodity aid program. In his first month in office, he ordered that, under Eisenhower's unused 1959 authorization, a food stamp program be put into operation. In theory, the food stamp program seemed simple, workable, and a great improvement over the distribution of commodities. The eligible poor, as determined by the local county welfare department, were authorized to purchase a certain amount of food stamps each month. However, the administrative requirements of the program made it almost unusable for the neediest people. In the first place, the amount of money that a family had to pay was determined by its level of income and by the number of persons in the family, and each family had to buy the whole allotment of stamps. For many people, buying the whole allotment meant spending more than 50 percent of their income for the stamps, and they could not do this and have enough money left for other needs. In addition, the stamps had to be purchased on a monthly or semimonthly basis. Few families in poverty have a normal expenditure for food,

or budget for it as this required. Families in poverty simply purchase food with the funds that are left over after the most pressing bills are paid. Most of the eligible families were too poor to afford food stamps (Katz, 1969, pp. 169–180).

However, during the 1960s and 1970s the food stamp program has gradually increased coverage and raised benefit levels. The discontinuance of surplus commodities has contributed to the growth of the food stamp program to some extent. Administrative roadblocks have gradually been removed or altered. The food stamp program is no longer a voluntary program, but is now mandated in all counties in the nation. Although the program is available to all poor and is not limited to public assistance clients, the states administer the program through their public assistance agencies and share the costs of administration with the federal government. Over the years the food stamp program: (1) has stimulated the market for farm products; (2) has, despite its limitations, raised the nutritional level of low-income persons; and (3) has supplemented the income of persons in poverty (Weaver, 1977, pp. 1131–32).

✑§ The Great Society and the War on Poverty

While the years of the Kennedy and Johnson administrations may be considered the years of the Great Society, it was on June 26, 1964, that President Johnson declared a War on Poverty. The Economic Opportunity Act was passed on August 20, 1964. The title of the act was perhaps more accurate than the title Johnson gave his efforts. Underlying the promise to abolish poverty was an important shift in national policy: the efforts of the federal government were now to be directed not so much to increasing the income maintenance programs as to offering opportunities for the prevention of poverty. Thus, what was mounted was not so much a war on poverty, which might have called for an increase in money payments to those below the poverty line, as an economic opportunity offered the poor, by the provision of in-kind services, to join the mainstream of American life. The programs rested on the assumption that a combination of legislation to create jobs, opportunities for education, and other in-kind incentives could reduce the number of families living in poverty. Further, there was an acceptance of the notion that it was a governmental responsibility to provide such opportunities as an essential supplement to the marketplace economy. The programs that were mounted, though they were of immense help to many poor families and dramatically increased the federal, state, and local expenditures on social welfare programs, conformed to the basic principles of the 1930s (Morris, 1979, pp. 49–52).

Youth programs were developed to give minority young people and young people from low-income families the education, skills, and experiences deemed necessary for success. These included federally established Job Corps training centers for young people requiring both vocational education and help with social or physical difficulties in order to be employable, a work-training program that provided for the employment of young people still in school in various governmental and private, nonprofit service activities, and a work-study program enabling young people to continue their education in secondary schools, colleges, and universities. Special programs of employment and investment incentives were provided to combat poverty in rural areas not reached by the Area Redevelopment Act. Short-term training courses were set up to help parents of AFDC families find jobs. Volunteers in Service to America was created to establish a corps of adult volunteers who would help with the rehabilitation and improvement of slums and other impoverished areas.

But the provision of the act that got the most attention and generated the most controversy was the creation of Urban and Rural Community Action Programs by Title II. This provision of the act was based on the belief that people who lived in poverty and with discrimination were damaged and made apathetic by their lack of political and social power, by their lack of opportunities to participate in controlling their own lives and the community decisions that affected them. Community Action Programs (CAP) were locally developed programs,

operated by private, nonprofit or public community action organizations, that promised progress toward the elimination of poverty and provided for "the maximum feasible participation" of residents of poverty areas. This part of the OEO was very popular, as it was able to fund projects by either public or private agencies without requiring that the projects have the approval of either city hall or the united funds. The most popular of these programs were: Head Start (a preparatory educational program for preschool, low-income children), Upward Bound (an educational program designed to prevent school dropouts), day-care centers, and neighborhood recreational centers or health centers. These programs served several purposes. They were meant to compensate the children and youth involved for the failures of parental upbringing and the social effects of poverty and discrimination, they were seen as freeing parents from child care so that they could take jobs. Family unity was not furthered by providing parents with an active and decisive part in the operation of the programs.

The OEO very rapidly came under harsh attack. Mayors of cities could hardly be expected to welcome and support the funding of programs over which they had no control. Legal suits brought by government-funded legal services for the poor against discrimination and inequality in the operation of government programs angered members of Congress. The notion of "maximum feasible participation" supported the aggressiveness and hostility of the poor, and this tended to alarm and upset the citizens of the communities in which the programs were established. The War on Poverty was proving expensive—not only in economic costs, but in the political and social criticism and dissent it created. The race riots of the summer of 1967 could have been expected to bring renewed attention to the problems of minorities, but President Johnson was becoming both disenchanted with the War on Poverty, which did not seem to be achieving its goals, and increasingly involved with the problems of the Vietnam War. The OEO began to lose all political support.

The OEO and the War on Poverty made some

important contributions to change. It helped make the poor and members of minority groups more visible and more audible. It created jobs for educationally prepared minority people who might not have found such jobs open to them without the program. It greatly improved access to neighborhood-based health and legal clinics. Community legal services mounted under the Economic Opportunity Act had a tremendous impact on changes in the rights of the poor. The Welfare Rights Organization and other such groups became a force for change.

❧§ Summary

We have now come to the end of a long and complex chapter that traced the development of income maintenance through years of war and prosperity. This period was marked by rapid advances of federal involvement in social programs, especially income maintenance and social insurance. Although many advances were made during the period, in general the principles followed in developing and shaping social programs had been a part of American thinking since colonial times. These years resembled the Progressive era in their activity and in the rapid development of programs.

One interesting development was to have a critical impact on social work as a profession; the emphasis toward the middle 1960s on the participation of the poor, the discriminated against, and the citizens of the community in the development of programs to serve them. In some ways, this was a further expansion of the American belief in locality. In this instance, however, the emphasis was not on the smallest unit of government, but on the individual, often bypassing the local government units in the process. Initially, professionals were also suspect and open to the charges that

they had failed to understand and help the very people they were supposed to serve.

❧§ A look ahead

In the next chapter we shall deal with the development of personal social services during this time. Readers will need to remember that the developments traced in the next chapter were occurring at the same time as those detailed in this chapter. The social forces were the same.

❧§ Study questions

1. Find out from your public welfare agency the differences in eligibility for food stamps and AFDC.
2. Diagram or list the various programs that developed during this time within the public assistances.

❧§ Selected readings

Morris, Robert, ed. *Social Work Encyclopedia of 1971.* New York: National Association of Social Workers, 1971.

Students should be asked to get at least an overview of the topics covered in this book. Obviously in our account we cannot cover much that is of interest to individual students. In this book they can find some excellent material in most fields of interest to social workers.

Kotz, Nick. *Let Them Eat Promises.* New York: Prentice-Hall, 1969, or New York: Anchor Books, 1971.

An excellent discussion of the politics of poverty and hunger in America. It is recommended as required reading for every student.

Bremner, Robert. *Children and Youth in America.* Vol. 3. Cambridge, Mass.: Harvard University Press, 1974.

The earlier volumes of this work have already been recommended. This volume provides original documents covering the period discussed in this chapter.

U.S.D.A. Photograph by Jack Schneider

The theme of this chapter is illustrated by this scene from the Navajo Indian Reservation. These women are collecting food furnished through the USDA's Food and Nutrition Service Commodity Distribution Program. Certification for the program, and actual distribution of the supplies, are handled by the Navajo Tribal Council.

Chapter 22 🦢

🦢 Toward the Great Society: 🦢
The personal social services, 1940–1967

🦢 **Introduction**

During the years between 1940 and 1967 the size and importance of the personal social services grew, as did the profession that serves them—social work. However, an observer from outer space, looking at the situation, would have been hard-pressed to recognize the personal social services as a common system, given the way they were organized and the way they operated. First, these services could be classified as either public utilities or case services. *Public utilities* are services which are available at consumer initiative and to which certain consumers are considered to have a right because those consumers fall within certain groups: membership, age, residence, or some such status. Such services generally contribute to socialization or development or are needed by many people in the course of daily living. *Case services* on the other hand, are available after the applicant has met some criteria in a process of eligibility determination with a "gatekeeper" of some sort in order to establish need in some form. This process of establishing eligibility may involve a court adjudication, a medical review, a social study, or a psychiatric study (Kahn, 1973, pp. 69–88). These concepts may be compared with Wilensky and LeBeaux's concepts of residual and institutional programs, and Bell's discussion of universal and selective programs presented earlier. A personal social services system clearly requires both types of service. However, the classification is important to both the social worker and the consumer because the meaning of the service depends in part on the way in which access to the service is structured. Client-worker engagement will be a different process for a case service than for a public utility because of the differences that exist between being a client and being a member.

Confusion is caused by the fact that a similar program may be either a utility (for example, a day-care service available to all children and par-

463

ents in a particular neighborhood or to all employees of a particular industry) or a case service (for example, day care available to children from disorganized or abusive homes or to children who are showing certain behavior problems) (Kammerman and Kahn, 1976, p. 505). This confusion is compounded by the fact that similar types of service grew up and are continuing to develop under different auspices and different patterns of financial support: (1) public tax support and auspices, (2) private philanthropic support and auspices, (3) and industrial support and auspices. Social services supported by private philanthropic resources are often divided by religious affiliation. In addition to these divisions among what might be called the central social services (those organized as social service agencies dealing with individuals, families, and children), there are the much wider divisions found among the services lodged in the other systems of social welfare, such as health, corrections, and particularly income maintenance.

Another division of the personal social services is found in the differences between services that are community-based and services that are provided in institutions for the delinquent, the adult offender, and the mentally ill or retarded and other handicapped groups. When one considers this division in the abstract, it is easy to see that these community-based and institutional services are related because people come from the community into institutions and move back to the community from institutions. In addition, most of the people who receive personal social services in institutions are also served by community-based personal social services both before they enter the institution and after their discharge from it. However, developing policies to bridge this gap is frustrating indeed. And even more frustrating are the attempts to take actions to bridge the gaps with or on behalf of clients. The trend, especially in our next period (1968 to the present), has been toward a decreasing use of institutions. However, this trend has not been matched with an equal provision of the personal social services needed by the population that was served by institutions in the 1940s.

✺ Industrial services

A new development of the personal social services appeared during World War II. When people's patterns of life are badly disrupted by crisis, we find a greatly increased need of and call for the personal social services—that part of the social welfare system which addresses individual needs and institutional dysfunction. Thus, various systems of social services, such as the Red Cross, have come from the stress of war.

From World War II came the industrial personal social services, which as of the writing of this book are rapidly expanding. Industrial social services are those personal social services which are established and paid for either by an industry or by a union attached to that industry. During World War II a joint project was set up between a new personal social services organization, the United Seamen's Service, and a trade union, the National Maritime Union, to serve the seamen in the merchant marine. In March 1943, Bertha Capen Reynolds accepted the position of social worker charged with offering personal social services to members of the Seamen's Union. (Reynolds, 1951, pp. 1–10). This service lasted only four years, but it was the foundation for the establishment of personal social service programs under very different auspices than those of the earlier programs. In our next period, there was also a rapid trend toward the provision of social services through the private practice of social work, but given our definition of social welfare in Part I, we shall not discuss the private practice of social work as a part of the welfare social services.

✺ The auspices and support for the social services

One complication that plagued the development of the social services during this period and continues to plague us, was, and remains, the diversity of sponsors and funding. As we pointed out above, family and child welfare agencies, settlement houses, and community centers often had religious ties that persisted even though most or all of the financial support might come from funds raised by the community chest. These ties and ties to the political or economic power structure of a community influenced the chest's allocation of money and other community policies in relation to the operation of the personal social services.

During this period many of the private agencies began to serve people who could afford to pay fees for service. The question of fees for service became a very confused one for many agencies and for many social workers who still identified personal social services with the poor. However, agencies did begin to charge fees. The public utilities such as the community centers and the youth-serving agencies (for example, the YWCA) charged fees for "memberships." Once a utility's fee was paid, the "member" had a right to access to its services. The case services also gradually began to charge fees for services rendered. The family agencies and the mental health clinics usually charged a sliding fee based on ability to pay. People were charged for each interview. Adoption agencies might follow this practice, or they might charge a set fee per adoption. Thus, agencies within the personal social services system began to be supported to some extent by user fees as well as contributions.

Contributors to private social welfare organizations of all types, health and education as well as personal social services, were also changing during this time. Business corporations and labor unions became the new patrons of private philanthropy. Wealthy businessmen and their families had once been the primary support of philanthropy. Then the organization of the united fund or the community chest began to push for a wider dispersion of giving, and individuals of the middle class began giving through pledges at home or at work. Now, starting in the 1930s, corporate executives began giving from the corporate treasury rather than, or in addition to, their private funds. Legally this money was the property of the stockholders, not the executives, but the executives were able to show that such giving was in the interest of the business and the investors in that it would benefit

the community in which the company was located. The services paid for by a company's contributions were often utilized by its workers, and besides such giving was a sort of institutional advertising that improved the company's image. Legislation enacted in 1935 made corporate giving much more attractive in that it recognized the right of corporations to make philanthropic contributions from their profits and also allowed them to deduct up to 5 percent of their taxable income for such giving. Now much of the costs of private giving could be shifted to the general taxpayer, and the company could not only reap the benefits of being viewed as a generous member of the business community but could have considerable impact on the development of policies relating to private social welfare. A belief grew among influential businessmen that the professional managers and executives of business should exercise a sense of social responsibility. In addition, these enlightened executives saw a value in private philanthropy that paralleled the value of private business enterprise. Private was better, was more adaptable to local conditions, and was a good example of freedom and pluralism.

As the unions gained power and stability, their leaders were asked to support this or that service or cause. Union leaders found themselves invited to serve on various united fund committees and community boards. They could see that their members used many of the agencies supported by the community chest. In addition, many social welfare activities helped the working class as well as the poor and the minority groups. Moreover unions, like corporations, had a public relations problem. There was a widespread belief that they and their leaders were self-seeking and often corrupt. They, too, could benefit from the image of a responsible community citizen that was created by philanthropic giving.

With the support of corporations and unions, the community chests or united funds were able to collect an increasing amount of money to support private personal social services. Clearly the chest and the agencies it supported—largely the local private personal social service agencies—

were unlikely to offend their most generous givers (Leiby, 1978, pp. 277–79).

Increasing prosperity, increasing population, the great social and geographic mobility of the population, and the increased attention that public agencies gave to the use of personal social services all increased the demand for such services during the 1950s and had tremendous impact on the way in which the services developed. In fact, the increased demand for the personal social services by the middle class and the increased demand generated by the Service Amendments to the Social Security Act, which mandated services for the poor and the indigent, were the two forces that had perhaps the greatest impact on the personal social services during this time.

◄§ The growth of psychotherapy

Most immediately affected by the social, economic, and geographic mobility of the 1950s were the business and professional families who made up the middle class. These people were interested in health, education, and self-development as developed and offered in a scientific and professional climate. In the 1930s and before, social welfare was associated with the poor and the working classes and with protective labor legislation. After 1950, personal social services began to be linked most often to health and education. In the conservative climate of the postwar years it was the ideas of the middle class that would dominate the development and the provision of personal social services. In discussing this movement, Leiby writes:

> Part of the conservative climate was that they were so absorbed in their work, home, and families. They loved the suburbs, the communities of nice houses each on its own plot, the lawn and garden, the outdoor life, the shopping center, the fine new school and church. That was where they chose to raise their children. . . . [the appeal of suburban life] grew with affluence and among the broad overlapping class of prosperous skilled workers
> . and white-collar functionaries who moved into the developments and tracts that lined the freeways. Poor people could not afford these communities—

this was the attraction—and the residents were not directly involved with the traditional clientele of social work. (1978, p. 273)

Leiby then discusses the migration of rural people to the urban centers, pointing out that many of them blended into the white society quite well.

> Much more conspicuous were the blacks, and to a lesser extent the Mexican-Americans and Puerto Ricans, who filled up the cities as suburbanites moved out. They came, like other migrants, seeking opportunity and security. . . . Nevertheless they appeared disproportionately among the dependent, sick, mentally disordered, and delinquent. . . . They too were interested in education and health, but their first concern was access to service, rather than to its content or delivery (1978, p. 274).

> So while the logic of direct services pointed toward an expansion of local programs, and while an affluent society could afford to pay for such expansion, there was lacking a sense of community that would encompass the suburbs and the city, the upward mobile and the poor migrants. Nor was there a sense of political urgency that would dramatize the problems of disorganization amid affluence (1978, p. 274).

Given the situation discussed above, the development of personal social services within the voluntary organizations and the development of the social work profession took a turn that could hardly have been predicted earlier. Perhaps the development would not have proceeded as it did without two other forces that particularly affected the educated middle class. One was the rapid dissemination of psychological notions of human development that exaggerated the sense of individualism and personal responsibility which had always been a part of our society and introduced the notion that much of human behavior was irrational (stemming from early life experiences), putting tremendous emphasis on understanding oneself and meeting one's emotional needs. So the educated middle class became psychologically sophisticated, could speak about "anxiety" and "depression," and could, for the first time in our society, be candid and positive about individual needs for security and love. Parents began to feel a great need to understand the psychological aspects of the development of children and to learn about the skills of competent parenting. Middle-class people began to turn to personal social services, seeking a counseling service akin to psychotherapy through which they could understand the meaning behind their behavior in their intimate relationships. The idea of counseling or psychotherapy as the central activity of the personal social services, and the principal and most meaningful activity of professional social workers, took hold not just because it "fitted the inclinations of social workers but also and especially because it made sense to the people who sponsored and financed the agencies through which the private social services were delivered" (Leiby, 1978, p. 282).

The selectivity of the voluntary agency

This movement had a great impact on education for social work, which we shall discuss later, but it also had an overwhelming impact on the personal social services and on the kinds of help they offered. The private family agency, the clinics for children, and the community centers had always made up the central core of the personal social services. Being private, these agencies could be selective about their clientele. Clients whose problems did not fit the services offered were usually seen by these organizations as "untreatable." However, despite their rejection of the applications of untreatable clients, agencies did not have to be afraid that they were not meeting the needs of people for services. An increasing number of family service agencies and mental health clinics had waiting lists of clients that were weeks, if not months, long. Articles began to appear in the professional literature about the problems of "the waiting list."

Thus, as personal social services were defined in terms of psychotherapy (and professional education and professional practice focused on this type of activity) lower-class applicants found themselves unwelcome in the agencies that were central to the personal social services. Social workers were primarily prepared to offer "counseling." The needs and expectations of lower-class clients for material aid or direct advice were seen as inappropriate by most workers, and such clients were totally unprepared for using other types of service. Thus client and worker talked past each other, with neither understanding the other. As an example of what we are saying, a careful study of family service agencies in 1960 found that 9 percent of the applicants were upper class and 48 percent were middle class (Beck, 1962, pp. 26–31). Thus, as the demand for personal social services grew in the middle class and as the organizations through which these services were offered became increasingly interested in the "treatable" clients, who were generally better able to support and finance such services in the community, the paradox arose that those who needed help the most and who faced the most complex and difficult life problems were being ignored and that the personal social services as practiced in private agencies had lost contact with the needs of the most vulnerable groups in our population.

Public assistance and personal social services

Perhaps a part of this development was supported and made possible by the development of public assistance and social insurance. Although these did not reach all persons in need (black families and children in the South and migrants and minorities in the cities suffered terribly), and in any case they were hardly to be considered minimally adequate, they, along with movement to the suburbs, contributed to the forces that made the distressed poor invisible, even to the social workers.

However, there were still professionally educated social workers who took positions in the public services. These practitioners knew intimately the need for helping clients with information about and access to needed services and supports; the urgency and importance of assuring to a wide range of clients a basic level of social care and aid in functioning with some satisfaction in the community; the importance of developing and utilizing the already developed networks of mutual aid, self-help, and participatory activities; and the importance of integrating the varieties of personal social services, income maintenance, and other social welfare services so that they were usable by clients. Casework practice in public assistance, corrections, and institutions was more often likely to involve the performance of selected tasks related to the services listed above than to involve longtime therapeutic relationships with individuals.

In public assistance the worker was supposed to administer both the financial aspects and personal social services. In public hospitals and institutions the social worker was more likely to be involved in the admission, discharge, placement, and financial arrangements of patients, all of which are important aspects of social services, than to be involved in even brief psychotherapy with families and patients. In either case, the pressure on the worker in public social services was likely to be aimed at keeping people out of the systems involved than at engaging in the processes by which individuals in need of service were helped with their problems. Another problem in the public services, which is almost as great today as it was in the past, was that the direct provision of public personal social services was more likely to be provided by subprofessional personnel than by professional personnel. As we have pointed out earlier, personal social services began to be split into two groups according to the agencies through which the services were offered. Unfortunately, most of the literature of the profession was being produced by practitioners in private agencies.

It was into this confusing and disorganized picture that leaders in social work and in public welfare pushed for the establishment of special provision for and recognition of the personal social services as a part of the public assistance worker's job. No one was able to define satisfactorily what personal social services should consist of. There was no conceptualization of the services that should be included. But there was a promise to achieve a specified goal—to get people off welfare. In our earlier discussion of public assistance, we have examined the problems that this commitment brought to the personal social services. The individual worker fac-

ing the daily tasks of delivering social services seldom expects the impossible. But the farther one gets from direct service to the client, the more grandiose one's goals become. In their eagerness to further their profession and in their recognition of the difficulty involved in getting adequate services for the "multiproblem" client, social work leaders have often been free and easy in espousing unrealistic goals. But the place of goals in social work practice, the effect of these goals on the offering of personal social services, and the place of personal social services in public welfare were not critically examined at this point. Instead, there was only the argument as to whether social services belonged in public assistance.

The problem of overlap

The movement toward changing the Bureau of Public Assistance to the Bureau of Family Services and the accompanying emphasis on personal social services to families resulted in some question on the part of the private agencies about the differences between public personal social services and the personal social services offered to families by the private family agencies. Was there to be a further overlap in the functions of agencies?

The problem of overlap among various agencies offering personal social services and the lack of effective boundaries and patterns of coordination and integration were, of course, of concern to many communities at the level of the social planning and financing of services. Yet each agency defended its boundaries very strongly, and though much was written, little was done. In St. Paul, Minnesota, in the early 1950s there was a community decision to look at what was really involved in the community's use of social services. Eventually this effort was to stretch over ten years. It was later named the Family Centered Project, and we shall call it the FCP in our discussion.

✑ The Family Centered Project

The first stage of the project began in 1948, when Bradley Buell of the Community Research

Associates of New York, with the support and co-operation of Charles Birt, executive director of the Greater St. Paul Community Chest and Council, and A. A. Heckman, executive director of the Family Service Association of St. Paul, proposed a study that was to take stock of all the families served by all the social agencies, the health and welfare agencies, and the recreational agencies of the community during the month of November 1948. Isaac Hoffman, research director of the Wilder Foundation of St. Paul, assisted with the planning, the research, and the data analysis. Birt, Heckman, and Buell had had long experience in the community organization efforts of social agencies, and they were convinced that advancement in social services rested on social planning. Accurate planning was dependent on securing information that could be provided by a reporting system which could measure the extent and the manner in which community social services were utilized. Birt, Heckman, and Buell believed that such measurements could contribute to social service delivery planning, coordinating the efforts among social agencies through the sharing of information and providing some accountability regarding the effectiveness of the services provided.

The study involved the completion of about 58,000 case schedules by the health, welfare, and recreational agencies of the community, reflecting the use of these resources by some 44,000 families. A crucial aspect of the research plan was to focus on families (which might be better designated as households), which gave the title Family Unit Report Study (FURS) to this part of the project. The findings of this study could be summarized as follows: 40 percent of the community's families used public and private social services during the month of November, and 6,000 families, or about 6 percent of the community's families, were suffering from such a compounding of serious problems that they were absorbing well over half of the combined services of the community's agencies.

At Buell's suggestion a National Conference on Appraising Family Needs was held in St. Paul in September 1949. Twenty-five local social work leaders and 125 social work leaders from other parts of the country were invited. The purpose of the conference was to discuss the findings of FURS. Particular attention focused on the "multiagency" families. Buell, supported by Birt and Heckman, felt that it was important to centralize services in such a way that the central core of the family troubles of these families could be attacked in an orderly and coordinated way. The study supported the idea that fragmented services in the community were not helpful to these families.

The findings of the community case-load analysis were published in 1952 by Buell and Community Research Associates under the title *Community Planning for Human Services*. Actually, the book reported little of the research, but rather used the research as a foundation for the conclusions of the CRA staff. The book proposed that human pathology, as found in the "hard-core seriously disorganized families," be prevented and controlled through early identification and through the coordinated treatment of the family unit. Buell also believed that social breakdown could be measured best, not by professional judgments, but by counting the number of official disorders found in a family. Official disorders were defined as contacts with the community agencies set up to deal with family troubles, such as courts, welfare agencies, institutions, health care facilities, and private social agencies.

In July 1954, five St. Paul agencies—Family Service, Bureau of Catholic Charities, Jewish Family Service, Wilder Child Guidance Clinic, and the Ramsey County Welfare Department—signed agreements to participate in the Family Centered Project. These agencies were later joined by two more; School Social Workers and the Probation Office. Under the terms of the signed agreement, the agencies agreed to lend the Family Centered Project a certain number of caseworkers and supervisors for the duration of its operation. These caseworkers were to carry a case load of 20 project cases and to consult with the central staff of the project while remaining under the full jurisdiction of their own agencies, participating in their own staff meetings, and remaining subject to their own agencies' administrative policies and regulations.

The families selected for the project were selected as follows: one half of the families came from the cases in the 1948 study that were still active, and one half came from the Ramsey County Welfare Department's Division of Protective Services. Later, families were screened into the project by the central staff after they had been referred by a participating agency. The families selected had to have at least one child under 18 in clear and present danger, either through delinquency or verified neglect. In addition, the family had to have a behavior problem which had a negative impact on children, had to have a problem in either the health or economic area, and had to be considered unreachable by active agencies.

According to a study of 150 of the closed cases, conducted by Ludwig Geismar, director of research, and Beverly Ayres, his associate, families received an average of two years of treatment efforts and 65.3 percent of the families showed a positive change, 18.7 percent showed no change, and 16.0 percent showed a negative change. The typical pattern of change for each family was not one of spectacular improvement but of small gains in several areas of family life.

The work with families could be summarized as primarily involving immediate access to services that the families needed, a concern with the total family and its needs as a unit, social care services and support, and active attention to the integration of services so that they were usable and "made sense" to the family. In other words, the worker offered the families, as a unit, the total range of personal social services as they seemed to be needed and the worker served as an active advocate of the family and as an integrative agent. The worker was careful to identify with the family in the beginning of service the problems the family saw and the goals for their solution. Once the family and the worker had agreed on what the family's goals were, the worker was very active and often directive as to what had to be done to achieve them.

The last major step of the project called for an increasing effort in research, toward the development of a community reporting system based on a family unit count to provide current data as to types of problems, trends, and results in the field of social work in the community, and for a revision of the working agreement established in 1956 in the project among the several agencies whereby the family-centered worker was accepted as the coordinator of treatment.

Many professional community leaders developed a great deal of hostility to this last effort of the project. Agency executives were not happy about the notion of accountability and control of their offers of service. They did not like the idea of having the project treatment staff instruct their workers in treatment methods. The schedule that agency workers were asked to fill out ran 16 pages, and they perceived it as being imposed on them and as being totally irrelevant to their work with clients. The casework and research staff of the project had serious questions about the definition of "pathology" that was being utilized, and the treatment staff strongly resisted the idea that the major effort of agencies should go to those families that were rated on the schedule as being the least troubled and thus "treatable" (Compton, 1979, pp. 1–8).

Thus, the effort to organize one community's personal social services into an effective and efficient system, with a factor of accountability built into the plan, came to a rather disappointing end. The boundaries of the various organizations within which the personal social services are lodged may be quite vague, but they are nonetheless important to, and defended by, the managers and the practitioners in every organization. Even where, as in the Family Centered Project, the mood favors collaboration, it may be difficult to formulate decision rules which grow out of solid knowledge as to what works best. Yet for the most vulnerable of clients the stress of integrating the services needed becomes too much when that stress is added to these clients' other life stresses. In addition, few clients had the skill and knowledge to sort out and independently use a complex array of services. The social casework methods that were demonstrated as important in the delivery of social services were also argued about by the profession, but they did not filter into the actual work with clients or extend the efforts of agencies to effectively reach vulnerable people in any important way.

⋖§ The private family agency

Readers will remember that the movement of public assistance to the public agencies during the depression presented the private family agencies with the problem of what services they would now offer. However, as a result of the efforts of the middle class to obtain professional counseling, the private family agencies found a great demand for their services from a new population group. In the *Encyclopedia of Social Work* the purpose of the private family agency is identified as that of "providing casework and related services to families whose functioning is impaired by strains in their interpersonal interrelationships" (Beatt, 1971, p. 394). The problems that were the focus of the family agency tended to be marital conflict, disturbed parent-child relationships, and strains between family members of different generations. The services offered were identified as marriage counseling, parent-child counseling, individual personality counseling, homemaker service, counseling service to the aged, and counseling related to economic need and to mental health. Given these new services, the family agency might now be duplicating services that were available through the rapidly growing mental health clinics (Beatt, 1971, p. 394).

The national organization of family services changed its name in 1946 from the National Association for Organizing Charities to the Family Association of America. This organization had grown over the years into the chief standard-setting body in the field of family social work. Statistics from this body revealed that in 1968 342 family service agencies around the country served more than 488,000 families with 1.7 million members and employed 2,600 MSW workers. The national association, through a carefully constructed democratic process, served as a national spokesman on matters of social welfare and legislative policy, particularly as they related to families. The national association also offered its member agencies field service guid-ance, personnel assistance, educational programs, public relations materials, publications and research, and data recording centers.

⋖§ Child welfare services

The *Encyclopedia of Social Work* defines child welfare as "referring to a variety of measures on the national, state, and local levels designed to promote healthy development of children" (Fanshel, 1971, p. 99). As we have seen, throughout our history the welfare of children in all areas, including the social, emotional, and physical, has been viewed increasingly as a matter of concern to the general society and less and less as the exclusive burden of individual families. The *Encyclopedia* outlines the shape of child welfare services during the 1950s and 1960s as directed toward solving problems connected with dependence, neglect, delinquency, physical and mental handicaps, and emotional disturbances. We have seen in previous chapters how these services developed from the complete separation of children from their parents, to casework with parents to help them to maintain children in their own homes, to the provision of concrete resources that parents might use to supplement their own resources for the care of children, such as public assistance, day care, homemaker services. We have seen how adoption and foster care grew as services to the child. We have seen the increasing concern with the development of services that would protect children against physical abuse or the neglect of their welfare. The one important change in child welfare during this period was the growth of public child welfare services. Established as a program for rural children, these services were steadily expanded. Our aim in this chapter is to bring readers up to date on child welfare services in these various areas during the period with which we are concerned at present.

The scope of child welfare services

In early 1968 the state and local departments of public welfare were providing services to about 656,000 children, or 80 out of every 10,000 children in our country. About 50 percent of these children lived with either their parents or relatives; 33 percent were in foster family homes; 10 percent were in institutions; and 7 percent were in adoptive homes. At this time, voluntary child welfare agencies and institutions were serving a total of 219,000 children. Of these children, 27 percent were living with parents or relatives; 21 percent were in foster family homes; 1 percent were in group homes; 33 percent were in institutions; and 18 percent were in adoptive homes. Thus the total number of children served by both voluntary agencies and public agencies in 1968 was about 824,000.

We do not have comparable figures across the same time periods for all child welfare services, so we cannot give readers a complete picture. However, it is estimated that during 1967 about 50,000 children who were members of 13,500 families received homemaker service from public child welfare agencies. In addition, an unknown number of children were receiving such service through voluntary agencies. In March 1968, 438,000 children could be accommodated by licensed day-care centers and 97,000 could be accommodated in licensed day-care homes. State and local public welfare agencies spent $499.7 million for child welfare services in the fiscal year ending June 30, 1968, a 13 percent increase over 1967. Of this total, 55 percent ($275.6 million) came from state funds, 36 percent ($177.2 million) came from local funds, and 9 percent ($46.9 million) came from federal funds. More than 60 percent of the total ($313.4 million) represented payments for foster care. The costs for-day care services came to $14.7 million.

In February 1970, there were 5.6 million children in families that were receiving assistance from AFDC. This represented an increase of 900,000 over the figure for 1969.

About 30,200 social workers were employed in child welfare programs of state and local public welfare agencies in June 1968. These were divided about equally between voluntary agencies and public agencies. About 25 percent of the social workers in all child welfare services had completed an MSW, and about two thirds of these were in agencies accredited by the Child Welfare League of America (Fanshel, 1971, pp. 100–101). Two major national agencies furnished leadership in the field during these years: the Children's Bureau, a public agency that we have discussed at length; and the Child Welfare League of America, which serves the same purposes for voluntary children's agencies that the Family Service Association of America serves for voluntary family agencies.

In discussing child welfare services Fanshel points out that a major problem of these services arises from the fact that throughout the history of their development there has been a lack of integration of the services. Writing at the very end of this period, Fanshel identified some of the following trends in child welfare services:

1. Public services increasingly loom large as the major source of services to children.
2. Reliance is shifting from a single method of help (casework) to multiple methods of intervention, including group work and community organization and action forms of intervention as well as individualized social services.
3. Increased effort is being made to develop greater integration and coherence in service delivery. Computer-based information systems are becoming an important component in the administration of services.
4. There is special concern with past and present neglect of children of minority ethnic and racial groups and a reexamination of services that might be affected by institutional racism.
5. An increasingly strong commitment is being made to support the family as the base in which child welfare needs are met. Thus day care and improved income maintenance are being looked to as the first line of defense for families threatened with disability and breakup.
6. There are signs of movement away from heavy reliance on foster family care to increased use of small group homes for children who need such care. (1971, pp. 102–3)

Foster family care and adoptions

During the years that followed the depression, the methods of offering substitute care changed.

The use of foster care increased, and the institutionalization of children decreased. The number of children placed by voluntary agencies decreased, while the number placed by public agencies increased. It was generally agreed by those working in foster care that at the end of this period more children were coming into foster homes from disturbed and disorganized homes. Also, as might be expected, the children placed in foster homes were themselves more disturbed. Since these children were coming from more disturbed homes, at the end of this period children were tending to stay in foster care longer. A greater percentage of the children tended to live out their entire childhood in foster care once they entered the system. Also, the longer a child remained in foster care, the more likely the child was to remain there.

One of the needs that seems to have been greatly neglected throughout the history of child care, and remained neglected during this period, was the provision of services to the parents of the children who were placed. A survey conducted by the Child Welfare League of America in 1969 indicated that the three factors adversely affecting the quality of foster home service were: (1) the lack of adequate foster homes, (2) the lack of staff, and (3) inadequate financing of the service. Most people involved with the program felt that the system as organized was not meeting the needs of children. Readers will remember that initially free homes were recruited for children needing placement but that agencies very quickly moved to paying foster families for their care. However, the amount paid has always been extremely low, barely, if at all, covering the expenses assumed by the foster parents in caring for the child. Nationwide, the board rates in 1967 ranged from $25 to $150 a month. In some instances, families willing to accept children with special problems might be paid more.

The status of foster parents has always been ambiguous. Historically, there has always been confusion as to the differences between the roles of foster parents and natural parents and as to the professional role of the worker. In some cities and states, foster parents organized themselves into pressure groups, asking that they be recognized as agency employees, that there be explicit job descriptions of their work and of the responsibilities they assumed, that there be better training opportunities for foster parents, and that the pay for the job be more adequate. Foster parents were becoming more difficult to recruit, and once recruited, they were difficult to retain, the average foster home being active for two to six years.

Group homes for the care of children in foster placement developed rapidly in the 1960s. However, these homes cared for only about 1 percent of the foster children. Usually the children cared for in such homes are in the 12–16 age range, so that it is almost impossible to find individual foster homes for them. Group homes took two forms—foster families licensed to care for more than four children and agency-operated homes in which unrelated persons rather than foster parents were often hired as child care staff (Kadushin, 1971, pp. 103–111).

Adoptions. Readers will remember the early discussions of adoptions, in which the primary focus was on the legal relationship and the gradual development of a study of the adoptive home in order to offer some protection to the child being adopted. Increasingly adoption has grown as an acceptable way of providing parents for children rather than providing children for parents. In the ten-year period 1957–67 there was a continuous increase in adoptions, though the increase began to level off toward the end of the period. Thus adoption appeared to become a more and more acceptable way of completing a family. During this period voluntary agencies accounted for most agency placements but the number of placements made by public agencies increased steadily. An increasing number of the children placed for adoption had been born out of wedlock. From 1958 to 1968 the ratio between the number of applicants and the number of children declined steadily. For each 100 children, there were 158 applicants in 1958, and 104 applicants in 1967. There was a steady trend away from assessing and evaluating adoptive applicants to helping them qualify as adoptive parents (Kadushin, 1971, pp. 103–11).

Institutions and residential treatment centers

On any given day during the 1960s one could find approximately 306,000 children living in institutions: 23.0 percent of these children were there as neglected and dependent children; 33.1 percent were in some kind of correctional institution; 25.6 percent were in homes and schools for the mentally handicapped; 7.2 percent were in mental hospitals or residential treatment centers; and 9.3 percent were institutionalized because of physical disabilities. Although the actual number of children in institutions increased from 1964 to 1967, the rate of increase apparently slowed from 1965–1969. This was probably accounted for by the increase in alternative ways of caring for children, coupled with the greater understanding of the needs of children for family relationships, and by the growing federal legislation and funding that encouraged other ways of dealing with children's problems. Establishment and use of institutions for the care of children has always followed other societal changes.

The special institutions for children gave way to widespread use of adoption and foster homes. However, adoption or foster homes could not meet the special needs of certain children. From 1946 to 1967 the children's institutions that were developed were intended to serve emotionally disturbed, psychiatrically ill, and delinquent children. The development of these institutions reflected the growing concern of professionals for children who had special needs that could not be met on the basis of intuition and warm family relationships. In 1965, private sources supported almost all of the maternity homes, the residential treatment centers for disturbed children, the institutions for dependent and neglected children, and the homes for the mentally retarded. Public funds largely supported juvenile correctional institutions, hospitals for mentally retarded and physically handicapped children, and psychiatric inpatient facilities (Matushima, 1971, pp. 120–128).

Although we did not discuss maternity homes earlier, and although we have some reservations about labeling them as institutions for children, we need to point out that the first two decades of

the 20th century were marked by the establishment of maternity homes (as well as by an increase in specialized homes for dependent and neglected children). A brief look at the development of the Crittenton Association over the years will give readers a notion of how specialized services for children changed. On April 19, 1883, Charles N. Crittenton, grieving because of the loss of his own daughter, established a mission to aid prostitutes. Gradually this movement became national, and with more lenient attitudes toward illegitimacy, the institutions gradually became homes for unwed mothers. In 1950 the Florence Crittenton Homes were founded. By 1956, the association was providing casework services for unwed women and also serving as an adoption agency. Throughout the 1960s the association was moving away from residential treatment homes and into the community. In 1969 it decided to call its homes "services." The Booth homes for unwed mothers, supported by the Salvation Army, followed a somewhat similar pattern.

Day care

At the end of the 1960s (and today as well), the lack of good day-care facilities probably affected more children than did the aggregate of unmet needs for all other services for children. In 1965, 3.5 million children of working mothers were in urgent need of day-care services. Statistics did not exist then (nor do they today) concerning children who needed or could benefit from day-care services but whose mothers did not work. Although it has been recognized since before World War II that day-care services should be used as a preventive measure to reduce the frequency of foster home or institutional placement by intervening before problems get out of hand in families with children who are handicapped or emotionally ill, day care has developed very slowly.

We discussed earlier the need for day care during World War II. At that time the Lanham Act, as legislation to help communities meet war-related needs, provided the first federal funds for day care. Because of the constant conflict that surrounded the use of these funds for such services and because organized public support for day care was discontinued with the end of the war, one can hardly say that the act provided support for publicly funded day care.

Efforts to establish day-care facilities seem always to get involved with our conflict over woman's place in our national life. Questions that always come to the fore are: Should mothers work, and does day care intrude into family life in an inappropriate way? The gradual accumulation of evidence that children of working mothers develop and cope as well as children of nonworking mothers seldom gets a clear hearing. Probably no other issue of personal social services shows the impact of values and ideological positions more clearly than the debate over day care that has taken place since 1946. This debate clearly indicates the problem that professionals encounter in social welfare development. If people behave contrary to the general mores, the tendency of the public is to deny such people the services necessary to deal with the results of their behavior. The public sees establishing such services as possibly encouraging the undesired behavior. It is difficult to get acceptance for the fact that the behavior continues or even increases in the absence of services and that not having services to deal with the results of the behavior only increases the social problems that may stem from it. Thus many opponents of day care focus on the behavior and life choices of the mother rather than the needs of the children.

Day-care homes (privately arranged care of children in the caretaker's own home) are often better accepted by parents than day-care centers, but day-care homes are often more expensive for parents, as the parents usually pay for the full cost of care. A day-care home is cheaper for the community than a good day-care center, which requires a high ratio of professionally trained staff to children. Thus the problems of funding and the complexity of funding have slowed the development of day-care centers. As of 1968, some 61 different authorities provided some support for certain aspects of day-care services. For example, the department of Agriculture provided funding for food pro-

grams and the purchase of kitchen equipment, and the Department of Housing and Urban Development provided support through its Model Cities Program. Day care, today, is found under a confusing array of programs and arrangements: child development centers; Head Start programs; nursery schools; day nurseries; kindergartens; family day-care homes; before-school, after-school, and vacation programs; and other facilities for a full day's care. In addition, day care may be a service for infants, toddlers, and school-age children as well as for children aged three to five, the traditional age group served. There has also been confusion over whether the profession central to day care should be social work or education. In general, day-care centers with a focus on educational development, whose services are often offered for part of a day, have been used by families in which mothers do not work and have been staffed primarily by educators, whereas day-care centers for working parents have been seen as a province of social work (Lansburgh, 1971, pp. 114–20).

The homemaker service

The homemaker service grew rapidly during the 1950s and 1960s. The basic goal of the service is to restore or sustain functioning and to prevent or reverse individual or family deterioration when, for whatever reason, the person who ordinarily takes care of the family is unable to do so or when individuals need help in self-care. Under this program, qualified persons are employed, trained, and supervised by local agencies and sent into homes to take care of the daily tasks of family, or individual, living. There are many circumstances in which the homemaker service is invaluable: when a mother is ill and the father cannot both work and take care of the children; when an aging couple need some help with cooking, cleaning, and shopping if they are to remain in their own homes; when a mother neglects her children but is open to learning through a warm relationship combined with specific teaching through daily task performance.

Although voluntary funds were used for the first

homemaker programs and have continued to be utilized, federal funds became increasingly available during this period. The 1962 amendments to the Social Security Act made homemaker funds available to public assistance clients. This program has grown rapidly, but there have never been enough homemakers, or funds to support them, to meet the rapidly growing need.

Protective services

Earlier we discussed the beginning of the child protection movement in the United States, when the Society for the Prevention of Cruelty to Animals intervened in a situation of extreme abuse of a little girl. We further traced the development of a network of private agencies that operated to protect children. Gradually, over the years after 1942, the protection of children became the responsibility of child welfare services of the public welfare agencies at either the state or county level. The aim of children's protective services moved away from a focus on punishing the parents and removing the children to a focus on preserving the home for the child, if at all possible, through work with the parents. Social workers in protective services intervene in family situations in which parents have not been able to offer adequate care and protection to their children, and these workers attempt to correct such situations by providing direct help based on the individual needs of the parents involved.

During the 1960s several studies aroused public concern about child abuse. As a result of that concern and of efforts made by the U.S. Children's Bureau and other groups, all 50 states ultimately enacted legislation that provided for the mandatory reporting of suspected cases of child abuse to either the police or the welfare boards by various professionals who come in contact with children, such as teachers, social workers, doctors, and nurses. Although it is generally believed that child abuse is a problem of considerable magnitude, its real extent was not known in the 1960s and is not known today. Even mandatory reporting laws are relatively ineffective in bringing all cases to public attention.

Further, the reporting of cases is but one aspect of the total problem, since follow-up with social services is necessary if adequate protection is to be achieved. In the 1960s it became increasingly evident that abusing and neglecting parents were not predominantly in the low-income strata/low social strata of society. It also became evident that parents who abused or neglected their children could be helped through adequate social service treatment and that the removal of the child from the abusive parent was not always desirable. Since, during the 1960s, 50 percent of the children in foster care were there because of neglect by their parents, it was being asked why millions of dollars were spent on foster care for children but an equal amount was not spent on protective services and appropriate resources that could greatly reduce the number of children needing such placement.

✌§ Personal social services and other social welfare systems

Health

National health organizations. One of the most remarkable examples of voluntary action on a national level after the depression was the growth of national voluntary health organizations on the model of the National Foundation for Infantile Paralysis. President Roosevelt had begun this effort in 1934 in order to raise funds for a treatment center in Warm Springs, Georgia. Himself a polio victim, Roosevelt was deeply interested in the establishment of this center. This effort was successful, and soon the movement, separated from its personal association with the president, became the National Foundation for Infantile Paralysis and was supported by the March of Dimes, an annual event conducted with great publicity to raise money to defend children against polio. The foundation helped polio victims and their families, worked with health authorities to improve methods of preventing and treating the disease, engaged in the education of both lay and professional people, and funded research. The success of such an effort depended on: (1) a core of interested people with a strong commitment to the cause that usually came from personal experience with the disease or from activity in work with it, (2) an effective national leadership, (3) extensive publicity emphasizing the tragedy of the disease and its unpredictability in choosing its victims and, (4) a big annual fund drive and a broad program of service (Leiby, 1978, p. 275).

There had been earlier organizations of a somewhat similar character: the National Tuberculosis Association (1904), the American Cancer Society (1913), the National Society for Crippled Children (1921), the American Heart Association (1924), and the National Committee for Mental Hygiene (1909). Some of these organizations were revived by the new interest and the new methods. The National Committee for Mental Hygiene was reorganized as the National Association for Mental Health in 1953. Groups were also established to deal with the problems of retarded children (1953), multiple sclerosis (1946), arthritis and rheumatism (1948), and kidney disease (1950). Most of these associations utilized large numbers of middle-class women to solicit modest amounts of funds from their neighbors once a week. These drives were seen as threats by the united funds. In many communities there were attempts to get the health organizations to join the united fund, but without much success. Most of the health organizations could do better on their own, and besides they did not want to submit their fund-raising methods and costs to the discipline of the funds (Leiby, 1978, pp. 276–278).

The Public Health Service. We have already traced the battle for health insurance under *social insurance.* This section will discuss other federal actions in relation to health. Readers will remember our discussion of both the beginning of public health as the oldest federal welfare agency, with the establishment of marine hospitals for sailors, and the maternal and child health programs located in the Children's Bureau. Also attached to the bureau was a second program for crippled children. In 1935, under the Social Security Act, substantial grants-in-aid were made to the states to increase their public health services. The Public Health Ser-

vice and the Children's Bureau were transferred to the Federal Security Agency in 1939. They continued the small grants-in-aid program. During the period 1946–67 however, federal support of public health programs grew with great rapidity. By 1960 the greatest medical research facility in the world had been built at Bethesda, Maryland. It housed the National Institutes of Health (NIH), which had a budget of $430 million. The money went to research in Washington and to scientists in universities throughout the country. Under the NIH and the National Institute of Mental Health (NIMH), established in 1946, funds were also made available for traineeships and fellowships to build up the pool of scientific personnel. These fellowships and traineeships, particularly those given through the NIMH, were critically important in supporting students in graduate schools of social work throughout the country. Grants were usually awarded through reviews of groups of professionals or scientists in special fields (known as peer review groups) (Leiby, 1978, pp. 286–88).

An important health measure enacted under the pressure of war needs was the Emergency and Maternity and Infant Care Act, a national health care program operating under the Children's Bureau to protect the health of servicemen's wives during pregnancy and delivery and to protect the health of servicemen's children. The benefits provided by the program were available to the wives of servicemen at the enlisted grades. These benefits, which included hospital and emergency costs, were benefits in kind. Cash payments were not made to the beneficiaries. The program was the responsibility of the states, with the federal government sharing the costs and the Children's Bureau responsible for supervising the administration. As part of its supervision, the Children's Bureau was empowered to set limits to the fees that could be charged for specified procedures (Morris, 1978, pp. 79–80).

Hospital care. The hospital care of the poor in the major cities of the country was generally offered through tax-supported city hospitals. In Chapter 9 we discussed the founding of some of the early hospitals. Thus, from an early time in our history local governments in the urban areas were involved in the direct administration and delivery of health care. In some instances, extensive locally administered ambulatory outpatient clinics were operated by the city hospitals. Many of these hospitals were highly respected for the care they offered and as teaching facilities for doctors, nurses, social workers, and many other health personnel.

In 1946 Congress, concerned about making hospital facilities available in rural areas, passed the Hospital Survey and Construction Act, familiarly known as the Hill-Burton Act. Through the Public Health Service, the act offered to pay the states one third to two thirds of the cost of planning and expanding their health facilities. Private or public organizations were eligible for planning and construction grants. The act made no provision for funds to operate the facilities (Morris, 1978, p. 76).

The most interesting part of the Hill-Burton Act was its provision that a state agency had to establish need for additional hospitals in relation to the areas of the state and to consider what types of facilities were needed. Statewide and regional councils were established through which determinations of need could be made and priorities set. Neither proprietary nor nonprofit groups could raise their own funds and build where and when they wished. Over time this legislation was amended to include nursing homes, chronic disease facilities, and finally urban areas in which many of the older facilities badly needed replacement. The legislation had the desired effect in that by the mid-1970s the rural Southeast, which had been the most deprived region, was close to the national average in hospital beds. However, this growth in facilities did not result in redistributing physicians to needier areas, as had been hoped. Today the southern states still have the fewest physicians relative to population and the north-central states still have the largest number.

Health planning. In 1966 Congress passed a measure to provide for the utilization of federal funds to stimulate the development of health-planning agencies throughout the nation. This act is known as the Partnership of Health Act or the Comprehensive Health Planning and Public Health Services Amendments. The act required that hospitals receiving federal funds be involved with a state or local government planning agency called a comprehensive health-planning agency. These agencies were usually composed of various representatives of the health-care systems, local political leaders, and lay citizens. The rapid increase in the costs of hospital construction and in the facilities needed in hospitals caused the states to begin to use these agencies to set priorities and attempt some control over hospital costs. New hospitals could not be built without a certificate of need from such an agency (Morris, 1978, pp. 85–88).

Mental retardation and mental health

Mental retardation. In 1948 Albert Deutsch wrote *The Shame of the Cities,* a description of the overcrowded, understaffed, and dilapidated institutions for the mentally retarded at the end of World War II. Neglect of the mentally retarded stemmed both from the vast dimensions of the problem and from lack of knowledge. Other factors that contributed to the neglect of the retarded were the lack of financial rewards, the scarcity of personnel, and attitudes of fear and rejection that were rooted in superstitious beliefs about the retarded. In the 1950s the National Association for Retarded Children (now known as the National Association for Retarded Citizens) was formed. This was an organization of parents of retarded children whose purpose was to arouse public interest in the problems of the mentally retarded.

President Kennedy was especially interested in mental retardation and mental health. Some results of that interest will be discussed below. However, in 1962 a report of a panel established by President Kennedy, *A Proposed Program for National Action to Combat Mental Retardation,* brought the planning and financial resources of the federal government to focus on the problem more intensively than ever before. In 1963 the Department of Health, Education, and Welfare expended approximately $130 million for activities related to mental retardation. In 1969 the HEW appropriations act allotted almost $510 million for such activities. The activities were in the categories of preventive services, basic and supportive services, the training of personnel, research, the construction of residential facilities, and income maintenance. The emphasis was on strengthening maternity and infant care programs, especially for the care of prospective mothers in high-risk populations; establishing screening programs to uncover metabolic disease; extending health and welfare services to the mentally retarded; increasing the number of clinics and trained personnel; extending and strengthening rehabilitation services; increasing the comprehensiveness of health programs; constructing facilities; improving the quality of state institutions; and overcoming the acute shortage of personnel.

Mental health. During World War II, mentally ill patients suffered from the serious neglect of the state services responsible for their care. In 1946, however, Congress established the Department of Medicine and Surgery in the Veterans Administration. Its provision for mentally ill veterans offered care that set a new standard for the states. In 1946 Congress passed the National Mental Health Act, which not only established the National Institute of Mental Health, as discussed above, but also provided states with grants-in-aid to develop their mental health services, presumably up to VA standards. This act created problems for the states in that the difficulties of bringing the care of the mentally ill up to acceptable standards were almost overwhelming. In 1954 Alfred Stanton and Morris Schwartz published a study of mental hospitals which took the position that the organization and milieu of the traditional state hospital actually made patients worse.

In the midst of this very discouraging situation, there came a breakthrough of new knowledge and new technology. The tranquilizing drugs were introduced on a large scale in 1954. Suddenly, the whole approach to the care of the mentally ill changed. It became possible to discharge many of the persons in state hospitals and to greatly improve the lives of those who remained. A whole new prospect for the care of the mentally ill opened up. If the states could discharge most of their mental patients, they could not only save the costs of con-

structing huge institutions, but they could support persons who were unable to function because of mental illness through the public assistance program of Aid to the Permanently and Totally Disabled, and the federal government would pay about half of the maintenance costs. By 1957, despite an increase in first admissions, the populations of state mental institutions were being reduced.

In 1955 Congress established a Joint Commission on Mental Illness and Health. Its report, made in 1960, emphasized community care to keep, or get, people out of the big state hospitals. For many psychiatrists, however, community care as an auxiliary of medical and hospital treatment of the obviously sick was not enough. These psychiatrists held that the focus should be on primary prevention, which meant that the community practice of psychiatry ought to concern itself with housing, unemployment, and other sources of stress for people. This view came to be called "community psychiatry" to distinguish it from efforts focused on curing the illnesses of patients. Studies of the community services available to people revealed terrible gaps and inadequacies of resources in income maintenance, health education, corrections, and recreation.

After taking office, President Kennedy appointed a cabinet-level committee to consider the problem of mental health. On February 5, 1963, he sent a message to Congress with recommendations based on the report of the committee, the first such message ever sent to Congress by a president. In 1963 the Mental Retardation Facilities and Mental Health Centers Construction Act authorized funds to public or voluntary groups to build community mental health centers. This act was much like the Hill-Burton Act in requiring a plan and community involvement. It required that the centers offer comprehensive services, including working with the community around planning, education, and consultation. The AMA successfully opposed grants for staffing the community mental health centers until 1965. It was clear that a new model of mental health and illness was taking shape, with the community seen as the unit within which mental illness is treated and mental health is developed (Margolis and Favazza, 1971, pp. 773–82; Leiby, 1978, pp. 288–89 and 308–9).

Corrections

Beginning in about the 1930s and continuing throughout this period, many questions arose about the role of social workers in correctional settings. Questions were raised about the incongruity between social work values and the punitive stance taken by many correctional agencies. There were many theories about the causes of crime and delinquency and many theories about treatment. A general trend could perhaps be seen in the continued movement of prison administrations toward the notion of rehabilitation, not punishment, and in the increased use of probation and parole for adult offenders. In relation to juvenile offenders, questions were being asked about juvenile "status offenders" and about whether such children should be before the court at all. A status offender is a child who has violated laws that are directed specifically at children, such as absenting oneself from home (running away) or refusing to attend school. Such behavior would not be considered an offense in an adult. Other questions related to the definition of delinquency itself. There were many who pointed out that a juvenile delinquent was a person below the age of 18 who had been caught by the police, brought to court, and found to be a delinquent. At every stage of this process, there were children—often upper- and middle-class children—who escaped the net. There were those who were not caught, who were dismissed by the police, or who were dismissed by the court.

None of these questions were resolved during the 1950s and 1960s. However, there were interesting developments in the field of corrections, of which we shall discuss only one, Mobilization for Youth, which was carried out on the Lower East Side of New York City. The project was essentially a plan for reducing delinquency. It was an example of comprehensive community planning and cooperation among relevant agencies and resources. It was mounted under the auspices of the Henry Street Settlement, the Columbia University School of Social Work, the mayor's office, NIMH, the Ford Foundation, and other organizations. It was founded on the notion that many youths living in poverty or in the midst of discrimination and severe limitations of opportunity became delinquents because crime was the only avenue to success open to them. It aimed at providing such youths with opportunity, at helping them to build strengths, at challenging racism and poverty, and at using the powers of the youths. In essence, the project used the usual social work helping methods.

In 1961, at President Kennedy's urging, Congress passed the Juvenile Delinquency and Youth Offenses Control Act. The appropriations were small—$10 million a year for three years. However, the people responsible for the administration of the act wanted projects that were aimed at the social causes of delinquency. They felt that the persons working with delinquent youths did not understand the problems of poverty and discrimination faced by such youths. Their idea was to involve the poor and to provide them with opportunities to build a better life in the community. In some ways, this idea was close to notion that had been developed in Chicago in the 1930s which held that delinquency was caused by disorganized neighborhoods and aimed at developing a sense of integration and competence in the community. In the 1960s the work was to be focused more on involving neighborhood residents in the community as planners and as consumers. Thus, in delinquency prevention, as in the mental health movement, we see the notion of the community as the cause of the problem and the changing of the community as the cure.

Housing

The depression years had brought into sharp question the notion that decent housing for low-income families could be provided by private enterprise at a profit. As readers will remember, federally subsidized housing was initiated in 1937. In the late 1940s and early 1950s it became clear that public aid was needed for the middle-income homeowner because of the failure to build in sufficient quantity during the depression, the mobilization for World War II, and the war itself. This problem was made more critical by the large number of new families that had been created during the war.

The Federal Housing Act of 1949 aimed at providing a decent house and a suitable living environment for every American family. The basic guideline that shaped the act, however, was the notion that government should function in this area by providing stimulation and incentive to the private market through mortgage and construction guarantees. It was assumed that if mortgage guarantees for middle- and upper-income families were instituted, those guarantees would spur the building of new homes and the older homes would then be free for occupation by lower-income families.

Large concentrations of public housing were constructed for the poor. This experiment proved disastrous because the sterile, sanitary housing that was erected did not take into account the social and group relationships of the poor or the decayed neighborhoods outside the housing complexes and because it ignored in many ways the problems and needs of the people who would occupy the housing.

The failure of this experiment in public housing resulted in a new approach to urban renewal. We would just get rid of the slums by bulldozing them out of existence. This led to reducing the supply of low-income housing instead of increasing it. Not only was no replacement housing provided for the people who were displaced, but when they eventually found something, it inevitably cost more.

During these years, federal expenditures for housing increased dramatically. In 1966 the Model Cities Program was developed under the Demonstration Cities and Metropolitan Development Act as an attempt to rehabilitate whole neighborhoods. This program helps selected cities plan and administer comprehensive efforts to upgrade both the physical environment and the personal welfare of people in the slums. It utilizes grants and other assistance from other federal programs that are coordinated at the federal and local levels to focus on target neighborhoods. The act mandates that,

wherever possible, neighborhood groups be consulted in planning and be employed in the construction of new buildings and programs. The neighborhood groups are eligible to receive federal funds to hire their own architects and engineers.

In 1966 the various housing programs were consolidated into one federal agency, the Department of Housing and Urban Development (HUD). At that time the federal housing programs could be roughly clustered into four categories by objectives, as follows:

1. Urban renewal programs developed to halt the deterioration of the central city. Such programs were used mainly to tear down slums and to construct middle-class housing. There are accusations of attempting to improve the environment through removal of the poor and construction of expensive housing.
2. Mortgage guarantee programs for all income classes. These programs widely used to support the construction of housing in suburban areas and even the experimental construction of new cities. They have resulted in the dispersion of middle-class populations, but were never funded at a level to significantly increase the amount of housing available to the poor.
3. Programs to provide congregate housing units at low cost to the poor through publicly administered housing and later through various subsidy devices for builders (such as low interest rates, tax write-downs, and incentives in the acquisition of land). These programs were intended to reduce the ultimate rental or sale price paid by the consumer.
4. Limited programs for specially identified groups, especially the aged and the disabled.

Although the above programs were in some respects addressed to special groups (the poor and the elderly), the definition of policy objectives remained general: to improve the physical quarters of all persons living in substandard housing. The focus on the objective of physical housing ignored the actual social consequences of the programs: the conflicting claims of different economic groups on the distribution of income, the disruption of groups with more or less homogeneous economic-class conditions, the relocation of persons of different status to common neighborhoods in the inner city, and the segregation of populations by income class in suburban areas (Morris, 1978, pp. 102–3).

Education

In some ways, the system of education breached the old principles of social welfare programs more than did any other social welfare system. During this period, educational opportunities for vulnerable children became a critical focus of much legislation. Education became clearly a matter of national responsibility in matters of social relationships, if not in the details of the school structure or the school curriculum. On May 17, 1954, in *Brown v. Board of Education,* the Supreme Court ruled unanimously that school segregation was unconstitutional since "separate educational facilities are inherently unequal." By fifteen years later, a federal survey revealed that almost 80 percent of black youth were still attending segregated schools. In fact, there had been an increase in *de facto* segregation in the North. The Supreme Court decision brought the federal government into various efforts to enforce desegregation of the schools. The effect on national life was considerable, and the arguments about the control and financing of the schools heated up considerably. Questions about the rights of parents to control the education and socialization of their children again came to the fore.

Federal aid to education for the purpose of equalizing educational opportunities for disadvantaged students increased dramatically in the 1960s. Head Start, which we have mentioned earlier, was a part of this act, as was a work-study program to assist college students from low-income families. But perhaps the most important part of the act was an allocation of funds to local school districts based on the number of schoolchildren from low-income families and the average expenditure per school-age child.

✎ Summary

We have now completed tracing the development of the social services during the years following World War II, a period of conservativism in the development of income maintenance programs, and during the great upsurge that came in the Kennedy and Johnson years. The years of conservatism in the public services were an active time for the personal social services in the voluntary agencies. During those years the voluntary agencies became very active in offering "social services above the poverty line." This was the time when social work consolidated its competence in the offering of "therapy," a service aimed more at self-understanding than at problems of social deprivation.

The Great Society years and the participation of the poor had a critical impact on the personal social services and resulted in an increase in the outreach of the voluntary agencies, but there was no great change in the way those agencies offered services. This led organizations of clients to raise the question: "Is social work relevant?" and thus triggered some of the problems that we will discuss in the next chapter.

✎ A look ahead

In the next chapter—the last chapter in this part of the book—we shall deal with two processes of disenchantment. One is the disenchantment of many critics and of minorities with social work. That disenchantment began in the early 1960s and came to a head at the end of the Johnson administration. The other is the disenchantment with what was considered the failure of the Great Society to reach its objectives. Thus we had a disenchantment both with the public social programs and with the profession that was central to the personal social services.

✑§ Study questions

1. Diagram or list the various programs that developed during this time within the various systems in social welfare.
2. Use the *Social Work Yearbook* of 1949 and 1957 and the *Social Work Encyclopedia* of 1971 as the basis for a written discussion of the changes in the programs developed within a system other than income maintenance from 1949 to 1968 or 1969.

✑§ Selected readings

Reynolds, Bertha Capen. *Social Work and Social Living.* Reprinted. New York: National Association of Social Workers, 1975.

This book is short and reads easily. It gives students an excellent view of the social work practice of the 1950s. In addition, it is the first account of an expansion of personal social services into industrial settings.

Kahn, Alfred J. Issues in American Social Work. New York: Columbia University Press, 1959.

The various papers in this book give students a good view of some concerns of the personal social services during the conservative years.

Hollis, Florence. *Social Casework in the Fifties: Selected Articles, 1951–1960.* New York: Family Association of America, 1962.

This is another book that will give students a sample of the concerns of the social workers within the voluntary family agencies.

A social welfare program in action: Food Stamps have been used by thousands of people to increase their ability to purchase an adequate diet.

Our photos show the progression from buying Food Stamps at a local distribution center, to using them at the grocery check-out counter.

Chapter 23 ❦

❦ Disenchantment and social welfare, 1960–1979 ❦

❦ Introduction

In Chapter 21 we traced the dramatic acceleration during the 1960s of governmental efforts to ensure the basic economic well-being of all citizens and to open opportunities to the minorities and the poor. The Supreme Court (known then as the Warren Court) decisions made at that time supported this activism in a number of historic decisions. Although there were those who predicted that the attempt to create a Great Society would lead to disaster, most of the public believed with Johnson in the possibility of creating a just and secure society. He was elected to his first full term as president with the greatest plurality of votes in our history. But during the four years of Johnson's administration, things changed drastically. Johnson did not run for a second term, sensing, perhaps accurately, that he would be defeated by a suspicious, angry, and frustrated electorate. Nixon won a narrow victory with promises of a return to normalcy, control of the violence of the cities, a proper end to the Vietnam War, and a dismantling of the Great Society and its visions.

The conflict over the handling of the Vietnam War undermined the country's sense of integration, mutuality of purpose, and moral authority. The riots in the cities challenged the social order of society and came at a time when many citizens felt that they were making real sacrifices of their own interests in behalf of others. There was a sense of injustice and a lack of appreciation and understanding on both sides. On one side were those who thought that they had waited long enough—who felt that the Great Society had come too late and offered too little; who in distrust and anger maintained that its programs had only been developed to "cool out the mark" and control people; who were made even more impatient by those who pointed out that such societal changes took time. On the other side were those who looked at the ever-growing public assistance budget and saw the way of life that they had built at great personal sacrifice and self-discipline threatened by the violence in the cities and the growing tax rates. These people felt that the Great Society, whigh had never really been fully implemented, had failed utterly. Further they viewed this failure as proof that governmental programs never worked but only caused greater troubles across the land. They, too, were impatient with those who pointed out that social changes took time and sacrifice, that such goals were not achieved overnight. The booming economy of the 1960s both made possible the activism of youth and minorities and provided the resources for the expanded social welfare vision. But the resources needed for full implementation of the War on Poverty were used instead to fight a war that increasingly divided the American people. The conflicts over the Great Society programs were made worse by a downturn of the economy in the 1970s. The price of social supports for those in need became more and more onerous, and the opposition to such supports became ever more strident and powerful.

The position that many people took in relation to social welfare advances was, in part, a reaction to the student protests of the late 1960s and early 1970s. Many people who had themselves been unable to attend college, but who were conscious of the amount that they paid in taxes to support institutions of higher learning, felt that the young who were enjoying an opportunity they never had should be grateful to the society that supported such institutions. Also, these people viewed the university as an organization that should be involved in the socialization and training of youth for future jobs, and this led them to the expectation that it was the task of the university to control and discipline youth, not to participate in the search for verified knowledge when that led to criticism of the accepted social structure and the accepted way of doing things.

✑§ Student protest

Black student protest

Student protests were lumped together although the black student unrest was not identical with the white student unrest and should have been viewed separately. The black student movement represented the development of a heightened awareness and consciousness of black culture and black achievements that led to black pride and a sense of black unity. With this heightened awareness a new generation of young blacks began the pursuit of social justice, equity, and parity in American society. "In the movement for civil rights, one could say that the battle was fought largely in terms of being American citizens, but in the new and developing struggle for social justice it is regarded as being waged in terms of being human beings" (*The Report of the President's Commission on Campus Unrest,* 1970, as quoted in Bremner, 1974, p. 296). Few white Americans understood that the depth of alienation and bitterness among black students was based on personal experience with the operation of the system. Although there were black revolutionaries, many black students, instead of wanting to destroy the university, wanted to shape it so that it could provide the education that they saw as needed if they were to help their people. These black students saw higher education as the best avenue to their personal development. Thus the black student movement was not a generational conflict but a movement for full political and social equality.

Other student protest

The student protest movements that swept the university campuses began at Berkeley as a complex phenomenon consisting in part of a rebellion against university attempts to limit certain political expressions on campus. In the beginning that rebellion did not attack the great issues of discrimination and injustice but was directed against a liberal university administration. The University of California added its part to the explosion by calling in the police and engaging in repressive measures. The escalating war in Vietnam and the problems of civil liberties in the broader society, combined with student dissatisfaction with their experiences as students, pushed the radicals on campus to an increasingly political view of the university. In addition, the reactions of police and other forces of social control were so brutal and excessive that a growing number of students began to see themselves as victimized by the very society of which they were a part. This feeling was also focused on the university and was a part of the increasing demands that the universities should be transformed into political weapons in the struggle for a just society. Threats were made against university administrators and officials, and acts of terrorism resulted in the destruction of property and loss of life. Increasingly, the goals were not to make the universities more open intellectually and more neutral politically but to make them revolutionary political weapons. Outraged by the violence on campus, and frightened by its possible implications, the great majority of Americans came to believe that only the harshest measures would control the problem. There was a tendency to see the student rebellion as being caused by the failure of parents and public authorities to control the young and to view the growth of social welfare programs, especially AFDC, as a symbol of this lack of control, as a part of the "permissiveness and softness" of society.

The culture of self-involvement

Influenced by the student unrest, a new youth culture developed which expressed itself in a special art and music, the use of drugs, distinctive dress, and changes in the patterns of social relationships. There was an accent on authenticity and alienation. Youth movements have come and gone in the history of most countries, but "never in the past has one been taken so seriously. Never in the past has an older generation been so disconcerted by the onslaught of the young" (Laqueur, 1969, p. 41). The new psychological knowledge of the importance of parental actions to the development of the child led to feelings of guilt on the part of parents and a sense of uncertainty regarding their own value system.

This led to a conviction among the educated and the middle class about the importance of self-actualization and personal happiness. For the first time in the history of the world a significant number of parents felt that they owed their children happiness and self-actualization, and many of the young were only too eager to push the issue. As a result, many parents joined their children in the belief that the primary purpose in life was self-fulfillment. The notion of responsibility to and concern for others was resented as an intrusion on this narcissistic involvement. It became popular to be suspicious of benevolence as only a disguised attempt to control, because if benevolence and concern for others were really of value, then the complete immersion in self and one's own needs would become selfishness, not self-actualization. This movement to put one's own needs first and to be concerned first with oneself obviously stands in contradiction to the social reform efforts which demand a transfer of money from those who have to those who have not, which involve a higher tax rate upon those who have in the interests of social justice. All of these forces led in 1968 to the election of a president pledged to reduce the governmental commitment to social welfare. It was to be expected that both the great income maintenance programs and the profession of social work would be affected by these forces.

There are many aspects of the turbulent 1960s and the disenchanted 1970s that we could examine, but our space in this text is limited. Therefore, we are going to limit this chapter largely to two themes. One of the themes is of President Nixon's attempt to reform the welfare system. Nixon was elected on the statement that governmental programs for social welfare purposes had been total failures and that he would reform the system, and we can learn a great deal about social change by examining the fate of his program. The other theme is the impact of the movement to restrict welfare activities and of the riots and the anger of the blacks and the students on the profession of social work. We did not have space in the last chapter to discuss the development of the profession during the 1940s and 1950s. Therefore, we shall include some discussion of the profession during that period as well as a discussion of the problems of the profession during the 1960s and 1970s. We shall begin our account with a discussion of what was happening over these years in education for the profession.

✑§ Social work education

Readers will remember the discussions in Chapters 19 and 20 about the beginning of education for social work practice: (1) in 1919 the leaders of 15 schools of social work met and established an association to support social work education; (2) in 1927 this organization became the American Association of Schools of Social Work with the purpose of formulating and maintaining standards of education for all schools of social work; (3) by 1932 a minimum curriculum had been developed which required at least one year of professional education that included both classwork and field-work; (4) by 1935 the AASSW had ruled that it would accredit only schools which were a part of an institution of higher learning accredited by the Association of American Universities, forcing the older independent schools to move rapidly to affiliate with universities; and (5) in 1939 the AASSW, supported by a general consensus about the need for graduate-level work as a part of competent professional development, began to require a two-year program leading to an MSW as a condition of accreditation.

The founding of the CSWE

This decision by AASSW came largely from the older schools and the voluntary agencies, and it was far from unanimous. In fact, it generated the first formal split within social work education. In order to meet the tremendous demand for social work personnel in the public agencies, during the 1930s and 1940s some public universities developed a program that combined four years of undergraduate education with one year of graduate work for a master's degree in social work. As these programs did not meet the minimum accrediting standards developed by the AASSW, the schools offering the programs split from the AASSW and established their own organization, the National

Association of Schools of Social Administration (NASSA). The development of two sets of standards for an accredited degree in social work could hardly be tolerated, and in 1946 a National Council on Social Work Education brought together representatives of both groups to consider the situation. A study of social work education mounted by the National Council on Social Work Education, with the support of the Carnegie Corporation, led to a merger of the two groups as the Council on Social Work Education in July 1952. Since 1952, CSWE has been the major national organization responsible for the development of social work education and the sole accrediting body for schools of social work in the United States. In addition, CSWE is active in considering the developmental issues of social work education. It publishes monographs and the *Journal of Education for Social Work*. From 1952 until 1970, CSWE also served as the accrediting body for Canadian schools. But in 1970 the Canadian Association of Schools of Social Work developed an independent accreditation association.

The CSWE authority to accredit is recognized by the U.S. Office of Education and the Council on Postsecondary Accreditation, a national organization to which all postsecondary educational accrediting organizations belong. The accreditation process is made up of a variety of standards, policies, and criteria that are based on policies adopted by the House of Delegates of CSWE and approved by its board of directors. Both the House of Delegates and the board are elected by the individual faculty members who are members of the association. The criteria for accreditation are set forth in the *Manual of Accrediting Standards* and responsibility for accreditation is carried by the Commission on Accreditation, which is a semiautonomous body appointed by the president of the board. Social work education encompasses four levels of formal degree programs—associate, baccalaureate, master's, and doctoral—as well as programs of continuing education. As we have mentioned earlier, prior to 1952 the two-year MSW program required a curriculum based on the inclusion of eight subject areas plus field instruction under the supervision of a qualified professional. During the 1950s many schools began to experiment with combining the traditional methods courses of casework, group work, and community organization into one course designed to develop certain competences in the student for work across the usual "method" lines with all clients, from individuals to communities. The focus also moved away from teaching various courses related to a specific field of practice. In 1962 the CSWE curriculum policy statement reflected some of the changes by requiring work toward the MSW to include social work methods, human behavior and social environment, social welfare history and policy, research, and field instruction (Bernard, 1977, pp. 290–300).

The 1960s were a difficult time for social work education and for social work faculty, many of whom had worked for years against the racial and economic inequality in our society and the lack of planning in the use of resources to alleviate human problems. Many faculty found themselves in the difficult position of agreeing with the students and other faculty who clearly pointed out the immorality and irresponsibility of our society but of being deeply troubled by the courses of action that such students urged on them, courses of action which these faculty saw as immoral and irresponsible. It was a time when analysis and argumentation were replaced by unquestioning affirmation of slogans. The *Journal of Social Work Education for Social Work* more than any other journal reflected the "new militancy" (Specht, 1972, p. 5). In classrooms and other meetings, faculty who differed with the most extreme statements of the militants had to deal with personal confrontations, harassment, and intimidation that in the name of rights denied them theirs. Holding that social work had been ineffective in dealing with social problems, that work with individuals only led to adaptation to "the system" rather than change, many faculty and students made an attack on social casework as the cause of all the world's troubles. Many other faculty were faced with the unwelcomed choice between social action and concern for individuals—as though they were mutually exclusive activities (Perlman, 1967, pp. 22–25).

The attack on casework

The attack on social casework as an effective method of helping people reached a peak with the publication of *Girls at Vocational High: An Experiment in Social Work Intervention*. The book reported an evaluation of a special project offering social casework and group counseling to girls whose records at a New York high school indicated that they were "potential problem cases." The book was widely accepted and was frequently cited as demonstrating the ineffectuality of social work in one or more of its methods. The results of the study were irresponsibly generalized far beyond what the data would support. It is interesting to ask how so much could be proved to the satisfaction of so many by this one study. It sounded suspiciously as though many people had now found support for a bias that they had cherished all along. This publication was followed by a series of works questioning, in the name of "science," the effects of social casework. Most of these efforts simply demonstrated that the effectiveness of social work in general was poorly documented, that we had good scientific proof of neither effectiveness nor ineffectiveness. However, because of these critical publications coming from within the social work profession itself, a very significant force was added to those who wanted to cut the financial support for social welfare.

These publications contributed to attacks on social casework that were made by faculty and students of schools of social work. Although most of the students coming into the schools still stated their career goals as those of direct practice within the personal social services, the academic knowledge which had formed the base in developing the competences for such work was sharply cut in favor of new knowledge about social structure and organizational theory. Among the more thoughtful faculty there was a recognition that the social problems of society itself could not be most directly attacked through individualized approaches. Such faculty recognized that the failure to solve social problems by applying the established methods of social work in specific instances arose not so much from the supposed shortcomings of those methods as from the fact that the problems themselves required an additional and different form of attack. They also recognized that all students needed some acquaintance with the social factors underlying individual difficulties. At the same time, knowledge had been accumulating since World War II through social science research which emphasized the social factors in community systems that acted to sustain such social problems as delinquency and mental illness. Social work students, no matter what their practice goals, needed to be acquainted with this thinking. The problem that faculties faced in integrating this material was similar to the problem that they had faced earlier in integrating borrowed psychological knowledge.

All professions borrow from the basic sciences their basic knowledge of the phenomena that are their concern. The question is: How do the professions select, order, and use such knowledge in developing their own practice theories? Just as early social workers borrowed unwisely from psychological knowledge, they now often borrowed unwisely from social science knowledge, which, after all, offered no guidelines for using the knowledge in designing and carrying out effective programs of social change and development. Social science knowledge gave us new insights into the structural and process aspects of social systems. The differences between these two types of knowledge were not adequately considered. There was a tendency in the 1960s to borrow more from the structural aspects than from the process aspects that would have been more helpful to the tasks of social work. Structural theory, however, supported the trend of the times to displace all problems and evils onto "the system," "the structure," or the "power elite." Being able to identify a target to blame may help us feel knowledgeable and in control of the situation, but it does not help us in deciding what needs change, what to do, or how to do it. For that we need a different kind of knowledge. Specht, writing about this tendency at the time, said: "All of these constructs are useful when guided by a knowledge of their limitations and of individual behavior and complex social processes. But they are

dangerously misleading when used without the mechanism of self-correction. For then what is left is an ideology which says that there is nothing in us that must change, nothing we can learn" (Specht, 1971, p. 11).

Among the other forces that had to be dealt with by troubled faculties were the agencies charged with delivering personal social services. These agencies complained to the schools of social work that the new curriculum was resulting in less competent graduates to staff their programs. Students who were being more broadly educated came with less direct practice skill. Perhaps Perlman summed up the conflict and defined the importance of casework best when she wrote:

> The attackers of casework had—and have—a point; more than that, they have a just cause. Because of many good and bad reasons . . . the casework method for too many years had come to dominate social work and to be mistakenly equated with it. From nationwide governmental programs to two-person family agencies, there was an implicit belief that if only there were enough well-trained caseworkers, people in trouble would be enabled to cope with their problems. . . . As the spokesmen for social work, caseworkers had tacitly promised more than could be delivered by *any one* profession, whatever its nature and modes of operation. Those who attacked it, therefore, were attacking our sometimes naive and unwitting pretenses. They were calling for forms of social action based on reforms of social policy and programs, some of which were within social work's long-marked-out (but scarcely scratched) turf, and some of which called for social work alliances with popular and political as well as with other professional sources of power.
>
> It is a long-needed movement that is sweeping through social work now. With some growing sense of their direction and some lessening of their romanticism, the "social actionists"—whether they are community workers, social program planners and developers, consultants and stimulators or grass roots organizations, or government officials—are directing their energies now toward fighting the real enemy. The real enemy is not casework. It is social conditions that pollute social living, not only among the poor—although there

is where the social smog is thickest—but across total communities.

This I propose as our perspective in casework: that man is not only worth our belief and faith in him, that he is not only worth our best help when he is troubled, but that he is worth our curious and wondering study of the nature of his adaptability, aspirations, and experiences and opportunities that can enrich his daily life. With the accumulation of this further knowledge we may be able to propose more surely what men need by way of social provisions beyond the fill-in of deficits. . . . Even if it yields less than we hope, in at least one small corner of the modern world— the life-space of the social agency that focuses on individuals and families—there would be in process the effort to enhance rather than diminish man's image of himself.

I am reminded that on the empty space of the moon the astronauts, guided by scientists, bent down and laboriously picked up piece by piece of pebble, rock, and stone. "What's in them?" they asked. "When we examine their fine particles what might we understand further about the nature of the universe?" No one thought that trivial or useless. (1970, pp. 216 and 224)

The forces of the 1960s and the rapid expansion of governmental programs calling for management and planning skills resulted in the rapid development of a new social welfare curriculum built on development and social change. The curriculum designs of schools of social work tended to develop along lines of micro (direct service), mezzo (supervision, consultation, and staff development), and macro (agency administration, planning, analysis, and evaluation) specializations for the MSW.

Curriculum changes

Faced by all the conflict and confusion in social work education, CSWE issued a new curriculum policy statement, effective in 1969, which moved away from a standard prescription on how curricula should be organized and called upon schools to state a set of objectives and develop appropriate learning experiences that would lead to the

achievement of such goals. It was hoped that such a curriculum would have a greater flexibility in recognizing regional differences, variations in student backgrounds and experiences, the role of the oppressed, and changing social conditions. At the same time, greater flexibility always results in less security. Thus schools in the midst of conflict had less clear guidelines to curriculum development. In 1971 a new standard was adopted that called for special efforts to enrich programs by providing racial and cultural diversity in the student body, faculty, and staff. In 1973, when the requirement was added that curriculum content should reflect racial and cultural diversity, the 1971 standard became mandatory.

The BSW program

During the 1960s undergraduate programs in social work education grew rapidly, and this expansion was followed by a demand both for recognition of these new workers and for increased professional accountability in education. Members of the faculty of undergraduate departments of social work held membership in CSWE, and in 1962 the council prepared a guide suggesting content and learning experiences appropriate for undergraduate social work education. In 1970 NASW admitted baccalaureate-holders as members of the professional association, and in 1971 CSWE agreed to review all programs that had the objective of preparing students for practice and to issue a statement of "approved status" for schools that seemed to be meeting certain standards for undergraduate education.

As a result of the recognition of the BSW degree for public employment, instead of the more interdisciplinary BA, CSWE sought authority to accredit the BSW programs. This was granted, and in 1974 the council issued the current *Standards for the Accreditation of Baccalaureate Degree Programs in Social Work*. The accreditation of undergraduate programs is limited to programs that prepare students for practice. In addition to the required classroom experiences, students' academic programs must include at least 300 clock hours of educationally directed field instruction experience. When standards for approved status were being developed, in 1971, CSWE approved permitting advanced standing of up to one year for students holding baccalaureates from CSWE-approved programs when they sought the MSW. This standard has been continued. Most graduate programs give some recognition of BSW work by allowing some advanced credit. Schools differ as to how much is allowed.

Since 1950 doctoral education for social work has grown rapidly. Two types of doctoral programs are offered—the PhD and the DSW. Essentially the different titles reflect the way in which the programs were developed within the individual universities rather than differences in programs. The minimum length of time required to complete a doctoral program is usually considered to be two to three years. Some schools admit persons into the doctoral program directly from the MSW program, but other schools make two or three years of successful social work employment after the MSW degree a condition for admission. At present, it appears that schools of social work are asking increasingly that candidates for teaching positions present several years of social work employment as well as the doctorate. Almost all doctoral programs prepare candidates for teaching, research, and social policy analysis and planning. A few doctoral programs prepare candidates for advanced direct practice. Doctoral programs are not accredited by CSWE.

Levels of social work education

Our description of the development of the different levels of social work education has not dealt with some of the problems of the distinctions and orderly progress between the various levels of education. These are difficult questions that the profession itself, in cooperation with the schools of social work, needs to address. Although the general objectives of social work education—socializing to the value system of the profession, providing basic knowledge, and offering opportunities to develop skill in professional practice—are the accepted

overall objectives, where and when these objectives are met, and what objectives are appropriate at what level, has still not been determined. It is thus impossible as of the time of this writing to discuss with any clarity what the BSW practitioner will do that is different from what the MSW one does. If one were to make a generalization, one could perhaps say that the BSW workers are more likely to hold direct practice positions and that the MSW workers are preferred for the positions of supervisor and administrator as well as for positions requiring policy and planning skills. The difference between the function of the holder of the doctoral degree and the MSW worker is somewhat clearer. Universities increasingly seek persons with doctorates for teaching, and agencies are likely to look for such persons for research and planning positions. The basic question of what levels of education are appropriate for what positions is a question for the profession. It relates to the necessity for offering the client systems the competent service we promise.

✑ The social work profession

The social work profession and social work practitioners did not escape the challenge of the 1960s. The workers within the public welfare system were probably more visible, accountable, and vulnerable than the workers of any other system. On behalf of their clients, many of these workers had struggled for years with the oppression of local policies that they were unable to change. Many of these workers had also felt ignored by the professional social work community, including the schools of social work and the private agencies. Now they were also attacked by their clients, and they found little support within the profession.

In addition, the profession found itself under attack on the ground that professionalism was constricting to many people of good intent. The idea was promoted that clients were competent to help themselves and one another and that the knowledge of the professional was not relevant to the life of the urban poor. Various rationales were advanced for using nonprofessional personnel in both direct services and community change programs. There was a broad and uncritical acceptance of the notion that the individual human being was uncompromisingly good, that only the structures individuals created were bad. Thus there was strong support of the notion that helping took only openness and honesty, not competence gained from knowledge and skill. The notion that a professional person should be limited by the function of the profession was strongly questioned. As a result, there was a fragmentation of professional practice that is still an issue.

During this period there was a growing separation between the direct service practitioners and the social workers who were involved in planning and policy. This division was not new in social work, as Porter Lee's 1929 paper pointed out (this was discussed in Chapter 19). In that paper he had written: "An outstanding problem of social work at the present time is that of developing its service as a function of well-organized community life without sacrificing its capacity to inspire in men enthusiasm for a cause" (Lee, 1937, p. 5). The relative importance of cause and function in social work has a great deal to do with the national climate and what it will support in the way of reform. In the 1920s the national crisis of depression followed the great reform movements in which many reforms had been shaped into programs calling for direct practitioners. Then came years of prosperity and self-satisfaction, and the direct practice of social work grew and blossomed, especially above the poverty line. This was followed by the vision of the Great Society, when the reformers again arose to challenge the profession and force it to rethink its direction. During the period from 1930 to 1960, change and development were always a part of the profession. There were always important members of the profession who played prominent roles in developing the social welfare system, and the broader reform and environmental approach was never without its advocates.

Now, at the end of the 1970s, there is a renewed push toward clinical practice. This movement will be discussed as one of the issues of the future in the last part of the text. For now, we need to examine the profession as it developed in an era of disenchantment.

The National Association of Social Workers (NASW)

Readers of earlier chapters will remember our discussion of the beginning of various membership organizations among social workers. By 1955 there were seven separate groups of considerable strength: the Association for the Study of Community Organization, American Association of Group Workers, American Association of Medical Social Workers, American Association of Psychiatric Social Workers, American Association of Social Workers, National Association of School Social Workers, and Social Work Research Group. The largest and strongest of these was the general membership association (AASW), whose founding we discussed in Chapter 19. There were some significant differences between AASW and the other organizations. The other organizations concerned themselves with the development of practice skills in relation to the various "fields of practice" that they represented, whereas AASW concerned itself with social policy, the legal regulation of social work, personnel practices, and public relations. It was not easy to bring all of these groups together. Seven years of study and negotiation were required.

Eventually, each of the older organizations was given a staff member and a budget and recognition as a "section" within the larger association. The programs of these sections were only loosely connected with the ongoing business of the association, as they continued to focus on the development of practice methods of casework, group work, and community organization (client welfare) as found within their fields of practice, while the larger association concentrated on issues relating to the welfare of the social worker rather than the client. Over the years since 1955, there have been at least two major reorganizations of the NASW structure. Each reorganization has moved toward the

dissolution of special interest groups and the bringing of all social workers into one large national
group. This objective was furthered when CSWE
ceased to accredit specialties within social work
education and took the position that the MSW degree represented social work practice and not a
special kind of practice. From the perspective of
the individual practitioner and of the teacher of
practice, however, there needs to be more emphasis on defining the common elements of all social
work practice, with a complementary effort to define the way in which those elements are utilized
and differences are developed within the particular
settings. From 1955 to 1961, NASW built membership and support within the profession by appealing
to the practitioner's need for status and better salaries. Today the NASW program deals primarily with
economic and status needs of professionals through
concern with defining the levels of social work
practice, through consideration of policy and social
change, and through the advancement of direct
practice skills (casework, group work, and community organization) (Beck, 1977, pp. 1084–93).

Professional standards

When NASW was founded it established the
possession of an MSW from an accredited school
of social work as a membership requirement. This
was considered a major step forward. However,
as we have discussed earlier, the problem of determining who is a social worker has never been
within the control of the professional organization.
The Bureau of the Census lists over 80 job titles,
from adoption worker to welfare visitor, under its
"social worker" job classification. In an effort to
regulate the practice of social work, NASW has
engaged actively in supporting moves toward the
licensing of social workers. The model licensing
statutes proposed by NASW provide that licensed
practitioners must present certain educational credentials and pass examinations to test practice
competence. (see Chapters 7 and 8).

In 1970, NASW took a step that had probably
never before been taken by a professional association when it actually lowered its membership stan-

dards to include persons holding a bachelor's degree with a CSWE-approved social work major and
to provide associate membership for persons with
any bachelor's degree who were employed in a
social agency. This development might be considered a result of some of the forces of the 1960s.
At this time, social welfare and social work were
stressing such themes as participation of the poor
in the antipoverty programs, the value of using indigenous personnel in providing services, the limitations of professionals in helping lower-class
clients, the wide use of nonprofessionals, and the
increased employment of persons trained in other
social science disciplines in the new government
programs. Critics inside and outside the profession
were challenging the notion of the professional social worker and the competence that such a worker
exhibited. One response was to change the definition of eligibility for NASW membership, and by
such action to change the definition of the professional social worker. Later, NASW defined six different levels of social work personnel and the functions appropriate to each level (see Chapter 8).

At present, in addition to persons with a master's
or a doctor's degree in social work, three categories
of originally excluded persons are now admitted
to regular NASW memberships: (1) BSW degree
holders, (2) full-time students in accredited graduate schools of social work, and (3) persons with
doctoral degrees in fields related to social work
and demonstrated competence in social work research. Persons who are employed in social work
positions but hold a baccalaureate degree other
than the BSW are admitted to associate membership.

In 1961 NASW formed a separate corporation
known as the Academy of Certified Social Workers
(ACSW). Membership in the academy was open
to all social workers who possessed an MSW, were
members in good standing of NASW, and had been
supervised by an ACSW member for two years.
ACSW members were issued a certificate attesting
to their membership and were allowed the exclusive use of the letters ACSW after their name. In
the early 1970s, the separate corporation was abolished; a stringent examination was added, with the

provision that the candidate for membership was eligible to take it after the two years of qualifying practice; and NASW itself became the certifying agent. Today, the use of ACSW after one's name indicates that a person is an NASW member, has an MSW, has had two years of ACSW supervision after the MSW, and has passed a national examination.

As of September 1976, 19 states and the Commonwealth of Puerto Rico had some type of legal regulation of social work practice. Such laws can be viewed as being both in the interests of the consumers of professional services and in the economic and status interests of the professional. In NASW there seems to be particular controversy over the legal regulation of social work practice because many minority groups and many persons involved in social change see it as an infringement of the individual rights of those who would engage in activities labeled social work, while those who are more concerned with direct practice in the personal social services support it.

Besides its work to define social work and determine who should practice in the name of the profession, NASW has been interested in raising the economic position of the profession. From time to time the organization sets minimum starting salaries for social workers at different levels of practice competence. In 1974 NASW recommended that salaries for BSW workers should start at $10,000 and that salaries for MSW workers should start at $12,500. In addition to being interested in the pay levels of salaried workers, NASW has been interested in the economic needs of private practitioners. Since 1972 NASW has been successful in getting some major insurance companies to accept NASW members who met certain standards as eligible for reimbursement under the medicare program (Beck, 1977, pp. 1090–92).

Social policy

The NASW staff includes persons with skills in social planning and policy implementation whose major responsibility is to influence legislation and administration to implement policies that have been approved by the Delegate Assembly. The Delegate Assembly, which consists of delegates from local chapters, meets biennially.

As a result of the considerable impact of the protest movements of the 1960s on NASW, the organization became more active in social policy issues. In the 1970s a system called ELAN (Educational Legislative Action Network) was organized to provide support and information that would help local chapters keep in touch with congressional representatives. NASW members who are interested in influencing policy or are active in supporting social welfare measures receive information about important social policy issues and legislation through *The Advocate for Human Services,* a newsletter of NASW. As a nonprofit, professional association, NASW could not engage directly in elections without endangering its preferred tax status. Therefore, in 1976 the organization formed a political arm known as PACE (Political Action for Candidate Election), which solicits members for contributions to aid the campaigns of candidates who back policies congruent with those of NASW.

Supports for social work practice

Perhaps the major means by which NASW supports the development of social work practice are the various publications available to members. The bimonthly journal *Social Work,* one of the leading professional publications available to social workers, is included in NASW membership. Other social work journals are available on subscription: *Social Work Research and Abstracts, The Practice Digest,* and *Health and Social Work.* In addition, *The Encyclopedia of Social Work,* a basic reference work, is published every five years and other publications are available from time to time.

Other characteristics of the social work profession

Growth. In spite of the fact that no other profession was attacked by as many different groups as was social work during the 1960s, the profession continued to grow at a rather rapid rate. We base this statement on the NASW membership statistics, though not all persons holding social work degrees are members of the professional association. In 1976 NASW reported a total membership of 70,046. This represented an increase of 17,000 members since 1970. Between 1970 and 1975, 43,000 social workers earned MSW degrees, though many of these new MSWs may have been workers who returned to school to upgrade their competence rather than newcomers to the social work field. However, figures provided by the Bureau of Labor Statistics show that between 1970 and 1976 the number of persons employed as social service workers increased by 79,000 (Meyer and Seigel, 1977, p. 1070).

Sex ratio. There is a traditional notion abroad that social work is a women's profession. This is far from true. Although most social work professionals are women (69 percent according to 1973–75 data), male social workers occupy leadership roles far in excess of their proportion in the profession. Men are far more likely than women to be found in visible status and decision-making positions. Officers and committee chairmen of the several national organizations, executives of both local and national organizations, deans of schools of social work and faculty above the rank of assistant professor are far more likely to be men than women. It is also interesting that women outnumber men as students in schools of social work except in the doctoral programs.

It also appears that men advance in their social work careers far more rapidly than do women, which may mean that men receive promotions without having to present the years of experience that women require for advancement. It is difficult to study salary equality in social work along sex lines because of the more rapid promotion of men, which may in itself be more evidence of discrimination than are salary levels. However, it appears that within similar categories men tend to report higher salaries than women. In both graduate and undergraduate social work programs, male faculty members are more highly paid than female faculty members according to salary data for full-time faculty members (Meyer and Seigel, 1977, pp. 1970–71; Fanshel, 1976, pp. 448–54).

Minority social work organizations

In the years from 1968 through 1971, four national organizations were founded by minorities in social work as a result of greater consciousness of ethnicity. Many of the members of these groups are also members of NASW. The National Association of Black Social Workers was formed in 1968 to deal with "problems peculiar to the black community that have not been dealt with adequately by the prevailing social work organizations and agencies." The organization appointed a paid executive director in 1974, and it has a paid professional and clerical staff. NABSW has a code of ethics, publishes the journal *Black Caucus,* and holds an annual conference. The Association of Puerto Rican Social Service Workers was founded in New York City in 1968. Although it emphasizes the interests of Puerto Ricans, it is open to all Spanish-speaking persons who are actively involved in the social welfare interests of the Spanish-speaking community. The Asian American Social Workers was organized in California in 1968. It focuses on the development of social welfare programs for Pacific-Asian people, and it seeks to protect the rights of these people. In addition, it works to encourage the professional development of Pacific-Asian social workers and to achieve proper professional recognition of such workers through affirmative action.

The Association of American Indian Social Workers was founded in 1971 to serve the interests of persons of American Indian or Alaskan Native descent who have a degree from an accredited school of social work, are students in such a school, or are employed in social work in a recognized social agency. The goals of AAISW fall into four general areas: to promote the welfare of American Indians by influencing legislation; to identify sources of financial support for Indians; to provide sensitive social workers of other races with guidance on Indian life-styles, customs, and needs; to conduct research and consult with the Indian people serving Indian populations; to influence the curriculum in schools of social work so as to make it more responsive to Indian needs; and to recruit Indian students to graduate social work education and to support such students in their efforts (Kurzman, 1977, pp. 1095–96).

Other social work organizations

Although NASW may be the central professional association serving individual social workers, social workers are also served by a wide variety of national special interest professional associations. We have discussed earlier the forming of such associations as the Child Welfare League of America and the Family Association of America. These two groups were formed primarily to assist in improving the work of local agencies, but both publish an extensive literature for individual social workers, such as *Social Casework,* which has its roots in the late 1800s. Such associations as the National Conference of Social Welfare (which readers will remember began as the Conference of Charities and Corrections) and the American Public Welfare Association serve both individual members and organizations. Readers will find a comprehensive listing of social work associations in the *Directory of Agencies: U.S. Voluntary, International Voluntary, and Intergovernmental.*

In addition to the above organizations, in 1971 the National Federation of Societies for Clinical Social Work was founded. Individuals become members of state societies, which then may affiliate with NFSCSW. The minimum requirement for membership in state societies is a master's degree from an accredited school of social work. The group began as a protest against the movement in schools of social work, and in the profession, toward what the members saw as a weakening of interest in—and support of—clinical (psychotherapy with individuals and families) practice; and in protest against the acceptance of the BSW. The emphasis of the group is on the advancement of competence in the treating of individuals or families, and many of its members engage in private practice. It publishes a journal, *Clinical Social Work Journal.*

✑ Public assistance and personal social services

Throughout the major portion of this book we treated personal social services and income maintenance separately. It was difficult to do this because up to the enactment of the Service Amendments in 1962, personal social services were implicitly assumed to go along with income maintenance in the public welfare agencies. Little consideration was given to what those services should involve, and the implicit model of such services was that found in the social services administered through social workers in the voluntary agencies. With the apparent failure of the explicit offering of personal social services in combination with income maintenance services, there developed a considerable controversy around the issue of the relationship between these two major services. Therefore, this section will consider that relationship as well as what was happening in income maintenance programs as a response to the disenchantment and frustration of the 1970s.

The disenchantment of the Right

One of the best discriptions of the disenchantment and reaction that were impacting social welfare programs in the late 1960s and the early 1970s is found in an editorial by Alvin L. Schorr in the January 1971 issue of *Social Work.* Schorr was speaking of social work as a profession, but as he implicitly recognized, two opposing forces were endangering not only the profession but the programs that served clients. He wrote:

> . . . criticism of social work from the Left continues unheeding, even while anti–social work sentiment rises now powerfully from the Right. The new criticism of social work blames it for sympathy for young people and welfare recipients, for squeamishness about applying harsh measures, and for overly humanitarian values. While criticism

from the Left made its mark on the feelings of social workers and even produced changes here and there [see the first part of this chapter], the new criticism comes from people who control public and private purses. More is to be hurt than our feelings. For at least a little while, we seem likely to be trying to defend ourselves at the same time from charges of representing anarchy and representing the establishment. We will find little comfort in assuming that, because we occupy some central ground, we must be right. More likely we are entering a chaotic period in which it will be terribly hard to know what we should be doing. What are the compromises that do not contravene our basic purposes? What is a role for social work in a community that may not value its purposes?

We shall discuss some possible issues raised by the last two questions in our two concluding chapters. For now, having discussed the impact of the criticism of the Left on its primary targets of social work education and the profession of social work, we shall discuss the impact of the disenchantment of the Right with the income maintenance and personal social services programs which were their primary target.

The Great Society revisited

By the beginning of the 1970s the social welfare tapestry that we discussed in the first chapter of this text was truly a mass of complex threads and colors. The Great Society's expansion of in-kind programs and special opportunities had added immensely to the complexity of the social welfare programs. Four fifths of the persons who received public assistance for the aged and three fourths of the pensioned veterans also received OASDI. Most of these people also received subsidized health care from medicare, medicaid, or veterans' programs. Most of the families receiving AFDC also received food stamps and free medical care. Subsidized housing and school lunches might add to the overlap of programs for these families. Recipients of unemployment compensation often supplemented this benefit with food stamps. During 1974 the separate social welfare programs provided over

$125 billion to beneficiaries. If one added together the lists of beneficiaries of the various programs, the total would be 130 million names, yet it has been estimated that less than half this many individuals were actually involved, as most recipients participated in two or more programs (Levitan and Taggart, 1976, p. 70).

Escalating costs. Obviously, the new approaches of the Great Society resulted in the rapid growth of federal social welfare expenditures. Federal social welfare expenditures were 4.0 percent of the gross national product in fiscal 1950, 5.8 percent in fiscal 1965, and 11.2 percent in fiscal 1975. These expenditures increased from 26 percent of the federal budget in fiscal 1955 to 33 percent in 1965 (Levitan and Taggart, 1976, p. 20). Beginning in 1967 and accelerating with the economic downturn of the 1970s, there was more and more concern over the level of federal spending for social welfare purposes. As citizens became aware of the tax costs of the social welfare programs as a whole, they charged increasingly that there must be abuses as they found it hard to believe that so many needed to be helped so much by the contributions of others. Such criticism of the social welfare programs mounted by the Great Society was a significant new factor. Before the 1960s the primary concern had been to see that welfare programs were operated honestly, that fraud was kept at a minimum.

New evaluation techniques. However, during the Great Society years new techniques for evaluating large social programs and decision making had been developing rapidly. For the first time, programs and policies could be tested on the basis of performance and results. Initially, numerous evaluators documented the successes of the new ventures. "A few years later when gainsaying had become fashionable and profitable, there was an equal number of pundits, some of them disenchanted proponents, who proclaimed the failure of the same programs and policies" (Levitan and Taggart, 1976, p. 6). Thus in the late 1960s a flood of analyses allegedly demonstrated the failures of the social welfare programs of the Johnson administration.

Whether there was convincing proof that these programs were failures and whether compelling reasons were advanced to reject similar approaches to social welfare problems remain questions of importance. However, the "proof" of the Great Society's shortcomings became a major obstacle to the continuance of social welfare activism. Evaluations did not have to show failure. If they could not conclusively prove the value of governmental programs, then the programs must have been a failure. "Many critics confused high cost with inefficiency, charging that any solution that was expensive was wasteful. In buying cosmetics, or medical care, or automobiles the consumer usually associates high price with high quality, but this does not apply to government activities where parsimony is considered a virtue" (Levitan and Taggart, 1976, p. 9). Little allowance was made for the fact that the discovery of problems may lead to a continuing process of improvement. The grandiose promises of the Great Society contributed their own part to the reaction of disenchantment. Nothing could have reached the level of those goals.

Proposals for reform

By 1969, when President Nixon took office, pledged to correct the mistakes of the Great Society, welfare reform generally focused on AFDC and its appendage of aid to unemployed parents. The various proposals for reform that were heard in the land generally fell into three types: (1) to improve the existing system by establishing a federal minimum in all states or by an outright federalization of the system and by expanding the unemployed parent program; (2) to grant children's allowances to all parents, whether they were poor or affluent, so that the affluent would return their allowance in income taxes and the poor would avoid the means test or the stigma of welfare; and (3) to establish a federally guaranteed minimum annual income for everyone and to arrange tax rates in such a way that work was still worthwhile for the working poor. In its most common form, this last proposal was called a "negative income tax" because it would be administered through the

Internal Revenue Service. Interestingly, this plan was advocated by Milton Friedman, an influential conservative economist, because he saw it as minimizing federal bureaucracy and because he envisioned a minimum that would be set much below the generally accepted poverty level for a family.

Nixon's Family Assistance Plan

On August 8, 1969, President Nixon proposed to replace the AFDC program with a guaranteed minimum cash income to every family with children that needed it. Called the Family Assistance Plan, the proposal provided that every family with children, whether headed by a male or a female, employed or unemployed, would be eligible for an annual grant of $500 for each of the first two family members and $300 for each additional family member. Thus a family of four would be entitled to receive an annual total of $1,600. These benefits would decline as family income increased. To preserve the work incentive the reduction would not be dollar for dollar but would decline by 50 cents for each dollar of earnings above $60 a month. Thus a family of four with an income of $720 or under per year would receive the full $1,600. The assistance would continue at a declining rate until the annual family earnings totaled $3,920.

Because the level of income provided through FAP would be considerably below that already provided to AFDC recipients in 42 out of 50 states, the proposal also included a requirement that states supplement the basic benefit so that AFDC recipients would not suffer any decline in income. But as a boon to the states, it included a provision guaranteeing that under the new system no state would have to pay more than 90 percent of what it had spent on public assistance in 1970, thus ensuring a minimum 10 percent reduction to every state. In addition, the proposal sought to forestall conservative hostility by including a requirement that recipients register for work or training and accept it when offered, as well as provisions for expanded training and day-care facilities to help make this possible. Although the penalties for violation of this work requirement were to be relatively mild—the primary breadwinner only, and not the entire family, would be required to forfeit his or her benefits—the requirement allowed Nixon to portray the proposal as something other than a guaranteed income which many conservatives vigorously opposed. Finally as a complement to the proposed revision of AFDC, the Nixon proposal would have established a basic national minimum standard for state payments under the adult assistance categories (the aged, blind, and disabled) though in this case the payment would continue to be a joint federal-state responsibility. (Salamon, 1978, p. 93)

The proposal cleared the house by a comfortable majority, but it ran into trouble in the Senate Finance Committee, where conservatives pointed out that because FAP continued the link between participation in the in-kind assistance programs and public assistance, the last dollar of earnings that resulted in a cutoff of FAP would cost the family its in-kind benefits as well as its cash assistance. Using the case of a welfare mother with three children in Chicago, it was demonstrated that through the loss of medicaid and food stamps, and the need to pay income and social security taxes, she would lose $19 in income by raising her earnings from $750 to $5,560 in a year. An attempt was made to deal with this problem by eliminating or reducing the benefits of the other programs that would interact with FAP. But this move lost the support of the Senate liberals.

Failure of the Family Assistance Plan

But the president was persistent, and FAP was introduced again when Congress convened in 1971. The reworked proposal was somewhat more conservative than the original proposal. It too failed to pass.

Much has been written about why such a promising effort in welfare reform by a conservative president failed so badly. In attempting to account for the failure, Salamon (1978, pp. 95–97) makes three major points. "First, FAP came very close to passing, despite many explanations as to why it failed." It cleared the House by substantial margins both

times it was introduced, and it would have passed in the Senate if eight Senators had switched their votes. Many analysts have attributed the defeat of the proposal to the opposition of liberals who felt that it was inadequate. However, Salamon says that study of the congressional voting patterns shows that liberal support for the proposal was overwhelming, with over 75 percent of the liberals in both the House and the Senate supporting it. He also points out that the supporters of FAP in both chambers were legislators from the states that would have benefited least from it—the northern and western industrial areas, where AFDC benefit levels already exceeded the FAP levels and where private wage rates kept far larger proportions of the labor force out of the class of working poor. The legislators from the states with the most to gain from FAP—such as the southern states—voted most consistently against it.

Salamon attributes the failure of FAP in part to the loss of the support of Senate moderates. Moderates are most likely to be open to persuasion. In the House there was leadership and persuasion for the bill, but in the Senate there was no such leadership and the Senate Finance Committee members were opposed to passage. A central factor in the southern senators' failure to support the bill was the lack of leadership on the part of the poor southern blacks and whites. Without the active involvement of their most affected constituents, the southern senators were left free to oppose the bill. This also weakened the position of the northern liberals, who were faced with opposition to the bill by the National Welfare Rights Organization in their states.

The public assistance improvements of the 1960s also contributed to the defeat of FAP. It has become increasingly difficult, yet politically important, to fit a comprehensive income maintenance program to the existing distribution of benefits in kind without leaving anyone worse off. Conservatives insist on the inclusion of a work incentive feature in income maintenance bills. Yet in order to maintain a meaningful work incentive it is necessary to set the level of benefits below what recipients in some states are already receiving. The only way not to deprive those recipients of present benefits is to require the states to supplement the payments. But the states are reluctant to support a measure that does nothing to relieve their welfare burden.

Although FAP was defeated, it did accomplish some advancements. It raised the notion of a guaranteed annual income from the status of an interesting academic proposal to a concrete subject of practical politics. A uniform federal income guarantee for the needy aged, blind, and disabled did pass. It became known as the Supplementary Security Income (SSI) program, and we shall discuss it below. In addition, after 1970 the food stamp program was expanded so that it provided a kind of income floor for persons in need.

Supplemental Security Income (public assistance)

In October 1972 legislation was passed to establish a program of uniform national minimum cash income to aged, blind, and disabled individuals. It was to replace the programs of Old-Age Assistance, Aid to the Blind, and Aid to the Permanently and Totally Disabled. The administration of the new program was to be lodged in the Social Security Administration of HEW. Except for state supplementation, which will be discussed below, SSI is 100 percent federally funded through open-ended appropriations from general tax revenues. Persons aged 65 or over, or blind or disabled persons as defined by the act, whose resources are below the limits set by the act are eligible for benefits. Applicants may have no more than $1,500 in liquid assets ($2,250 for a couple). Several kinds of assets, such as a home valued at not more than $25,000 and a car with a market value of less than $1,200, are excluded.

Eligibility requirements. There are no work requirements for SSI, though blind and disabled individuals below 65 must accept referral to the state vocational rehabilitation service or forfeit their grants. Beneficiaries must reside in the United States and be citizens or legally admitted aliens. There is no direct requirement that relatives contribute to the needs of the applicant, but the income

of a spouse with whom the applicant lives, or the income of the parents if the applicant is a child, are considered to be resources of the applicant. If the applicant lives in the home of others and receives some support or maintenance in kind, the applicant's benefit level is reduced by one third. Social security benefits count as income in determining the level of the SSI grant. As of July 1, 1975, the monthly level of the SSI grant was $158. In figuring the grant, the first $20 of monthly income from any source and the first $65 of monthly earned income are not counted; all other income is deducted from the $158. The grant is the difference between the deducted income and $158.

As we mentioned earlier, all states except Texas are required to provide supplements to the SSI program that are not counted as income to the recipient. All states are required to make supplementary payments to persons receiving assistance under the OAA, AB, or AD programs as of December 1973 whose income would have been reduced under the new program. A state may make these supplementary payments directly to the beneficiary through the public welfare offices, or it may request that the social security offices administer the payments. When the state's supplementation exceeds the amount it spent in 1972 on the old programs, the costs of state supplementation become a federal obligation.

> SSI started out as a simple, straightforward concept—that of a new federal program for the adult categories, funded by the general revenue of the federal government and administered by the Social Security Administration. The program would establish nationally uniform standards of eligibility and provide for a single national benefit schedule. The benefit reduction schedule would also be precise. Intergovernmental funding conflicts would disappear, interstate differences in benefits would vanish, and the intercase differences created by caseworker-determined "basic need schedules" . . . would no longer plague welfare administrators. In addition, the measure would provide fiscal relief to the states. A program of such promise had to disappoint some people and it did. (Heffernan, 1977, p. 1139)

Problems and strengths. There have been enormously complex problems involved in getting the SSI program under way. Federal social security administrators have found that a program based on a means test is very different from the OASDI program. Also, the program in no way provides for adequate income for its beneficiaries, so that the states are called upon to supplement the SSI amounts and food stamps still play an important part in adequate maintenance of SSI recipients. Thus the program is still an undesirable mix of federal, state, and local policy, financing, and administration. The responsibility for the program has not been removed from the states. In addition, many individual recipients complain, sometimes bitterly, about the cool, businesslike, and unfeeling treatment that they receive in the social security offices. Since the SSA offices are accustomed only to administering financial benefits according to a set formula and are unaccustomed to participating in personal problem solving with recipients, recipients go without needed services. It is necessary to establish more effective ways through which SSI recipients may receive the other social welfare services they need.

The SSI program has many strengths. Probably the most important is that it established the principle of a national minimum standard of living attached to the costs of living. Although this standard may seem very inadequate, in many instances the benefits are substantially higher than those received under the old programs. Another important strength of the SSI program is that the population it covers has been rising more rapidly than the populations covered by other programs. This increase may be due in part to the fact that larger numbers in the population are becoming eligible for coverage, but it may also be due in part to the fact that SSI is considered more as a right than the programs it replaced since SSI is administered through the social security office rather than the welfare office.

AFDC (public assistance)

As we have discussed earlier, there are few defenders of AFDC, the only categorical assistance program which is still administered in somewhat the same form as that in which it was originated. AFDC is the most extended, the most costly though its individual benefits are lower than those of the other income maintenance programs), and the most controversial of the income maintenance programs. It undoubtedly continues to exist in its present form because (as the experience with FAP indicates) agreement cannot be reached on a plan of reform. When people speak of welfare reform, they are usually thinking of AFDC.

As was indicated above, despite the costs of AFDC, the average per recipient payment is, and always has been, less than that of other public assistance programs. Although there is considerable public concern over the low level of income available to many aged persons and there seems to be a general consensus that the aged need more benefits, the poor families with children, especially those families headed by a single woman, receive less. The state supplementation to a couple receiving SSI is higher than the benefit level to a two-person AFDC family in 45 states and is higher than the amount available to an AFDC family of four in 22 states. The differences were somewhat similar under the older OAA, AB, and AD. Possibly one factor in this problem is the lack of effective organization and political activity on the part of AFDC families (the OEO Act was concerned in part with this). On the other hand, older citizens, and now the handicapped, have developed or are developing strong and vocal organizations to lobby for their interests.

Bell estimated in early 1973 that 92 percent of AFDC families were poor without the welfare check and that 76 percent were still poor after it arrived. Bell reproduced two tables in her article that are of particular interest because they show that critical demographic factors are related to the adequacy of AFDC grants. Bell also stated that there was some evidence that, at least in the South, AFDC was helping poorer families more than it once did.

> . . . while the chances of receiving welfare are still lowest in the South, states in that region are now more likely than northern and western states

&§ Table 23-1
Poverty deficit before AFDC and percentage reduction after AFDC, 1973*

	Mean pre-AFDC deficit†	Reduction in deficit after AFDC‡
All families	$3,533	72%
Size of family		
2	2,410	79
3	2,868	78
4	3,670	72
5	4,337	69
6	4,697	68
7 or more	5,838	66
Race or ethnicity		
White (excluding Spanish origin)	3,241	75
Spanish origin	3,789	77
Black	3,720	69
American Indian	3,599	73
Residence		
Inside SMSA	3,578	75
Outside SMSA	3,299	61
Education of head		
Elementary	3,848	67
1–3 years high school	3,582	72
High school graduate	3,187	75
College	3,113	78
Region		
Northeast	3,568	89
North central	3,594	74
South	3,547	42
West	3,387	78

* Estimate based on 65 percent sample of 1973 AFDC Survey; excludes Puerto Rico, Virgin Islands, and Guam.

† AFDC income in this analysis includes cash value imputed to income in kind and a miscellaneous item, "other cash income," together consisting of less than 1 percent of total income.

‡ Reduction in gross deficit before and after AFDC, including that part of the AFDC check necessary to take family income to the threshold for families that moved above the threshold. Monthly income annualized. 1972 poverty threshold. AFDC families and income as recorded in welfare record as of January 1973.

Source: U.S. Department of Health, Education, and Welfare, Social and Rehabilitation Service, National Center for Social Statistics, AFDC Survey, 1973. Derived in Center for Studies in Income Maintenance Policy, New York University.

to extend aid to the poorest of the poor. This may well reflect several significant legal decisions during the sixties . . . [that] had the effect of making hundreds of thousands of children, especially in the South, eligible for AFDC. In this connection, the remarkable gain of black children in the southern case load in recent years is noteworthy—from 53 percent in 1962 to 67 percent in 1973 (p. 182).

Bell also pointed out that the earnings policy enacted by Congress in 1967 had resulted in a change of case load not experienced in other parts of the country in that there was a sizable reduction of working mothers. She wrote:

Historically, black mothers were more likely than white ones to be fully employed. If this group now tends to be disqualified for AFDC in the South and nonetheless the proportions of black children have risen so drastically, it could be inferred that southern states have opened the program . . . to some extremely poor families that once were simply outside the bounds of community compassion. In this sense, a poorer case load may reflect a

๛§ Table 23-2
Families above poverty threshold receiving AFDC grant, 1973, for regions*

	Proportion of families above threshold†			
	NE	NC	S	W
All families	38%	24%	9%	22%
Size of family				
2	43	31	13	21
3	56	28	12	24
4	30	20	9	24
5	19	18	7	17
6	21	18	7	23
7 or more	24	16	3	13
Race or ethnicity				
White (excluding Spanish origin)...................	43	31	11	24
Spanish origin	35	16	3	14
Black	35	17	9	19
American Indian	31	22	2	9
Residence				
Inside SMSA	37	22	10	21
Outside SMSA	43	36	8	25
Education of head				
Elementary	29	16	5	12
1–3 years high school	35	17	10	19
High school graduate	43	32	17	27
College	49	38	17	27

* Estimate based on 65 percent sample of 1973 AFDC Survey; excludes Puerto Rico, Virgin Islands, and Guam.

† AFDC monthly income annualized. AFDC income includes cash value imputed to income-in-kind and a miscellaneous item "other cash income," together consisting of less than 1 percent of total income. Poverty threshold, 1972; AFDC families and income as recorded in welfare record as of January 1973.

Source: U.S. Department of Health, Education, and Welfare, Social and Rehabilitation Service, National Center for Social Statistics, AFDC Survey, 1973. Derived in Center for Studies in Income Maintenance Policy, New York University.

civil rights victory for one group of families at the possible expense of their slightly better off neighbors (p. 182).

Statistics related to income maintenance programs in the United States seem to indicate that the persons who receive the least adequate resources relative to need are the children dependent for some part of their need on AFDC. Despite overwhelming evidence that physical and mental damage stemming directly from deprivation in childhood produces adults who are prime candidates for remaining in poverty and starting a new poverty generation, we are unwilling to take the steps necessary to remedy this situation. Probably the great-

est change in the AFDC program was the explicit recognition and incorporation of the Service Amendments of 1962 as a part of the program. Since 1962 there has been a basic and persistent controversy relative to this issue. The other important issue in public assistance has been the increased use of vendor payments. We shall discuss these two issues below.

Public assistance and social services

The Service Amendments of 1962 provided that the federal government would reimburse the states for 75 percent of the costs of the social services that they gave public assistance clients. This law did not define social services or their function. It only defined the purpose of social services, which was to move people toward self-support. (See the efforts to define social services discussed in Chapter 8.) This resulted in an open-ended authorization which was subject to significant abuse as state welfare departments began charging the federal program for services that had always been furnished by the states. By 1972 there had been a huge increase in the costs of services as states took advantage of the legislation. In September 1972 Congress moved to close the open-ended 75 percent match by establishing a $2.5 billion limit on what could be spent for social services. Interestingly enough, Congress did not evaluate whether the services had been effective or whether the sharply increased costs had been the result of abuse (Randall, 1975, pp. 191–207). It simply acted to limit federal participation in the program, a decision that meant a real decrease in federal participation. Although state expenditures for social services increased slightly following this action, the consequence seems to have been a decline in personal social service programs.

By the end of 1973 it was very clear that social service programs throughout the United States were rapidly deteriorating. During 1974 there were efforts by many interests in public welfare to develop a plan that would encourage the states to develop sound programs of personal social services and at the same time would place some safeguards on the fiscal participation of the federal government. Finally, a new title to the Social Security Act assured a reasonably firm foundation for a continuing federal support for the development of a personal social services network as a public welfare program. This act, which is commonly known as Title XX, was achieved at the cost of a limit on federal participation. It requires that the states assume the primary responsibility for planning and developing social services.

Title XX. The federal guidelines state that the social services must be directed toward at least one of the following goals: (1) achieving economic self-support or reducing dependence; (2) achieving or maintaining self-sufficiency (in other words, offering services that would help people toward self-care); (3) preventing or remedying the neglect, abuse, or exploitation of children and adults unable to protect their own interests, or preserving, rehabilitating, and reuniting families; (4) preventing or reducing inappropriate institutional care by providing for community-based, home-based, or other forms of less intensive care; and (5) securing referral or admission for institutional care when other forms are not appropriate and providing services for individuals in institutions. At least one personal social service must be provided for each objective, and at least three personal social services must be directed toward recipients of Supplemental Security Income.

Once again personal social services were not defined, but the states were directed to devote at least one half of the funds to programs aimed at the recipients of public assistance, SSI, or medicaid. Medical or remedial care, room and board for more than six consecutive months, child day care that does not meet federal standards, generally available educational services, capital expenditures, and case payments are not eligible for federal funding. There was an attempt to make these services available to a broader population than public assistance recipients. Individuals and families that do not receive assistance but have a family income of less than 115 percent of the state's median income for a family of similar size are eligible for service. In addition, information and referral services and protective functions for children and adults may be offered by states without an income test.

Vendor payments

We will discuss the implications of Title XX later in this chapter. Before we move further into some of the complexities of that program, we need to discuss two other issues that were developing in the 1970s. First, we want to discuss vendor payments as a way of securing personal social services for public assistance and SSI recipients. A vendor payment is a payment made for the purchase of a service by the government for a third party—in the case of our present concern, for a public assistance or SSI recipient. Thus a vendor payment is an in-kind benefit furnished by someone outside the public welfare agency to supplement cash assistance and other benefits that are furnished by the public agency. Such services must be purchased for recipients by the agency because the recipients are unable to purchase the services from their own income. Vendor payments are usually found in two program areas: personal social services and medicaid. We do not consider food stamps as meeting the definition of vendor payments.

Although they may not have been known by the term *vendor payments,* such third-party payments had been used throughout our social welfare history to purchase services that the public programs did not provide—for example, the use of private children's institutions for the care of dependent children in the 19th century and the public agency's purchase of homemaker services from the private family agency in more recent times. However, the 1962 and 1967 Service Amendments broadened the use of service purchases. By 1969, public agencies were increasingly using the option of purchasing necessary services for their clients from other agencies, usually community chest agencies or profit-making organizations, rather than mount and staff such programs within their own boundaries. Between 1969 and 1971, the purchase of services by the public welfare agencies skyrocketed. This method of acquiring services for clients declined in use when a cap was put on expenditures for personal social services, but the initiation of Title XX may again increase its use.

The largest and best-known vendor program and the most costly is medicaid, the federal-state medical care program for AFDC and SSI recipients and certain other persons who are determined to be medically needy. Medicaid expenditures consist of payments to physicians, hospitals, nursing homes, and pharmacists as well as the administrative costs of the program. These expenditures reached a total of $12.7 billion in 1975.

> Increased eligibility, participation, and utilization, coupled with spiraling costs of medical care, have been the primary factor in the program's immense growth and complexity. At present Medicaid ab-

sorbs over half of all public assistance costs. Moreover, poor management of the program has led to abuses on the part of vendors and clients. The escalation and inept management of the program have harmed many people and are the chief factors behind efforts to reshape the health care system. (Weaver, 1977, p. 1131)

The relationship between public assistance and personal social services

In the last chapter we discussed briefly the Services Amendment, which joined social services and financial aid in the public assistances. However, this policy had no sooner been enacted than a great controversy broke out over two issues. The first issue was whether personal social services actually helped recipients to "achieve employment and self-sufficiency." Certainly the rolls continued to increase, and the general impression was that increased personal social services did not achieve the goals set for them. However, no systematic national study was ever made that rigorously evaluated the program. Many people condemned the effort as an embarrassing failure, but this seemed to be a good example of the earlier problem we discussed: If you can't prove that something works well, then it must be a failure. Using HEW data, Ronald Randall attempted to take certain steps toward the evaluation of the social services that were provided to AFDC recipients in 1967. His conclusions were that the services were not without value, but that it would be impossible to demonstrate whether or not they justified their cost until clearly defined goals and improved measures were formulated (Randall, 1975, p. 205).

Two findings of Randall's study are of interest to us: (1) Randall puzzles over the fact that workers with graduate education tended to refer fewer clients for work training than did workers without such education; and (2) he notes that when case loads were heavy, there were more referrals to training. One way to interpret these findings is to conclude that graduate workers referred fewer recipients to training and rehabilitation because, with greater skills of assessment and with greater respect for clients' goals, graduate workers exercised greater discrimination about such referrals, knowing that referrals which failed only added to clients burdens. This interpretation fits in with Randall's second finding, that referrals increase when case loads are heavy. When workers are too busy to get to understand their clients and the clients' abilities and goals, they refer simply in order to be doing something. These interpretations also fit with the concern we expressed earlier over the setting of mass goals for clients instead of developing individualized ones. Thus, whereas social workers far removed from direct contact with clients set goals related to employment and self-sufficiency, graduate workers in actual contact with clients made individual decisions congruent with clients' desires and capacities but not necessarily congruent with the overall program goals. Thus it is entirely possible that the increase in the costs of assistance were entirely in accord with the basic purpose of personal social services, which is individualized help to the client.

The second issue centers on the belief that the administration of financial aid and the provision of personal social services are inherently different functions and should be separated as a matter of principle. This follows from the belief that public assistance should be available as a matter of legal right, that it is wrong to attach conditions requiring any kind of behavior to the acceptance of assistance because this makes special demands on the poor that are not made on the nonpoor. Exponents of this point of view argue that no one should have to accept social services because of poverty. The acceptance of social services should be voluntary except when a legal mandate applies their acceptance to every citizen (as in cases of child abuse or child neglect) and their use is justified by their intrinsic merit. Hoshino, who takes this stand, sets forth the following principles:

> (1) An individual should be able to claim maintenance as a legal entitlement unconditioned by the judgments of others about his behavior, (2) personal services that involve behavioral change should be provided only on the basis of free and voluntary acceptance by the individuals con-

cerned, and (3) if intervention is necessary, irrespective of the individual's wishes, in order to protect his, his family's or community's interests, it should be according to specific statutory provisions that apply to all citizens. (1971, p. 23)

There are persons who would agree totally with Hoshino's statement, yet would feel that there is no inherent contradiction in having social services offered by the same worker who deals with income maintenance. Income maintenance is one service, and needed personal social services are simply another array of services that can and should be made available. Whether or not the client accepts either of these types of services should be the decision of the client, and each type of service may be accepted separately or in combination with the other.

People who would combine these two types of services point out that it is often difficult for recipients to be sent from one source of aid to another (just as it may be difficult for any one of us to be sent to three doctors' offices to get the needed specialized services from each doctor), that the rigid division of these services simply does not make much sense to burdened people who see them as all of a piece in their lives. The concern is that many people will not receive needed services if they must initiate the request for them, because they neither know about the services and how to request them nor have the strength to approach another bureaucracy. Many workers who have direct contact with the very old, the very ill, the very confused, and the distrusting are only too painfully aware that bureaucratic hurdles deny access to services to these populations as surely as does any administrative rule.

Those who point to such repressive measures as the "man in the house rule" as examples of how workers oppress clients should recognize that this rule was an administrative rule, not a decision of the personal social services workers. They should be aware that many workers resigned or were fired for refusal to enforce the rule. The rule was eventually held illegal in part because of the efforts of professional social workers who were unwilling to administer it.

Helping all clients to gain access to needed services should be a charge to all social workers, whether they are administering income maintenance services or offering other social services. The important variable here is not the combination of services but the mistaken notion that administrative authorities can set class goals that are to be achieved by one group of people for another. If people are to change and grow, it will be because such change and growth is in line with their goals for themselves.

In line with the goals of the Great Society and the beliefs of social workers, in an attempt to make public assistance programs more available and less demeaning, there were a number of experiments with simplifying the process of applying for public assistance. Several of these experiments simply required the client to fill out a declaration of need which was accepted as a valid statement with no further investigation. In this type of program, there was a widespread use of nonprofessional staff, called eligibility technicians, to administer the simplified procedures. The duties and expectations of these workers were more or less clerical and were differentiated from the activities of other workers who gave the necessary services. These experiments strengthened the notion that income maintenance should be separated from social services, perhaps in part because eligibility workers came cheaper than social workers. In 1967, John Gardner, secretary of HEW, announced the principle that social services and income maintenance should be separated. In 1972, federal regulations mandated the separation of aid and services. The regulations required that the two systems be entirely separated, with separate staffs for determining eligibility and providing services, supervised by their own supervisors and working within separate administrative structures. Separate monitoring and accounting systems were also to be set up (Hoshino, 1977, p. 1153).

The division between personal social services and public assistance functions was furthered by the establishment of SSI and by the fact that this program was lodged in the Social Security Adminis-tration. Social services for the SSI recipients remained as a part of the programs of local agencies. For this group of people, separation was completed by placing the two programs under two totally different federal administrative structures.

Title XX

We are now prepared to discuss Title XX in somewhat more detail. Title XX eliminates previous services provisions in the Social Security Act and thus moves us further toward the separation of services and income maintenance. However, Title XX is limited to low-income families and thus is a program for the poor rather than a universal program. It also continues the notion that social services are to be directed toward enabling the poor to achieve and maintain economic self-support and to prevent dependence. We have not yet reached the point of suggesting that personal social services should be available to all of our people in order to increase their satisfaction in living. Title XX still imposes administrative goals rather than demanding that the effectiveness of social services be tied to their ability to aid individual recipients in achieving individual goals.

Title XX does not represent the totality of the personal social services that are available through public funding. Federally supported activities which are also considered a part of personal social services are: rehabilitation services, other services for children and youths, work incentive programs, programs for the aging, refugee services, and other services for Native Americans. Although the total expenditures for these programs are small the programs are an important development in that they are a commitment to a federal policy of support for attention to the personalized needs of certain groups. However, there are many unresolved problems in the development of these services.

First, there has been a substantial widening of the mandate to states to provide increased services, but the sums of money available are very limited. Thus the states are being asked to spread limited funds over an ever-widening spectrum of demands.

The procedures required under Title XX demand that public hearings on state and local plans be held and that the participation of consumers be solicited. This is easily seen as a positive step, but it also means that an increased number of special-interest groups are legally able to assert claims on the available funds. It does not resolve the conflicts between service providers and consumer groups that we saw in the previous categorical assistance programs. The difference is that we may now have new claimants for the same funds and that once again the voices of the most vulnerable and the neediest may not be heard, as they have not been heard in the past.

Morris introduces an important dilemma when he asks whether "the new program and its policies [should] be used to lay the foundations for a network of tax-supported personal social services throughout the country, or . . . used solely to underwrite a variety of services already provided by existing public, private, and proprietary agencies" (1978, p. 126). Does the increasing use of vendor services mean that existing service providers are using these funds to shore up their present operating costs, or does it mean that they are using these funds to expand their present programs? Are federal funds being used in such a way that local appropriations are displaced? Does the increasing use of vendor services mean that the private agency system will increasingly become a part of the public agency system and will be more concerned with developing services in line with federal guidelines and with services to a carefully defined population than to developing pioneering services or serving different populations? We will come back to some of these questions in the last chapter.

⇜ Social security

There seemed to be a general agreement in the 1960s that social security, like welfare reform, needed a new look. The concerns seemed to center on the adequacy of social security benefits in a time of sharply increasing inflation and on the ability of the social security program to continue in the face of a growing population of the aged and a decreasing population of the younger people whose contributions were needed to support the program. These concerns were met by the adoption of various automatic provisions that were designed to keep OASDI up to date with rising prices and rising wages and by a sharp increase both in the rates of social security taxes and in the amount of salary subject to those taxes.

Improvements in social security

Beginning in 1968, a series of changes in the level of social security benefits and in the way the relationship of those benefits to wages was computed, promised to go a long way toward assuring recipients in the years ahead of a reasonably adequate replacement for their earnings. From 1968 through 1977, the level of benefits was increased by about 130 percent. As prices rose approximately 75 percent during this period, the real value of social security benefits increased about 55 percent. Even more important, the laws were changed so that benefit levels were tied to the cost of living.

But another important change was made in the way benefits are computed. For the worker who reaches age 62 or becomes disabled or dies in 1979 or later, benefits will be based on the worker's lifetime average wage updated to reflect the current level of wages just before eligibility for benefits is established. The overall effect of basing benefits on average earnings indexed to the level of wages at the time one reaches one's 62d birthday will result in benefits that will ordinarily increase more than the increase in prices. This is an example of the way in which indexing works:

. . . if a worker earned $3000 in 1954, retired at age 62 in 1970, and earnings levels were . . . [on the average] three times higher in 1979 than in 1954, the $3000 would be increased three times to $9000. Benefits would be based on the worker's earnings brought up to date in this way and averaged over the period since 1950 to age 62 [minus the five years of lowest earnings that workers are permitted to drop out] . . . benefits are not held down by the generally lower level of rates in the past. (Ball, 1978, p. 233)

Social security benefits were increased at a time when there was considerable concern about whether the social security system was in danger of "bankruptcy." There was considerable discussion about the financing of the program and proposals that the financing pattern be changed. Two proposals put forward were those considered earlier: (1) employers should pay a greater proportion of the cost than employees; and (2) some costs of the program, perhaps medicare, should be paid from general revenue. Both of these plans were rejected in favor of continuing the original pattern. The only changes made were the rather significant increases in tax rates and in the level of wages covered.

In discussing the changes in OASDI, most administrators prefer to discuss the greatly increased benefits that the retirees will eventually receive. However, this does not deal with the problems that wage and payroll taxes bring to low-income earners and to families which require two wage earners in order to obtain adequate income. In many of these families the costs of social security increased by twice the amount that is generally shown in tables. Wilcox estimated in 1969 (p. 132) that social security taxes took $1.5 billion a year from people below the poverty line. He pointed out that these taxes took more money than did the income tax from three fifths of those who paid both. If this was true under the much lower tax rates of 1969, how much truer must it be today? Is it possible that social security tax rates have approached the limits of political tolerance?

✌§ Child welfare

During the 1960s and 1970s, at least five major trends affected child welfare services: (1) an increasing concern with the rights of children; (2) a rapid increase in teenage pregnancies and in the number of teenagers who kept their children; (3) controversy over abortion; (4) a rediscovery of the old problem of child abuse, particularly sexual

abuse; and (5) an increase in the number of working mothers.

The rights of children

In the 1970s there was an increasing emphasis on the law as the protector of children's rights and an increasing emphasis on the law as an instrument for the reform of services to children. Several Supreme Court cases, such as *In re Gault* in 1967 and *In re Winship* in 1970, strengthened the procedural safeguards available to children who were before the juvenile court for offenses and introduced legal aid for children into juvenile court practice. As a consequence the juvenile court became more and more adversarial. There has also been a growing literature which urges that the rights of children be considered more important than the righs of parents.

In addition, several important court decisions ruled that state and local agencies were obliged to offer education, help, or treatment when they accepted a child in placement. In some states this ruling was extended to community-based educational programs for certain types of handicapped children.

All of the above changes have affected the functioning of all agencies relating to the welfare of children—public and private social agencies, educational institutions, and correctional systems. The ultimate outcome for the welfare of children and the implications for the role and functions of agencies are still not fully clear. These changes all pose questions for the future.

A rapid increase in teenage pregnancies and in the number of unwed teenagers keeping their children

According to reports from the National Center for Health Statistics, there were 418,100 births to unwed mothers in 1974, or 13.2 percent of all live births. This percentage was up from 3.5 percent in 1940 and 10.0 percent in 1969. As the percentage of such births increased, the ages of the mothers decreased. In 1974, 221,400 out-of-wedlock babies, or 53 percent of all out-of-wedlock births, were born to girls under 19 years old. Almost 30 percent of these births were to girls under age 17. From 1971 to 1974, for girls aged 15 to 19, unwed parenthood increased by 12 percent among white girls and by 5 percent among black girls. For girls under 15, it increased by 35 percent. In the large cities, almost one out of two babies are born to an unmarried, usually adolescent, mother.

Less than 10 percent of unmarried mothers now release their babies for adoption. Those who do give up their babies may well view this action with the shame and guilt that previous generations of unwed mothers felt in relation to the pregnancy itself. The concern about the legal rights of fathers has led to recent court decisions giving unwed fathers a claim to their babies. The father's consent may now be required before a baby can be given up for adoption. Although this may be a very positive step, it has complicated the process of releasing an out-of-wedlock child for adoption both for the mother and for the agencies that are involved.

No one associated with unmarried parents would claim that all parents are alike or that pregnancy has a similar meaning for all adolescent unwed mothers. It is interesting that in an era when so many girls aspire to higher individual goals than did girls in the past, many girls have no goal other than motherhood. It may be that many adolescent girls need a baby to reassure themselves about their sexuality. Having a baby is easily accomplished and may appear to give focus to a life that seems aimless and undirected otherwise.

> Although no statistics exist, all authorities attribute recent increases in cases of child abuse and neglect and of foster care of young children of adolescent parents. . . . In the past, grandmothers would have cared for the babies. While parental roles might be vague, the child still grew with relative stability and mothering. Economic pressures may force many grandmothers to work while other still-young and liberated grandmothers are disinclined to raise a second generation of children. . . . Urban living makes life more difficult than the simple rural environment of the past. . . . Consequently, many such children are expressing mul-

tiple problems at home, in school and in the community. (Schwartz, 1977, p. 1565)

Faced with the problems of the unwed mother and her child, agencies have been active in developing new programs. Pregnant girls can now continue their education by remaining in their regular classes or by attending special classes. Many schools are providing day care for the babies. The medical risks for adolescent mothers and their babies are significantly greater than the risks for more mature pregnant women. As a result, hospitals are focusing on better and more responsive care for such mothers. Although sex education and parent-effectiveness training are increasing, there is still much community opposition to such programs for fear that they will encourage unwed pregnancies (Schwartz, 1977, pp. 1564–66).

Family planning and the abortion controversy

At the beginning of the 20th century there developed an active advocacy for planned parenthood. The movement was controversial, and it has remained so, despite a growing acceptance. The federal government's concern with such programs first developed during the 1960s. In 1965 Secretary of the Interior Stewart Udall directed the BIA to make population planning services available for Indians. In 1966 the Children's Bureau was enabled to support family planning services through formula grants to the state health departments. In 1967 the amendments to the Economic Opportunity Act included family planning among a group of special programs for the poor, such as Head Start, Follow Through, Legal Services, and Comprehensive Services.

In 1973 the Supreme Court found that laws prohibiting abortion during the first two trimesters of a pregnancy were unconstitutional. This decision has met with much conflict. A struggle immediately developed over the right of the federal government and/or the states to provide funds for abortions for poor women. Candidates for political office often found their capacity for office judged on their stand on this issue. Those who oppose the provision of such funds feel that public funds should not be utilized for purposes that they regard as immoral. Others feel that the Supreme Court decision is meaningless for poor women unless they are given funds with which to exercise the choice that the Court has held is a woman's right.

Child abuse and child neglect

The complex and difficult problem of child abuse became a focus of concern during the 1960s. It was one program that continued to receive increased funding into the 1970s. However, with the movement to develop the public programs of personal social services there was an effort to reintegrate the child abuse services into the general child welfare services and to integrate the general child welfare services into the general personal social services.

In 1975 the Office of Child Development initiated a number of research and demonstration projects that attempted to deal with a number of major issues related to child abuse and protective services. The establishment of the National Center for Abuse and Neglect and the work of other groups interested in this problem seem to indicate an ongoing interest in the needs of abused and neglected children and their families.

The need for day care

The fundamental issue in day care may be seen as the issue of how the optimal nurturance of today's children can be provided at a time when the American family is undergoing many changes, but for many people the fundamental issue is seen as the issue of whether mothers should work. There has been great reluctance to address this issue clearly on a national level. Yet it is being addressed in pieces that pose serious obstacles to the expansion of day care. There are something over 61 separate authorities under which day-care services can be funded. None of these programs, except perhaps Title XX, makes a dent on the needs of day care. It is estimated that only 10 to 20 percent

of the day-care services needed by working women are actually available.

In 1971 Congress passed the Comprehensive Child Development Act, which would have provided funds for comprehensive high-quality day care and support for other supporting services for children. The bill was vetoed by President Nixon, and it has not been reintroduced into Congress. President Nixon's veto message was in substantial agreement with other arguments against the funding of day-care programs: (1) such programs would destroy the family; (2) they would duplicate already existing services, and thus the need for them had not been established; (3) they would establish communal child-rearing approaches that were contrary to American values; and (4) the bill as written did not respect the role of the states in welfare measures.

✌§ Other systems

Mental health

By 1972 the community mental health centers were in serious trouble. The original appropriation had envisioned that the communities would take up the costs of the centers when the seed money was exhausted. Communities were very reluctant to take on this expense, and President Nixon was opposed to further national funding. Consumer organizations and other groups were questioning the traditional mental health model, and there was a strong feeling that individual psychotherapy was not helpful to the working class and the poor, the very groups which the centers were developed to help. The various studies which found the results of psychotherapy to be questionable at best had an impact on the community mental health centers.

At the same time, those who had originally fostered the movement for community mental health centers as a preventive one on the public health model and who had visions of community psychiatry seemed unable to transmit their visions to the professionals in the centers. These professionals were puzzled by the notion that the centers should be leaders in community action and community reform, should act as advocates for social justice, and should work for programs that promised to support good mental health in citizens in general rather than in individual patients.

Perhaps the greatest opportunity for the centers to be of service was offered by the rapid discharge of institutionalized mental patients into the community that was taking place. Many of these patients were not really capable of developing a satisfying, or even a safe, life for themselves. They generally lived in drab boarding homes or old hotels, unable to cope with the complexities of life. These people desperately needed supporting services, and the community mental health centers might have rallied to provide these, but they did not. The staff of such centers, accustomed to providing clinical counseling services, had neither skill nor interest in giving the social care services which were the type of personal social services needed by the former patients.

Many of the centers saw their charge to the community as one of providing expert advice to other community agencies. They had little understanding of how to engage in cooperative efforts or of how to participate in community problem-solving efforts on the basis of equality. Thus much of their help was neither appropriate to where the community was nor acceptable when presented from the position of the expert.

Corrections

Corrections, like other human welfare systems in the 1960s, was confronted with findings that the reform and rehabilitation efforts that had been supported for more than two centuries by reformers did not work. The notion was introduced that the process of rehabilitation might actually be crueler than a simple and definite punishment. Court decisions were both affirming the rights of the accused and of convicts and expanding the responsibilities of the correctional authorities.

At the same time that interest was being expressed in the rights of the offender and concern was being expressed that rehabilitation efforts failed to really help, public opinion was moving in another

direction. Law and order became a popular conservative platform from which to demand that the rights of the community be protected and that heavier penalties be imposed on offenders. In 1968 Congress established the Law Enforcement Assistance Administration in the Department of Justice (LEAA). This was to operate somewhat on the model of the National Institutes of Health—to conduct and fund research, promote efforts to improve personnel in the field of corrections, and encourage demonstration projects. Largely under the impact of the law and order movement, between 1969 and 1972 its budget rose from $60 million to $700 million. But the research mounted under this program only seemed to support the notion that various rehabilitation efforts did not work. There were suggestions that perhaps some demonstration and research efforts should be conducted to determine whether old-fashioned deterrence did not work better.

In 1971 the American Friends Service Committee published an influential report, *Struggle for Justice,* which called for a return to a fixed sentence and was highly critical of the indeterminate sentence. This argument fitted very well into the law and order position and soon won many supporters.

An important by-product of this new emphasis on punishment and deterrence was the notion that many minor offenses should be "decriminalized" and removed entirely from the courts. Juvenile offenses that would not be considered crimes if committed by adults, usually called "status offenses," were no longer to be considered appropriate for court intervention. And such adult behavior as drunkenness, vagrancy, prostitution, and minor drug offenses were to be handled in ways other than court action so that the courts could concentrate on really serious crime. It was suggested that such behavior was appropriate for "treatment" and should be separated from the criminal justice system.

Education

The schools were also under attack. Questions were raised about the inability of many students to handle the life tasks of adults in our society, and the blame for this deficiency was laid squarely on the schools and on the professionals who worked in them. In addition, the problems of integration in the schools, particularly in the urban North, came to full bloom. Courts ordered forced busing in order to achieve racial balance in the schools, and if the school administrators did not comply, the courts themselves sometimes took over the administration of the schools.

Yet in the midst of this turmoil there was evidence that even the most disadvantaged students could learn and that with appropriate work their learning rates could be improved. There was also evidence that added years of education did result in increased earnings for disadvantaged groups.

Summary

The late 1960s and the 1970s were years of confusion—years when many of those who worked in social welfare felt that they had no friends. They were attacked on one side by the far Left and on the other by the far Right, and their clients were critical as well. It was a time when newly found evaluative methods were used with great abandon. It was assumed, contrary to good research principles, that if something could not be proved to be of significant help, it was a failure. The possibility that certain evaluative efforts were themselves questionable and that they did not support the generalizations that were drawn from them was not raised. The result of all this was that programs for the poor were curtailed. Not only were such programs curtailed, but the general feeling arose that the poor had had an opportunity through the Great Society and that it had been proved that they could not be helped.

President Nixon's general stance with regard to social welfare was "to give it back to the states." He wanted to take the money that went into federal grants-in-aid and give it to the states and cities to develop their own ways of dealing with social problems. Revenue sharing was a key to Nixon's New Federalism. Nixon got what he wanted with the

passage of the State and Local Financial Assistance Act of 1972. He then moved with vigor to cut back on as many of the social programs of the 1960s as possible. In this he faced stiff congressional resistance. It was plain that thinking about social welfare faced a change. Conservatives were once again affirming their concern with the state and local governments and the principle of locality. But now they had the support of the radicals who were preaching participatory democracy and community control.

A look ahead

We have come to the end of our consideration of the development of social work and of social welfare programs. This may seem a discouraging note on which to end, but in the next part we shall try to introduce some notion of the issues before us. Thus, though we may not be able to end this text with any definitive answers, we hope that we can point to some directions for defining the problems. We have deliberately left the discussion of President Carter's welfare proposal for our next part, as it will help shape our summary of where we are today.

Study questions

1. Look back through the chapter at some of the social welfare programs that failed. Identify where the resistance was located in our political system—Congress, the presidential veto, court decisions.

2. How do these blocks relate to the thinking of the men who drafted our Constitution?

3. If you were president, would you continue Nixon's focus on having the community make its own social welfare decisions, or do you believe that federal participation in terms of financing should be accompanied by attention to national human rights? Support your position.

4. What do you think about the separation of personal social services and public assistance? Draw up a list of principles that would support your position.

ఆ Selected readings

Leiby, James. *A History of Social Welfare and Social Work in the United States.* New York: Columbia University Press, 1968.

Chap. 16 deals with the disenchantment of the period 1967–72. It will expand the material in this chapter. We recommend it as supplementary reading.

Levitan, Sar A., and Taggart, Robert. *The Promise of Greatness.* Cambridge, Mass.: Harvard University Press, 1976.

We strongly recommend that this book be used as supplementary reading for this chapter. It details what the authors see as the real achievements of the Great Society.

~§ Part IV

~§ Toward
social welfare ₷~

One of the many ways of assuring better nutrition for the young and the old, is a hot lunch program (or a hot breakfast, or hot dinner program).

In the 1930s Dorothea Lange chronicled the migration of impoverished farm families from the dust bowl of the Southwest to California. Contrast her stark portrait of a worried mother and her tired, hungry children, huddled in a migrant refugee camp of that era—with the generous trays of food given to older adults and young children in today's hot lunch programs.

The desperate fears of poor parents for the welfare of their children have been somewhat alleviated, but not yet eradicated.

Chapter 24 ॐ

ॐ Current problems and issues in income maintenance programs ॐ

✑ Introduction

In this chapter we shall attempt to discuss the problems and issues in our present approach to income maintenance. We shall begin the chapter with a description of President Carter's proposal for a revision of the means-tested income maintenance program (commonly known as welfare reform, though Carter managers to avoid using the words). We shall describe the present operation of the income maintenance programs administered by public welfare agencies. The welfare agencies also administer personal social services, but we shall leave those for the next chapter. Finally, we shall discuss the present concerns about welfare, issues that need to be considered in changing our present welfare system, and the role of social work in income maintenance programs.

✑ President Carter's program for better jobs and income

It appears that every candidate for national office feels a need to promise the people a reform of the welfare program. Perhaps this is because the issue of welfare (by which we mean the means-tested assistances) is one that unites people everywhere—everyone is against welfare. But in his proposal to restructure the public and general programs of assistance, Carter managed to avoid even mentioning the word *welfare*. In considering social welfare, or other difficult and divisive programs, it is always interesting to note the use of language. At one time we attempted to do away with poverty by substituting the words *inadequate income* for the word *poverty*. Carter's program, presented on August 6, 1977, was called the Program for Better Jobs and Income. As presented by the president, this proposal did not deal with two important programs found in public welfare: medicaid and social services. The program was to "increase job opportunities for the low-income population and consolidate our major income support programs into one simple and efficient system" (*New York Times,* 1977, p. 40). Carter's program followed tradition in two out of three basic elements; (1) it retained

the concept of categorization and the notion that some of the poor are more deserving than others; (2) it retained the idea that relief must be designed in such a way as to avoid interference with the private labor market; however (3), it moved away from the concept of local responsibility for income maintenance programs. Carter proposed that welfare recipients be divided into two groups—those expected to work and those not expected to work—and that different benefit levels be established for the two groups. There have been other attempts to put welfare recipients to work—the unique feature of Carter's proposal was the creation of jobs for welfare recipients who were unable to find jobs in the regular economy.

The Carter proposal was an extremely complex one, and it did not deal with either medicaid or the personal social service programs of public welfare. It did require that the principal wage earner in each family applying for assistance engage in an intensive five-week job search, during which the family would be eligible for limited cash benefits. If after five weeks no job had been found, the family would become eligible for a subsidized public service job. During the next three weeks every effort would have to be expended to try to provide such a job. If the principal wage earner refused a job, his or her benefits would be cut off, though benefits would continue to the rest of the family. If no job were found or created after eight weeks, during which benefits would be $44 a week for a family of four, the family would begin receiving a higher cash benefit for as long as the principal wage earner was unemployed. Once placed in a public service job, this person would be eligible to hold it for 12 months, after which another job must again be sought in the private job market. If that search proved unsuccessful, the person would again become eligible for a public service job.

Eligibility for subsidized jobs was to be limited to the principal wage earner in single-parent and two-parent families with children. The basic wage paid on the public service jobs was to be limited to the higher of the federal or the state minimum wage. Participants in the job program would also be eligible for cash assistance if their wages could not support the family. In addition to paying the wages of those in the jobs program, the federal government would provide 30 percent over the basic wage to cover fringe benefits and administrative costs. Although no specific plans were offered for job training programs, the Carter proposal made several references to training.

The cash assistance program for those not expected to work

In addition to the jobs program, the Carter plan proposed that the three existing cash assistance programs—AFDC, SSI, and food stamps—be consolidated into a single, universal program. For those not expected to work, the plan provided cash benefits to all in need, including, for the first time, single individuals, childless couples, and low-wage earners. Those not expected to work under the plan included the aged, the blind, and the disabled, plus single parents with children under seven. Single parents with children aged 7 through 13 were not expected to work if no day-care facilities were available.

For those not expected to work because of child care responsibilities the basic benefit for a family of four with no other income was $4,200 in 1978 dollars. This was lower than the existing benefits in 38 states. An aged, blind, or disabled person with no other income would receive $2,500 a year, and a couple would get $3,750. This would be slightly more than they now receive under SSI, but it would be about the same as the amount that many actually receive from a combination of SSI and food stamps.

If a person in the not-expected-to-work category did in fact work, his or her cash benefits would be reduced 50 cents for each dollar earned. Thus the benefits for a family of four would phase out completely when earnings reached $8,400 (Shapiro, 1979, pp. 179–80).

Cash benefits for those expected to work

For those who were expected to work but who did not earn enough to support their families, either a direct cash benefit, called a work benefit, or an expanded earned income tax credit would be available. For an expected-to-work family of four, the basic benefit would be $2,300 per year. This would consist of $1,100 for the spouse and $600 per child. The expected-to-work adult or principal wage earner would receive nothing during the initial eight-week job search or if he or she refused a proffered regular or subsidized job. If the family member secured a regular or a subsidized job, the family would be able to keep $3,800 of earned income. After that, the federal cash benefits would be reduced 50 cents for each dollar. If no job were found, the family would move up to the same level of assistance as the one for a family that was not expected to work.

The president also proposed to supplement low-income wages while strengthening the push to leave public service jobs by providing a 10 percent income tax credit on the first $4,000 of annual earnings in the labor market, thus saving a family a maximum of $400. The amount of EITC would be reduced by $1 for each $10 of earnings over $4,000, thus disappearing completely when, adjusted gross income reached $8,000. There would be an added 5 percent income tax credit on earnings between $4,000 and $9,100. The credit would phase out at the rate of $1 for each $10 of income beyond $9,100, thus providing some benefits for a family of four with income up to $15,650. This part of the plan would be administered by the Internal Revenue Service (Shapiro, 1979, pp. 180–81).

Questions about the Carter proposal

Some persons were concerned that the Carter proposal infringed on tax and employment programs. Others were concerned that the proposal failed to deal with medicaid and the increasing demand for social services. There were questions about the complexity of the proposal. Many felt that it was too complex to legislate, too complex to implement, and too intricate to operate successfully. There were fewer complaints about the heavy emphasis on work than one would have expected, given the fact that previously many liberals had strongly opposed work requirements, feeling that these made income maintenance a support of inadequate wage levels and practices. The recently changed attitudes toward work requirements were particularly important for women. Only a few years earlier the notion that mothers should work would have aroused a storm of protest from many. Although putting people to work seems to have developed an appeal among liberals as well as conservatives, these two groups hold very different notions about the meaning of work. The conservatives see work as a punitive measure to extract something from reluctant and perhaps lazy applicants in return for aid. The liberals tend to see work as a means of enhancing the self-respect of workers and enhancing their sense of having a place in the community.

The sharpest criticism of the Carter proposal was reserved for its heavy emphasis on requiring subsidized workers to work for a minimum wage with no fringe benefits and no vacation time. Another major criticism had to do with the level of benefits. The lower benefits for those expected to work would be only $5 above the benefits currently provided for families by the food stamp program and were clearly inadequate. Some people felt that the proposal was all structure and without any sense of human need.

❧ Problems in welfare reform

Although almost everyone is against welfare, the opponents of welfare are against it for different reasons, and many of the reasons are in conflict. If we want to reduce the inequities in welfare, we are likely to end up extending the coverage. If we believe that welfare recipients need more adequate support, we will increase welfare grants and also increase the cost of welfare programs. If we want to give some relief to taxpayers, we will have to reduce benefits to the recipients. As a consequence we seem only slightly closer to consensus on the direction that welfare should take than we were a century ago—or perhaps two centuries ago. However, we do seem to be increasingly united

on the notion that people in need are entitled to some minimum help (Salamon, 1978, p. 4).

One of the things that impede reform is the sheer complexity of the income assistance programs. "At last count, no fewer than 62 separate federal programs were providing social insurance and aid to the needy, and several of these must be multiplied by 50 to reflect the fact that they are run differently—in terms of eligibility provisions, benefit levels, administrative procedures—from state to state" (Salamon, 1978, p. 4). As most recipients receive benefits from more than one program, a proposed change in any program has to be considered for its effects on all other programs. Furthermore, this complexity of programs is institutionalized in the structure of the congressional committee system and the executive branch of government. "Jurisdiction over the 62 federal income assistance programs is split among no fewer than 11 House committees and ten Senate committees, and nine executive departments and agencies," each of which operates according to its own sense of mission and its own priorities (Salamon, 1978, p. 4).

Another factor that has made it increasingly difficult to change the welfare system is the fear of those concerned with the poor that a reformed system will be even less generous. Despite gaps, inequities, and inconsistencies, the changes since 1930 have made increasingly adequate benefits available to a sizable portion of the poor. "By increasing benefits, the recent changes have created a set of implicit entitlements that inevitably complicate the task of reform" (Salamon, 1978, p. 9). An example of this was evident during the argument over FAP, when welfare mothers from the high-benefit states strongly opposed the program because it would decrease *their* benefits, although aiding a far larger group of needy mothers elsewhere. Thus, as the scope and level of benefits increase, the difficulty of structuring a comprehensive welfare program that would leave everybody better off greatly increases.

A factor that has been with us since the first welfare acts in England is the problem of adapting welfare programs to the needs of the larger economic order. Reform measures are forced to measure up to two separate standards that are really in conflict with each other: (1) How well do they relieve suffering? (2) How effectively do they protect the work system that welfare is thought to endanger? It is extremely difficult to provide adequate benefits and an effective work requirement without extending coverage and expanding costs to a level that many consider unacceptable.

ᴥᔓ Operation of the public welfare programs

Public welfare is difficult to discuss because it is not a uniform concept, but rather should be seen as a collection of a half dozen or more discrete programs operated by over 1,200 separate public welfare agencies. As readers of this book should recognize by now, public welfare programs represent compromises between conflicting political and social ideologies and interests. In addition, specific policies in local agencies and interpretations in actual practice with clients are affected by the basic beliefs and competences of the administrative and direct practice staff of the local agencies. The policies covering different programs at the state or national level differ widely, and such differences and lack of coordination present many difficulties for both clients and workers in utilizing the available programs effectively. As an example, the criteria of eligibility for food stamps and for AFDC vary substantially and are actually formulated by two separate federal agencies. Readers should understand by now something of the complex structure involving the federal, state, and local governmental levels of the various programs. In addition, administrative patterns vary from state to state (see Chapter 20). Thus in some states a program may be state administered, with the state agency in full control over the development of policy and procedure, of administrative actions, and of all operations, whereas in other states the county may be responsible for administrative matters and operations and the state may merely set broad policy and exercise supervision of the program.

Public welfare agencies are responsible for the following programs, which may be offered by the public welfare agency itself or by other agencies under arrangements with the public welfare agency:

Assistance payments, public assistance, income security, security welfare payments. This is the payment of money to or on behalf of eligible needy individuals and families to help them meet their basic needs for food, clothing, shelter, and personal and household necessities. Three programs of income maintenance are provided: Aid to Families with Dependent Children (AFDC), Supplemental Security Income (SSI), and General Assistance (GA).

Medical assistance for the poor (medicaid). This is for the provision of medical services for public assistance recipients and medically indigent persons.

Food stamps. These are provided to low-income households to help finance basic food needs for the family.

Cuban refugee assistance. This provides financial assistance and a wide variety of helping services to Cuban refugees to achieve their resettlement, adjustment, self-support, and self-sufficiency in the United States. More recently, 1975–78, it also covered Vietnamese and Cambodian refugees.

Assistance to repatriated U.S. nationals. This provides travel, temporary financial assistance, and helping services to U.S. citizens and their dependents who are destitute or mentally ill in a foreign country.

Social services. These include a wide variety of helping services for individuals and families, including public assistance recipients and applicants and other specified low-income persons. The services are intended to help eligible individuals and families to attain or retain their capability of self-sufficiency and self-support or to strengthen family life.

Child welfare services. These services, now considered a part of social services, are for homeless, delinquent, neglected, abused, or dependent children and their families. They provide a wide variety of helping services for preventing, remedying, and solving problems of children, protecting children, promoting their welfare, strengthening family life, providing for adequate care of children in foster homes, day care and other child care facilities.

The Work Incentive Program (WIN). This provides supportive services, day care, employment training, and development and employment services to registered youth and heads of households of AFDC families to help them become self-supporting (Spindler, 1979, pp. 25–29).

We can divide the above programs into programs that are mandated by law to all state and local public welfare agencies—that is, all public welfare agencies must offer the programs—and other programs. The other programs can be divided into services that must be offered but can be offered under the auspices of agencies other than county welfare agencies (these agencies often have such names as Family and Rehabilitation Services, Human Services, and Family Services), services that may be mandated only for certain sections of the country, and services that states may elect to include with the mandated services under a common agency administration. For example, recent legislation provides for the administering of child welfare services by the same agency that administers social services for individuals and families, except in certain instances in which the state has had a long history of separate administration of the two programs. Although the county welfare agency must determine eligibility for medicaid, the state can offer the actual services through another agency. Spindler divides the programs as follows:

Mandated functions

Cash assistance—eligibility determinations and payments administration.

Social services—eligibility determinations and the provision of services.

Medical assistance—eligibility determinations and administration and distribution of food stamps.

Work incentives—referrals to the WIN agencies and the provision of supporting social services and day care.

Other functions

Child welfare services. Some state governments (e.g., Ohio, Pennsylvania) have assigned responsibility for this program to separate county agencies. Federal regulations under the Social Security Act provide that federal policy is that the state agency responsible for the state plan approved under Title XX (social services for individuals and families) will also administer or supervise the administration of the child welfare services plan (under Title IVB), except that if on January 2, 1968, the two programs were administered by separate agencies, the programs may continue to be administered separately.

Medical assistance program administration. Title XIX of the Social Security Act, which authorizes the medical assistance program, gives the states the option of selecting the agency to be made responsible for administering the program. However, the act requires that the eligibility determination function be conducted by the state or local agency administering income maintenance and social services for recipients of old-age assistance, that is, the public welfare agency. Eleven states make a separate agency, usually the state public health agency, responsible for program administration.

Cuban refugee assistance. This program is administered by the city of Miami, Dade County, and the state of Florida in conjunction with the U.S. Department of Health, Education, and Welfare. The resettlement of Cuban refugees throughout the country has made many state and local public welfare agencies responsible for their financial assistance and social services. With the number of refugees diminishing and the program winding down, this program will gradually end within the next few years.

Assistance to repatriated U.S. nationals. Services by state and local public welfare agencies are being provided to repatriated citizens under this program, primarily at the points of entry for foreign travelers, namely New York, Boston, San Francisco, New Orleans, Miami, Los Angeles, and Washington, D.C. The agencies in these cities are called upon to provide emergency help for these persons.

Income maintenance for the needy aged, the

blind, and the disabled. With the passage on January 1, 1974, of the Supplemental Security Income Program under the Social Security Amendments of 1972 to provide financial assistance to aged, blind, and disabled persons, the responsibility of state and local public welfare agencies for this case load changed. Payments are made by the Social Security Administration, and those states with a payments level in 1973 greater than the new uniform national standard are required to provide supplemental amounts to their former aged, blind, and disabled recipients. Other states are no longer required to make provision for state maintenance assistance for these groups of recipients, though most do. This marks an exception to the provision of core functions for income maintenance found in all state and local public welfare agencies.

Other human service functions

The third category of public welfare functions comprises other human service programs and activities that are assigned to state and local public welfare agencies authorized in the given jurisdictions. Examples found in state, county, and city agencies include the operation of institutions for the aged or the mentally retarded, programs for crippled children, mental health programs, juvenile delinquency prevention programs, services for the blind, correctional rehabilitation, day care, employment development, vocational rehabilitation, and community programs.

The term *public welfare* does not appear in the names of federal government organizations responsible for the public welfare functions and activities described above, and it is found in only nine states. A few states include the term *welfare* in their agency titles. Various other terms for public welfare agencies in different states and counties include social and rehabilitation services, social services, family services, public aid, economic security, human resources, and institutions.

No single executive agency of the federal government is responsible for the public welfare system in its entirety. The federal agencies responsible for the different public welfare programs include the Department of Health, Education, and Welfare, primarily the Health Care Financing Administration, the Office of Human Development Services,

and the Social Security Administration; the Food and Nutrition Service of the Department of Agriculture; and the Employment and Training Administration of the Department of Labor (Spindler, 1979, pp. 25–29).

As a summary, the following outline sets forth the ten core programs of public welfare divided into the four types of services:

1. *Income maintenance programs (cash programs)*

    Aid to Families with Dependent Children (AFDC)
    Supplemental Security Income (SSI)
    General Assistance (GA)

2. *Social services programs*

    Social services to individuals and families—Title XX
    Child welfare services

3. *Income maintenance programs (in-kind programs)*

    Health: Medical assistance (medicaid)
    Food: Food stamps
    Manpower training and employment: Work Incentive Program (WIN)

4. *Special programs for population groups*

    Cuban refugee assistance
    Assistance to repatriated U.S. nationals (Spindler, 1979, p. 75)

It may help readers to grasp the complexity of the job in public welfare if they realize that any client who meets the worker across the intake desk of a public welfare agency may have problems, or needs, or be served in some way by programs developed under the following federal laws:

Public welfare	Social Security Act of 1935, as amended
	Food Stamp Act of 1964, as amended
	Migration and Refugee Assistance Act

Education	
Preschool	Community Services Act of 1974 (Head Start)
Elementary and secondary	Elementary and Secondary Education Act of 1965, as amended
	Head Start–Follow-Through Act of 1974
Vocational	Vocational Education Act of 1963, as amended
Higher	Higher Education Act of 1965, as amended
	Educational Amendments of 1972
Adult	Adult Education Act of 1966, as amended
Minority group	Emergency School Act of 1972, as amended
	Bilingual Education Act of 1936
Handicapped children	Education of the Handicapped Act of 1968, as amended
Indian	Indian Education Act
	Indian Adult Vocational Training Act of 1956

Food and nutrition	
Commodity food distribution	Agricultural Adjustment Act of 1938, as amended
	Agricultural Act of 1949, as amended
	Food and Agricultural Act of 1965
School food programs: School lunch, breakfast, milk; women's, infants', and children's supplemental food program (WIC); child care food program; and so on	National School Lunch Act of 1946, as amended
	Child Nutrition Act of 1966, as amended
Nutrition program for the aged	Older Americans Act of 1965, as amended

Housing and community development	
Public housing	Housing Act of 1937, as amended
Housing for low-income families	National Housing Act of 1934, as amended
	Housing and Urban Development Act of 1965, as amended
Community planning and development	Housing and Community Development Act of 1974
Indian housing improvement	Snyder Act of 1921

Employment and training	
Comprehensive employment and training	Comprehensive Employment and Training Act of 1973
Apprenticeship training	National Apprenticeship Act of 1937
Employment services	Wagner-Peysner Act of 1933, as amended
Senior community service employment	Older Americans Act of 1965, as amended
Minimum wage and hours standards	Fair Labor Standards Act of 1938, as amended
Age discrimination in employment	Age Discrimination in Employment Act of 1967, as amended
Farm labor contractor registration	Farm Labor Contractor Registration Act of 1963
Job discrimination	Civil Rights Act of 1964, as amended

Health	
Family planning	Public Health Service Act of 1912, as amended
Community mental health centers	Community Mental Health Centers Amendments of 1975
Alcohol and drug abuse education	Alcohol and Drug Abuse Education Act of 1970, as amended
Drug abuse prevention and treatment	Comprehensive Drug Abuse Prevention and Control Act of 1970
	Drug Abuse Office and Treatment Act of 1972
Alcohol abuse and alcoholism prevention, treatment, and rehabilitation	Comprehensive Alcohol Abuse and Alcoholism Prevention, Treatment, and Rehabilitation Act of 1970, as amended
Health maintenance organizations	Health Maintenance Organization Act of 1973
Childhood lead-based paint poisoning control	Lead-Based Paint Poisoning Prevention Act of 1971

Veterans' health services	Veterans Health Care Expansion Act of 1973 and the veterans' legislation
Appalachian health programs	Appalachian Regional Development Act of 1965, as amended
Civilian health and medical program of the uniformed services (CHAMPUS)	Military Medical Benefits Amendments of 1966

Vocational rehabilitation	Rehabilitation Act of 1973

Aging	
Special programs for the aging	Older Americans Act of 1965, as amended
Foster grandparents and retired senior volunteers	Domestic Volunteer Service Act of 1973

Administration of justice	
Juvenile delinquency	Juvenile Justice and Delinquency Prevention Act of 1974, as amended
Law-enforcement assistance	Omnibus Crime Control and Safe Streets Act of 1968, as amended
Narcotics and drug abuse	Comprehensive Drug Abuse Prevention and Control Act of 1970, as amended
Community relations services	Civil Rights Act of 1964, as amended

Income security and benefit payments	
Disabled coal miners' benefits	Federal Coal Mine Health and Safety Act of 1969, as amended by the Black Lung Benefits Act of 1972
Veterans' benefits	Veterans Benefits Act, as amended
Railroad retirement benefits	Railroad Retirement Act of 1971, as amended
Longshoremen's and harbor workers' compensation	Longshoremen's and Harbor Workers' Compensation Act of 1927, as amended
Indian assistance payments	Snyder Act of 1921

Other federal programs	
Community action	Community Services Act of 1947, as amended
VISTA volunteers	Domestic Volunteer Service Act of 1973
Federal youth and handicapped employment	Civil Service Act of 1883, as amended
Small business assistance	Small Business Act of 1953, as amended
Legal services corporation	Legal Services Corporation Act of 1974
Indian social services	Snyder Act of 1921
Federal income taxes	Federal income tax legislation

(Spindler, 1979, pp. 36–39)

State plans

As we mentioned briefly in Chapter 20, each state is required to submit to the federal government a plan of how it intends to conform with federal policy relative to the operation of a particular federal program. Each separate federal program will have separate specific requirements for what has to be in the state plans, but such plans must meet the following minimum criteria:

1. The state must provide that the program will be in effect in all political subdivisions of the state.

2. The state must participate financially in the program.
3. The state must establish or designate a single state agency to administer or supervise the administration of the plan.
4. The state must grant opportunities for a fair hearing to any individuals who claim that their applications for assistance have been unjustly denied or have not been acted upon with reasonable promptness.
5. The state must provide the methods of administration necessary for the proper and efficient operation of the plan, including the establishment and maintenance of personnel standards on a merit basis.

6. The state must provide for the training and effective use of paid subprofessional staff, with priority given for the full- or part-time employment of recipients and other poor persons and the use of unpaid partly paid volunteers.
7. The state agency must make the reports prescribed by the U.S. Department of Health, Education, and Welfare (Spindler, 1979, p. 42).

These state plans are very important. Once a state plan has been approved it becomes the criterion by which the state's continued eligibility for federal funding is determined. The various divisions of the federal government make a periodic review of the state's administration of its plan. The state also make checks of its own, as it is essential that the criteria of the various laws and the requirements of the state plan be met. Failure to meet a federal or state plan requirement may result in the withholding of federal funds from a state. Such withholding of funds is a very drastic step that will affect both the welfare of individual clients and the state program. Because of the seriousness of this step, various procedures of negotiation and appeal are provided for in the case of federal withholding of funds.

The individual and the agency

The individual applying to the agency, the worker who takes the application, and the worker who continues to serve the recipient each have certain obligations and responsibilities. In addition, the client has certain rights that must be observed by the worker and the agency. An important characteristic of public welfare is that the relationship that is developed between workers and clients will inevitably affect the clients' feeling about themselves and their use of the resources available. In addition, in most programs the client's life may be affected in irreversible ways, for good or ill, by relationship with the worker. In general, the following is a statement of the criteria that shape their relationship:

Any individual citizen or alien lawfully in this country may request that another person apply in his behalf to a state or local agency and receive

a prompt decision upon his request for assistance or services with no discrimination by reason of race, sex, religion, national origin, political belief, citizenship, or durational residency requirement. The only exception is the Social Security Act provision under the SSI program which permits a state to exclude an individual who has been absent from its borders for a period in excess of 90 consecutive days until he has been present in the state for 30 consecutive days.

No individual is required to apply for assistance or services or is required to accept them if offered. This needs to be qualified in a number of instances, however. In the case of a dependent child removed from his home or the home of a relative by a judicial determination and placed in a foster home or child care institution, foster care or institutional services must be provided under the state law as prescribed by the court. This same concept also applies to delinquent, abused, and neglected children placed under court supervision and receiving child welfare services, in which the state or local agency serves as agent for the court. For another group of persons, including heads of households and youth from families receiving AFDC required to register for the WIN program, failure to register or undergo training, employment or other required social services, unless for good cause, will result in the state or local agency discontinuing income payments for themselves, but not the children in their families.

Recipients receiving payments are free to spend them as they wish without government intervention. Although payments are made to help cover their basic needs for food, clothing, shelter, and other necessities, they may be used for purchases of other items, or be used for necessities in different proportions or amounts than those on which the payments are based.

Any individual has the right to appeal the action of the state or local agency to deny assistance payments or services in the amount or type he deems he is entitled to, and must be provided with a fair hearing and legal assistance for such hearing.

In fiscal year 1975, 133,058 requests for fair hearings were received by 48 state agencies. Three-fourths of these were filed under the AFDC program, with another one-fourth under the Medicaid program. About three-fourths of the requests were disposed of by a formal hearing. More than a quarter of the requests resulted in a change in favor of the claimant.

Any individual is entitled to examine state and local agency program manuals, rules, and regulations concerning eligibility, need standards, and amounts of assistance payments, recipient rights, and responsibilities and services offered by the agency. He is also entitled to a copy of such materials without cost, or at a reasonable charge to cover the cost of reproducing the material.

Agency procedures and methods must be designed and executed to give full respect for the rights and dignity of applicants and recipients of the agency's programs. Moreover, the confidentiality of records and information about individual applicants and recipients and agency actions in specific cases is assured and the disclosure of such information is proscribed, usually through an order issued by a court having jurisdiction to issue such orders in a legal matter in which the information is indispensable to its resolution.

All individual applicants and recipients have an implicit obligation to provide the agency complete, honest, and current information which the agency requires to make an initial determination of eligibility for assistance payments, services, or food stamps or to confirm continued eligibility. Individuals are also obligated to cooperate with the agency in its activities to corroborate the information they supply. On its part, the agency has an obligation to limit its requests for applicant or recipient information to essentials in order to make agency determinations of eligibility and entitlement for payments or services.

Misrepresentation of information by an individual with the intent to defraud a government in receiving assistance payments or services is punishable under federal and state law by a fine not exceeding $1,000, or by imprisonment not exceeding one year, or both.

In fiscal year 1975, state agencies reported there were over 144,000 AFDC cases which involved questions of recipient fraud disposed of by administrative action. Of these, 81,000 cases were determined to be sufficient to support a question of fraud. Another 40,000 cases, or 49 percent, were referred to law enforcement officials for action. During the year, 38,000 cases were disposed of by legal action. An additional 18,000 prosecu-

tions were initiated and, in 5,570 cases, reimbursement of amounts falsely paid was arranged.

Over 27,000 recipient fraud cases were disposed of without referral to law enforcement officials. In more than half of these (58 percent), reimbursement by the recipient was made. The trend in fraud cases has risen as state public welfare agencies continue improvement in detecting and reporting suspected fraud, initiate procedures to assist in correcting agency practices in eligibility determination processes leading to overpayments, and stressing to clients their legal responsibilities as recipients of assistance payments and services. (Spindler, 1979, pp. 46–48)

How an applicant becomes a recipient

To discuss each program in detail would take more space than we have in this introductory text. Also, changes in various details come so rapidly in public welfare programs that the specifics of a program learned today will not be applicable tomorrow. In addition, to be completely specific about each program would require 51 separate accounts, as each state and territory has differing requirements. Something of the impact of the differences among the states may be understood by comparing the following tables, which set forth the average payment in the five states with the highest levels of AFDC payments and in the five states with the lowest levels. The five states with the highest average AFDC payment per family were:

Massachusetts	$381.94
New York	356.55
Hawaii	338.53
Wisconsin	298.07
Michigan	287.04

The five states with the lowest average payment per family were:

Mississippi	$ 48.61
South Carolina	89.77
Alabama	94.58
Georgia	100.48
Tennessee	104.72

(Spindler, 1979, p. 83)

Instead of giving the details of each program, we are going to discuss the process and generalized principles of eligibility requirements and benefit determination. This will give readers a general notion of the workings of the programs.

Intake. The intake process is the process in which the worker and the applicant engage immediately after the applicant makes contact with the agency. Its purpose is to provide applicants with information about the program, to establish the eligibility of applicants for assistance and/or services, or to aid applicants in finding other sources of help if they are ineligible for agency assistance and/or services. As was noted earlier, an applicant may request assistance in a number of ways. Applicants may be assisted in the intake process by an individual of their choice (Spindler, 1979, p. 344).

Application. Individuals asking about assistance become formal applicants when an application form has been completed and signed. Although the details on the form will differ from program to program, from time to time, and from state to state, in general the form may request the following: personal details about the applicant; about each individual family member; and about the family's legal relationships, race, financial needs, income sources, working experience, education, housing conditions, eating practices, kinds and value of assets, health and life insurance, and potential resources, such as tax refunds and back pay. The application form requires that the applicant certify to the completeness, accuracy, and truthfulness of the application, and informs applicants of their rights. Applicants are required to furnish an assortment of documents, such as birth certificates, that may be used to verify the statements made on the application form. Most applicants will not have the necessary materials with them at the time of the first interview, so the worker will make another appointment and will help the applicant to consider how to obtain the necessary documentation. Several interviews may be needed to complete the process (Spindler, 1979, pp. 344–47).

Verification. It is now the responsibility of the eligibility worker to establish the truthfulness and completeness of the material provided. Spindler has estimated that more than 100 individual decisions must be made by the worker in processing an application. The verification is expected to be completed within 45 days, but agencies do not always meet this deadline. Because of the slow, inefficient process of such work, in 1970 it was made possible for the agency to rely almost wholly upon the applicant's written declaration as to the truthfulness of the information. However, this method contributed so substantially to errors and fraud that it was discontinued in August 1973.

Methods of control; accountability. All agencies have some methods, usually very detailed and complicated ones, for assuring that applicants are served, that verifications are made, and that payments are properly made in the proper amount.

Income maintenance programs (all programs). The agencies must determine whether the applicant is financially needy. The federal social security legislation does not define "need." When the Social Security Act was originally introduced in Congress, it was decided that to define standards of need was to invite rejection of the legislation. Therefore, the definition of need was left to the states, each of which has established its own standard of need as expressed in a money amount. This standard is expected to represent the cost of basic needs. To this amount it is possible to add the costs of any special needs, such as a diabetic diet or special school needs. Federal regulations require that each state establish uniform standards of need throughout the state except for the costs of shelter, which may vary widely from urban to rural areas. No two states have the same standards.

All of the income and resources available to the applicants are taken into consideration in determining need except for certain amounts that are disregarded, such as the earnings of dependent children who are full-time students. Some of these so-called disregards are mandated under federal regulations, and some are state-determined. In addition to meeting an income test, applicants must meet an assets test. All states set limits to the resources and assets that applicants may own and still be eligible for the programs. For example, a top limit is set on savings, equity in a home, a car, and so on. And there may be other conditions, such as that an applicant must not have transferred property within the last six months or the last year.

Income maintenance (financial aid). The difference between the applicant's available income and the need standard represents the budget deficit. In 19 states and the Virgin Islands, that deficit is met in full. This means that applicants' resources are subtracted from applicants' needs, and applicants are given the difference between what they have and what they need. However, not all states give the full amount of need. Eighteen states set maximums by family size. Thus a family of four might not be able to receive more than $150, no matter what its amount of need. If a family's budget deficit is less than the maximum amount allowed, then the family would receive only the deficit.

Twenty-eight states, Puerto Rico, and the District of Columbia never have sufficient funds appropriated by the legislature to meet the full needs of their AFDC clients. Thus they reduce the standards of need, or the budget deficit, on a percentage basis. For example, a family needs $250 a month. However, the state reduces the needs of all families by 10 percent. Thus the amount allowed for this family's needs would be $250 − $25, or $225. If the family had an income of $25, this amount would then be deducted, and the family would receive $200. Another way to accomplish the same goal would be to take a percentage of the budget deficit rather than a percentage of need. In this instance, the family's income of $25 would be deducted from its total needs of $250. The deficit would be $225. The agency would then reduce this amount by 10 percent, and the family would receive $202.50 (Spindler, 1979, pp. 356–58).

Methods of payment. Assistance payments are usually mailed to recipients once a month. The agency is forbidden to restrict the recipient's use of funds in any way. However, if the recipient is held to be unable to manage money properly, the agency may make payments for such services as rental housing and heat directly to the vendors of the services. Federal regulations limit the proportion of recipients who can be subjected to this restriction to 10 percent of the case load in the state in any one month.

This completes our account of the process of establishing an individual applicant's eligibility and the amount of benefits received.

Concerns about public welfare income maintenance programs

One of the important things to remember when we discuss welfare is that the vast majority of income assistance expenditures are made, not for the means-tested programs, but for social insurance programs whose larger benefits go to the relatively affluent. In fact, the social insurance programs outspend the means-tested programs by more than two to one. The largest social insurance program is OASDI. But two other social insurance programs are also very expensive. One is medicare, which we have discussed at some length. The other is unemployment insurance, which we have only touched on. Although the basic unemployment insurance benefit is given for 26 weeks, a number of special extensions increase the duration of aid to as long as 65 weeks. Among the means-tested income assistance programs, almost one third of the total outlays are spent on in-kind programs. About half of the in-kind expenditures now go for two sizable programs—medicaid and food stamps. Of the $21.8 billion spent on cash transfer means-tested programs in 1976, about half went for the SSI programs and about half for the AFDC programs (Salamon, 1978, pp. 10–16).

Cost

Perhaps the principal concern about welfare is its cost. The rapid rise of expenditures has raised many fears of the possibility of overwhelming welfare costs. These fears become particularly evident during periods of high employment and strong economic growth, when people assume that those on welfare should find work.

It was the growth in the expenditures of the AFDC program that first touched off the present major concern with the costs of welfare programs. There are three ways in which the costs of AFDC can increase over time: (1) the number of those who are eligible can increase; (2) more of those who are eligible can decide to use the program; and (3) benefits can be increased to those who apply. During the 1960s most people seemed to assume that AFDC costs were increasing because more children were being left without adequate parental support as a result of deterioration in family life. However, a careful look at the AFDC applications reveals that the growth was not in the number of *eligible* families but in the decision of the families that were eligible to use the system for temporary assistance. The OEO programs and other community assistance programs may have helped people who were eligible for AFDC to understand their eligibility and the workings of the program so that they were willing and able to apply for something they should have had all along. It is estimated that by 1971 94 percent of those eligible for AFDC were receiving assistance, so growth from this source will probably not continue at the earlier rate. In spite of the emphasis on "getting people off welfare" the recipients of AFDC do not constitute a group of people who are trapped forever in dependence on welfare. It has been estimated that only about 20 percent of AFDC recipients remain on the rolls for longer than four years (Rein and Rainwater, 1978, pp. 511–35). The Rein and Rainwater study seems to indicate that the longtime AFDC recipient is a mother who not only lacks education and work experience but is also deprived of any "supporting network" of family or friends. Obviously, there are also families that move off AFDC only to reapply when an unskilled job evaporates and to move off again when another unskilled job is found.

Perhaps the most important increase in the costs of the means-tested programs came from the rapid increase of the in-kind programs. This increase came about largely because the in-kind programs were new or substantially increased programs and thus demanded support in areas where there had been no expenditures previously. It is estimated that in some situations the in-kind programs will probably not continue to increase at the start-up rate. However, for other in-kind programs, such as the housing program, the definitions of eligibility have established a population so large that the need cannot possibly be met. The pressure on such programs will probably persist as eligible people struggle to get their benefits.

We need to recognize that as inflation continues, the costs of welfare will continue to go up in actual dollars. If our GNP declines, as it has recently, our present system and level of benefits will take an increasing share of our output. Thus, even maintaining the present level of welfare may become a heavier burden on the citizens of the country, and the pressure on in-kind programs may cause a continuing rise in welfare costs. Although the growing costs of welfare do not appear to be the disaster that some would have us believe, welfare costs will continue to be a significant part of governmental spending.

Two other problems of welfare costs need to be considered. First, administrative costs in the means-tested programs are high. This is because of the necessity of proving need. The verification of eligibility, discussed earlier in this chapter, is a costly process. Second, welfare costs have an excessive impact on state and local budgets because of the complicated and intricate funding arrangements that seem to be necessitated by the division of powers among various levels of governments. The federal grants-in-aid that must be matched by the states mean that the poorer states are usually able to command less federal assistance than the wealthier states, which can afford to appropriate enough matching funds to claim maximum federal funds (Salamon, 1978, pp. 18–30).

Adequacy

While one group of citizens express despair and fear over one side of the welfare equation, another group are equally concerned about the other side. Are benefits, no matter what their costs, adequate? This becomes an ever more difficult question to answer. What do we mean when we talk about adequacy? Do we mean programs that will provide a family with a bare minimum of survival needs? Or do we mean programs that will enable a family to live at a decent level in comparison with the country's general level of living at the time? These questions also relate to an earlier discussion on how we define poverty. Is poverty absolute, pegged at the minimum amount of money to purchase a bare minimum of food, clothing, and shelter? Or do we mean by poverty some amount that expresses a ratio between what is available to the well-off in our society and what is available to the less well-off? Readers may want to go back to Chapter 20 and review the problems in the absolute definition of poverty that we now use.

One of the problems with adequacy concerns what Salamon has called "gaps" and "leaks" (Salamon, 1978, pp. 34–35). Salamon points out that "except for food stamps (and Medicaid to a lesser extent) none of the major income assistance programs provides benefits solely on the basis of need." The social insurance programs in which benefits are based on age, or disability, or prior or present work experience, or dependence on a prior worker, provide benefits to a large number of recipients who live far above the poverty line. The means-tested programs, except as noted above, do not give assistance simply on the basis of need. Because access to these programs rests on inclusion in particular population groups as well as on need, the programs exclude more needy people than they include—there are massive gaps in their coverage. The largest of these particular population groups are families in which there is a male who is considered the family head and the chief wage earner. It is estimated that 15–20 percent of assistance from the means-tested programs goes to the nonpoor (Salamon, 1978, p. 37). A recent study based on census data shows that the major income maintenance programs helped 44 percent of the poor escape poverty. However, it appears that most of this help was provided to the aged through the social security program. The public assistance programs helped only 5 percent out of poverty.

Such studies have two significant problems. First, the census studies, and most other studies as well, do not take into consideration the value of in-kind benefits. The intricate, cumbersome, and wide variety of in-kind benefits makes measurement almost impossible. In an effort to deal with this problem some studies estimate the distribution of in-kind benefits. One such study shows that 83 percent of the poor are helped out of poverty when in-kind transfers are included (Plotnick and Skidmore, 1976, p. 140). However, there are two problems with this type of analysis. The first is that leaks occur in in-kind programs just as they do in cash programs. Thus one cannot assume that in-kind benefits are really distributed in such a way that all of them can be assigned to the relief of poverty. Second, a serious problem, is the assumption that in-kind benefits are worth as much to the poor as they cost the government (see Chapters 5 and 6). The food stamp program is a good example in that it forced families to do without other things (for example, many mothers could not give their children money for the subsidized lunch at school) so that they could participate in the program, which required that they spend a certain amount in a lump sum for such stamps. Another example is the poor family with a member who has a severe and unusual illness. If the value of the in-kind medical care that the family receives is added to its budget, the family will appear to have an income far above the poverty line, but it will not have seen a penny of this, and, in fact, given trips to the hospital to visit the sick member or the need to use the pay telephone on the corner with increasing frequency, the family may have far less money available to it because of this illness which has so significantly increased its income on paper.

Inequity

In the face of the social problems of the past decade, we have added incrementally to the welfare programs instead of reshaping them. There are many who feel that this may be the best way to deal with the welfare problem—gradual change rather than a complete reform. However, this way of dealing with our welfare problem has created an almost insurmountable problem: the problem of equity, of the basic fairness of the system. Salamon (1978, pp. 42–43) has identified two important dimensions of this problem—horizontal inequity, or disparities in the treatment of different segments of the poor, and vertical inequity, or the advantages that the system sometimes provides for the poor as compared to the nonpoor.

Horizontal inequity. The food stamp program, which is available to all in need, whatever their family situation, has helped reduce the disparity between female-headed families and all other families, but there are still problems in the fact that families equally poor are treated differently because of the status of their members. Also, because AFDC and medicaid leave the decision about benefit levels and eligibility to the various states, there are tremendous disparities in the assistance available to similar families based on where they live. Thus, although the in-kind programs relieve some of the inequities among the poor, they also produce other inequities based on residence or on the fact that access to in-kind programs may rest on the receipt of the cash benefits as well. Also, the benefits of the in-kind programs are rarely available to all who are technically eligible to participate, both because of the limited funds of the programs and because of the limited knowledge of the poor who are eligible to receive these benefits.

Vertical inequity. Perhaps even more politically damaging than the horizontal inequities in the welfare system are the so-called vertical ones, those that result in a higher income after welfare for those who start off poor than is ultimately available to those who start off non-poor (Salamon, 1978, p. 46). For example, a woman who earned $5,300 per year, out of which she paid social security and income taxes plus her work expenses, ended the year with far less than a neighbor receiving AFDC who had access to a subsidized home and medicaid and, in addition, drew $750 in cash per month, determined on the basis of her large family's need. Her income for the year totaled more than $9000 in untaxed benefits.

This presents a very interesting puzzle. This concern that welfare recipients are now better off than the working poor goes back to the principle of "less eligibility" (discussed in Chapter 9), which was first raised in England in the 19th century in the report of the British Poor Law Commission of 1834. This principle grew out of a wish to support the workings of the labor market by avoiding any competition of relief with low-paying jobs. However, much of the present rise in AFDC welfare benefits comes about because of an effort to build in an incentive to work. As an example of this, let us assume that our $5,300-a-year woman has a friend who works beside her. This friend is receiving AFDC and is able to claim $1,000 per year in work-related expenses (taxes, child care, transportation). She ends the year with a gross income of $7,473, or $2,000 more than the other woman. If she buys food stamps and uses medical services during the year, she could easily end the year with a great deal more income and less expenses than our $5,300 woman, who uses the same amount of medical care, unless that woman's medical expenses are covered by a company-paid medical plan. This example illustrates the relationship between adequacy and equity. It leads Congresswoman Griffiths to argue: "The theory of comparing what is given in welfare with what is needed is foolish. 'What is needed' is a phony standard set up by a paternalistic middle class. The real standard is what similar people earn, and how they are treated" (Salamon, 1978, p. 47).

Readers may be wondering about the woman who earns the $5,300. Should she be excluded from welfare benefits? Are her needs for an adequate standard of living changed by the fact that she is not a widowed mother of two children two and four years of age but is providing care for a widowed mother, 60 years old, who does not work because of her age and her lack of skills? People who focus on the problem of inequities between the poor and the near-poor ignore a far more important problem that needs to be addressed: the difference between the poor and the near-poor and the rest of the population.

Disincentive to work and other social factors

One of the troubling questions in relation to equity centers on the concept of disincentive to work. What level of income maintenance will discourage work? Or will people work regardless of income? And, on the other side, what level of incentives will encourage family breakup? And what level of incentives will encourage an in-migration of welfare recipients from a less generous state to a more generous one?

Work. By this time, readers of this book will have recognized that one of the primary concerns about welfare has been that it should not reduce the supply of labor. In earlier times, when employable individuals were not entitled to aid and recipients of aid were considered unemployable, it seemed very simple and logical to deduct anything that a welfare recipient earned from the amount of the welfare grant. This meant that unless welfare recipients got jobs paying more than the welfare grant, they gained no economic advantage by working. In the past 30 years, however, two changes have significantly affected the nature of this problem. First, the rapid entry of women into the labor market, especially the entry of mothers of small children, has challenged our notion of mothers as unemployable. In addition, the fact that the typical AFDC mother was not a widow but was a woman who had never been married or had been deserted by her husband raised questions about whether she deserved the privilege of staying home (work as a punishment?). Second, AFDC benefits have been extended to unemployed fathers.

These two changes, added together, resulted in a tremendous change in public attitudes about the employability of AFDC recipients and a tremendous concern (stimulated by disapproval of the morality of AFDC mothers and the picture of such women as black and therefore inevitability irresponsible) with the possibility that most such women and their husbands were shirking their responsibilities. As a result, there was a move to provide work incentives by allowing AFDC recipients to exclude certain income from consideration in figuring the grant. Salamon describes the operation of this disregard of income as follows:

> Many of these work incentives have been cancelled out by the operation of other programs. Each of the in-kind programs supplementing AFDC had its own marginal tax rate, so that the combined loss in benefits from an additional dollar of earnings could, theoretically at least, be greater than one dollar. As one example, while AFDC taxes net earnings at a 67 percent rate (benefits decline $2 for every $3 in earnings in excess of expenses and $30 per month), the food stamp program taxes participants an additional 30 percent. Based on program operations in 100 areas, the Joint Economic Committee concluded that this can mean in practice that the income left, after work expenses and benefit reductions for employed AFDC and food stamp recipients, can average as little as 20 cents per dollar earned.
>
> Beyond these marginal-tax-rate problems is a whole series of so-called notch problems. A notch is a point in the public assistance benefit scale where an additional dollar of earnings makes a recipient ineligible for other public programs.
>
> . . . Perhaps the most severe of these notches occurs in eligibility for Medicaid. AFDC and food stamp benefits decline somewhat gradually as earnings increase, but Medicaid benefits click off suddenly at the point where the family ceases to be eligible for AFDC, or passes beyond the cutoff point for coverage for the medically indigent. An additional dollar of income can thus spell financial disaster for a recipient family, denying it access to $500–$1,000 in medical care. Similarly, in states with AFDC coverage for families with unemployed fathers, moving from part-time to full-time work automatically means the loss of all benefits. (Salamon, 1978, pp. 49–50)

Although there has been considerable exploration of this problem, the results are far from definite. Most of the studies seem to add up to the following: (1) not as many people will seek work if the economic return from such work does not exceed what could be secured from income maintenance programs; (2) this is much likelier to be true for women than for men; (3) for most AFDC mothers, working really means taking on two jobs: being away from the home at tiring work eight hours or more a day and also having to manage the home and the children—jobs made heavier because shopping, business, medical care, and so forth, have to be attended to at odd and difficult-to-arrange times; (4) most AFDC mothers do not have the qualifications for interesting and personally satisfying jobs but must do the most physically exhausting work; and (5) the pay levels, fringe benefits, and promotion opportunities are much lower for uneducated, unskilled, or black women than for their husbands. The WIN program seems to bear out these observations.

Family stability. For many years there has been a steady stream of criticism of the AFDC program as rewarding family instability. This criticism was prompted by the realization that a large proportion of AFDC funds was going to families broken by separation or desertion. There was a feeling that AFDC might be encouraging such breakups in that AFDC funds were available, and only available, to a family when the man had left the home. This is probably a good example of how the force of social change affects welfare programs, and of how even the best of programs may have unanticipated consequences. Moreover, it is easier in social welfare to identify problems than to develop programs or put them into effective operation. One effort to deal with this problem was to extend AFDC to unemployed fathers. It is almost impossible to establish the impact of assistance upon behavior as complicated as the separation of parents in a family. In summary, it would appear doubtful that much of the growth in the number of female-headed families is realted to the existence of the AFDC program.

Migration. From time to time, particularly during the 1960s, when there was considerable in-migration from the southern states to northern states with better benefits, it has been suggested that in-migration may be caused by welfare benefits. Were people moving to secure larger welfare benefits? In part, this concern is undoubtedly a reflection of racism. The view of blacks as lazy and dependent reinforces this false concern. If there is any relationship at all between larger benefits and in-migration, it is a very tenuous one that holds for whites only. Studies of black in-migration reveal that only 14 percent of AFDC mothers received relief during their first 23 months in New York, a state with no residence requirements. Most of the increase in welfare rolls came from the growth of the population already within the state (Steiner, 1971, p. 88).

Perhaps the concern with the in-migration of possible welfare recipients stems from the threats of business to leave states in which taxes are high or from the movement of firms to states with low wage rates in order to maximize profits. If business moves for such reasons, why not individuals?

Administrative complexity

A very real problem with income maintenance programs is their administrative complexity, which comes largely from attempts to deal with the issues raised above. Income maintenance programs are an unbelievable administrative nightmare. The administrative complexity is caused by several factors: (1) the use of both means-tested and demographic criteria for determining eligibility; (2) the complexity of state and federal relationships in which Congress, the executive, and the Supreme Court all have a part in a confusing federal process which combines with an unpredictable political and bureaucratic local process to make decisions; (3) these problems affect many programs, and they affect each program differently; (4) many programs have different administrative structures (readers might well consider what Carter's proposal would mean when parts of it are administered by HEW, parts by the Department of Labor, and parts by the Internal Revenue Service; and (5) the welfare population is not static—people move off welfare and onto it over relatively short periods of time.

Much of the administrative complexity of income maintenance programs has been introduced into the programs as a way of protecting the public from possible cheaters or from misuse of the programs. It is really doubtful that such procedures save much. First, the direct costs of administration consume approximately 12 percent of the total costs of the programs. In addition to these direct costs, there are significant indirect costs of errors that inevitably increase with the increasing complexity of the programs. HEW Secretary John Veneman put it as follows: "It is not welfare recipients cheating the system that constitutes the big problem. It is a chaotic, do-it-yourself system that is cheating the whole nation" (Veneman, 1974, p. 76). Many feel that, given the complexity of the programs, quality control to eliminate errors would cost nearly as much as the costs of the errors.

A significant cost of administrative complexity that cannot be easily measured, but is far from insignificant, is the confusion and misperception of potential program recipients. A system so complex and difficult to negotiate that it discourages applicants seriously challenges the claim that programs have become more equitable in recent years. A complex system denies benefits to eligible people just as effectively as a system that limits eligibility.

There is serious question whether any program that maintains categorical and means-tested eligibility can really be simplified in administration. When SSI was originally proposed, one of the strong selling points for its adoption was that it would be much better administered under the Social Security Administration, which was certainly more efficient than the welfare agencies. After all, it was going to require only a means test. Salamon discusses this experience as follows:

> Despite pressures for simplicity, the SSI law retained a host of special exclusions from income that vary depending on individual circumstances, and that require consideration of over a dozen rules to compute eligibility and benefit levels. Elaborate checks are still required to assess the value of applicants' personal property and resources. State variations that were purged from benefit determination by the adoption of SSI then crept back in via permission—and later requirements—for state supplementation in states where the federal payment is below what recipients were getting under the old categorical programs. Although the federal Social Security Administration typically administers these state supplement programs in addi-

tion to basic benefits, it has been obliged to retain the confusing array of state benefit determination criteria for the supplements and to graft these onto the standard criteria used for the SSI benefit. The upshot has been widespread dissatisfaction with the changeover from the categorical programs to SSI, persistent errors, and very limited progress in achieving the reduction in administrative costs anticipated from this switch. The Social Security Administration originally estimated that it would need only half as many employees to administer the simplified, centralized, computerized SSI program as were needed by the states in the old categorical programs. Within a year, however, the agency was back before Congress seeking authority to add 50 percent more permanent employees, as well as more temporary and overtime help, than originally anticipated.

> . . . All in all, there is a certain irony, in view of the claims made for SSI, in the fact that "the No. 1 problem facing the program," in the eyes of its administrators, is "excessive complexity." Even after making adjustments for the tight deadlines under which the program went into operation and for the legislative changes made just prior to implementation, the experience cannot help leaving us less sanguine about the prospects for reducing administrative costs and complexity elsewhere in the public assistance system. While the existing system leaves room for improvement in this regard, SSI makes it clear that even simplification has its limits as long as public assistance remains means tested. (Salamon, 1978, pp. 56–68)

Food stamps

One of the important in-kind means-tested income maintenance programs administered by the public welfare agencies has been, as we have discussed, the food stamp program. In 1977 this program was changed substantially. The new provisions of the act were to take effect beginning on January 1, 1979. The objectives of the changes were: (1) to make the program more accessible to the neediest individuals, (2) to eliminate nonneedy persons from the program, (3) to improve program administration and reduce fraud, and (4) to control program costs.

Perhaps the single most important change in the new act was its elimination of the purchase requirement. Thus the poor family that is eligible for food stamps no longer has to get together the cash to purchase them. The plan provides that each eligible household will receive the full allotment of food stamps for a household of its size minus a reduction representing 30 percent of the household's net income. The net income eligibility limit is set at the poverty line as updated semiannually to reflect price increases.

The itemized deductions of the old act were eliminated in favor of standard deductions that were expected to reduce errors in computing benefits and to prevent high-income households from receiving food stamps by submitting inflated lists of deductions from income. The new act provided for work registration requirements, and it significantly restricted the eligibility of students for stamps. The act placed a ceiling on federal expenditures for the food stamp program. However, this has been a controversial provision and President Carter has recommended its removal in 1980. The act will expire in 1981, at which time Congress will have to consider its reauthorization.

✑ Other systems of social welfare that serve income maintenance functions

Earlier, we pointed out that there are a number of freestanding social welfare systems which are not really a part of income maintenance or personal social service systems, yet may serve as an in-kind support of income and often include personal social service divisions within their boundaries. We are going to discuss certain income maintenance functions of these systems in this chapter and the functions of personal social services within these systems in the next chapter. However, readers should be sure to understand that the social work profession is not the profession central to the programs and policies of these systems.

Public health policy and medical care

The development of public policy related to health and medical care reflects the values and principles underlying the development of income maintenance programs. Readers will remember that social work's interest in a program of publicly supported medical care begain in the early 1900s and that there has been a constant effort in Congress to establish some kind of national health care program since President Truman's administration.

However, society has been remarkably resistant to any departure from the delivery of medical care via the private marketplace. The notions that the marketplace is a superior means for delivering medical care and that the professional medical association ought to have absolute charge of health care policy development have persisted despite accumulating evidence that serious deficiencies result from basing programs of health care on these notions. It is argued that the doctor is an individual practitioner who must be left free to practice medicine as she/he sees fit. Yet the American Medical Association and the hospitals impose significant restrictions on the individual practitioner. It is believed that care financed privately produces the greatest advances. Yet all major breakthroughs in medical knowledge and practice have been accomplished by people working in salaried positions within bureaucratic structures. There is a generally accepted notion that our health care is the best in the world. Yet for certain measures of health we rank below some 12 or 15 nations with publicly financed health care.

Our present programs of publicly financed medical care tend to follow our established welfare principles in that only specifically limited populations are eligible for care and in that the programs are based on the principle of purchasing care from the private sector without interfering with it. Today our public expenditures on the health system fall into the following programs: medicare, medicaid, benefits for injured workers (workers' compensation), preventive health programs for mothers and children, rehabilitation of the injured and the disabled, special medical services for the poor in selected ghetto areas, medical care for veterans, and the support of medical research. Medicare and medicaid represent about 60 percent of all our public expenditures on health care.

Of the above programs, only the Veterans Administration medical care programs give us a model for a national health service. These programs were originally designed for a special segment of the veteran population, but over the years the ambulatory and hospital care that the programs provide have been extended so that in practical terms all veterans are now eligible for such care. Although the extension of care to veterans with non-service-connected medical needs was originally intended to aid veterans who could not afford to pay for private care, in practice few questions about ability to pay are raised. The VA administers an almost self-contained health system, directly maintaining over 100 hospitals with some 100,000 beds, as well as outpatient medical clinics, nursing homes, and social services for veterans who can be treated outside a hospital. The system is administered and operated by the federal government through full-time publicly paid employees. These characteristics of the VA health care system are the characteristics of a national health service rather than those of an insurance program (Morris, 1979, p. 88).

The program of adequate medical care at an affordable cost remains a central issue of our social welfare policies. Among the reasons why the problem continues to be an active political issue are the rapidly increasing costs of medical care. Over the last decade those costs have escalated sharply, rising to over 7.7 percent of the GNP. This rise in costs has resulted from the rising cost of hospitalization (charges to individuals may now run more than $200 a day, exclusive of physicians' fees or diagnostic costs) and increases in doctors' fees rather than from the increased use of medical services. Although the aged make more visits to physicians than do other parts of the population, their number of visits per capita has declined since 1964. Physician visits per capita have also declined in the last decade for the population as a whole. They have risen slightly for minority groups, which may indicate slightly better access to care for minority groups. However, the number of physician visits may have little or no relationship to health needs or the adequacy of health care (Klarman, 1974, pp. 110–11). In any case, hospitals and physicians have certainly benefited from increases in income as a result of the present programs of medical care.

What social effects have resulted from the programs of medical care that we have developed since 1965? Morris writes as follows:

> Medical care has been more and more institutionalized and is now predominantly delivered in hospitals. Home visits and the delivery of medical care in any form to the patient's home have been significantly reduced. Hospitals have become larger and often less personal. Physicians' offices are often crowded and replace outpatient clinics of earlier times. The prescription of drugs and chemical therapies have increased enormously, with both great benefits and possible damage. With the rapid expansion in scientific means made possible in part by public support for the purchase of services of payment for research, the capacity to monitor and control the use of noxious or dangerous medicines has diminished. Attention to preventive health methods has declined as hospitals and physicians' offices have become the dominant focus of health services, while public health, sanitation, supervision of water supply have diminished in importance in health policy. . . .
>
> Thus, while the preamble of health legislation has argued that the purpose of the public policies adopted has been to improve and maintain the health of the people, the policies in effect have concentrated only on giving the population access to whatever services have been developed by the private providers—hospitals, physicians, the pharmaceutical companies, and so on (1979, pp. 91–92).

In his 1976 election campaign President Carter promised to introduce a comprehensive health care bill. But the primary emphasis in Congress has been on cost constraint and on either modifying or extending existing programs. A number of health care proposals have been put forward in Congress. The Long-Ribicoff Bill would cover catastrophic health needs and federalize the medicaid program. The Dole-Long Bill would require employers to provide catastrophic health coverage for their employees. The most complete health coverage plan is that of Senator Kennedy, which would have employers provide comprehensive health coverage for all employees and would have the government provide health coverage for all other persons. The Carter administration prefers to phase in a program that would generally give the entire population coverage through private insurance companies or under HealthCare, a new health insurance program.

Although the enactment of comprehensive national health insurance remains only a distant possibility, there has been some movement toward various incremental changes in health policy. The National Health Planning and Resource Development Act of 1974 was passed to replace earlier health planning provisions. This act seeks to prevent: (1) shortages and surpluses of resources, for example, a lack of inner-city doctors, an excess of hospital beds, and so on; (2) wrong mixes of services; and (3) inefficient use of resources. Essentially the act created a network of health planning agencies with the goal of making health services available to everyone at a minimum cost to the consumer. There are three levels of administration: federal, state, and local. Each state is required to establish a State Health Planning and Development Agency that would play a significant role in the review and coordination of local plans, the preparation of a state health plan, and the monitoring of local budgets. A majority of the council members are supposed to be consumers. The local organization is the Health System Agency, which is responsible for planning, coordinating, and developing health services in its area. The HSA can be a nonprofit corporation, a public regional planning body, or a unit of local government. However, its governing board must be composed of a majority of consumers plus providers. The continued spiraling costs of health care through 1977 and 1978 resulted in an extension of and amendments to the 1974 Health Planning Act. The amendments provided for the following significant changes:

> The effects of health planning goals on the health care delivery system must now be documented in periodic reports.
>
> Doctors must obtain state approval, under certain conditions, to purchase major medical equipment for their offices.
>
> Prepaid group health plans are exempted from requirements for state approval.
>
> Through a $155 million program, more hospitals will be encouraged to close underused

acute care facilities or convert them to other uses.

> Competition among institutional and services health care agencies will be fostered.
>
> Regional and state health plans must be coordinated with the planning of drug, alcohol abuse, and mental health agencies.
>
> State agencies must now consider in their "appropriateness reviews" the criteria of need for services, accessibility, agencies' financial stability, cost effectiveness, and quality of services provided. (NASW, 1979, pp. 1–4)

The government has attempted to exercise some control over health care in other ways. The Hill-Burton Act (discussed in Chapter 21) has been altered and expanded so that for all practical purposes federal policy determines what hospital and nursing home facilities will be built and where. All medical facilities are now required to provide for the review of physicians' practices by professional review committees. The Health Manpower Act of 1975 now determines the volume and types of medical education, and utilization reviews by such insurers as the Blue Cross associations now determine what health services will be paid for. In *The Advocate,* NASW recently took the position that the spiraling costs of medical care are pushing the United States at an ever-increasing pace toward some type of planned system of health care, furthered by the determination of Congress to curb the rising costs of health care through some type of regulation of the health industry.

What basic questions have to be answered in developing a national health care plan? Who needs publicly financed health care? Can we extend medical care to the entire population without means tests? How do we contain the costs of a national health care plan? How do we know, determine, and control the quality of medical care offered, and how do we regulate the quantity of care available? What do we do about long-term care? What do we do about care for long-term or permanent disabilities that impair social functioning? Do we continue to develop privately owned, profit-making nursing homes? We have not really faced these problems yet. Consumers themselves are often unable to evaluate how good their present medical care is and how much of it they need. Our present inability to evaluate the quality of health care, and thus our inability to help consumers make informed decisions as to what they want, is not a small detail in health care planning.

Instead of seeking to regulate and control our present system, should we abandon it and develop a national health service on the model of the VA or the English health service? Should doctors be employees of the government, or should they be paid on the basis of the number of patients they serve? Both these methods differ from our present system in which doctors are paid for each service rendered. Will our present plans of monitoring and establishing a "usual and customary fee" for service result in good care and containment of costs? Should hospitals remain as nonprofit, voluntary, and/or proprietary organizations, or should they become public utilities, owned and administered by the federal government or by local governments? Other industrialized countries around the world have various plans through which they attempt to assure their populations access to the vital resource of health care. In some instances, doctors are salaried employees—as they are in the VA or in some university settings in the United States. In other instances, doctors remain private practitioners who are paid through various arrangements. In some countries, hospitals and clinics are publicly owned; in other countries, these essential utilities are provided by means of other arrangements. These are some of the matters on which critical decisions regarding health care have to be made in the United States.

Housing programs

The goals of our public housing policies as set forth in legislation over the last 20 years have been ambiguous, conflicting, inflated, and impossible to relate to outcome. Certainly, the public housing programs have often had unexpected consequences. We summarize the housing policies below. In this summary we state the major objectives of a policy first, the programs that were developed within the policy second, and the consequences of the policy third.

To assure enough new housing to meet the needs of the population. Programs to meet this objective have generally involved increasing the supply of housing by encouraging the private housing industry through mortgage guarantee programs and other programs influencing monetary, fiscal, credit, and tax policies that were aimed at general targets, such as fighting inflation or maintaining prosperity. On the whole, these programs have increased the supply of housing available to middle- and upper-income people but have done little to relieve the need of the poor for adequate housing. In fact, one of their unexpected consequences has been the segregation of various socioeconomic, racial, and ethnic groups by making it possible for those with more economic resources to build in the suburbs or other locations remote from the central cities.

There are hidden assumptions in these programs: (1) that individual home ownership is superior to rental units as a way to house the population and (2) that as older housing units are abandoned by people moving into new homes, they would be renovated and made available to new occupants. The tax policies related to housing provided hidden subsidies to the affluent and discriminated against renters, who were more likely to be poor and to be members of minority racial or ethnic groups.

To reduce housing costs so that more households could afford decent units. The programs developed to meet this objective involved the construction of publicly administered housing and, increasingly, various subsidy devices for builders. Public housing projects were constructed without giving consideration to the social and emotional needs of people. As a result, living conditions in Housing Authority projects became impossible in many instances.

Direct subsidy programs to enable builders to construct low-cost dwelling units for the poor resulted in corrupt practices and in the bilking of poor families by unscrupulous speculators. Many of the poor who purchased such units were unable to keep up the required payments, and there was widespread repossession of homes. The high cost of subsidizing the new housing units over the lifetime of their mortgages troubled authorities, though these direct subsidies, which appeared in the federal budget, were smaller than the indirect subsidies of tax credits to middle- and upper-income buyers, which did not appear in the budget. The low-cost housing units were constructed primarily in urban areas, and rural needs for low-cost housing were largely ignored.

To bring present buildings up to code. This policy was implemented by granting low-interest loans to homeowners and business tenants in targeted neighborhoods in order to bring existing buildings up to present standards of decency and to make some other improvements. The policy appears to have been moderately successful in meeting its objectives.

To permit low-income renters to occupy decent units. Under this program the government subsidizes the construction and rent payments of low-income people. The participants in the program pay from 15 to 25 percent of their income in rent, and public financing makes up the remainder of the "fair market rent." Such subsidies are paid directly to the landlord. The elderly occupy nearly one half of all HUD-assisted housing. This program appears to be an effective way to assist the poor renter. However, the funds for the program have never been adequate and it appears that they may be cut further.

The National Housing Act provides for financial assistance to enable nonprofit corporations such as labor unions, churches, and fraternal associations to construct low-cost housing for the poor. This is a very modest program that operates through interest-free loans and technical assistance.

To improve central city environments and living conditions. A number of programs have been developed with this objective in mind: Model Cities, Urban Renewal, and so on. There have been many criticisms of some of these programs as primarily assisting middle- and upper-income people to move back into the city. The construction of new upper-income units caused the poor to be pushed out of old neighborhoods and priced out

of the new units. However, out of these earlier programs have come some more effective programs.

The Neighborhood Self-Help Development program provides for grants and assistance to enable neighborhood organizations to conduct housing, economic, and community development programs. These grants are targeted to low- and moderate-income neighborhoods and stress partnership between the public and the private interests involved. However, it is anticipated that in 1980 only 120 grants will be made under this program.

Community Development Block Grants is a program that replaced the earlier Urban Renewal and Model Cities Program. It provides funds for physical, economic, and social development projects in cities and counties. These funds are to be spent according to local priorities. Activities under this program must have as their principal purpose the improvement of the living environment of low- and moderate-income people. Susan E. Rees, NASW legislative consultant, made the following evaluation of the program:

> Early studies of the impact of this program found funds channeled disproportionately to high- and moderate-income parts of cities.Very little money was being used for the improvement of such community services as day care, youth and elderly services, job and housing counseling and legal aid, which are eligible activities. Since then, a new formula was adopted favoring older, more distressed cities. In 1978, Congress strengthened requirements that local plans principally assist low- and moderate-income neighborhoods. The budget includes $400 million for Urban Development Action Grants (the same level as in 1978 and 1979) which are used to encourage private investment in the upgrading of the economic base of distressed cities which have proven their ability to improve housing and employment opportunities for minorities and low- to moderate-income people. (1979, p. 6)

Housing problems are excellent examples of the complexity of social problems. It is almost impossible to deal with objectives for housing without getting involved in the entire range of social and economic policies. Housing is realted to poverty, business cycles, inner-city decay, crime, the national financial structure, racial and ethnic discrimination and preferences, the location of employment opportunities, and so on. The results of housing efforts brought into question the notion that changing only physical conditions will significantly change people's lives. Improvements in housing did not necessarily improve the lives of the people living in it. People's living patterns, needs (in some public housing there were no bathroom facilities near the playground, so that children had to walk blocks and take an elevator to the upper floors in order to find bathroom facilities), social resources, and so on, must be considered. However, the continued existence of widespread substandard housing and the concentration of racial groups within such housing are also important considerations. Morris has identified the issues that we need to confront in developing housing policies and plans as follows: (1) high-density concentration, (2) elimination of the slums, (3) integration of social and ethnic classes, and (4) integration of age groups (Morris, 1979, pp. 113–15).

Work force policies

Since the beginning of the industrial revolution, as readers will remember, work and welfare have not been considered separately. In fact, it is often difficult to determine whether we are concerned with poverty or unemployment in our welfare policies. In spite of this link, the problem of finding employment remained primarily that of the individual until the 1930s, though there had been aid to the states for vocational education since the Smith-Hughes Act of 1917.

In considering unemployment, one can assume that the problem arises because more persons are seeking work than there are jobs. On this basis, one can consider stimulating the economy so that more jobs will become available or one can consider reducing the number of workers by persuading persons to leave the labor force. This was the early social security thinking—older workers would have support and so could retire, leaving places

for younger workers. Educational programs and support for education can reduce unemployment by delaying the entry of young workers into the job market. Certainly the GI Bill accomplished this for thousands of returning veterans after World War II. One can also spread the available work—and thus hold down unemployment—by reducing the regular workweek and by making overtime on the job so expensive for employers that they will prefer to hire additional labor.

A possible reason for high unemployment is that technological changes in industry have caused demands for skills that older workers do not have. In this case retraining might be helpful. Or if employment opportunities are greater in one area than another, shifting people to the area affording greater opportunities might be considered. As a last resort, the government itself can provide jobs in public employment.

A federal employment policy probably began with the establishment of the U.S. Employment Service in the 1930s. However, the modern federal manpower programs began with the enactment of the Manpower Development and Training Act (MDTA) in 1962 and of the Economic Opportunity Act in 1964, supplemented by the Emergency Employment Act (EEA) in 1970. This earlier legislation was replaced in 1974 by the Comprehensive Employment and Training Act (CETA). As the names indicate, the principal focus of these programs was job training, with supportive services and income support for trainees, efforts at coordinating employment programs and opportunities, and—later on—efforts at job creation.

This legislation assumed that the principal task was to find, train, and place the unemployed, particularly young, urban, minority job seekers. The principal efforts made were to train such persons for entry-level jobs. If regular jobs were not available, efforts were made to find summer jobs. Training, counseling, an a variety of special services were brought together to prepare the unemployed for the labor market. Some programs were directed at specific subgroups: the Work Incentive Program (WIN) for AFDC recipients, the Job Corps for School dropouts. The JOBS program, which was inaugurated in 1967, sought to involve the private sector in administering training and employment contracts. The Neighborhood Youth Corps sought summer jobs. But for the bulk of the MDTA enrollees, work skills were taught either through on-the-job training or through educational programs in the classroom. In 1970 the EEA was passed to provide for the creation of public jobs for the unemployed. It was the first law since the 1930s which provided for the government's assumption of the role of employer. This reaffirmation of the federal obligation to respond in this way in times of economic distress was carried further in subsequent legislation.

Programs of general revenue sharing were proposed in the mid-1960s. Under such programs federal assistance to the states takes the form of block grants that are spent and administered in accordance with local decisions relative to local needs rather than the grant-in-aid types of categorical assistance that had previously been relied on in federal assistance to the states. The first general revenue-sharing act was enacted in 1972, and CETA represented the first significant use of this new funding device in a specific program area. Manpower programs were selected for this effort in part because the existing programs were so complex administratively and because they were really not meeting their objectives. But this shift could also be considered a response to growing social pressures to increase the authority of state and local governments and to shift the focus of social programs from the problems of the poor and minority groups to the problems of the "forgotten Americans" of the white majority.

Under revenue sharing, CETA provided block grants to states and local governments for purposes that they were free to determine, within broad guidelines. The responsibility for establishing programs was placed in the hands of local governments, with the exception of the Job Corps program and programs for such special groups as the American Indians, migrant workers, and criminal offenders, which remained the responsibility of the federal government.

CETA went into effect at the same time that

an economic reversal began. Thus the viability of its approach is difficult to evaluate. CETA was expanded in 1974 by the enactment of emergency job legislation, and its expansion has again been suggested. It has been proposed that industry councils be established at the local level to work with CETA prime sponsors to develop more private sector jobs for hard-core unemployed and to encourage industry involvement in all employment and training activities. Greater emphasis will be placed on on-the-job training programs and on shifting workers from public employment to private industry. Also employers of a CETA-referred workers are to get tax credits of $2,000 the first year and $1,500 the second year for each such worker to a maximum of 50 percent and 25 percent of wages, respectively. In 1978, 100,000 public service jobs established under CETA went unfilled. Consequently Congress wanted to cut the program. The result was CETA reauthorization that was targeted more specifically to the disadvantaged and established a permanent program to be triggered by high unemployment. However, the summer youth jobs, making up one third of the CETA program, were eliminated from it (Rees, 1979, p. 3).

America has never accepted a national goal of full employment. And until it does, employment efforts will remain narrow in scope and short term and will neglect integration with other social policies. In addition, such efforts will ignore important groups of people who want to work, especially older workers and women. It is somehow consistently assumed, despite all statistics to the contrary, that women can go back home and live on a husband's support if they do not find work. However, our efforts to create an employment policy since the 1970s have heightened awareness of the unequal distribution of employment and career opportunities, have improved the capacities of some youth, and have encouraged the involvement of employers, labor unions, and educational institutions in the problem.

Among the changes in the economic situation that we must reckon with in public employment policies are the following: during the 1970s job growth was most rapid outside the central cities, with corresponding higher unemployment in such cities as Boston, New York, Detroit, and Los Angeles; urban areas had a higher proportion of lower-skilled jobs than did other areas; economic growth shifted geographically to the West and the South, areas in which 70 percent of all workers, 54 percent of black workers, and 45 percent of Spanish-speaking workers were high school graduates; women workers continued to increase in numbers, with 45.7 percent of women in the labor market; the males among blacks and other minority groups continued to experience unemployment rates double those of white males. A comprehensive manpower program should be developed that would at a minimum: (1) minimize unemployment and alleviate its impact and hardship; (2) equip workers for life-long advancement in skills, earnings, and mobility; (3) improve the geographic match between where workers live and where jobs are; (4) minimize institutional forms of discrimination; (5) improve workers' knowledge about where jobs are available and what the opportunities are; (6) improve workers' geographic mobility and minimize the costs of relocation; and (7) determine what skills and knowledges are needed in what jobs so that the educational credentials required match the job requirements (Rees, 1979, p. 7).

Education

We saw earlier that because of conflicting interests and the lack of a constitutional allocation of responsibility for education, education has remained primarily a local responsibility. The federal funds available for education have been allocated largely to specific programs of vocational or higher education. For example, the GI Bill of Rights was a tremendous program of aid to colleges. Thus the passage of an act that provided elementary and secondary public schools with substantial supplementary funds for educating disadvantaged children was an impressive political achievement. The Elementary and Secondary Education Act of 1965 made provision for financial assistance to local educational agencies serving areas with concentrations of children from low-income families. Most local schools had not analyzed the complex problems of disadvantaged children, and thus the first programs introduced under this act were awkward and simplistic. By the mid-1970s, however, positive results were being reported from the programs that eventually evolved.

The increased concern with the education of poor children resulted in a growing understanding of the critical importance of the early years in children's development. As a result we had legislation that authorized the use of federal funds to support community programs to provide early educational experiences (Head Start); programs to promote better health through physical examinations, nutritious lunches, rest, and exercise; and programs to provide a safe environment for disadvantaged preschoolers. Experience with these programs has been varied, as the programs themselves began with a variety of approaches, varying degrees of conscious planning, and great differences in the attempts to learn from experience. Funds for these programs have been reduced continuously, and it is not likely that the programs will be expanded without years of effort.

The present legislation continues to provide for regular aid to low-income school districts plus supplementary services to disadvantaged students in places with high concentrations of low-income residents. In three cities a program has been established that aims at the integration of education and human services for disadvantaged students through highly individualized assistance. In 1980 this program will be expanded to ten cities.

Recent federal educational activities have also been concerned with programs such as the Job Corps and with vocational education to prepare disadvantaged youth for better job opportunities. In addition, the federal government has been concerned with broadening the access of disadvantaged students to higher education. Its activities along these lines have taken the form of assisting existing institutions to expand their capacity of to serve such students and of providing direct support for the individual students. These activities took the form of work-study programs and low-cost loans to students.

Legislative provisions of importance for schools and their students were contained in Titles IV and VI of the Civil Rights Act of 1964, which authorized the desegregation of schools and colleges. The two major values seen in educational desegregation were: (1) it would provide truly equal educational opportunities for persons of all races; and (2) it would create opportunities to teach respect for the dignity and worth of all children and to develop an appreciation of the varied contributions to America that are made by different peoples and groups. Desegregation problems still plague many of our larger cities as parents resist governmental efforts to establish a racial and socioeconomic mix of children in the learning environment.

Federal efforts during the last two decades have furnished significant assistance to education by mounting programs helpful to disadvantaged children, by broadening access to higher education, by providing education for the world of work, and by beginning a movement toward the desegregation of schools.

⇜ Issues in income maintenance policy

Before we conclude our discussion of the development of income maintenance programs and policies in the United States, we need to consider the basic issues in developing such policies and programs. The first question that confronts us in attempting this task is the question of *purpose*. What are the goals and purposes of the various systems within social welfare? Are these systems developed to eliminate poverty, or at least to protect people from the ravages of being poor? Are they aimed at ensuring the provision of a certain amount of security for all people? And what about establishing an equality of opportunity, an equal access to the resources from which we can construct a satisfying life? When we raise the question of equality, we also raise the question of social justice. Should we seek to equalize income and wealth among different groups of people not only as an exercise in social justice but in order to make our society a stronger unit? Certainly, we recognize that in the

United States there are great extremes of wealth which apparently coincide with enormous concentrations of power. "One need not be wildly committed to equality to question whether such patterns of distribution augur well for political stability or the general welfare in a democratic society" (Bell, 1974, p. 3).

Every day, government decisions taken in relation to social welfare systems and the other institutions of our society shift income among various segments of our population. "Taxes, subsidy regulations, special benefits for such favored industries as mineral extraction and farming, revenue-sharing formulas, wage-price controls, public welfare eligibility clauses, highway trust fund restrictions, and affirmative action employment commitments of corporations, are a few of the many public interventions in the flow of income and wealth" (Bell, 1974, p. 2). These decisions to shift income among various groups reinforce or alter social relationships and have profound consequences for family welfare and the quality of community life. Yet these decisions tend to be made without considering national goals for the welfare of our people and without considering the effects of the decisions on those goals. Both absolute and relative poverty exist in the United States. There is a prevailing divisiveness and distrust in our society. This must mean that people feel that they are not getting their fair share of the services and supports of our society. We need to consider how to translate the values of a democratic society into specific public policies and programs. This requires a rationalization of the whole interlocking network of cash transfers and in-kind benefits, including those within the social service system, which we will discuss in the next chapter.

We have discussed the impact of available knowledge on the development of social welfare programs, in particular the impact of a growing knowledge about human behavior and development. An important advance in knowledge that greatly increases our ability to do rational planning is the development of a science of administration and planning that makes use of our sophisticated computer technology and other statistical data collection and analysis methods. Recent technical innovations in this area have allowed a more adequate and accurate look at the impact of taxes and transfer payments (though we are still unable to evaluate the impact of in-kind programs). Table 24–1 shows, by population quintile, the percentage distribution of income for 1970 before federal and state income taxes and after taxes and cash income transfers (Okner, 1973, p. 16). Okner concludes from his study of the impact of taxes and transfers that if we should decide that the best way of assuring an equalization of opportunity and protection from poverty and insecurity is to distribute income more equitably, then we will have to adopt policy changes that would either increase the progressivity of existing taxes or expand transfer payments, or both (1972, pp. 29–32).

We believe that people need to be aware of six central issues if they desire to analyze our present social welfare policies and programs: (1) coverage and eligibility, (2) the mode of transfer (cash or in-kind services), (3) the benefit levels of programs (adaptive or fixed), (4) the funding or programs, (5) the methods of administration, and (6) accountability.

Coverage

The first basic issue in any welfare program is who is to receive assistance or benefits. Our pro-grams have tended to be organized exclusively for the poor or for groups of people with some common characteristic or condition other than poverty. Programs developed for the poor only are called *selective* in that they require a definition of poverty and a method for screening (selecting) the poor from the nonpoor. Readers will easily recognize that SSI and AFDC are selective programs. *Universal* programs, on the other hand, are organized solely in relation to individual characteristics or conditions—for example, age, disability, or parenthood. In developing programs of this kind, a group known as a universe is identified. Once this group has been identified, the benefits of such a program—OASDI is an example—are available to everyone in the group irrespective of income status. A universal system of benefits can be as important an antipoverty measure as any selective program. Planners simply need to identify qualities or conditions that may make people poverty-prone. For example, all single parents who are responsible for children under the age of 18 may be poverty-prone. In many countries, including our neighbor Canada, all mothers of minor children receive monthly allowances for the support of the children. In the United States, to be sure, we have a tax exemption for families with children, but this type of tax action is of much more benefit to high-income families than it is to low-income families or to families with no income at all. What would happen if we eliminated the tax deduction for children and instituted a universal payment to help parents cover the costs of supporting their children? This would be more equitable than tax deductions. In recent years much of the push has been toward selective programs, with the rapid growth of in-kind programs furthering such programs.

The strong push toward selectivity in recent years has been promoted by arguments about efficiency. It has been reasoned that antipoverty efforts will be more efficient if all of the money appropriated for anti-poverty measures goes to the poor. Yet past experience teaches us that programs prosper and grow based on their mix of beneficiaries. It is the programs for the poor and the public assistance, public housing, and medicaid programs that

❧ Table 24–1

Percentage distribution of before-tax income and income after taxes and transfers, by population quintile, 1970

Before-tax and transfer population quintile	Before-tax income	1970 income after taxes and transfers
Lowest fifth	1.80	5.29
Second fifth	6.82	8.84
Third fifth	14.67	14.97
Fourth fifth	24.09	23.27
Highest fifth	52.62	47.63
Top 5 percent	22.06	19.03
Top 1 percent	9.07	7.27
Total	100.00	100.00

Source: Okner, p. 16.

have been the most criticized and most condemned by our society. It appears that programs which spread benefits among people who are identified as in danger of poverty or insecurity, unlike programs which confine their benefits to the poor, are popular and accepted. For example, a rise in AFDC benefits is strongly resisted by most people in our society and is certainly politically unpopular. Yet a rise in OASDI income is greeted with great rejoicing. In discussing these two different types of coverage, Bell says

> The record provides ample evidence that appropriations for selective programs are never sufficient to help all eligible people, usually too low to provide adequate benefits to even limited groups, and yet are regarded in many quarters as a fantastic drain on the public treasury. . . . by conferring a right to benefits upon everyone falling in a prescribed category universal programs not only have the far simpler and cheaper administrative task, but when overall funding is insufficient everyone shares the consequences according to whatever rules were laid down to guide distribution, and intended beneficiaries have a legal right to protest administrative decisions that appear inequitable under the rules. Not so with selective programs where tight rationing has generated a host of whimsical, arbitrary, administrative judgments. In practice, the record shows, some "worthy" applicants are first screened into the system, while the "unworthy" are set away. When fiscal pressures mount, even the "worthy" are subdivided. (1974, p. 32)

Recent discussions of reductions in the food stamp program confirm Bell's last point. The rapid increase in the program has resulted in consideration of how it should or could be cut. One proposal is that the aged, the blind, and the handicapped be protected against cuts, which means that families with children would receive less.

Within the American system of values, which regards poverty as proof of personal inadequacy, any programs that provide benefits only to people below the poverty line are likely to become suspect. It appears that a mix of program beneficiaries

serves to safeguard a program and to permit its expansion. If a program's funds are to be channeled to poor families with able-bodied members who could conceivably be in the work force, two primary factors affect the program: (1) the fear of subverting the work effort and (2) the wish to avoid exploitation and abuse, which are seen as strong possibilities. This results in a very vigorous screening applicants, as we have seen, and in a series of awards to maintain the work effort, and in a clarification of unworthy (able to work) and worthy (generally considered as out of the labor market). As an example, the aged in our society are not without economic stress, but they are better protected than the young or the middle-aged. There are good ways to extend universal programs to all people. Bell discussed the possibility of expanding definitions of disability in OASDI to include all groups of persons with handicaps that might restrict their earning power now or in the future, temporarily or permanently. Unemployment compensation could be improved to cover all segments of the labor force, including youths and women who are seeking jobs, and to provide decent levels of support that keep up with earnings levels. A family allowance, or some other grant of funds based on a population characteristic, could be established at a level that would raise the income of all persons so that poverty and financial insecurity are no longer a threat to our population. Such programs would serve to limit selective programs to small programs to cover emergencies and to unusual situations not easily or readily covered by universal programs.

As we have seen, from the very earliest times the major constraint on the development of income maintenance programs has been the concern about the effect of publicly supplied support on the work efforts of the poor. However, it should be recognized that the best possible work incentive is the assurance of a *decently paying* job. If there are not enough decently paying jobs to go around, this is hardly the fault of the poor, and attempts to correct this problem can be made by the establishment of adequately paid, long-term public employment. We are also facing the new problem of increasing energy costs, and how we will structure programs to see that the poor and near-poor are to survive this new stress. In relation to the problem, Hoshino recently wrote

> What seems to be overlooked—indeed, the label is being studiously avoided—is that all of the current proposals are, in effect, welfare. They are all proposals to add another welfare program—specifically, an income maintenance program—to the already existing programs: SSI, AFDC, Food Stamps, Medicaid, General Assistance—regardless of the name or title under which they parade.

> All are—to view them conceptually—federally-aided, state-administered, residual, selective, means or income tested, in-cash or in-kind (depending on the proposal) income maintenance programs; in other words, public assistance.

> It is, indeed, ironic that for several administrations and Congresses the cry has been "welfare reform"; to simplify and consolidate the plethora of welfare programs, to make them more equitable, to extend protection to the major group historically excluded (the working poor whose only income maintenance is food stamps since they are excluded from all cash programs, except in New York). The President in his election campaign promised to clean up the welfare mess and did submit a welfare reform bill. Congress has had before it a series of welfare reform bills, including President Nixon's. After all the dust and hot air; another welfare program!

> One bill would make the program essentially an extension of the food stamp program and it would be administered in the same way and by the same agencies that administer food stamps. That clearly would be "welfare." All make AFDC and SSI recipients automatically eligible and extend eligibility to other lower income groups, as does the food stamp program. All programs are selective means or income tested. None takes an alternative "institutional" "universal" non–means test route, probably because, like children's allowances, the alternative would mean too drastic and fundamental changes in the present way of rationing goods and services, that is, the market and the price system. (As Sen. Hayakawa said, "Raise the price; the poor don't have any place to go anyway.")

> In other words, price control and rationing—or an even more drastic measure, nationalization, don't square with our basic values.

> So, we go the welfare route, and so another welfare program to add to those we already have. All of the proposals and their authors assume that the program will be "temporary" thus, they are all labelled "emergency." That's what they said about food stamps, AFDC, Old Age Assistance, Aid to the Blind, and Aid to the Disabled (the latter three now SSI—bigger and better welfare), Medicaid. Medicaid and Food Stamps are now larger than the AFDC. There must be a lesson in all this somewhere. (1979, pp. 1–2).

The opponents of this position argue that the insurance programs are designed to cover the non-needy as well as the needy and thus are an inefficient and costly way to deal with problems of poverty. Increasing coverage under social security would only increase "leakage" to the nonpoor. If social insurance were extended to numerous new situations, its costs would probably destroy the integrity of the present system of financing and the use of general revenue funds would destroy the illusion of recipients that they have paid for their benefits. This would result in the loss of the privileged place that social security has heretofore held in American thought.

Benefit levels

There is a serious problem in the attempt to determine what benefit levels are adequate. Only in the past ten years have we had any measure of poverty, and that measure is far from perfect. Using a specific measure of poverty to determine the adequacy of financial levels presents great problems, but it is a measure. Also, even if it were agreed that this is a good measure, in many states there would be opposition to its use because of the effect that this could have on the work effort. In states with low wage levels, persons can work full time and still not have a family income above the poverty level. However, in a number of states the level of aid is now above the poverty level, and certainly recipients in these states would oppose reduction in their benefits.

Modes of supports

The kind of program through which aid is given may be as important as the benefit level. Are cash payments or in-kind services more effective as antipoverty measures, as ways of guarding against insecurity, as ways of providing for equality of opportunity? If we believe that services are better, which ones should be given priority? And do we subsidize demand or supply? In stating its position on welfare reform, the American Public Welfare Association made the following points:

> The payment of cash to individuals is not only simpler administratively, but is also beneficial to those who receive assistance. It reduces the stigma which attaches to those who currently purchase necessities with in-kind benefits which clearly identify them as "welfare recipients." Furthermore it allows poor people to spend their money in a manner which is most responsive to their own needs and priorities. In-kind benefits and vendor payments often hinder rather than promote efficient management of resources. For these reasons, the Committee endorses, as a general rule, the conversion of in-kind benefits into cash payments wherever feasible. (1976, p. 2)

It is interesting that since the beginning of the 20th century, reformers have almost unconditionally condemned in-kind programs. The early reformers expended much effort to establish cash programs as giving the recipients of welfare a better control of their own life choices. However, during the Great Society years one of the ways in which advances were made was through the use of in-kind programs. Moreover, the food stamp program has made a greater contribution to the economic well-being of the very poor than has any other program. There is evidence that in general the children of the very poor do not show the evidences of malnutrition that they showed ten years ago. Much of the credit for this is given to the food stamp program. Salamon summarizes this position as follows:

The second argument for continued use of in-kind assistance is far less debatable, however. For whatever reasons, it seems that the public is willing to support greater outlays for in-kind assistance than it is for outright cash grants. The image of providing food or shelter, rather than the cash that will buy food and shelter, reduces the hostility of many people toward welfare. What is more, it generates support among the affected provided groups (for example, home builders). To the extent this continues to be true, therefore, reliance on in-kind modes of assistance may be the price that has to be paid to achieve an adequate level of benefits. (Salamon, 1978, p. 126)

However, these income maintenance services are not the only services that contribute to people's sense of well-being. Educational and recreational services, parks, and libraries tend to be utilized far less by the poor than by the better-off. Parks are seldom linked to public transportation in ways that make them accessible to the poor. When user charges or special equipment is needed, as with some museums, tennis courts, golf links, or skating facilities, the poor are discouraged. Higher education is certainly far more accessible to the better-off than to the poor, as are the private social services. The Community Action Programs, Model Cities, and Neighborhood Legal Services were programs that were intended to stimulate and assure access of the poor to their rights in the access to and use of certain services.

Actually, for the poor the issue is not cash or services but that, having been shortchanged in both, the poor are in need of both. Just as families need an income floor, so they need a wide range of services. A very important characteristic of cash programs is the fact that entitlement to cash programs is more easily established and protected than are rights to services. Also, public investment goes more fully to the poor in cash programs.

Another question in this area is whether it is better to subsidize demand or supply. For example, subsidies for the construction of public housing increase the housing supply, whereas rent supplements increase the demand for rental units. Housing is an interesting example in that it raises the question of whether supplying a rental allowance to persons of marginal income would increase the availability of decent housing or would simply result in the payment of higher rentals for the units already available. Certainly our experience with medicaid and medicare should have demonstrated that merely subsidizing demand without paying attention to service delivery patterns and effective cost controls can be foolish and expensive. In discussing this question, Bell points out that there are important exceptions to the belief of many that competition in the social welfare marketplace would result in better services. She points out that for some services, such as housing, there is discrimination against certain groups regardless of their possession of the resources to purchase; that other services are so terribly expensive and essential that subsidizing demand so that more of those services will be developed for profit is both wasteful and foolish; that such services as adoption or nursing homes are utilized by vulnerable populations and thus require supervision; and that when national values are at risk the public provision of services is to be preferred (Bell, 1974, pp. 41–43).

Costs

In the face of the pressure to curtail the welfare programs, it is interesting that the problem of the direct costs of welfare reform has really not been given serious consideration. It may be that people see reform as cutting down on waste, inefficiency, overlap, fraud, and abuse, and assume that this will lower costs. Yet it is undoubtedly inevitable that reform of the welfare system, particularly in the direction of universalism, will bring increased costs. One question that will be of primary importance in welfare reform will be the relative participation of the federal government and the states in funding. If the federal government simply takes over the present programs from the states, matching the levels of the highest-paying states, there would be a huge increase in costs. For example, Carter's proposal of a $4,200 minimum payment would have been below payments now being made to recipients in 23 states representing 60 percent of the welfare population. Such a move would probably demand a reform of our tax system, which now provides so many hidden and unacknowledged subsidies.

In addition to considering these problems of direct costs, it is important to consider the indirect costs of continuing with our present programs. The current programs seem to have contributed to a growing stigmatization of the poor, who are blamed for the troubles of the system on which they are forced to rely. The part that the present general disillusionment with welfare has to do with destroying the confidence in government also needs to be considered. Finally, the impact of many welfare procedures on the poor is certainly a problem that any movement toward social justice should take into account (Shapiro, 1979, p. 198).

Administration and funding

The direct cash transfer is certainly the easiest and simplest to administer. Cost and impact are easier to assess and more predictable. Services are always more difficult to design, with questions of personnel training and recruitment and methods of delivery and control looming large. Our complicated structure of local, state, and federal administration creates tremendous complexity in both administration and funding. Cash transfers are probably better administered if they are placed at the federal level of both administration and funding. Certain programs of social services, however, may be better administered if they are placed at the smallest level of government, where the community has some imput into the system.

Three proposals for reform

There is certainly no royal road to welfare reform. Welfare reform is an area in which there are strong tendencies to believe the impossible. But reform will never be achieved by good intentions or large platitudes. It requires a willingness to make hard choices, and those choices cannot be made on technical grounds only. As we said in Part I of this book, the basic question is a question of values exercised through political choice in a democratic society.

Every proposal made in welfare reform requires choices in one sphere that by their very nature rule out choices in other spheres. There are basically three groups of proposals that are now being advanced by concerned people.

The first group would have the goal of replacing the existing programs with a uniform system of demogrants, which would involve the payment of a flat grant to every person or family in the country, regardless of need. The money would be treated as ordinary income, and it would be taxed at whatever rate applied to the taxpayer in question. Thus, wealthier persons would return the grant in the form of taxes. The poor would keep most or all of their grant. This system would avoid the stigma of relief, and it would be simple to administer. The costs, however, would be substantial.

Another proposal that some people would place in this group is the negative income tax. This is perhaps most popular in that it requires a means test. People who fall below a certain level of income would receive a grant instead of making an income tax payment—hence the name. This tax-free cash benefit would be based on the level of income and would not vary with family composition or other personal situations of the taxpayer. As earnings rise and income increases, the grant would be reduced, but the reduction would be less than dollar for dollar below a certain cutoff point.

Proposals of this type offer opportunity for administrative efficiency equity and work equity. They eliminate the problems of categorical distinctions and establish a single, integrated program structure. They would reduce the stigma of welfare. However, they pose problems in the areas of adequacy and target efficiency.

There are significant drawbacks to these proposals. In order to preserve work incentive, the proposals must include higher benefits that will extend coverage and increase costs. If we attempt to keep the costs down, the result would be a severe hardship on persons who cannot work since they would have to subsist on a lower basic benefit. The pro-

posals tend to assume that everyone has a choice between work and leisure and that all one has to do to increase employment is to manipulate the benefit levels of public assistance. This assumption appears to be questionable. Also, such plans would probably have to be pegged at a level below what many states are already paying, and this would certainly generate much political pressure to introduce supplementations of some kind.

The second group of proposals resemble Carter's plan in that they would consolidate the existing categorical programs and expand coverage. These proposals would divide the poor into those who can work and those who are not expected to work. Those who can work would be still further subdivided into those who have jobs and those who do not. In general, the benefits would be divided into three types: supplements to low wages for the working poor, jobs and job training for the unemployed, and cash assistance for persons who are not expected to work.

These proposals provide for adequate benefits to unemployables without having to cut back on the financial incentives to work. The benefit cutoff point for those who work could be lower, benefits could be better targeted to those in need, and costs could be controlled better. These proposals uphold the generally acceptable work ethic and thus lessen the stigma that attaches to relief. However, they raise questions regarding the link between public and private jobs, and they raise issues of equity between those on the welfare track and those on the work track. For example, welfare benefits are adjusted to family size, but doing this for work benefits would violate the principle of equal pay for equal work. If jobs were not guaranteed, the same frustrations that have plagued the previous training programs would also plague the new ones. A guaranteed jobs program paying decent wages would undoubtedly attract to the labor force a number of persons who had not worked previously, especially women. Some difficult decisions would have to be made as to who would be entitled to the new jobs, what the new jobs should pay, and how many should be created.

The third group of reform proposals would not

revamp the present welfare system but would make some adjustments in the way it works. In general, the people who advocate this incremental approach believe that the growth in the welfare programs over the past decade has tremendously reduced the poverty in the nation. They see the existing multiple programs, not as something to be deplored, but as a natural consequence of a pluralistic society involving many people with many different needs. They believe that this approach would avoid the pressures to reduce benefits in order to provide work incentives. They believe that the claims for the administrative efficiency of other programs are exaggerated. Among the reforms that the supporters of this approach would like to see are the establishment of a federally funded minimum payment for AFDC families combined with an extension of the Unemployed Parent Program for AFDC parents. The proponents of the incremental approach would eliminate the requirement that food stamps must be purchased and would simply give each eligible family the bonus value of the stamps to which it is entitled. Thus a family of four with an income of $350 that pays $95 to receive food stamps with a value of $182 would simply be given $87 in food stamps. The incrementalists have also proposed that new benefits be added, one being a means-tested housing supplement. Some of them have proposed a small refundable tax credit in which the per capita tax credit would be enlarged and would be refundable to persons whose tax liabilities fell below this amount.

Summary

We have taken a very brief look at the problems involved in our means-tested income maintenance programs of today. We do not expect the readers of a beginning book such as this to explore all the details and all the technical ramifications of the finer points of the issues raised. We simply hope that readers have finished this chapter with some understanding of the complexity of this part of our social welfare programs. To illustrate the balance of spending in our economy, we are reproducing,

Table 24-2

	1979 ($ billions)	1980 ($ billions)
Defense	$117.7	$129.9
International affairs	6.1	8.4
Science, space	5.0	5.7
Energy	6.8	7.25
Natural resources	12.2	11.9
Agriculture	6.0	2.55
Commerce, housing	2.7	2.85
Transportation	17.5	18.6
Community development	9.3	8.35
Education, jobs, social services	29.7	31.0
Health	49.7	54.45
Income security	160.4	190.0
Veterans' benefits	19.9	20.8
Justice	4.2	4.4
General government	4.3	4.2
General fiscal aid	8.4	9.05
Interest	52.3	58.1
Allowances	−0.2	−0.2
Undistributed receipts	−18.5	−19.7
Totals:		
Outlays	493.6	547.6
Revenue	465.9	517.8
Deficit	27.7	29.8

Note: Details of the table may not add to totals because of rounding of the numbers involved.
Source: *Minneapolis Tribune,* November 19, 1979, p. 13A.

in Table 24–2, a breakdown of the proposed national budget for 1980.

A look ahead

In our next chapter we shall examine some of the issues in the personal social services and the profession of social work.

Study questions

1. If you had the task of designing a welfare program for this country, how would you change our present system? Deal with the six issues that are set forth in this chapter.

2. Find out from your welfare board what the average family payment for AFDC is, and where your state falls in relation to other states in such payments.

3. Find out how many people in your county receive

food stamps. What is the average value of those stamps to the average family that receives them?

4. Find out whether your state has the Unemployed Parent Program of AFDC.

5. Are you eligible for any benefits from any income maintenance programs in your community?

6. Look at the table reproduced in the summary of the chapter (Table 24–2). What classes of spending are a part of social welfare? What is the total cost of such spending?

◄§ Selected readings

Spindler, Arthur. *Public Welfare.* New York: Human Sciences Press, 1979.

This book is an excellent account of public welfare—the laws and court decisions under which it operates, its eligibility requirements for various programs, its methods, and its problems.

Ball, Robert M. *Social Security Today and Tomorrow.* New York: Columbia University Press, 1979.

This book is written by the former commissioner of social security. It supports the present funding and operation of the program and therefore may need to be accompanied by some discussion. Its question and answer format is interesting. Its recommendations for change should give excellent material for class discussion.

Turner, Jonathan H., and Starnes, Charles E. *Inequality: Privilege and Poverty in America.* Pacific Palisades, Calif.: Goodyear, 1976.

This is a book that can be utilized to acquaint students with the operation of certain policies that offer significant ''wealthfare'' to the wealthy in our society. It has some excellent tables on the distribution of assets, income, and wealth in our society.

Greenblatt, Michael, and Richmond, Steven. *Public Welfare: Notes from the Underground.* Cambridge, Mass.: Schenkman, 1979.

This very interesting little book was written by two former caseworkers in Massachusetts' welfare agencies. They attempt to describe in concrete terms the public welfare worker's job.

United Press International

Two segments of the population often in need of special protection and social care services are those pictured here: The mentally retarded and the aged.

U.S. Department of Housing and Urban Development

Chapter 25 🦆

🦆 Current programs and issues in personal social services and the profession of social work 🦆

🦆 Introduction

As we begin a summary of personal social services and social change activities, we are again confronted with the fact that there is no accepted definition of what we are discussing. Elizabeth Wickenden's discussion of the definition of personal social services appears to be a useful one: "For my part, I find my best understanding to lie in the interaction of three phases: 'social welfare' to describe a broad functional field; 'social service' to describe the personal service element of that function; and 'social work' to describe the profession which directs, supervises, or performs these services" (1976, p. 573). Wickenden points out another problem in considering the social services: the fact that such services are themselves a mixture of concrete in-kind benefits and services relying on the helpful effects of professional interaction with the client or with others on behalf of the client. She asks whether in-kind benefits should be considered income maintenance in that they often perform that function for the recipients. Her conclusion, which is the rough distinction we have made implicitly in this text, is that a benefit is considered to be a personal social service when professional interaction is critical to effective use of the service. Day care is a good example of this conflict. Should the provision of day care for a sliding fee based on a working parent's ability to pay be considered a social service or income maintenance? Certainly, day care helps support the parental function and serves as a developmental resource for the child and therefore could well be considered a social service. However, if day care is offered only in order to permit parents to work as an income maintenance measure, perhaps it is not a social service.

If readers will go back to Chapter 5, they will find the beginning discussion of personal social services in which the services are at least classified into four groups: (1) protection services, which offer services to individuals who are seen as needing

557

succor or protection from the exploitation of others because of particular vulnerabilities; (2) social care services, which essentially involve making services available to people in such a way that they can utilize the services available with some personal satisfaction; (3) development and maintenance services, which involve fairly traditional services and social work activities aimed at enhancing normal development; and (4) rehabilitation or psychotherapeutic services, which are aimed at change in the functioning of people. This comes as close to explaining what we mean by the personal social services as is possible at this point. Of course, another way to define such services would be to say that they are services offered to individuals, families, and small groups by social workers for purposes of supporting, developing, enhancing, or changing the social functioning of the recipients. This definition is somewhat cyclical as it defines social services as these things that social workers do. The definition presents us with several problems. Some immediate questions are: Is it personal social service if it doesn't involve social workers? What is the position of the profession in such services? Are personal social services analogous to medical services, which probably would not be recognized as medical services if they were not offered under the auspices of medical professionals? Wickenden seems to imply that social services need to be "directed, supervised, or performed by social workers."

In the above definition, we have included a statement of the purpose of personal social services. Readers should note that the definition is broad and that it does not state any specific objective, such as "getting people off welfare" or "decreasing dependence." It is our considered opinion that such large and encompassing objectives are inappropriate for the personal social services and for the profession involved in their delivery—social work. Our definition gives us enough trouble in that the purpose of personal social services is defined as supporting, developing, enhancing, or changing social functioning. The question immediately raised by the use of such terms is: In whose view? From whose perspective do we approach

the supporting, developing, enhancing, and changing?

✍ The classification of social services

By source of funding

There are many ways to organize a discussion of social services. For example, as was discussed in Chapter 5, one can divide them into services that are supported by public funds and services that are supported by voluntary agencies. While the income maintenance functions of social welfare have been taken on increasingly by the government and funded increasingly by tax revenues, two separate and overlapping groups of personal social services have developed: those funded by voluntary contributions, fees, and so on, and those financed by the government from tax revenues. Over the years, as the public responsibility for income maintenance has grown, the voluntary or private agencies have increasingly limited their services to clients who voluntarily apply for social services (see Chapter 23). At the same time, the public agencies have been developing an increasing range of social services both for voluntary clients and for involuntary clients whose problem is usually identified by a force outside the client system. Thus one might say that we now have two overlapping systems of personal social services in this country—the public and the private, or voluntary.

The private or voluntary agencies are usually financed at least in part by the United Way, though small agencies serving limited groups may receive no United Way funding, and many sectarian agencies, funded in part by the Way, may also receive support from their sponsoring groups. In order to help readers grasp the complexity of the system of voluntary social services in an urban community, Table 25–1 lists appropriations by United Way to privately supported agencies in Minneapolis, Minnesota. Most of the agencies listed deliver personal social services to individuals, families, and communities. However, some of the agencies have programs of social development and change. This list-

United Way charity amounts and increases

	1980 budget	Increase	Change
American Cancer Society	$451,111	$40,861	10%
American Heart Association	240,592	22,792	10
American Red Cross	1,438,000	93,953	7
Carver Red Cross	4,250	0	0
Dakota Red Cross.....................	3,300	0	0
American Social Health Association	7,500	1,500	25
Anoka Association for			
Retarded Citizens	47,305	5,050	12
Arthritis Foundation	66,000	8,000	14
Big Brothers	146,100	9,675	7
Big Sister Association	146,900	10,025	7
Boy Scouts	358,000	25,208	8
Bridge for Runaway Youth	27,000	2,000	8
Camp Fire...........................	144,000	8,226	6
Catholic Charities	713,101	55,980	9
Centro Cultural			
Chicano	60,000	*	*
Children's Dental Association	13,439	2,286	21
Children's Home Society	125,243	46,656	59
Chrysalis Center	27,400	2,400	10
The City, Inc.	136,377	25,903	23
Community Action Council	25,772	7,922	44
Community nursing:			
Anoka	43,451	1,576	4
Bloomington	14,000	400	3
Suburban	69,500	4,500	7
Minneapolis	183,514	4,514	3
Correctional Service			
of Minnesota........................	34,300	2,300	7
Courage Center	343,355	18,414	6
Dakota Association for			
Retarded Citizens	21,021	2,270	12
Division of Indian Work	50,251	22,693	82
East Side Neighborhood			
Service	385,201	20,996	6
Family and Children's			
Service	1,099,257	63,361	8
Girl Scouts	204,000	17,974	10
Glenwood-Lyndale			
Community Center	55,000	*	*
International Institute			
of Minnesota........................	25,000	4,498	22
Jewish Community Center	174,000	15,255	10
Jewish Family and			
Children's Service....................	262,500	28,390	12
Johnson Institute	42,000	−3,441	−8
Legal Advice Clinics	8,000	1,000	14
Legal Aid Society of Minneapolis	268,100	35,442	15
Legal Rights Center	21,000	*	*
Loring Nicollet-Bethlehem			
Community Centers	157,057	27,000	21
Lorraine Black Child Care			
Resource Center	25,000	*	*
Lutheran Social Service of Minnesota	441,761	28,159	7
Mental Health Association of Minnesota	108,000	8,000	8
Minneapolis Association for Retarded			
Citizens	188,242	7,994	4
Minneapolis Society for the Blind	151,734	5,000	3
Minneapolis Urban League	321,526	56,356	21

◆§ Table 25-1 *(continued)*

Minnesota Association for Children with Learning Disabilities	59,000	5,855	11
Minnesota Charities Review Council	19,977	3,004	18
Minnesota Epilepsy League	37,000	5,000	16
Minnesota Foundation for Better Hearing and Speech	56,000	4,000	8
Minnesota Social Services Association	1,200	0	0
Multi Resource Centers	150,000	0	0
National Council on Aging	3,000	2,000	200
National Council on Crime and Delinquency	2,000	0	0
The Neighborhood Center	74,083	38,336	107
Neighborhood Involvement	46,954	26,704	132
Northside Settlement Service	398,998	38,692	11
Opportunity Workshop	60,000	0	0
Phyllis Wheatley Community Center	258,988	23,762	10
Pillsbury-Waite Neighborhood Services	657,711	46,348	8
Plymouth Christian Youth Center	18,500	−4,000	−18
Public and Parochial School Child Welfare	7,000	2,000	40
Relate, Inc.	66,043	20,245	44
Rise, Inc.	32,321	2,467	8
Sabathani Community Center	205,990	24,762	14
Salvation Army	383,556	58,556	18
Senior Citizens of Greater Minneapolis	212,088	23,088	12
Suburban Community Service	120,000	8,000	7
Twin Cities Diabetes Association	74,000	7,000	10
United Cerebral Palsy, Minneapolis	156,453	9,240	6
United Service Organization	6,000	−3,000	−33
Upper Midwest American Indian Center	86,000	2,443	3
The Way—Opportunities Unlimited	132,107	0	0
YMCA	826,400	63,704	8
YWCA	453,302	35,077	8

* Newly funded agency in 1980.
Source: *Minneapolis Tribune,* November 28, 1979, p. 5A.

ing also illustrates the process of development and change in social welfare services in that it names four new programs which received funding in 1980 (they are the programs that show no increase or percentage of change). All of these new programs serve minority neighborhoods and the economically disadvantaged. Although this is not shown by the table, existing agencies added new programs that were also funded. However, more than half of the United Way dollar in Minneapolis goes to support the "top 10" traditional United Way agen-

cies. The Red Cross, consistently on top in Minneapolis United Way spending, stays there in 1980, with more than 11 percent of the total ($1.4 million). Other agencies which each account for at least 5 percent of the United Way Budget rank just as they did ten years ago: the Family and Children's Service, the YMCA, the Catholic Charities, and the Pillsbury-Waite Neighborhood Services. These agencies and the next five biggest spend 53 percent of all the United Way money that is allocated to charities. The other 65 agencies share the remainder of the money. In discussing the use of United Way funds, the *Minneapolis Tribune* stated:

> Several things happen to the United Way dollar from the time it is promised on a pledge card (250,000 such pledges were made this year) until it reaches community groups.
>
> Many pledges aren't honored when employees leave the companies they worked for when they filled out a pledge card. In 1980, an estimated $1.1 million will be lost in uncollected pledges.
>
> Then, the United Way will keep about $2.8 million—17 percent—of the income it collects in 1980 for administrative costs and fund-raising, for two referral services it operates itself and to pay for training it offers to member charities.
>
> That leaves $13.6 million for the United Way board to divide among the 75 community agencies. In addition to contributions, that fund also includes money from investment income, grants and service fees—about $800,000 worth.
>
> Some of the agencies depend on the United Way for only a small share of their support, but more than one-third get most of their money from United Way.
>
> Some of that money, too, is spent on administration or fund-raising, by the charities themselves.
>
> Traditionally, about a half-dozen United Way member groups spend more than 30 percent of their budgets on administration and fund-raising and about a half dozen spend less than 10 percent on such costs. The remainder fall in between.

The divisions between public delivery systems of personal social services and voluntary or privately supported delivery systems are no longer as clear-cut as they once were. Readers should remember that amendments written into the Social Security Act during the 1960s enable public agencies to utilize "purchase of service agreements." The use of such agreements by public agencies to secure services from voluntary agencies for clients of the public agencies has grown extremely rapidly. There are several reasons for this growth. Funds from private sources have not kept pace with inflation and with the growing needs of the private agencies. Thus the voluntary agencies have been under great pressure to find money to support their present programs, to say nothing about devel-

oping new programs. The private agencies have therefore been only too glad to accept public money which allows them to expand and upgrade services to clients as well as support the growth of their community influence. The inability of public agencies to recruit competent staff and to offer adequate developmental activities to staff has resulted in the feeling that clients can be served better by voluntary agencies. There has always been a suspicion of the public agency in our society. Many people take it as a given that the private agency inevitably offers better service.

Our society's trust in technology leads to the conclusion that people are better served by specialists than by generalists. Thus there is a strong tendency to expect that better service will result if the public agency practitioner specializes in the establishment of eligibility and "case management" and if another vendor offers "services" to the client. Further, there has been a constant concern in social welfare about the overlap of services (since the early 1800s in America, as readers will remember). Many efforts have been made to organize services so that they are more efficient and therefore less costly to the community. The purchase of services appears to offer an ideal way to avoid duplication of services and thus to pave the way for a new breakthrough in the efficient organization of community services. In addition to the above factors, which apply to services organized and delivered through agencies, there has been a growing tendency in social work for social workers to function as private practitioners offering therapeutic services to their own clients. As a result, NASW has become very interested in the development of legislation that will allow vendor payments to be made directly to social workers as private practitioners.

Vendor payments. A number of problems are associated with the move toward the use of vendor payments. These include specialization, referral procedures, the concept of case management, accountability, the importance of client choice, and the need for an appeals process. Although there is a basic assumption that the prevention of overlap leads to more efficient service, we have not examined whether it really offers the client more effective service. Should clients have a choice among a number of agencies and a number of ways of approaching their problems—a choice that would be unavailable if there were only one source of help? The notion that, in working with people, help is better offered by specialized services should be seriously questioned. Our own position is that with certain problems and certain clients specialization furthers the probability that the client will not receive help. We have little literature that deals with the referral process and with ways of effectively using this process, which is absolutely necessary when only specialized services are offered. It is interesting that medicine, as a human service has become increasingly concerned with the failure of specialized medical practice to meet the health needs of people.

Case management. We are using a new phrase in social services—case management—without a very good understanding of what we mean. Our value system is such that the very term *case management* troubles us. It carries the connotation that the client is a "case" and that the professional is the manager of what happens to the "case." We are further troubled by the possibility that this approach, which sounds so very efficient, will mean that the least competent of social work personnel, or perhaps personnel with no social work training, will be put in charge of administering services, so that we will develop only another layer of bureaucratic structure which will further remove clients from active participation in working out their problems in a manner congruent with their goals.

A severe problem of accountability appears to be involved in the purchase of services. Should public funds be used to pay for services by nonpublic delivery organizations without a system of accountability? If a really effective accountability process is established, how does that affect the independence and autonomy of the private agency? Ordinarily the private agency is accountable to a privately elected board which usually holds itself accountable only to selected elements within the community, not to a public authority.

The final question relates to the appeals process. Public agencies that serve clients usually provide for a process through which clients can appeal agency decisions with which the clients disagree. However, very few private agencies provide for appeal processes.

By client group and/or problem

A second way to classify personal services is by the population groups that use the services, such as children and the aged. Many agencies have titles that indicate such classifications—Children's Services, Golden Age Center, and so on. Social services may also be classified by problem, such as services for troubled families, or care for disturbed children. Unfortunately, such classifications are not very specific and they often overlap.

By delivery system and/or function

A common way to classify personal social services is by the delivery system (as we have done throughout the book) that offers the service, such as family services, corrections, school social work, medical social work, child welfare services. Historically, services have been classified in this way. In the literature, one often finds the term *field of practice.* This is an older way of saying "delivery systems."

In Part I of this book we classified social services by function, such as protection and social care services. In this summary we will also follow that pattern.

✑ The current context of personal social service operations

Populations at risk and life-style changes

We are no longer a country with a growing population. We reached a zero-population-growth birthrate in December 1972, and we are maintaining that rate. At present our concern with population demographics is a concern with the shifts in the number of various groups within our population and what those shifts may mean for the future of personal social services. We need to be concerned with the number of persons within our population who can be identified as being more vulnerable to the risks of life. It appears that the decrease in the number of children in the population will result in an upward shift in the average age of the population. The decrease in the number of children seems to be related to the greater number of couples who choose to remain childless and who have the resources and the capacity to implement that choice. In addition, both men and women seem to be delaying marriage and more people are choosing to remain single.

At the same time that the proportion of children is decreasing, the number of aged persons in our population is increasing. What makes the increase in the number of old people important for social services is not only the fact that never before in history have there been so many old people but that never before have so many people been so old. The elderly represent several generational strata—the "young old," the middle group of old people and the "very old old." The young old and the very old old are separated by at least a generation. It is the very old old, the most vulnerable segment of the older population, whose numbers are increasing most rapidly. It is estimated that between now and the year 2000, persons aged 65–74 will increase by 23 percent but persons 75 and over will increase by 60 percent and will comprise some 44 percent of the total elderly population. It is not generally recognized that the aging phase of life can encompass a longer time span (an estimated 30 percent of an individual lifetime) than any other phase of life. An important consideration is that the elderly are a constantly changing group because of attrition by death and because of the entry of new people into this category. Each new group that enters this population group will have experienced a different period of history and different life conditions (Brody, 1977, pp. 55–76).

There has been concern about the meaning for productive adults of the growth of the perhaps nonproductive elderly population group. However, the growth of this group needs to be considered along with the decrease in the number of dependent children. Although the size of the aged group has grown, the size of the dependent childhood group has decreased. By 1974, there was a more favorable ratio of dependent population to productive adults than there had been in the immediate past, and it appears that this more favorable ratio will continue to be maintained.

Changes in Populations at risk

The very old old. Obviously, as a result of the increase in the very old old population, a larger number of persons will need long-term care. Also, the difference in life expectancy between men and women means that many women who have spent many years in marriage will spend their later years in an increasingly vulnerable state because of loss and separation from a life companion.

Out-of-wedlock births. There has been a steady rise in out-of-wedlock births since 1950. Whatever the changes that may be taking place at present, out-of-wedlock births among both white and nonwhite teenage mothers have increased more rapidly than have out-of-wedlock births among older mothers. A disproportionately high number of out-of-wedlock births occur among minority teenagers, and the rate of out-of-wedlock births is higher among minority women than among white women. However, the percentage of increase of out-of-wedlock births has been greater for whites than for nonwhites.

Teenage mothers are particularly vulnerable to problems with pregnancies, and their babies are more likely to have physical difficulties than are the babies of more mature mothers. Thus the increase in teenage mothers represents an increase in two vulnerable populations.

Divorce. After remaining relatively unchanged during the decade between 1955 and 1965, the divorce rate began to move steadily upward in the late 1960s. Nonwhite families have experienced a much higher separation rate than white families. Many reasons have been advanced for the increase in the divorce rate, and there has been much argument as to whether this really represents a breakdown of family life. However that may be, the separation of parents is never easy for children.

This and the stress and loneliness that at least one of the partners may experience following divorce may increase the number of parents and children who will need some type of social service as a result of the increase in divorce.

Single-parent families. In the last ten years, the number of children living in single-parent families has increased significantly. The majority of these families are headed by a female. Single-parent families more than doubled between 1974 and 1960. The growth was greatest for families of young mothers with young children. Marriage and remarriage rates for such women are high, so some families are only temporarily single-parent families. However, it has been predicted that for "children born in the 1970s two out of five will live for some period with a single parent" (Fleming, 1976, p. 60). Although the largest number of children living in single-parent households were white, a much larger proportion of black children were living in such households.

We do not mean to imply that the single-parent family is an inherently unhealthy environment for children. Most children who grow up in such homes live satisfying adult lives. However, it is more difficult to achieve healthy child rearing in single-parent families than in two-parent families. First, the levels of income for female-headed families are significantly lower than those of two-parent families, and thus the single-parent family is more likely to live in poverty. In a single-parent family a heavy burden of tasks and responsibilities is imposed on the one parent. Any significant increase in situational stress, such as physical illness that impairs the parent's ability to meet his enlarged burden, may mean a need for outside help.

Working mothers. An increasing number of mothers with small children are working outside the home. This is not necessarily a problem for either the working mother or her family, but as with the single-parent family, it may well call for an increase in the personal social services available to the mother and her family.

People who live alone. As with the other situations identified above, living alone is not necessarily pathogenic. However, persons who live alone may also be without close supportive networks. When this is true, such persons are more vulnerable to situational stress and to health problems than are people who live with other members of their families.

►§ Present trends in personal social services

Protection services

Some of the more important recent developments in personal social services have been in this area. We have become increasingly aware of the importance of violence in the family. For a hundred years, as we have written earlier, there has been a certain amount of concern about the abuse of children. However, the abused child has been seen as an exception, and professionals other than social workers, such as teachers and doctors, have tended to avoid dealing with this issue. Within the last decade, however, there has been an awakening to the amount and seriousness of child abuse.

As professional people have felt freer about entering the family to protect children, and as women have become more aware of their rights, there has been a growing concern with the abuse of women. There is a growing recognition that the abused wife does not remain in a relationship involving beating out of a psychological need to be beaten but because she has no other alternative. The uncovering of the problems of wife abuse has led to concern with other types of family violence—the battered husband, the aged parent who is mistreated, children who mistreat parents. There has also been a growing awareness of the sexual abuse of children.

Identification of these problems has resulted in a rapid development of various programs aimed at doing something about them. Some of these programs are new efforts to offer emergency shelter to the victims of violence. Some are programs of therapy aimed at the family unit and at the correction of identified family problems.

One of the present issues in protective services is the problem of foster placement of minority children. All of the statistics indicate that minority children are found in foster care far more often than white children. The association of American Indian Affairs stated that Indian children are disproportionately represented in foster care in states with significant Indian populations. For example, currently, South Dakota has 16 times as many Indian as white children in foster care; in Minnesota, the ratio is 5 Indians in foster care to 1 Anglo child; and in North Dakota, South Dakota, and Nebraska, Indian children are placed out of their homes at a rate more than 20 times the national average. A study of foster care in New York revealed that although the absolute number of children in foster care had declined, the number of black children in foster care had more than doubled and the number of Puerto Rican children in foster care had doubled. Statistics of this kind have led to recent (1979) enactment of the Indian Child Welfare Act which mandates the involvement of the tribe and the tribal court in placement of Indian children.

Many minority people believe that foster care workers judge parents' behavior from the perspective of the values of middle-class whites rather than asking whether the children involved are really in danger. The interrelationship between poverty and parental treatment has not been established, but most theories of human behavior and the social environment would lead us to expect the stress that comes with poverty interferes with parental nurturing of children. Proportionately more minority parents than Anglo parents live in poverty. Once problems in the parental care of children have been identified, fewer resources may be available to aid minority children than are available to aid white children. We need more minority social workers to serve minority families and to participate in evaluating services to minority children. We also need to be sure that minority parents are offered all the advantages available to other parents. It may be especially important to consider the use of community support networks for minority parents.

Adoption programs are no longer as large as they were in earlier years. As more and more unwed pregnant women have either opted for abortion or have decided to keep their children, there have been fewer "adoptable" babies. This has re-

sulted in the development of programs to stimulate the adoption of handicapped children or children with behavior problems, who would previously have been considered "unadoptable." Programs of interracial adoption and international adoption have been developed. These programs have not been without controversy. Blacks in particular have raised questions about the identity of self-esteem problems of a child raised in a racially different family. These blacks have been concerned about the preservation of black culture.

Agencies which offer personal social services in child welfare have a new population of concern—the teenage mothers. Many agencies have developed important programs of help to such mothers. These programs usually focus on helping teenagers with the role transition involved in becoming a mother and with development and socialization, and on providing protection for teenage mothers, who are often at extreme risk from both physical and emotional problems.

Social care services

It is probably in the area of social care services that we fail most. We have not done nearly enough to offer personal care services to those who need them. It is interesting to speculate on the reasons why fewer social workers are interested in such services, which may be the most important and needed services in our society. One reason may relate to our continuing need to "cure"—to offer services aimed at change. We do not value services aimed at helping people preserve their present functioning and comfort nearly as highly. Another reason may be that we find the investigation of and the work aimed at internal change more fascinating than the work aimed at access to and change in the service procedures of other agencies and groups. Perhaps it still goes back to our feeling that people really ought to be able to accomplish such details for themselves.

Whatever the reasons for our relative inactivity in the area of social care services, we desperately need to turn our attention in this direction. In corrections, mental health, and mental retardation, there has been a movement toward community care. We are rapidly deinstitutionalizing certain populations. However, there is considerable doubt that the community is ready to accept these people back and to supply adequate resources for a satisfying way of life. People are now discharged from mental institutions, given only minimum financial support, and left to shift for themselves in small rooms, with little human companionship, to say nothing of experiencing an ongoing nurturing relationship. We must be willing to invest a great deal more in the way of caring services for such clients.

The aged are another group which desperately needs such services. With SSI and OASDI administered by an agency that is concerned only with making financial payments, older people seldom come in contact with organizations that offer social care services. We have found many examples of older people, without family or friends, who spend two weeks or more at a time in their rooms, with no outside contact or exercise. These people are alone and are fearful of going out. Their patterns of relationship have been broken, and they do not know how to establish new ones.

None of these populations are going to be "cured" by our services, and none are going to respond quickly to help. They need personal social services that are provided over years by nurturing practitioners who give social care services.

All personal social service agencies should be alert to the needs of people for social care services, and the patience, skill in resources development, and ability to support and nurture that these services demand should be highly valued by agencies. It would appear, however, that community mental health delivery systems and medical social work should be especially central to developing social care services. Community mental health agencies have tended to consider themselves as treatment centers rather than as care givers, but it would appear that this stance needs to be reexamined. Perhaps medical social work should move beyond the hospital walls. In some cases this is already being done, but the possibilities need to be considered more actively.

Development and socialization services

These services entered the stream of social services with the beginning of the settlements. Group work arose primarily from the attempt to provide development and socialization services. We have continued an orderly evolution in this area. One new trend has been the movement toward the use of social services combined with certain community supports and programs to aid in the socialization or resocialization of the offender. There are exciting programs of community corrections and programs of restitution to the victim by the offender that offer promise.

One of the new concerns in corrections has been with status offenders—the youths whose offenses (truancy, running away from home, curfew violations, and so on) would not be considered a matter of concern were they adults. There has been a movement toward considering status offenders as needing protection and socialization services rather than court action. Increasingly, such youths are being diverted from the juvenile court and handled by child welfare services without legal mandate. There appears to be considerable controversy as to whether moving away from legally mandated services for such youths makes for a denial of needed services to a population of desperate families and youths at a time of crisis. Certainly, many of these families and youths have already been unable to obtain effective aid from a wide array of voluntary social services. Will it help to channel them once again into these service systems? It appears that at the very least we need to be concerned about the level of professional social work help that is available to such persons and about seeing that quality service to meet the individualized needs of the specific case is readily available.

Rehabilitation or psychotherapeutic services

These services are the oldest of the personal social services. But there is a new concern with the notion of the individual as a part of a social system, a new concern that perhaps we cannot really help individuals unless we also attempt to deal with the intimate social systems in which they find themselves. This has resulted in a movement toward working with families rather than individuals. It has also resulted in an increasing attempt of the voluntary agency to reach out to vulnerable populations.

A possible problem for personal social services in this area is the tendency of social work practitioners to adopt certain organized treatment methods and to apply them to all comers. This results in less emphasis on differential service to clients.

Personal social services as a right

Increasing concerns have been expressed by clients that they should have a part in the evaluation of services, that services are not a gift to them but a right. Thus strong consumer movements are developing within the personal social services. These movements may be furthered by the growing tendency of industry to establish programs of personal counseling for employees in industry.

Client participation

Starting in the 1960s, clients have been increasingly demanding a part in determining the types of help that they receive and in evaluating the services that they are given.

✎§ The social work profession

To continue with our discussion above, social work has not developed a literature that deals with the methods of social work practice within the total range of social work roles. The literature available to social change professionals is often borrowed from the social sciences or public administration, and the work with individuals, groups, and families often focuses on methods of rehabilitation. These methods are often discussed as therapy and are often assigned the highest status within the profession. This is perhaps accounted for by the fact that the social work professionals with the highest credentials have over the years gravitated to the personal social service programs whose primary offering has been psychotherapy.

There are movements toward change. As a result of the movement to recognize the right of clients to participate in their evaluation of services, the agencies offering personal social services have been taking a new look at their heavy reliance on only one direct practice role. Also, the attack on social work has had some positive results in that it forced agencies to establish new types of personal social services that were initiated on the basis of exploring new methods.

Another problem confronting social work is the distinction and differentiation between the BSW and MSW level of preparation and practice competence. The failure to resolve this issue is a disservice both to the profession and to the client. Obviously the achievement of this task requires considerable work on the knowledge and skill needed for certain social work roles. We certainly do not deal honestly with the BSW workers if we continue to view such workers as second-class citizens who are used to fill in for scarce MSW personnel. The BSW workers need to have an area of practice carved out for them which allows them to act with competence and pride as a part of a profession. Both the job assignments and the educational curriculum that prepare the BSW worker need to be realistic in terms of what can be achieved.

The push toward the licensing of social workers has forced us toward some consideration of the differentiation of social work from similar professions. To discuss social work under the rubric of the human service professions does not seem helpful to us. We desperately need to be able to answer the question of what is different about social work practice at any level of intervention.

At the level of direct practice we are once again involved in the consideration of specialities within social work practice. NASW has been working hard on this problem and has recently issued a statement on specialization.

An example of the problem of social work specialization is the existence of the clinical societies within NASW and outside the profession. These societies began to develop during the attack on social work in the 1960s, when social work education eliminated some education for psychotherapy in order to include some social science content. Many workers, proud of their skills in psychotherapeutic methods and very aware that the competent practice of psychotherapy makes heavy demands on workers for differential assessment and the differential use of skills, organized their own societies. These societies are open only to MSW social workers who are involved directly in client system change. The problem of whether "clinical social work" is a special method or includes all of personal social service practice has tended to begin some fragmentation within the profession. Also, the position of "clinical" workers that the services they render are of greater value than other services, or require something that is more difficult to learn, is also a problem. This is in no way to deny that psychotherapy requires special skills. The question raised is whether psychotherapy is a "higher" or "more demanding" type of social work service.

✒ Summary

In this chapter we have attempted to briefly develop some notions of the issues in personal social services and in the development and social change activities of social workers. One of the principal concerns of the social work profession and of education for the profession should be to formulate a recognized system of development and change activities staffed by social workers within the social welfare institution. There is a growing tendency to assign many of these activities to people from other disciplines who are able to demonstrate certain technical competences. However, policy and planning activities involve values and a knowledge of individuals and the working of human social systems that appear to be found primarily within the profession of social work.

We have also presented in this chapter a very brief overview of the issues in the profession of social work. We are still plagued as a profession by the breadth of our assigned function and by the sense of separateness that grows among social workers who are working in the separate systems of social welfare.

✒ A look ahead

Our next and last chapter attempts to trace certain themes found in social welfare.

✒ Study questions

1. In a movement toward client participation in the social services, a number of new "storefront" agencies have developed in the last decade. If you live in a community large enough for a united fund, explore the fund's knowledge of this movement and find out how many of these storefront agencies it supports. If you live in a smaller community, visit the local welfare agency and ask its staff whether they can identify new, consumer-oriented agencies that have developed recently.

2. Identify the positions within your local welfare institution that entail making policy decisions and carrying through on planning. How many of these positions are filled by social workers?

3. Visit your public welfare agency and find out what types of problems are brought to its division of personal social services.

4. Find out what positions in your community tend to be filled by BSW workers and what position are held by MSW workers. Can you estimate how many positions that call for "social workers" are filled by people without either a BSW degree or an MSW degree?

✒ Selected readings

Meyer, Carol. *Social Work Practice: The Changing Landscape.* (2d ed.) New York: Free Press, 1976.

It is our conviction that this book addresses many of the issues raised in this chapter. We believe that students can profit from being exposed to Meyer's thinking.

Department of Health, Education, and Welfare. *Child Welfare Strategy in Coming Years.* Washington, D.C.: U.S. Department of Health, Education, and Welfare, 1979.

This discussion of child welfare services in today's world is an excellent source book that could be used to form a base for discussion of development and change in the personal social services.

Urban Renewal in Hartford, Connecticut—the old and the new!
But, do those new buildings shelter the residents of the old buildings?

Chapter 26 ❧

❧ Themes of social welfare development ❧

❧ Introduction

The account of the development of the institution of social welfare is a fascinating record of social change. In this concluding chapter we shall try very briefly to set forth the themes that we feel have been a part of, and have been developed by, the process of change. In spite of the many back and forth surges of change, in spite of excrutiatingly slow progress and the great distance that we still have to go, in spite of the terrible sufferings of vulnerable individuals throughout history, social welfare has followed an upward spiral toward social justice and human welfare.

The central trends over 400 or 500 years have been from the absolute political power of kings and nobles (status rights) to citizen participation based on the central notion of contact; from aid given as a favor, with no recourse on the part of the recipient, to aid given as a right with a prescribed course of appeal. During those years, constant progress has been made in setting limits to economic exploitation but less progress has been made in equalizing wealth. There has been constant progress toward increasing individual security, a gradual mastery of the problems of poverty, and a slow increase in equality of opportunity. These improvements have been built both on the desire of society for stability and on the caring response to the needs of individuals. We must also remember that the struggle of society for stability and for the preservation of the existing social order is a necessary condition for individual welfare. In times of great instability, it is often the most vulnerable who are most badly hurt.

An underlying theme in the development of American social welfare has been a belief that causes of social and individual problems can be discovered and that once the cause of such a problem is discovered, it will be possible to invent a simple solution to the problem. Our search for simple and easy answers to complex social problems has probably hindered the development of more adequate programs. Our search for simple explanations of social problems began with the notion that those explorations would be found in the morality of individuals. After all, at that time most problems were ascribed to the hands of God. Then we came to believe that the cause of social problems was social and could be found through the methods of scientific inquiry. New knowledge changed the notion of cause—now it was to be found in the pathology or internal struggle of the individual— but there was little loss of faith in the search for a cause through science. If we could only understand that the causes of social problems are both social and individual, that these problems come from the interpenetration of social and psychological factors, that they differ from person to person and from situation to situation, and that the best solutions are social programs that move us toward security, equality of opportunity, and social justice we might make more rapid progress.

The beginnings

We will remember that the beginning of modern welfare came out of the massive social change that occurred as feudal society gave way to mercantilism and the industrial revolution. This change affected all social institutions—it was linked to rapid economic change and the growth of new sources of economic power; to new political developments that changed the base of political power and involved a broader participation based on economic power rather than status; a change in the position and power of the church, particularly in interaction with the economic and political institutions; to the breakdown and change of people's relationship with each other as the notion of contract replaced the notion of status. For perhaps the first time in human history, there was a massive movement of people as individuals rather than as tribes or extended families. This loosened the integrative and control forces in society and threatened the very existence of society. It is understandable that such upheavals gave rise to frantic efforts to establish some stability.

Thus the first welfare policies and programs came out of the need of society for stability. The first institution that needed stability was the economic institution, because it was undergoing the greatest change and because individuals perish if they cannot gain access to food, clothing, and shelter. The first welfare programs and policies established principles that were to have a tremendous effect on the development of social welfare in the United States. Those principles were aimed at the control of individuals and their movement. They included the notions of local responsibility, family responsibility, classification of the poor based primarily on the concepts of employability and individual responsibility for one's troubles, concern with the impact of aid on the availability of a work force for industrial growth, and lesser eligibility. This last notion was probably based both on views regarding the moral virtues of work and on concern over the impact of aid on the motivation to work.

The colonies and social welfare

These principles of welfare policy were brought to the United States by the first English settlers. There were, however, some differences in the new country: an optimism about change, less respect for status and a rebellion against old patterns of status, fear of the power of government to control that translated into the need to locate the decision-making power on welfare close to local people, a belief in private voluntary efforts both in the marketplace and in charity, and a sense of the importance of benevolence and a concern for the plight of the vulnerable. Despite the generally held picture of the colonists as being equal in economic status and as engaging in an open political process, from the beginning great wealth was concentrated in the hands of a few families (some of these families are still among our wealthiest citizens) and participation in the decision-making process was generally limited to white, male property owners.

The programs that developed were a mixture of various ingredients. This is important to remember. Never were our welfare policies or programs the result of monolithic factors, nor were they ever of one piece. On the whole, our early efforts were local and individual, based both on concern for the sufferings of others and on the need of a pioneer society to survive, and limited by the knowledge and resources of the time. There developed programs that gave aid to individuals, that sold the poor, that boarded the poor out, and that boards out children for purposes of maintenance and socialization. Mixed with these local efforts and programs were programs of statewide aid. These statewide programs were available to veterans on the basis that they had earned their benefits through earlier service to society (present veterans' and social insurance programs reflect this notion). Statewide programs were also made available with some reluctance to individuals who were without a local settlement, and special statewide programs were developed in times of crisis.

The Constitution

The Constitution, a document that reflected the economic and social thinking of its time and the values of its authors and supporters, has had tremendous impact on the development and the structure of our welfare programs. In essence, the Constitution was concerned with limiting the police powers of the federal government. This was done by specifying what the police powers of the federal government were and by reserving all other police powers to the states and by dividing the powers of the federal government among three separate branches.

Institutions, federal partnership, vendor payments

Since the establishment of the federal government, there has been federal participation in social welfare. In general, that participation has followed principles that were developed when the states gave aid to communities. First, the aid given by the federal government to the veterans of the Revolutionary War established veterans' aid as a federal responsibility. Second, the federal government assumed responsibility for people without a settle-

ment by establishing an agency to control and aid immigrants. This has continued in our present federal assistance to refugees. Third, the federal government offered aid in crisis, as we see, for example, in the establishment of the Freedmen's Bureau at the close of the Civil War. The federal government also began to make assistance available to certain organizations and provided aid for education. In contrast to its limited federal participation in social welfare, the federal government offered much more substantial assistance to the developing economic institution. Aid to the poor was seen as a drain on resources, whereas aid to the economic institution, which often translated into aid to the wealthy and the powerful, was considered an investment in society's welfare.

As urbanization developed, there came organizations that removed the poor and the deviants from the community. The first of these institutions was the almshouse, which was often combined with a house of correction and which served informally as a hospital. As the problems of the almshouse began to be recognized, there were moves toward a finer categorization of the poor and toward the development of a more individualized approach through the creation of specialized institutions. Thus prisons for adult offenders and Houses of Refuge for juvenile offenders began to be established. Hospitals for the treatment of physical and mental illness were established. Reformers made strenuous efforts to remove children from the almshouses and to put them in institutions (organizations) for children. Schools and other institutions for the handicapped developed. Most of these institutions were treated under state auspices and with state support. With these developments, especially in relation to the care of children, came the use of vendor payments. State or local governments often contracted with privately established institutions for the care of special populations.

However, almost as soon as such institutions were well established, they were charged with failure to deal with the social problems. State boards of control were set up to offer some criteria of good operation. And programs to move people back to the community began to develop. This shift began with the foster home program for children, and it has culminated in the present tendency to deny any utility to the use of institutions. The question of the adequacy of community care has remained a problem for all institutionalized persons. The institutions may have offered poor care and damaging experiences, but once again we have bought a quick solution. Move them back to the community, but do not accept the responsibility that should accompany such a move.

Private philanthropy

From the beginning of our nation, there has been a steady growth in the private funding of efforts to solve social problems. Originally, this giving was almost entirely by the wealthy. With the coming of the united fund movement, however, giving began to be spread across the community. Then came the development of corporate and union contributions. Giving has always had an appeal as a private rather than a governmental activity. However, with the establishment of the income tax deductions for private giving, it has become possible for larger contributors to acquire important decision-making power relative to community programs at a minimum cost to themselves and at significant cost to the public programs. The impulse to give is a complex one, and it is simplistic to assign any one or two reasons as an explanation for all giving. People undoubtedly give because of a real desire to help others; they give because doing so increases their sense of well-being; they give because of social pressure; they give because of the desire to control others; they give in many instances as a way of promoting their own welfare in case they should be in need. This last is certainly one of the reasons for the appeal of the great health foundations. People often cannot imagine themselves as being without funds, or as offenders, but they can picture themselves or their family members as victims of dreaded physical illnesses, so they give generously.

The organization of private social welfare organizations has been a constant theme of social welfare efforts through the years. Attempts to organize the private philanthropies of the community began in America in the early 1800s and are still of concern. Also of concern since the end of the 1800s has been the relationship between private social welfare and public social welfare.

Scientific welfare

In all of this there has been a constant search for the cause of poverty and social malfunctioning. As knowledge of human beings and their development was accumulated, two important trends developed: the notion that the cause and cure of poverty would be found through scientific effort and some movement away from the notion that poverty was caused by moral deviations. The cause of poverty began to be seen as being in the social environment. This resulted in the development of our systems of social welfare—health and housing were seen as important determinants of poverty; education became important, as both a socialization factor and a gateway to equality of opportunity; the recognition of the importance of working conditions lead to full employment and labor legislation. Efforts were made to define poverty and to develop a standard of living necessary to adequate human development. Problems began to be defined as social problems—crime, illegitimacy, public health, education, housing, and so on. There began to be a consciousness of racism and other problems of discrimination, some of which centered on the place assigned to women.

The efforts of the reformers to use the powers of the federal government were an important part of the reform movement of the early 1900s. Finding access to the forces of change at the local level blocked by entrenched local power structures, the reformers of the early 1900s tried to organize in such a way as to have impact at the federal level. This was far from successful, but it worked well enough to develop a tendency on the part of those interested in reform to prefer attempts to bring national forces to bear on movements for change.

The depression and social insurance

Then came the crisis of the 1930s. The major themes of the 30s represented both some change and some continuance of slightly altered old patterns. Work continued to be emphasized in the development of programs, but a new thread was woven into this policy. Work began to be emphasized as a necessity for human dignity rather than as a punishment. Social insurance programs were developed, inadequate and still built on classification of the poor and on attachment to the work force, but in this development a long step was taken toward the notion that people had a right to security and to freedom from poverty. Although there are critical limitations to social security programs built on the contributions of employees and employers, such programs have been a way of giving people the feeling that they have a right to assistance.

The Great Society and reaction

The 1960s were marked by a great surge of social welfare development. There was an accelerated acceptance of the notions that people had the right to security, to a living standard above the poverty line, and to equal access to opportunity. This change came in large part from the development of the civil rights movement and from the effort of the Great Society to ensure citizens the participation of in community decision making. The belief spread that poverty was damaging to individuals' sense of their ability to participate in the community and that participation in community decision making would help the poor feel that they were a part of our society.

Despite a sense of frustration and failure in relation to the Great Society programs, certain achievements of those programs, or certain changes in our ways of dealing with things, are still important to us. There was a movement toward a concern with the rights of people rather than the needs of people. Such a movement is not an unmixed blessing if a concern for rights totally displaces the consideration of human needs. There was a new emphasis on local efforts and on community decision making. This was in part an offshoot of the notion of rights and of the importance of participation. It remains to be tested whether this movement really serves people well. The period of the Great Society programs was marked by a tremendous growth in the knowledge and tools of data collection, data processing, and data analysis. This, too, has not been an unmixed blessing in that we have used those tools with some degree of irresponsibility. The notion developed that science is value-free and, above all, that its answers are truth. The fact that efforts could not be proved of value with the new scientific tools came to be seen as meaning that the efforts were obviously of no value. However, these tools have provided us with means of collecting data and engaging in analysis that we have never had before. Much of our understanding of the real problem of poverty came from our access to such tools.

In the frustration of the 1970s there were strong attacks on professionalism because of the belief that professionals had failed in their claims to expertness and because of the growing belief in the importance of client participation. These attacks have been damaging in their denial of the importance of knowledge and competence in dealing with human problems. Doing what comes naturally has never solved serious social problems, and it may contribute to their spread. On the other hand, such attacks have forced professionals to reexamine their positions and their behavior. There have been many positive changes in social work and social work education as a result of these challenges. Professions, too, can become entrenched. This offers client and community stability and an assurance of consistency in service but it also means that sometimes it takes strong weapons to force them to examine themselves.

One of the severe problems that we face today is the exhaustion of resources. We are beginning to recognize that we face a scarcity of many things that we have taken for granted as important to our well-being. If we have problems in providing for security, well-being, and equality of opportunity in times of affluence, what choices will we make? It is becoming increasingly important that we understand the complexity of the choices before us. Although we may each individually wish that changes could come more rapidly, we need to recognize that concern with poverty did not originate with the 1960s. We need to understand that the roots of change may lie in our past, and that even if they do not lie there, we will need to understand the past in any case in order to avoid its mistakes. We have been engaged in a struggle with the problems of insecurity, poverty, and inequality of opportunity throughout our history. We should recognize that this struggle has taken place in part because of a real need to preserve the stability of society and in part because of a real concern for the well-being of others.

◈§ Conclusions

What are some of the conclusions about social change and development that can be drawn from our account of the development of the social welfare institution in America? Perhaps the first conclusion is that given the values of American society, the public will accept large-scale programs of social support or intervention only at long intervals of time. Although there appears to be nothing inherently cyclical about this pattern, changes do come about at certain intervals. However, the changes appear to develop out of special circumstances, such as a national crisis or a sudden spurt of accepted knowledge. If these special circumstances are to result in major social reform, there must be an individual or a group that can give strong leadership. In recent years such leadership has generally been provided by the president or other public leaders. In earlier times it was provided by social workers and other private reformers.

Given the public's limited tolerance for reform, a piecemeal approach may be the only way to move toward reform. Piecemeal reforms can often come at an administrative level, as large policies are translated into service programs. Thus social work administrators should be aware of ways in which program design can advance reform. We certainly have ample evidence that the prolonged neglect of social problems is costly to both society and the individual. Social problems do not simply fade away—when neglected, they become more complex and acute.

In a democracy whose social and political institutions are functioning reasonably well, social legis-

lation and social reform activities will always need the participation of groups that will not be direct beneficiaries of such activities, as those who can expect to gain from social legislation and social reform will always be a weak and powerless minority by themselves. At times of major national crises, when all people suffer alike, the situation is different. Even then, however, older structures and older value positions operate to limit what can be accomplished. Even in times of crises, those who will have to pay a price for progress will still resist change that leaves them less well-off. At such times, when great promises are made to rescue people from their troubles, the expectations of the beneficiaries are likely to be greater than the improvements in their circumstances, and as a result there is some backlash from the very persons for whom reforms are developed.

Thus promises and goals should be realistic. If we are engaged in reform activities, we must be careful to promise no more than we can deliver. This has been a problem with many social work efforts. There is no firm body of knowledge that tells us how to develop and structure social programs. We must act while we learn, generating knowledge as we go along. The causes of social problems are extremely complex, and we understand those causes only dimly. Thus most of our reform activities have unexpected consequences. More of our effort should be devoted to assessing the possibility of such consequences of our proposals. We need to be especially careful not to embark on a course of reform without sufficient funds. The availability of funds is critical to all efforts at change, and the probable success of our efforts can perhaps be better estimated by the size of our budget than by any other factor. There is no inherent law that the programs of state and local governments, or private efforts, are better than federal programs. Social legislation can deal with social problems.

And finally, people in need have benefited from the social reform efforts that have been made over the years of our history. There may have been troubling and unwanted or unintended side effects, but the movement has been forward. We may often find less than admirable motivations among those who have led our efforts toward social change and the expansion of social services, but we should be sure always to remember that all human actions stem from complex motivations. Thus, the reforms and forward movements in social welfare rest, in the final analysis, on our concern for others—on our willingness to be, in the best sense of the phrase, our brother's keeper.

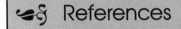 References

Abbott, E. Clara Barton. In *Encyclopedia of the Social Sciences.* Vol. 2. New York: Macmillan, 1935.

Abbott, E. *Women in Industry: A Study of American Economic History.* New York: Arno Press, New York Times, 1969. Originally published in 1909.

Abbott, G. *The Child and the State.* 2 vols. Chicago: University of Chicago Press, 1938.

Addams, J. Child Labor and Pauperism. In *Proceedings of the National Conference of Charities and Corrections,* 1903, pp. 114–21.

Addams, J. *The Spirit of Youth and The City Streets.* New York: Macmillan, 1909.

Addams, J. *Twenty Years at Hull House: With Autobiographical Notes.* New York: Macmillan, 1935. Originally published 1910.

American Heritage Dictionary of the English Language, The. Boston: Houghton Mifflin Company, 1979. © 1979 by Houghton Mifflin Company. Excerpts reprinted by permission from *The American Heritage Dictionary of the English Language.*

American Public Welfare Association. American Public Welfare Position on Income Maintenance. In *Report of the Committee on Income Maintenance Policy.* Washington, D.C.: American Public Welfare Association, 1976. Pp. 12–20.

Apthekar, H., ed. *The Negro People in the United States.* New York: Citadel Press, 1957.

Aptheker, H., ed. *A Documentary History of the Negro People, 1933–1945.* Secaucus, NJ: Citadel Press, 1974.

Axinn, J., and Levin, H. *Social Welfare: A History of the American Response to Need.* New York: Harper & Row, 1975.

Baer, B. L., and Federico, R. C. *Educating the Baccalaureate Social Worker.* Cambridge, Mass.: Ballinger, 1978.

Ball, R. M. *Social Security: Today and Tomorrow.* New York: Columbia University Press, 1978.

Bartlett, H. M. *The Common Base of Social Work Practice.* New York: National Association of Social Workers, 1970.

Barton, W. E. *Life of Clara Barton, Founder of the American Red Cross.* Boston: Houghton Mifflin, 1922.

Baxandall, R.; Gordon, L.; and Reverby, S., eds. *America's Working Women: A Documentary History— 1600 to the Present.* New York: Vintage Books, 1976.

Beath, E. J. Family Services: Family Service Agencies. In. R. Morris, ed., *Encyclopedia of Social Work, 1971.* Vol. 1. New York: National Association of Social Workers, 1971.

Beck, B. M. Professional Associations: National Association of Social Workers. *Encyclopedia of Social Work.* New York: National Association of Social Workers, 1977.

Beck, D. F. *Patterns in the Use of Family Agency Service.* New York: Family Service Association of America, 1962.

Becker, D. G. The Visitor to the New York City Poor, 1843–76. *Social Service Review, 35*(3) (1961):382–96.

Becker, D. G. Early Adventures in Social Casework: The Charity Agent, 1880–1910. *Social Casework, 44*(5) (1965):255–62.

Becker, D. G. Clara Barton. In J. B. Turner, ed., *Encyclopedia of Social Work, 1977.* New York: National Association of Social Workers, 1977.

Beers, C. *A Mind That Found Itself.* New York: Longman's Green, 1909.

Bell, W. Services for People: An Appraisal. *Social Work, 15*(3) (1970):5–12.

Bell, W. and Bushe, D. M. The Economic Efficiency of AFDC. *Social Service Review, 49*(2) (1975): 175–90.

Bell, W., Lekachman, R., and Schorr, A. *Public Policy and Income Distribution.* New York: Center for Studies in Income Maintenance, New York School of Social Work, 1974.

Bennett, L., Jr. *Before the Mayflower: A History of the Negro in America, 1619–1962.* Chicago: Johnson Publishing, 1962.

Bergman, P. M. *The Chronological History of the Negro in America.* New York: Harper and Row, 1969.

Bernard, J. The United States. In J. B. Turner, ed., A. Rose, ed., *The Institution of Advanced Societies.* Minneapolis: University of Minnesota Press, 1958.

Bernard, L. D. Education for Social Work. In *Encyclopedia of Social Work, 1977.* New York: National Association of Social Workers, 1977.

Billingsley, A., and Giovannoni, J. *Children of the Storm.* New York: Harcourt Brace Jovanovich, 1972.

Bisno, H. A Theoretical Framework for Teaching Social Work Methods and Skills with Particular Reference to Undergraduate Social Welfare Education. *Journal of Education for Social Work, 5*(2) (1969):5–17.

Boehm, B. Review of *Girls at Vocational High. Social Service Review, 38*(4) (1965):479–80.

Boehm, W. W. The Nature of Social Work. *Social Work, 3*(2) (1958):10–19.

Boorstin, D. J. *The Americans: The Colonial Experience.* New York: Random House, 1958.

Boorstin, D. J. *The Americans: The National Experience.* New York: Vintage Books, 1965.

Bowers, S. Nature and Definition of Social Casework. *Journal of Social Casework, 30*(8) (1949):311–17.

Brace, D. L. *The Dangerous Classes of New York and Twenty Years' Work among Them.* New York: National Association of Social Workers, 1978. Reprinted from New York: Wynkoop & Hollenbeck, 1872.

Breckinridge, S. P. *Public Welfare Administration in the United States.* Chicago: University of Chicago Press, 1935.

Bremner, R. H. *From the Depths: The Discovery of Poverty in the United States.* New York: New York University Press, 1956. Copyright © 1956 by New York University Press.

Bremner, R. H. *America Philanthropy.* Chicago: University of Chicago Press, 1960.

Bremner, R. H., ed. *Children and Youth in America: A Documentary History.* Vol. 1. Cambridge, Mass.: Harvard University Press, 1970.

Bremner, R. H., ed. *Children and Youth in America: A Documentary History.* Vol. 2. Cambridge, Mass.: Harvard University Press, 1971.

Bremner, R. H., ed. *Children and Youth in America: A Documentary History.* Vol. 3. Cambridge, Mass.: Harvard University Press, 1974.

Brieland, D.; Costin, L. B; and Atherton, D., eds. *Contemporary Social Work.* New York: McGraw-Hill, 1975.

Brockway, Z. R. *Fifty Years of Prison Service: An Autobiography.* New York: Charities Publication Committee, 1912.

Brody, E. M. Aging. *Encyclopedia of Social Work.* New York: National Association of Social Workers, 1977.

Brogden, M. S. The Johns Hopkins Hospital Department. *Social Service Review, 38*(1) (1964):88–98.

Brown, J. C. *Public Relief, 1929–1939.* New York: Holt, 1940.

Bruno, F. J. *Trends in Social Work, 1874–1956.* New York: Columbia University Press, 1957.

Burns, E. M. Some Economic Aspects of Welfare as an Institution. In J. M. Romanyshny, ed., *Social Science and Social Welfare.* New York: Council on Social Work Education, 1974.

Cabot, R. *Social Service and the Art of Healing.* New York: National Association of Social Workers, 1978. Reprinted from New York: Moffat, Yard & Co., 1915.

Carey, M. *Appeal to the Wealthy of the Land, Ladies as Well as Gentlemen, on Character, Conduct, Situation and Prospects of Those Whose Sole Dependence for Subsistence is on the Labour of Their Hands.* Philadelphia: Stereotyed by L. Johnson, No. 6 George Street, 1833.

Carroll, P., and Noble, D. W. *The Free and the Unfree: A New History of the United States.* New York: Penguin Books, 1977.

Chafe, W. H. *The American Woman: Her Changing Social, Economic, and Political Roles, 1920–1970.* New York: Oxford University Press, 1972.

Chambers, C. A. *Seedtime of Reform: American Social Service and Social Action, 1918–1933.* Minneapolis: University of Minnesota Press, 1963.

Chambers, C. A. *New Deal at Home and Abroad.* New York: Free Press, 1965.

Chambers, C. A. *Paul U. Kellogg and the Survey.* Minneapolis: University of Minnesota Press, 1972.

Clarke, H. I. *Social Legislation.* 2d ed. New York: Appleton-Century-Crofts, 1957.

Cohen, N. E. *Social Work in the American Tradition.* New York: Holt, Rinehart & Winston, 1958.

Cohen, W. J. Social Insurance. In R. H. Kurtz, ed., *Social Work Year Book.* New York: National Association of Social Workers, 1957.

Cohen, W. J. Social Insurance. In R. Morris, ed., *Encyclopedia of Social Work, 1971.* New York: National Association of Social Workers, 1971.

Coit, S. *Neighborhood Guilds. An Instrument of Social Reform.* London: Swan Sonnenschlint, 1891.

Coll, B. D. *Perspectives in Public Welfare: A History.* Washington, D.C.: U.S. Department of Health, Education, & Welfare, 1969.

Commager, H. S. *The American Mind.* New Haven: Yale University Press, 1950.

Commager, H. S. *Living Ideas in America.* New York: Harper, 1957.

Commission on Private Philanthropy and Public Needs. *Giving in America: Toward a Stronger Voluntary Sector.* Washington, D.C.: Commission on Private Philanthropy and Public Needs, 1975.

Commission on Social Work Practice, National Association of Social Workers. Working Definition of Social Work Practice. *Social Work, 3*(2) (1958):5–8.

Compton, B. R. The Family Centered Project Revisited. Mimeographed paper. Minnesota: University of Minnesota, 1980.

Compton, B. R., and Galaway, B. *Social Work Processes.* Homewood, Ill.: Dorsey Press, 1975.

Compton, B. R., and Galaway, B. *Social Work Processes.* Rev. ed. Homewood, Ill.: Dorsey Press, 1979.

Coser, L. *The Functions of Social Conflict.* Glencoe, Ill.: Free Press, 1956.

Crampton, H., and Keiser, K. *Social Welfare: Institution and Process.* New York: Random House, 1970.

Davis, H. E., Jr. Letters. *Social Work, 16*(1) (1971):128.

Delliquadri, F. Child welfare. In R. H. Kurtz, ed., *Social Work Year Book, 1957.* New York: National Association of Social Workers, 1957.

de Schweinitz, E., and de Schweinitz, K. *The Content of the Public Assistance Job.* New York: National Association of Social Workers, 1950.

de Schweinitz, K. *The Art of Helping People out of Trouble.* New York: Houghton Mifflin, 1924.

de Schweinitz, K. *England's Road to Social Security.* New York: A. S. Barnes, 1943.

Deutsch, A. *The Mentally Ill in America.* 2d ed. New York: Columbia University Press, 1949.

Dewey, J. Liberty and Social Control. *Social Frontier, 11*(2) (1935):41.

Dillard, D. *Economic Development of the North Atlantic Community.* New York: Prentice-Hall, 1967.

Douglas, P. *Real Wages in the United States, 1890–1926.* Boston: Houghton Mifflin, 1930.

Du Bois, W. E. B. *Black Reconstruction: An Essay Toward A History of the Part Which Black Folk Played in the Attempt to Reconstruct Democracy in America, 1860–1880.* 1935. Reprinted, New York: Russell and Russell, 1956.

Duffy, J.   *Epidemic in Colonial America*. Baton Rouge: Louisiana State University Press, 1953.

Duffy, J.   *A History of Public Health in New York City, 1625–1866*. New York: Russell Sage Foundation, 1968.

Earle, A. M.   *Home Life in Colonial Days*. Stockbridge, Mass.: Berkshire Traveller Press, 1974. Originally published in 1898.)

Epstein, I.   Organizational Careers, Professionalization, and Social Work Radicalism. *Social Work Review, 44*(4) (1970):123–31.

Erikson, E. H.   Identity and the Life Cycle. *Psychological Issues, 1*(1) (1959). Monograph 1.

Fanshel, D.   Status Differentials: Men and Women in Social Work, *Social Work, 21*(6) (1976): 448–54.

Farrell, G.   *The Story of Blindness*. Cambridge, Mass.: Harvard University Press, 1956.

Feagin, J. R.   *Subordinating the Poor*. Englewood Cliffs, N.J.: Prentice-Hall, 1975.

Federico, R.   *The Social Welfare Institution*. 2d ed. Lexington, Mass.: D. C. Heath, 1976.

Fitch, J. A.   In *American Labor Legislation Review, 10*(1) (1920):61.

Flemming, V.   *America's Children 1976—A Bicentennial Assessment*. Washington, D.C.: National Council of Children and Youth, 1976.

Folks, H.   *The Care of Destitute, Neglected, and Delinquent Children*. New York: National Association of Social Workers, 1978. Originally published in 1902.

Frankel, C.   The Moral Framework of Welfare. In J. S. Morgan, ed., *Welfare and Wisdom*. Toronto: University of Toronto Press, 1968.

Frankel, C.   The Transformation of Welfare. In J. S. Morgan, ed., *Welfare and Wisdom*. Toronto: University of Toronto Press, 1968.

Frankel, Emil.   *Poor Relief in Pennsylvania: A State-Wide Survey*. Harrisburg, Pa.: Commonwealth of Pennsylvania, Public Board of Welfare, 1925.

Franklin, J. H.   *From Slavery to Freedom*. New York: Alfred A. Knopf, 1947.

Franklin, J. H.   *Reconstruction after the Civil War*. Chicago: University of Chicago Press, 1961.

Friedlander, W. A.   *Introduction to Social Welfare*. New York: Prentice-Hall, 1955.

Friedson, E.   Dominant Professions, Bureaucracy, and Client Services. In W. R. Rosengren and M. Lefton, eds., *Organizations and Clients: Essays in the Sociology of Service*. Columbus, Ohio: Charles E. Merrill, 1970. Pp. 71–92.

Gartland, R.   Editorial Notes. *The Family, 21*(4) (1940):125–26.

Gaylin, W.   In the Beginning: Helpless and Dependent. In W. Gaylin, I. Glasser, S. Marcus, and D. Rothman, *Doing good: The Limits of Benevolence*. New York: Pantheon Books, 1975.

Gil, D.   *Unraveling Social Policy*. Cambridge, Mass.: Schenkman, 1976.

Gilbert, N., and Specht, H.   *Dimensions of Social Welfare Policy*, © 1974. Englewood Cliffs, N.J.: Prentice-Hall, Inc. Material reprinted by permission of Prentice-Hall, Inc.

Gilbert, N., and Specht, H.   *The Emergence of Social Welfare and Social Work*. Itasca, Ill.: F. E. Peacock, 1976.

Gitterman, A., and Germain, C.   Social Work Practice: A Life Model. In B. Compton and B. Galaway, Social Work Processes. Rev. ed. Homewood Ill.: Dorsey Press, 1979. Reprinted from *Social Service Review, 50*(4) (1976):601–10.

Glasser, I.   Prisoners of Benevolence: Power versus Liberty in the Welfare State. In W. Gaylin, I. Glasser, S. Marcus, and D. Rothman, *Doing Good: The Limits of Benevolence*. New York: Pantheon Books, 1975.

Glueck, S.   *The Problem of Delinquency*. Boston: Houghton Mifflin, 1959.

Goldstein, H.   *Social Work Practice: A Unitary Approach*. Columbia: University of South Carolina Press, 1973.

Gordon, W. E.   Knowledge and Value: Their Distinction and Relationship in Clarifying Social Work Practice. *Social Work, 10*(3) (1965):33.

Gordon, W. E.   Basic Constructs for an Integrative and Generative Conception of Social Work. In G. Hearn, ed., *The General Systems Approach: Contributions toward an Holistic Conception of Social Work*. New York: Council on Social Work Education, 1969. Pp. 5–11.

Gould, J., and Kolb, W. L.   *A Dictionary of the Social Sciences*. Glencoe, Ill.: Free Press, 1964.

Griscom, J.   The first annual report of the managers of the Society for the Prevention of Pauperism in the City of New York as quoted in R. E. Pumphrey and M. W. Pumphrey, *The Heritage of American Social Work*. New York: Columbia University Press, 1961. Pp. 59–62.

Grob, G. N. *The State and the Mentally Ill.* Chapel Hill: University of North Carolina Press, 1966.

Grob, G. N. *Mental Institutions in Social Policy to 1875.* New York: Free Press, 1973.

Guggenbühl-Craig, A. Power in the Helping Professions. Zurich, Switzerland: Spring Publications, 1976.

Gyarfas, M. Social Science, Technology, and Social Work: A Caseworker's View. *Social Service Review, 43*(3) (1969):259–73.

Haas, T. H. The Legal Aspects of Indian Affairs from 1887 to 1957. *Annals of the American Academy of Political and Social Science, 311* (1957):12–22.

Hagan, W. T. *American Indians.* Chicago: University of Chicago Press, 1961.

Hagar, Alice Rogers. Occupations and Earnings of Women in Industry. *Annals of the American Academy of Political and Social Science, 143* (1929):31–39.

Halleck, S. Family Therapy and Social Change. *Social Casework, 57*(8) (1976):483–93.

Hawes, J. *Children in Urban Society: Juvenile Delinquency in Nineteenth Century America.* New York: Oxford University Press, 1971.

Heffernan, W. J. Public Assistance and Supplemental Security Income: Administration of. Copyright 1977, National Association of Social Workers, Inc. Material reprinted with permission from, J. B. Turner, ed., *Encyclopedia of Social Work,* 17th ed. New York: National Association of Social Workers, 1977.

Heffernan, W. J. *Introduction to Social Welfare: Power, Scarcity, and Human Needs.* Itasca, Ill.: F. E. Peacock, 1979.

Hollis, F. *Casework: A Psychosocial Approach.* New York: Random House, 1964.

Hoshino, G. Money and Morality: Income Security and Personal Social Services. Copyright 1971, National Association of Social Workers, Inc. Reprinted with permission, from *Social Work, 16*(2) (April 1971): 23.

Hoshino, G. Public Assistance and Supplemental Security Income: Social Services. In J. B. Turner, ed., *Encyclopedia of Social Work, 1977.* New York: National Association of Social Workers, 1977.

Hunter, R. *Poverty.* New York: Grosset and Dunlap, 1904.

Jarrett, M. C. The Psychiatric Thread Running through All Social Case Work. In *Proceedings of Conference of Charities and Corrections, 1919.* Chicago: National Conference of Charities and Corrections, 1919.

Jeffers, C. *Living Poor.* Ann Arbor, Mich.: Ann Arbor Publishers, 1971.

Jennings, W. *A History of Economic Progress in the United States.* New York: Thomas Y. Crowell, 1926.

Jernegan, M. W. *The American Colonies, 1492–1750: A Study of Their Political, Economic, and Social Development.* New York: Frederick Ungar, 1929.

Jernegan, M. W. *Laboring and Dependent Classes in Colonial America, 1607–1783.* New York: Frederick Ungar, 1931.

Jordan, W. K. The English Background of Modern Philanthropy. *American Historical Review, 66*(1) (1961):401–8.

Kadushin, A. Child Welfare: Adoption and Foster Care. In R. Morris, ed., *Encyclopedia of Social Work, 1971.* New York: National Association of Social Workers, 1971.

Kahn, A. J. *Social Policy and Social Services.* New York: Random House, 1973.

Kammerman, S. B., and Kahn, A. J. *Social Services in the United States: Policies and Programs.* Philadelphia: Temple University Press, 1973.

Katz, N. *Let Them Eat Promises.* New York: Anchor Books, 1969.

Keith-Lucas, A. *The Giving and Taking of Help.* Chapel Hill: University of North Carolina Press, 1972. Copyright 1972, The University of North Carolina Press. Excerpts reprinted by permission of the publisher.

Kelso, R. *The Science of Public Welfare.* New York: Henry Holt, 1928.

Kidneigh, J. C. Letters. *Social Work, 15*(4) (1970):119.

Klein, P. *From Philanthropy to Social Welfare.* San Francisco: Jossey-Bass, 1968.

Kurzman, P. A. Professional Associations: Special Interest Organizations. In J. B. Turner, ed., *Encyclopedia of Social Work, 1977.* New York: National Association of Social Workers, 1977.

Lansburgh, T. W. Child Welfare: Day Care of Children. In R. Morris, ed., *Encyclopedia of Social Work, 1971.* New York: National Association of Social Workers, 1971.

La Queur, W. Reflections on Youth Movements. Commentary, 47(6) (1969):396–41.

Lathrop, Julia C. The Background of the Juvenile Court

in Illinois. In *The Child, the Clinic, and the Court.* New York: New Republic, 1925. Pp. 290–95.

Lee, P. R. *Social Work as Cause and Function.* New York: Columbia University Press, 1937.

Leiby, J. *History of Social Welfare and Social Work in the United States.* New York: Columbia University Press, 1978.

Lens, S. *Poverty: America's Enduring Paradox.* New York: Thomas Y. Crowell, 1969.

Levine, M., and Levine, A. *A Social History of the Helping Services.* New York: Appleton-Century-Crofts, 1970.

Levine, M.; Moulton, H. G.; and Warburton, C. *America's Capacity to Consume.* Washington, D.C.: Brookings Institution, 1934.

Levitan, S. A., and Taggart, R. *The Promise of Greatness.* Cambridge, Mass.: Harvard University Press, 1976.

Levy, C. S. Social Work Values and Planned Change. *Social Casework, 54*(10) (1972):488–93.

Levy, C. S. *Social Work Ethics.* New York: Human Sciences Press, 1976.

Lewis, H. Morality and the Politics of Practice. *Social Casework, 53*(7) (1972):404–17.

Lewis, O. F. *The Development of American Prisons and Prison Customs, 1776–1845.* Albany: Prison Association of New York, 1922.

Loewenburg, F. M. Toward a Sociological Perspective on Social Welfare Strategies. In J. M. Romanyshyn, ed., *Social Science and Social Welfare.* New York: Council on Social Work Education, 1974.

Lowry, F. Objectives in Social Casework. *The Family, 18*(8) (1937):261–66.

Lubove, R. *The Professional Altruist: The Emergence of Social Work as a Career.* Cambridge, Mass.: Harvard University Press, 1965.

Lundberg, E. O. *Unto the Least of These: Social Services for Children.* New York: Appleton-Century-Crofts, 1947.

Lynch, J. J. *The Broken Heart: The Medical Consequences of Loneliness.* New York: Basic Books, 1977.

Macarow, D. *The Design of Social Welfare.* New York: Holt, Rinehart & Winston, 1978.

MacDonald, M. E. Reunion at Vocational High. *Social Service Review, 40*(2) (1966):175–89.

Marcus, G. Social Work and Mental Health. *The Family, 19*(4) (1938):101–6.

Margolis, P. M. and Favazza, A. R. In J. B. Turner, ed., *Encyclopedia of Social Work, 1977.* New York: National Association of Social Workers, 1977.

Matushima, J. Child Welfare: Institutions for Children. In R. Morris, ed., *Encyclopedia of Social Work, 1971.* New York: National Association of Social Workers, 1971.

Meier, A., and Rudwick, E. *From Plantation to Ghetto.* 3d ed. New York: Hill and Wang, 1976.

Meier, M. S., and Rivera, F. *Readings on La Raza: The Twentieth Century.* New York: Hill and Wang, 1974.

Mencher, S. *Poor Law to Poverty Program.* Pittsburgh: University of Pittsburgh Press, 1967.

Meyer, C. *Social Work Practice: The Changing Landscape.* 2d ed. New York: Free Press, 1976.

Meyer, H. J. and Siegel, S. Profession of Social Work: Contemporary Characteristics. In J. B. Turner, ed., *Encyclopedia of Social Work, 1977.* New York: National Association of Social Workers, 1977.

Mindes, R. H. P. Theory Heroes and Theory Villains: Reflections on the Boundaries of Reason. In J. M. Romanyshyn, ed., *Social Service and Social Welfare.* New York: Council on Social Work Education, 1974.

Morales, A., and Bradford, C. S. *Social Work: A Profession of Many Faces.* Boston: Allyn & Bacon, 1977.

Morgan, B. Four Pennies to My Name: What It's Like on Welfare. *Public Welfare, 37*(2) (1979):13–22.

Morgan, J. S. *Welfare and Wisdom.* Toronto: University of Toronto Press, 1968.

Morris, R., ed. *Encyclopedia of Social Work.* New York: National Association of Social Workers, 1971.

Morris, R. *Social Policy of the American Welfare State.* New York: Harper & Row, 1979.

Morse, N. C., and Wiese, R. S. The Function and Meaning of Work and the Job. In S. Nosow and W. H. Form, *Man, Work, and Society.* New York: Basic Books, 1962.

Mostwin, D. Letters. *Social Work, 15*(4) (1970):119.

National Association of Social Workers. *Standards for Social Service Manpower.* New York: National Association of Social Workers, 1973.

Nicolay, J. G., and Hay, J., eds. *Abraham Lincoln: Complete Works.* New York: Century, 1894.

Nosow, S., and Form, W. H. *Man, Work, and Society.* New York: Basic Books, 1962.

Okner, B. The Role of Demogrants as an Income Maintenance Alternative. In U.S. Congress, Joint Economic Committee, Subcommittee on Fiscal Policy. *Studies in Public Welfare,* Paper No. 9, Concepts in Welfare Program Design, 93rd Cong., 1st ss. August 20, 1973, pp. 1–30.

Olds, V. The Freedmen's Bureau: A Nineteenth Century Federal Welfare Agency. *Social Casework, 44*(5) (1963):247–55.

Otis, J. Liberty, Social Work, and Public Policy Development. From *The Social Welfare Forum, 1976,* New York: Columbia University Press, (c) 1977, National Conference on Social Welfare. Used by Permission of the publisher.

Owen, J. Letters. *Social Work, 15*(4) (1970):119.

Paine, T. The Rights of Man. Part 2. In T. Paine, *Basic Writings of Thomas Paine.* New York: John Wiley, 1942.

Perlman, H. H. *Social Casework: A Problem-Solving Process.* Chicago: University of Chicago Press, 1957.

Perlman, H. H. *So You Want to Be a Social Worker.* New York: Harper, 1962.

Perlman, H. H. Social Casework. In N. V. Lurie, ed., *Encyclopedia of Social Work, 1965.* New York: National Association of Social Workers, 1965.

Perlman, H. H. Casework Is Dead. *Social Casework, 48*(1) (1967):22–26.

Perlman, H. H. Casework and the Diminished Man. *Social Casework, 57*(4) (1970):216–24.

Pessen, E. *Jacksonian America: Society, Personality, and Politics.* Rev. ed. Homewood, Ill.: Dorsey Press, 1978.

Peterson, J. A. From Social Settlement to Social Agency: Settlement Work in Columbia, Ohio, 1898–1958. *Social Service Review, 39*(2) (1965):191–208.

Piccard, B. J. *An Introduction to Social Work: A Primer.* 2d ed. Homewood, Ill.: Dorsey Press, 1979.

Pincus, A., and Minahan, A. *Social Work Practice: Model and Method.* Itasca, Ill.: F. E. Peacock, 1973.

Plotnick, R. D., and Skidmore, F. *Progress against Poverty.* New York: Academic Press, 1975.

Pruger, R. The Good Bureaucrat. *Social Work, 18*(4) (1973):26–32.

Pumphrey, M. W. *The Teaching of Values and Ethics in Social Work Education.* Vol. 13 of the Curriculum Study. New York: Council on Social Work Education, 1959.

Pumphrey, R. E., and Pumphrey, M. W. *The Heritage of American Social Work.* New York: Columbia University Press, 1961.

Pusic, E. The Political Community and the Future of Welfare. In J. S. Morgan, ed., *Welfare and Wisdom.* Toronto: University of Toronto Press, 1968.

Queen, S. A. *Social Work in the Light of History.* Philadelphia: J. B. Lippincott, 1922.

Randall, R. Social Services in AFDC. *Social Service Review, 49*(2) (1975):191–207.

Random House College Dictionary, The, rev. ed. New York: Random House, Inc., 1975. Copyright © 1975, 1979, 1980 by Random House, Inc.

Rees, S. E. Carter's Urban Policy and Budget Chart. *The Advocate for Human Services, 8*(3) (1979): 3–6.

Rein, M., and Rainwater, L. Patterns of Welfare Use. *Social Service Review, 52*(4) (1978):511–34.

Reisler, M. *By the Sweat of Their Brow: Mexican Immigrant Labor in the United States, 1900–1940.* Westport, Conn.: Greenwood Press, 1976.

Reynolds, B. C. *Social Work and Social Living.* New York: National Association of Social Workers, 1951. Republished, 1975.

Rich, M. E. *A Belief in People: A History of American Social Work.* New York: Family Service Association of America, 1956.

Richmond, M. E. The Social Caseworker in a Changing World. In *Proceedings of the National Conference of Charities and Corrections, 1915.* Chicago: National Conference of Charities and Corrections, 1915.

Richmond, M. E. *The Long View.* New York: Russell Sage Foundation, 1917.

Richmond, M. E. *What Is Social Casework?* New York: Russell Sage Foundation, 1922.

Romanofsky, P., ed. *Social Service Organizations.* 2 vols. Westport, Conn.: Greenwood Press, 1978.

Romanyshyn, J. M. *Social Welfare: Charity to Justice.* New York: Random House, 1971.

Romanyshyn, J. M., ed. *Social Science and Social Welfare.* New York: Council on Social Work Education, 1974.

Rooney, J. L. Public Assistance. In R. H. Kurtz, ed.,

Social Work Year Book. New York: National Association of Social Workers, 1957. Copyright 1957, National Association of Social Workers, Inc. Excerpts reprinted with permission.

Rose, A. M.   *The Institutions of Advanced Societies.* Minneapolis: University of Minnesota Press, 1958.

Rosengren, W. R., and Lefton, M.   *Hospitals and Patients.* 1st ed. New York: Atherton Press, 1969.

Rosenheim, M. K.   Wards of the Court: A Perspective on Justice for Children. In A. L. Schorr, ed., *Children and Decent People.* New York: Basic Books, 1974.

Rothman, D. J.   The State as Parent. In W. Gaylin, I. Glasser, S. Marcus, and D. Rothman, eds., *Doing Good: The Limits of Benevolence.* New York: Pantheon Books, 1978.

Rubinow, I. M.   *Social Insurance.* New York: Henry Holt, 1913.

Russell, W.   *The New York Hospital: A History of the Psychiatric Service, 1771–1936.* New York: Columbia University Press, 1945.

Salamon, L. M.   *Welfare the Elusive Consensus.* New York: Praeger Publishers, 1978.

Shapiro, H. D.   An Analysis of President Carter's Program. In Salamon, L. M., *Welfare the Elusive Consensus.* New York: Praeger Publishers, 1978.

Schneider, D. M.   *History of Public Welfare in New York, 1609–1866.* Chicago: University of Chicago Press, 1938.

Schneider, D. M., and Deutsch, A.   *The Road Upward.* New York: New York State Dept. of Social Welfare, 1939.

Schneider, D. M., and Deutsch, A.   *The History of Public Welfare in New York State, 1876–1940.* Chicago: University of Chicago Press, 1941.

Schorr, A.   Editorial. *Social Work, 16*(1) (1971):2.

Schorr, A.   Comments. *Social Work, 15*(3) (1970): 102–3.

Schwartz, B. A.   Unwed Parents. Copyright 1977, National Association of Social Workers, Inc. Excerpts reprinted with permission from, J. B. Turner, ed., *Encyclopedia of Social Work,* 17th ed. New York: National Association of Social Workers, 1977.

Schwartz, W.   Private Troubles and Public Issues: One Social Work Job or Two? In *Proceedings of the National Conference on Social Welfare: Social Welfare Forum.* New York: Columbia University Press, 1969.

Schwartz, W.   The Social Worker in the Group. In B. R. Compton and B. Galaway, *Social Work Processes.* Rev. ed. Homewood, Ill.: Dorsey Press, 1979. Reprinted from National Conference on Social Welfare, *Social Welfare Forum, 1961.* New York: Columbia University Press, 1961.

Siegel, S.   *Social Service Manpower Needs: An Overview to 1980.* New York: Council on Social Work Education, 1975.

Skolnik, M., and Dales, S. R.   Social Welfare Expenditures, 1850–1915. *Social Security Bulletin, 35*(1) (1965):3–20.

Smith, R., and Zeitz, D.   *American Social Welfare Institutions.* New York: John Wiley, 1970.

Sowers, W. J., Jr.   Letters. *Social Work, 16*(1) (1971): 128.

Spargo, J.   *The Bitter Cry of the Children.* New York: Macmillan, 1906.

Spindler, A.   *Public Welfare.* New York: Human Sciences Press, 1979.

Specht, H.   The Deprofessionalization of Social Work. *Social Work, 17*(2) (1972):3–15.

Stein, H. D.   Social Work's Developmental and Change Function. *Social Service Review, 50*(1) (1976):1–11.

Steiner, G.   *The State of Welfare.* Washington, D.C.: Brookings Institution, 1971.

Teeters, N. K., and Reinemann, J. O.   *The Challenge of Delinquency: Causation, Treatment, and Prevention of Juvenile Delinquency.* Englewood Cliffs, N.J.: Prentice-Hall, 1950.

Tilgher, A.   Work through the Ages. In S. Nosow and W. H. Form, *Man, Work, and Society.* New York: Basic Books, 1962.

Towle, C.   Social Casework. In R. Kurtz, ed., *Social Work Year Book.* New York: National Association of Social Workers, 1947.

Trapp, E.   Three Problematic Concepts: Client, Help, Worker. *Social Casework, 55*(1) (1974):19–29.

Trattner, W.   *From Poor Law to Welfare State: A History of Social Welfare in America.* New York: Free Press, 1974.

Turner, J. B., ed.   *Encyclopedia of Social Work.* Vol. 1. New York: National Association of Social Workers, 1977.

Turner, J. H., and Starnes, C. E.   *Inequality: Privilege and Poverty in America.* Pacific Palisades, Calif.:

Goodyear, 1976. Copyright © 1976 by Goodyear Publishing Co. Material reprinted by permission.

Turney, B.   *Medieval Poor Law: A Sketch of Canonical Theory and Its Application in England.* Berkeley: University of California Press, 1959.

United Nations, Department of Social Affairs.   *Training for Social Work: An International Survey.* New York: United Nations, 1950.

U.S. Department of Health, Education, and Welfare, Social Security Administration.   *Social Security Bulletin, 39*(1) (1976):6–8.

Webster's Seventh New Collegiate Dictionary.   Springfield, Mass.: G. & C Merriam, 1970.

Weinberger, P. E.   *Perspectives on Social Welfare.* New York: Macmillan, 1969.

Whittaker, J. K.   *Planning for Child Care Institutions.* Unpublished doctoral dissertation, University of Minnesota, 1970.

Wickenden, E.   *Social Welfare in a Changing World.* Washington, D.C.: Department of Health, Education, and Welfare, 1965.

Wickenden, E.   A Perspective on Social Services: An Essay Review. *Social Service Review, 50*(4) (1976):570–85.

Wilcox, C.   *Toward Social Welfare.* Homewood, Ill.: Richard D. Irwin, 1969.

Wilcox, P.   Letters. *Social Work, 16*(1) (1971):128.

Wilensky, H. L., and Leeaux, C. N.   *Industrial Society and Social Welfare.* New York: Free Press, 1965.

Wilsnack, W. H.   Handling Resistance in Social Case Work. *American Journal of Orthopsychiatry, 16*(1) (1946):297–311.

Wolins, M.   The Societal Function of Social Welfare. *New Perspectives: The Berkeley Journal of Social Welfare, 1* (1967):1–18.

Woodward, S. W.   A Businessman's View of Child Labor. *Charities and Commons, 15* (1905–6):798–801.

Wright, H.   Three against Time: Edith and Grace Abbott and Sophonisba P. Breckinridge. *Social Service Review, 28*(1) (1957):41–53.

Yates, J. V. N.   Report of the Secretary of State on the Relief and Settlement of the Poor. In *Poverty, U.S.A.: The Almshouse Experience.* New York: Arno Press, New York Times, 1971.

Zastrow, C.   *Introduction to Social Welfare Institutions.* Homewood, Ill.: Dorsey Press, 1978.

ᵉ⧸ Index

A

Abbott, E., 181, 186, 228, 258
Abbott, Grace, 200, 241–42, 292, 297, 305, 362, 364, 372–73
Abortion, 296–97, 511–12
Academy of Certified Social Workers, 133, 494
Acceptance, 121
Addams, Jane, 289, 291, 323, 333, 335–36, 343, 347
Adler, Felix, 333
Adoption, 241–42
Agencies, 59, 66–69
 funding, 66–67
 organizational structure, 67–68
 policy, 67
 private, 68–69
 programs and functions, 67
 public, 68, 427–29
Agency-client relationship, 97
Agency specialization, 129
 duplication of services, 131
 segregation, 130–31
 stigmatization, 130–31
Aging, 54
Agricultural cooperatives, 328
Agriculture, 327
 aid through education, 327
 government aid, 328
Aid to the Blind (AB), 419
Aid for Dependent Children (ADC), 10, 419
Aid for Families with Dependent Children (AFDC), 10, 425, 453–57, 502–4, 532
 federal participation, 451
 in-kind approach, 457
 reforms in 1960s, 454
 rise in number of recipients, 453
 unemployed fathers, 454
 work approach, 457
The Alliance, 276
Almshouse, 197
 children, 297
Almshouse hospitals, 247
Altgeld, John, 275
Altmeyer, Arthur, 427
Amalgamated Clothing Workers of America, 329
American Aid Association, 298
American Antislavery Society, 224

American Association of Group Workers, 431
American Association of Hospital Social Workers, 405
American Association of Medical Social Workers, 405, 431
American Association for Organizing Charities, 401
American Association for Organizing Family Social Work, 402
American Association of Psychiatric Social Workers, 431
American Association of Social Workers, 388, 431
American Association for the Study of the Feeble-Minded, 307
American Colonization Society, 223
American Farm Bureau Federation, 328
American Federation of State, County and Municipal Employees, 432
American Indian Movement (AIM), 441
American Indians, 178–79
 Bureau of Indian Affairs, 221
 child care, 242
 children's education in pre-Civil War period, 251–52
 Civil War, 266
 depression, 432–33
 domestication, 187
 education, 203, 399–410
 laws of 1834, 221
 period 1940–1967, 440–41
 relationship with whites, 219
 removal to the West, 220
 Revolutionary War, 220
American Medical Association, founding, 248
American Public Health Association, 307
American Public Welfare Society, 497
American Revolution, 174–75, 191
 Indian relationships, 220
American Social Science Association, 304
American value system, 86–89
 capitalist-puritan, 86
 humanist-positivist-utopian, 86
 Judeo-Christian, 86–87
Antipoverty budget, 44
Antitrust movement, 326
Apprenticeship, 187, 201–3
Aptheker, Herbert, 223, 256
Archives of Pediatrics, 307
Asian American Social Workers, 496
Assistance to repatriated U.S. nationals, 523–24
Association of American Indian Social Workers, 496

Association of Catholic Day Nurseries, 403
Association of Medical Superintendents of American Institutions for the Insane, 301
Association of Puerto Rican Social Service Workers, 496
Association of Schools of Social Work, 488
Association for the Study of Community Organization, 431
Attucks, Crispus, 190
Augustus, John, 250, 312, 315
Authority in social worker-client relationships, 121–22
Awl, William M., 301
Axinn, J., 197, 229, 247, 265, 270–71, 322, 325–26, 416–18, 436, 444–45, 452
Ayres, Beverly, 470

B

Baer, B. L., 108, 113
Bailey v. *Drexel Furniture Company,* 333
Ball, Robert M., 423, 448–49, 510
Banks, Dennis, 441
Bard, Samuel, 247
Barkley, Alben W., 364
Barnard, Henry, 308
Barnett, Ida B. Wells, 344
Barnett, Samuel A., 288
Barton, Clara, 257–58
Baxandall, R., 186, 206, 229, 257
Beard, James, 173
Becker, D. G., 258
Bell, Winifred, 104, 546, 548
Bellamy, Edward, 279
Bellecourt, Clyde, 441
Bellecourt, Vernon, 441
Bellevue hospital, 247
Benefits in cash, 93–94
Benefits in kind, 93–94
Benezet, Anthony, 177
Bennett, L., Jr., 190, 224–25, 256–57, 260–62, 264
Bentham, Jeremy, 165
Bergman, P. M., 204
Bernard, Jessie, 49, 489
Bethune, Mary, 438
Beveridge, Albert J., 333
Big Brothers, 13
Biggs, Herman M., 306
Billingsley, A., 242, 265–66, 349
Birt, Charles, 469
Birth control, 296–97
Birtwell, Charles W., 298

This book has been set VideoComp, 10 and 9 point Roma, leaded 2 points. Part numbers and titles are 36 point Avant Garde Extra Light and chapter numbers and titles are 16 point Avant Garde Gothic Book. The size of the type page is 37½ by 48 picas.